For selected older vintages

ITALY	04									
Barolo, Barbaresco	9									
Chianti Classico Ris.	9									
Brunello	9	8	5	9	8	9	8	10	6	8
Amarone	9	8	5	7	9	7	7	10	6	10
SPAIN										
Ribera del Duero	8	8	4	8	7	8	7	6	9	8
Rioja (red)	8	7	7	6	8	7	6	7	8	8
PORTUGAL										
South	8	6	5	8	9	8	6	6	8	7
North	8	8	5	8	9	7	6	8	8	7
Port	8	9	6	7	9	7	6	8	7	7
USA										
California Cabernet	8	8	7	8	8	9	7	8	7	9
California Chardonnay	8	9	8	8	7	8	7	8	6	8
Oregon Pinot Noir	8	8	8	7	9	9	8	5	7	5
Wash. State Cabernet	9	8	7	8	9	9	8	8	9	8
AUSTRALIA										
Coonawarra Cabernet	8	8	9	9	6	8	10	7	9	5
Hunter Semillon	8	9	7	7	9	8	10	8	9	7
Barossa Shiraz	9	7	10	9	8	8	10	8	10	7
Marg. River Cabernet	8	8	9	10	8	10	7	8	10	9
NEW ZEALAND										
M'lborough Sauvignon	7	8	6	9	9	8	5	8	9	3
H'kes Bay Cab/Merlot	7	5	9	7	8	7	10	7	7	8
SOUTH AFRICA										
Stellenbosch Cabernet	8	9	5	9	8	7	8	9	6	9
S'bosch Chardonnay	9	8	6	7	7	8	6	8	6	8

Numerals (1–10) represent an overall rating for each year. ◑ Not ready
● Just ready ● At peak ◐ Past best ○ Not generally declared

D0307186

Oz Clarke's
Pocket Wine
Book 2006

the world of wine from a-z

Wine Guide of the Year 2004 LE PRIX DU *Lanson* CHAMPAGNE

**TIME WARNER
BOOKS**

WEBSTERS

A TIME WARNER/WEBSTERS BOOK

This edition first published in 2005 by
Time Warner Book Group UK
Brettenham House
Lancaster Place
LONDON WC2E 7EN
www.twbg.co.uk

Created and designed by
Websters International Publishers Limited
Axe and Bottle Court
70 Newcomen Street
London SE1 1YT
www.websters.co.uk
www.ozclarke.com

14th edition. First published in 1992.
Revised editions published annually.

A CIP catalogue for this book is available from the
British Library.

ISBN 0-316-73056-4

Printed and bound in China

Thanks are due to the following people for their invaluable help with
the 2006 edition and the generous spirit in which they have shared
their knowledge: Nicolas Belfrage MW, Dan Berger, Stephen Brook, Bob
Campbell MW, Bill Evans, Giles Fallowfield, Peter Forrestal, Roger
Harris, James Lawther MW, John Livingstone-Learmonth, Angela Lloyd,
Dan McCarthy, Dave McIntyre, Richard Mayson, Jasper Morris MW,
Victor de la Serna, Stephen Skelton MW, Patricio Tapia, Roger Voss.

CONTENTS

HOW TO USE THE A–Z

The **A–Z** section starts on page 44 and includes over 1600 entries on wines, producers, grapes and wine regions from all over the world. It is followed on page 289 by a **Glossary** of some of the more common winemaking terms that are often seen on labels.

Detailed **Vintage Charts**, with information on which of the world's top wines are ready for drinking in 2006, can be found on the inside front and back covers; the front chart features vintages back to 1995; the back chart covers a selection of older vintages for premium wines.

Glass Symbols   These indicate the wines produced.

❢ Red wine   ❢ Rosé wine   ♀ White wine

The order of the glasses reflects the importance of the wines in terms of volume produced. For example:

🍷 White followed by rosé wine

🍷 Red followed by white wine

🍷 Red followed by rosé, then white wine

Grape Symbols   These identify entries on grape varieties.

∷ Red grape   ⁖ White grape

Star Symbols   These indicate wines and producers that are highly rated by the author.

★   A particularly good wine or producer in its category

★★   An excellent wine or producer in its category – one especially worth seeking out

★★★   An exceptional, world-class wine or producer

Best Years   Recommended vintages are listed for many producer and appellation entries. Those listed in bold, e.g. **2004**, **99**, indicate wines that are ready for drinking now, although they may not necessarily be at their best; those appearing in brackets, e.g. (2004), (01), are preliminary assessments of wines that are not yet ready for drinking.

Cross References   To help you find your way round the A–Z, wine names, producers and regions that have their own entries elsewhere in the A–Z are indicated by SMALL CAPITALS. Grape varieties are not cross-referred in this way, but more than 70 varieties, from Albariño to Zinfandel, are included.

Special Features   The A–Z section includes special 2-page features on the world's most important wine styles, regions and grape varieties. These features include recommended vintages and producers, as well as lists of related entries elsewhere in the A–Z.

Index   The Index, starting on page 297, will help you find over 4000 recommended producers, including all of those that don't have their own entry in the A–Z. Some of the world's most famous brand names are also included.

INTRODUCTION

I judged the Wines of Chile Awards this year, along with a bunch of other British judges. I thought we did a pretty good job, seeking out wines with the most vibrant fruit, the most alluring scent. We had a strong idea of what we thought Chilean Sauvignon Blanc, Chardonnay and Riesling could and should be. We were enthusiastic supporters of the cassis and occasionally mint- and leaf-perfumed Cabernets and I was thrilled by the exotic but immensely attractive mix of ripe fruit, floral scent and peppery fire that characterizes Carmenère. So we sniffed and slurped through the samples in front of us, awarding top marks to wines that fitted our pre-conceived idea of beauty and pleasure. We've also been getting tired recently of over-ripe, over-alcoholic Shirazes and Syrahs, so when we found the haunting floral perfume and the herbs and blackberry flavours of a good cool climate Syrah – Viña Falernia's Alta Tierra Syrah – well, we gave it a gold medal; in fact we gave it a trophy, Best Wine in Show.

And that's a prime example of globalization at work. I mean it. We were there to praise and reward the best that Chile had to offer, but we weren't necessarily rewarding what the *Chileans* thought were their best wines. Indeed, many Chilean producers and critics were puzzled and sometimes upset by our decisions, because the mainstream styles – the Maipo Cabernets, the chunky Colchagua reds, the cool-climate Casablanca whites and Pinot Noirs – weren't collecting the medals, weren't being appreciated by this bevy of foreign judges. We told the Chileans what *we* thought were best – and at least half of our gold medals were from unlikely places or for unheralded wine styles – and that left many Chileans wondering, had they got it wrong, should they change their style to please us, and in any case, what *was* the real flavour of Chile?

Now, I'd say ours was an attempt to be really positive. The last thing we were likely to reward was a Napa Valley Cabernet or McLaren Vale Chardonnay look-alike. We were seeking the Chilean point of difference. But were we actually helping? Because you could say we were in fact imposing our northern European views on the Chileans. The views of a group from the USA, or Australia, Italy or China could be completely different. Who to believe? Well, eventually, producers have to believe in themselves and their particular talents.

But they have to sell the wine. And nowadays, with a global surplus that has more than doubled in the last 12 months alone, and global consumption that continues to decline, export has become a matter of life or death for most wine companies in most wine countries. So shouldn't they listen to the export markets and say – yes, we'll make what you want?

People object to Robert Parker and his unhealthy omnipotence in the world of fine wine criticism, but didn't he set out to democratize wine and improve the standards of winemaking through his self-confident opinions? People criticize Michel Rolland for creating a worldwide style of red based on his own Pomerol roots – but they forget how poor many of the world's wines were before Rolland bustled up and said let's do it my way. Is Parker wrong? Is Rolland wrong? Were *we* wrong? The road to hell is paved with good intentions.

Globalization comes in many forms nowadays. Certainly I dislike and regret the multinational drinks giants who treat wine like washing powder, who neither know nor care about flavour and personality any more than they care about whether the people who grow the grapes for their wretched brands earn enough money to send their kids to school or call out the doctor when they're sick. But is globalization all bad? Hasn't globalization brought us a whole swathe of products – at the bottom and the top ends of the market – that we can enjoy without the need to comprehend them? They are wine – top and bottom – for an 'instant gratification' generation.

But is globalization all bad? Well, no. When it means an attempt by worldly-wise wine people to persuade producers to make the best of their fruit and their particular growing conditions – well, I'll buy that. But what does 'make the best of' mean? I admit, I do prefer the 'modern' route, so by all means emphasize the fruit, but make sure the wine tastes of *your* fruit – not Bordeaux's, or California's, or Australia's. And how do you do that? By employing methods of vine cultivation and winemaking that have been invented then honed to a shining state of efficiency – in Bordeaux, or California, or Australia. Globalization.

But I must drink wine, and drink wine I shall. And I'll start with **Chilean** wine – red and white. Merlot, Carmenère and Cabernet, scented Pinot and Shiraz and remarkable cool-climate whites of every sort. **Argentina** seems to be marking time and **Uruguay** is still playing catch-up, but I'll keep an eye on them. In North America, I've been drinking better and better **California** Pinot Noirs for several years, but the revelation this year is how California has re-discovered the art of outstanding Chardonnay. These will nicely balance powerhouse **Washington** Cabernet, Merlot and Shiraz.

Chardonnays are pretty good from **South Africa** too, but it's the Sauvignon Blancs I like best; and Pinotage, Shiraz and Pinot Noir when they're not smothered in oak. **New Zealand** should give me Pinot Noir, and definitely could give me some stunning Shiraz, along with some of the world's best Chardonnay and Sauvignon. **Australia** could offer the world's best in almost any grape, but too many of the Big Company offerings lack heart. So I'll be looking to independent producers for brilliant Victoria Shiraz, Margaret River Cabernet, Eden and Clare Valley and Tasmanian Riesling and any other grape variety that tastes of place and people and not boardroom bottom line.

Back in Europe, I'm going to seek out some of the revolutionary new wines from **Greece** and keep encouraging the producers in Sicily and **Italy**'s far south to give us their fascinating warm-hearted reds. **Portugal**'s reds have a different flavour but they do the same job brilliantly. And **Spain**'s reds seem to have gone through a period of over-oaking to emerge now as some of Europe's tastiest and best.

In **France**, exports are down and producers are wailing and weeping, but quality is generally up. The **Loire**, the **Rhône** and the **Languedoc** are producing fabulous wines and I'll be drinking them. **Bordeaux** and **Burgundy** have some lovely stuff. Burgundy I'll drink anyway, Bordeaux if they give us all a break on price.

And that just leaves the chilly North. Traditionally chilly in 2004, eye-poppingly warm in 2003. **Austria**'s and **Germany**'s cool 2004s and exotic 2003s I'll drink, and as for **England** – roll out those warm climate 2003s; I can't wait!

SOME OF MY FAVOURITES

The following are some of the wines I've enjoyed most this year. They're not definitive lists of 'best wines', but all the wines, regions and producers mentioned here are on an exciting roll in terms of quality. Some are easy to find; others are very rare or expensive, but if you get the chance to try them, grab it! You can find out more about them in the A–Z on pages 44 to 288: the cross-references in SMALL CAPITALS will guide you to the relevant entries.

WORLD-CLASS WINES THAT DON'T COST THE EARTH
- Tim ADAMS Shiraz, CLARE VALLEY, Australia
- CARMEN, Nativa Cabernet Sauvignon, Chile
- Heartland Director's Cut Shiraz, LIMESTONE COAST, Australia
- HIDALGO La Gitana Manzanilla, Spain
- SANTA RITA Triple C, MAIPO, Chile
- STEENBERG Merlot, CONSTANTIA, South Africa
- VILLA MARIA Reserve Merlot-Cabernet, HAWKES BAY, New Zealand

BEST LOOKALIKES TO THE CLASSICS
Bordeaux-style red wines
- ANDREW WILL Sorella, WASHINGTON STATE, USA
- CULLEN Cabernet Sauvignon-Merlot, Australia
- STONYRIDGE Larose, New Zealand
- VERGELEGEN, South Africa

Burgundy-style white wines
- CA' DEL BOSCO Chardonnay, Italy
- FROMM, Clayvin Vineyard Chardonnay, New Zealand
- LEEUWIN ESTATE Art Series Chardonnay, Australia
- TE MATA, Elston Chardonnay, New Zealand

Champagne-style wines
- Jansz Vintage, YALUMBA, Australia
- NYETIMBER, England
- RIDGEVIEW, England
- ROEDERER ESTATE L'Ermitage, CALIFORNIA, USA

TOP-VALUE WINES
- CAVA fizz from Spain
- Vin de Pays des COTES DE GASCOGNE whites, France
- Heartland Shiraz, LIMESTONE COAST, Australia
- Inycon FIANO, SICILY, Italy
- Peter LEHMANN whites, Australia
- Marqués de Casa Concha range, CONCHA Y TORO, Chile
- MONTANA Sauvignon Blanc, New Zealand
- Old Vines Garnacha (Grenache Noir) from Calatayud and Campo de Borja, ARAGON, Spain
- Trincadeira, ALENTEJO, Portugal

REGIONS TO WATCH
- ARAGON, Spain
- CENTRAL OTAGO, New Zealand
- CORBIERES, France
- GREAT SOUTHERN, Australia
- Leyda, SAN ANTONIO, Chile
- MINERVOIS, France
- Santa Lucia Highlands, MONTEREY COUNTY, California
- SICILY, Italy
- Sussex, England
- UCO VALLEY, MENDOZA, Argentina

PRODUCERS TO WATCH
- Clos de los Siete, UCO VALLEY, Argentina
- CRAGGY RANGE, HAWKES BAY, New Zealand
- FERNGROVE, GREAT SOUTHERN, Australia
- GIRARDIN, Burgundy, France
- Henry's Drive (reds), PADTHAWAY, Australia
- PLANETA, SICILY, Italy
- João Portugal RAMOS, Portugal
- Telmo RODRIGUEZ, Spain
- Tabalí (SAN PEDRO), Limarí, Chile
- Trivento, Argentina (see CONCHA Y TORO)

AUSTRALIA
- Tim ADAMS Aberfeldy Shiraz
- CAPE MENTELLE Cabernet Sauvignon
- GROSSET Watervale Riesling
- HENSCHKE HILL OF GRACE Shiraz
- HOUGHTON Gladstones Shiraz
- LEEUWIN ESTATE Art Series Chardonnay

- MORRIS Old Premium Liqueur Tokay
- PETALUMA Tiers Chardonnay
- PLANTAGENET Shiraz
- TYRRELL'S Vat 1 Semillon

BORDEAUX
- Ch. CHEVAL BLANC (red)
- Ch. DUCRU-BEAUCAILLOU (red)
- Ch. GRAND-PUY-LACOSTE (red)
- Les Forts DE LATOUR (red)
- Ch. LEOVILLE-BARTON (red)
- Ch LYNCH-BAGES (red)
- Ch. MARGAUX (red)
- Ch. PICHON-LONGUEVILLE-LALANDE (red)
- Ch. SMITH-HAUT-LAFITTE (white)
- Ch. SUDUIRAUT (sweet)

BURGUNDY
- CARILLON, Bienvenues-BATARD-MONTRACHET (white)
- R Chevillon, NUITS-ST-GEORGES les Perrières (red)
- COCHE-DURY, CORTON-CHARLEMAGNE (white)
- B Dugat-Py, Charmes-CHAMBERTIN (red)
- J-N GAGNARD, BATARD-MONTRACHET (white)
- Anne GROS, CLOS DE VOUGEOT (red)
- LAFON, VOLNAY Santenots (red)
- Denis MORTET, GEVREY-CHAMBERTIN Lavaux-St-Jacques (red)
- M Rollin, CORTON-CHARLEMAGNE (white)
- TOLLOT-BEAUT, CORTON-Bressandes (red)

CALIFORNIA
- AU BON CLIMAT Chardonnay Les Nuits Blanches
- Cline Cellars Small Berry Mourvèdre, SONOMA COUNTY
- LAUREL GLEN Cabernet Sauvignon
- Long Meadow Ranch, NAPA VALLEY
- NEWTON Le Puzzle
- Pahlmeyer Red, NAPA VALLEY
- RIDGE Santa Cruz Mountains Chardonnay
- Saucelito Canyon Zinfandel, SAN LUIS OBISPO COUNTY
- SHAFER Hillside Select Cabernet Sauvignon
- Viader, NAPA VALLEY

ITALIAN REDS
- ALLEGRINI AMARONE
- Fattoria di Basciano CHIANTI RUFINA Riserva
- BOSCARELLI
- Caggiano, TAURASI
- GAJA LANGHE Sperss
- ISOLE E OLENA Cepparello
- PLANETA Santa Cecilia
- POLIZIANO Le Stanze
- SELVAPIANA CHIANTI RUFINA Riserva Bucerchiale

RHÔNE AND SOUTHERN FRANCE
- Ch. de BEAUCASTEL Roussanne Vieilles Vignes (white)
- Dom. du Chêne, ST-JOSEPH
- CLOS DES PAPES, CHATEAUNEUF-DU-PAPE
- CUILLERON, CONDRIEU les Chaillets
- GRAILLOT, CROZES-HERMITAGE la Guiraude
- JAMET, COTE-ROTIE
- Dom. de la Janasse, CHATEAUNEUF-DU-PAPE Vieilles Vignes
- Ch. de St-Cosme, CONDRIEU

CABERNET SAUVIGNON
- CAPE MENTELLE, MARGARET RIVER, Western Australia
- CLOS QUEBRADA DE MACUL, Domus Aurea, MAIPO Valley, Chile
- GAJA Darmagi, PIEDMONT, Italy
- Ch. GRAND-PUY-LACOSTE, PAUILLAC, France
- Forts de LATOUR, PAUILLAC, France
- Long Meadow Ranch, NAPA VALLEY, CALIFORNIA, USA
- RIDGE Monte Bello, CALIFORNIA, USA
- STAG'S LEAP WINE CELLARS SLV, CALIFORNIA, USA
- TERRAZAS DE LOS ANDES, Gran Cabernet Sauvignon, MENDOZA, Argentina

CHARDONNAY
- CARILLON, Bienvenues-BATARD-MONTRACHET, France
- COCHE-DURY, CORTON-CHARLEMAGNE, France
- CONCHA Y TORO Amelia, Chile
- Diamond Valley Vineyards, YARRA VALLEY, Australia
- J-N GAGNARD, BATARD-MONTRACHET, France
- GIACONDA, VICTORIA, Australia
- GROSSET Piccadilly, ADELAIDE HILLS, Australia

8

- KISTLER Kistler Vineyard, CALIFORNIA
- KUMEU RIVER, AUCKLAND, New Zealand
- NEWTON Unfiltered, CALIFORNIA, USA
- M Rollin, CORTON-CHARLEMAGNE, France

MERLOT

- ANDREW WILL, WASHINGTON, USA
- Ch. ANGELUS, ST-EMILION, France
- Ch. AUSONE, ST-EMILION, France
- CASA LAPOSTOLLE Cuvée Alexandre, Chile
- CONO SUR 20 Barrels, Chile
- LEONETTI CELLAR, WASHINGTON, USA
- ORNELLAIA Masseto, TUSCANY, Italy
- Ch. PETRUS, POMEROL, France

PINOT NOIR

- ATA RANGI, MARTINBOROUGH, New Zealand
- R Chevillon, NUITS-ST-GEORGES les St-Georges, France
- FELTON ROAD, CENTRAL OTAGO, New Zealand
- FLOWERS Camp Meeting Ridge, CALIFORNIA, USA
- Freycinet, TASMANIA, Australia
- Anne GROS, CLOS DE VOUGEOT, France
- LAFON, VOLNAY Santenots, France
- Viña Leyda, SAN ANTONIO, Chile
- SAINTSBURY Reserve, USA
- E Rouget, ECHEZEAUX, France

RIESLING

- BRUNDLMAYER, KAMPTAL, Austria
- H DONNHOFF Niederhäuser Hermannshöhle, NAHE, Germany
- GROSSET Watervale, CLARE VALLEY, Australia
- GUNDERLOCH Nackenheimer Rothenberg, RHEINHESSEN, Germany
- Fritz HAAG Brauneberger Juffer Sonnenuhr, MOSEL, Germany
- Dr LOOSEN Erdener Prälat, MOSEL, Germany
- MOUNT HORROCKS, CLARE VALLEY, Australia
- Horst SAUER Escherndorfer Lump, FRANKEN, Germany

SAUVIGNON BLANC

- Lucien Crochet, SANCERRE, France
- Didier DAGUENEAU, POUILLY-FUME, France
- Neil ELLIS Groenekloof, South Africa

- Forrest Estate, MARLBOROUGH, New Zealand
- PALLISER ESTATE, MARTINBOROUGH, New Zealand
- Ch. SMITH-HAUT-LAFITTE, PESSAC-LEOGNAN, France
- STEENBERG, CONSTANTIA, South Africa
- VERGELEGEN, STELLENBOSCH, South Africa
- VILLA MARIA Reserve Clifford Bay, MARLBOROUGH, New Zealand

SYRAH/SHIRAZ

- Tim ADAMS Aberfeldy, CLARE VALLEY, Australia
- BOEKENHOUTSKLOOF, FRANSCHHOEK, South Africa
- BROKENWOOD Graveyard, HUNTER VALLEY, Australia
- CHAVE, HERMITAGE, France
- HENSCHKE HILL OF GRACE, Eden Valley, Australia
- JAMET, COTE-ROTIE, France
- MONTES Folly, COLCHAGUA, Chile
- PENFOLDS GRANGE, Australia
- Tyrrell's Rufus Stone, HEATHCOTE, Australia

FORTIFIED WINE

- BARBADILLO Amontillado Principe
- Blandy's Vintage Bual, MADEIRA
- CHAMBERS, RUTHERGLEN Muscat
- GONZALEZ BYASS Noé Pedro Ximénez
- GRAHAM'S Vintage Port
- HENRIQUES & HENRIQUES 15-year-old Madeira
- NIEPOORT Vintage Port

SPARKLING WINE

- BILLECART-SALMON Cuvée N-F Billecart CHAMPAGNE, France
- CLOUDY BAY Pelorus, MARLBOROUGH, New Zealand
- DEUTZ Blanc de Blancs CHAMPAGNE, France
- Alfred GRATIEN Vintage CHAMPAGNE, France
- Charles HEIDSIECK Mis en Caves CHAMPAGNE, France
- Charles MELTON Sparkling Red, BAROSSA, Australia
- Jansz, YALUMBA, Australia
- POL ROGER Vintage CHAMPAGNE, France
- ROEDERER ESTATE L'Ermitage, CALIFORNIA, USA

MODERN WINE STYLES

Not so long ago, if I were to have outlined the basic wine styles, the list would have been strongly biased towards the classics – Bordeaux, Burgundy, Sancerre, Mosel Riesling, Champagne. But the classics have, over time, become expensive and unreliable – thus opening the door to other, less established regions, and giving them the chance to offer us wines that may or may not owe anything to the originals. *These* are the flavours to which ambitious winemakers the world over now aspire.

WHITE WINES

Ripe, up-front, spicy Chardonnay Fruit is the key here: round, ripe, apricot, peach, melon, pineapple and tropical fruits, spiced up with the vanilla and butterscotch richness of some new oak – often American oak – to make a delicious, approachable, easy-to-drink fruit cocktail of taste. Australia and Chile are best at this style.

Green, tangy Sauvignon New Zealand was the originator of this style – all zingy, grassy, nettles and asparagus and then green apples and peach – and South Africa now has its own tangy, super-fresh examples. Chile has the potential to produce something similar, and there are hopeful signs in southern France. Bordeaux and the Loire are the original sources of dry Sauvignon wines, and at last we are seeing an expanding band of committed modern producers matching clean fruit with zippy green tang. Riesling in Australia is often lean and limy.

Bone-dry, neutral whites This doesn't sound very appetizing, but as long as it is well made it will be thirst-quenching and easy to drink. Many Italian whites fit this bill. Southern French wines, where no grape variety is specified, will be like this; so will many wines from Bordeaux, South-West France, Muscadet and Anjou. Modern young Spanish whites and Portuguese Vinho Verdes are good examples, as are Swiss Fendant (Chasselas) and southern German Trocken (dry) wines. I don't like seeing too much neutrality in New World wines, but cheap South African and California whites are 'superneutral'.

White Burgundy By this I mean the nutty, oatmealy-ripe but dry, subtly oaked styles of villages like Meursault at their best. Few people do it well, even in Burgundy itself, and it's a difficult style to emulate. California makes the most effort. Washington, Oregon and New York State each have occasional successes, as do top Australian and New Zealand Chardonnays.

Perfumy, off-dry whites Gewürztraminer, Muscat and Pinot Gris from Alsace will give you this style and in southern Germany Gewürztraminer, Scheurebe, Kerner, Grauburgunder (Pinot Gris) and occasionally Riesling may also do it. In New Zealand Riesling and Gewürztraminer can be excellent. Irsai Oliver from Hungary and Torrontés from Argentina are both heady and perfumed. Albariño in Spain is leaner but heady with citrus scent.

Mouthfuls of luscious gold Good sweet wines are difficult to make. Sauternes is the most famous, but the Loire, and sometimes Alsace, can also come up with rich, intensely sweet wines that can live for decades. Germany's top sweeties are stunning; Austria's are similiar in style to Germany's, but weightier. Hungarian Tokaji has a wonderful sweet-sour smoky flavour. Australia, California and New Zealand also have some exciting examples.

RED WINES

Spicy, warm-hearted reds Australia is out in front at the moment through the ebullient resurgence of her Shiraz reds – ripe, almost sweet, sinfully easy to enjoy. France's Rhône Valley is also on the up and the traditional appellations in the far south of France are looking good. In Italy Piedmont is producing delicious beefy Barbera and juicy exotic Dolcetto. Spain's Ribera del Duero and Toro and Portugal's south also deliver the goods, as does Malbec in Argentina. California Zinfandel made in its most powerful style is spicy and rich.

Juicy, fruity reds The excellent 2003 vintage brought Beaujolais' come-hither charms back into the spotlight. Even so, Grenache and Syrah vins de pays are often better bets, as are grassy, sharp Loire reds. Modern Spanish reds from Valdepeñas and La Mancha, and some Garnachas from Aragón, do the trick, as do young Chianti and Teroldego in Italy. Argentina has some good examples from Sangiovese, Tempranillo and other Italian and Spanish grape varieties.

Blackcurranty Cabernet Chile has climbed back to the top of the Cabernet tree, knocking Australia off its perch, though there are still some good examples from Australia. New Zealand strikes the blackcurrant bell in a much greener, sharper way. California only sometimes hits the sweet spot, and often with Merlot rather than Cabernet. Northern Spain is getting better. And what about Bordeaux? Only a few of the top wines reach the target; for the price, Tuscan Cabernet is often more exciting.

Tough, tannic long-haul boys Bordeaux does lead this field, and the best wines are really good after 10 years or so – but don't expect wines from minor properties to age in the same way. It's the same in Tuscany and Piedmont – only the top wines last well – especially Brunello di Montalcino, Vino Nobile di Montepulciano, some DOCG and IGT wines from Chianti Classico, Barolo and Barbaresco. In Portugal there are some increasingly good long-lasting Douro reds.

Soft, strawberryish charmers Good Burgundy definitely tops this group. Rioja in Spain can sometimes get there, as can Navarra and Valdepeñas. Pinot Noir in California, Oregon and New Zealand is frequently delicious, and Chile and Australia increasingly get it right too. Germany hits the spot with Spätburgunder (Pinot Noir) now and then. Italy's Lago di Caldaro often smooches in; and over in Bordeaux, of all places, both St-Émilion and Pomerol can do the business.

SPARKLING AND FORTIFIED WINES

Fizz This can be white or pink or red, dry or sweet, and I sometimes think it doesn't matter what it tastes like as long as it's cold enough and there's enough of it. Champagne can be best, but frequently isn't – and there are lots of new-wave winemakers making good-value lookalikes. Australia is tops for tasty bargains, followed by California and New Zealand. Spain pumps out oceans of good basic stuff.

Fortified wines For once in my life I find myself saying that the old ways are definitely the best. There's nothing to beat the top ports and sherries in the deep, rich, sticky stakes – though for the glimmerings of a new angle look to Australia, California and South Africa. The Portuguese island of Madeira produces fortifieds with rich, brown smoky flavours and a startling acid bite – and don't forget the luscious Muscats made all round the Mediterranean.

11

MATCHING FOOD AND WINE

Give me a rule, I'll break it – well, bend it anyway. So when I see the proliferation of publications laying down rules as to what wine to drink with what food, I get very uneasy and have to quell a burning desire to slosh back a Grand Cru Burgundy with my chilli con carne.

The pleasures of eating and drinking operate on so many levels that hard and fast rules make no sense. What about mood? If I'm in the mood for Champagne, Champagne it shall be, whatever I'm eating. What about place? If I'm sitting gazing out across the shimmering Mediterranean, hand me anything, just as long as it's local – it'll be perfect.

Even so, there are some things that simply don't go well with wine: artichokes, asparagus, spinach, kippers and mackerel, chilli, salsas and vinegars, chocolate, all flatten the flavours of wines. The general rule here is avoid tannic red wines and go for juicy young reds, or whites with plenty of fruit and fresh acidity. And for chocolate, liqueur Muscats, raisiny Banyuls or Italy's grapy, frothy Asti all work, but some people like powerful Italian reds such as Barolo or Amarone. Don't be afraid to experiment. Who would guess that salty Roquefort cheese and rich, sweet Sauternes would go together? But they do, and it's a match made in heaven. So, with these factors in mind, the following pairings are not rules – just my recommendations.

FISH

Grilled or baked white fish
White Burgundy or other fine Chardonnay, white Bordeaux, Viognier, Australian and New Zealand Riesling and Sauvignon.
Grilled or baked oily or 'meaty' fish (e.g. salmon, tuna, swordfish) Alsace or Austrian Riesling, Grüner Veltliner, fruity New World Chardonnay or Semillon; reds such as Chinon or Bourgueil, Grenache/Garnacha, or New World Pinot Noir.
Fried/battered fish Simple, fresh whites, e.g. Soave, Mâcon-Villages, Verdelho, Pinot Gris, white Bordeaux, or a Riesling Spätlese from the Pfalz.
Shellfish Chablis or unoaked Chardonnay, Sauvignon Blanc, Pinot Blanc; *clams and oysters* Albariño, Aligoté, Vinho Verde, Seyval Blanc; *crab* Riesling, Viognier; *lobster, scallops* fine Chardonnay, Champagne, Viognier; *mussels* Muscadet, Pinot Grigio.
Smoked fish Ice-cold basic fizz, manzanilla or fino sherry, Riesling, Sauvignon Blanc, Alsace Gewurztraminer or Pinot Gris.

MEAT

Beef and lamb are perfect with just about any red wine.
Beef/steak *Plain roasted or grilled* tannic reds, Bordeaux, New World Cabernet Sauvignon, Ribera del Duero, Chianti Classico, Pinotage.
Lamb *Plain roasted or grilled* red Burgundy, red Bordeaux, especially Pauillac or St-Julien, Rioja Reserva, New World Pinot Noir, Merlot or Malbec.
Pork *Plain roasted or grilled* full, spicy dry whites, e.g. Alsace Pinot Gris, lightly oaked Chardonnay; smooth reds, e.g. Rioja, Alentejo; *ham, bacon, sausages, salami* young, fruity reds, e.g. Beaujolais, Lambrusco, Teroldego, unoaked Tempranillo or Garnacha, New World Malbec, Merlot, Zinfandel/Primitivo, Pinotage.
Veal *Plain roasted or grilled* full-bodied whites, e.g. Pinot Gris, Grüner Veltliner, white Rioja; soft reds, e.g. mature Rioja or Pinot Noir; *with cream-based sauce* full, ripe whites, e.g. Alsace Pinot Blanc or Pinot Gris, Vouvray, oaked New World Chardonnay; *with rich red-wine sauce* (e.g. *osso*

buco) young Italian reds, Zinfandel.

Venison *Plain roasted or grilled* Barolo, St-Estèphe, Pomerol, Côte de Nuits, Hermitage, big Zinfandel, Alsace or German Pinot Gris; *with red-wine sauce* Piedmont and Portuguese reds, Pomerol, St-Émilion, New World Syrah/Shiraz or Pinotage, Priorat.

Chicken and turkey Most red and white wines go with these meats – much depends on the sauce or accompaniments. Try red or white Burgundy, red Rioja Reserva, New World Chardonnay.

Duck Pomerol, St-Émilion, Côte de Nuits or Rhône reds, New World Syrah/Shiraz (including sparkling) or Merlot; also full, soft whites from Austria and southern Germany.

Game birds *Plain roasted or grilled* top reds from Burgundy, Rhône, Tuscany, Piedmont, Ribera del Duero, New World Cabernet or Merlot; also full whites such as oaked New World Semillon.

Casseroles and stews Generally uncomplicated, full-flavoured reds. The thicker the sauce, the fuller the wine. If wine is used in the preparation, match the colour. For strong tomato flavours see Pasta.

HIGHLY SPICED FOOD

Chinese Riesling, Sauvignon, Pinot Gris, Gewürztraminer, unoaked New World Chardonnay; fruity rosé; light Pinot Noir.

Indian Aromatic whites, e.g. Riesling, Sauvignon Blanc, Gewürztraminer, Viognier; non-tannic reds, e.g. Valpolicella, Rioja, Grenache.

Mexican Fruity reds, e.g. Merlot, Cabernet Franc, Grenache, Syrah/Shiraz, Zinfandel.

Thai/South-East Asian Spicy or tangy whites, e.g. Riesling, Gewürztraminer, New World Sauvignon Blanc, dry Alsace Muscat. Coconut is tricky: New World Chardonnay may work.

EGG DISHES

Champagne and traditional-method fizz; light, fresh reds such as Beaujolais or Chinon; full, dry unoaked whites; New World rosé.

PASTA, PIZZA

With tomato sauce Barbera, Valpolicella, Soave, Verdicchio, New World Sauvignon Blanc; *with meat-based sauce* north or central Italian reds, French or New World Syrah/Shiraz, Zinfandel; *with cream- or cheese-based sauce* gently oaked Chardonnay, though the Italians would drink unoaked whites from northern Italy; Valpolicella or soft Merlot; *with seafood/fish sauce* dry, tangy whites, e.g. Verdicchio, Vermentino, Grüner Veltliner, Muscadet; *with pesto* New World Sauvignon Blanc, Dolcetto, Languedoc reds.
Basic pizza, with tomato, mozzarella and oregano juicy young reds, e.g. Grenache/Garnacha, Valpolicella, Austrian reds, Languedoc reds.

SALADS

Sharp-edged whites, e.g. New World Sauvignon Blanc, Chenin Blanc, dry Riesling, Vinho Verde.

CHEESES

Hard Full reds from Italy, France or Spain, New World Merlot or Zinfandel, dry oloroso sherry, tawny port.

Soft LBV port, Zinfandel, Alsace Pinot Gris, Gewürztraminer.

Blue Botrytized sweet whites such as Sauternes, vintage port, old oloroso sherry, Malmsey Madeira.

Goats' Sancerre, Pouilly-Fumé, New World Sauvignon Blanc, Chinon, Saumur-Champigny.

DESSERTS

Chocolate Australian Liqueur Muscat, Asti, Banyuls.

Fruit-based Sauternes, Eiswein, fortified European Muscats.

MATCHING WINE AND FOOD

With very special bottles, when you have found an irresistible bargain or when you are casting around for culinary inspiration, it can be a good idea to let the wine dictate the choice of food.

Although I said earlier that rules in this area are made to be bent if not broken, there are certain points to remember when matching wine and food. Before you make specific choices, think about some basic characteristics and see how thinking in terms of grape varieties and wine styles can point you in the right direction.

In many cases, the local food and wine combinations that have evolved over the years simply cannot be bettered (think of ripe Burgundy with *coq au vin* or *boeuf bourguignon*; Chianti Riserva with *bistecca alla Fiorentina*; Muscadet and Breton oysters). Yet the world of food and wine is moving so fast that it would be madness to be restricted by the old tenets. Californian cuisine, fusion food, and the infiltration of innumerable ethnic influences coupled with the re-invigoration of traditional wines, continuous experiment with new methods and blends and the opening up of completely new wine areas mean that the search for perfect food and wine partners is, and will remain, very much an on-going process.

Here are some of the characteristics you need to consider, plus a summary of the main grape varieties and their best food matches.

Body/weight As well as considering the taste of the wine you need to match the weight or body of the wine to the intensity of the food's flavour. A heavy alcoholic wine will not suit a delicate dish; and *vice versa.*

Acidity The acidity of a dish should balance the acidity of a wine. High-acid flavours, such as tomato, lemon or vinegar, need matching acidity in their accompanying wines. Use acidity in wine to cut through the richness of a dish but for this to work, make sure the wine is full in flavour.

Sweetness Sweet food makes dry wine taste unpleasantly lean and acidic. With desserts and puddings find a wine that is at least as sweet as the food (sweeter than the food is fine). However, many savoury foods, such as carrots, onions and parsnips, taste slightly sweet and dishes in which they feature prominently will go best with ripe, fruity wines that have a touch of sweetness.

Salt Salty foods and sweet wines match, but salty foods and tannin are definitely best avoided.

Age/Maturity The bouquet of a wine is only acquired over time and should be savoured and appreciated: with age many red wines acquire complex flavours and perfumes and a similar degree of complexity in the flavour of the food is often a good idea.

Tannin Rare red meat can have the effect of softening tannic wine. Avoid eggs and fish.

Oak Oak flavours in wine vary from the satisfyingly subtle to positively strident. This latter end of the scale can conflict with food, although it may be suitable for smoked fish (white wines only) or full-flavoured meat or game.

Wine in the food If you want to use wine in cooking it is best to use the same style of wine as the one you are going to drink with the meal (it can be an inferior version though).

RED GRAPES

Barbera Wines made to be drunk young have high acidity that can hold their own with sausages, salami, ham, and tomato sauces. Complex older or oak-aged wines from the top growers need to be matched with rich food such as beef casseroles and game dishes.

Cabernet Franc Best drunk with plain rather than sauced meat dishes, or, slightly chilled, with grilled or baked salmon or trout.

Cabernet Sauvignon All over the world the Cabernet Sauvignon makes full-flavoured reliable red wine: the ideal food wine. Cabernet Sauvignon seems to have a particular affinity for lamb, but it partners all plain roast or grilled meats and game well and would be an excellent choice for many sauced meat dishes such as beef casserole, steak and kidney pie or rabbit stew and substantial dishes made with mushrooms.

Dolcetto Dolcetto produces fruity purple wines that go beautifully with hearty meat dishes such as calves' liver and onions or casseroled game with polenta.

Gamay The grape of red Beaujolais, Gamay makes wine you can drink whenever, wherever, however and with whatever you want – although it's particularly good lightly chilled on hot summer days. It goes well with pâtés, bacon and sausages because its acidity provides a satisfying foil to their richness. It would be a good choice for many vegetarian dishes.

Grenache/Garnacha Generally blended with other grapes, Grenache nonetheless dominates, with its high alcoholic strength and rich, spicy flavours. These are wines readily matched with food: barbecues and casseroles for heavier wines; almost anything for lighter reds and rosés – vegetarian dishes, charcuterie, picnics, grills, and even meaty fish such as tuna and salmon.

Merlot Merlot makes soft, rounded, fruity wines that are some of the easiest red wines to enjoy without food, yet are also a good choice with many kinds of food. Spicier game dishes, herby terrines and pâtés, pheasant, pigeon, duck or goose all team well with Merlot; substantial casseroles made with wine are excellent with top Pomerols; and the soft fruitiness of the wines is perfect for pork, liver, turkey, and savoury foods with a hint of sweetness such as honey-roast or Parma ham.

Nebbiolo Lean but fragrant, early-drinking styles of Nebbiolo wine are best with local salami, pâtés, *bresaola* and lighter meat dishes. Top Barolos and Barbarescos need substantial food: *bollito misto*, rich hare or beef casseroles and *brasato al Barolo* (a large piece of beef marinated then braised slowly in Barolo) are just the job in Piedmont, or anywhere else for that matter.

Pinot Noir The great grape of Burgundy has taken its food-friendly complexity all over the wine world. However, nothing can beat the marriage of great wine with sublime local food that is Burgundy's heritage, and it is Burgundian dishes that spring to mind as perfect partners for the Pinot Noir: *coq au vin*, *boeuf bourguignon*, rabbit with mustard, braised ham, chicken with tarragon, *entrecôtes* from prized Charolais cattle with a rich red-wine sauce ... the list is endless.

Pinot Noir's subtle flavours make it a natural choice for complex meat dishes, but it is also excellent with plain grills and roasts. New World Pinots are often richer and fruitier – excellent with grills and roasts and a good match for salmon or tuna.

In spite of the prevalence of superb cheese in Burgundy, the best Pinot Noir red wines are wasted on cheese.

Sangiovese Tuscany is where Sangiovese best expresses the qualities that can lead it, in the right circumstances, to be numbered among the great grapes of the world. And Tuscany is very much 'food with wine' territory. Sangiovese wines such as Chianti, Rosso di Montalcino, Vino Nobile di Montepulciano, and the biggest of them all, Brunello, positively demand to be drunk with food. Drink them with *bistecca alla Fiorentina*, roast meats and game, calves' liver, casseroles, hearty pasta sauces, *porcini* mushrooms and Pecorino cheese.

Syrah/Shiraz Whether from France (the Rhône Valley and Languedoc), Australia, California, South America or South Africa, this grape always makes powerful, rich, full-bodied wines that are superb with full-flavoured food. The classic barbecue wine, Shiraz/Syrah also goes with roasts, game, hearty casseroles and charcuterie. It can also be good with tangy cheeses such as Manchego or Cheshire.

Tempranillo Spain's best native red grape makes juicy wines for drinking young, and matures well in a rich (usually) oaky style. Tempranillo is good with game,

cured hams and sausages, casseroles and meat grilled with herbs; it is particularly good with lamb. It can partner some Indian and Mexican dishes.

Zinfandel California's much-planted, most versatile grape is used for a bewildering variety of wine styles from bland, slightly sweet pinks to rich, succulent, fruity reds. And the good red Zinfandels themselves may vary greatly in style, from relatively soft and light to big and beefy, but they're always ripe and ready for spicy, smoky, unsubtle food: barbecued meat, haunches of lamb, venison or beef, game casseroles, sausages, Tex-Mex or anything rowdy – Zin copes with them all.

WHITE GRAPES

Albariño Light, crisp, aromatic in a grapefruity way, this goes well with crab and prawn dishes as well as Chinese-style chicken dishes.

Aligoté This Burgundian grape can, at its best, make very versatile food wine. It goes well with many fish and seafood dishes, smoked fish, salads and snails in garlic and butter.

Chardonnay More than almost any other grape, Chardonnay responds to different climatic conditions and to the winemaker's art. This, plus the relative ease with which it can be grown, accounts for the marked gradation of flavours and styles: from steely, cool-climate austerity to almost tropical lusciousness. The relatively sharp end of the spectrum is one of the best choices for simple fish dishes; most Chardonnays are superb with roast chicken or other white meat; the really full, rich, New World blockbusters need rich fish and seafood dishes. Oaky Chardonnays are, surprisingly, a good choice for smoked fish.

Chenin Blanc One of the most versatile of grapes, Chenin Blanc makes wines ranging from averagely quaffable dry whites to the great sweet whites of the Loire. The lighter wines can be good as aperitifs or with light fish dishes or salads. The sweet wines are good with fruit puddings and superb with those made with slightly tart fruit.

Gewürztraminer Spicy and perfumed, Gewürztraminer has the weight and flavour to go with such hard-to-match dishes as *choucroute* and smoked fish. It is also a good choice for Chinese or any lightly spiced oriental food and pungent soft cheeses.

Grüner Veltliner In its lightest form, this makes a peppery, refreshing aperitif. Riper, more structured versions keep the pepper but add peach and apple fruit, and are particularly good with grilled or baked fish.

Marsanne These rich, fat wines are a bit short of acidity, so match them with simply prepared chicken, pork, fish or vegetables.

Muscadet The dry, light Muscadet grape (best wines are *sur lie*) is perfect with seafood.

Muscat Fragrant, grapy wines coming in a multitude of styles, from delicate to downright syrupy. The drier ones are more difficult to pair with food, but can be delightful with oriental cuisines; the sweeties really come into their own with most desserts. Sweet Moscato d'Asti, delicious by itself, goes well with rich Christmas pudding or mince pies.

Pinot Blanc Clean, bright and appley, Pinot Blanc is very food-friendly. Classic white wine dishes, modern vegetarian dishes, pasta and pizza all match up well.

Pinot Gris In Alsace, this makes rich, fat wines that need rich, fat food: *choucroute*, *confit de canard*, rich pork and fish dishes. Italian Pinot Grigio wines are light quaffers. New World Pinot Gris is often delightfully fragrant and ideal with grilled fish.

Riesling Good dry Rieslings are excellent with spicy cuisine. Sweet Rieslings are best enjoyed for their own lusciousness but are suitable partners to fruit-based desserts. In between, those with a fresh acid bite and some residual sweetness can counteract the richness of, say, goose or duck, and the fuller examples can be good with oriental food and otherwise hard-to-match salads.

Sauvignon Blanc Tangy green flavours and high acidity are the hallmarks of this grape. Led by New Zealand, New World Sauvignons are some of the snappiest, tastiest whites around. Brilliant with seafood and Oriental cuisine, they also go well with tomato dishes and goats' cheese.

Sémillon/Semillon Dry Bordeaux Blancs are excellent with fish and shellfish; fuller, riper New World Semillons are equal to spicy food and rich sauces, often going even better with meat than with fish; sweet Sémillons can partner many puddings, especially rich, creamy ones. Sémillon also goes well with many cheeses, and Sauternes with Roquefort is a classic combination.

Viognier Viognier is at its best as an aperitif. It can also go well with spicy Indian dishes.

MAKING THE MOST OF WINE

Most wine is pretty hardy stuff and can put up with a fair amount of rough handling. Young red wines can knock about in the back of a car for a day or two and be lugged from garage to kitchen to dinner table without coming to too much harm. Serving young white wines when well chilled can cover up all kinds of ill-treatment – a couple of hours in the fridge should do the trick. Even so, there are some conditions that are better than others for storing your wines, especially if they are on the mature side. And there are certain ways of serving wines which will emphasize any flavours or perfumes they have.

STORING

Most wines are sold ready for drinking, and it will be hard to ruin them if you store them for a few months before you pull the cork. Don't stand them next to the central heating or the cooker, though, or on a sunny windowsill.

Light and extremes of temperature are also the things to worry about if you are storing wine long-term. Some wines, Chardonnay for instance, are particularly sensitive to exposure to light over several months, and the damage will be worse if the bottle is made of pale-coloured glass. The warmer the wine, the quicker it will age, and really high temperatures can spoil wine quite quickly. Beware in the winter of garages and outhouses, too: a very cold snap – say –4°C (25°F) or below – will freeze your wine, push out the corks and crack the bottles. An underground cellar is ideal, with a fairly constant temperature of 10°–12°C (50°–53°F). And bottles really do need to lie on their sides, so that the cork stays damp and swollen, and keeps out the air.

TEMPERATURE

The person who thought up the rule that red wine should be served at room temperature certainly didn't live in a modern, centrally heated flat. It's no great sin to serve a big, beefy red at the temperature of your central heating, but I prefer most reds just a touch cooler. Over-heated wine tastes flabby, and may lose some of its more volatile aromas. In general, the lighter the red, the cooler it can be. Really light, refreshing reds, such as Beaujolais, are nice lightly chilled. Ideally, I'd serve Burgundy and other Pinot Noir wines at larder temperature (about 15°C/59°F), Bordeaux and Rioja a bit warmer (18°C/64°F), Rhône wines and New World Cabernet at a comfortable room temperature, but no more than 20°C/68°F.

Chilling white wines makes them taste fresher, emphasizing their acidity. White wines with low acidity especially benefit from chilling, and it's vital for sparkling wines if you want to avoid exploding corks and a tableful of froth. Drastic chilling also subdues flavours, however – a useful ruse if you're serving basic wine, but a shame if the wine is very good. A good guide for whites is to give the cheapest and lightest a spell in the fridge, but serve bigger and better wines – Australian Chardonnays or top white Burgundies – perhaps half-way between fridge and central-heating temperature. If you're undecided, err on the cooler side, for whites or reds. To chill wine quickly, and to keep it cool, an ice bucket is more efficient if filled with a mixture of ice and water, rather than ice alone.

OPENING THE BOTTLE

There's no corkscrew to beat the Screwpull, and the Spinhandle Screwpull is especially easy to use. Don't worry if bits of cork crumble into the wine – just fish them out of your glass. Tight corks that refuse to budge might be loosened if you run hot water over the bottle neck to expand the glass. If the cork is loose and falls in, push it right in and don't worry about it.

Opening sparkling wines is a serious business – point the cork away from people! Once you've started, never take your hand off the cork until it's safely out. Remove the foil, loosen the wire, hold the wire and cork firmly and twist the bottle. If the wine froths, hold the bottle at an angle of 45 degrees, and have a glass at hand.

AIRING AND DECANTING

Scientists have proved that opening young to middle-aged red wines an hour before serving makes no difference whatsoever. The surface area of wine in contact with air in the bottle neck is too tiny to be significant. Decanting is a different matter, because sloshing the wine from bottle to jug or decanter mixes it up quite thoroughly with the air. The only wines that really need to be decanted are those that have a sediment which would cloud the wine if they were poured directly – mature red Bordeaux, Burgundy and vintage port are the commonest examples. Ideally, if you are able to plan that far in advance, you need to stand the bottle upright for a day or two to let the sediment settle in the bottom. Draw the cork extremely gently. As you tip the bottle, shine a bright light through from underneath as you pour in a single steady movement. Stop pouring when you see the sediment approaching the bottle neck.

Contrary to many wine buffs' practice, I would decant a mature wine only just before serving; elderly wines often fade rapidly once they meet with air, and an hour in the decanter could kill off what little fruit they had left. By contrast, a good-quality young white wine can benefit from decanting.

GLASSES

If you want to taste wine at its best, to enjoy all its flavours and aromas, to admire its colours and texture, choose glasses designed for the purpose and show the wine a bit of respect. The ideal wine glass is a fairly large tulip shape, made of fine, clear glass, with a slender stem. When you pour the wine, fill the glass no more than halfway to allow space for aromas. For sparkling wines choose a tall, slender glass, as it helps the bubbles to last longer.

KEEPING LEFTOVERS

Leftover white wine keeps better than red, since the tannin and colouring matter in red wine is easily attacked by the air. Any wine, red or white, keeps better in the fridge than in a warm kitchen. And most wines, if well made in the first place, will be perfectly acceptable, if not pristine, after 2 or 3 days re-corked in the fridge. But for better results it's best to use one of the gadgets sold for this purpose. The ones that work by blanketing the wine with heavier-than-air inert gas are much better than those that create a vacuum in the air space in the bottle.

FRANCE

I've visited most of the wine-producing countries of the world, but the one I come back to again and again, with my enthusiasm undimmed by time, is France. The sheer range of its wine flavours, the number of wine styles produced, and indeed the quality differences, from very best to very nearly worst, continue to enthral me, and as each year's vintage nears, I find myself itching to leap into the car and head for the vineyards of Champagne, of Burgundy, of Bordeaux and the Loire. France is currently going through a difficult period – aware that the New World is making tremendous strides and is the master of innovation and technology, yet unwilling to admit to the quality and character of this new breed of wines. But the best French producers learn from the newcomers while proudly defining their Frenchness.

CLIMATE AND SOIL

France lies between the 40th and 50th parallels north, and the climate runs from the distinctly chilly and almost too cool to ripen grapes in the far north near the English Channel, right through to the swelteringly hot and almost too torrid to avoid grapes overripening in the far south on the Mediterranean shores. In the north, the most refined and delicate sparkling wine is made in Champagne. In the south, rich, luscious dessert Muscats and fortified wines dominate. In between is just about every sort of wine you could wish for.

The factors that influence a wine's flavour are the grape variety, the soil and climate, and the winemaker's techniques. Most of the great wine grapes, like the red Cabernet Sauvignon, Merlot, Pinot Noir and Syrah, and the white Chardonnay, Sauvignon Blanc, Sémillon and Viognier, find conditions in France where they can ripen slowly but reliably – and slow, even ripening always gives better flavours to a wine. Since grapes have been grown for over 2000 years in France, the most suitable varieties for the different soils and meso-climates have naturally evolved. And since winemaking was brought to France by the Romans, generation upon generation of winemakers have refined their techniques to produce the best possible results from their different grape types. The great wines of areas like Bordeaux and Burgundy are the results of centuries of experience and of trial and error, which winemakers from other countries of the world now use as role models in their attempts to create good wine.

WINE REGIONS

White grapes generally ripen more easily than red grapes and they dominate the northern regions. Even so, the chilly Champagne region barely manages to ripen its red or white grapes on its chalky soil. But the resultant acid wine is the ideal base for sparkling wine: with good winemaking and a few years' maturing, the young still wine can transform into a golden honeyed sparkling wine of incomparable finesse.

Alsace, on the German border, is warmer and drier than Champagne (the vineyards sit in a rain shadow created by the Vosges mountains that rise above the Rhine Valley) but still produces mainly dry white wines, from grapes such as Riesling, Pinot Gris and Gewurztraminer that are not widely encountered elsewhere in France. With its clear blue skies, Alsace can provide ripeness, and therefore the higher alcoholic strength of the warm south, but also the perfume and fragrance of the cool north.

South-east of Paris, Chablis marks the northernmost tip of the Burgundy region, and the Chardonnay grape here produces very dry wines, usually with a streak of green acidity, but nowadays with a fuller softer texture to subdue any harshness.

It's a good 2 hours' drive further south to the heart of Burgundy – the Côte d'Or, which runs between Dijon and Chagny. World-famous villages such as Gevrey-Chambertin and Vosne-Romanée (where the red Pinot Noir dominates) and Meursault and Puligny-Montrachet (where Chardonnay reigns) here produce the great Burgundies that have given the region renown over the centuries. Lesser Burgundies – but they're still good – are produced further south in the Côte Chalonnaise, while between Mâcon and Lyon are the white Mâconnais wine villages (Pouilly-Fuissé and St-Véran are particularly tasty) and the villages of Beaujolais, famous for bright, easy-going red wine from the Gamay grape. The 10 Beaujolais Crus or 'growths' are the most important communes and should produce wine with more character and structure.

South of Lyon, in the Rhône Valley, red wines begin to dominate. The Syrah grape makes great wine at Hermitage and Côte-Rôtie in the north, while in the south the Grenache and a host of supporting grapes (most southern Rhône reds will include at least Syrah, Cinsaut or Mourvèdre in their blends) make full, satisfying reds, of which Châteauneuf-du-Pape is the most famous. The white Viognier makes lovely wine at Condrieu and Château-Grillet in the north.

21

The whole of the south of France has undergone considerable change over the last 20 years and is still improving at a bewildering rate, often prompted by a new generation or a change in ownership. Provence and the scorched Midi vineyards are learning how to produce exciting wines from unpromising land and many of France's tastiest and most affordable wines now come under a Vin de Pays label from the south. In the Languedoc the red wines from traditional vineyards of Grenache, Syrah, Mourvèdre and Carignan can be exceptional, and in the Roussillon the sweet Muscats and Grenache-based fortifieds are equally fine.

The South-West of France is dominated by the wines of Bordeaux, but has many other gems benefiting from the cooling influence of the Atlantic. Dry whites from Gascony and Bergerac can be exciting. Jurançon down in the Basque country produces some remarkable dry and sweet wines, while Madiran, Cahors and Bergerac produce good to excellent reds.

But Bordeaux is the king here. The Cabernet Sauvignon and Merlot are the chief grapes, the Cabernet dominating the production of deep reds from the Médoc peninsula and its famous villages of Margaux, St-Julien, Pauillac and St-Estèphe on the left bank of the Gironde river. Round the city of Bordeaux are Pessac-Léognan and Graves, where Cabernet and Merlot blend to produce fragrant refined reds. On the right bank of the Gironde estuary, the Merlot is most important in the plump rich reds of St-Émilion and Pomerol. Sweet whites from Sémillon and Sauvignon Blanc are made in Sauternes, with increasingly good dry whites produced in the Entre-Deux-Mers, and especially in Graves and Pessac-Léognan.

The Loire Valley is the most northerly of France's Atlantic wine regions but, since the river rises in the heart of France not far from the Rhône, styles vary widely. Sancerre and Pouilly in the east produce tangy Sauvignon whites and some surprising reds; the centre of the river produces fizzy wine at Vouvray and Saumur, sweet wine at Vouvray and the Layon Valley (Chenin Blanc is used for everything here, from sparkling wines to botrytized ones), red wines at Chinon and Bourgueil, and dry whites virtually everywhere; while down at the mouth of the river, as it slips past Nantes into the Atlantic swell, the vineyards of Muscadet produce one of the world's most famous and often least memorable dry white wines.

CLASSIFICATIONS

France has an intricate but eminently logical system for controlling the quality and authenticity of its wines. The system is divided into 4 broad classifications (in ascending order): Vin de Table, Vin de Pays, VDQS (Vin Délimité de Qualité Supérieure) and AC (Appellation Contrôlée). Within the laws there are numerous variations, with certain vineyards or producers singled out for special mention. The 1855 Classification in Bordeaux or the Grands Crus of Alsace or Burgundy are good examples. The intention is a system which rewards quality. Vin de Pays and VDQS wines can be promoted to AC, for example, after a few years' good behaviour. However, the AC system is now under increasing attack from critics, both inside and outside France, who feel that it is outmoded and ineffectual and that too many poor wines are passed as of Appellation Contrôlée standard.

2004 VINTAGE REPORT

After the extraordinary heatwave of 2003 Bordeaux was back to normal in 2004. A dry, sunny September and early October assisted the ripening, relieving anxiety after a spell of rain in August. The major problem was over-production, grapes everywhere, so producers really had to be out in the vineyards thinning the crop and tending the vines. Expect a fresher, more 'classic' style of red Bordeaux but a very mixed bag in terms of quality. The dry whites are fruity and zingy with good acidity. As for sweet wines, a tiny crop of botrytized grapes was picked in September but late October rain put paid to this being considered a memorable year.

In Burgundy, a fine September and October saved the day after a fairly miserable summer. Repeated hailstorms damaged the crop in some red wine villages, but the whites mostly escaped and look to be the better bet this year: healthy grapes with respectable sugar levels, correct acidity and fine aromas look set to produce some attractive wines. In Beaujolais, 2003 was limited in production and acidity was quite low; even so, Georges Duboeuf says it's the best vintage in his lifetime. 2004 was plentiful and generally light in colour; some really good wines have been made, but the general standard is mediocre.

In the Rhône the year was very dry until August rain. The vintage was saved by a dry, sunny September with beneficial winds. The northern reds have good, clear fruit and will be long-lived. Northern whites were very successful. Southern Rhône reds have good stuffing and are wholesome, well-filled wines. They should be long-lived, too.

In Languedoc the harvest was two weeks later than average. The problem was rot after a wet spring and cool summer, and it was a year in which attention in the vineyards paid off. Generally, reds are better than whites in both Languedoc and Provence. In the South-West, huge quantities of wine have filled the cellars with good reds and great whites.

The Loire reverted to tricky, uneven weather after the hot, dry vintage of 2003. Producers who worked hard in the vineyard and thinned their crops were rewarded with excellent wines showing typical Loire freshness but higher than average alcohol levels; the rest suffered rot, overcropping and underripeness. From the best expect very ripe, fresh and powerful Muscadets; pure, aromatic Sauvignons; intense, long-lived reds; excellent dry Chenins; and perfectly poised sweet wines.

In Alsace, too, crop thinning was essential to avoid both rot and excessive yields – but only the best producers were sufficiently rigorous in the wake of two small vintages. Riesling and Pinot Gris show the most initial promise among the very successful dry wines, with good fruit and balance. October rains dashed hopes for late-harvest and sweet wines.

The largest harvest on record in Champagne; unusually, it was also high in quality. Following a very wet and cool August, the harvest was saved by a dry and sunny September. Good, perhaps excellent, vintage wines are predicted.

See also ALSACE, BORDEAUX RED WINES, BORDEAUX WHITE WINES, BURGUNDY RED WINES, BURGUNDY WHITE WINES, CHAMPAGNE, CORSICA, JURA, LANGUEDOC-ROUSSILLON, LOIRE VALLEY, MIDI, PROVENCE, RHONE VALLEY, ROUSSILLON, SAVOIE, SOUTH-WEST FRANCE; and individual wines and producers.

ITALY

The cultivation of the vine was introduced to Italy around 3000 years ago, by the Greeks (to Sicily and the south) and by the Etruscans (to the north-east and central zones). Despite this great tradition, Italian wines as we know them today are relatively young. New attitudes have resulted, in the last 30 years or so, in a great change in Italian wine. The whole industry has been modernized, and areas like Tuscany are now among the most dynamic of any in the world. With her unique characteristics, challenging wine styles and mass of grape varieties, Italy is now ready again to take on the role of leadership she has avoided for so long.

GRAPE VARIETIES AND WINE REGIONS

Vines are grown all over Italy, from the Austrian border in the north-east to the island of Pantelleria in the far south, nearer to North Africa than to Sicily. The north-west, especially Piedmont, is the home of many of the best Italian red grapes, like Nebbiolo (the grape of Barolo and Barbaresco), Dolcetto and Barbera, while the north-east (Friuli-Venezia Giulia, Alto Adige and the Veneto) is more noted for the success of native white varieties like Garganega and Ribolla, reds like Corvina, and imports like Pinot Grigio, Chardonnay and Sauvignon.

The Po Valley is Lambrusco country west of Bologna, while San-giovese rules in the hills to the east. Tuscany is best known for its red Chianti and other wines from the native Sangiovese grape as well as its famed Super-Tuscans. South of Rome, where the Mediterranean climate holds sway, modern winemakers are revelling in the chance to make exciting wines from varieties of long tradition, such as Negroa-maro and Primitivo (Puglia), Aglianico, Fiano and Greco (Campania, Basilicata) and Gaglioppo (Calabria). The islands have their own vari-eties: red Nero d'Avola and white Inzolia in Sicily, red Cannonau and Carignano and white Vermentino in Sardinia.

CLASSIFICATIONS

Vino da Tavola, or 'table wine', is used for a wine that is produced either outside the existing laws, or in an area where no delimited zone exists. Both cheap, basic wines and inspired innovative creations like Tignanello, Sassicaia and other so-called Super-Tuscans used to fall into this anonymous category. Now the fancy wines have become either DOC (particularly in Piedmont with its Langhe DOC) or IGT. Remaining Vino da Tavola are labelled simply as *bianco, rosso* or *rosato* without vintages or geographical indications.

IGT (Indicazione Geografica Tipica) began taking effect with the 1995 vintage to identify wines from certain regions or areas as an equiv-alent of the French Vin de Pays. A great swathe of both ordinary and premium wines traded their Vino da Tavola status for a regional IGT.

DOC (Denominazione di Origine Controllata) is the main classification for wines from designated zones made following traditions that were historically valid but often outdated. Recently the laws have become more flexible, encouraging producers to reduce yields and modernize techniques, while bringing quality wines under new appellations that allow for recognition of communes, estates and single vineyards. If anything, the problem today is a surfeit of DOCs.

DOCG (Denominazione di Origine Controllata e Garantita) was con-ceived as a 'super-league' for DOCs with a guarantee of authenticity that promised high class but didn't always provide it. Wines are made under stricter standards that have favoured improvements, but the best guarantee of quality remains the producer's name.

2004 VINTAGE REPORT

After two very short harvests in 2002 and 2003, 2004 proved both abundant and of consistently high quality. Temperatures throughout the land remained moderate during the growing season, with positive day/night fluctuations, and rainfall was well spaced out, holding off at vintage time, in most cases, until picking was over, despite the gener-ally late harvest. The exception was along the east coast, from Abruzzo down to Puglia, where later-harvested vineyards got caught in the del-uge. White wines everywhere fared extremely well and the classics – Barolo, Barbaresco, Chianti, Brunello and Vino Nobile – were balanced and elegant. Generally a year to buy with confidence.

See also ABRUZZO, ALTO ADIGE, BASILICATA, CALABRIA, CAMPANIA, EMILIA-ROMAGNA, FRIULI-VENEZIA GIULIA, LAZIO, LIGURIA, LOMBARDY, MARCHE, PIEDMONT, PUGLIA, ROMAGNA, SARDINIA, SICILY, TRENTINO, TUSCANY, UMBRIA, VALLE D'AOSTA, VENETO; and individual wines and producers.

GERMANY

Dull, semi-sweet wines with names like Liebfraumilch, Niersteiner Gutes Domtal and Piesporter Michelsberg used to dominate the export market, but they are rapidly vanishing off all but the most basic radar screens. Though producers at present find exports difficult, single-estate wines, with a greatly improved quality, are now the focus of sales abroad. Throughout Germany, both red and white wines are year by year, region by region, grower by grower, becoming fuller, better balanced and drier.

GRAPE VARIETIES

Riesling makes the best wines, in styles ranging from dry to intensely sweet. Other white wines come from Grauburgunder/Ruländer (Pinot Gris), Weissburgunder (Pinot Blanc), Gewürztraminer, Silvaner and Scheurebe, although Müller-Thurgau produces much of the simpler wine. In the past decade, plantings of red grape varieties have doubled to fully 30% of the nation's vineyard. Good reds can be made in the south of the country from Spätburgunder (Pinot Noir), Dornfelder and Lemberger.

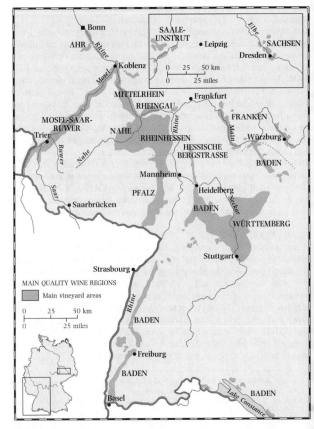

WINE REGIONS

Many of the most delectable Rieslings come from villages such as Bernkastel, Brauneberg, Ürzig and Wehlen on the Mosel, and Kiedrich, Johannisberg and Rüdesheim in the Rheingau. The Nahe makes superb Rieslings in Schlossböckelheim and Traisen, and Niederhausen has the best vineyards in the entire region. Rheinhessen is unfortunately better known for its sugary Niersteiner Gutes Domtal than it is for the excellent racy Rieslings produced on steep riverside slopes in the villages of Nackenheim and Nierstein. Franken is the one place the Silvaner grape excels, often made in a powerful, dry, earthy style. The Pfalz is climatically similar to Alsace and has a similar potential for well-rounded, dry whites, plus rapidly improving reds. Baden also produces fully ripe wine styles, which appeal to an international market increasingly reared on fuller, drier wines. In Württemberg most of the red wines are thin and dull, but there are a few producers who understand the need for weight and flavour. The other smaller wine regions make little wine and little is exported.

CLASSIFICATIONS

Germany's classification system is based on the ripeness of the grapes and therefore their potential alcohol level.

Tafelwein (table wine) is the most basic term, used for any blended wine, accounting for only a tiny percentage of production.

Landwein (country wine) is a slightly more up-market version, linked to 17 regional areas. These must be Trocken (dry) or Halbtrocken (medium-dry).

QbA (Qualitätswein bestimmter Anbaugebiete) is 'quality' wine from one of 13 designated regions, but the grapes don't have to be very ripe, and sugar can be added to the juice to increase alcoholic content.

QmP (Qualitätswein mit Prädikat) or 'quality wine with distinction' is the top level. There are 6 levels of QmP (in ascending order of ripeness): Kabinett, Spätlese, Auslese, Beerenauslese, Eiswein, Trockenbeerenauslese. The addition of sugar is strictly forbidden.

Since 2000, there have been 2 designations for varietal dry wines: **Classic** for 'good' wines and **Selection** for 'top-quality' wines. And an increasing number of good estates are using lengthy single-vineyard names only on their top selections.

The Rheingau has introduced an official classification – Erstes Gewächs (First Growth) – for its best sites. Other regions are evolving similar classifications – currently called Grosses Gewächs – to indicate top wines from top sites.

2004 VINTAGE REPORT

Despite a wet summer the grapes remained healthy, and ripened fully during a fine September and Indian summer. The result is a large but classic vintage – for producers who didn't overcrop – ripe and with good acidity levels, and a range of wines from dry styles to sweet rarities such as Trockenbeerenauslese.

See also AHR, BADEN, FRANKEN, HESSISCHE BERGSTRASSE, MITTELRHEIN, MOSEL-SAAR-RUWER, NAHE, PFALZ, RHEINGAU, RHEINHESSEN, SAALE-UNSTRUT, SACHSEN, WURTTEMBERG; and individual wine villages and producers.

AUSTRIA

I can't think of a European nation where the wine culture has changed so dramatically over a generation as it has in Austria. Austria still makes great sweet wines, but a new order based on world-class medium- and full-bodied dry whites and increasingly fine reds has emerged, including Austria's first territorial appellation, Weinviertel.

WINE REGIONS AND GRAPE VARIETIES

The Danube runs through Niederösterreich, scene of much of Austria's viticulture. The Wachau produces great Riesling and excellent pepper-dry Grüner Veltliner. Next along the Danube are Kremstal and Kamptal, also fine dry white regions with a few good reds. Burgenland, south of Vienna, produces the best reds and also, around the Neusiedler See, superb dessert wines. Further south, in Steiermark, Chardonnay and Sauvignon are increasingly oak-aged.

CLASSIFICATIONS

Wine categories are similar to those in Germany, beginning with **Tafelwein** (table wine) and **Landwein** (country wine). **Qualitätswein** must come from one of the 16 main wine-producing regions. Like German wines, quality wines may additionally have a special category: Kabinett, Spätlese, Auslese, Beerenauslese, Ausbruch, Trockenbeerenauslese. Since most Austrian wines are dry, these categories count for less than in Germany. The first Austrian appellations, known as DAC, are starting to appear.

2004 VINTAGE REPORT

Excellent conditions in the Burgenland resulted in outstanding dry white wines and some very good reds. For sweet wines it was a late vintage but a good one. Conditions were more problematic along the Danube in the Wachau and Kremstal.

See also BURGENLAND, CARNUNTUM, DONAULAND, KAMPTAL, KREMSTAL, STEIERMARK, THERMENREGION, WACHAU, WIEN; and individual wine villages and producers.

SPAIN

The late 1990s provided a dramatic turnaround in the quality of Spain's long-neglected wines. A drastic modernization of winemaking technology has now allowed regions like Priorat, Ribera del Duero, Rueda, Bierzo, Toro and La Mancha to muscle into the limelight, alongside Rioja and Jerez, with potent fruit-driven wines with the impact and style to convert the modern consumer.

WINE REGIONS

Galicia in the green, hilly north-west grows Spain's most aromatic whites. The heartland of the great Spanish reds, Rioja, Navarra and Ribera del Duero, is situated between the central plateau and the northern coast. Further west along the Duero, Rueda produces fresh whites and Toro good ripe reds. Cataluña is principally white wine country (much of it sparkling Cava), though there are some great reds in Priorat and increasingly in Terra Alta and new DO Montsant. Aragón's reds and whites are looking good too. The central plateau of La Mancha makes mainly cheap reds and whites, though non-DO producers are improving spectacularly. Valencia in the south-east can rival La Mancha for fresh, unmemorable but inexpensive reds and whites. Andalucía's specialities are the fortified wines – sherry, Montilla and Málaga.

CLASSIFICATIONS

Vino de Mesa, the equivalent of France's Vin de Table, is the lowest level, but is also used for a growing number of non-DO 'Super-Spanish'.
Vino de la Tierra is Spain's equivalent of France's Vin de Pays.
DO (Denominación de Origen) is the equivalent of France's AC, regulating grape varieties and region of origin.
DOCa (Denominación de Origen Calificada) is a super-category. For a long time Rioja was the only region to have been promoted to DOCa, but it has now been joined by Priorat.

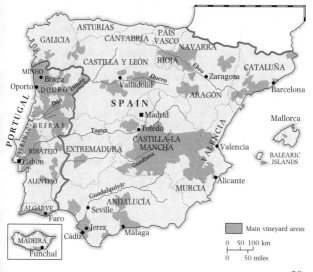

2004 VINTAGE REPORT
After the wet 2002 and the hot 2003, 2004 was uneven, particularly in eastern Spain. A cool summer and late August rains, with outbreaks of grey rot, were followed by fierce drought in September and October, which caused grape-shrivelling and ultimately high alcohol contents. A vintage in which grape selection was essential. Ribera del Duero came out on top, with uneven results in Rioja.

PORTUGAL

Investment and imagination are paying off in this attractive country, with climates that vary from the mild, damp Minho region in the north-west to the subtropical island of Madeira. Innovative use of native grapes and blending with international varieties means that Portugal is now a rich source of inexpensive yet characterful wines.

WINE REGIONS
The lush Vinho Verde country in the north-west gives very different wine from the parched valleys of the neighbouring Douro, with its drier, more continental climate. The Douro, home of port, is also the source of some of Portugal's best unfortified red wines. In Beiras, which includes Bairrada and Dão, soil types are crucial in determining the character of the wines. Estremadura and Ribatejo use native grape varieties to supply generous quantities of wine from regions either influenced by the maritime climate or softened by the river Tagus. South of Lisbon, the Terras do Sado and Alentejo produce some exciting table wines – and the Algarve is waking up. Madeira is unique, a volcanic island 850km (530 miles) out in the Atlantic Ocean.

CLASSIFICATIONS
Vinho Regional (9 in number) is equivalent to French Vin de Pays, with laws and permitted varieties much freer than for IPR and DOC.
IPR (Indicação de Proveniência Regulamentada) is the intermediate step for wine regions hoping to move up to DOC status. Many were promoted in 1999, leaving just 9 IPRs. Their wines are referred to as Vinhos de Qualidade Produzidos em Região Determinada (VQPRD).
DOC (Denominação de Origem Controlada) Equivalent to France's AC. Following necessary rationalization, there are now 23 DOC regions.

2004 VINTAGE REPORT
After the extremes of the previous two years, 2004 proved to be more amenable, though not without risks. The wettest August for over a century nearly ruined the vintage, but fine late summer weather in September saved the day. The Touriga Nacional grape produced particularly fine and fragrant reds in Dão and the Douro, and overall, 2004 has produced many well-balanced reds with intensity and acidity, which should hold them in good stead for years to come.

See also (SPAIN) ANDALUCIA, ARAGON, BALEARIC ISLANDS, CANARY ISLANDS, CASTILLA-LA MANCHA, CASTILLA Y LEON, CATALUNA, GALICIA; (PORTUGAL) ALENTEJO, ALGARVE, BEIRAS, ESTREMADURA, PORT, RIBATEJO, TERRAS DO SADO, TRAS-OS-MONTES; and individual wines and producers.

USA

The United States has more varied growing conditions for grapes than any other country in the world, which isn't so surprising when you consider that the 50 states of the Union cover an area that is larger than Western Europe; and although Alaska doesn't grow grapes in the icy far north, Washington State does in the north-west, as does Texas in the south and New York State in the north-east, and even Hawaii, lost in the pounding surf of the Pacific Ocean, manages to grow grapes and make wine. Every state, even Alaska (thanks to salmonberry and fireweed), now produces wine of some sort or another; it ranges from some pretty dire offerings, which would have been far better distilled into brandy, to some of the greatest and most original wines to be found in the world today.

GRAPE VARIETIES AND WINE REGIONS

California is far and away the most important state for wine production. In its determination to match the best red Bordeaux and white Burgundy, California proved that it was possible to take the classic European role models and successfully re-interpret them in an area thousands of miles away from their home. However, there is more to California than this. The Central Valley produces the majority of the simple beverage wines that still dominate the American market. Napa and Sonoma Counties north of San Francisco Bay do produce

great Cabernet and Chardonnay, but grapes like Zinfandel and Merlot also make their mark and the Carneros and Russian River Valley areas are highly successful for Pinot Noir, Chardonnay and sparkling wines. In the north, Mendocino and Lake Counties produce good grapes. South of San Francisco, in the cool, foggy valleys between Santa Cruz and Santa Barbara, Chardonnay, Pinot Noir and Syrah are producing exciting cool-climate but ripe-flavoured wines.

Oregon, with a cooler and more capricious climate than most of California, perseveres with Pinot Noir, Chardonnay, Pinot Gris, Pinot Blanc and Riesling with patchy success. Washington, so chilly and misty on the coast, becomes virtual desert east of the Cascade Mountains and it is here, in irrigated vineyards, that superb reds and whites can be made, with thrillingly focused fruit.

New Yorkers are showing that Long Island has all the makings of a classic region: this warm, temperate claw of land to the east of New York City is well suited to Merlot, Cabernet Franc and Chardonnay. Finger Lakes and the Hudson Valley have made a name with Riesling, Chardonnay and sparklers, and improved vineyard management has led to advances with reds, especially Pinot Noir and Cabernet Franc.

Of the other states, Texas has the most widespread plantings of classic vinifera wine varieties, but producers of excellence also exist in Virginia, Maryland and Pennsylvania on the east coast, and Idaho, Arizona and New Mexico in the west.

CLASSIFICATIONS
The AVA (American Viticultural Area) system was introduced in the 1980s. It does not guarantee a quality standard, but merely requires that at least 85% of grapes in a wine come from a specified area. There are over 135 AVAs, nearly 90 of which are in California.

2004 VINTAGE REPORT
Most of northern California experienced a warm spring in 2004, getting the vines off to a fast start. There followed two months of cool weather, and most growers expected an early, easy harvest. By late August, Cabernet Sauvignon in the Napa Valley was ripening well and growers thought they could pick in a few days. Then came the first of eight straight days of temperatures over 39°C (102°F). As a result, many growers irrigated to keep photosynthesis going. Still, in some areas of Napa and Sonoma, it was one of the earliest harvests in decades, running three to four weeks ahead of normal. The first grapes, for sparkling wine, were picked on 23 July. Quality was initially rated as excellent, but could be patchy.

In Washington, for a second year, a (2003) Halloween night freeze weakened vines. A hard freeze on 5 January left many vineyards severely damaged in the Yakima and Walla Walla Valleys, and crop levels across the state were affected. Cold, wet weather in early summer caused uneven flowering and fruit set. July and August were hot, with temperatures reaching 32°C (90°F) for days in a row. The hot weather broke in early September and there was a long cool spell of two weeks. A late blast of sunny weather brought on the harvest under ideal conditions. Merlot seemed to perform extremely well.

In Oregon, a cold spell in January and wet weather in early summer resulted in reduced yields: Pinot Noir down by as much as 25%, Chardonnay and Pinot Gris by 10–15%. After a hot summer, rainy, cold conditions lasted from 21 August to mid-September. A hot spell of two weeks was followed by more rain and then very cold weather. Most wines have high alcohol levels and lots of flavour.

The Eastern US had another soggy vintage, though not as rainy as 2003. New York's Finger Lakes region suffered a devastating winter, with entire vineyards wiped out by prolonged sub-zero temperatures.

See also CALIFORNIA, NEW YORK STATE, OREGON, TEXAS, VIRGINIA, WASHINGTON STATE; and individual wine areas and wineries.

AUSTRALIA

Australian wine today enjoys a reputation still well out of proportion to the quantity of wine produced (total output is about one-fifth that of France), though volumes are mushrooming. The New World wine revolution – emphasizing ripe, rich fruit, seductive use of oak, labelling by grape variety and consumer-friendly marketing – has been led by wine warriors from the southern seas. There's more than enough sunshine and not nearly enough rain to grow the grapes, so most growers are guaranteed ripeness but rely heavily on irrigation for their vines to survive. Dynamic and innovative winemakers ensure a steady supply of new wines, wineries and even regions, but consolidation and internationalization of larger operators seems to be causing an unwarranted and unwelcome dumbing down of flavour.

GRAPE VARIETIES
Varietal wines remain more prized than blends. Shiraz has long been a key varietal and is more fashionable than Cabernet Sauvignon, while the position of Chardonnay remains unchallenged. Pinot Noir, Semillon and Riesling lead the pack of alternative varieties.

WINE REGIONS
Western Australia is a vast state, virtually desert except for its southwestern coastal strip. The sun-baked region near Perth was best suited to throaty reds and fortified wines but winery and vineyard expertise is so sophisticated that good dry whites are now being made. The most exciting wines, both red and white, come from Margaret River and Great Southern down towards the coast.

South Australia dominates the wine scene – it grows the most grapes, makes the most wine and is home to most of the nation's biggest wine companies. There is more to it, however, than attractive, undemanding, gluggable wine. The Clare Valley is an outstanding producer of cool-climate Riesling, but some sites in the region produce excellent Shiraz and Cabernet. The Barossa is home to some of the planet's oldest vines, particularly Shiraz and Grenache. Eden Valley, in the hills to the east of Barossa, excels at crisp, steely Rieslings and scented Shiraz. Coonawarra also makes many thrilling reds.

Victoria was Australia's major producer for most of the 19th century until her vineyards were devastated by the phylloxera louse. It's only recently that Victoria has regained her position as provider of some of the most startling wine styles in the country: stunning liqueur Muscats; the thrilling dark reds of Central Victoria; and the urbane Yarra Valley and Mornington Peninsula reds and whites.

New South Wales was home to the revolution that propelled Australia to the front of the world wine stage (in the Hunter Valley, an area that remains a dominant force). However, the state is a major bulk producer in Riverina, and a clutch of new regions in the Central Ranges are grabbing headlines.

Tasmania, with its cooler climate, is attracting attention for top-quality Pinot Noirs and Champagne-method sparkling wines. Riesling and Gewürztraminer would almost certainly be excellent, if the producers would give them a chance.

CLASSIFICATIONS
Formal appellation control, restricting certain grapes to certain regions, is virtually unknown; regulations are more of a guarantee of authenticity than a guide to quality. In a country so keen on inter-regional blending for its commercial brands, a system resembling France's AC could be problematic. However, the Label Integrity Program (LIP) guarantees all claims made on labels and the Geographical Indications (GI) committee is busy clarifying zones, regions and sub-regions – albeit with plenty of lively, at times acrimonious, debate about where some regional borders should go.

2005 VINTAGE REPORT
An outstanding harvest for Australia – a record 1.96 million tonnes and exceptional quality, thanks to disease-free conditions and a mild growing season. In most areas, winter rainfall was adequate and any rain that fell during the growing season did so early on, and was therefore a positive influence. The exceptions to this were heavy summer rains in New South Wales and eastern Victoria and heavy April rainfall in Western Australia; the latter adversely affected reds in regions south of Margaret River. Aromatic whites (especially Sauvignon Blanc, Semillon and Riesling) did very well. Some reds were affected by warm dry conditions towards the end of the harvest, which brought on ripeness a little too quickly, but many producers believe that quality will be the best in 30 years.

See also NEW SOUTH WALES, QUEENSLAND, SOUTH AUSTRALIA, TASMANIA, VICTORIA, WESTERN AUSTRALIA and individual wineries.

NEW ZEALAND

New Zealand's wines, though diverse in style, are characterized by intense fruit flavours, zesty acidity and pungent aromas – the product of cool growing conditions and high-tech winemaking.

GRAPE VARIETIES AND WINE REGIONS
Nearly 1600km (1000 miles) separate New Zealand's northernmost wine region from the country's (and the world's) most southerly wine region, Central Otago. In terms of wine styles it is useful to divide the country into two parts. Hawkes Bay and regions further north produce the best Cabernet Sauvignon, Merlot, Cabernet Franc and Syrah. From Martinborough and further south come the best Sauvignon Blanc, Riesling, Pinot Noir and fizz. Chardonnay, Gewürztraminer and Pinot Gris perform well everywhere, with riper, fleshier styles in the north and finer, zestier styles to the south.

CLASSIFICATIONS
Labels guarantee geographic origin. The broadest designation is New Zealand, followed by North or South Island. Next come the 10 or so regions. Labels may also name specific localities and individual vineyards.

2005 VINTAGE REPORT
Wet, cold weather during flowering reduced crop levels in every region, but new plantings bearing their first crops limited the impact. A warm, dry ripening period gave Auckland one of its best ever seasons. Heavy rain early in the season in Hawkes Bay affected the quality of white wine, although reds are reported to be very good. Marlborough Sauvignon Blanc enjoyed a very good vintage.

NORTH ISLAND

Matakana

AUCKLAND
Kumeu/Huapai
Henderson
Auckland

Waiheke Island

BAY OF PLENTY
WAIKATO
GISBORNE

HAWKES BAY

Nelson
WELLINGTON
Wairarapa
NELSON
Martinborough
Blenheim
Wellington
MARLBOROUGH

CANTERBURY
Waipara
Christchurch

SOUTH ISLAND

OTAGO

Dunedin

Main vineyard areas

0   100   200 km

0   100 miles

See also AUCKLAND, CANTERBURY, CENTRAL OTAGO, GISBORNE, HAWKES BAY, KUMEU/HUAPAI, MARLBOROUGH, MARTINBOROUGH, NELSON, WAIHEKE ISLAND; and individual wineries.

SOUTH AMERICA

The only two countries to have proved their ability to make fine wine are Chile and Argentina, though Uruguay is clearly trying to join them. Elsewhere it's largely a story of heat, humidity and the indifference of a local population much keener on spirits than wine.

ARGENTINA

Argentina is the fifth largest producer in the world but political and economic circumstances used to discourage foreigners from attempting to do business with her. The economic turmoil took a welcome respite during the 1990s and the wine industry took the opportunity to modernize, but the collapse of 2002 plunged the country into uncertainty. Now, with a stronger economy, wines seem set to shine again. The upper Mendoza region has impressive Malbec from old vines, as well as rich, creamy Chardonnay from the high altitudes of Uco Valley. Cafayate in the north produces wildly aromatic Torrontés and concentrated Malbec, while further south, Río Negro is producing crisp Semillons and intensely perfumed Malbec. Even deeper in Patagonia, the new Chubut area, developed by Bodega Weinert, is worth watching out for.

CHILE

Over the years Chile has boasted of having the world's most perfect conditions for grape growing. Reliable sunshine, no rain, irrigation from the Andes – and almost no disease in the vineyards. Which is all

Main vineyard areas

0   250   500 km
0   250 miles

very well, but most of the world's great wines have been made from grapes grown in far more taxing conditions, and until recently you could accuse Chile of simply having things too easy to excel. There is now a new generation of wine people in charge here, keen to meet the challenge of upping quality, and results get more exciting every year. Though vineyards extend for over 1100 km (685 miles) north to south, the majority of grapes are grown from just north of Santiago at Aconcagua, down to Maule, with the most important quality areas being Maipo, Aconcagua, Rapel and cool-climate Casablanca. San Antonio, south of Casablanca, is a great new discovery offering crisp Sauvignon Blanc and cool-climate Syrah, while the brandy regions of the Limarí and Elqui Valleys, more than 400 km (250 miles) north of Santiago, have some exciting reds and whites. Cabernet Sauvignon, especially from Maipo, is still the top grape, scented and richly fruity, but Carmenère is increasingly making some of Chile's most individual wines, either on its own or blended with Merlot. Syrah is a new star, both from warm areas like Aconcagua and Colchagua, and from cool coastal regions where Pinot Noir is also starting to shine.

URUGUAY

The majority of Uruguay's vines are on clay soil in Canelones, around Montevideo, which has relatively high rainfall in a relatively cool, humid climate. This may explain why the thick-skinned, rot-resistant black Tannat grape from South-West France is the leading variety. However, there is a clutch of modern wineries working hard at adapting vineyard practices and winemaking technology to the conditions; they are beginning to have some success with greatly improved, snappy Sauvignon Blanc and full, balanced Chardonnay as well as Merlot, Cabernet Franc – and even Nebbiolo. Best producers include Carrau, Castillo Viejo, Filgueira, Juanico, de Lucca, Pisano, Stagnari, and the small Bodega Bouza.

OTHER COUNTRIES

Look at Brazil, how vast it is. Yet in all this expanse, running from 33° South to 5° North, there's nowhere ideal to site a vineyard. The best attempts are made down towards the Uruguayan border. Peru has seemingly good vineyard sites in the Ica Valley south of Lima, but nothing exciting winewise. Bolivia has few vineyards, but they're good, and incredibly high. Venezuela's chief claim to fame is that some of her subtropical vines give three crops a year!

2005 VINTAGE REPORT

Excellent quality in Chile, but only where growers took care. March and April rains caused some rot, but allowed most grapes to ripen slowly and fully. Cabernet Sauvignon and Carmenère are elegant and fresh in the style of 2001. Very good Sauvignon Blanc, but in reduced quantities. Argentina has reduced volumes due to frosts and hail in Mendoza (especially the high vineyards), but good quality. Rio Negro in the south had no problems and fine quality.

See also (ARGENTINA) CAFAYATE, MENDOZA, UCO VALLEY; (CHILE) CASABLANCA, CENTRAL, COLCHAGUA, CURICO, MAIPO, MAULE, RAPEL, SAN ANTONIO; and individual wineries.

SOUTH AFRICA

Many highly reputed wine people from across the globe have been attracted to invest and make wine in South Africa. Confidence and optimism among local winegrowers is also high and new, quality-focused private wineries open at a rate of one a week, although co-operatives still process nearly 80% of the crop. The strength of the Rand and the recent flavourant scandal have put pressure on exports, but the wines have been transformed as many new, virus-free vineyards start to bear fruit.

GRAPE VARIETIES AND WINE REGIONS
The Cape's winelands run roughly 400km (250 miles) north and east of Cape Town, although small pockets of new vineyards are extending the winelands into exciting virgin territory. From a mere 18% eight years ago, red varieties now account for nearly 41% of the vineyards, while white varieties have declined from 82% to 59%. Chenin Blanc, still decreasing, remains the dominant variety. Cabernet Sauvignon, Shiraz, Sauvignon Blanc, Merlot and Chardonnay increase their share every year, with Pinotage holding steady. Some new clone Grenache and old bush-vine Cinsaut support the unabated excitement with Rhône varieties, and there are small quantities of Viognier, Verdelho, Mourvèdre, Malbec, Nebbiolo and Sangiovese. There is little typicity of origin, although some areas are historically associated with specific varieties or styles. Stellenbosch makes some of the best red wines; maritime-influenced Constantia produces exhilarating Sauvignon Blancs, a variety also showing great promise in Durbanville, Darling and upland Elgin. Cooler areas also include Walker Bay, where the focus is Pinot Noir, and Elim (at the tip of Africa). There are distinctive limy Chardonnays from inland Robertson, although these warmer areas are noted for fortifieds, both Muscadel (Muscat) and port styles.

CLASSIFICATION
The Wine of Origin (WO) system divides wine-producing areas into regions, districts and wards. Wines can be traced back to their source, but quality is not guaranteed. Varietal wines for export must be made from at least 85% of the named grape. Estate wines are no longer part of the WO system; from 2005, the Estate has been supplanted as the smallest unit of production by the single vineyard designation.

2005 VINTAGE REPORT
The 2005 harvest has been described as the driest, wettest, earliest and hottest ever; such was the difference, even within short distances, that generalizations are impossible. The Cape is in the grip of a drought cycle – even with a burst of spring rain, those without irrigation struggled. After early heat, a December downpour in Robertson and a prolonged electric storm in coastal areas in late January caused rot among white varieties, reducing the crop by 15–25% but producing abundant botrytis dessert styles. Those who harvested before the rain or were ultra-selective have made fruity, fuller-bodied Sauvignon Blancs and Chardonnays. The rain, however, benefited coastal reds.

See also CONSTANTIA, ELGIN, FRANSCHHOEK, PAARL, ROBERTSON, STELLENBOSCH, WALKER BAY; and individual wineries.

OTHER WINE COUNTRIES

ALGERIA With many vines over 40 years old, there should be great potential here, but political uncertainty hinders progress despite government support. The western coastal province of Oran produces three-quarters of Algeria's wine, including the soft but muscular Coteaux de Tlemcen wines and dark, beefy reds of the Coteaux de Mascara.

BULGARIA After success in the 1980s and disarray in the 90s, the roller coaster seems to have stopped, with an annual fall in vineyard acreage and loss of sales. New World influences are having some effect, but few wines shine. International varieties dominate, but local grapes – plummy Mavrud, meaty Gamza, deep Melnik, fruity white Dimiat and Misket – can be good. A few estate wines are now being made and exported. Best wineries include BOYAR, Khan Krum and SUHINDOL.

CANADA The strict VQA (Vintners Quality Alliance) maintains high standards in British Columbia and Ontario, and there has been enormous progress in the 2 most important regions – OKANAGAN VALLEY in British Columbia and the NIAGARA PENINSULA in Ontario – where the move from hybrid to vinifera varieties has been rapid. Sweet icewine is still Canada's trump card. Pinot Gris, Chardonnay, Riesling and Gewürztraminer lead the way in non-sweet whites; Merlot, Cabernet Franc, Cabernet Sauvignon, even Syrah, show potential in red wines.

CHINA Though China officially promotes wine, its potential remains unfulfilled as the majority of Chinese are reluctant to drink it. Plantings, mainly international grapes with some traditional Chinese, German and Russian varieties, are expanding rapidly, yet only 15% of the harvest is crushed for wine. But there are now home-grown premium wines emerging and foreign investment proceeds apace with continual improvements in viticulture and winemaking. Major producers include Changyu, Dynasty, Great Wall, HUADONG and newcomer Xintian, which has 10,000ha (25,000 acres) under vine.

CROATIA Inland Croatia has an undercurrent of rising potential: bulk whites dominate but small private producers are emerging. Initiatives to sow vines in former minefields are helping to restore Croatia's viticultural heritage. What the country needs now is more investment, more technology in the vineyard and winery and a fair price for the grapes. The best vineyards are on the Dalmatian coast, where international varieties are being planted alongside gutsy indigenous grapes: deep, tannic Plavac Mali – related to Zinfandel – has long produced the top red wines. GRGICH of California has a winery on the Peljesac peninsula. Very few wines are exported.

CYPRUS This island has not had a high reputation for wine since the Crusades, when COMMANDARIA was reputedly a rich, succulent nectar worth risking your neck for. However, Cyprus is modernizing and, supported by the government, regional press houses and wineries are being built in or near the vineyards. A 3-year restructuring plan and investment by companies like Etko, Keo, Loel and Sodap is at last producing tasty modern reds and whites (for the first time we are seeing varietal wines). The first efforts with grapes like Cabernet Sauvignon and Sémillon are impressive. EU membership should support these improvements.

THE CZECH REPUBLIC The vineyards of Bohemia in the north-west and Moravia in the south-east are mainly planted with white varieties – Grüner Veltliner, Müller-Thurgau, Riesling, Pinot Blanc – with pockets of red such as St-Laurent and Lemberger. Quality is erratic, though EU membership and Western investment and consultancy should help.

ENGLAND In 2003 the UK's winegrowing industry celebrated its 50th vintage since the 'revival' of commercial vineyards in the early 1950s. However, with around 800ha (2000 acres) of vines, 330 vineyards (many very small), 115 wineries and an average annual output of around 2 million bottles, it is still minute. Nevertheless, producers have learnt which varieties are successful (Bacchus, Schönburger and Seyval Blanc for whites, Rondo, Dornfelder and Pinot Noir for reds, and Chardonnay, Pinot Noir and Meunier for quality sparklings), how to train and trellis them to cope with the (usually) cool summers and – most importantly – how to make sound, sometimes excellent, wines. In particular, sparkling wines have shown they can equal Champagne in quality. Growers are seeking out new disease-resistant varieties with some success: Regent (red) and Phoenix (white) are two of the best. The most popular winemaking counties are: Kent (CHAPEL DOWN, Biddenden, Sandhurst), East Sussex (Battle, Davenport), West Sussex (BREAKY BOTTOM, NYETIMBER, RIDGEVIEW), Berkshire (VALLEY VINEYARDS), Gloucestershire (THREE CHOIRS), Hampshire (Wickham) and Surrey (DENBIES). 2003 was an exceptional vintage: a long, warm and dry September and October resulted in the ripest grapes for 20 years.

GEORGIA Georgia faces many challenges – lack of regulation, resistance to change, counterfeiting – but its diverse climates (from subtropical to moderate continental) and soils could produce every style imaginable. International and indigenous varieties abound; the peppery, powerful red Saperavi shows promise. Most wine is still pretty rustic, but investment is beginning to have an effect, with GWS (Georgian Wines & Spirits Company, 75% owned by Pernod Ricard) leading the way.

GREECE Sadly, the Athens Olympics made little difference to our minimal enthusiasm for Greek wines. That's a shame, because a new generation of winemakers and grape growers, many of them trained in France, Australia or California, have a clear vision of the flavours they want to achieve and their wines are modern but marvellously original too. Polarization between cheap bulk and expensive boutique wines continues, but large companies such as Boutari, Kourtakis and Tsantalis are upping the quality stakes and flavours improve every vintage. More vineyard and marketing work – many labels are still difficult to understand – is needed. International plantings have led to surprising and successful blends with indigenous varieties such as the red Agiorgitiko, Limnio and Xynomavro, and white Assyrtiko, Moschofilero and Roditis. Quality areas: Naousa and Nemea for reds, SAMOS for sweet Muscats, Patras for dessert Mavrodaphne. Wineries to watch include: Aidarinis, Argyros, ANTONOPOULOS, Gentilini, GEROVASSILIOU, Hatzimichali, Kyr Yanni, Domaine Constantin LAZARIDI, Mercouri, Papaïoannou, Strofilia and Tselepos.

HUNGARY Hungary makes good whites, improving reds and out-standing sweet wines, and has joined the EU, yet few of us have much idea about her as a wine country. Stringent regulations and investment/advice from Australian and western European companies and consultants, particularly in TOKAJI, have put Hungary, with its 22 designated appellations, back on the international wine map. There is renewed interest in native varieties such as Furmint, Irsai Oliver, Kékfrankos and Kadarka, and top Hungarian winemakers – the late Tibor Gál, Akos Kamocsay, Vilmos Thummerer and others – are now a solid force. But price and reputation remain low and Hungary's great potential remains underrated.

INDIA This large country has a tiny wine industry, partly due to its climate. Only 1% of the 50,000ha (123,500 acres) of vines is used for wine; both international varieties and ancient Indian ones, such as Arkesham and Arkavati, are planted. CHATEAU INDAGE, with vineyards in the Maharashtra hills east of Mumbai (Bombay), controls 75% of the market and produces still and sparkling wines. The Sula winery, north-east of Mumbai, is a promising new winery. Bordeaux superstar Michel Rolland advises Grover Vineyards in Bangalore.

ISRAEL More small wineries continue to open and existing ones consolidate and enlarge. A lack of a decent labelling regime and regulatory authority means that quality is variable and labels not always 100% accurate. Most wine is locally consumed and only a few of the best are exported. Besides GOLAN HEIGHTS, some of Israel's most promising wines now come from Castel in the Judean Hills, Galil Mountain in Galilee and Tishbi in Shomron.

JAPAN Wine can be made from locally grown or imported grapes, juice or wine – the labels don't tell you which. One has to assume that the present situation suits most growers/wineries who continue to sell almost all their wines locally. At the first national wine show in 2003, only 2 gold medals were awarded, showing how quality remains a problem. Despite humid conditions, wine is produced in almost every province. SUNTORY is in the best region, Yamanashi. Other main players are Mercian, Sapporo, Manns and Domaine Sogga.

LEBANON CHATEAU MUSAR, Kefraya and Ksara survived the 25-year war. Peace has brought a new generation of producers and improved quality from the older companies – new releases from Kefraya, Massaya, Musar and Ksara are vastly superior to those produced just a few years ago.

LUXEMBOURG Co-operatives dominate here and quality is about what you would expect. Elbling and Rivaner (Müller-Thurgau) continue to decline, to be replaced with quality varietals such as Riesling, Pinot Noir, Chardonnay and Gewürztraminer.

MEXICO In the far north-west of Mexico, in Baja California, some good reds are made by L A CETTO as well as by smaller companies such as Monte Xanic. In the rest of the country, only high-altitude areas such as the Parras Valley and Zacatecas have the potential for quality wines. Casa Madero, in the Parras Valley, has some success with Cabernet Sauvignon. Other promising grape varieties include Nebbiolo, Petite Sirah, Tempranillo, Zinfandel and Barbera, with Viognier and Chardonnay also planted.

MOLDOVA Standards of winemaking and equipment still leave much to be desired, but fruit quality is good, and international players, including PENFOLDS and winemakers Jacques Lurton, Hugh Ryman and Alain Thiénot, have worked with local wineries to make encouraging whites. However, chaotic social conditions have led to many attempts being abandoned. You may find sparkling wines from the Cricova winery.

MONTENEGRO This red-wine-dominated part of the former Yugoslavia shows some potential in the beefy Vranac grape with its bitter cherry flavours. Navip is a producer you might come across.

MOROCCO Known for big, sweet-fruited reds that once found a ready blending market in France. Since the 1990s massive investment by

41

Castel Frères is instigating a rebirth: the first results are tasty Syrah and Cabernet reds at very reasonable prices. A country to watch.

ROMANIA This ancient wineland, of enormous potential, 10th in world production, is slowly getting the message that its strength lies in its *terroir*: Dealul Mare, MURFATLAR and COTNARI all have ancient reputations. International-backed ventures are a sign of the mini-revolution, but challenges remain. Huge investment from Halewood, as in the cautiously improving Prahova Valley range, may help, but there is a long way to go. Impending EU membership may help.

SLOVAKIA The eastern part of the old Czechoslovakia, with its cool-climate vineyards, is dominated by white varieties: Pinot Blanc, Riesling, Grüner Veltliner, Irsai Oliver. Western investment at the state winery at Nitra and smaller wineries such as Gbelce and Hurbanovo near the Hungarian border at Komárno, is rapidly improving the quality. With EU membership we may now see a few examples.

SLOVENIA Many of the old Yugoslav Federation's best vineyards are here. On the Italian border, Brda and Vipava have go-ahead co-operatives, and Kraski Teran is a red wine of repute. The Movia range, from the Kristancic family, looks promising. A well-policed quality wine scheme allows only the best to be bottled and exported. Potential is considerable, and some interesting reds and whites are emerging, but quality is still erratic. With EU membership, Slovenia could rapidly make a name for itself.

SWITZERLAND Fendant (Chasselas) is the main grape for spritzy but neutral whites from the VAUD and VALAIS. Like the fruity DOLE reds, they are best drunk very young. German-speaking cantons produce light reds and rosés from Pinot Noir (Blauburgunder), and whites from Müller-Thurgau. Italian-speaking TICINO concentrates on Merlots that have been increasingly impressive since 2000. Serious wines, especially in Valais, use Cabernet, Syrah, Chardonnay and traditional varieties like Amigne and Petite Arvine. See also NEUCHATEL.

THAILAND I first tasted Thai wine a few years ago: it was a light and fruity red and impressive for what I thought of as sub-tropical conditions. Since then, serious Shiraz and Chenin wines have shown that Thailand's high-altitude vineyards are capable of some tasty offerings.

TUNISIA Ancient wine traditions have had an injection of new life from international investment, and results so far are encouraging.

TURKEY The world's sixth-largest grape producer, but 97% ends up as table grapes or raisins. However, with EU membership pencilled in for 2012 and with vast vineyards, good growing conditions and cheap labour on hand, Turkey could become a major player if the will-power and the investment are harnessed. Producers such as Diren, Kavaklidere, Turasan and Doluca are using modern technology to produce very drinkable wines. Local variety Buzbag can be good.

UKRAINE The Crimea's vineyards, producing hearty reds, are the most important. Muscatels are considered to be a cause for national pride, especially the Massandra brand. The Odessa region is successful with its sparkling wines, the 3 most well-known facilities being the Inkerman winery, Novyi Svet and Zolota Balka. Future European investment is said to be in the pipeline.

ZIMBABWE Despite the present political and economic upheaval, the small wine industry is doing quite well. Summer rain can be more of a problem. There are just two companies: Mukuyu and Stapleford.

A–Z

OF WINES, PRODUCERS, GRAPES & WINE REGIONS

In the following pages there are over
1600 entries covering the world's top wines, as well as
leading producers, main wine regions and grape
varieties, followed on page 289 by a glossary of wine
terms and classifications.

*On page 4 you will find a full explanation of
How to Use the A–Z. On page 297 there is an index
of all wine producers in the book, to help you find the
world's best wines.*

AALTO *Ribera del Duero, Spain* Former VEGA SICILIA winemaker Mariano García and former RIBERA DEL DUERO appellation boss Javier Zaccagnini have teamed up to create this new winery. From the outset, they have challenged top Spanish producers with their dense but elegant reds, Aalto★★ and old vines cuvée Aalto PS★★. Best years: (2001) 00 **99**.

ABRUZZO *Italy* This region stretches from the Adriatic coast to the mountainous Apennine interior. White Trebbiano d'Abruzzo DOC is usually dry and neutral; the MONTEPULCIANO D'ABRUZZO DOC is generally a strapping, peppery red of real character, but sometimes a rosé called Cerasuolo. Overproduction has been a problem, but quality is on the increase with the gradual lowering of vineyard training height and the establishment of new DOCs and sub-zones.

ACACIA *Carneros AVA, California, USA* Leading producer of Chardonnay and Pinot Noir from the CARNEROS region for 2 decades. The regular Carneros Chardonnay★ is restrained but attractive. Pinot Noirs include the superb Beckstoffer Vineyard★★ and a Carneros★ – the wines have moved to a riper, meatier style of late. Best years: (Pinot Noir) 2002 **01 00 99 97 96 95**.

ACCADEMIA DEI RACEMI *Manduria, Puglia, Italy* Premium venture from the Perrucci family, long-established bulk shippers of basic Puglian wines. Quality, modern-style reds mainly from Primitivo and Negroamaro under various producers' names: Felline (Vigna del Feudo★★), Pervini (PRIMITIVO DI MANDURIA Archidamo★★), Masseria Pepe (Dunico★★). Best years: (reds) 2004 03 **01 00 98 97 96**.

ACHAVAL-FERRER *Uco Valley, Mendoza, Argentina* Garage winery created by a group of friends in 1998 and today one of Argentina's most sought-after labels. 80-year-old vines in the La Consulta area of UCO VALLEY produce Finca Altamira★★★, a Malbec bursting with personality and a real sense of place. Red blend Quimera★ is also good. Best years: (2003) 02 **01 99**.

TIM ADAMS *Clare Valley, South Australia* Important maker of fine, old-fashioned wine from his own and bought-in local grapes. Classic dry Riesling★★, oaky Semillon★★, and rich, opulent Shiraz★★ (sometimes ★★★) and Cabernet★★. The botrytis Semillon★ can be super, The Fergus is a glorious Grenache-based blend, and minty, peppery Aberfeldy Shiraz★★★ is a remarkable, at times unnerving, mouthful of brilliance from 100-year-old vines. Best years: (Aberfeldy Shiraz) (2002) 01 00 99 98 **96 94**.

Tim Adams

2003
RIESLING
CLARE VALLEY

WINE OF AUSTRALIA FROM CLARE VALLEY
750mL   12.0%Vol

ADELAIDE HILLS *South Australia* Small and exciting region 30 minutes' drive from Adelaide. High altitude affords a cool, moist climate ideal for fine table wines and superb sparkling wine. Consistently good Sauvignon Blanc and Chardonnay, plus promising Pinot Noir, Cabernet Franc, Shiraz and even Zinfandel. Best producers: Ashton Hills★, Bird in Hand, Chain of Ponds, HENSCHKE★★, KNAPPSTEIN LENSWOOD★★, Nepenthe★★, PETALUMA★★, SHAW & SMITH★★, Geoff WEAVER★★.

ADELSHEIM VINEYARD *Willamette Valley AVA, Oregon, USA* Over the past 3 decades, Adelsheim has established a reputation for excellent, generally unfiltered, Pinot Noir – especially cherry-scented Elizabeth's Reserve★★ and Bryan Creek Vineyard★ – and for rich Chardonnay

Stoller Vineyard★★. Also a bright, fresh Pinot Gris★. Best years: (Elizabeth's Reserve) (2003) 02 01 **00 99 98 96**.

AGLIANICO DEL VULTURE DOC *Basilicata, Italy*   Red wine from the Aglianico grape grown on the steep slopes of Mt Vulture. Despite the zone's location almost on the same latitude as Naples, the harvest here is sometimes later than in BAROLO, 750km (470 miles) to the north-west, because the Aglianico grape ripens very late. The best wines are structured, complex and long-lived. Best producers: Basilium★, Consorzio Viticoltori Associati del Vulture (Carpe Diem★), D'Angelo★★, Cantine del Notaio★★, Paternoster★★, Le Querce★. Best years: (2004) (03) 01 00 **98 97 95 93 90 88**.

AHR *Germany*   The Ahr Valley is a small (520ha/1285-acre), mainly red wine region south of Bonn. Chief grape varieties are the Spätburgunder (Pinot Noir) and (Blauer) Portugieser. Most Ahr reds used to be made sweet, but this style is on the way out. Meyer-Näkel and Deutzerhof are the best of a growing band of serious producers.

AIRÉN Spain's – and indeed the world's – most planted white grape can make fresh modern white wines, or thick, yellow, old-fashioned brews. Airén is grown all over the centre and south of Spain, especially in La MANCHA, VALDEPENAS and ANDALUCIA (where it's called Lairén).

ALBAN *Edna Valley AVA, California, USA*   A Rhône specialist in the Arroyo Grande district of Edna Valley, John Alban first produced Viognier in 1991. Today he offers 2 bottlings, Estate★★ and Central Coast★. Roussanne★★ from estate vineyards is laden with honey notes. Syrah is represented by 3 bottlings: Reva★★ and the more expensive Lorraine★★ and Seymour's Vineyard★★. Intense Grenache★★ and Pandora★★, a blend of about 60% Grenache, 40% Syrah, round out the line-up. Best years: (Syrah) 2002 01 **00 99 98 97 96**.

ALBANA DI ROMAGNA DOCG *Romagna, Italy*   In the hills south of Bologna and Ravenna, Italy's first white DOCG was a 'political' appointment that caused outrage among wine enthusiasts because of the totally forgettable flavours of most Albana wine. Though also made in dry and sparkling styles, the sweet *passito* version is really the only one that justifies the lofty status. Best producers: (passito) Celli, Conti, Ferrucci, Giovanna Madonia (Chimera★), Paradiso, Riva, Tre Monti, Uccellina★, Zerbina (Scacco Matto★★).

ALBARIÑO Possibly Spain's most characterful white grape. It grows in GALICIA in Spain's rainy north-west and, as Alvarinho, in Portugal's VINHO VERDE region. When well made, Albariño wines have fascinating flavours of apricot, peach, grapefruit and Muscat grapes, refreshingly high acidity, highish alcohol – and unrefreshingly high prices.

ALEATICO Rarely seen, ancient, native Italian grape that produces sweet, scented, high-alcohol dessert wines in central and southern Italy. Best producers: AVIGNONESI, Candido (delicious Aleatico di Puglia★).

ALENQUER DOC *Estremadura, Portugal*   Maritime-influenced hills north of Lisbon, producing wines from (mostly) local grape varieties, but also Cabernet and Chardonnay. Many wines are simply labelled ESTREMADURA. Best producers: Quinta do Carneiro★, Quinta da

45

Cortezia★/ALIANCA, D F J VINHOS★, Quinta de Monte d'Oiro★★, Quinta de Pancas★★, Casa SANTOS LIMA★. Best years: (reds) 2003 01 **00**.

ALENTEJO *Portugal* A large chunk of southern Portugal east of Lisbon and, along with the DOURO, one of Portugal's fastest improving red wine regions. Has its own DOC, and there are also 8 sub-regions: Borba, Évora, Granja-Amareleja, Moura, Portalegre, Redondo, Reguengos and Vidigueira. Potential is far from realized, but already some of Portugal's finest reds come from here. Best producers: (reds) Quinta da Terrugem★★/ALIANCA, Fundação Eugénio de Almeida (Cartuxa★, Pera Manca★★), Borba co-op, Quinta do CARMO★, Herdade dos Coelheiros★, CORTES DE CIMA★★, Vinha d'Ervideira★, ESPORAO★★, José Maria da FONSECA★, J P VINHOS★, Mouchão★★, Quinta do Mouro★, João Portugal RAMOS★★, Reguengos de Monsaraz co-op. Best years: (reds) 2004 01 **00**.

ALEXANDER VALLEY AVA *Sonoma County, California, USA* Important AVA, centred on the Russian River, which is fairly warm, with only patchy summer fog. Cabernet Sauvignon is highly successful here, with lovely, juicy fruit not marred by an excess of tannin. Chardonnay may also be good but is often overproduced and lacking in ripe, round flavours. Zinfandel and Merlot can be outstanding from hillside vineyards. Best producers: Alexander Valley Vineyards★, CLOS DU BOIS★, De Lorimier★, GEYSER PEAK★, JORDAN★, Murphy-Goode★★, SEGHESIO★★, SILVER OAK★★, SIMI★, Trentadue★★. See also Russian River Valley AVA, Sonoma County. Best years: (reds) (2002) 01 00 **99 97 95 94 93 91 90**.

ALGARVE *Portugal* Holiday region with feeble-flavoured, mostly red wines in 4 DOCs: Lagoa, Lagos, Portimão and Tavira. The Vinho Regional Algarve classification suffices for D F J VINHOS' chunky but tasty Esplanada. Look out for Vida Nova red from Sir Cliff Richard, made by David Baverstock.

ALIANÇA, CAVES *Beira Litoral, Portugal* Based in BAIRRADA, Aliança makes crisp, fresh whites and soft, approachable red Bairradas★. Also made, either from its own vineyards or bought-in grapes or wines, are reds from the DAO and DOURO; Quinta dos Quatro Ventos★★ from the Douro is a blend of Tinta Roriz, Touriga Franca and Tinta Barroca. The top reds, however, are those from an estate in ALENTEJO, Quinta da Terrugem★★.

ALIGOTÉ French grape, found mainly in Burgundy, whose basic characteristic is a lemony tartness. It can make extremely refreshing wine, especially from old vines, but is generally rather dull and lean. In ripe years it can resemble Chardonnay, especially if a little new oak is used. The best comes from the village of Bouzeron in the COTE CHALONNAISE, where Aligoté has its own appellation. Occasionally also found in Moldova and Bulgaria. Drink young. Best producers: (Burgundy) M Bouzereau★, COCHE-DURY★, A Ente★, J-H Goisot, JAYER-GILLES★, Denis MORTET★, TOLLOT-BEAUT, Villaine★.

ALL SAINTS *Rutherglen, Victoria, Australia* Old winery revived with great flair since 1998 by Peter Brown of the BROWN BROTHERS family. Superb fortifieds Rare Tokay★★ and Rare Muscat★★ have rediscovered past glory. Other fortifieds★ are good but still finding their best form. Table wines have shown significant improvement recently.

ALLEGRINI *Valpolicella, Veneto, Italy* High-profile producer in VALPOLICELLA
Classico, making single-vineyard La Grola★★ and Palazzo della
Torre★★. These are now sold under the regional Veronese IGT – partly
to distance them further from the continuing low regard in which
much of Valpolicella is held. These, and the barrique-aged La Poja★★★
(made solely with the Corvina grape), show the great potential that
exists in Valpolicella. Outstanding AMARONE★★★ and RECIOTO Giovanni
Allegrini★★. Best years: (Amarone) (2003) 01 **00 97 95 93 90 88 85.**

THIERRY ALLEMAND *Cornas AC, Rhône Valley, France* Thierry
Allemand has a smallholding of some 4ha (10 acres) of vines. He is
determined to keep yields low, uses little sulphur and seeks to avoid
making harsh, tannic wines. With careful vinification he produces 2
intense, unfiltered expressions of CORNAS at its dense and powerful
best: Chaillot★★ is marginally the lighter; Reynard★★ is from a
parcel of very old Syrah. Best years: (Reynard) (2004) 03 01 00 99 98
97 96 95 94 91 90.

ALLENDE *Rioja DOCa, Rioja, Spain* The ebullient Miguel Angel de
Gregorio has made his winery into one of the most admired new
names in RIOJA. Scented, uncompromisingly concentrated reds include
Aurus★★★, Calvario★★ and the affordable Allende★. There is also a
delicate white★. Best years: (reds) (2002) 01 00 **99 98 97 96.**

ALMAVIVA★★★ *Valle del Maipo, Chile* State-of-the-art joint venture
between CONCHA Y TORO and the Baron Philippe de Rothschild company
(see MOUTON-ROTHSCHILD), located in MAIPO Valley's El Tocornal vineyard
at the foot of the Andes and – after a slow start – producing a
memorably powerful red from old Cabernet Sauvignon vines planted
in alluvial, stony soils. It can be drunk at 5 years but should age for
10. Best years: (2002) 01 00 99 **98 97 96.**

ALOXE-CORTON AC *Côte de Beaune, Burgundy, France* An important
village at the northern end of the CÔTE DE BEAUNE producing mostly red
wines from Pinot Noir. Its reputation is based on the 2 Grands Crus,
CORTON (mainly red) and CORTON-CHARLEMAGNE (white only). Other
vineyards in Aloxe-Corton used to be a source of tasty, good-value
Burgundy, but nowadays the reds rarely exhibit their former
characteristic blend of ripe fruit and appetizing savoury dryness.
Almost all the white wine is sold as Grand Cru; straight Aloxe-Corton
Blanc is very rare. Best producers: CHANDON DE BRIAILLES★★, M
Chapuis★, Marius Delarche★, Dubreuil-Fontaine★, Follin-Arvelet★,
Antonin Guyon★, JADOT★, Rapet★, Comte Senard★, TOLLOT-BEAUT★★,
Michel Voarick★. Best years: (reds) (2004) 03 02 **01 99 97 96** 95 **90.**

DOM. ALQUIER *Faugères, Languedoc, France* The estate which shows best
how good FAUGÈRES can be. Barrel aging of all the wines, and low
yields for the special cuvées, Les Bastides★★ and La Première★. Also a
good white Vin de Pays blend of Marsanne and Roussanne. Best years:
(Bastides) 2003 **01 00 98.**

ALSACE AC *Alsace, France* Tucked away on France's eastern border with
Germany, Alsace produces some of the most individual white wines of
all, rich in aroma and full of ripe, distinctive flavours. Alsace is almost
as far north as Champagne, but its climate is considerably warmer
and drier. The 50 best vineyard sites can call themselves Grands Crus,
and account for 4% of production; quality regulations are more
stringent and individual crus can add further local rules. Riesling,
Muscat, Gewurztraminer and Pinot Gris are generally considered the
finest varieties in Alsace and have been the only ones permitted for

47

Grand Cru wines, although Sylvaner is now legal in Zotzenberg and further changes may follow. Pinot Blanc can produce good wines too. Reds from Pinot Noir are improving fitfully. Alsace was one of the first regions to label its wines by grape variety. Apart from Edelzwicker (a blend) and CREMANT D'ALSACE, all Alsace wines are made from a single grape variety, although blends from Grand Cru sites

are an emerging possibility. Medium-dry or sweeter wines are now, as of the 2004 vintage, labelled *moelleux*. Vendange Tardive means 'late-harvest'. The grapes (Riesling, Muscat, Pinot Gris or Gewurztraminer) are picked late and almost overripe, giving higher sugar levels and potentially more intense flavours. The resulting wines are usually rich and mouthfilling and often need 5 years or more to show their personality. Sélection de Grains Nobles – late-harvest wines made from superripe grapes of the same varieties – are invariably sweet and usually affected by noble rot; they are among Alsace's finest, but are very expensive to produce (and to buy). Best producers: L Albrecht, Barmès-Buecher★★, J Becker, Léon Beyer★ (Vendange Tardive★★), P BLANCK★★ (Vendange Tardive★★★), Bott-Geyl (Vendange Tardive★★★), A Boxler, E Burn★ (Vendange Tardive★★★), DEISS★★★, Dirler-Cadé, HUGEL★ (Vendange Tardive★★), Josmeyer★★, Kientzler★ (Vendange Tardive★★★), Klur★, Kreydenweiss (Vendange Tardive★★★), S Landmann★, A MANN★★ (Vendange Tardive★★★), Jean-Louis & Fabienne Mann, Meyer-Fonné, Mittnacht Frères★, MURE★ (Vendange Tardive★★), Ostertag★ (Vendange Tardive★★), Pfaffenheim co-op, Ribeauvillé co-op, Rolly Gassmann (Vendange Tardive★★), M Schaetzel, Schlumberger★, SCHOFFIT★★, Louis Sipp, Bruno Sorg★, M Tempé★, TRIMBACH★ (Vendange Tardive★★), TURCKHEIM co-op★, WEINBACH★★, ZIND-HUMBRECHT★★★. Best years: (2004) 03 02 **01 00 98 97 96 95**.

ALTARE *Barolo DOCG, Piedmont, Italy* Elio Altare crafts some of the most stunning of Alba's wines: excellent Dolcetto d'Alba★★ and BARBERA D'ALBA★ and even finer BAROLO Vigneto Arborina★★★ and Barolo Brunate★★★. Though he is a professed modernist, his wines are intense, full and structured while young, but with clearly discernible fruit flavours, thanks largely to tiny yields. He also makes 3 barrique-aged wines under the LANGHE DOC: Arborina★★★ (Nebbiolo), Larigi★★★ (Barbera) and La Villa★★ (Nebbiolo-Barbera). Also one of 7 producers that make a version of L'Insieme★★ (a Nebbiolo-Cabernet-Barbera blend). Best years: (Barolo) (2004) (03) (01) (00) 99 **98** 96 **95 93 90 89 88 85**.

ALTO ADIGE *Trentino-Alto Adige, Italy* A largely German-speaking province, originally called Südtirol. The region-wide DOC covers 25 types of wine. Reds are almost invariably varietal and range from light and perfumed when made from the Schiava grape, to fruity and more structured from the Cabernets or Merlot, to dark and velvety if Lagrein is used. Excess oak can mar their delightful fruit. Whites include Chardonnay, Pinot Bianco, Pinot Grigio, Riesling and Sauvignon, and are usually fresh and fragrant. There is also some good sparkling wine. Much of the wine comes from well-run co-ops. Sub-zones include the previously independent DOCs of Santa Maddalena and Terlano. Best producers: Abbazia di Novacella★, Casòn Hirschprunn★, Peter Dipoli★, Egger-Ramer★, Franz Haas★★,

Hofstätter★★, Kränzl★, LAGEDER★★, Laimburg★, Loacker★, Franz Gojer★, Muri-Gries★, Nalles-Magré, Josephus Mayr★, Ignaz Niedriest★, Plattner Waldgries★, Peter Pliger-Kuenhof★★, Prima & Nuova/Erste & Neue★, Hans Rottensteiner★, Heinrich Rottensteiner★, Tiefenbrunner★, Elena Walch★, Wilhelm Walch, Baron Widmann★; (co-ops) Caldaro★, Colterenzio★★, Girlan-Cornaiano★, Gries★, San Michele Appiano★★, Santa Maddalena ★, Terlano★, Termeno★. See also Trentino.

ALTOS LAS HORMIGAS *Mendoza, Argentina*   A rising star in Argentina, founded in 1995 by a group of Italians and Argentines. Altos Las Hormigas Malbec★ is an opulent example of the grape, while Reserva Viña Hormigas★★ is packed with pure, dense blackberry and cherry flavours. Colonia Las Liebres is one of Argentina's best Bonardas.

ALVARINHO   See Albariño.

AMA, CASTELLO DI *Chianti Classico DOCG, Tuscany, Italy*   Model estate of CHIANTI CLASSICO, with outstanding Chianti Classico, plus single-vineyard Riservas★★ (Bellavista and La Casuccia). L'Apparita★★★ is one of Italy's best Merlots; less impressive Il Chiuso is made from Pinot Nero. Also good Chardonnay Al Poggio★. Best years: (Chianti Classico) (2004) (03) 01 **00 99 98 97 95 93 90 88 85.**

AMARONE DELLA VALPOLICELLA *Valpolicella DOC, Veneto, Italy*   A brilliantly individual, bitter-sweet style of VALPOLICELLA made from grapes shrivelled on mats for months after harvest. The wine, which can reach 16% of alcohol and more, differs from the sweet RECIOTO DELLA VALPOLICELLA in that it is fermented to near-dryness. Wines from the Classico zone are generally the best, with exceptions from DAL FORNO, Corte Sant'Alda and Roccolo Grassi. Best producers: Stefano Accordini★★, ALLEGRINI★★★, Bertani★★, Brigaldara★, Brunelli★, BUSSOLA★★★, Michele Castellani-I Castei★★, Corte Sant'Alda★★, DAL FORNO★★★, Guerrieri-Rizzardi★★, MASI★, QUINTARELLI★★★, Le Ragose★★, Roccolo Grassi, Le Salette★★, Serègo Alighieri★, Speri★★, Tedeschi★★, Tommasi★, Villa Monteleone★★, VIVIANI★★, Zenato★★. Best years: (2003) 01 **00 97 95 93 90 88.**

AMIGNE   Swiss grape variety that is virtually limited to the region of Vétroz in the VALAIS. The wine has an earthy, nutty intensity and benefits from a few years' aging. Best producers: Jean-René Germanier, Caves Imesch.

ANDALUCÍA *Spain*   Fortified wines, or wines naturally so strong in alcohol that they don't need fortifying, are the speciality of this southern stretch of Spain. Apart from sherry (JEREZ Y MANZANILLA DO), there are the lesser, sherry-like wines of Condado de Huelva DO and MONTILLA-MORILES DO, and the rich, sweet wines of MALAGA DO. These regions also make some modern but bland dry whites; the best are from Condado de Huelva. Red wine is now appearing from producers in Málaga, Granada and Almeria provinces.

ANDERSON VALLEY AVA *California, USA*   Small appellation (less than 245ha/600 acres) in western MENDOCINO COUNTY that produces brilliant wines. Most vineyards are within 15 miles of the Pacific Ocean, making this one of the coldest AVAs in California. Delicate Pinot Noirs and Chardonnays, and one of the few places in the state for first-rate Gewürztraminer. Superb sparkling wines with healthy acidity and creamy yeast are highlights as well. Best producers: Brutocao★,

Greenwood Ridge★, HANDLEY★★, Lazy Creek★, Navarro★★★, ROEDERER ESTATE★★, SCHARFFENBERGER CELLARS★.

ANDREW WILL WINERY *Washington State, USA* Winemaker Chris Camarda makes delicious blends of Bordeaux varietals from a range of older WASHINGTON vineyards. At the top are the complex Champoux Vineyard★★★, the opulent Ciel du Cheval★★★ and the tannic yet age-worthy Klipsun Vineyard★★. Wines from 2 newer vineyards, Sheridan Vineyard★ and Two Blondes Vineyard★, still show young vine character. Sorella★★★, a blend of the best barrels each vintage, is outstanding with age. White wines seem more a pastime than a portfolio. Best years: (reds) (2003) 02 01 **00 99 97 96 95**.

CH. ANGÉLUS★★★ *St-Émilion Grand Cru AC, 1er Grand Cru Classé, Bordeaux, France* One of the best-known ST-EMILION Grands Crus, with an energetic owner and talented winemaker. Increasingly gorgeous wines throughout the 80s and 90s, recognized by promotion to Premier Grand Cru Classé in 1996. Best years: 2003 02 **01** 00 **99** 98 **97** 96 **95** 94 93 92 90 89 88 85.

MARQUIS D'ANGERVILLE *Volnay AC, Côte de Beaune, Burgundy, France* 2003 sadly saw the passing of Jacques d'Angerville after half a century's experience and meticulous attention to detail. He produced an exemplary range of elegant Premiers Crus from VOLNAY, the classiest of the COTE DE BEAUNE's red wine appellations. Clos des Ducs and Taillepieds are ★★★. All should be kept for at least 5 years. Best years: (top reds) 2003 02 99 98 **97** 96 **95 93 91** 90.

CH. D'ANGLUDET★ *Margaux AC, Cru Bourgeois, Haut-Médoc, Bordeaux, France* This English-owned château makes a gentle, unobtrusive but generally attractive red that can be of Classed Growth standard and is never overpriced. It ages well for at least a decade. Best years: 2003 02 00 **98 96 95** 94 90 89 88 86 85 83 82.

ANJOU BLANC AC *Loire Valley, France* Ill-defined AC; ranges from bone dry to sweet, from excellent to dreadful; the best are dry. Up to 20% Chardonnay or Sauvignon can be added, but many of the leading producers use 100% Chenin. Best producers: M Angeli/Sansonnière★★, Cady, des Chesnaies★, Fesles★, Richard Leroy★, Montgilet/V Lebreton, Mosse★, Ogereau★, Pierre-Bise★, J Pithon★★, RICHOU★, Soucherie/P-Y Tijou★, Yves Soulez★. Best years: (top wines) 2004 **03** 02 **01 00 99 97 96**.

ANJOU ROUGE AC *Loire Valley, France* Anjou reds (from Cabernets Sauvignon and Franc or Pineau d'Aunis) are increasingly successful. Usually fruity, easy-drinking wine, with less tannin than ANJOU-VILLAGES. Wines made from Gamay are sold as Anjou Gamay. Best producers: Brizé★, Chamboureau, Fesles★, Putille, RICHOU★. Best years: (top wines) 2004 03 02 **01 00 97 96 95**.

ANJOU-VILLAGES AC *Loire Valley, France* Superior Anjou red from 46 villages, and made from Cabernet Franc and Cabernet Sauvignon. Some extremely attractive dry, fruity wines are emerging, with better aging potential than ANJOU ROUGE. Anjou-Villages Brissac is an exciting sub-appellation. Best producers: P Baudouin, Brizé★, P Delesvaux★, Fesles★, Montgilet/V Lebreton★, de la Motte★, Ogereau★, Pierre-Bise★, Putille★, RICHOU (Vieilles Vignes★★), Rochelles/J-Y Lebreton★★, du Prieuré, Tigné★. Best years: 2004 03 02 **01 00 97 96 95**.

ANSELMI *Veneto, Italy* Roberto Anselmi (and PIEROPAN) has shown that much-maligned SOAVE can have personality when carefully made. Using ultra-modern methods he has honed the fruit flavours of his San

Vincenzo★ and Capitel Foscarino★★ and introduced small-barrel-aging for single-vineyard Capitel Croce★★ and luscious, Sauternes-like I Capitelli★★ (sometimes ★★★), as well as the Cabernet Sauvignon Realdà. All sold under the regional IGT rather than Soave DOC. Best years: (I Capitelli) (2004) (03) 01 **00 99 98 97 96 95 93 92 90 88**.

ANTINORI *Tuscany, Italy* World-famous Florentine family firm that has been involved in wine since 1385, but it is Piero Antinori, the current head, who has made the Antinori name synonymous with quality and innovation. The quality of its CHIANTI CLASSICO wines like Badia a Passignano★ (Riserva★★), Pèppoli★, Tenute Marchese Antinori Riserva★★ and Villa Antinori★ is consistently good, but it was its development of the SUPER-TUSCAN concept of superior wines outside the DOC that launched a quality revolution during the 1970s. Introducing small-barrel-aging to Tuscany, TIGNANELLO★★ (Sangiovese-Cabernet) and SOLAIA★★★ (Cabernet-based) can be great wines. Other Tuscan wines include VINO NOBILE La Braccesca★★, BRUNELLO DI MONTALCINO Pian delle Vigne★★, BOLGHERI's Guado al Tasso★★ (Cabernet-Merlot), and Bramasole, a new Syrah-Merlot blend from Cortona DOC. Interests further afield include PRUNOTTO in Piedmont, Tormaresca in PUGLIA, FRANCIACORTA's Monte Nisa and Bátaapáti in Hungary. Best years: (reds) (2004) (03) 01 **00** 99 **98 97 95 93 90**. See also Castello della Sala.

ANTONOPOULOS *Patras AO, Peloponnese, Greece* Boutique winery producing barrel-fermented Chardonnay★★, Cabernet Nea Dris (New Oak)★, a blend of Cabernets Sauvignon and Franc, and Private Collection★, a promising Agiorgitiko-Cabernet blend.

ARAGÓN *Spain* Aragón, stretching from the Pyrenees south to Spain's central plateau, used to be responsible for much of the country's cheap red wine. Winemaking has improved markedly, first of all in the cooler, hilly, northern SOMONTANO DO, and now also further south, in Campo de Borja DO, Calatayud DO and CARIÑENA DO; these 3 areas have the potential to be a major budget-price force in a world mad for beefy reds.

ARAUJO *Napa Valley AVA, California, USA* Boutique winery whose great coup was to buy the Eisele vineyard, traditionally a source of superb Cabernet under the Joseph PHELPS label. Araujo Cabernet Sauvignon★★★ is now one of California's most sought-after reds, combining great fruit intensity with powerful but digestible tannins. There is also an attractively zesty Sauvignon Blanc★ and a tiny amount of impressive estate Syrah★★.

ARBOIS AC *Jura, France* The largest of the specific ACs in the Jura region. The majority of wines are red or rosé, but most widely seen outside the region are the whites, made from Chardonnay or the local Savagnin, which can give the wines a sherry-like flavour that is most concentrated in *vin jaune*. There is also a rare, sweet *vin de paille*. Good sparkling CREMANT DU JURA is made mainly from Chardonnay. Best producers: Ch. d'Arlay★, Aviet★, Bourdy★, Désiré★, Dugois★, M Faudot★, F Lornet★, H Maire★, P Overnoy★, la Pinte★, J Puffeney★, Pupillin co-op★, Renardière★, Rijckaert★, Rolet★, A & M Tissot★, J Tissot★, Tournelle★. Best years: 2003 02 **01 00 99 98 97 96**.

ARCHERY SUMMIT *Willamette Valley AVA, Oregon, USA* Based in the renowned Dundee Hills of WILLAMETTE VALLEY, this winery has more than 40ha (100 acres) in 4 estate vineyards. The focus is on deeply coloured, heavily oaked Pinot Noir; single-vineyard bottlings from Archery Summit Estate★, Red Hills★, Renegade Ridge★ and Arcus Estate★ top the list. Best years: (Pinot Noir) (2004) (03) 02 **01 00 99 98**.

ARGIOLAS *Sardinia, Italy* Sardinian star making DOC wines Cannonau (Costera★), Monica (Perdera) and Vermentino (Costamolino★) di Sardegna, but the best wines are the IGT Isola dei Nuraghi blends – Turriga★★ and Korem★ are powerful, spicy reds, Angialis★★ a golden, sweet white. All the wines are good value.

ARGYLE *Willamette Valley AVA, Oregon, USA* In 1987, Brian Croser and Rollin Soles planned a world-class New World sparkling wine firm; the cool WILLAMETTE VALLEY was ideal for late-ripened Pinot Noir and Chardonnay. Argyle sparkling wine★ was soon followed by barrel-fermented Chardonnay★ and Pinot Noir★. The Reserve★★ and Spirithouse★★ bottlings show just how much potential this large winery possesses. Best years: (Pinot Noir) 2002 01 **00 99**.

ARNEIS Italian grape grown in the ROERO hills in PIEDMONT. Arneis is DOC in Roero, producing dry white wines which, at best, have an attractive (appley, herbal) perfume. Good ones can be expensive, but cheaper versions rarely work. Best producers: Araldica/Alasia★, Brovia★, Cascina Chicco★, Correggia★, Deltetto★, GIACOSA★, Malvirà★, Angelo Negro★, PRUNOTTO★, Vietti★, Gianni Voerzio★.

CH. L'ARROSÉE★★ *St-Émilion Grand Cru AC, Grand Cru Classé, Bordeaux, France* This small property, just south-west of the small historic town of ST-EMILION, makes really exciting wine: rich, chewy and wonderfully luscious, with a comparatively high proportion (40%) of Cabernet Sauvignon. Drink after 5 years, but may be cellared for 10 or more. Best years: 2003 02 00 **98 96 95 94 90 89 88 86 85**.

ARROWOOD *Sonoma Valley AVA, California, USA* Dick Arrowood was the winemaker at CHATEAU ST JEAN during its glory years of Chardonnay, and in 1986 he started his own winery. The wines have mostly been tip-top – beautifully balanced Cabernet★★, superb Merlot★★, deeply fruity Syrah (Saralee's★★, Kuljian★★), lovely, velvety Chardonnay★ (Alary Ranch★★) and fragrant Viognier★★. Best years: (Cabernet Sauvignon) (2002) (01) 00 **99 97 96 95 94 91 90**.

ARTADI *Rioja DOCa, País Vasco, Spain* This former co-op is now producing some of RIOJA's deepest, most ambitious reds. These include Grandes Añadas★★★, Viña El Pisón★★★, Pagos Viejos★★ and Viñas de Gain. Best years: 2001 00 **99 98 96 95 94 91**.

ASCHERI *Piedmont, Italy* Winemakers in PIEDMONT for at least 5 centuries. The Ascheri style is forward and appealingly drinkable, whether it be BAROLO (Vigna dei Pola★, Sorano★★), Dolcetto d'Alba (Vigna Nirane★) or NEBBIOLO D'ALBA. Montalupa Rosso and Bianco are made from Syrah and Viognier. The Cristina Ascheri MOSCATO D'ASTI is delightful.

ASTI DOCG *Piedmont, Italy* Asti Spumante, the world's best-selling sweet sparkling wine, was long derided as light and cheap, though promotion to DOCG signalled an upturn in quality. Made in the province of Asti south-east of Turin, under the new appellation (which includes the rarer MOSCATO D'ASTI) the wine is now called simply Asti. Its light sweetness and refreshing sparkle make it ideal with fruit and a wide range of sweet dishes. Drink young. Best producers: Araldica, Bera★, Cinzano★, Contero, Giuseppe Contratto★, Cascina Fonda★, FONTANAFREDDA, Gancia★, Martini & Rossi★, Cascina Pian d'Or★.

ATA RANGI *Martinborough, North Island, New Zealand* Small, high-quality winery run by 2 families. Stylish, concentrated wines include big, rich Craighall Chardonnay★, seductively perfumed cherry/plum Pinot Noir★★★ and an impressive Cabernet-Merlot-Syrah blend called Célèbre★★. Young Vines Pinot Noir is not of the same standard, but new Syrah★★, delicately luscious Lismore Pinot Gris★ and a concentrated and succulent Sauvignon Blanc★ are exciting. Best years: (Pinot Noir) 2003 02 **01 00 99 98 97**.

ATLAS PEAK *Atlas Peak AVA, Napa, California, USA* Established in 1987 by ANTINORI of Italy, this mountaintop winery in the south-east corner of NAPA VALLEY has been a leader in Californian Sangiovese without ever managing to achieve a consistent style. Consenso★ is a tasty Cabernet-Sangiovese blend; excellent Chardonnay★ also is grown in these cool, high vineyards. Allied Domecq, which now owns the winery brand, is retooling it and looking to make more of a Cabernet statement. Best years: (reds) (2002) (01) **99 97 95**.

AU BON CLIMAT *Santa Maria Valley AVA, California, USA* Pace-setting winery in this cool region, run by the talented Jim Clendenen, who spends much time in BURGUNDY and PIEDMONT. The result is a range of lush Chardonnays★★ and intense Pinot Noirs★★ (Isabelle and Knox Vineyard bottlings can be ★★★), plus BORDEAUX styles under the Vita Nova label. Watch out for Italian varietals under the Il Podere dell' Olivos label and Cold Heaven Viognier made by Clendenen's wife, Morgan. QUPE operates from the same winery. Best years: (Pinot Noir) 2002 **01 00 99 98 97 96 95 94**; (Chardonnay) 2002 **01 00 99 98 97 95**.

AUCKLAND *North Island, New Zealand* Vineyards in the region of Auckland are concentrated in the districts of Henderson, KUMEU/HUAPAI, Matakana and WAIHEKE ISLAND. Clevedon, south of Auckland, is a fledgling area that shows promise. Best producers: Heron's Flight, KUMEU RIVER★. Best years: (Cabernet Sauvignon) (2004) 02 **00 99 98 96 94 93**.

CH. AUSONE★★★ *St-Émilion Grand Cru AC, 1er Grand Cru Classé, Bordeaux, France* This beautiful property is situated on what are perhaps the best slopes in ST-EMILION. Since the involvement of Michel Rolland in the mid-1990s, the wines have greatly increased in texture and ripeness, if not in elegance. A high proportion (50%) of Cabernet Franc adds complexity. Production is just 2500 cases a year (CHEVAL BLANC makes 12,000). Second wine: La Chapelle d'Ausone. Best years: 2003 02 01 00 99 98 **97** 96 **95 94 90 89 88 86 85 83 82**.

AUXEY-DURESSES AC *Côte de Beaune, Burgundy, France* Auxey-Duresses is a backwater village up a valley behind MEURSAULT. The reds should be light and fresh but can often lack ripeness. At its best, and at 3–5 years, the white is dry, soft, nutty and hinting at the creaminess of a good Meursault, but at much lower prices. Of the Premiers Crus, Les Duresses is the most consistent. Best producers: (reds) Comte Armand★★, J-P Diconne★, Jessiaume Père et Fils, Maison LEROY, Duc de Magenta★, M Prunier★, P Prunier★; (whites) R Ampeau★, d'Auvenay (Dom. LEROY)★★, J-P Diconne★, DROUHIN★, J-P Fichet★, Gras, Olivier LEFLAIVE★, Maison LEROY★, M Prunier★. Best years: (reds) (2004) 03 02 **99 96**; (whites) (2004) **03 02 00 99**.

AVIGNONESI *Vino Nobile di Montepulciano DOCG, Tuscany, Italy* The Falvo brothers led Montepulciano's revival as one of TUSCANY's best zones. Although international wines like Il Marzocco★ (Chardonnay) and Desiderio★★ (Merlot-Cabernet) at one time received more attention, today the focus is back on the top quality classics, VINO NOBILE★ and its superior version, made only in top years, Grandi Annate★★. The VIN SANTO★★★ is the most sought-after in Tuscany; there's also a rare red version from Sangiovese, Occhio di Pernice★★★. Best years: (Vino Nobile) (2004) (03) 01 **00 99 98 97 95 93 90 88**.

BABICH *Henderson, North Island, New Zealand* Family-run winery with some prime vineyard land in MARLBOROUGH and HAWKES BAY. Irongate Chardonnay★ is an intense, steely wine that needs plenty of cellaring, while intense, full-flavoured varietal reds under the Winemakers Reserve label show even greater potential for development. Flagship label The Patriarch features Chardonnay★★ and Cabernet Sauvignon★★, both from Hawkes Bay. Marlborough wines include a stylish Sauvignon Blanc★, a tangy Riesling and a light, fruity Pinot Gris. Best years: (premium Hawkes Bay reds) 2002 **00 98**.

BAD DÜRKHEIM *Pfalz, Germany* This spa town has some good vineyards and is the headquarters of the dependable Vier Jahreszeiten co-op. Best producers: DARTING★, Fitz-Ritter, Pflüger, Karl Schaefer★. Best years: (2004) 03 02 01 **99 98 97 96 93**.

BADEN *Germany* Very large wine region stretching from FRANKEN to the Bodensee (Lake Constance). Its dry whites and reds show off the fuller, softer flavours Germany can produce in the warmer climate of its southerly regions. Many of the best non-Riesling German wines come from here, as well as many of the best barrel-fermented and barrel-aged wines. Good co-operative cellars at Achkarren, Bickensohl, Bötzingen, Durbach, Königs-schaffhausen, Pfaffenweiler and Sasbach.

BAGA Important red grape in BAIRRADA, which is one of the few regions in Portugal to rely mainly on one variety. Also planted in much smaller quantities in DAO and the RIBATEJO. It can give deep, blackberryish wine, but aggressive tannin is a continual problem.

BAIRRADA DOC *Beira Litoral, Portugal* Bairrada, along with the DOURO and ALENTEJO, can be the source of many of Portugal's best red wines. These can brim over with intense raspberry and blackberry fruit, though the tannin levels are severe and may take quite a few years to soften. The whites are coming on fast with modern vinification methods. With an Atlantic climate, vintages can be very variable. Best producers: (reds) Caves ALIANCA★, Quinta das Bágeiras★, Quinta do Carvalhinho★, Gonçalves Faria★, Caves Messias (Garrafeira★), Caves Primavera (Garrafeira★), Quinta da Rigodeira★, Casa de Saima★★, Caves SAO JOAO★, SOGRAPE, Sidónio de Sousa★★; (whites) Quinta da Rigodeira★, Casa de Saima★, SOGRAPE (Reserva★, Quinta de Pedralvites★). Best years: (reds) 2003 01 00 **97**.

BALATONBOGLÁR WINERY *Transdanubia, Hungary* Premium winery, in the Lake Balaton region, that has benefited from heavy investment and the expertise of viticulturist Dr Richard Smart and wine consultant Kym Milne, but still needs to work to improve quality, particularly in the inexpensive but dumbed-down range sold under the Chapel Hill label.

BALEARIC ISLANDS *Spain* Medium-bodied reds and soft rosés were the mainstays of Mallorca's 2 DO areas, Binissalem and Plà i Llevant, until the Anima Negra winery began turning out its impressive, deep reds from the native Callet grape. Best producers: Anima Negra★, Franja Roja (J L Ferrer), Hereus de Ribas, Miquel Gelabert, Miquel Oliver, Son Bordils★.

BANDOL AC *Provence, France* A lovely fishing port with vineyards high above the Mediterranean, producing some of the best reds and rosés in Provence. The Mourvèdre grape gives Bandol its character – gentle raisin and honey softness with a herby fragrance. The reds happily age for 10 years, sometimes more, but can be very good at 3–4. The rosés, delicious and spicy but often too pricy, should be drunk young. There is a small amount of neutral, overpriced white. Best producers: (reds) Bastide Blanche★, la Bégude★, Bunan★, Frégate★, le Galantin★, J P Gaussen★★, Gros' Noré★★, l'Hermitage★, Lafran-Veyrolles★, Mas Redorne★, la Noblesse★, PIBARNON★★, Pradeaux★★, Ray-Jane★★, Roche Redonne★, Romassan★, Ste-Anne★, Salettes★, de Souviou★, la Suffrène★, Tempier★, Terrebrune★, la Tour de Bon★, VANNIERES★★. Best years: (2003) 01 00 99 98 **97 96 95 90**.

BANFI *Brunello di Montalcino DOCG, Tuscany, Italy* High-tech American-owned firm which is now a force in Italy. Noted winemaker Ezio Rivella (here from 1977 to 1999) did much to establish Banfi's reputation. BRUNELLO★, Chardonnay (Fontanelle★), Cabernet (Tavernelle★★) and Merlot (Mandrielle★) are successful, but even better are Brunello Riserva Poggio all'Oro★★ and SUPER-TUSCANS Summus★★ (a blend of Sangiovese, Cabernet and Syrah) and Excelsus★★ (Cabernet-Merlot). Also has cellars (Vigne Regali) in PIEDMONT for GAVI and fizz. Best years: (top reds) (2004) (03) 01 **99 98 97 95 93 90**.

BANNOCKBURN *Geelong, Victoria, Australia* Under the direction of Gary Farr for the past 26 years, Bannockburn has been widely regarded as one of Australia's best medium-sized wineries. Its most famous wines so far have been the powerful, gamy and controversial Pinot Noir★, MEURSAULT-like Chardonnay★★ and my favourite, the complex and classy Alain GRAILLOT-influenced Shiraz★★. It'll be fascinating to see how these fare now that Farr has left to work with his son, Nick, at the family winery, By Farr. Best years: (Shiraz) (2003) 02 01 **00 99 98 97 96 94 92 91**.

BANYULS AC *Roussillon, France* One of the best *vins doux naturels*, made mainly from Grenache, with a strong plum and raisin flavour. Rimage – vintaged early bottlings – and tawny styles are the best. Generally served as an apéritif in France and deserves a wider audience. Try sampling it mid-afternoon with some macaroons. Best producers: Cellier des Templiers★, CHAPOUTIER, Clos des Paulilles★, l'Étoile★, Mas Blanc★★, la RECTORIE★★, la Tour Vieille★, Vial Magnères★.

BARBADILLO *Jerez y Manzanilla DO, Andalucía, Spain* The largest sherry company in the coastal town of Sanlúcar de Barrameda makes a wide range of good to excellent wines, in particular salty, dry manzanilla styles (Solear★★) and intense, nutty, but dry amontillados and olorosos, led by Amontillado Principe★★ and Oloroso Cuco★★. Neutral dry white Castillo de San Diego is a bestseller in Spain.

BARBARESCO DOCG *Piedmont, Italy* This prestigious red wine, grown near Alba in the LANGHE hills south-east of Turin, is often twinned with its neighbour BAROLO to demonstrate the nobility of the Nebbiolo grape. Barbaresco can be a shade softer and less powerful. The wine usually takes less time to mature and is often considered the more approachable of the two, as exemplified by the international style of GAJA. But, as in Barolo, traditionalists also excel, led by Bruno GIACOSA. Even though the area is relatively compact (575ha/1420 acres), wine styles can differ significantly between vineyards and producers. Best vineyards: Asili, Bricco di Neive, Costa Russi, Crichet Pajè, Gallina, Marcorino, Martinenga, Messoirano, Moccagatta, Montestefano, Ovello, Pora, Rabajà, Rio Sordo, San Lorenzo, Santo Stefano, Serraboella, Sori Paitin, Sorì Tildin. Best producers: Barbaresco co-op★★, Piero Busso★, CERETTO★★, Cigliuti★★, Stefano Farina★★, Fontanabianca★★, GAJA★★★, GIACOSA★★★, Marchesi di Gresy★★, Moccagatta★★, Fiorenzo Nada★★, Castello di Neive★★, Oddero★, Paitin★★, Pelissero★★, Pio Cesare★, PRUNOTTO★, Albino Rocca★★, Bruno Rocca★★, Sottimano★★, La Spinetta★★, Vietti★★. Best years: (2004) (03) 01 00 99 **98 97 96 95 93 90 89 88 86 85 82**.

BARBERA A native of north-west Italy, Barbera vies with Sangiovese as the most widely planted red grape in the country. When grown for high yields its natural acidity shows through, producing vibrant quaffers. Low yields from the top PIEDMONT estates create intensely rich and complex wines. Oaked versions can be stunning.

BARBERA D'ALBA DOC *Piedmont, Italy* Some outstanding Barbera comes from this appellation. The most modern examples are supple and generous and can be drunk almost at once. More intense, dark-fruited versions require at least 3 years' age, but might improve for as much as 8. Best producers: G Alessandria★★, ALTARE★, Azelia★★, Boglietti★★, Brovia★, Cascina Chicco★, CERETTO★, Cigliuti★, CLERICO★, Elvio Cogno★★, Aldo CONTERNO★★, Giacomo CONTERNO★, Conterno-Fantino★, Corino★, Correggia★★, Elio Grasso★, Giuseppe MASCARELLO★, Moccagatta★, M Molino★★, Monfalletto-Cordero di Montezemolo★★, Oberto★★, Parusso★★, Pelissero★, F Principiano★★, PRUNOTTO★★, Albino Rocca★★, Bruno Rocca★, SANDRONE★★, P Scavino★★, La Spinetta★★, Vajra★★, Mauro Veglio★★, Vietti★★, Gianni Voerzio★★, Roberto VOERZIO★★★. Best years: (2004) 03 **01 00 99 98 97 96 95**.

BARBERA D'ASTI DOC *Piedmont, Italy* While Dolcetto d'Asti is usually light and simple, wines made from Barbera show a greater range of quality. Unoaked and barrique-aged examples can compete with the best BARBERA D'ALBA and rival some of the better Nebbiolo-based reds. Best examples can be kept for 5–6 years, occasionally longer. Best producers: Araldica/Alasia★, La Barbatella★, Pietro Barbero★, Bava★, Bertelli★★, Braida★★, Cascina Castlèt★, Coppo★, Hastae (Quorum★), Martinetti★★, Il Mongetto★★, PRUNOTTO★★, Cantine Sant'Agata★, Scarpa★★, La Spinetta★★, Vietti★★, Vinchio-Vaglio Serra co-op★. Best years: (2004) 03 **01 00 99 97 96 95**.

BARDOLINO DOC *Veneto, Italy* Substantial zone centred on Lake Garda, giving, at best, light, scented red and rosé (chiaretto) wines to be drunk young, from the same grape mix as neighbouring VALPOLICELLA. Bardolino Superiore is now DOCG. Best producers: Cavalchina★, Corte Gardoni★, Guerrieri-Rizzardi★, MASI, Le Vigne di San Pietro★, Fratelli Zeni.

BAROLO DOCG *Piedmont, Italy* Renowned red wine, named after a village south-west of Alba, from the Nebbiolo grape grown in 1455ha (3595 acres) of vineyards in the steep LANGHE hills. For a time its austere power, with tough, chewy tannins that took years of cask-aging to soften, was considered too much for modern palates. But for more than 2 decades, many winemakers have applied new methods to make Barolo that is fresher, cleaner, better balanced and ready sooner, with greater colour, richer fruit, softer tannins, and the distinctive 'tar and roses' character so beloved of Barolo fans. Distinct styles of wine are made in the zone's villages. Barolo and La Morra make the most perfumed wines; Monforte and Serralunga the most structured; Castiglione Falletto strikes a balance between the two. Barolo is nowadays frequently labelled by vineyards, though the producer's reputation often carries more weight. Best vineyards: Bricco delle Viole, Brunate, Bussia Soprana, Cannubi Boschis, Cerequio, Conca dell'Annunziata, Fiasco, Francia, Gavarini, Giachini, Ginestra, Monfalletto, Monprivato, Rocche dell'Annunziata, Rocche di Castiglione, Santo Stefano di Perno, La Serra, Vigna Rionda, Villero. Best producers: C Alario★★, G Alessandria★★, ALTARE★★, Azelia★★, Boglietti★★, Bongiovanni★★, Brovia★★, Cappellano★★, CERETTO★★, CHIARLO★, CLERICO★★★, Poderi Colla★★, Aldo CONTERNO★★★, Giacomo CONTERNO★★★, Conterno-Fantino★★, Corino★★, Luigi Einaudi★★, GIACOSA★★★, Elio Grasso★★, M Marengo★★, Bartolo MASCARELLO★★, Giuseppe MASCARELLO★★★, Monfalletto-Cordero di Montezemolo★★, Oberto★★, Oddero★★, Parusso★★, Pio Cesare★★, Pira★★, E Pira & Figli★★, F Principiano★, PRUNOTTO★★, Renato RATTI★, Revello★★, Giuseppe Rinaldi, Rocche dei Manzoni★★, SANDRONE★★★, P Scavino★★, M Sebaste★★, Vajra★★, Mauro Veglio★★, Vietti★★, Vigna Rionda★★, Gianni Voerzio★★, Roberto VOERZIO★★. Best years: (2004) (03) (01) 00 99 **98 97 96 95 93 90 89 88 86 85**.

BAROSSA VALLEY See pages 58–9.

BAROSSA VALLEY ESTATE *Barossa, South Australia* Half owned by local grapegrowers and half by industry giant HARDY. The contracted growers own some of the best sited vineyards in BAROSSA. Flagship reds are huge, gutsy Barossa beauties E&E Black Pepper Shiraz★★, Ebenezer Shiraz★★ and E&E Sparkling Shiraz★★, all of them bursting with ripe plum fruit, spice and plenty of vanilla oak. Other Ebenezer wines include intense, full-flavoured sparkling Pinot Noir. Some of the Barossa's best value is found in the Moculta and Spires ranges. Best years: (E&E Black Pepper Shiraz) (2002) 01 **98 96**.

JIM BARRY *Clare Valley, South Australia* Traditionally a source of perfumed, classy Rieslings★. However, it is for rich and complex reds such as Cabernet Sauvignon, McCrae Wood Shiraz★ and the heady, palate-busting Armagh Shiraz★★ that it is now best known. Best years: (Armagh Shiraz) (2003) 02 01 99 98 **96** 95 92 **89**.

BARSAC AC *Bordeaux, France* Barsac, lying close to the river Garonne and with the little river Ciron running along its eastern boundary, is the largest of the 5 communes in the SAUTERNES AC, also has its own AC, which is used by most, but by no means all, of the top properties. In general, the wines are a little less luscious than other Sauternes, but from good estates they can be marvellous. Best producers: CLIMENS★★★, COUTET★★, DOISY-DAENE★★, Doisy-Dubroca★, DOISY-VEDRINES★★, Myrat★, NAIRAC★★, Piada, Suau★. Best years: 2003 02 01 **99 98 97 96 95 90 89 88 86 83**.

BASILICATA *Italy* Southern Italian region best known for one wine, the potentially excellent, gutsy red called AGLIANICO DEL VULTURE.

BAROSSA

South Australia

The Barossa Valley, an hour or so's drive north of Adelaide in South Australia, is the heart of the Australian wine industry. Penfolds, Orlando, Beringer Blass, Seppelt, Yalumba and other giants have their headquarters here, alongside around 50 or so smaller wineries, producing or processing up to 60% of the nation's wine. However, this percentage is based mostly on grapes trucked in from other regions, because the Barossa's vineyards themselves grow less than 10% of Australia's grapes. Yet Barossa-grown grapes, once rejected as uneconomical for their low yields, are now increasingly prized for those same low yields.

Why? Well, it's highly likely that the world's oldest vines are in the Barossa. The valley was settled in the 1840s by Lutheran immigrants from Silesia, who brought with them vines from Europe, most importantly, as it turned out, cuttings from the Syrah (or Shiraz) variety of France's Rhône Valley. And because Barossa has never been affected by the phylloxera louse, which destroyed many of the world's vineyards in the late 19th century, today you can still see gnarled, twisted old vines sporting just a few tiny bunches of priceless fruit that were planted by refugees from Europe all of a century and a half ago, and are still tended by their descendants. A new wave of winemakers has taken up the cause of the Barossa vines with much zeal and no small amount of national pride, and they now produce from them some of the deepest, most fascinating wines, not just in Australia, but in the world.

GRAPE VARIETIES

Shiraz is prized above all other Barossa grapes, able to conjure headswirling, palate-dousing flavours. Barossa is the main source of Shiraz grapes for Penfolds Grange, the wine that began the revolution in Australian red wine in the 1950s. Cabernet Sauvignon is also excellent and similarly potent, as are the Rhône varieties of heady Grenache and deliciously earthy Mourvèdre; some of the most exciting examples are from the original vines planted in the 19th century. All these varieties are largely grown on the hot, dry, valley floor, but just to the east lie the Barossa Ranges, and in these higher, cooler vineyards, especially in those of the neighbouring Eden Valley, some of Australia's best and most fashionable Rieslings are grown, prized for their steely attack and lime fragrance. But even here you can't get away from Shiraz, and some thrilling examples come from the hills, not least Henschke's Hill of Grace and Mount Edelstone.

CLASSIFICATIONS

The Barossa was among the first zones to be ratified within the Australian system of Geographical Indications and comprises the regions of Barossa Valley and Eden Valley. The Barossa lies within South Australia's collective 'super zone' of Adelaide.

See also GRANGE, SOUTH AUSTRALIA; and individual producers.

(Barossa Valley Shiraz) (2004)
(03) 02 **01 99 98 97 96 94 91 90
88**; (Eden Valley Riesling) 2003
02 **01 00 99 98 97 96 95 94 92
91 90 87**

BEST PRODUCERS

Shiraz-based reds
BAROSSA VALLEY ESTATE, Bethany,
Grant BURGE, Burge Family,
Elderton (Command), GLAETZER,
Greenock Creek (Block Shiraz,
Seven Acres), HENSCHKE,
Hewitson, Jenke, Trevor Jones,
Kies Family, Peter LEHMANN,
Charles MELTON, Miranda
(Family Reserve), ORLANDO,
PENFOLDS (RWT, GRANGE),
ROCKFORD, ST HALLETT, Schild
Estate, Tim Smith, Thorn Clarke,
Three Rivers, TORBRECK, Turkey
Flat, Two Hands, VERITAS, The
Willows, YALUMBA (Octavius).

Riesling
Bethany, Grant BURGE, Leo
Buring (Leonay), HENSCHKE,
Hewitson, Peter LEHMANN,
ORLANDO (Steingarten,
St Helga), Ross Estate,
ST HALLETT, YALUMBA (Heggies,
Mesh/with Jeffrey GROSSET,
Pewsey Vale).

Cabernet Sauvignon-based
reds
Grant BURGE, Greenock Creek,
HENSCHKE, Peter LEHMANN,
ST HALLETT, VERITAS.

Other reds (Grenache,
Mourvèdre, Shiraz)
Burge Family (Olive Hill), Grant
BURGE, Charles Cimicky
(Grenache), Elderton (CSM),
HENSCHKE (Johann's Garden,
Henry's Seven), Jenke
(Mourvèdre), Peter LEHMANN,
Charles MELTON, PENFOLDS
(Bin 138 Old Vine), TORBRECK
(Juveniles, The Steading), Turkey
Flat (Butcher's Block, Grenache
Noir), Two Hands, VERITAS.

Semillon
Grant BURGE, HENSCHKE,
Heritage, Jenke, Peter LEHMANN,
ROCKFORD, Turkey Flat,
The Willows.

BASSERMANN-JORDAN *Deidesheim, Pfalz, Germany* Since the arrival of winemaker Ulrich Mell in 1996, this famous estate has resumed making rich yet elegant Rieslings of ★ and ★★ quality from Deidesheim and FORST. Best years: (2004) 03 02 01 **99 98 97 96 90 89 88 86 76 71**.

CH. BATAILLEY★ *Pauillac AC, 5ème Cru Classé, Haut-Médoc, Bordeaux, France* A byword for reliability and value for money among the PAUILLAC Classed Growth estates. Marked by a full, obvious blackcurrant fruit, not too much tannin and a luscious overlay of creamy vanilla. Lovely to drink at only 5 years old, the wine continues to age well for at least 15 years. Best years: 2003 02 **00 96 95 94 90 89 88 86 85 83 82**.

BÂTARD-MONTRACHET AC *Grand Cru, Côte de Beaune, Burgundy, France* This Grand Cru produces some of the world's greatest whites – they are full, rich and balanced, with a powerful mineral intensity of fruit and fresh acidity. There are 2 associated Grands Crus: Bienvenues-Bâtard-Montrachet and the minuscule Criots-Bâtard-Montrachet. All can age for a decade – indeed, they ought to. Best producers: Blain-Gagnard★★, CARILLON★★★, DROUHIN★★★, Fontaine-Gagnard★★, J-N GAGNARD★★★, JADOT★★★, V & F Jouard★★, Louis LATOUR★★, Dom. LEFLAIVE★★★, Olivier LEFLAIVE★★★, Marc Morey★★★, Pierre Morey★★★, Michel Niellon★★★, RAMONET★★★, SAUZET★★★, VERGET★★★. Best years: (2004) 03 02 01 00 99 **97** 96 **95 92 90 89**.

DOM. DES BAUMARD *Coteaux du Layon, Loire Valley, France* Excellent domaine with well-sited vineyards in both the Layon Valley and SAVENNIERES. The heart of the domaine is its sweet wines: sensational QUARTS DE CHAUME★★★ which requires aging, as well as rich, honeyed, impeccably balanced COTEAUX DU LAYON Clos de Ste Catherine★★. Also fine steely, mineral-scented Savennières Clos du Papillon★★ and Clos St-Yves★★, with a late-harvest Trie Spéciale★★ in top years. CREMANT DE LOIRE and ANJOU reds are OK but unexciting. New is an experimental sweet Verdelho. Best years: (Quarts de Chaume) 2002 01 00 99 97 **96 95 93 90 89 88 85 83 78 76 71 62 59 47**.

LES BAUX-DE-PROVENCE AC *Provence, France* This AC has proved that organic farming can produce spectacular results, mainly due to the warm dry climate. Good fruit and intelligent winemaking produce some of the more easily enjoyable reds in Provence. Best producers: Hauvette★, Mas de la Dame★, Mas de Gourgonnier★, Lauzières, Mas Ste-Berthe★, Romanin★, Terres Blanches★. Best years: (2003) **02 01 00 99 98 97 96**.

BÉARN AC *South-West France* While the rest of South-West France has been busy producing some unusual and original flavours in recent years, Béarn hasn't managed to cash in. The wines (90% red and rosé) just aren't special enough, despite some decent grape varieties. The 2000 vintage saw an improvement in quality. Best producers: Bellocq co-op, Cauhapé, Guilhemas, Lapeyre★, Nigri.

CH. DE BEAUCASTEL *Châteauneuf-du-Pape AC, Rhône Valley, France* François Perrin makes some of the richest, most tannic reds★★★ in CHATEAUNEUF-DU-PAPE, with an unusually high percentage of Mourvèdre and Syrah, which can take at least a decade to show at their best. The white Roussanne Vieilles Vignes★★★ is exquisite, too. Perrin also produces COTES DU RHONE Coudoulet de Beaucastel red★ and white★ and a range of increasingly good southern reds, including several Rhône villages, like Vinsobres, under the Domaines Perrin label. Best years: (reds) (2004) 03 01 00 99 98 **97** 96 **95 94** 90 89 88 86 85 83 81; (whites) (2004) 03 01 00 99 **98 97 96 95 94** 93 90 89 88.

BEAUJOLAIS AC *Beaujolais, Burgundy, France* Wine region in the beautiful hills that stretch down from Mâcon to Lyon, producing predominantly red wine from the Gamay grape in prolific quantities. Beaujolais is best known for BEAUJOLAIS NOUVEAU, which accounts for 40% of the production. The better quality reds, each having their own appellation, come from the north of the region and are BEAUJOLAIS-VILLAGES or the 10 single Cru villages; from north to south these are ST-AMOUR, JULIENAS, MOULIN-A-VENT, CHENAS, FLEURIE, CHIROUBLES, MORGON, REGNIE, BROUILLY and COTE DE BROUILLY. Simple Beaujolais comes from the extreme south, and in good vintages is light, fresh, aromatic and delicious to drink, but in poorer vintages the wine can be drab and excessively acidic. A little rosé is also made from Gamay, while a small quantity of Beaujolais Blanc is made from Chardonnay. To combat falling sales, a new Vin de Pays is being discussed. Best producers: (reds) L & J-M Charmet/La Ronze★, DUBOEUF, J-F Garlon★, JADOT (Dom. de la Madone★), Terres Dorées/J-P Brun, Vissoux/P-M Chermette★.

BEAUJOLAIS NOUVEAU *Beaujolais AC, Burgundy, France* Also known as Beaujolais Primeur, this is the first release of bouncy, fruity Beaujolais on the third Thursday of November after the harvest. Once a simple celebration of the new vintage, then over-hyped, and now enjoyed by the true Beaujolais lover. Quality is generally reasonable and the wine is delicious until Christmas and the New Year, but thereafter, while drinkable, is likely to throw a slight sediment.

BEAUJOLAIS-VILLAGES AC *Beaujolais, Burgundy, France* Beaujolais-Villages can come from one of 38 villages in the north of the region, many of the best examples rivalling the quality of the BEAUJOLAIS Crus, having more body, character, complexity and elegance than simple Beaujolais and representing all the excitement of the Gamay grape at its best. Best villages in addition to the 10 Crus are Lancié, Quincié and Perréon. Best producers: (reds) Ch. de Belleverne★, G Descombes★, DUBOEUF, Manoir du Pavé★, P Sapin (Dom. St-Cyr).

BEAULIEU VINEYARD *Napa Valley AVA, California, USA* The late André Tchelistcheff had a major role in creating this icon for Napa Cabernet Sauvignon as winemaker from the late 1930s to the late 60s. After he left, Beaulieu lived on its reputation for too long. However, recent bottlings of Private Reserve Cabernet Sauvignon★ signal a return to form. A meritage red called Tapestry★ is good, as are Chardonnay★ and Pinot Noir★ from CARNEROS, and Syrah★. Best years: (Private Reserve) (2002) 01 00 99 98 97 96 95 94 **92 91 90 87 86 84**.

BEAUMES-DE-VENISE *Rhône Valley, France* Area famous for its sweet wine, MUSCAT DE BEAUMES-DE-VENISE. The local red wine is also very good, one of the meatier COTES DU RHONE-VILLAGES, with a ripe, plummy fruit in warm years. Best producers: (reds) Beaumes-de-Venise co-op, Bernardins, Cassan, Durban, les Goubert★, Redortier.

BEAUNE AC *Côte de Beaune, Burgundy, France* Most of the wines are red, with delicious, soft red-fruits ripeness. There are no Grands Crus but some excellent Premiers Crus, especially Boucherottes, Bressandes, Clos des Mouches, Fèves, Grèves, Marconnets, Teurons, Vignes Franches. White-wine production is increasing – DROUHIN makes outstanding, creamy, nutty Clos des Mouches★★★. Best producers: (growers) Germain★★, LAFARGE★★, Albert Morot★★, Rateau, TOLLOT-BEAUT★★; (merchants) BOUCHARD PERE ET FILS★★, Champy★★, Chanson★, DROUHIN★★, Camille Giroud★★, JADOT★★, Jaffelin, LABOURE-ROI, THOMAS-MOILLARD★. Best years: (reds) (2004) 03 02 **01 99 96**; (whites) (2004) 02 **01 00 99**.

61

CH. BEAU-SÉJOUR BÉCOT★★ *St-Émilion Grand Cru AC, 1er Grand Cru Classé, Bordeaux, France* Demoted from Premier Grand Cru Classé in 1986 and promoted again in 1996, this estate is now back on top form. Brothers Gérard and Dominique Bécot produce firm, ripe, richly textured wines that need at least 8–10 years to develop. Best years: 2003 02 01 00 98 **96 95 94 90 89 88 86 85**.

BEAUX FRÈRES *Willamette Valley AVA, Oregon, USA* Wine critic Robert Parker is co-owner with winemaker Mike Etzel, his brother-in-law (hence the winery name). The aim has been to make ripe, unfiltered Pinot Noir★★ that expresses the essence of the grape and vineyard. Its immediate success has attracted a cult following. Second label Belles Soeurs★ is also good. Best years: (2004) (03) 02 **01 00 99 98 97**.

GRAHAM BECK WINES *Robertson WO, South Africa* A vibrant 2-cellar operation. In ROBERTSON, Pieter Ferreira highlights the area's potential for Cap Classique sparkling, with an elegant, rich NV Brut from Chardonnay and Pinot Noir, a toastily fragrant, creamy, barrel-fermented Blanc de Blancs★ and an occasional, quirky sparkling Pinotage★. The Ridge Syrah★ and flavourful, balanced Chardonnay★ carry the flags for red and white table wine respectively.

Charles Hopkins runs the FRANSCHHOEK cellar: his Graham Beck Coastal range – much from old-vine STELLENBOSCH fruit – is making waves with Shiraz, The Old Road Pinotage★ and Cabernet Sauvignon★. The William★, a Cabernet Sauvignon-Cabernet Franc-Pinotage blend from both cellars, shows much promise and aging potential. Viognier is good, too.

J B BECKER *Walluf, Rheingau, Germany* Hajo Becker makes some of the raciest and longest-living dry Rieslings – usually ★, some Spätlese trocken ★★ – in the RHEINGAU. He also makes impressive dry Spätburgunder★ (Pinot Noir) reds matured without any new oak. Best years: (Riesling Spätlese trocken) (2004) 03 02 01 **99 98 97 96**.

BEDELL CELLARS *Long Island, New York State, USA* Winemaker Kip Bedell earned a reputation in the 1980s for high-quality, BORDEAUX-styled Merlot★ (Reserve★★), Cabernet Sauvignon★ and a red blend called Cupola★★. In the 90s, other wineries began imitating Bedell's vineyard management techniques, contributing to a quality increase throughout the region. Bedell sold the winery in 2000, but remains as winemaker. Best years: (reds) (2002) 01 **00 98 97**.

BEECHWORTH *Victoria, Australia* Beechworth was best known as Ned Kelly country before Rick Kinzbrunner planted the hilly slopes of sub-Alpine North-East Victoria and started making wines so successfully at GIACONDA. Now boutique wineries produce tiny volumes at high prices and are on a steep learning curve. BROKENWOOD has staked its future expansion on a large new vineyard at Beechworth. Best producers: Amulet (Shiraz★★), Castanga★ (Shiraz★★), Cow Hill★, GIACONDA★★★, Savaterre (Chardonnay★★), Sorrenberg★.

BEIRAS *Portugal* This large, central Portuguese province includes the DOCs of DAO, BAIRRADA, Távora-Varosa and Beira Interior. A number of important wines are made at the Vinho Regional level, using Portuguese red and white grape varieties along with international grapes such as Cabernet Sauvignon and Chardonnay. Best producers: Caves ALIANCA

(Galeria), D F J VINHOS (Bela Fonte), Figueira de Castelo Rodrigo co-op, Quinta de Foz de Arouce★, Luís PATO★★, Rogenda, Caves SAO JOAO (Quinta do Poço do Lobo). Best years: (2004) 03 01 **00**.

CH. BELAIR★★ *St-Émilion Grand Cru AC, 1er Grand Cru Classé, Bordeaux, France* Belair is next to AUSONE on ST-EMILION's limestone plateau. Under owner-winemaker Pascal Delbeck the estate has been run biodynamically since 1994, and the soft, supremely stylish wines are currently on top form. Best years: 2003 02 01 00 98 **95 94 90 89 88 86 85 83 82**.

BELLAVISTA *Franciacorta DOCG, Lombardy, Italy* Winemaker Mattia Vezzola specializes in FRANCIACORTA sparkling wines with a very good Cuvée Brut★★ and 4 distinctive Gran Cuvées★★ (including an excellent rosé). Riserva Vittorio Moretti Extra Brut★★ is made in exceptional years. Also produces lovely still wines, including white blend Convento dell'Annunciata★★★, Chardonnay Uccellanda★★ and red Casotte★ (Pinot Nero) and Solesine★★ (Cabernet-Merlot).

BELLET AC *Provence, France* A tiny AC in the hills behind Nice; the wine, mostly white, is usually overpriced. Ch. de Crémat★ and Ch. de Bellet★ are the most important producers but my favourite is Delmasso★. Best years: (2004) 03 **01 00**.

BENDIGO *Central Victoria, Australia* Warm, dry, former gold-mining region, which produced some decent wines in the 19th century, and is now home to more than 20 small-scale, high-quality wineries. The best wines are rich, ripe, distinctively minty Shiraz and Cabernet. Best producers: Balgownie, Chateau Leamon, Passing Clouds, Water Wheel. Best years: (Shiraz) (2002) 01 00 99 98 **97 95 94 93 91 90**.

BERBERANA *Rioja DOCa, Rioja, Spain* Now part of one of RIOJA's largest companies, Arco Bodegas Unidas, incorporating Lagunilla, Marqués de Monistrol and Dominio de Súsar, Berberana makes a pleasant, lightly oaked Crianza and respectable Reservas and Gran Reservas. Best years: (Reserva) **1998 96 95 94**.

BERCHER *Burkheim, Baden, Germany* The Bercher brothers run one of the top estates of the KAISERSTUHL. The high points are the powerful oak-aged Spätburgunder★★ (Pinot Noir) reds, Grauburgunder★★ (Pinot Gris) dry whites, which marry richness with perfect balance, and their dry Muskateller★, which is firm, elegant and tangy. Drink young or cellar for 3–5 years or more. Best years: (whites) (2004) 03 02 01 **99 98 97 96**; (reds) (2004) 03 02 01 **99 97 96**.

BERGERAC AC *South-West France* Bergerac is the main town of the southern Dordogne and the overall AC for this underrated area on the eastern edge of Bordeaux. The grape varieties are mostly the same as those used in the BORDEAUX ACs. The red is generally like a light, fresh claret, a bit grassy but with a good, raw blackcurrant fruit and hint of earth. Recent vintages have shown more ripe fruit character. Côtes de Bergerac AC wines have a higher minimum alcohol level. In general drink young, although a few estate reds can age for at least 3–5 years. Whites are generally fresh and dry for early drinking. Best producers: l'Ancienne Cure★, Bélingard, la Colline★, Court-les-Mûts, Eyssards, Gouyat, Monestier, Ch. les Nicots, Panisseau, TOUR DES GENDRES★★, Tour des Verdots★, Tourmentine. Best years: (reds) 2003 02 **01 00 98 96 95**.

BERINGER *Napa Valley AVA, California, USA* Beringer produces a full range of wine, but, in particular, offers a serious range of top-class Cabernet Sauvignons. The Private Reserve Cabernet can be ★★★ and is one of NAPA VALLEY's finest yet most approachable; the Chabot Vineyards★★, when released under its own label, can be equally impressive. The Knight's Valley Cabernet Sauvignon is made in a lighter style and is good value. Beringer makes red★★ and white★ Alluvium (meritage wines) from Knight's Valley. The powerful Private Reserve Chardonnay★★ is ripe and toasty. HOWELL MOUNTAIN Merlot★★ from Bancroft Ranch is also very good. Best years: (Cabernet Sauvignon) (2001) 00 99 **98 97 96 95 94 93 91 90 87 86 84 81**.

BERNKASTEL *Mosel, Germany* Both a historic wine town in the Middle Mosel and a large Bereich. Top wines, however, will come only from vineyard sites within the town – the most famous of these is the overpriced Doctor vineyard. Many wines from the Graben and Lay sites are as good or better and cost a fraction of the price. Best producers: Dr LOOSEN★★, Pauly-Bergweiler, J J PRÜM★★, S A PRÜM★★, Dr H Thanisch★, WEGELER★★. Best years: (2003) 02 01 **99** 98 **97** 95 **93 90 88**.

BEST'S *Grampians, Victoria, Australia* Viv and Chris Thomson run this historic winery, with vineyards dating back to 1868. There have been more recent plantings in the GRAMPIANS and at Lake Boga in the Murray Darling region. There are three ranges: the As the Crow Flies quaffers from Lake Boga, the medium-priced Kindred Spirits and the premium Great Western wines. Of these the Bin No. 0 Shiraz★★ is superb, the Cabernet★ is good, and the Riesling★ shows flashes of brilliance. The Thomson Family Shiraz★★ is an outstanding cool-climate Shiraz. Best years: (Thomson Family Shiraz) (2004) 01 99 98 **97 96 95 94 92**.

CH. BEYCHEVELLE★ *St-Julien AC, 4ème Cru Classé, Haut-Médoc, Bordeaux, France* At its best, this beautiful château can make wine of Second Growth quality. The wine has a charming softness even when young, but takes at least a decade to mature into the cedarwood and blackcurrant flavour for which ST-JULIEN is famous. In the best years it is worth its high price and, after a period of inconsistency, quality has become more regular since the late 1990s. Second wine: Amiral de Beychevelle. Best years: 2003 01 00 **99** 98 **96 95 90 89**.

BEYERSKLOOF *Stellenbosch WO, South Africa* Red-wine maestro Beyers Truter's energies are now focused on this range. All bar the striking Cabernet Sauvignon-based Beyerskloof★★ are built around Truter's favourite Pinotage. Reserve versions of the juicy Pinotage★★ and Synergy★, a succulent Pinotage-Cabernet-Merlot, raise the level of refinement. There's also a flavoursome dry Pinotage rosé. A black empowerment grouping, including the farm workers, shares an interest in nearby Bouwland. Best years: (Beyerskloof) 2002 01 **00 99 98 97 96 95 94 93**.

BIANCO DI CUSTOZA DOC *Veneto, Italy* Dry white wine from the shores of Lake Garda, made from a blend of grapes including Soave's GARGANEGA. Drink young. Best producers: Cavalchina★, Gorgo★, Montresor★, Le Vigne di San Pietro★, Fratelli Zeni★.

BIENVENUES-BÂTARD-MONTRACHET AC See Bâtard-Montrachet.

BIERZO DO *Castilla y León, Spain* Sandwiched between the rainy mountains of GALICIA and the arid plains of CASTILLA Y LEON, Bierzo used to make mostly commonplace reds. However, the recent arrival of Alvaro PALACIOS, of PRIORAT fame, with his inspired Corullón★★ red, sheds an entirely new and exciting light on the potential of the Mencía grape. Best producers: Pérez Caramés, Castro Ventosa, Estefania, Paixar★★, Descendientes de José Palacios★★, Pittacum★, Prada a Tope, Dominio de Tares★, Valtuille★.

JOSEF BIFFAR *Deidesheim, Pfalz, Germany* Gerhard Biffar runs this reliable estate, making dry and sweet Rieslings from top sites in Deidesheim, Ruppertsberg and WACHENHEIM. Consistent ★ quality from recent vintages. Drink young or cellar for 5 years or more. Best years: (2004) 03 02 01 **99 98 97 96 93**.

BILLECART-SALMON *Champagne AC, Champagne, France* Top-notch family-controlled CHAMPAGNE house which makes extremely elegant wines that become irresistible with age. I do hope that a label revamp and new, non-family investment don't herald a style change, because currently non-vintage Brut★★, non-vintage Brut Rosé★★, Blanc de Blancs★★★, vintage Cuvée N-F Billecart★★★ and Cuvée Elisabeth Salmon Rosé★★ are all excellent. Clos Saint-Hilaire, a single-vineyard 1995 vintage Blanc de Noirs, was launched in 2003. Best years: 1997 96 **95 90 89 88 86 85 82**.

BINGEN *Rheinhessen, Germany* This is a small town and also a Bereich, the vineyards of which fall in both the NAHE and RHEINHESSEN. The best vineyard in the town is the Scharlachberg, which produces some exciting wines, stinging with racy acidity and the whiff of coal smoke. Best producer: Villa Sachsen. Best years: (2004) 03 02 01 **99 98 97 96**.

BIONDI-SANTI *Brunello di Montalcino DOCG, Tuscany, Italy* Franco Biondi-Santi's Il Greppo estate has created both a legend and an international standing for BRUNELLO DI MONTALCINO. The modern dynamism of the zone owes more to other producers, however, since quality has slipped over the last 2 decades. Yet the very expensive Riserva★★, with formidable levels of extract, tannin and acidity, deserves a minimum 10 years' further aging after release before serious judgement is passed on it. Franco's son, Jacopo, has created his own range of wines, including Sassoalloro★★, a barrique-aged Sangiovese, and Sangiovese-Cabernet-Merlot blend Schidione★★. Best years: (Riserva) (2003) (01) (99) (97) (95) 90 88 85 **83 82 75 64 55 45 25**.

BLAGNY AC *Côte de Beaune, Burgundy, France* The red wine from this tiny hamlet above MEURSAULT and PULIGNY-MONTRACHET can be fair value, if you like a rustic Burgundy. Actually much more Chardonnay than Pinot Noir is grown here, but this is sold as Puligny-Montrachet, Meursault Premier Cru or Meursault-Blagny. Best producers: R Ampeau★, Lamy-Pillot★, Matrot★. Best years: (2004) 03 02 **99 96**.

DOM. PAUL BLANCK *Alsace AC, Alsace, France* Philippe Blanck and his winemaker cousin Frédéric run one of Alsace's most interesting and reliable domaines, although real character only shows in the Grand Cru wines. From a range of 30 or more different wines, Riesling★★ and Vieilles Vignes Gewurztraminer★★ from the Furstentum Grand Cru (also the source of super-rich Pinot Gris SGN★★★) stand out. Riesling Schlossberg★★ and Pinot Gris Altenbourg★★ offer depth and finesse. Best years: (Grand Cru Riesling) 2004 03 02 01 **00 98 97 96 95 94 93 92 90 89 88**.

BLANQUETTE DE LIMOUX AC *Languedoc-Roussillon, France* Sharp, refreshing fizz from the Mauzac grape, which makes up a minimum 90% of the wine and gives it its striking 'green apple skin' flavour – the balance is made up of Chardonnay and Chenin Blanc. The traditional (CHAMPAGNE) method is used to create the sparkle. The more rustic *méthode rurale*, finishing off the original fermentation inside the bottle, is used under a separate appellation – Blanquette Méthode Ancestrale. Best producers: Collin, Fourn★, Guinot, Martinolles★, SIEUR D'ARQUES★, les Terres Blanches. See also Crémant de Limoux AC and pages 258–9.

WOLF BLASS *Barossa Valley, South Australia* Wolf Blass, with its huge range, is the cornerstone of Beringer Blass, one of the big 4 Aussie companies. The wines do still faintly reflect the founder's dictum that they must be easy to enjoy, though I think they could do better. The reds show overt oak, sometimes clumsy, and occasionally capture the traditional Blass mint and blackcurrant charm. Whites are on the oaky side, except for the Rieslings, which are good, though sweeter and less vibrant than they used to be, including star Gold Label Riesling★. Black Label★, a red blend released at 4 years old, is expensive but good. Ultra-expensive Platinum Label reds are quite impressive. Regional varietals under the Blass label reflect the winemaking style rather than regional taste, whatever the label says. The Eaglehawk range is reliable quaffing wine. Best years: (Black Label) (2002) 01 **99 98 97** 96 95 91 **90** 88 86.

BLAUBURGUNDER See Pinot Noir.

BLAUER LEMBERGER See Blaufränkisch.

BLAUFRÄNKISCH Good, ripe Blaufränkisch has a taste similar to raspberries and white pepper or even beetroot. Hungarian in origin, it does well in Austria, where it is the principal red grape of BURGENLAND. The Hungarian vineyards (where it is called Kékfrankos) are mostly just across the border on the other side of the Neusiedlersee. Called Lemberger in Germany, where almost all of it is grown in WURTTEMBERG. Also successful as Lemberger in WASHINGTON STATE.

BLAYE See Premières Côtes de Blaye AC.

BOEKENHOUTSKLOOF *Franschhoek WO, South Africa* Perched high in the FRANSCHHOEK mountains, this small winery is named after the surrounding Cape beech trees. It also gives its name to Marc Kent's flagship trio: punchy, savoury Syrah★★; deep, long-lived Cabernet Sauvignon★★; and sophisticated, individual Semillon★★ from 100-year-old vines. Placed between these and the fruit-focused, value Porcupine Ridge★ range is the burly, expressive Chocolate Block★, a Cabernet Sauvignon-Shiraz blend with Grenache and Cinsaut. Best years (premium reds): 2002 01 **00 99 98** 97.

BOISSET *Burgundy, France* Jean-Claude Boisset bought his first vineyards in 1964 and began a négociant company whose extraordinary success has enabled him to swallow up many other long-established names such as Jaffelin, Ponelle, Ropiteau and Héritier Guyot in the COTE D'OR, Moreau in CHABLIS, Cellier des Samsons and Mommessin in BEAUJOLAIS and others elsewhere in France. None of these companies has delivered much in the way of quality wine to date, though there are big changes at last, happening under the Boisset name itself. Also projects in LANGUEDOC, Canada, Chile and Uruguay. See also Domaine de la Vougeraie.

BOLGHERI DOC *Tuscany, Italy* In 1994, this zone in the MAREMMA extended its DOC beyond simple white and rosé to cover red wines based on Cabernet, Merlot or Sangiovese, while creating a special sub-zone category for SASSICAIA. The DOC Rosso Superiore now covers wines from the prestigious estates of Grattamacco★★, Le MACCHIOLE★★, ORNELLAIA★★★, Michele Satta★★ and ANTINORI's Guado al Tasso★★. Best years (since 1994): (reds) (2004) (03) (01) 00 99 **98 97 96 95 94**.

BOLLINGER *Champagne AC, Champagne, France* One of the great CHAMPAGNE houses, with good non-vintage (Special Cuvée★) and vintage wines (Grande Année★★★), made in a full, rich, rather old-fashioned style. (Bollinger is one of the few houses to ferment its base wine in barrels.) It also produces a range of rarer vintages, including a Vintage RD★★★, and a Vieilles Vignes Françaises Blanc de Noirs★★ from ancient, ungrafted Pinot Noir vines. Bollinger bought Champagne Ayala, a near neighbour in Ay, in early 2005. Best years: (Grande Année) 1997 96 95 **92 90 89 88 85 82 79**.

CH. LE BON PASTEUR★★ *Pomerol AC, Bordeaux, France* Small château which has established an excellent reputation under the ownership of Michel Rolland, one of Bordeaux's leading winemakers. The wines are expensive, but they are always deliciously soft and full of lush fruit. Best years: 2003 01 00 **99** 98 **96 95 94** 93 90 89 88 85 83 82.

BONNES-MARES AC *Grand Cru, Côte de Nuits, Burgundy, France* A large Grand Cru straddling the communes of CHAMBOLLE-MUSIGNY and MOREY-ST-DENIS, commendably consistent over the last few decades. Bonnes-Mares generally has a deep, ripe, smoky plum fruit, which starts rich and chewy and matures over 10–20 years. Best producers: d'Auvenay (Dom. LEROY)★★★, BOUCHARD PERE ET FILS★★, DROUHIN★★, Drouhin-Laroze★★, DUJAC★★★, Robert Groffier★★★, JADOT★★★, D Laurent★★, J-F Mugnier★★, ROUMIER★★, VOGUE★★★, VOUGERAIE★★★. Best years: (2004) 03 02 01 00 99 98 **97** 96 **95 93 90 89 88**.

CH. BONNET *Entre-Deux-Mers AC, Bordeaux, France* This region's pioneering estate for quality and consistency. Large volumes of good, fruity, affordable Entre-Deux-Mers★, and BORDEAUX AC rosé and red, particularly the barrel-aged Merlot-Cabernet Réserve★. Drink this at 3–4 years and the others young. A new special cuvée, Dominus★, was launched with the 2000 vintage. Owner André Lurton is also the proprietor of La LOUVIERE and other properties in PESSAC-LEOGNAN.

BONNEZEAUX AC *Loire Valley, France* One of France's great sweet wines, Bonnezeaux is a zone within the larger COTEAUX DU LAYON AC. Like SAUTERNES, the wine is influenced by noble rot, but the flavours are different, as only Chenin Blanc is used. Extensive recent plantings have made quality less reliable. It can age very well in good vintages. Best producers: M Angeli/Sansonnière★★★, Fesles★★★, Godineau★★, des Grandes Vignes★★, Petit Val★★, Petits Quarts★★, René Renou★★, Terrebrune★★, la Varière★★. Best years: 2004 03 02 01 **99 97 96 95 90 89 88 85 83 76 71 61 59 47**.

BONNY DOON *Santa Cruz Mountains AVA, California, USA* Randall Grahm revels in the unexpected. He has a particular love for RHONE, Italian and Spanish varietals and for fanciful brand names: Le Cigare Volant★★ is a blend of Grenache and Syrah and is Grahm's homage to CHATEAUNEUF-DU-PAPE. Old Telegram★★ is 100% Mourvèdre. Particularly delightful are his Ca' del Solo Italianate wines, especially a bone-dry Malvasia Bianca★. He also makes a lovely Syrah★★, Cardinal Zin★ Zinfandel and various Rieslings, including one entirely from WASHINGTON, and one a blend of Washington and MOSEL fruit. Grahm has now spread his net even wider and has 6 wines from European vineyards: a MADIRAN★, a Vin de Pays d'Oc Syrah and 4 Italian wines, including an Uva di Troia from PUGLIA. Best years: (Old Telegram) 2002 01 00 **98 97 96 95 94 91**.

BORDEAUX RED WINES

Bordeaux, France

This large area of South-West France, centred on the historic city of Bordeaux, produces a larger volume of fine red wine than any other French region. Wonderful Bordeaux-style wines are produced in California, Australia, South Africa and South America, but the home team's top performers still just about keep the upstarts at bay. Around 800 million bottles of red wine a year are produced here. The best wines, known as the Classed Growths, account for a tiny percentage of this figure, but some of their lustre rubs off on the lesser names, making this one of the most popular wine styles.

GRAPE VARIETIES

Bordeaux's reds are commonly divided into 'right' and 'left' bank wines. On the left bank of the Gironde estuary, the red wines are dominated by the Cabernet Sauvignon grape, with varying proportions of Cabernet Franc, Merlot and Petit Verdot. At best they are austere but perfumed with blackcurrant and cedarwood. The most important left bank areas are the Haut-Médoc (especially the communes of Margaux, St-Julien, Pauillac and St-Estèphe) and, south of the city of Bordeaux, the ACs of Pessac-Léognan and Graves. On the right bank, Merlot is the predominant grape, which generally makes the resulting wines more supple and fleshy than those of the left bank. The key areas for Merlot-based wines are St-Émilion and Pomerol.

CLASSIFICATIONS

Red Bordeaux is made all over the region. At its most basic, the wine is simply labelled Bordeaux or Bordeaux Supérieur. Above this are the more specific ACs covering sub-areas (such as the Haut-Médoc) and individual communes (such as Pomerol, St-Émilion or Margaux). Single-estate Crus Bourgeois are the next rung up on the quality ladder, followed by the Crus Classés (Classed Growths) of the Médoc, Graves and St-Émilion. The famous classification of 1855 ranked the top red wines of the Médoc (plus one from Graves) into 5 tiers, from First to Fifth Growths (Crus); there has been only one change, in 1973, promoting Mouton-Rothschild to First Growth status. Since the 1950s the Graves/Pessac-Léognan region has had its own classification, for red and white wines. St-Émilion's classification (for red wines only) has been revised several times, the last modification being in 1996; the possibility of re-grading can help to maintain quality. Curiously, Pomerol, home of Château Pétrus, arguably the most famous red wine in the world, has no official pecking order. Many top Bordeaux châteaux also make 'second wines', which are cheaper versions of their Grands Vins.

See also BORDEAUX, BORDEAUX-COTES DE FRANCS, BORDEAUX SUPERIEUR, CANON-FRONSAC, COTES DE BOURG, COTES DE CASTILLON, FRONSAC, GRAVES, HAUT-MEDOC, LALANDE-DE-POMEROL, LISTRAC-MEDOC, LUSSAC-ST-EMILION, MARGAUX, MEDOC, MONTAGNE-ST-EMILION, MOULIS, PAUILLAC, PESSAC-LEOGNAN, POMEROL, PREMIERES COTES DE BLAYE, PREMIERES COTES DE BORDEAUX, PUISSEGUIN-ST-EMILION, ST-EMILION, ST-ESTEPHE, ST-GEORGES-ST-EMILION, ST-JULIEN; and individual châteaux.

BEST PRODUCERS

Graves, Pessac-Léognan Dom. de CHEVALIER, HAUT-BAILLY, HAUT-BRION, la LOUVIERE, MALARTIC-LAGRAVIERE, la MISSION-HAUT-BRION, PAPE-CLEMENT, SMITH-HAUT-LAFITTE.

Margaux BRANE-CANTENAC, FERRIERE, MALESCOT ST-EXUPERY, Ch. MARGAUX, PALMER, RAUZAN-SEGLA.

Pauillac GRAND-PUY-LACOSTE, LAFITE-ROTHSCHILD, LATOUR, LYNCH-BAGES, MOUTON-ROTHSCHILD, PICHON-LONGUEVILLE, PICHON-LONGUEVILLE-LALANDE, PONTET-CANET.

Pomerol le BON PASTEUR, Certan-de-May, Clinet, la CONSEILLANTE, l'EGLISE-CLINET, l'EVANGILE, la FLEUR-PETRUS, GAZIN, LAFLEUR, LATOUR-A-POMEROL, PETIT-VILLAGE, PETRUS, le PIN, TROTANOY, VIEUX-CHATEAU-CERTAN.

St-Émilion ANGELUS, l'ARROSEE, AUSONE, BEAU-SEJOUR BECOT, BELAIR, CANON, CANON-LA-GAFFELIERE, CHEVAL BLANC, Clos Fourtet, la Dominique, FIGEAC, Grand Mayne, MAGDELAINE, MONBOUSQET, La Mondotte, PAVIE, PAVIE-MACQUIN, Rol Valentin, TERTRE-ROTEBOEUF, TROPLONG-MONDOT, VALANDRAUD.

St-Estèphe CALON-SEGUR, COS D'ESTOURNEL, HAUT-MARBUZET, LAFON-ROCHET, MONTROSE.

St-Julien BRANAIRE, DUCRU-BEAUCAILLOU, GRUAUD-LAROSE, LAGRANGE, LANGOA-BARTON, LEOVILLE-BARTON, LEOVILLE-LAS-CASES, LEOVILLE-POYFERRE, ST-PIERRE, TALBOT.

BORDEAUX WHITE WINES

Bordeaux, France

This is France's largest fine wine region but, except for the sweet wines of Sauternes and Barsac, Bordeaux's international reputation is based solely on its reds. From 52% of the vineyard area in 1970, white wines now represent only 12% of the present 118,000ha (291,460 acres) of vines. Given the size of the region, the diversity of Bordeaux's white wines should come as no surprise. There are dry, medium and sweet styles, ranging from dreary to some of the most sublime white wines of all. Bordeaux's temperate southern climate – moderated by the influence of the Atlantic and of 2 rivers, the Dordogne and the Garonne – is ideal for white wine production, particularly south of the city along the banks of the Garonne.

GRAPE VARIETIES

Sauvignon Blanc and Sémillon, the most important white grapes, are varieties of considerable character and are usually blended together. They are backed up by smaller quantities of other grapes, the most notable of which is Muscadelle (unrelated to Muscat), which lends perfume to sweet wines and spiciness to dry.

DRY WINES

With the introduction of new technology and new ideas, many of them influenced by the New World, Bordeaux has become one of France's most exciting white wine areas. The wines have improved beyond recognition over the last decade. At their best, dry Bordeaux whites have fresh fruit flavours of apples, peaches and apricots, balanced by a light grassiness.

SWEET WINES

Bordeaux's most famous whites are its sweet wines made from grapes affected by noble rot, particularly those from Sauternes and Barsac. The noble rot concentrates the flavours, producing rich, honeyed wines replete with pineapple and peach flavours, and which develop a nut-oiliness and greater honeyed richness with age. On the other side of the Garonne river, Cadillac, Loupiac and Ste-Croix-du-Mont also make sweet wines; these rarely attain the richness or complexity of a top Sauternes, but they are considerably less expensive.

CLASSIFICATIONS

The two largest dry white wine ACs in Bordeaux are Bordeaux Blanc and Entre-Deux-Mers. There are plenty of good dry wines in the Graves and Pessac-Léognan regions; the Pessac-Léognan AC, created in 1987, contains all the dry white Classed Growths. The great sweet wines of Sauternes and Barsac were classified as First or Second Growths in 1855.

See also BARSAC, BORDEAUX, BORDEAUX-COTES DE FRANCS, BORDEAUX SUPERIEUR, CADILLAC, CERONS, COTES DE BLAYE, COTES DE BOURG, ENTRE-DEUX-MERS, GRAVES, GRAVES SUPERIEURES, LOUPIAC, PESSAC-LEOGNAN, PREMIERES COTES DE BLAYE, PREMIERES COTES DE BORDEAUX, STE-CROIX-DU-MONT, SAUTERNES; and individual châteaux.

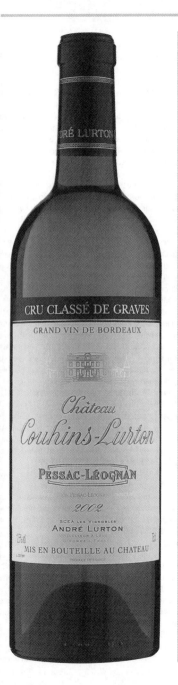

BEST YEARS

(dry) (2004) **02 01 00 99 98 96 95**; (sweet) 2003 02 01 **99 98 97 96 95** 90 89 88 86 83

BEST PRODUCERS

Dry wines

Pessac-Léognan Dom. de CHEVALIER, Couhins-Lurton, FIEUZAL, HAUT-BRION, LATOUR-MARTILLAC, LAVILLE-HAUT-BRION, la LOUVIERE, MALARTIC-LAGRAVIERE, SMITH-HAUT-LAFITTE; *Graves* Archambeau, Ardennes, Brondelle, Chantegrive, Clos Floridène, Magneau, Rahoul, Respide-Médeville, St. Robert (Cuvée Poncet-Deville), Vieux-Ch.-Gaubert, Villa Bel Air.

Entre-Deux-Mers BONNET, de Fontenille, Nardique-la-Gravière, Ste-Marie, Toutigeac, Turcaud.

Bordeaux AC l'Abbaye de Ste-Ferme, CARSIN, DOISY-DAENE (Sec), LYNCH-BAGES, Ch. MARGAUX (Pavillon Blanc), REYNON, Roquefort, Thieuley, Tour de Mirambeau.

Premières Côtes de Blaye Charron (Acacia), Haut-Bertinerie, Cave des Hauts de Gironde co-op, Tourtes (Prestige).

Sweet wines

Sauternes and Barsac CLIMENS, Clos Haut-Peyraguey, COUTET, DOISY-DAENE, DOISY-VEDRINES, FARGUES, GILETTE, GUIRAUD, LAFAURIE-PEYRAGUEY, NAIRAC, Raymond-Lafon, RIEUSSEC, Sigalas-Rabaud, SUDUIRAUT, la TOUR BLANCHE, YQUEM.

Cadillac Cayla, Manos, Mémoires.

Cérons Ch. de Cérons, Grand Enclos du Ch. de Cérons.

Loupiac Clos Jean, Cros, Mémoires, Noble.

Ste-Croix-du-Mont Loubens, Pavillon, la Rame.

BORDEAUX AC *Bordeaux, France* One of the most important ACs in
France. It can be applied to reds, rosés and the dry, medium and sweet
white wines of the entire Gironde region. Most of the best wines are
allowed more specific district or commune ACs (such as MARGAUX or
SAUTERNES) but a vast amount of Bordeaux's wine – delicious, atrocious
and everything in between – is sold as Bordeaux AC. At its best,
straight red Bordeaux is marked by bone-dry grassy fruit and an
attractive earthy edge, but far more frequently the wines are tannic
and raw – and often overpriced. Good examples usually benefit from a
year or so of aging. Bordeaux Blanc is joining the modern world with
an increasing number of refreshing, pleasant, clean wines. These may
be labelled as Bordeaux Sauvignon. Drink as young as possible.
Bordeaux Clairet is a pale red wine, virtually rosé but with a little more
substance. Best producers: (reds) BONNET★, Dourthe (Numéro 1), Ducla,
Fontenille★, Sirius, Thieuley★, Tour de Mirambeau, le Trébuchet; (whites)
l'Abbaye de Ste-Ferme★, CARSIN★, DOISY-DAENE★, Dourthe (Numéro 1),
d:vin★, LYNCH-BAGES★, MARGAUX (Pavillon Blanc★★), Premius, REYNON★,
Roquefort★, Thieuley★, Tour de Mirambeau★. See also pages 68–71.

BORDEAUX-CÔTES DE FRANCS AC *Bordeaux, France* There's been
quite a bit of investment in this tiny area east of ST-EMILION, and the top
wines are good value. The Thienpont family (Ch. Puygueraud) is the
driving force. Best producers: les Charmes-Godard★, Francs (Les
Cerisiers★★), Laclaverie★, Marsau, Moulin la Pitié, Pelan★, la Prade★,
Puygueraud★. Best years: 2003 01 **00 98 97 96 95 94 90**.

BORDEAUX SUPÉRIEUR AC *Bordeaux, France* Covers the same area as
the BORDEAUX AC but the wines must have an extra 0.5% of alcohol, a
lower yield and a longer period of maturation. Many of the best petits
châteaux are labelled Bordeaux Supérieur. Best producers (reds):
Barreyre★, de Bouillerot★, de Courteillac★, Grand Village★, Parenchère★,
Penin★, le Pin Beausoleil★, Reignac★, de Seguin, Tire-Pé★.

LUIGI BOSCA *Mendoza, Argentina* Founded by the Arizú family in 1901
and still family-owned, this winery has more than 600ha (1500 acres)
in LUJAN DE CUYO and Maipú, planted mainly with Malbec, Caberne
Sauvignon, Syrah, Chardonnay and Sauvignon Blanc. Try the mineral
Finca Los Nobles Chardonnay★, the dense and chocolaty Finca Los
Nobles Malbec★★, or the recently released Malbec-based blend Gala
1★ and Cabernet-based Gala 2★. Best years: (2003) 02 **01 99**.

BOSCARELLI *Vino Nobile di Montepulciano DOCG, Tuscany, Italy*
Arguably Montepulciano's best producer, Paola de Ferrari and her
sons Luca and Niccolò, with guidance from star enologist Maurizio
Castelli, craft rich and stylish reds. VINO NOBILE★★, Riserva del Nocio★★
and the barrique-aged Sangiovese Boscarelli★★ are all brilliant. Best
years: (2004) (03) (01) 00 **99 98 97 95 90 88 85**.

BOUCHARD FINLAYSON *Walker Bay WO, South Africa* Pinotphile Peter
Finlayson produces classy Pinot Noirs Galpin Peak★ and barrel
selection Tête de Cuvée★. His love of Italian varieties is reflected in
Hannibal, a multi-cultural mix led by Sangiovese with Pinot Noir,
Nebbiolo, Mourvèdre, Barbera and Syrah. Chardonnays
(Kaimansgaat/Crocodile's Lair★ and home-grown Missionvale★) are
full, nutty and passably Burgundian. Sauvignon Blanc★ is elegant and
fresh. Best years: (Pinot Noir) (2004) 03 **02 01 00 99 98 97 96 95**.

BOUCHARD PÈRE ET FILS *Beaune, Burgundy, France* Important
merchant and vineyard owner, with vines in some of Burgundy's most
spectacular sites, including CORTON, CORTON-CHARLEMAGNE, Chevalier-

Montrachet and le MONTRACHET. The firm is owned by Champenois Joseph HENRIOT, who is now realizing the full potential here. Wines from the company's own vineyards are sold under the Domaines du Château de Beaune label. Don't touch anything pre-1996. Best years: (top reds) (2004) 03 02 01 **00 99 98 97 96**.

BOUCHES-DU-RHÔNE, VIN DE PAYS DES *Provence, France* Wines from 3 areas: the coast, a zone around Aix-en-Provence and the Camargue. Mainly full-bodied, spicy reds, but rosé can be good. Best producers: Ch. Bas, de Boujeu, l'Île St-Pierre, Mas de Rey, TREVALLON★★, Valdition. Best years: (reds) 2003 **01 00 99 98**.

BOURGOGNE AC *Burgundy, France* Bourgogne is the French name anglicized as 'Burgundy'. This generic AC mops up all the Burgundian wine with no AC of its own, resulting in massive differences in style and quality. The best wines will usually come from a single grower's vineyards just outside the main village ACs of the COTE D'OR; such wines may be the only way we can afford the joys of fine Burgundy. If the wine is from a grower, the flavours should follow a regional style. However, if the address on the label is that of a négociant, the wine could be from anywhere in Burgundy. Pinot Noir is the main red grape, but Gamay from a declassified BEAUJOLAIS cru is, absurdly, allowed. Red Bourgogne is usually light, fruity in an upfront strawberry and cherry way, and should be drunk young (within 2–3 years). The rosé (from Pinot Noir) can be pleasant, but little is produced. Bourgogne Blanc is a usually bone-dry Chardonnay wine and most should be drunk within 2 years. Bourgogne Passe-tout-Grains is made from Gamay with a minimum 33% of Pinot Noir, while Bourgogne Grand Ordinaire is the most basic appellation of all – rarely more than a quaffing wine, drunk in local bars. Best producers: (reds/growers) COCHE-DURY★, Dugat-Py★★, Germain★, LAFARGE★, MEO-CAMUZET★★, Pierre Morey★, Patrice RION★★, ROUMIER★; (reds/merchants) DROUHIN★, GIRARDIN★, JADOT★, LABOURE-ROI, Maison LEROY★★, N Potel★★, VOUGERAIE; (reds/co-ops) BUXY★, Caves des Hautes-Côtes★; (whites/growers) M Bouzereau★, Boyer-Martenot★, COCHE-DURY★★, J-P Fichet★, P Javillier★★, Ch. de Meursault★, Guy Roulot★, (whites/merchants) DROUHIN★, FAIVELEY, JADOT★, Olivier LEFLAIVE, RODET★; (whites/co-ops) BUXY, Caves des Hautes-Côtes. Best years: (reds) (2003) **02 01 99**; (whites) **2002 01 00**. See also pages 76–9.

BOURGOGNE ALIGOTÉ AC See Aligoté.

BOURGOGNE-CÔTE CHALONNAISE AC *Côte Chalonnaise, Burgundy, France* These vineyards have gained in importance, mainly because of spiralling prices on the COTE D'OR to the north. This AC covers vineyards to the west of Chalon-sur-Saône around the villages of Bouzeron, RULLY, MERCUREY, GIVRY and MONTAGNY. Best producers: X Besson, BUXY CO-OP★, Villaine★. Best years: 2004 **03 02**.

BOURGOGNE-HAUTES-CÔTES DE BEAUNE AC *Burgundy, France* The hills behind the great COTE DE BEAUNE have been a source of affordable Burgundy since the 1970s. The red wines are lean but drinkable, as is the slightly sharp Chardonnay. Best producers: D & F Clair★, Caves des Hautes-Côtes★, J-Y Devevey★, L Jacob★, J-L Joillot★, Ch. de Mercey★/RODET, Naudin-Ferrand★, C Nouveau★. Best years: (reds) (2004) **03 02**; (whites) (2004) **03 02**.

BOURGOGNE-HAUTES-CÔTES DE NUITS AC *Burgundy, France* Attractive, lightweight wines from the hills behind the COTE DE NUITS. The reds are best, with an attractive cherry and plum flavour. The whites tend to be rather dry and flinty. Best producers: (reds)

Bertagna★, FAIVELEY★, A-F GROS★, M GROS★, A Guyon★, Caves des Hautes-Côtes★, B Hudelot★, JAYER-GILLES★★, THOMAS-MOILLARD★; (whites) Caves des Hautes-Côtes★, Y Chaley★, Champy★, B Hudelot★, JAYER-GILLES★★, Thévenot-le-Brun★, THOMAS-MOILLARD★, A Verdet★. Best years: (reds) (2004) **03 02 99**; (whites) (2004) **03 02**.

BOURGUEIL AC *Loire Valley, France* Fine red wine from between Tours and Angers. Made with Cabernet Franc, topped up with a little Cabernet Sauvignon; in hot years results can be superb. Given 5–10 years of age, the wines can develop a wonderful raspberry fragrance. Best producers: l'Abbaye★, Y Amirault★★, Audebert (estate wines★), T Boucard★, P Breton★, la Butte★, la Chevalerie, Max Cognard, DRUET★★, Forges★, Lamé-Delisle-Boucard★, la Lande/ Delaunay★, Nau Frères★, Ouches★, Raguenières★. Best years: 2004 03 02 01 **00 97 96 95**. See also St-Nicolas-de-Bourgueil.

BOUVET-LADUBAY *Saumur AC, Loire Valley, France* Sparkling wine producer owned by the Champagne house TAITTINGER. The basic range (Bouvet Brut, Bouvet Rosé) is good. Cuvée Saphir, the top-selling wine, is over-sweet, but Trésor (Blanc★ and Rosé★), fermented in oak casks, is very good. Now also a good Brut Zéro. Weird and wonderful Rubis★ sparkling red is worth trying. The expanded Nonpareils★ range of still wines are pricy for the quality.

BOUVIER Austrian and Slovenian grape short on acidity and so mainly used for sweet to ultra-sweet wines, where it achieves richness but rarely manages to offer any other complexity. Best producers: KRACHER★, Münzenrieder, OPITZ★, Velich★.

BOWEN ESTATE *Coonawarra, South Australia* Doug Bowen – now joined in the winemaking team by daughter Emma – can make some of COONAWARRA's best peppery Shiraz★★ and vibrant blackcurranty Cabernet★. Tough tannins in the 1999s (which have since softened) and a tricky vintage for Cabernet in 2000 suggested that things might have been on the slide. Not so: as subsequent vintages show. Best years: (Shiraz) (2003) 02 01 00 **98 97 96 94 93 92 91**.

BOYAR ESTATES *Bulgaria* The leading distributor of Bulgarian wines, selling more than 65 million bottles worldwide each year. It also has extensive vineyard holdings of 1000ha (2470 acres), and wineries at Iambol, Shumen, Sliven (state-of-the-art Blueridge) and – following its merger with Vinprom – at Rousse. Quality is still far too erratic: many reds are raw and tannic, whites are merely decent.

BRACHETTO Piedmontese grape revived in dry versions and in sweet, frothy types with a Muscat-like perfume, as exemplified by Brachetto d'Acqui DOCG. Best producers: (dry) Contero, Correggia★, Scarpa★; (Brachetto d'Acqui) BANFI★, Braida★, G Marenco★.

CH. BRANAIRE★★ *St-Julien AC, 4ème Cru Classé, Haut-Médoc, Bordeaux, France* After a long period of mediocrity, 1994 and subsequent vintages have confirmed a welcome return to full, soft, chocolaty form. Best years: 2003 02 01 00 **99** 98 96 **95 94**.

BRAND'S *Coonawarra, South Australia* COONAWARRA firm, owned by MCWILLIAM'S, with 100ha (250 acres) of new vineyards as well as some ancient vines now over 100 years old. Improved viticulture, greater investment in oak and chief winemaker Jim Brayne's influence have lifted standards dramatically. Ripe Cabernet★★ and Cabernet-Merlot★ are increasingly attractive; Patron's Reserve Cabernet★★ is excellent. New life has been breathed into Shiraz★, and the opulent Stentiford's Reserve★★ shows how good Coonawarra Shiraz can be. Special Release Merlot★★ is among Australia's best examples of the variety. Best years: (reds) (2004) (03) 02 01 00 **99 98 97 96 94 90**.

CH. BRANE-CANTENAC★★ *Margaux AC, 2ème Cru Classé, Haut-Médoc, Bordeaux, France* After a drab period, Brane-Cantenac returned to form during the late 1990s. Henri Lurton has taken over the family property and is making some superb wines, particularly the 2000, and I am delighted that I can once more enjoy what used to be one of my favourite Bordeaux. Best years: 2003 02 01 00 **99** 98 **96 95** 90.

BRAUNEBERG *Mosel, Germany* Small village with 2 famous vineyard sites, Juffer and Juffer Sonnenuhr, whose wines have a honeyed richness and creamy gentleness rare in the Mosel. Best producers: Bastgen★★, Fritz HAAG★★★, Willi Haag★, Paulinshof★, M F RICHTER★★. Best years: (2004) 03 02 01 **99 98 97** 95 **93 90**.

BREAKY BOTTOM *Sussex, England* Small vineyard in the South Downs near Lewes. Peter Hall is a quirky, passionate grower, making dry, nutty Seyval Blanc★ that becomes creamy and BURGUNDY-like after 3–4 years. Sparkling Seyval Blanc★ is delicious, but there is a shift to fizz made from more classic varieties, using early-ripening clones of Chardonnay and Pinot Noir.

GEORG BREUER *Rüdesheim, Rheingau, Germany* Estate run, until his untimely death in 2004, by Bernhard Breuer, producing intense dry Riesling from RUDESHEIM Berg Schlossberg★★, Berg Rottland★★ and RAUENTHAL Nonnenberg★★. He also created a remarkable Sekt in 1987 from barrel-fermented Pinot Gris, Pinot Blanc and a dash of Riesling – a blend both distinctive and surprisingly successful. Best years: (Berg Schlossberg) (2004) 03 02 01 00 99 **98 97** 96 **94 93 90**.

BRIGHT BROTHERS *Ribatejo, Portugal* The Fiúza-Bright winemaking operation is located in the town of Almeirim in the RIBATEJO and Fiúza-labelled wines are from local vineyards planted to both Portuguese and French varieties. Australian Peter Bright also sources grapes (exclusively Portuguese varieties) from, chiefly, Palmela (Reserva★) and DOURO (TFN★) for the Bright Brothers label. Bright also makes a range of wines for Peñaflor in Argentina.

JEAN-MARC BROCARD *Chablis AC, Burgundy, France* Dynamic wine-maker who has built up this 80ha (200-acre) domaine almost from scratch, and is now one of Chablis' most reliable and satisfying producers. The Premiers Crus (including Montée de la Tonnerre★★, Montmains★★) and slow-evolving Grands Crus (les Clos★★★ stands out) are tremendous, while the basic Chablis, especially Vieilles Vignes★★, are some of the best on the market. Brocard also produces a range of BOURGOGNE Blancs★ from different soil types. Now adopting an increasingly organic – and in some cases biodynamic – approach to his vineyards. Best years: (2004) **03 02 00**.

BROKENWOOD *Hunter Valley, New South Wales, Australia* High-profile winery with delicious aged HUNTER Semillon★★ and Chardonnay★. Best wine is classic Hunter Graveyard Vineyard Shiraz★★★; MCLAREN VALE Rayner Vineyard Shiraz★★ is also stunning. Cricket Pitch reds and whites are cheerful, fruity ready-drinkers. New vineyard at BEECHWORTH will be worth following. Best years: (Graveyard Vineyard Shiraz) 2003 02 00 99 98 **96 95 94 93 91 90 89 88 86**.

BURGUNDY RED WINES

Burgundy, France

 Rich in history and gastronomic tradition, the region of Burgundy (Bourgogne in French) covers a vast tract of eastern France, running from Auxerre, south-east of Paris, down to the city of Lyon. As with its white wines, Burgundy's red wines are extremely diverse. The explanation for this lies partly in the fickle nature of Pinot Noir, the area's principal red grape, and partly in the historical imbalance of supply and demand between growers – who grow the grapes and make and bottle much of the best wine – and merchants, whose efforts originally established the reputation of the wines internationally.

WINE STYLES

Pinot Noir shows many different flavour profiles according to climate, soil and winemaking. The reds from around Auxerre (Épineuil, Irancy) in the north will be light, chalky and strawberry-flavoured. Also light, though more rustic and earthy, are the reds of the Mâconnais in the south, while the Côte Chalonnaise offers solid reds from Givry and Mercurey.

The top reds come from the Côte d'Or, the heartland of Burgundy. Flavours sweep through strawberry, raspberry, damson and cherry – in young wines – to a wild, magnificent maturity of Oriental spices, chocolate, mushrooms and truffles. The greatest of all – the world-famous Grand Cru vineyards such as Chambertin, Musigny, Richebourg and Clos de Vougeot – are in the Côte de Nuits, the northern part of the Côte d'Or from Nuits-St-Georges up toward Dijon. Other fine reds, especially Volnay, Pommard and Corton, come from the Côte de Beaune. Some villages tend toward a fine and elegant style (Chambolle-Musigny, Volnay), others toward a firmer, more tannic structure (Gevrey-Chambertin, Pommard).

The Beaujolais should really be considered as a separate region, growing Gamay on granitic soils rather than Pinot Noir on limestone, though a small amount of Gamay has also crept north to be included in the lesser wines of Burgundy.

CLASSIFICATIONS

A large part of Burgundy has 5 increasingly specific levels of classification: regional ACs (e.g. Bourgogne), specified ACs covering groups of villages (e.g. Côte de Nuits-Villages), village wines taking the village name (Pommard, Vosne-Romanée), Premiers Crus (good village vineyard sites) and Grands Crus (the best individual vineyard sites).

See also ALOXE-CORTON, AUXEY-DURESSES, BEAUJOLAIS, BEAUNE, BLAGNY, BONNES-MARES, BOURGOGNE, BOURGOGNE-COTE CHALONNAISE, BOURGOGNE-HAUTES-COTES DE BEAUNE/NUITS, CHAMBERTIN, CHAMBOLLE-MUSIGNY, CHASSAGNE-MONTRACHET, CHOREY-LES-BEAUNE, CLOS DE LA ROCHE, CLOS ST-DENIS, CLOS DE VOUGEOT, CORTON, COTE DE BEAUNE, COTE DE NUITS, COTE D'OR, CREMANT DE BOURGOGNE, ECHEZEAUX, FIXIN, GEVREY-CHAMBERTIN, GIVRY, IRANCY, LADOIX, MACON, MARANGES, MARSANNAY, MERCUREY, MONTHELIE, MOREY-ST-DENIS, MUSIGNY, NUITS-ST-GEORGES, PERNAND-VERGELESSES, POMMARD, RICHEBOURG, la ROMANEE-CONTI, ROMANEE-ST-VIVANT, RULLY, ST-AUBIN, ST-ROMAIN, SANTENAY, SAVIGNY-LES-BEAUNE, la TACHE, VOLNAY, VOSNE-ROMANEE, VOUGEOT; and individual producers.

BEST YEARS

(2004) 03 02 01 99 **98 97** 96
95 93 90

BEST PRODUCERS

Côte de Nuits B Ambroise,
Dom. de l'Arlot, Robert
Arnoux, Denis Bachelet,
G Barthod, Bertagna,
A Burguet, S Cathiard,
Charlopin, R Chevillon, CLAIR,
J-J Confuron, C Dugat,
B Dugat-Py, DUJAC, R Engel,
Sylvie Esmonin, Geantet-
Pansiot, Gouges, GRIVOT, GROS,
Hudelot-Noëllat, JAYER-GILLES,
Dom. LEROY, H Lignier,
MEO-CAMUZET, Denis MORTET,
Mugneret-Gibourg,
J-F Mugnier, Perrot-Minot,
Ponsot, RION, Dom. de la
ROMANEE-CONTI, Roty,
E Rouget, ROUMIER, ROUSSEAU,
Sérafin, THOMAS-MOILLARD,
de VOGUE, VOUGERAIE.

Côte de Beaune Ampeau,
d'ANGERVILLE, Comte Armand,
J-M Boillot, CHANDON DE
BRIAILLES, COCHE-DURY, Courcel,
Germain, Michel LAFARGE,
LAFON, Montille, Albert Morot,
Pousse d'Or, TOLLOT-BEAUT.

Côte Chalonnaise Brintet,
H & P Jacqueson, Joblot,
M Juillot, Lorenzon, Raquillet,
Thénard, Villaine.

Merchants BOUCHARD PERE ET
FILS, Champy, DROUHIN,
DUBOEUF, FAIVELEY, Féry-
Meunier, V GIRARDIN, Camille
Giroud, JADOT, LABOURE-ROI,
D Laurent, Maison LEROY,
Nicolas POTEL, RODET.

Co-ops BUXY, Caves des
Hautes-Côtes.

77

BURGUNDY WHITE WINES
Burgundy, France

White Burgundy has for generations been thought of as the world's leading dry white wine. The top wines have a remarkable succulent richness of honey and hazelnut, melted butter and sprinkled spice, yet are totally dry. Such wines are all from the Chardonnay grape and the finest are generally produced in the Côte de Beaune, the southern part of the Côte d'Or, in the communes of Aloxe-Corton, Meursault, Puligny-Montrachet and Chassagne-Montrachet where limestone soils and the aspect of the vineyard provide perfect conditions for even ripening of grapes.

WINE STYLES

However, Burgundy encompasses many more wine styles than this, even if no single one quite attains the peaks of quality of those 4 villages on the Côte de Beaune.

Chablis in the north traditionally produces very good steely wines, aggressive and lean when young, but nutty and rounded – though still very dry – after a few years. Modern Chablis is frequently a softer, milder wine, easy to drink young, and sometimes enriched (or denatured) by aging in new oak barrels.

There is no doubt that Meursault and the other Côte de Beaune villages can produce stupendous wine, but it is in such demand that unscrupulous producers are often tempted to maximize yields and cut corners on quality. Consequently white Burgundy from these famous villages must be approached with caution. Lesser-known villages such as Pernand-Vergelesses and St-Aubin often provide good wine at lower prices. There are also good wines from some villages in the Côte de Nuits, such as Morey-St-Denis, Nuits-St-Georges and Vougeot, though amounts are tiny compared with the Côte de Beaune.

South of the Côte d'Or the Côte Chalonnaise is becoming more interesting for quality white wine now that better equipment for temperature control is becoming more widespread and oak barrels are being used more often for aging. Rully and Montagny are the most important villages, though Givry and Mercurey can produce nice white, too. The minor Aligoté grape makes some attractive, if acidic, wine, especially in Bouzeron.

Further south, the Mâconnais is a large region, two-thirds planted with Chardonnay. There is some fair sparkling Crémant de Bourgogne, and some very good vineyard sites, in particular in St-Véran and in Pouilly-Fuissé. Increasingly stunning wines can now be found, though there's still a lot of dross.

See also ALOXE-CORTON, AUXEY-DURESSES, BATARD-MONTRACHET, BEAUJOLAIS, BEAUNE, BOURGOGNE, BOURGOGNE-COTE CHALONNAISE, BOURGOGNE-HAUTES-COTES DE BEAUNE/NUITS, CHABLIS, CHASSAGNE-MONTRACHET, CORTON, CORTON-CHARLEMAGNE, COTE DE BEAUNE, COTE DE NUITS, COTE D'OR, CREMANT DE BOURGOGNE, FIXIN, GIVRY, LADOIX, MACON, MACON-VILLAGES, MARANGES, MARSANNAY, MERCUREY, MEURSAULT, MONTAGNY, MONTHELIE, MONTRACHET, MOREY-ST-DENIS, MUSIGNY, NUITS-ST-GEORGES, PERNAND-VERGELESSES, POUILLY-FUISSE, POUILLY-VINZELLES, PULIGNY-MONTRACHET, RULLY, ST-AUBIN, ST-ROMAIN, ST-VERAN, SANTENAY, SAVIGNY-LES-BEAUNE, VIRE-CLESSE, VOUGEOT; and individual producers.

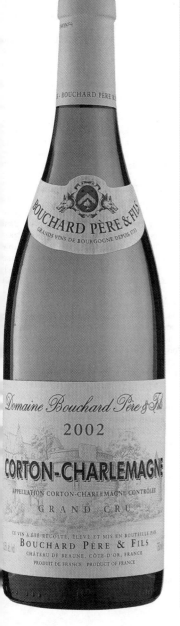

BEST YEARS

(2004) 03 02 **01 00 99 97 95**

BEST PRODUCERS

Chablis Barat, J-C Bessin, Billaud-Simon, A & F Boudin, J-M BROCARD, D Dampt, R & V DAUVISSAT, D & E Defaix, Droin, DURUP, W Fèvre, J-P Grossot, LAROCHE, Malandes, Louis MICHEL, G Picq, RAVENEAU, Vocoret.

Côte d'Or (Côte de Beaune) G Amiot, R Ampeau, d'Auvenay (LEROY), Blain-Gagnard, Jean Boillot, J-M Boillot, Bonneau du Martray, M Bouzereau, Y Boyer-Martenot, CARILLON, CHANDON DE BRIAILLES, COCHE-DURY, Marc Colin, Colin-Deléger, Arnaud Ente, J-P Fichet, J-N GAGNARD, P Javillier, F Jobard, R Jobard, LAFON, H & O Lamy, R Lamy-Pillot, Dom. LEFLAIVE, Dom. Matrot, F Mikulski, Bernard Morey, Marc Morey, Pierre Morey, M Niellon, P Pernot, J & J-M Pillot, RAMONET, M Rollin, G Roulot, SAUZET, VERGET.

Côte Chalonnaise S Aladame, H & P Jacqueson.

Mâconnais D & M Barraud, Bonhomme, Corsin, Deux Roches, J A Ferret, Ch. Fuissé, Guffens-Heynen (VERGET), J-J Litaud, O Merlin, Robert-Denogent, Ch. des Rontets, Saumaize-Michelin, Soufrandière, Thévenet, Valette.

Merchants BOUCHARD PERE ET FILS, Champy, DROUHIN, FAIVELEY, V GIRARDIN, JADOT, LABOURE-ROI, Louis LATOUR, Olivier LEFLAIVE, Maison LEROY, Rijckaert, RODET, VERGET.

Co-ops BUXY, la CHABLISIENNE, Lugny, Viré.

BROUILLY AC *Beaujolais, Burgundy, France* Largest of the 10 BEAUJOLAIS Crus; at its best, the wine is soft, fruity, rich and brightly coloured. Best producers: Ch. de la Chaize★, DUBOEUF (Ch. de Nervers★), A Michaud★, Ch. Thivin★★. Best years: **2003**.

BROWN BROTHERS *North-East Victoria, Australia* Highly successful family winery, producing a huge range of varietal wines, which have improved significantly in recent years. Good fizz and fine stickies★★. Top-of-the-range Patricia wines (Cabernet★★) are Brown's best yet. Focuses on cool King Valley and mountain-top Whitlands for its premium grapes. Exciting new vineyard at HEATHCOTE.

BRÜNDLMAYER *Kamptal, Niederösterreich, Austria* Willi Bründlmayer makes wine in a variety of Austrian and international styles, but his outstanding dry Riesling (Alte Reben★★★) from the great Heiligenstein vineyard and Grüner Veltliner (Ried Lamm★★★) are the best; high alcohol is matched by superlative fruit and mineral flavours. Good Sekt★. Best years: (Zöbinger Heiligenstein Riesling) (2004) 03 02 01 **99 98 97 95 94**.

BRUNELLO DI MONTALCINO DOCG *Tuscany, Italy* Powerful red wine produced from Sangiovese (known locally as Brunello). Traditionally needed over 10 years to soften, but modern practices result in more fruit-rich wines, yet still tannic enough to age spectacularly. Best producers: Altesino★ (Montosoli★★), BANFI★, Barbi★ (Riserva★★), BIONDI-SANTI★★, Gianni Brunelli★★, Camigliano★, La Campana★, Caparzo★ (La Casa★★) Casanova di Neri★★, Casanuova delle Cerbaie★★, Case Basse★★★, CASTELGIOCONDO (Riserva★), Centolani★ (Pietranera★★), Cerbaiona★★, Ciacci Piccolomini d'Aragona★★, Donatella Cinelli Colombini★, Col d'Orcia★★, COSTANTI★★, Fuligni★★, La Gerla★★, Le Gode★★, Gorelli-Due Portine★, Greppone Mazzi★★, Maurizio Lambardi★★, Lisini★★, Mastrojanni★★ (Schiena d'Asino★★★), Siro Pacenti★★★, Pian delle Vigne★★/ANTINORI, Piancornello★★, Agostina Pieri★★, Pieve Santa Restituta★★, La Poderina★★, Poggio Antico★★, Poggio San Polo★★, Il Poggione★★ (Riserva★★★), Salvioni★★, Livio Sassetti-Pertimali★★, Talenti★★, La Togata★★, Valdicava★, Villa Le Prata★★. Best years: (2004) (03) (01) (00) 99 **98 97 95 93 90 88 85**.

BUCELAS DOC *Estremadura, Portugal* A tiny but historic DOC. The wines are whites based on the Arinto grape (noted for its high acidity). For attractive, modern examples try Quinta da Murta or Quinta da Romeira (Morgado de Santa Catherina★).

VON BUHL *Deidesheim, Pfalz, Germany* Large estate, leased to the Japanese Sanyo group. Winemakers Frank John, and now Jan Kux, have dramatically improved quality at all levels. Best years: (Grosses Gewächs Rieslings) (2004) 03 02 01 99 **98 96 95**.

BUITENVERWACHTING *Constantia WO, South Africa* Time slows down at this beautiful property, part of the Cape's original CONSTANTIA wine farm. The traditional, Old World-style wines also take time to unfold; a ripe, fruit-laden Chardonnay★★, penetrating, zesty Sauvignon Blanc★ and light, racy Riesling. Recent vintages of aristocratic red blend Christine★ show ripe, deeper flavours thanks to new, virus-free vineyards. Firmly structured and dry, it remains one of the Cape's most accurate BORDEAUX lookalikes. Best years: (Christine) (2001) 00 **99 98 96 95 94**.

BULL'S BLOOD *Hungary* Kékfrankos (Blaufränkisch) grapes sometimes replace robust Kadarka in the blend, thinning the blood; some producers blend with Cabernet Sauvignon, Kékoporto or Merlot. New stringent regulations should improve the quality of Bikavér ('bull's blood') in the 2 permitted regions, Eger and Szekszárd. Winemakers such as Vilmos Thummerer are working hard on this front, and are putting some balls back into the wine.

GRANT BURGE *Barossa Valley, South Australia* The largest landowner and a leading producer in the BAROSSA, with a wide range, including chocolaty Filsell Shiraz★ and rich Meshach Shiraz★★, Cameron Vale Cabernet★ and Shadrach Cabernet★ (which includes some COONAWARRA fruit), the continually improving RHONE-style Grenache-Shiraz-Mourvèdre blend Holy Trinity★, fresh Thorn Riesling★, oaky Zerk Semillon, and the excellent-value Barossa Vines range. Recent vintages have shown a most welcome reduction in oak. Best years: (Meshach) (2002) (01) 99 **98 96 95 94 91 90**.

BURGENLAND *Austria* 4 regions: Neusiedlersee, including Seewinkel for sweet wines; Neusiedlersee-Hügelland, famous for sweet wines, now also big reds and fruity dry whites; Mittelburgenland, for robust Blaufränkisch reds; and Südburgenland, for good reds and dry whites. Best producers: FEILER-ARTINGER★★, Gernot Heinrich★★, Juris★, Kollwentz★★, KRACHER★★★, Krutzler★★, M & A Nittnaus★★, OPITZ★, Pöckl★★, Prieler★, Schandl, Schröck★, Ernst Triebaumer★★, UMATHUM★★, VELICH★★, Robert Wenzel★.

BURGUNDY See Bourgogne AC and pages 76–9.

BÜRKLIN-WOLF *Wachenheim, Pfalz, Germany* With nearly 100ha (250 acres) of vineyards, this is one of Germany's largest privately owned estates. Under director Christian von Guradze, a champion of vineyard classification, it has shot back up to the first rank of the region's producers since the 1994 vintage. The powerful, spicy dry Rieslings are now ★★ to ★★★. Best years: (Grosses Gewächs Rieslings) (2003) 02 01 98 **97** 96 **95**.

BURMESTER *Port DOC, Douro, Portugal* Shipper established since 1730, and now owned by cork giant Amorim. Vintage PORT★★ is much improved, as is the Vintage released under the Quinta Nova de Nossa Senhora do Carmo★ label, a quinta purchased by Burmester in 1991. As well as refined 10- and 20-year-old tawnies, there are some outstanding old colheitas★★ which extend back over 100 years. Also good recent Late Bottled Vintage★ and oak-aged DOURO red, Casa Burmester★. Gilbert is the second label. Best years: (Vintage) 2000 97 **95 94**.

TOMMASO BUSSOLA *Valpolicella DOC, Veneto, Italy* Tommaso Bussola learned the art of tending vines from his uncle Giuseppe, but in the art of making wine he is self-taught. His AMARONE Vigneto Alto★★★ combines elegance with stunning power. Amarone Classico TB★★ is similar with slightly less finesse, and even the basic Amarone BG★ is a challenge to the palate. The Ripasso VALPOLICELLA Classico Superiore TB★★ is one of the best of its genre, and the RECIOTO TB★★★ is consistently excellent. Best years: (2004) (03) (01) 00 99 **97 95**.

BUXY, CAVE DES VIGNERONS DE *Côte Chalonnaise, Burgundy, France* Based in the Côte Chalonnaise and now rechristened 'La Buxynoise', this ranks among Burgundy's top co-operatives, producing affordable, well-made Chardonnay and Pinot Noir. The light, oak-aged BOURGOGNE Pinot Noir★ and the red and white Clos de Chenôves★, as well as the nutty white MONTAGNY★, are all good, reasonably priced, and best with 2–3 years' age.

BUZET AC *South-West France*   Good Bordeaux-style red wines from the same mix of grapes and at a lower price. There is very little rosé and the whites are rarely exciting. Best producers: les Vignerons de Buzet (especially Baron d'Ardeuil and Ch. de Gueyze), Dom. du Pech.

BYRON *Santa Maria Valley AVA, California, USA*   Since the 1990s, with a new winery and expansion and replanting of vineyards, Ken Brown (whose real first name is Byron) has been making better-than-ever Pinot Noir and Chardonnay. His Nielson Vineyard Pinot★★ is full of spicy cherry fruit, and the Nielson Vineyard Chardonnay★★ with mineral notes and fine balance can age for several years. Regular Chardonnay is often good value, as is a vibrant Pinot Gris★★. Io★, a robust RHONE blend, looks good too. Best years: (Nielson Pinot Noir) (2002) **01 00 99 98 95**.

CA' DEL BOSCO *Franciacorta DOCG, Lombardy, Italy*   Model estate, headed by Maurizio Zanella, making some of Italy's finest and most expensive wines: outstanding sparklers in FRANCIACORTA Brut★★, Dosage Zero★, Satén★★ and the prestige Cuvée Annamaria Clementi★★★; good Terre di Franciacorta Rosso★, remarkably good Chardonnay★★★, Pinero★★ (Pinot Nero) and BORDEAUX blend, Maurizio Zanella★★★. Also promising varietal Carmenère, Carmenero★.

CABARDÈS AC *Languedoc, France*   Next door to MINERVOIS but, as well as the usual French Mediterranean grape varieties, Cabernet Sauvignon and Merlot are allowed. At best, full-bodied, chewy and rustically attractive. AC status granted in 1999 and quality has improved since. Wines are attractively priced. Best producers: Cabrol★, Jouclary, Pennautier★, Salitis, Ventenac. Best years: 2003 **02 01 00**.

CABERNET D'ANJOU AC *Loire Valley, France*   Rosé made from both Cabernets; generally medium dry or semi-sweet. Drink young. Best producers: Hautes-Ouches, Ogereau, Petites Grouas, Terrebrune.

CABERNET FRANC   Often unfairly dismissed as an inferior Cabernet Sauvignon, Cabernet Franc comes into its own in cool zones or areas where the soil is damp and heavy. It can have a leafy freshness linked to raw but tasty blackcurrant-raspberry fruit. In France it thrives in the LOIRE VALLEY and BORDEAUX, especially ST-EMILION and POMEROL where it accounts for 19% of the planting. Successful in northern Italy, especially ALTO ADIGE and FRIULI, although some plantings here have turned out to be Carmenère, and increasingly preferred to Cabernet Sauvignon in Tuscany. Experiments with Cabernet Franc on CALIFORNIA's North Coast and in WASHINGTON STATE show promise. There are also some good South African, Chilean and Australian examples.

CABERNET SAUVIGNON See pages 84–5.

CADENCE *Red Mountain AVA, Washington State, USA*   Cadence produces vineyard-specific reds. Tapteil Vineyard★★★, a powerful, Cabernet Sauvignon-dominated blend, is the flagship until their own vineyard, adjacent to Tapteil, has mature fruit. Ciel du Cheval Vineyard★★★, with a higher percentage of Merlot and Cabernet Franc, is more forward and juicy. Klipsun Vineyard★★ shows the characteristic firm tannins of the site. Best years: (2003) 02 01 **00 99 98**.

CADILLAC AC *Bordeaux, France*   Sweet wine from the southern half of the PREMIERES COTES DE BORDEAUX. Styles vary from fresh, semi-sweet to richly botrytized. The wines have greatly improved in recent vintages. Drink young. Best producers: CARSIN, Cayla★, Ch. du Juge/Dupleich, Manos★, Mémoires★, REYNON. Best years: 2003 **02 01 99 98**.

CAFAYATE VALLEY *Salta , Argentina*   At almost 2000m (6500 ft) above
sea level – a few are even higher – the vineyards of Cafayate are some
of the highest in the world. Located 700km (435 miles) north of
Mendoza, this region is known for its aromatic and intense Torrontés.
Don't miss the perfumed, fruity Malbec, fruity yet dense Tannat and
spicy Cabernet Sauvignon. Best producers: Etchart, San Pedro de
Yacochuya, Michel Torino.

CAHORS AC *South-West France*   Important South-West red wine region.
This dark, often tannic wine is made from at least 70% Auxerrois
(Malbec) and has an unforgettable, rich plummy flavour when ripe
and well made – which is less often than I'd wish. Ages well. Best
producers: la Caminade★, Cayrou, CEDRE★★, Clos la Coutale★, Clos de
Gamot★, Clos Triguedina★, Gaudou, Gautoul★, Haut-Monplaisir, Haute-
Serre, les Ifs, LAGREZETTE★, Lamartine★, les Laquets★, Primo Palatum,
les Rigalets★. Best years: (2003) 01 00 **98 96 95 94 90 89**.

CAIRANNE *Rhône Valley, France*   One of the best of the 16 Rhône villages
entitled to the COTES DU RHONE-VILLAGES appellation, offering full, herb-
scented reds and solid whites. Best producers: D & D Alary★★,
Ameillaud★, Brusset★, Cave de Cairanne★, Les Haute Cances★,
ORATOIRE ST-MARTIN★, Rabasse-Charavin★, M Richaud★★. Best years
(reds): 2004 03 **01 00 99 98 95**.

CALABRIA *Italy*   One of Italy's poorest regions. CIRO, Donnici, Savuto and
Scavigna reds from the native Gaglioppo grape, and whites from Greco, are
much improved thanks to greater winemaking expertise. The leading
producers are the Librandi family – who have recently added Magno
Megonio★★, from the obscure Magliocco variety, to an already fine range
– and Odoardi, with their excellent Scavigna Vigna Garrone.

CALERA *San Benito, California, USA*   A pace-setter for California Pinot
Noir with 4 estate wines: Reed Vineyard★★, Selleck Vineyard★★,
Jensen Vineyard★★ and Mills Vineyard★★. They are complex,
fascinating wines with power and originality and capable of aging. Mt
Harlan Chardonnay★★ is excitingly original too. CENTRAL COAST
Chardonnay★ and Pinot Noir★ are good value. Small amounts of
Viognier★★ are succulent with sensuous fruit. Best years: (Pinot Noir)
(2002) 01 **00 99 97 96 95 91 90**; (Chardonnay) 2002 01 **00 99 98 97 96**.

CALIFORNIA *USA*   California's importance is not simply in being the
fourth largest wine producer in the world (behind Italy, France and Spain).
Most of the revolutions in technology and style that have transformed the
expectations and achievements of winemakers in every country of the
world – including France – were born in the ambitions of a band of
Californian winemakers during the 1960s and 70s. They challenged the
old order, with its regulated, self-serving elitism, and democratized the
world of fine wine, to the benefit of every wine drinker. This revolutionary
fervour is less evident now. And there are times when Californians seem
too intent on establishing their own particular New World old order. A few
figures: there are around 178,000ha (440,000 acres) of wine grape
vineyards, producing around 20 million hectolitres (500 million gallons) of
wine annually, about 90% of all wine made in the USA. A large proportion
comes from the hot, inland CENTRAL VALLEY. See also Central Coast,
Mendocino County, Monterey County, Napa Valley, San Luis Obispo
County, Santa Barbara County, Sonoma County.

CABERNET SAUVIGNON

Wine made from Cabernet Sauvignon in places like Australia, California, Chile, Bulgaria, even in parts of southern France, has become so popular now that many people may not realize where it all started – and how Cabernet has managed to become the great, all-purpose, omnipresent red wine grape of the world.

WINE STYLES

Bordeaux Cabernet It all began in Bordeaux. With the exception of a clutch of Merlot-based beauties in St-Émilion and Pomerol, all the greatest red Bordeaux wines are based on Cabernet Sauvignon, with varying amounts of Merlot, Cabernet Franc, and possibly Petit Verdot also blended in. The blending is necessary because by itself Cabernet makes such a strong, powerful, aggressive and assertive wine. Dark and tannic when young, the great Bordeaux wines need 10–20 years for the aggression to fade, the fruit becoming sweet and perfumed as fresh blackcurrants, with a fragrance of cedarwood, of cigar boxes, mingling magically among the fruit. It is this character which has made red Bordeaux famous for at least 2 centuries.

Cabernet worldwide When winemakers in other parts of the world sought role models to try to improve their wines, most of them automatically thought of Bordeaux and chose Cabernet Sauvignon. It was lucky that they did, because not only is this variety easy to grow in almost all conditions – cool or warm, dry or damp – but that unstoppable personality always powers through. The cheaper wines are generally made to accentuate the blackcurrant fruit and the slightly earthy tannins. They are drinkable young, but able to age surprisingly well. The more ambitious wines are aged in oak barrels, often new ones, to enhance the tannin yet also to add spice and richness capable of developing over a decade or more. Sometimes the Cabernet is blended – usually with Merlot, sometimes with Cabernet Franc, and occasionally with other grapes: Shiraz in Australia, Sangiovese in Italy.

European Cabernets Many vineyards in southern France now produce good, affordable Cabernet Sauvignon. Spain has produced some good Cabernet blends, and Portugal has also had success. Italy's red wine quality revolution was sparked off by the success of Cabernet in Tuscany, and all the leading regions now grow it. Eastern Europe grows lots of Cabernet, but of widely varying quality, while the Eastern Mediterranean (Cyprus, Lebanon, Israel) and North Africa are beginning to produce tasty examples. Germany has tried it but is returning to Pinot Noir. Austria has had more success but is also returning to Blaufränkisch and Zweigelt.

New World Cabernets California's reputation was created by its strong, weighty Cabernets. Recently some producers have eased up, making examples that bring out the fruit flavours and can be drunk young, while others have intensified their styles. Both Australia and New Zealand place more emphasis on upfront fruit in their Cabernets. Chile has made the juicy, blackcurrany style very much her own, and Argentina is showing it wants to join in too. New clones, producing riper fruit and tannins, show South Africa will be capable of mixing with the best.

84

BEST PRODUCERS

France
Bordeaux Dom. de CHEVALIER, COS D'ESTOURNEL, GRAND-PUY-LACOSTE, GRUAUD-LAROSE, LAFITE-ROTHSCHILD, LATOUR, LEOVILLE-BARTON, LEOVILLE-LAS-CASES, Ch. MARGAUX, MOUTON-ROTHSCHILD, PICHON-LONGUEVILLE, RAUZAN-SEGLA; *Midi* TREVALLON.

Other European Cabernets
Italy BANFI, CA' DEL BOSCO, Col d'Orcia (Olmaia), GAJA, ISOLE E OLENA, LAGEDER, LE MACCHIOLE, MACULAN, ORNELLAIA, RAMPOLLA, SAN LEONARDO, SASSICAIA, SOLAIA, TASCA D'ALMERITA, TUA RITA.

Spain Blecua, MARQUES DE GRINON, TORRES.

New World Cabernets
Australia CAPE MENTELLE, CULLEN, HOUGHTON (Jack Mann), HOWARD PARK, LEEUWIN (Art Series), MAJELLA, MOSS WOOD, MOUNT MARY, PARKER ESTATE, PENFOLDS (Bin 707), PENLEY ESTATE, PETALUMA, SANDALFORD, WENDOUREE, WIRRA WIRRA.

New Zealand BABICH, Esk Valley, GOLDWATER, STONYRIDGE, TE MATA, VILLA MARIA.

USA (California) ARAUJO, BERINGER, Bryant Family, CAYMUS, CHIMNEY ROCK, DALLA VALLE, DIAMOND CREEK, DOMINUS, DUNN, Grace Family, HARLAN, HARTWELL, LAUREL GLEN, Long Meadow Ranch, Peter MICHAEL, MINER, MONDAVI, NEWTON, PHELPS, RIDGE, SCREAMING EAGLE, SHAFER, SILVER OAK, SPOTTSWOODE, STAG'S LEAP, Viader; (Washington) ANDREW WILL, DELILLE, LEONETTI, QUILCEDA CREEK, WOODWARD CANYON.

Chile ALMAVIVA, CARMEN (Nativa), CASABLANCA (Santa Isabel), CLOS QUEBRADA DE MACUL, CONCHA Y TORO, SANTA RITA (Floresta), Miguel TORRES.

Argentina CATENA, TERRAZAS DE LOS ANDES (Gran).

South Africa BEYERSKLOOF, BOEKENHOUTSKLOOF, BUITEN-VERWACHTING, Neil ELLIS, KANONKOP, MEERLUST, RUSTEN-BERG, SAXENBURG, THELEMA, VEENWOUDEN, VERGELEGEN.

CH. CALON-SÉGUR★★ *St-Estèphe AC, 3ème Cru Classé, Haut-Médoc,*
Bordeaux, France Long considered one of ST-ESTEPHE's leading
châteaux, but in the mid-1980s the wines were not as good as they
should have been. Recent vintages have been more impressive, with
better fruit and a suppler texture. Second wine: Marquis de Ségur.
Best years: 2003 02 01 00 98 96 **95 90 89 86 82**.

CAMPANIA *Italy* Three regions – PUGLIA, SICILY and Campania – lead the
revolution in Italy's south. In Campania moves toward quality have been
underpinned by the likes of enologist Riccardo Cotarella. Other producers
besides the venerable MASTROBERARDINO have finally begun to realize the
potential of its soil, climate and grapes, especially the red Aglianico. DOCs
of note are FALERNO DEL MASSICO, Fiano di Avellino, Greco di Tufo, Ischia,
TAURASI and VESUVIO. The leading wines are Montevetrano★★★ (Cabernet-
Merlot-Aglianico) and Galardi's Terra di Lavoro★★★ (Aglianico-
Piedirosso), but also look for top Aglianico reds from Antonio Caggiano★★,
De Conciliis★, Feudi di San Gregorio★★, Luigi Maffini★, Orazio Rillo★,
Cantina del Taburno★ and others that fall outside the main DOCs.

CAMPILLO *Rioja DOCa, País Vasco, Spain* An up-market subsidiary of
Bodegas FAUSTINO, producing some exciting new red RIOJAS★. The wines
are often Tempranillo-Cabernet Sauvignon blends, with masses of ripe,
velvety fruit. Best years: (Reserva) (2001) **99 98 96 95 94**.

CAMPO VIEJO *Rioja DOCa, Rioja, Spain* The largest producer of RIOJA.
Reservas★ and Gran Reservas★ are reliably good, as are the elegant,
all-Tempranillo Reserva Viña Alcorta and the barrel-fermented white
Viña Alcorta. Albor Tempranillo is a good modern young Rioja, packed
with fresh, pastilley fruit. Best years: (Reserva) (2001) **98 96 95 94**.

CANARY ISLANDS *Spain* The Canaries have a total of 10 DOs – there's
local politics for you! The sweet Malvasia from Lanzarote DO and La Palma
DO is worth a try, otherwise stick with the young reds. Best producers: El
Grifo, Monje, Viña Norte, Tenegría, Viñátigo.

CANBERRA DISTRICT *New South Wales, Australia* Cool, high altitude
(800m/2600ft) may sound good, but excessive cold and frost can be
problematic. Lark Hill and Helm make exciting Riesling, Lark Hill and
Brindabella Hills some smart Cabernet blends and Clonakilla
increasingly sublime Shiraz (with a dollop of Viognier). HARDY is
pouring money in here. Best producers: Brindabella Hills★, Clonakilla★
(Shiraz★★), Doonkuna★, Helm★, Lake George★, Lark Hill★, Madew★.

DOM. CANET-VALETTE *St-Chinian AC, Languedoc, France* Marc Valette
is uncompromising in his quest to make great wine: organic
cultivation, low yields, gravity-fed grapes and traditional *pigeage* (foot-
stomping) are just some of his methods. The wines offer an enticingly
rich expression of ST-CHINIAN's French Mediterranean grape varieties
and clay-limestone soils. Cuvées include Mille et Une Nuits (1001
Nights)★ and the powerful, complex Syrah-Grenache Le Vin
Maghani★★. Best years: (Le Vin Maghani) (2003) 02 01 00 **99 98 97**.

CANNONAU Sardinian grape variety, essentially the same as Spain's
Garnacha and France's Grenache Noir. In SARDINIA it produces deep,
tannic reds but lighter, modern, dry red wines are gaining in popularity,
although traditional sweet and fortified styles can still be found. Best

producers: (modern reds) ARGIOLAS, SELLA & MOSCA; Dolianova, Dorgali, Jerzu, Ogliastra, Oliena, Santa Maria La Palma and Trexenta co-ops.

CANOE RIDGE VINEYARD *Columbia Valley AVA, Washington, USA*
Outpost of California's CHALONE group, with reliable and tasty Chardonnay, but the focus is on fruit-filled Merlot★ and powerful, ageworthy Cabernet Sauvignon★. Best years: (reds) (2003) (02) 01 **00 99 98 97**.

CH. CANON★ *St-Émilion Grand Cru AC, 1er Grand Cru Classé, Bordeaux, France* Canon can make some of the richest, most concentrated ST-EMILIONS, but it went into steep decline before being purchased in 1996 by Chanel. Signs are that things have returned to form. The 3.5ha (8.65-acre) vineyard of Grand Cru Classé Ch. Curé-Bon has recently been added to the estate. In good vintages the wine is tannic and rich at first but is worth aging 10–15 years. Second wine: Clos J Kanon. Best years: 2003 02 01 00 98 **95 90 89 88 86 85 83 82**.

CANON-FRONSAC AC *Bordeaux, France* This AC is the heart of the FRONSAC region. The wines are quite sturdy when young but can age for 10 years or more. Best producers: Barrabaque (Prestige★), Canon de Brem★, Cassagne Haut-Canon★, la Fleur Cailleau, Gaby, Grand-Renouil★, Lamarche Canon Candelaire, Moulin Pey-Labrie★, Pavillon, Vrai Canon Bouché. Best years: 2003 **01** 00 **98 97 96 95 94 90 89 88**.

CH. CANON-LA-GAFFELIÈRE★★ *St-Émilion Grand Cru AC, Grand Cru Classé, Bordeaux, France* Owner Stephan von Neipperg has placed this property, located at the foot of the town of ST-EMILION, at the top of the list of Grands Crus Classés. The wines are firm, rich and concentrated. Under the same ownership are Clos de l'Oratoire★, Ch. l'Aiguilhe★★ in the CÔTES DE CASTILLON, and the remarkable *micro-cuvée* La Mondotte★★. Best years: 2003 02 01 00 **99** 98 **97 96 95 94 93 90 89**.

CH. CANTEMERLE★ *Haut-Médoc AC, 5ème Cru Classé, Bordeaux, France* With la LAGUNE, the most southerly of the Crus Classés. The wines are delicate in style and delightful in ripe vintages. Second wine: Villeneuve de Cantemerle. Best years: 2003 **01 00 98 96 95 90 89**.

CANTERBURY *South Island, New Zealand* The long, cool ripening season of the arid central coast of South Island favours white varieties, particularly Chardonnay, Pinot Gris, Sauvignon Blanc and Riesling, as well as Pinot Noir. The northerly Waipara district produces Canterbury's most exciting wines, especially from Riesling and Pinot Noir. Best producers: Mountford★, PEGASUS BAY★★, Daniel Schuster★, Waipara West★. Best years: (Pinot Noir) (2004) **02 01 00 99 98**; (Riesling) (2004) **02 01 00 98**.

CAPE MENTELLE *Margaret River, Western Australia* Leading MARGARET RIVER winery, owned by LVMH. Question of the moment is how it will fare without founder David Hohnen. Rugged independence has always been the Cape Mentelle way, so I hope that winemaker John Durham and his team continue to produce superb, cedary Cabernet★★★, impressive Shiraz★★ and Chardonnay★★, tangy Semillon-Sauvignon Blanc★★ and wonderfully chewy Zinfandel★★. All wines benefit from cellaring – whites up to 5 years, reds 8–15. Best years: (Cabernet Sauvignon) (2003) (02) 01 00 99 **98 96 95 94 92 91 90**.

CAPEL VALE *Geographe, Western Australia* Dr Peter Pratten's winery sources fruit from its own vineyards in Geographe, Mount Barker, PEMBERTON and MARGARET RIVER. Many of its CV and White Label wines represent good value, especially Sauvignon Blanc-Semillon★ and Riesling★. The top Black Label range has lacked consistency, except for the classy Whispering Hill Riesling★★. Rebecca Catlin has continued the clearer focus on regionality begun when she was working with former winemaker, Nicole Esdaile. Best years: (Whispering Hill Riesling) 2004 03 **02 01 00 98 97**.

CARIGNAN The dominant red grape in the south of France is responsible for much boring, cheap, harsh wine. But when made by carbonic maceration, the wine can have delicious spicy fruit. Old vines are capable of thick, rich, impressive reds, as shown by the odd success in France, California, Chile and South Africa. Although initially a Spanish grape (as Cariñena or Mazuelo), it is not that widespread there, but is useful for adding colour and acidity in RIOJA and CATALUÑA, and has gained unexpected respect in PRIORAT.

CARIGNANO DEL SULCIS DOC *Sardinia, Italy* Carignano is now producing wines of quite startling quality. Rocca Rubia★, a barrique-aged Riserva from the co-op at Santadi, with rich, fleshy and chocolaty fruit, is one of SARDINIA's best reds. In a similar vein, but a step up, is Baie Rosse★★; even better is the more structured and concentrated Terre Brune★★. Best producer: Santadi co-op. Best years: (reds) (2004) (03) 01 **00 99 98 97 96 95**.

LOUIS CARILLON & FILS *Puligny-Montrachet AC, Côte de Beaune, Burgundy, France* Excellent family-owned estate in PULIGNY-MONTRACHET. The emphasis is on traditional, finely balanced whites of great concentration, rather than new oak. Look out for Premiers Crus les Referts★★, Champs Canet★★ and les Perrières★★★, and the tiny but exquisite production of Bienvenues-BATARD-MONTRACHET★★★. Reds

from CHASSAGNE-MONTRACHET★, ST-AUBIN★ and MERCUREY★ are good, too. Best years: (whites) (2004) 03 02 **01 00 99 97 96 95 92**.

CARIÑENA DO *Aragón, Spain* The largest DO of ARAGON, baking under the mercilessly hot sun in inland eastern Spain, Cariñena has traditionally been a land of cheap, deep red, alcoholic wines from the Garnacha grape. Since the late 1990s, however, temperature-controlled fermentation has been working wonders with this unfairly despised grape. International grape varieties like Cabernet Sauvignon are being planted widely. Best producers: Añadas, San Valero (Monte Ducay, Don Mendo), Solar de Urbezo.

CARMEN *Maipo, Chile* Led by Pilar González, this winery has some of the best reds in MAIPO, including Reserve Carmenère-Cabernet★★, balanced, complex Wine Maker's Reserve★★ and organic Nativa Cabernet Sauvignon★★ from a project started by Alvaro Espinoza (now at VOE).

CARMENÈRE An important but forgotten constituent of BORDEAUX blends in the 19th century, historically known as Grande Vidure. Planted in Chile, it was generally labelled as Merlot until 1998. When ripe and made with care, it has rich blackberry, plum and spice flavours, with an unexpected but delicious bunch of savoury characters – grilled meat, soy sauce, celery, coffee – thrown in. A true original. Also found in northern Italy and China, and now being replanted in ST-EMILION.

CARMENET See MOON MOUNTAIN.

CARMIGNANO DOCG *Tuscany, Italy* Red wine from the west of Florence, renowned since the 16th century and revived in the 1970s by Capezzana. The blend (Sangiovese, plus 10–20% Cabernet) is one of Tuscany's more refined wines and can be quite long-lived. Although Carmignano is DOCG for its red wine, DOC applies to a lighter red Barco Reale, a rosé called Vin Ruspo and fine VIN SANTO. Best producers: Ambra★ (Vigne Alte★★), Artimino★, Capezzana★★, Le Farnete/E Pierazzuoli★ (Riserva★★), Il Poggiolo★, Villa di Trefiano★. Best years: (2004) (03) 02 01 **00 99 98 97 95 90 88 85**.

CARMO, QUINTA DO *Alentejo, Portugal* Well-established estate, part-owned by Domaines Rothschild since 1992. Estate red★ used to be complex and ageworthy, but in the 1990s quality slumped badly. However, a large replanting programme seems at last to be bringing quality up again, and wines since the 2000 vintage are likely to restore the Quinta's reputation. Second label: Dom Martinho. Best years: (2004) 01 **00**.

CARNEROS AVA *California, USA* Hugging the northern edge of San Francisco Bay, Carneros includes parts of both NAPA and SONOMA Counties. Windswept and chilly with morning fog off the Bay, it is a top cool-climate area, suitable for Chardonnay and Pinot Noir as both table wine and a base for sparkling wine. Merlot and even Syrah are also coming on well, but too much vineyard expansion is beginning to worry me. Best producers: ACACIA★★, Buena Vista★, Carneros Creek★, DOMAINE CARNEROS★★, David Ramey★★, RASMUSSEN★★, SAINTSBURY★★, Truchard★★. Best years: (Pinot Noir) (2002) **01 00 99 98 97 96 95 94**.

CARNUNTUM *Niederösterreich, Austria* 890ha (2200-acre) wine region south of the Danube and east of Vienna, with a strong red wine tradition. Best producers: Glatzer, G Markowitsch★, Pitnauer★.

CH. CARSIN *Premières Côtes de Bordeaux AC, Bordeaux, France* With wine made by an Australian winemaker until 2003 and a winery built by an Australian engineering company, what could you expect other than aromatic and fruity New World-style wines? Carsin delivers the goods with well-oaked, drink-young white Cuvée Prestige★ and red Cuvée Noire★. Also peach and citrus vin de table Etiquette Gris★ and a sweet CADILLAC. Best years: (Cuvée Noire) 2003 **01 00**.

CASA LAPOSTOLLE *Rapel, Chile* Leading Chilean winery owned by Marnier-Lapostolle of France, and with consultancy from leading BORDEAUX winemaker Michel Rolland. Cuvée Alexandre Merlot★★, a Carmenère-based wine from the acclaimed Apalta area in COLCHAGUA, was its first hit back in 1994, now eclipsed by red blend Clos Apalta★★★. Also rich, creamy Cuvée Alexandre Chardonnay★ from the CASABLANCA Valley.

CASA MARÍN *San Antonio, Chile* Owner-winemaker María Luz Marín produces an impressive collection of whites, led by single-vineyard Sauvignon Blancs: Laurel★★ is a powerful wine, full of mineral and intense fruit flavours, while Cipreses★★ shows the influence of the Pacific Ocean in its citrus aromas. Casona Vineyard Gewürztraminer★ and Estero Sauvignon Gris★ are good too.

CASABLANCA, VALLE DE *Aconcagua, Chile* Coastal valley with a cool-climate personality that is Chile's strongest proof of regional style. Whites dominate, with best results from Chardonnay, Sauvignon Blanc and Gewürztraminer. Even so, the Pinot Noir is some of Chile's best, and Merlot and Carmenère are very good. Best producers:

(whites) Casas del Bosque, CASA LAPOSTOLLE★, CASABLANCA★, CONCHA Y TORO★★, ERRAZURIZ★, Morandé★, MONTES, Veramonte★★, VOE★. Best years: (whites) 2004 03 02 01.

CASABLANCA, VIÑA *Casablanca, Chile* This much-acclaimed estate owes its reputation to Ignacio Recabarren, now departed to CONCHA Y TORO, but Spanish guru Joseba Altuna from GUELBENZU is continuing the upward direction. The cool Santa Isabel Estate in CASABLANCA is the source of top wines such as quince-edged Chardonnay★, minty, exotic Merlot★★ and Cabernet Sauvignon★★. White Label wines use vineyards in Lontué and MAIPO: there is rose- and lychee-filled Gewürztraminer★, excellent tangy, intense Sauvignon Blanc★, inky-black Cabernet Sauvignon★ and low-yield Merlot★. Joseba Altuna's first major project has been the flagship red blend Neblus★, made only in the best years.

DOM. CASENOVE *Côtes du Roussillon AC, Roussillon, France* Former photojournalist Étienne Montès, with the help of consultant enologist Jean-Luc COLOMBO, has developed an impressive range of wines, including a perfumed white Vin de Pays Catalan made from Macabeu and Torbat, MUSCAT DE RIVESALTES★, RIVESALTES★ and 2 red COTES DU ROUSSILLON: La Garrigue★ and the predominantly Syrah Commandant François Jaubert★★. Drink this with at least 5 years' bottle age. Best years: (Commandant François Jaubert) (2003) 01 **00 98 97 96**.

CASSIS AC *Provence, France* A picturesque fishing port near Marseille. Because of its situation, its white wine is the most overpriced on the French Riviera. Based on Ugni Blanc and Clairette, the wine can be good if fresh. The red wine is dull, but the rosé can be pleasant (especially from a single estate). Best producers: Bagnol★, Clos Ste-Magdelaine★, Ferme Blanche★, Fontblanche, Mas de Boudard, Mas Fontcreuse, Paternel. Best years: (white) 2004 **02 01 00 99 98 97 96**.

CASTEL DEL MONTE DOC *Puglia, Italy* An arid, hilly zone, and an ideal habitat for the Uva di Troia grape, producing long-lived red wine of astonishing character. There is also varietal Aglianico, some good rosé, and the whites produced from international varieties are improving. Best producers: RIVERA★, Santa Lucia, Tormaresca/ANTINORI, Torrevento★. Best years: (2004) (03) 01 **00 98 97 96 95 93**.

CASTELGIOCONDO *Brunello di Montalcino DOCG, Tuscany, Italy* FRESCOBALDI's Castelgiocondo estate is the source of merely adequate BRUNELLO, good Brunello Riserva★ and Merlot Lamaione★★. The vineyards are also providing grapes for the much-trumpeted Luce, a Sangiovese-Merlot blend, which has greatly improved of late, but which is hardly value for money. The second wine, Lucente, is somewhat better from that point of view.

CASTELLARE *Chianti Classico DOCG, Tuscany, Italy* Publisher Paolo Panerai's fine estate in the west of the Classico zone produces excellent CHIANTI CLASSICO★ and deeper, richer Riserva★★. Canonico di Castellare★ (Chardonnay), Coniale di Castellare★★ (Cabernet Sauvignon) and Spartito di Castellare★ (Sauvignon Blanc) are all ripe and fruity. Top wine I Sodi di San Niccolò★★ is an unusual Sangiovese-Malvasia blend, intense but finely perfumed.

CASTILLA-LA MANCHA *Spain* The biggest wine region in the world; hot, dry country with poor clay-chalk soil. The DOs of the central plateau, La MANCHA and VALDEPENAS, make white wines from the Airén grape, and some good reds from the Cencibel (Tempranillo). Méntrida DO, Manchuela

DO, Ribera del Júcar DO and Almansa DO make mostly rustic reds. The most ambitious wines made here are those from MARQUES DE GRIÑON's Dominio de Valdepusa★★ estate and the Dehesa del Carrizal★ estate, both in the Toledo mountains. Uribes Madero's Calzadilla★ in Cuenca province, Finca Sandoval★ from Manchuela and Manuel Manzaneque's Cabernet-based reds★ and Chardonnay from Sierra de Alcaraz in Albacete province are full of promise. Manzaneque now has his own DO, Finca Élez, as does the Marqués de Griñón: Dominio de Valdepusa DO.

CASTILLA Y LEÓN *Spain* This is Spain's harsh, high plateau, with long cold winters and hot summers (but always cool nights). A few rivers, notably the Duero, temper this climate and afford fine conditions for viticulture. After many decades of winemaking ignorance, with a few exceptions like VEGA SICILIA, the situation has changed radically for the better in 2 of the region's DOs, RIBERA DEL DUERO and RUEDA, and is rapidly improving in the other 3, BIERZO, Cigales and TORO. Dynamic winemakers such as Telmo RODRIGUEZ and Mariano García of AALTO and MAURO have won huge critical acclaim for the region.

CATALUÑA *Spain* Standards vary among the region's DOs. PENEDES, between Barcelona and Tarragona, has the greatest number of technically equipped wineries in Spain, but doesn't make a commensurate number of superior wines. In the south, mountainous, isolated PRIORAT has become a new icon for its heady, raging reds, and the neighbouring DOs of Montsant and Terra Alta are following in its footsteps. Inland COSTERS DEL SEGRE and Conca de Barbera make potentially excellent reds and whites. Up the coast, Alella makes attractive whites and Ampurdán-Costa Brava (Empordá-Costa Brava), by the French border, is showing signs of life. Cataluña also makes most of Spain's CAVA sparkling wines. The Catalunya DO allows (generally) inexpensive blends from anywhere in the region.

CATENA ZAPATA *Mendoza, Argentina* Argentinian pioneer Nicolás Catena's admiration for California is evident in the ripe, gentle, oaky Alamos and Argento ranges. However, Catena has vines in some of the best terroirs in MENDOZA and the wines in the Alta range – Chardonnay★, Cabernet Sauvignon★★ and Malbec★★ – are developing a recognizable sense of place. Cabernet-based Nicolás Catena Zapata★★ from the Agrelo district is top-flight. Viñas, a collection of single-vineyard Malbecs from the Upper Mendoza River region, is the latest range from this winery. Caro, a joint venture with LAFITE-ROTHSCHILD, aims for elegance but still needs to prove its potential.

DOM. CAUHAPÉ *Jurançon AC, South-West France* Henri Ramonteu has been a major influence in JURANÇON, proving that the area can make complex dry whites as well as more traditional sweet wines. Dry, unoaked Jurançon Sec is labelled Chant des Vignes★; the oaked version is Sève d'Automne★. Top wines are sweet Noblesse du Temps★★ and barrel-fermented Quintessence★★★.

CAVA DO *Spain* Cava, the Catalan name for CHAMPAGNE-method fizz, is made in 159 towns and villages throughout Spain, but more than 95% are in CATALUÑA. Grapes used are the local trio of Parellada, Macabeo and Xarel-lo. The best-value, fruitiest Cavas are generally the youngest, with no more than the minimum 9 months' aging. Some good Catalan Cavas are made with Chardonnay and maybe Pinot Noir. A number of top-quality wines are now produced but are seldom seen abroad, since their prices are too close to those of Champagne to attract international customers. Best producers: Can Feixes, Can Ràfols dels Caus★, Castellblanch, Castell de Vilarnau, CODORNIU★, FREIXENET, JUVE Y CAMPS★, Marques de Monistrol, Parxet, RAIMAT, Raventós i Blanc, Rovellats, Agustí Torelló★, Jané Ventura.

CAYMUS VINEYARDS *Napa Valley AVA, California, USA* Caymus Cabernet Sauvignon is a ripe, intense and generally tannic style that is good in its regular bottling★ and can be outstanding as a Special Selection★★★. Conundrum★★ is an exotic, full-flavoured blended white. Also successful MONTEREY Chardonnay under the Mer Soleil★★ label. Best years: (Special Selection) 2002 01 00 **99 98 97 95 94 91 90 87 86 84**.

CAYUSE VINEYARDS *Walla Walla Valley AVA, Washington, USA* Winemaker Christophe Baron has created a cult label that now rivals all Washington producers in demand. His best work is done with Viognier★★★ which is crisp, floral and spicy, yet he is best known for his Syrahs. Using French clones, he farms a vineyard reminiscent of some in CHATEAUNEUF-DU-PAPE for its large stones, called Cobblestone Vineyard. Each parcel of the vineyard has a designation. Syrah Cailloux★★ has a distinctive mineral flavour, Syrah En Cerise★★ shows more cherry and raspberry flavour. The Syrah Bionic Frog★★ sports a cartoon-ish label but is a serious Syrah, reminding me of a northern Rhône version. Best years: (Syrah) 2002 01 00 **99**.

DOM. CAZES *Rivesaltes, Roussillon, France* The Cazes brothers make outstanding MUSCAT DE RIVESALTES★★, RIVESALTES Vieux★★ and the superb Aimé Cazes★★, but also produce a wide range of red and white table wines, mainly as COTES DU ROUSSILLON and Vin de Pays des Côtes Catalanes. Look out for the soft, fruity red Le Canon du Maréchal★, the Cabernet-based Le Credo★ and Ego★, and the small production of barrel-fermented Chardonnay.

CH. DU CÈDRE *Cahors AC, South-West France* Pascal Verheaghe is the leader of a new generation of CAHORS winemakers, producing dark, richly textured wines with a generous coating of chocolaty oak. There are 3 cuvées: Le Prestige★, the 100% Auxerrois (Malbec) Le Cèdre★★, which is aged in new oak barrels for 20 months, and from 2000 the Cuvée GC★, which is fermented and aged in oak. All 3 benefit from at least 5–6 years' bottle age. Best years: (Le Cèdre) (2003) 01 00 **99 98 97 96**.

CELLIER LE BRUN *Marlborough, South Island, New Zealand* CHAMPAGNE-method specialist, with vintage Blanc de Blancs★, and tasty blended vintage and non-vintage bubblies. Founder Daniel Le Brun has now sold up and established a new MARLBOROUGH winery, Le Brun Family Estate. Best years: (Blanc de Blancs) **1997 96 95 92 91**.

CENCIBEL See Tempranillo.

CENTRAL COAST AVA *California, USA* Huge AVA covering virtually every vineyard between San Francisco and Los Angeles, with a number of sub-AVAs, such as SANTA CRUZ MOUNTAINS, Santa Ynez Valley, SANTA MARIA VALLEY and Monterey. There is superb potential for Pinot Noir and Syrah in Santa Lucia Highlands in the western Monterey area. See also Monterey County, San Luis Obispo County, Santa Barbara County.

CENTRAL OTAGO *South Island, New Zealand* The only wine region in New Zealand with a continental rather than maritime climate. Technically the ripening season is long and cool, suiting Pinot Noir, Gewürztraminer, Chardonnay and even Shiraz, but there are usually periods of considerable heat during the summer to intensify flavour. Long autumns have produced some excellent Rieslings. There are already well over 30 wineries and an explosion of plantings, both in good areas like Bannockburn and Lowburn, and in marginal zones. Best producers: Akarua★, Carrick★, Chard Farm★, FELTON ROAD★★, Gibbston Valley★, Mt Difficulty★, Mount Edward★, Mount Maude, Nevis Bluff★, Peregrine★★, Quartz Reef★★, Rippon Vineyard★, Two Paddocks★. Best years: (Pinot Noir) **2003 02 01 99 98**.

CENTRAL VALLEY/VALLE CENTRAL *Chile* The heart of Chile's wine industry, encompassing the valleys of MAIPO, RAPEL, CURICO and MAULE. Most major producers are located here, and the key factor determining mesoclimate differences is the distance relative to the Coastal Ranges and the Andean Cordillera.

CENTRAL VALLEY *California, USA* This vast area grows 75% of California's wine grapes, used mostly for cheaper styles of wine, along with brandies and grape concentrate. Viewed overall, the quality has improved over the past few years, but it is a hot area, where irrigated vineyards tend to produce excess tonnages of grapes. It has often been said that it is virtually impossible to produce exciting wine in the Central Valley, but in fact the climatic conditions in the northern half are not that unlike those in many parts of Spain and southern France. Vineyards in the Lodi AVA have expanded to 26,500ha (65,000 acres), making Lodi the volume and quality leader for Chardonnay, Merlot, Zinfandel and Cabernet. Lodi Zinfandel shows most potential. Other sub-regions with claims to quality are the Sacramento Valley and the Delta area. Best producers: McManis★, RAVENSWOOD (Lodi★), Woodbridge/MONDAVI.

CENTRAL VICTORIA *Victoria, Australia* The Central Victoria zone comprises the regions of BENDIGO, Goulburn Valley, HEATHCOTE and the cooler Central Victorian High Country and Strathbogie Ranges. Central Victoria, with its mostly warm conditions, produces powerful and individual wines. The few wineries on the banks of the serene thread of the Goulburn River produce fine RHONE varieties, particularly white Marsanne, while reds from the high country are rich but scented and dry; whites are delicate and scented. Best producers: DELATITE★★, Jasper Hill★★, MITCHELTON★★, Paul Osicka★, TAHBILK★, Wild Duck Creek★.

CERETTO *Piedmont, Italy* This merchant house, headed by brothers Bruno and Marcello Ceretto, is one of the chief modern producers in BAROLO. With the help of enologist Donato Lanati, Barolo (Bricco Rocche★★, Brunate★★ and Prapò★★), BARBARESCO (Bricco Asili★★), BARBERA D'ALBA Piana★ and white Arneis Blangè are living up to their reputation. Ceretto also produces an oak-aged LANGHE red, Monsordo★★, from Cabernet, Merlot, Pinot Nero and Nebbiolo. An unusual white counterpart, Arbarei, is 100% Riesling. A good sparkler, La Bernardina, is made from Chardonnay and Pinot Noir.

CÉRONS AC *Bordeaux, France* An AC for sweet wine in the GRAVES region of Bordeaux. The soft, mildly honeyed wine is not quite as sweet as SAUTERNES and not so well known, nor so highly priced. Most producers now make dry wine under the Graves label. Best producers:

Ch. de Cérons★, Chantegrive★, Grand Enclos du Château de Cérons★, Seuil. Best years: 2003 02 **01 99 98 97 96 95 90 89.**

L A CETTO *Baja California, Mexico*   Mexico's most successful winery relies on mists and cooling Pacific breezes to temper the heat of the Valle de Guadalupe. Italian Camilo Magoni makes ripe, fleshy Petite Sirah★, oak-aged Cabernet Sauvignon, Zinfandel and Nebbiolo. Whites, led by Chardonnay and Chenin, are greatly improved. Also decent fizz.

CHABLAIS *Vaud, Switzerland*   A sub-region of the VAUD. Most of the vineyards lie on the alluvial plains but 2 villages, Yvorne and Aigle, benefit from much steeper slopes and produce tangy whites and good reds. Most of the thirst-quenchingly dry whites are made from Chasselas. The reds are from Pinot Noir, as is a rosé speciality, Oeil de Perdrix, an enjoyable summer wine. Drink whites and rosés young. Best producers: Henri Badoux, J & P Testuz.

CHABLIS AC *Burgundy, France*   Chablis, closer to CHAMPAGNE than to the COTE D'OR, is Burgundy's northernmost outpost. When not destroyed by frost or hail, the Chardonnay grape makes a crisp, dry white wine with a steely mineral fruit which can be delicious. Several producers are experimenting with barrel-aging for their better wines, resulting in some full, toasty, positively rich dry whites. Others are intentionally producing a soft, creamy, early-drinking style, which is nice but not really Chablis. The outlying areas come under the Petit Chablis AC and should be drunk young. The better straight Chablis AC should be drunk at 3–5 years, while a good vintage of a leading Chablis Premier Cru may take 5 years to show its full potential. About a quarter of Chablis is designated as Premier Cru, the best vineyards on the rolling limestone slopes being Fourchaume, Mont de Milieu, Montmains, Montée de Tonnerre and Vaillons. Best producers: Barat★, J-C Bessin (Fourchaume★★), Billaud-Simon (Mont de Milieu★★), Pascal Bouchard★, A & F Boudin★★, BROCARD★★, la CHABLISIENNE★, Collet★, Dampt★, R & V DAUVISSAT★★, D & E Defaix★, Droin★, DROUHIN★, Duplessis, DURUP★, W Fèvre★, J-P Grossot (Côte de Troesme★), LAROCHE★★, Long-Depaquit, Malandes (Côte de Léchêt★★), L MICHEL★★, Picq (Vaucoupin★★), Pinson★, RAVENEAU★★, Vocoret★★. Best years: (Chablis Premier Cru) (2004) **03 02 00 99 98 96 95 90.**

CHABLIS GRAND CRU AC *Burgundy, France*   The 7 Grands Crus (Bougros, les Preuses, Vaudésir, Grenouilles, Valmur, les Clos and les Blanchots) facing south-west across the town of Chablis are the heart of the AC. Oak barrel-aging takes the edge off taut flavours, adding a rich warmth to these fine wines. Droin and Fèvre are the most enthusiastic users of new oak, but use it less than they used to. Never drink young: 5–10 years is needed before you can see why you spent your money. Best producers: J-C Bessin★★, Billaud-Simon★★, BROCARD★★, la CHABLISIENNE★★, J Dauvissat★★, R & V DAUVISSAT★★★, D & E Defaix★★, Droin★★, Fèvre★★★, LAROCHE★★, Long-Depaquit★★, MICHEL★★★, Pinson★★, RAVENEAU★★★, Servin★, Vocoret★★. Best years: (2003) 02 00 99 98 **97** 96 **95 92 90.**

LA CHABLISIENNE *Chablis AC, Burgundy, France*   Substantial co-op producing nearly a third of all CHABLIS. The wines are reliable and can aspire to something much better. The best are the oaky Grands Crus – especially les Preuses★★ and Grenouilles (sold as Ch. Grenouille★★) – but the basic unoaked Chablis★, the Vieilles Vignes★★ and the numerous Premiers Crus★ are good, as is the red BOURGOGNE Épineuil. Best years: (whites) (2004) **03 02 00 99 98 97 96.**

CHALONE *Monterey County, California, USA* Producers of full-blown but slow-developing Chardonnay★ and concentrated Pinot Noir★★ from vineyards on the arid eastern slope of the Coastal Range in mid-MONTEREY COUNTY. Also very good Reserve Pinot Noir★ and Chardonnay★★, as well as Pinot Blanc★★ and Chenin Blanc★. Syrah★ is a promising recent addition. These are strongly individualistic wines. Best years: (Chardonnay) (2002) **01 00 99 98 97 96 95 94 93 91 90**; (Pinot Noir) 2001 **00 99 98 96 95 94 91 90**.

CHAMBERS *Rutherglen, Victoria, Australia* Legendary family winery making sheer nectar in the form of Muscat and Tokay. The secret is Bill Chambers' ability to draw on ancient stocks put down in wood by earlier generations. His 'Special'★★ and 'Rare'★★★ blends are national treasures. The Cabernet and Shiraz are good, the whites pedestrian.

CHAMBERTIN AC *Grand Cru, Côte de Nuits, Burgundy, France* The village of GEVREY-CHAMBERTIN, the largest COTE DE NUITS commune, has no fewer than 8 Grands Crus (Chambertin, Chambertin-Clos-de-Bèze, Chapelle-Chambertin, Charmes-Chambertin, Griotte-Chambertin, Latricières-Chambertin, Mazis-Chambertin and Ruchottes-Chambertin), which can produce some of Burgundy's greatest and most intense red wine. Its rough-hewn fruit, seeming to war with fragrant perfumes for its first few years, creates remarkable flavours as the wine ages. Chambertin and Chambertin-Clos-de-Bèze are neighbours on the slope above the village and the two greatest sites, but overproduction is a recurrent problem with some producers. Best producers: Denis Bachelet★★, BOUCHARD PERE ET FILS★★, Charlopin★, B CLAIR★★★, P Damoy★, DROUHIN★★, Drouhin-Laroze★★, C Dugat★★, Dugat-Py★★★, FAIVELEY★★, R Groffier★★, JADOT★★, D Laurent★★★, Dom. LEROY★★★, Denis MORTET★★★, H Perrot-Minot★★, Ponsot★★, Rossignol-Trapet★, J Roty★★, ROUMIER★★, ROUSSEAU★★★, J & J-L Trapet★★, VOUGERAIE★★. Best years: (2004) 03 02 01 00 99 98 **97** 96 **95 93 91 90 88**.

CHAMBERTIN-CLOS-DE-BÈZE AC See Chambertin AC.

CHAMBOLLE-MUSIGNY AC *Côte de Nuits, Burgundy, France* AC with the potential to produce the most fragrant, perfumed red Burgundy, when not over-cropped. Encouragingly, more young producers are now bottling their own wines. Best producers: G Barthod★★, J-J Confuron, DROUHIN★★, DUJAC★★, R Groffier★★, Hudelot-Noëllat★★, JADOT★★, Dom. LEROY★★, F Magnien, Marchand-Grillot★★, D MORTET★, J-F Mugnier★★, RION★★, ROUMIER★★ VOGUE★★. Best years: (2004) 03 02 01 00 **99 98 97** 96 **95 93 90**.

CHAMPAGNE See pages 96–7.

CHAMPAGNE ROSÉ *Champagne, France* Good pink CHAMPAGNE has a delicious fragrance of cherries and raspberries. The top wines can age well, but most should be drunk on release, as young as possible. Best producers: (vintage) BILLECART-SALMON★★, BOLLINGER★★, Gosset★★, Charles HEIDSIECK★★, JACQUESSON★★, LAURENT-PERRIER (Grand Siècle Alexandra★★★), MOET & CHANDON★★ (Dom Pérignon★★★), PERRIER-JOUET (Belle Époque★★), POL ROGER★★, POMMERY (Louise★★), Louis ROEDERER★★ (Cristal★★★), RUINART (Dom Ruinart★★★), TAITTINGER (Comtes de Champagne★★), VEUVE CLICQUOT★★ (Grande Dame★★★); (non-vintage) Paul Bara★, E Barnaut★★, Beaumont des Crayères★, BILLECART-SALMON★★, Egly-Ouriet★★, Jacquart★, KRUG★★, LANSON★, LAURENT-PERRIER★, MOET & CHANDON★, RUINART★, TAITTINGER★, Vilmart★. Best years: (1999) (98) 96 **95 91 90 89 88 85 82**. See also pages 96–7.

CHAMPAGNE AC

Champagne, France

The Champagne region produces the most celebrated sparkling wines in the world. It is the most northerly AC in France – a place where grapes struggle to ripen fully, but provide the perfect base wine to make fizz. Champagne is divided into 5 distinct areas – the best are the Montagne de Reims, where the Pinot Noir grape performs brilliantly, and the Chardonnay-dominated Côte des Blancs south of Épernay. In addition to Chardonnay and Pinot Noir, the only other grape permitted for the production of Champagne is Pinot Meunier.

The wines undergo a second fermentation in the bottle, producing carbon dioxide which dissolves in the wine under pressure. Through this method Champagne acquires its crisp, long-lasting bubbles and a distinctive yeasty, toasty dimension to its flavour. If you buy a bottle of Coteaux Champenois, a still wine from the area, you can see why they decided to make bubbly instead; it usually tastes mean and tart, but is transformed by the Champagne method into one of the most delightfully exhilarating wines of all.

That's the theory anyway, and for 150 years or so the Champenois have persuaded us that their product is second to none. It can be, too, except when it is released too young or sweetened to make up for a lack of richness. When that periodically happens you know that, once again, the powers of marketing have triumphed over the wisdom and skills of the winemaker. But as Champagne expertise begins to turn out exciting sparklers in California, Australia and New Zealand, the Champagne producers must re-focus on quality or lose much of their market for good.

The Champagne trade is dominated by large companies or houses, called négociants-manipulants, recognized by the letters NM on the label. The récoltants-manipulants (RM) are growers who make their own wine, and they are becoming increasingly important for drinkers seeking characterful Champagne.

STYLES OF CHAMPAGNE

Non-vintage Most Champagne is a blend of 2 or more vintages. Quality varies enormously, depending on who has made the wine and how long it has been aged. Most Champagne is sold as Brut, which is a dry, but rarely bone-dry style. Strangely, Extra Dry denotes a style less dry than Brut.

Vintage Denotes Champagne made with grapes from a single vintage. As a rule, it is made only in the best years, but far too many mediocre years were declared in the 1990s.

Blanc de Blancs A lighter, and at best highly elegant, style of Champagne made solely from the Chardonnay grape.

Blanc de Noirs White Champagne made entirely from black grapes, either Pinot Noir, Pinot Meunier, or a combination of the two.

Rosé Pink Champagne, made either from black grapes or (more usually) by mixing a little still red wine into white Champagne.

De luxe cuvée In theory the finest Champagne and certainly always the most expensive, residing in the fanciest bottles.

See also CHAMPAGNE ROSE; and individual producers.

(1999) (98) **96 95 90 89 88 85 83 82**

BEST PRODUCERS

Houses BILLECART-SALMON, BOLLINGER, Cattier, Delamotte, DEUTZ, Drappier, Duval-Leroy, Gosset, Alfred GRATIEN, Charles HEIDSIECK, HENRIOT, JACQUESSON, KRUG, LANSON, LAURENT-PERRIER, Bruno PAILLARD, Joseph PERRIER, PERRIER JOUET, Philipponnat, POL ROGER, POMMERY, Louis ROEDERER, RUINART, Salon, TAITTINGER, VEUVE CLICQUOT.

Growers Michel Arnould, Paul Bara, Barnaut, Beaufort, Beerens, Chartogne-Taillet, Paul Déthune, Diebolt Vallois, Daniel Dumont, Egly-Ouriet, René Geoffroy, Gimonnet, H Goutorbe, André Jacquart, Lamiable, Larmandier, Larmandier-Bernier, Launois, Margaine, Serge Mathieu, J Michel, Moncuit, Alain Robert, Secondé, Selosse, de Sousa, Tarlant, Vilmart.

Co-ops Beaumont des Crayères, H Blin, Nicolas Feuillatte, Jacquart, Mailly, Union Champagne.

De luxe cuvées Belle Époque (PERRIER-JOUET), N-F Billecart (BILLECART-SALMON), Blanc de Millénaires (Charles HEIDSIECK), Clos des Goisses (Philipponnat), Clos de Mesnil (KRUG), Comtes de Champagne (TAITTINGER), Cristal (Louis ROEDERER), Cuvée Josephine (Joseph PERRIER), Cuvée Sir Winston Churchill (POL ROGER), Cuvée William Deutz (DEUTZ), Dom Pérignon (MOET & CHANDON), Dom Ruinart (RUINART), Grand Siècle (LAURENT-PERRIER), Grande Dame (VEUVE CLICQUOT), Noble Cuvée (LANSON), Vintage RD (BOLLINGER).

CHANDON DE BRIAILLES *Savigny-lès-Beaune AC, Côte de Beaune, Burgundy, France* The de Nicolays – mother, son and daughter – combine modern sophistication with traditional values to produce rich but refined reds from SAVIGNY-LES-BEAUNE★, PERNAND-VERGELESSES★, ALOXE-CORTON★★ and CORTON★★, and an equally good range of whites from Pernand-Vergelesses★★, Corton★★ and CORTON-CHARLEMAGNE★★★. Best years: (reds) (2004) 03 02 **01 99 98 96 95 90**

CHAPEL DOWN *Kent, England* The UK's largest winery (the result of a merger with Lamberhurst Vineyards), producing around 30,000 cases from its own vineyards and bought-in grapes from contract growers in the south-east of England. Now embarking on major expansion by persuading growers to plant 400ha (1000 acres) over the next 5 years. A large and excellent range of wines includes Chapel Down sparkling, Curious Grape fruity whites (especially Bacchus), Rondo-based Epoch Reserve and Pinot Noir reds, Tenterden and Lamberhurst blends and varietals.

CHAPEL HILL *McLaren Vale, South Australia* New winemaker Michael Fragos looks set to continue Chapel Hill's range of powerful, classy wines. The Cabernet Sauvignon★★ is a successful blend of mature MCLAREN VALE and COONAWARRA fruit, while the Shiraz★★ is all McLaren Vale. Good Unwooded Chardonnay★ (Reserve★★) and fascinating, bone-dry, honey-scented Verdelho★★. Best years: (Shiraz) 2002 01 **00 98 97 96 95 94 93 91**.

CHAPELLE-CHAMBERTIN AC See Chambertin AC.

CHAPELLE L'ENCLOS *Madiran AC, South-West France* Patrick Ducournau has tamed the savage Tannat grape with his invention of controlled oxygenation during barrel aging. The Chapelle L'Enclos★★ and Dom Mouréou★ reds are ripe and concentrated, though they need at least 5 years to mature. Best years: (2003) 01 00 99 **98 96 95 94**.

M CHAPOUTIER *Rhône Valley, France* Chapoutier is very much in the vanguard of progress, both in viticulture and in winemaking, and is producing a full range of serious and exciting wines. The HERMITAGE la Sizeranne★★ and special Ermitages (Chapoutier's spelling) les Greffieux★★, l'Ermite★★, le Méal★★★ and le Pavillon★★★, white Hermitage de l'Orée★★ and l'Ermite★★★, CROZES-HERMITAGE les Varonniers★★, ST-JOSEPH les Granits★★ and CHATEAUNEUF-DU-PAPE Barbe Rac★ are all good, but some of them show a surfeit of new oak. Also BANYULS, COTEAUX DU TRICASTIN and Australian joint ventures. Best years: (la Sizeranne) (2003) 01 00 99 **98 95 94 91 90 89 88**.

CHARDONNAY See pages 100–101.

CHARMES-CHAMBERTIN AC See Chambertin AC.

CHASSAGNE-MONTRACHET AC *Côte de Beaune, Burgundy, France* Some of Burgundy's greatest white wine vineyards (part of le MONTRACHET and BATARD-MONTRACHET, all of Criots-Bâtard-Montrachet) are within the village boundary. The white Chassagne Premiers Crus are not as well known, but can offer nutty, toasty wines, especially if aged for 4–8 years. Ordinary white Chassagne-Montrachet is usually enjoyable; the red is a little earthy, peppery and plummy and can be an acquired taste. Look out for reds from the following Premiers Crus: Clos de la Boudriotte, Clos St-Jean and Clos de la Chapelle. Best producers: (whites) F d'Allaines★, G Amiot★, Blain-Gagnard★★, M Colin★★, Colin-Deléger★★, J-N GAGNARD★★, V GIRARDIN★★, V & F Jouard★, H Lamy★, B Morey★★, M Morey★★, Morey-Coffinet, M Niellon★★, RAMONET★★, VERGET★★; (reds) G Amiot★, CARILLON★, R

Clerget★, V GIRARDIN★★, B Morey★★, RAMONET★★. Best years: (whites) (2004) 03 02 **01 00 99 98 97 96 95** 92; (reds) (2004) 03 02 99 **98 97** 96 **95**.

CHASSELAS Chasselas is considered a table grape worldwide. Only in BADEN (where it is called Gutedel) and Switzerland (called Dorin, Perlan or Fendant) is it thought to make decent light, dry wines with a slight prickle. A few Swiss examples, notably from DEZALEY, rise above this.

CH. CHASSE-SPLEEN★ *Moulis AC, Cru Bourgeois, Haut-Médoc, Bordeaux, France* Chasse-Spleen is not a Classed Growth – but during the 1980s it built a tremendous reputation for ripe, concentrated and powerful wines under the late proprietor, Bernadette Villars. The château is now run by Villars' daughter Céline, and recent vintages are again finding the form of the old days. Second wine: l'Ermitage de Chasse-Spleen. Best years: 2003 02 01 00 **99 96 95 94 90 89 88 86 83 82**.

CHÂTEAU-CHALON AC *Jura, France* The most prized – and pricy – *vin jaune*, it is difficult to find, even in the Jura. But if you do find a bottle, beware – the awesome flavour will shock your tastebuds like no other French wine. Not released until 6 years after the vintage, it can be kept for much longer. Best producers: Baud★★, Berthet-Bondet★★, Bourdy★★, Chalandard★★, Credoz★, Durand-Perron★★, J Macle★★, H Maire★★. Best years: (1999) 97 96 95 94 **93 92 91 90 89 88 87**.

CHÂTEAU-GRILLET AC★★ *Rhône Valley, France* This rare and *very* expensive RHÔNE white, made from Viognier and aged in oak, has a magic reek of orchard fruit and harvest bloom when young but is best drunk after 5 years. More reserved in style than CONDRIEU. Best years: **2001 00 98 95**.

CHATEAU INDAGE *Maharashtra, India* India's first traditional-method sparkling wine appeared in the 1980s, with technical assistance from Champagne's PIPER-HEIDSIECK. Dry sparklers are firm, fresh and chunky – though quality is somewhat erratic. Omar Khayyám is produced from a blend of Chardonnay, Ugni Blanc, Pinot Noir and Pinot Meunier. A demi-sec and a good pink fizz are also produced. Red and white table wines use both international and indigenous Indian grape varieties such as Bangalore Purple and Arkavati.

CHATEAU MONTELENA *Napa Valley AVA, California, USA* Napa winery producing broad-shouldered Chardonnay★ and an estate Cabernet★★ that is impressive, if slow to develop. The Napa Valley Cabernet★ is an elegantly styled wine for younger consumption. Also impressive is the Briary Estate Zinfandel★★. Best years: (Chardonnay) 2002 01 **00 99 98**; (Cabernet) (2002) 01 00 **99 98 91 90 87 86 85 84**.

CHATEAU MUSAR *Ghazir, Lebanon* Founded by Gaston Hochar in the 1930s and now run by his Bordeaux-trained son Serge, Musar is famous for having made wine every year bar two (1976 and 84) throughout Lebanon's civil war. From an unlikely blend of primarily Cabernet Sauvignon and Cinsaut comes a wine of real, if wildly exotic, character, with sweet, spicy fruit and good aging potential: Hochar says that red Musar★ 'should be drunk at 15 years'. Some recent vintages have not quite lived up to expectations, but latest harvests are encouraging. There is also a rosé, and a white from local Chardonnay and Sémillon lookalikes Obaideh and Merwah. Hochar Père et Fils is not aged in oak and is ready to drink upon release; Musar Cuvée Reservée (red, white and rosé) is also young and light. Best years: (red) (1999) (98) (97) **96 95 94 93 91 89 88**; (white) **1997**.

99

CHARDONNAY

 I never thought I'd see myself write this. Yes, we are getting bored with Chardonnay. Not all Chardonnay: there's probably more top Chardonnay being produced right now than ever before. And for millions of wine drinkers the Chardonnay revolution (easy to pronounce, easy to swallow) has only just begun. But in the heart of the wine world – the middle market, where people care about flavour but also care about price – we're getting fed up. Far too much sugary, over-oaked, unrefreshing junk has been dumped into our laps recently, from countries and producers who should know better. Add to this the increasingly desperate dirt-cheap offerings at the rump end of the market, and you'll see why I think the great golden goose of Chardonnay has the carving knife of cynicism and greed firmly held against its neck. It's now the fourth most-planted variety in the world. The next few years will show whether it wishes to be the supremely versatile all-rounder or the sloppy jack of all trades and master of none.

WINE STYLES

France Although a relatively neutral variety if left alone (this is what makes it so suitable as a base wine for top-quality Champagne-method sparkling wine), the grape can ripen in a surprising range of conditions, developing a subtle gradation of flavours going from the sharp apple-core greenness of Chardonnay grown in Champagne or the Loire, through the exciting, bone-dry yet succulent flavours of white Burgundy, to a round, perfumed flavour in Languedoc-Roussillon.

Other regions Italy produces Chardonnay that can be bone dry and lean or fat, spicy and lush. Spain does much the same. California and Australia virtually created their reputations on great, viscous, almost syrupy, tropical fruits and spice-flavoured Chardonnays; the best producers are now moving away from this style. Some of the best New World Chardonnays, dry but ripe and subtly oaked, are coming from South Africa. New Zealand is producing rich, deep, but beautifully balanced Chardonnays, while Chile and Argentina have found it easy to grow and are rapidly learning how to make fine wine from it too. Add Germany, Austria, Canada, New York State, Greece, Portugal, Slovenia, Moldova, Romania, even China, and you'll see it can perform almost anywhere.

Using oak The reason for all these different flavours lies in Chardonnay's wonderful susceptibility to the winemaker's aspirations and skills. The most important manipulation is the use of the oak barrel for fermenting and aging the wine. Chardonnay is the grape of the great white Burgundies and these are fermented and matured in oak (not necessarily new oak); the effect is to give a marvellous round, nutty richness to a wine that is yet savoury and dry. This is enriched still further by aging the wine on its lees.

The New World winemakers sought to emulate the great Burgundies, planting Chardonnay and employing thousands of oak barrels (mostly new), and their success – and the enthusiasm with which wine drinkers embraced the wine – has caused winemakers everywhere else to see Chardonnay as the perfect variety – easy to grow, easy to turn into wine and easy to sell to an adoring public.

100

BEST PRODUCERS

France *Chablis* Billaud-Simon, A & F Boudin, DAUVISSAT, Fèvre, LAROCHE, MICHEL, RAVENEAU; *Côte d'Or* R Ampeau, J-M Boillot, Bonneau du Martray, M Bouzereau, CARILLON, COCHE-DURY, M Colin, DROUHIN, A Ente, J-N GAGNARD, V GIRARDIN, JADOT, F Jobard, R Jobard, LAFON, H Lamy, Louis LATOUR, Dom. LEFLAIVE, B Morey, M Niellon, RAMONET, M Rollin, G Roulot, SAUZET, VERGET; *Mâconnais* D & M Barraud, Guffens-Heynen (VERGET), O Merlin, Thévenet, Valette.

Other European Chardonnays
Austria TEMENT, VELICH.

Germany JOHNER, REBHOLZ.

Italy BELLAVISTA, CA' DEL BOSCO, GAJA, LAGEDER, Vie di Romans, Castello della SALA (Cervaro).

Spain CHIVITE, ENATE, Manzaneque, Señorío de Otazu, TORRES.

New World Chardonnays
Australia BANNOCKBURN, CAPE MENTELLE, CULLEN, GIACONDA, GROSSET, HOWARD PARK, LEEUWIN, KNAPPSTEIN LENSWOOD, Mountadam, PENFOLDS (Yattarna), PETALUMA, PIERRO, TARRAWARRA, TYRRELL'S, Voyager.

New Zealand BABICH, CLOUDY BAY, CRAGGY RANGE, DRY RIVER, FELTON ROAD, FROMM, ISABEL, KUMEU RIVER, MILLTON, MORTON, NEUDORF, PEGASUS BAY, SERESIN, TE MATA, VAVASOUR, Vidal, WITHER HILLS.

USA ARROWOOD, AU BON CLIMAT, BERINGER, CALERA, CHALONE, CHATEAU ST JEAN, FERRARI-CARANO, FLOWERS, KISTLER, MARCASSIN, MATANZAS CREEK, MERRYVALE, Peter MICHAEL, NEWTON, David Ramey, RIDGE, ROCHIOLI, SAINTSBURY, SANFORD, SHAFER, STEELE, TALBOTT.

South Africa BUITENVERWACHTING, Neil ELLIS (Elgin), GLEN CARLOU, HAMILTON RUSSELL, JORDAN, MEERLUST, MULDERBOSCH, SPRINGFIELD, THELEMA, VERGELEGEN.

South America CATENA, CONCHA Y TORO (Amelia), CONO SUR (20 Barrels), Tabalí/SAN PEDRO.

CHATEAU ST JEAN *Sonoma Valley AVA, California, USA* Once known almost entirely for its range of Chardonnays (Belle Terre★★ and Robert Young★★), St Jean has emerged as a producer of delicious reds including a BORDEAUX-style blend called Cinq Cépages★★ and a Reserve Merlot★★. Now owned by Beringer Blass. Best years: (Chardonnay) (2002) 01 00 **99 98 97 95 94 91 90**; (Cabernet) (2002) 01 00 **99 97 95 94**.

CHATEAU STE MICHELLE *Washington State, USA* Pioneering winery with an enormous range of wines, including several attractive vineyard-designated Chardonnays★, Cabernet Sauvignons★ and Merlots★, especially Cold Creek Vineyard★★ wines. Good Riesling, both dry and sweet, and increasingly interesting red Meritage★ and white Sauvignon. Partnership with Italy's ANTINORI and Germany's Ernst LOOSEN have produced dark, powerful red Col Solare★★, a lovely dry Riesling Eroica★ and a thrilling sweet version, TBA★★★, made in tiny quantities. Best years: (premium reds) (2003) (02) 01 00 **99 98 97**.

CHÂTEAUNEUF-DU-PAPE AC *Rhône Valley, France* A large (3350ha/ 8275-acre) vineyard area between Orange and Avignon. The red wine is based on Grenache, plus Syrah and Mourvèdre (10 other varieties are also allowed). Always choose Châteauneuf from a single estate, distinguished by the papal coat of arms or hat embossed on the neck of the bottle. Only 5% of Châteauneuf is white: made mainly from Grenache Blanc, Bourboulenc and Clairette, these wines can be surprisingly good. Top reds, particularly old-vine cuvées, will age for 8 years or more; whites are best young. Best producers: (reds) P Autard★, L Barrot★★, BEAUCASTEL★★★, Beaurenard★★, Bois de Boursan★★, H Bonneau★★, Bosquet des Papes★★, du Caillou★★, les Cailloux★★, Chante Perdrix★★, CHAPOUTIER★, la Charbonnière★★, L Charvin★, Clos du Mont Olivet★★, CLOS DES PAPES★★, Font du Loup★, FONT DE MICHELLE★★, Fortia★★, la Gardine★★, Grand Tinel★, la Janasse★★, Marcoux★★, Monpertuis★★, Mont-Redon★★, la Nerthe★★, Pégaü★★, RAYAS★★★, la Roquette★, Roger Sabon★★, Tardieu-Laurent★★, P Usseglio★★, la Vieille-Julienne★★, Vieux Donjon★★, VIEUX TELEGRAPHE★★★, Villeneuve★★; (whites) BEAUCASTEL★★★, CLOS DES PAPES★★, FONT DE MICHELLE★★, Grand Veneur★★, Marcoux★★, RAYAS★★, St-Cosme★★, VIEUX TELEGRAPHE★★. Best years: (reds) (2004) 03 01 00 99 **98 97 96 95 94 90 89 88**.

JEAN-LOUIS CHAVE *Rhône Valley, France* Jean-Louis Chave's red HERMITAGE★★★ is one of the world's great wines, surpassed only by the Cuvée Cathelin★★★, produced only in exceptional years. His wonderful, richly flavoured white Hermitage★★★ sometimes even outlasts the reds, as it quietly moves toward its honeyed, nutty zenith. Also produces a small amount of excellent red ST-JOSEPH★★ and an occasional stunning traditional sweet Vin de Paille★★. Expensive, but worth the money. Best years: (reds) (2004) 03 01 00 99 98 **97** 96 **95 94 92 91 90 89 88 86 85 83 82 79 78**; (whites) (2004) 03 01 00 99 98 **97** 96 **95 94 93 92 91 90 89 88 85 83**.

CHÉNAS AC *Beaujolais, Burgundy, France* The smallest of the BEAUJOLAIS Crus, Chénas, while little known, offers a range of styles from light and elegant to austere and needing time to develop Burgundian tones. Best producers: J Benon★★, G Braillon★, L Champagnon★, DUBOEUF (Manoir des Journets★), H Lapierre★, B Santé★. Best years: **2003 00 99**.

CHENIN BLANC One of the most underrated white wine grapes in the world. In the LOIRE VALLEY, where it is also called Pineau de la Loire, it is responsible for the great sweet wines of QUARTS DE CHAUME and

BONNEZEAUX, as well as for VOUVRAY, sweet, dry or sparkling, and much other Anjou white. In South Africa, vineyards continue to decrease but the best sites have been identified and retained; all-round improvements have led to the best wines being compared favourably with their Loire counterparts. Styles range from easy-drinking, dryish whites through modern barrel-fermented versions to botrytized dessert wines. New Zealand and Australia have produced good varietal examples, and it is also grown in California and Argentina.

CH. CHEVAL BLANC★★★ *St-Émilion Grand Cru AC, 1er Grand Cru Classé, Bordeaux, France* Along with AUSONE, the leading ST-EMILION estate. Right on the border with POMEROL, it seems to share some of its sturdy richness, but with an extra spice and fruit that is impressively, recognizably unique. An unusually high percentage (60%) of Cabernet Franc is often used in the blend. Best years: 2003 02 01 00 **99 98 97 96 95 94** 90 89 88 86 85 83 82.

CHEVALIER-MONTRACHET AC See Montrachet AC.

DOM. DE CHEVALIER *Pessac-Léognan AC, Cru Classé de Graves, Bordeaux, France* This estate, mainly devoted to red, can produce some of Bordeaux's finest wines. The red★★ always starts out firm and reserved but over 10–20 years gains heavenly cedar, tobacco and blackcurrant flavour. The brilliant white★★★ is both fermented and aged in oak barrels; in the best vintages it will still be improving at 15–20 years. Best years: (reds) 2003 02 01 00 **99 98 96 95** 90 89 88; (whites) (2004) 03 02 01 00 **99 98 97 96 95 94 90 89 88**.

CHEVERNY AC *Loire Valley, France* A little-known area south of Blois. The local speciality is the white Romorantin grape, which makes a bone-dry wine under the AC Cour-Cheverny, but the best whites are from Chardonnay. Also pleasant Sauvignon, Pinot Noir, Gamay and bracing CHAMPAGNE-method fizz. Drink young. Best producers: Cazin, Cheverny co-op, Courtioux, Gendrier/Huards★, Gueritte, H Marionnet, du Moulin, Salvard, Sauger, C Tessier/la Desoucherie, Tue-Boeuf★.

CHIANTI DOCG *Tuscany, Italy* The most famous of all Italian wines, but there are many styles, depending on what grapes are used, where they are grown, and by which producer. It can be a light, fresh, easy-drinking red wine with a characteristic hint of bitterness, or it can be an intense, structured yet sleek wine in the same league as the best BORDEAUX. The vineyards are scattered over central Tuscany, either simply as 'Chianti' or Chianti plus the name of one of the 8 sub-zones: Classico (with its own DOCG), Colli Aretini, Colli Fiorentini, Colli Senesi, Colline Pisane, Montalbano, Montespertoli and Rufina. Sangiovese is the main grape; traditionally it was blended with the red Canaiolo and white Malvasia and Trebbiano. Modern winemakers often make Chianti from Sangiovese alone or blended with 20% of Cabernet, Merlot, Syrah or, increasingly, with native grapes like Colorino. See also Chianti Colli Fiorentini, Chianti Colli Senesi, Chianti Rufina, Super-Tuscans.

CHIANTI CLASSICO DOCG *Tuscany, Italy* The original (if slightly enlarged) CHIANTI zone in the hills between Florence and Siena. Classico has led the trend in making richer, more structured and better-balanced wines. Nonetheless, many producers use their best grapes for high-profile SUPER-TUSCANS. Since the 96 vintage, Classico can be made from 100% Sangiovese, though winemakers all too often accept the option of including 20% 'international' grapes (see CHIANTI). Riserva must be aged at least 27 months (usually in barrel) and must use only red grapes. The finest Riserva wines can improve for a decade or more. Many of the estates also offer regular bottlings of red wine, round and fruity, for drinking about 2–5 years after the harvest. Best producers: Castello di AMA★★, ANTINORI★★, Badia a Coltibuono★★, Brancaia★, Cacchiano★, Capaccia★★, Carpineto★★, Casaloste★★, CASTELLARE★, Castell'in Villa★, Collelungo★★, Colombaio di Cencio★★, Dievole★, Casa Emma★★, FELSINA★★, Le Filigare★, FONTERUTOLI★★, FONTODI★★, ISOLE E OLENA★★, Il Mandorlo★★, La Massa★★, Melini★, Monsanto★★, Il Palazzino★★, Panseretta★★, Panzanello★★, Poggerino★★, Poggiopiano★★, Poggio al Sole (Casasilia★★★), Querceto★, QUERCIABELLA★★★, Castello dei RAMPOLLA★★, RICASOLI (Castello di Brolio★★), RIECINE★★, Rignana★★, Rocca di Castagnoli★★, RUFFINO★★, San Felice★★, San Giusto a Rentennano★★, San Polo in Rosso★, Casa Sola★★, Terrabianca★★, Vecchie Terre di Montefili★★, Verrazzano★, Vignamaggio★, Villa Cafaggio★★, VOLPAIA★★. Best years: (2004) (03) 01 **00 99 98 97 95 93 90 88**.

CHIANTI COLLI FIORENTINI *Chianti DOCG, Tuscany, Italy*   Colli Fiorentini covers the hills around Florence. The wines traditionally are made to drink young, though some estates make Riservas of real interest. Best producers: Baggiolino★, Le Calvane, Il Corno, Corzano e Paterno★, Lanciola★, Malenchini★, Pasolini dall'Onda★, Poppiano★, La Querce, Sammontana, San Vito in Fior di Selva.

CHIANTI COLLI SENESI *Chianti DOCG, Tuscany, Italy*   This CHIANTI sub-zone consists of a vast area of Siena province (including the towns of Montalcino, Montepulciano and San Gimignano). Wines range from everyday quaffers to fairly elegant Riservas. Best producers: Campriano, Carpineta Fontalpino★, Casabianca, Casale-Falchini★, Farnetella★, Ficomontanino★, Pacina★, Paradiso★, Pietraserena.

CHIANTI RUFINA *Chianti DOCG, Tuscany, Italy*   Smallest of the CHIANTI sub-zones, situated in an enclave of the Apennine foothills to the east of Florence, where wines were noted for exceptional strength, structure and longevity long before they joined the ranks of Chianti. Today the wines, particularly the long-lived Riserva Bucerchiale from SELVAPIANA and FRESCOBALDI's Montesodi, match the best of CHIANTI CLASSICO. Pomino DOC is a small (100ha/250-acre) high-altitude zone almost entirely surrounded by Chianti Rufina; dominated by Frescobaldi, it makes greater use of French varieties such as Merlot, Cabernet and Chardonnay. Best producers: (Riservas) Basciano★★, Tenuta di Bossi★, Colognole★, FRESCOBALDI★★, Grati/Villa di Vetrice★, Grignano★, Lavacchio★, SELVAPIANA★★★, Castello del Trebbio★. Best years: (2004) (03) 01 **00 99 98 97 95 93 90 88 85**.

MICHELE CHIARLO *Piedmont, Italy*   From his winery base south of Asti, Michele Chiarlo produces stylish wines from several PIEDMONT zones. Single-vineyard BAROLOS★★ and BARBARESCOS★ top the list, but BARBERA D'ASTI★ and GAVI★ are reliable, too. The Monferrato DOC embraces Countacc!★, a Nebbiolo-Barbera-Cabernet Sauvignon blend.

CHIMNEY ROCK *Stags Leap District AVA, California, USA*   Winemaker Doug Fletcher produces powerful yet elegantly sculpted Cabernet Sauvignon★★, Reserve Cabernet Sauvignon★★ and a meritage blend called Elevage★★. A tangy Fumé Blanc★ is also made. Best years: (Elevage) (2002) 01 00 99 **98** 97 **96 95 94 91 90**.

CHINON AC *Loire Valley, France* Best red wine of the LOIRE VALLEY, made mainly from Cabernet Franc. Lovely light reds full of raspberry fruit and fresh summer earth to drink young, and heavyweights for keeping; always worth buying a single-estate wine. Best producers: P Alliet★★, B Baudry★★, J & C Baudry★, Logis de la Bouchardière, P Breton★, Coulaine★, COULY-DUTHEIL★, J-P Crespin/Ch. de l'Aulée★, DRUET★★, La Grille★, C Joguet★, la Perrière★, Olga Raffault★, Raifault, Roncée★, Rouet, Ch. de St-Louand, Sourdais★. Best years: 2004 03 02 **01 00 97 96 95**.

CHIROUBLES AC *Beaujolais, Burgundy, France* The highest in altitude of the BEAUJOLAIS Crus, producing a light, fragrant, delicious Gamay wine capable of exhibiting all the attractions of a youthful Cru. Best producers: Cheysson★, Dom. de la Combe au Loup/Méziat★, Dom. de la Grosse Pierre/A Passot★, J Passot★. Best years: **2004** 03.

CHIVITE *Navarra DO, Navarra, Spain* The longtime leader in exports from NAVARRA, owned and run by the Chivite family. The Gran Feudo★ wines (red and rosé) are very good easy drinkers. However, the more upmarket reds could be a bit more lively. The top range is called Colección 125 and includes a red Reserva★, classy white Blanco★★ made from Chardonnay, and a characterful sweet Vendimia Tardía★★ from Moscatel (Muscat Blanc à Petits Grains).

CHOREY-LÈS-BEAUNE AC *Côte de Beaune, Burgundy, France* One of those tiny, forgotten villages that make good, if not great, Burgundy at prices most of us can afford, with some committed producers too. Can age for 5–8 years. Best producers: Arnoux★, DROUHIN★, Germain★, Maillard★, TOLLOT-BEAUT★★. Best years: (2004) **03 02** 01 99 96.

CHURCH ROAD *Hawkes Bay, North Island, New Zealand* Church Road is a premium-wine project owned by MONTANA/Allied Domecq. The reds seem a bit Bordeaux-obsessed, but top-of-the-range Tom★, austere but stylish, just about gets away with it. Reserve Chardonnay★ is rich and smooth with flavours of peach, grapefruit and hazelnut. Best years: (Tom) (2002) 00 **98 96**.

CHURCHILL *Port DOC, Douro, Portugal* Established in 1981, it was the first new PORT shipper for 50 years. The wines can be good, notably Vintage★, LBV★, Crusted★, single-quinta Agua Alta★ and a well-aged quirky dry white port★, but they aren't consistent. Quinta da Gricha (purchased in 1999) is a new source of Vintage port. Also new red unfortified DOURO wine, bottled under the name Churchill Estates. Best years: (Vintage) 2000 97 94 **91 85**; (Agua Alta) 1998 **96 95 92**.

CINSAUT Also spelt Cinsault. Found mainly in France's southern RHONE, PROVENCE and the MIDI, giving a light wine with fresh, but rather fleeting, neutral fruit. Ideal for rosé wine. Used in the blend for Lebanon's CHATEAU MUSAR. Popular as a bulk blender in South Africa, it is now being rediscovered by enthusiasts of the Rhône style.

CIRÒ DOC *Calabria, Italy* The legend that this was the wine offered to champions in the ancient Olympics has often seemed a more potent reason to buy it than for its quality. Yet Cirò Rosso, a full-bodied red from the Gaglioppo grape, has improved remarkably of late. Non-DOC Gaglioppo-based IGTs, like Librandi's Gravello★★ (an oak-aged blend with Cabernet), are genuinely exciting. The DOC also covers a dry

105

white from Greco and a rare dry rosé. Best producers: Caparra & Siciliani★, Librandi★ (Riserva★★), San Francesco★. Best years: (reds) (2004) (03) 01 **00 99 97 96 95 93**.

BRUNO CLAIR *Marsannay AC, Côte de Nuits, Burgundy, France* Bruno Clair produces excellent wines from vineyards in MARSANNAY, as well as in GEVREY-CHAMBERTIN and VOSNE-ROMANEE, SAVIGNY in the Côte de Beaune and GIVRY in the Côte Chalonnaise. Most of his wine is red, but there is a small amount of white (CORTON-CHARLEMAGNE★★) and a delicious Marsannay rosé★. Top wines are CHAMBERTIN Clos de Bèze★★★, Gevrey-Chambertin Clos St-Jacques★★★ and vineyard-designated Marsannay reds★★. Best years: (top reds) (2003) 02 **01 00** 99 **98** 96 **95** 90.

CLAIRETTE DE DIE AC *Rhône Valley, France* Sparkling wine made from a minimum of 75% Muscat, off-dry, with a creamy bubble and an orchard-fresh fragrance. The *méthode Dioise* is used, which preserves the Muscat scent. An ideal light aperitif. Drink young. Best producers: Achard-Vincent★, Clairette de Die co-op, D Cornillon, Jacques Faure, J-C Raspail★. See also Crémant de Die.

A CLAPE *Cornas, Rhône Valley, France* The leading estate in CORNAS – dense, tannic, consistently excellent wines, full of rich, roasted fruit and often★★★. Clape also makes fine COTES DU RHONE, both red★ and white★, and decent ST-PERAY★. Best years: (Cornas) (2004) 03 01 00 99 98 **97 96 95 94** 92 91 90 89 88 86 85 83.

LA CLAPE *Coteaux du Languedoc AC, Languedoc, France* The mountain of La Clape rises above the flat coastal fields south-east of Narbonne; its vineyards produce some excellent whites from Bourboulenc and Clairette, plus fine, herb-scented reds and rosés, mainly from Grenache, Syrah and Mourvèdre. The whites and reds can age. Best producers: Ch. Bouisset, Capitoul, L'HOSPITALET★, Mire l'Étang, Négly, Pech-Céleyran★, Pech Redon★, Vires. Best years: (reds) 2003 **01 00 99 98 96**.

CLARE VALLEY *South Australia* Historic upland valley north of Adelaide with a deceptively moderate climate, able to grow fine, aromatic Riesling, marvellously textured Semillon, rich, robust Shiraz and Cabernet blends and peppery but voluptuous Grenache. Best producers: (whites) Tim ADAMS★★, Jim BARRY★, Wolf BLASS (Gold Label★), Leo Buring (Leonay★★), Crabtree, GROSSET★★★, KNAPPSTEIN★, LEASINGHAM★, MITCHELL★, MOUNT HORROCKS★★, O'Leary Walker, PETALUMA★★, Pikes, Taylors/Wakefield★; (reds) Tim ADAMS★★, Jim BARRY★★, GROSSET★★, Kilikanoon★, LEASINGHAM★, MITCHELL★, Pikes★, Taylors/Wakefield, WENDOUREE★★★. Best years: (Shiraz) (2003) 02 **01 99 98** 97 96 94 93 92 91 90 88 86; (Riesling) 2003 **02 01 99 98** 97 96 95 94 93 92 90.

CLARENDON HILLS *McLaren Vale, South Australia* Winery with a name for high-priced, highly extracted, unfined, unfiltered and unobtainable reds. At the top is single-vineyard Astralis (a controversial ★★★), a hugely concentrated Shiraz from old vines, aged in 100% French new oak. Other Shiraz★★ labels offer slightly better value, while Merlot★★ and Cabernet Sauvignon★★ aim to rub shoulders with great red BORDEAUX – although I'm not sure which ones. Several cuvées of Old Vines Grenache★★ are marked by saturated black cherry fruit and high alcohol. Best years: (Astralis) 2003 02 00 99 98 96 **95 94**.

CH. CLARKE *Listrac-Médoc AC, Bordeaux, France* This property had millions spent on it by the late Baron Edmond de Rothschild during the late 1970s, and from the 98 vintage leading Bordeaux winemaker Michel Rolland has been consultant enologist. The wines can have an attractive blackcurrant fruit, though they never quite escape the typical LISTRAC earthiness. But with a name like Clarke, how could they possibly fail to seduce? There is also a small production of dry white wine, le Merle Blanc. Best years: 2003 **01 00 99 98 96 95 90**.

DOMENICO CLERICO *Barolo DOCG, Piedmont, Italy* Domenico Clerico produces consistently superlative BAROLO (Ciabot Mentin Ginestra★★★, Pajana★★★, Per Cristina★★★) and excellent BARBERA D'ALBA★ (Trevigne★★), all wonderfully balanced. His range also includes LANGHE Arte★★, a barrique-aged blend of Nebbiolo and Barbera. Best years: (Barolos) (2004) (03) (01) 00 99 **98 97** 96 **95 93 90 89 88**.

CH. CLIMENS★★★ *Barsac AC, 1er Cru Classé, Bordeaux, France* The leading estate in BARSAC, with a deserved reputation for fabulous, sensuous wines, rich and succulent yet streaked with lively lemon acidity. Easy to drink at 5 years, but a good vintage will be richer and more satisfying after 10–15 years. Second wine: les Cyprès (also delicious). Best years: 2003 02 01 **99 98 97 96 95 90 89 88 86 83 76 75**.

CLOS DE L'ANHEL *Corbières, Languedoc, France* In just a few years, Sophie Guiraudon and Philippe Mathias have started to produce remarkable wines with a power unusual even for the CORBIERES. Top wine is smooth, rich Les Dimanches★★; also Les Terrassettes★ and Le Lolo de l'Anhel. Best years (les Dimanches): 2003 **01 00**.

CLOS BAGATELLE *St-Chinian AC, Languedoc-Roussillon, France* Siblings Luc and Christine Simon produce various ST-CHINIANS: top wine La Gloire de Mon Père★ is made from Syrah, Mourvèdre and Grenache, and aged in 100% new oak barrels; Sélection in only 25%. Unoaked Marie et Mathieu★ is fruit-driven; Cuvée Camille has spicy, herbal aromas. Also a MUSCAT DE ST-JEAN-DE-MINERVOIS.

CLOS DU BOIS *Alexander Valley AVA, California, USA* I've always been partial to the house style here: gentle, fruit-dominated SONOMA Chardonnay, Merlot and Cabernet. Top vineyard selections can be exciting, especially the Calcaire★★ and Flintwood★ Chardonnays, as well as the rich, strong Briarcrest Cabernet Sauvignon★★ and Marlstone★★, a red BORDEAUX-style blend. Now owned by Allied Domecq. Best years: (reds) (2002) (01) 00 **99 97 96 95 94 91 90 88 86**.

CLOS CENTEILLES *Minervois AC, Languedoc-Roussillon, France* Daniel Domergue and his wife Patricia Boyer produce excellent MINERVOIS La Livinière and innovative vins de pays. Impressive Clos Centeilles★★ is their top wine; Capitelle de Centeilles★ and Carignanissime★ are 100% Cinsaut and Carignan respectively. Best years: (2003) **01 00 99 98 97 96**.

CLOS DE LA COULÉE-DE-SERRANT *Savennières AC, Loire Valley, France* Fine estate of only 7ha (17 acres) which merits its own AC within the boundaries of SAVENNIERES. The Joly family runs the property on fervently biodynamic lines, and the estate wine★★ is a concentrated, long-lived, very pricy Chenin Blanc with a honeyed, floral bouquet. Also produces better-value Savennières Roche aux Moines★★ and Becherelle★. Best years: (2003) 02 01 00 **97 96 95 93 90 89 88 85 83 82**.

CLOS ERASMUS★★★ *Priorat DOCa, Cataluña, Spain* Daphne Glorian's tiny estate turns out one of the most profound and personal reds in PRIORAT. Her small winery (formerly Alvaro PALACIOS') also makes a convincing second wine, Laurel★. Best years: (2002) 01 00 99 98 **97 96 94**.

CLOS MOGADOR★★★ *Priorat DOCa, Cataluña, Spain* René Barbier Ferrer was one of the pioneers who relaunched the reputation of PRIORAT in the 80s. The wine is a ripe, intense, brooding monster built to age. Best years: (2001) (00) 99 98 **97 96 95 94 93 92 91 90**.

DOM. DU CLOS NAUDIN *Vouvray, Loire Valley, France* Philippe Foreau
runs this first-rate VOUVRAY domaine. Depending on the vintage, he
produces a range of styles: dry★★, medium-dry★★ and sweet★★ (rare
Réserve★★★), as well as Vouvray Mousseux★★ and Pétillant★★. The
wines are supremely ageworthy. Best years: (Moelleux Réserve) 2003
97 96 **95 90 89 88 85 83 78 76 75 70**.

CLOS DES PAPES *Châteauneuf-du-Pape AC, Rhône Valley, France* The
red CHATEAUNEUF-DU-PAPE★★ has an unusually high amount of
Mourvèdre (20%), which gives structure and complexity, and potential
longevity. Nevertheless, there is enough Grenache to ensure the wine's
approachability in its youth and provide an initial blast of fruit. The
white★★ takes on the nutty character of aged Burgundy after 5 or 6
years. Best years: (red) (2004) 03 01 99 98 **97 96 95 94 90 89 88 83 81**.

CLOS QUEBRADA DE MACUL *Maipo, Chile* Located toward the east of
Santiago, at the foot of the Andes, this garage winery was created by
winemaker Ignacio Recabarren to produce superbly idiosyncratic
Cabernet Sauvignon-based Domus Aurea★★, a red packed with MAIPO
character. Recabarren left in 2002 and Bordelais Patrick Valette is
now in charge as a consultant winemaker. Best years: 2001 **99 97**.

CLOS DE LA ROCHE AC *Grand Cru, Côte de
Nuits, Burgundy, France* The best and
biggest of the 5 MOREY-ST-DENIS Grands Crus.
It has a lovely, bright, red-fruits flavour
when young, and should become richly
chocolaty or gamy with age. Best
producers: DROUHIN★★★, DUJAC★★★, Léchenaut★★★,
H Lignier★★★, Henri Perrot-Minot★★, Ponsot★★★, ROUSSEAU★★. Best
years: (2004) 03 02 01 00 99 **98 97** 96 **95 93 90** 89 88.

CLOS ST-DENIS AC *Grand Cru, Côte de Nuits, Burgundy, France* This
small (6.5ha/16-acre) Grand Cru, which gave its name to the village of
MOREY-ST-DENIS, produces wines that are sometimes light, but should
be wonderfully silky, with the texture that only great Burgundy can
regularly achieve. Best after 10 years or more. Best producers:
Bertagna★★, Charlopin★★, DUJAC★★★, JADOT★★, Ponsot★★★. Best
years: (2004) 03 02 01 00 99 **98 97** 96 **95 93 90**.

CLOS UROULAT *Jurançon AC, South-West France* Charles Hours makes
tiny quantities of stunningly good JURANÇON. Dry Cuvée Marie★★ has
ripe fruit yet a deliciously refreshing finish. The rich sweet Jurançon★★
pulls together lemon, lime, honey and apricot: enjoyable young, but
ages magnificently. Best years: (sweet) 2002 **01 00 99 98 96 95 93**.

CLOS DU VAL *Napa Valley AVA, California, USA* Elegant Cabernet
Sauvignon★ (STAGS LEAP DISTRICT★★), Chardonnay★, Merlot★ and
Zinfandel★. (The Reserve Cabernet★ can age well. Ariadne★★, a
Semillon-Sauvignon Blanc blend, is a lovely aromatic white. Best
years: (Reserve Cabernet) (2001) (00) 99 **97 96 95 94 91 90** 87 86 84.

CLOS DE VOUGEOT AC *Grand Cru, Côte de Nuits, Burgundy, France*
Enclosed by Cistercian monks in the 14th century, and today a
considerable tourist attraction, this large (50ha/125-acre) vineyard is
now divided among 82 owners. As a result of this division, Clos de
Vougeot has become one of the most unreliable Grand Cru Burgundies;
the better wine tends to come from the upper and middle parts. When
it is good it is wonderfully fleshy, turning deep and exotic after 10 years
or more. Best producers: B Ambroise★★, Amiot-Servelle★★, Chopin-
Groffier★★, J-J Confuron★★★, R Engel★★★, FAIVELEY★★, GRIVOT★★★,

The label reads:
CLOS DE LA ROCHE
GRAND CRU
2001
DOMAINE DUJAC

Anne GROS★★★, Haegelen-Jayer★, JADOT★★★, Dom. LEROY★★★, MEO-CAMUZET★★★, Denis MORTET★★★, Mugneret-Gibourg★★★, J Raphet★★, VOUGERAIE★★. Best years: (2004) 03 02 01 00 99 98 **97** 96 **95 93 91 90 88**.

CLOUDY BAY *Marlborough, South Island, New Zealand* New Zealand's most successful winery, Cloudy Bay achieved cult status with the first release of its zesty, herbaceous Sauvignon Blanc★★ in 1985. Sauvignon Blanc Te Koko★★ is very different: rich, creamy, oak-matured and bottle-aged. Cloudy Bay also makes Chardonnay★★, a late-harvest Riesling★★, a superb ALSACE-style Gewürztraminer★★, and good Pinot Noir★. Vintage Pelorus★★ is a high-quality old-style CHAMPAGNE-method fizz and non-vintage Pelorus★★ is excellent too. Best years: (Sauvignon Blanc) **2005 03 02 01 00**.

J-F COCHE-DURY *Meursault AC, Côte de Beaune, Burgundy, France* Jean-François Coche-Dury is a modest superstar, quietly turning out some of the finest wines on the CÔTE DE BEAUNE. His best wines are his CORTON-CHARLEMAGNE★★★ and MEURSAULT Perrières★★★, but even his BOURGOGNE Blanc★★ is excellent. His red wines, from VOLNAY★★ and MONTHELIE★, tend to be cheaper than the whites and should be drunk younger. Best years: (whites) (2004) 03 02 01 00 **99 97 96 95 92 90 89**.

COCKBURN *Port DOC, Douro, Portugal* Best known for its Special Reserve ruby, Cockburns has much more than that to offer. Vintage★★ is stylishly cedary and Quinta dos Canais★★ is a fine single quinta, while the aged tawnies★★ are refined and nutty. Best years: (Vintage) 2000 97 94 **91 70 63 60 55**; (dos Canais) 2001 00 **95 92**.

CODORNÍU *Cava DO, Cataluña, Spain* The biggest CHAMPAGNE-method sparkling wine company in the world. Anna de Codorníu★ and Jaume Codorníu★ are especially good, but all the sparklers are better than the CAVA average. Drink young for freshness. Codorníu also owns RAIMAT in COSTERS DEL SEGRE, Masía Bach in the PENEDES and Bodegas Bilbaínas in RIOJA, and has a stake in Scala Dei in PRIORAT. They also own Artesa in NAPA, CALIFORNIA.

COLCHAGUA, VALLE DE *Rapel, Chile* RAPEL sub-region and home to several exciting estates, such as the acclaimed Apalta vineyard, where CASA LAPOSTOLLE, MONTES and others have plantings. Syrah and Carmenère do very well here. Santa Cruz and Chimbarongo are the best-known sub-zones. Best producers: CASA LAPOSTOLLE★★, Casa Silva, CONO SUR★★, MONTES★★, MontGras, Viu Manent★.

COLDSTREAM HILLS *Yarra Valley, Victoria, Australia* Founded by Australian wine guru James Halliday; owned by Southcorp since 1996. Pinot Noir★ is usually good (Reserve★★): sappy and smoky with cherry fruit and clever use of all-French oak. Chardonnay★ (Reserve★★) has subtlety and delicacy but real depth as well. Reserve Cabernet★ can be very good, though not always ripe; Merlot★★ ripens more successfully. Plans to dramatically increase production don't make a lot of sense in a cool region like the YARRA VALLEY. Best years: (Reserve Pinot Noir) 2004 02 **00 98 97 96**.

COLLI BOLOGNESI DOC *Emilia-Romagna, Italy* Wines from this zone in the Apennine foothills near Bologna were traditionally slightly sweet and frothy. Today concessions are made to international taste, resulting in fine Cabernets★★ from Bonzara and Terre Rosse. Other good red wines are produced from Merlot, and increasing amounts of dry white wine are made from Sauvignon, Pignoletto and Pinot Bianco. Best producers: Bonzara (Cabernet★, Merlot★), Santarosa★, Terre Rosse★★, Vallona★. Best years: (reds) (2003) 01 00 **99 98 97 95 93**.

COLLI ORIENTALI DEL FRIULI DOC *Friuli-Venezia Giulia, Italy* This DOC covers 20 different types of wine. Best known are the sweet whites from Verduzzo in the Ramandolo sub-zone and the delicate Picolit, but it is the reds, from the indigenous Refosco and Schioppettino, as well as imports like Cabernet and dry whites, from Tocai, Ribolla, Pinot Bianco and Malvasia Istriana, that show how exciting the wines can be. Prices are high. Best producers: Ca' Ronesca★, Dario Coos★, Dorigo★, Dri★, Le Due Terre★★, Livio FELLUGA★★, Walter Filiputti★, Adriano Gigante★, Livon★, Meroi★, Miani★★, Davide Moschioni★, Rocca Bernarda★, Rodaro★, Ronchi di Cialla★, Ronchi di Manzano★★, Ronco del Gnemiz★★, Scubla★, Specogna★, Le Vigne di Zamò★★, Zof★. Best years: (whites) (2004) 02 01 **00 99 98 97**.

COLLI PIACENTINI DOC *Emilia-Romagna, Italy* Home to some of EMILIA-ROMAGNA's best wines, this DOC covers 11 different types, the best of which are Cabernet Sauvignon and the red Gutturnio (a blend of Barbera and Bonarda) as well as the medium-sweet white and bubbly Malvasia. Best producers: Luretta★, Lusenti, Castello di Luzzano/Fugazza★, Il Poggiarello★, La Stoppa★, Torre Fornello★, La Tosa (Cabernet Sauvignon★). Best years: (reds) (2004) 03 **01 00 99 98 97 95**.

COLLINES RHODANIENNES, VIN DE PAYS DES *Rhône Valley, France* Region between Vienne and Valence. The best wines are Gamay and, notably, Syrah, although there are some good juicy Merlots, too. Best producers: P & C Bonnefond★, COLOMBO★, CUILLERON (Viognier★), P Gaillard★, JAMET, R Jasmin, M Ogier★, Pochon★, ST-DESIRAT co-op, TAIN-L'HERMITAGE co-op, Vernay★, Vins de Vienne (Sotanum★★). Best years: (reds) (2004) 03 **01 00 99 98**.

COLLIO DOC *Friuli-Venezia Giulia, Italy* Some of Italy's best and most expensive dry white wines are from these hills on the Slovenian border. The zone produces 19 types of wine, from the local Tocai and Malvasia Istriana to international varieties. The best white and red wines are ageworthy. Best producers: Borgo Conventi★, Borgo del Tiglio★★, La Castellada★, Damijan★, Livio FELLUGA★★, Marco Felluga★, Fiegl★, GRAVNER★★, JERMANN★★, Edi Keber★, Renato Keber★★, Livon★, Primosic★, Princic★, Puiatti★, Roncùs★★, Russiz Superiore★, SCHIOPETTO★★, Matijaz Tercic★★, Venica & Venica★★, Villa Russiz★★, Villanova★, Zuani★★. Best years: (whites) (2004) 02 01 **00 99 98 97 96 95**.

COLLIOURE AC *Roussillon, France* This tiny fishing port tucked away in the Pyrenean foothills is also an AC, and makes a throat-warming red wine that is capable of aging for a decade but is marvellously rip-roaring when young. Best producers: (reds) Baillaury★, Cellier des Templiers★, Clos des Paulilles★, Mas Blanc★★, la RECTORIE★★, la Tour Vieille★, Vial Magnères★. Best years: (2003) **01 00 99 98 96 95**.

COLOMBARD In France, Colombard traditionally has been distilled to make Armagnac and Cognac, but has now emerged as a table wine grape in its own right, notably as a Vin de Pays des COTES DE GASCOGNE. At its best, it has a lovely, crisp acidity and fresh, aromatic fruit. The largest plantings of the grape are in California, where it generally produces rather less distinguished wines. South Africa can produce attractive basic wines and Australia also has some fair examples.

JEAN-LUC COLOMBO *Cornas AC, Rhône Valley, France* Colombo has caused controversy with his criticism of traditional methods. His powerful, rich CORNAS has far less tannic grip than some. Top cuvées are les Ruchets★★ and the lush late-harvest la Louvée★★, made in tiny quantities. Among négociant wines now produced, CHATEAUNEUF-DU-PAPE les Bartavelles★, red HERMITAGE★ and the white Hermitage le Rouet★ stand out, although some lesser labels don't always seem fully ripe. Also produces fragrant, expensive ST-PERAY la Belle de Mai★, good COTES DU RHONE★ and vins de pays from the RHONE, the Marseille area and ROUSSILLON. Best years: (Cornas) (2004) 03 01 00 **99 98 97 95 90**.

COLUMBIA CREST *Washington State, USA* Offshoot of CHATEAU STE MICHELLE, producing good-value, good-quality wines. Grand Estates Merlot★ and Grand Estates Chardonnay★ are strong suits. For fruit intensity, drink both with 2–3 years' age. Promising, intense Syrah★.

COLUMBIA VALLEY AVA *Washington State, USA* The largest of WASHINGTON's viticultural regions, covering a third of the landmass in the state and encompassing both the YAKIMA VALLEY and WALLA WALLA regions. It produces 98% of the state's wine grapes: Merlot is the most widely planted variety, with Cabernet Sauvignon and Chardonnay following close behind. Best producers: ANDREW WILL★★★, CADENCE★★, CAYUSE VINEYARDS★★, CHATEAU STE MICHELLE★, COLUMBIA CREST★, DELILLE CELLARS★★, Matthews Cellars★★, QUILCEDA CREEK★★★. Best years: (reds) (2003) 02 01 **00 99 98 97**.

COLUMBIA WINERY *Columbia Valley AVA, Washington State, USA* Under the guidance of David Lake MW, Columbia produces an assortment of decent wines along with several stand-outs from Red Willow Vineyard. The best include deeply fruited, built-to-last Cabernet Sauvignon★ and a fruity, smoky-styled Syrah★. Merlot★ has softened and improved in recent vintages. Best years: (Red Willow reds) (2003) 02 01 **00 99 98 97**.

COMMANDARIA *Cyprus* Dark brown, treacly wine made from red Mavro and white Xynisteri grapes, sun-dried for 2 weeks before vinification and solera aging. Pretty decent stuff but only potentially one of the world's great rich wines. A lighter, drier style is also produced.

CONCHA Y TORO *Maipo, Chile* Chile's biggest winery, Concha y Toro has 4500ha (12,000 acres) of vineyards and a talented group of winemakers, led by Ignacio Recabarren (ex-CASABLANCA) and the brilliant young Marcelo Papa. Casillero del Diablo★ is the excellent budget label and Marqués de Casa Concha is the next step up (reds★★). Higher up, Trio★ and Terrunyo★★ are good labels for reds and whites. Amelia★ is the top Chardonnay and small amounts of various excellent reds come out under the Winemaker's Lot label. The classic Cabernet Sauvignon-based Don Melchor★★ is back on form with the 2001 vintage. Trivento is an exciting Argentinian project. See also Almaviva.

CONDRIEU AC *Rhône Valley, France* Wonderfully fragrant but expensive wine, made entirely from Viognier. Ranging from full and opulent to sweet, late-harvested, Condrieu is a sensation everyone should try, but choose a good producer. Best drunk young. Best producers: G Barge★★, P & C Bonnefond★★, du Chêne★★, L Chèze★, COLOMBO★★, CUILLERON★★★, DELAS★★, P Dumazet★★, C Facchin★★, Faury★, Y Gangloff★★, GUIGAL★★ (Doriane★★★), F Merlin, Monteillet★★, R Niero★★, A Paret★★, A PERRET★★★, C Pichon★★, ROSTAING★★, St-Cosme★★, G Vernay★★★, F Villard★★.

CONO SUR *Rapel, Chile* Dynamic sister winery to CONCHA Y TORO, whose Chimbarongo Pinot Noir★ put both grape and region on the Chilean map. The largely CASABLANCA-sourced 20 Barrels Pinot★★ is rich and perfumed and the wholly Casablanca 20 Barrels Limited Edition★★

and Ocio★★ are positively unctuous. Chardonnay★★, Riesling★★, Merlot★★ and Cabernet Sauvignon★★, under 20 Barrels and Visión labels, are excellent. Isla Negra offers drier, more 'European' flavours.

CH. LA CONSEILLANTE★★ *Pomerol AC, Bordeaux, France* Elegant, exotic, velvety wine that blossoms beautifully after 5–6 years but can age much longer. Best years: 2003 02 01 00 **98 96 95 94 90 89**.

CONSTANTIA WO *South Africa* The historic heart of South African wine: three modern wine farms – KLEIN CONSTANTIA, BUITENVERWACHTING and Groot Constantia – were all part of Simon van der Stel's original 1685 land grant. STEENBERG was also one of the earliest wine farms. Despite the crowding of upmarket houses, new names and plantings are springing up, some on the steepest slopes. Sauvignon Blanc thrust this cool-climate area into the limelight, but Chardonnays are also good. Constantia-Uitsig's elegant, flavoursome Semillon-Sauvignon Blanc reflects growing trends for this blend. Best producers: BUITENVERWACHTING★, Constantia-Uitsig★, High Constantia, KLEIN CONSTANTIA★, STEENBERG★★. Best years: (whites) **2004 03 02 01 00 99**.

ALDO CONTERNO *Barolo DOCG, Piedmont, Italy* One of BAROLO's finest traditionalist producers. He makes good Dolcetto d'Alba★, excellent BARBERA D'ALBA Conca Tre Pile★★, a barrique-aged LANGHE Nebbiolo Il Favot★★, blended red Quartetto★★ and 2 Langhe Chardonnays: unoaked Printaniè and Bussiador★, fermented and aged in new wood. Pride of the range, though, are his Barolos from the hill of Bussia. In top vintages he produces Barolos Vigna Colonello★★★, Vigna Cicala★★★ and excellent Granbussia★★★, as well as a blended regular Barolo called Bussia Soprana★★. All these Barolos, though accessible when young, need several years to show their true majesty, but retain a remarkable freshness. Best years: (Barolo) (2004) (03) (01) (00) 99 **98 97** 96 **95 93 90 89 88 86 85 82**.

GIACOMO CONTERNO *Barolo DOCG, Piedmont, Italy* Aldo's late elder brother Giovanni, now followed by his son Roberto, took an even more traditional approach to winemaking. The flagship wine is BAROLO Monfortino★★★ (only released after some 5 or 6 years in large oak barrels) but Barolo Cascina Francia★★★ is also superb. Also excellent traditional BARBERA D'ALBA★. Best years: (Monfortino) (2004) (03) (01) (00) (99) 98 97 96 95 **90 89 88 85 82 79 78 74 71**.

CONTINO *Rioja DOCa, Rioja, Spain* An estate on some of the finest RIOJA land, half-owned by CVNE. The wines include a Reserva★, a single-vineyard Viña del Olivo★★ and an innovative Graciano★ varietal. Best years: (Reserva) (2002) (01) 00 **99 98 96 95 94 86 85**.

COONAWARRA *South Australia* On a flat limestone belt thinly veneered with terra rossa soil, Coonawarra can produce sublime Cabernet with blackcurrant leafy flavours and spicy Shiraz that age for years. Merlot, Chardonnay and Riesling can be good, too. An export-led boom has seen hundreds of new vineyards planted, many of which are outside the legendary terra rossa strip. In view of some disappointing light reds, I wonder if Coonawarra's reputation is not at risk. Best producers: Balnaves★, BOWEN★, BRAND'S★★, HOLLICK★, KATNOOK★, Leconfield, LINDEMANS★★, MAJELLA★★, ORLANDO★, PARKER★★, PENFOLDS★★, PENLEY★★, PETALUMA★★, WYNNS★★, Zema★★. Best years: (Cabernet Sauvignon) 2004 03 02 **01 00 99 98 97 96 94 91 90 86**.

COOPERS CREEK *Auckland, North Island, New Zealand* Successful HAWKES BAY Chardonnay★, especially Swamp Reserve Chardonnay★, and tangy MARLBOROUGH Sauvignon Blanc★. Dry Riesling★ and Late Harvest Riesling styles are also good. A smart range of Reserve reds from Hawkes Bay includes complex Merlot★ and elegant Cabernet Sauvignon★. Best years: (Chardonnay) (2004) **02 00 99 98**.

CORBIÈRES AC *Languedoc, France* This huge AC now produces some of the best reds in the LANGUEDOC, with juicy fruit and more than a hint of wild hillside herbs. Excellent young, but wines from the best estates can age for years. White Corbières can be tasty – drink as young as possible. Best producers: (reds) Baillat★, Caraguilhes★, Ch. Cascadais★, CLOS DE L'ANHEL★, Étang des Colombes★, Fontsainte★, Grand Crès★, Grand Moulin★, Haut-Gléon★, Hélène★, l'Ille★, LASTOURS★, Mansenoble★, MONT TAUCH co-op, Ollieux★, les Palais★, St-Auriol★, VOULTE-GASPARETS★. Best years: (reds) 2003 **01 00 99 98 96**.

CORNAS AC *Rhône Valley, France* Pure Syrah wines; attractive alternatives to pricy neighbours HERMITAGE and COTE-ROTIE. When young, the wines are a thick, impenetrable red, almost black in the ripest years. Many need 10 years' aging. Best producers: ALLEMAND★★, F Balthazar★★, CLAPE★★★, COLOMBO★★, Courbis★★, DELAS★, E & J Durand★★, Fauterie★, JABOULET★, J Lemenicier★, LIONNET/ Rochepertuis★★, R Michel★★, TAIN L'HERMITAGE co-op★, Tardieu-Laurent★★, Tunnel★, A Voge★★. Best years: (2004) 03 01 00 99 **98 97 96 95 94 91 90 89 88 85 83**.

CORSE, VIN DE *Corsica, France* Overall AC for CORSICA with 5 superior sub-regions: Calvi, Cap Corse, Figari, Porto Vecchio and Sartène. Ajaccio and Patrimonio are entitled to their own ACs. The most distinctive wines, mainly red, come from local grapes (Nielluccio and Sciacarello for reds, Vermentino for whites). There are some rich sweet Muscats – especially from Muscat de Cap Corse. Best producers: Arena★, Catarelli★, Clos d'Alzeto★, Clos Capitoro, Clos Culombu★, Clos Landry★, Clos Nicrosi★, Gentile★, Leccia★, Maestracci★, Orenga de Gaffory★, Comte Peraldi★, Renucci★, Torraccia.

CORSICA *France* This Mediterranean island has made some pretty dull and undistinguished wines in the past. The last decade has seen a welcome trend toward quality, with co-ops and local growers investing in better equipment and planting noble grape varieties – such as Syrah, Merlot, Cabernet Sauvignon and Mourvèdre for reds, and Chardonnay and Sauvignon Blanc for whites – to complement the local Nielluccio, Sciacarello and Vermentino. Whites and rosés are pleasant for drinking young; reds are more exciting and can age for 3–4 years. See also Corse AC.

CORTES DE CIMA *Alentejo, Portugal* Dane Hans Kristian Jørgensen and his American wife Carrie make excellent modern Portuguese reds in the heart of the ALENTEJO. Local grape varieties – Aragonez (Tempranillo), Trincadeira and Periquita – are used for spicy, fruity Chaminé★, oaked red Cortes de Cima★ and a splendid dark, smoky Reserva★★. A little Cabernet, Touriga and Syrah are also grown, the latter for Incógnito★★, a gutsy, black-fruited blockbuster. Best years: (2004) **03 01 00**.

CORTESE White grape variety planted primarily in south-eastern PIEDMONT in Italy; it can produce good, fairly acidic, dry whites. Sometimes labelled simply as Cortese Piemonte DOC, it is also used for GAVI.

CORTON AC *Grand Cru, Côte de Beaune, Burgundy, France* The only red Grand Cru in the COTE DE BEAUNE; ideally the wines should have the burliness and savoury power of the top COTE DE NUITS wines, combined with the seductively perfumed fruit of Côte de Beaune. Red Corton should take 10 years to mature, but many modern examples never get there. Very little white Corton is made. Best producers: B Ambroise★★, Bonneau du Martray★★, CHANDON DE BRIAILLES★★, Dubreuil-Fontaine★★, FAIVELEY★★, Guyon★★, JADOT★★★, Dom. LEROY★★★, MEO-CAMUZET★★★, Prince de Merode★, Rapet★★, Senard★★, TOLLOT-BEAUT★★★. Best years: (reds) (2004) 03 02 01 00 99 **98 97** 96 **95 93 90**.

CORTON-CHARLEMAGNE AC *Grand Cru, Côte de Beaune, Burgundy, France* Corton-Charlemagne, on the west and south-west flanks and at the top of the famous Corton hill, is the largest of Burgundy's white Grands Crus. It can produce some of the most impressive white Burgundies – rich, buttery and nutty with a fine mineral quality. The best show their real worth only at 10 years or more. Best producers: B Ambroise★★, Bonneau du Martray★★★, BOUCHARD PERE ET FILS★★, Champy★★, CHANDON DE BRIAILLES★★★, COCHE-DURY★★★, DROUHIN★★, FAIVELEY★★, V GIRARDIN★★★, JADOT★★, P Javillier★★, LATOUR★★, Rapet★★, M Rollin★★, ROUMIER★★, TOLLOT-BEAUT★★★, VERGET★★. Best years: (2004) 03 02 01 00 99 98 **97** 96 **95 92 90** 89.

CH. COS D'ESTOURNEL★★★ *St-Estèphe AC, 2ème Cru Classé, Haut-Médoc, Bordeaux, France* One of the leading châteaux of Bordeaux. Despite a high proportion of Merlot (just under 40%), the wine is classically made for aging and usually needs 10 years to show really well. Recent vintages have been dark, brooding, powerful and, but for a wobble in 1999, of the highest order. Second wine: les Pagodes de Cos. Best years: 2003 02 01 00 98 **97** 96 **95 94** 93 90 89 88 86 85 83 82.

COSTANTI *Brunello di Montalcino DOCG, Tuscany, Italy* One of the original, highly respected Montalcino estates making fine BRUNELLO★★ and Rosso★★, as well as Vermiglio★, a tasty partially barrique-aged Sangiovese. Costanti Riserva★★ is archetypal Brunello, austere, elegant and long-lived. New Calbello wines from the hill of Montosoli include excellent Rosso★★ and Merlot-Cabernet blend Ardingo★★. Best years: (Brunello) (2004) (03) (01) 99 97 **95 93 90 88 85 82**.

COSTERS DEL SEGRE DO *Cataluña, Spain* DO on the 'banks of the Segre' in western CATALUNA. A great array of grape varieties is grown, with the accent on French varieties. Quality is generally good and prices moderate. Best producers: Celler de Cantonella★, Castell del Remei★, RAIMAT★. Best years: (reds) 2001 **00 99 98 96 95 94**.

COSTIÈRES DE NÎMES AC *Languedoc, France* Improving AC between Nîmes and Arles. Reds are generally bright and perfumed, rosés are good young gluggers. Whites are usually tasty versions of Marsanne and Roussanne. Best producers: l'Amarine★, Grande Cassagne★, Mas des Bressades★, Mas Carlot, Mas Neuf, Mourgues du Grès★, Nages★, la Tuilerie★, Vieux-Relais★. Best years: (2004) **03 01 00 99 98**.

CÔTE DE BEAUNE *Côte d'Or, Burgundy, France* Southern part of the COTE D'OR; beginning at the hill of CORTON, north of the town of BEAUNE, the Côte de Beaune progresses south as far as les MARANGES, with white wines gradually taking over from red.

CÔTE DE BEAUNE AC *Côte de Beaune, Burgundy, France* Small AC, high on the hill above the town of Beaune, named to ensure maximum confusion with the title for the whole region. Best producers: Allexant, VOUGERAIE★. Best years: (2004) **03** 02 **00** 99.

CÔTE DE BEAUNE-VILLAGES AC *Côte de Beaune, Burgundy, France*
Red wine AC covering 16 villages, such as AUXEY-DURESSES, LADOIX, MARANGES. If the wine is a blend from several villages it is sold as Côte de Beaune-Villages. It can also cover the red wine production of mainly white wine villages such as MEURSAULT. Best producers: DROUHIN★, J-P Fichet★, JADOT★. Best years: (2004) 03 02 **01 99**.

CÔTE DE BROUILLY AC *Beaujolais, Burgundy, France*
Wine from the higher slopes of Mont Brouilly, a small but abrupt volcanic mountain in the south of the BEAUJOLAIS Crus area. The wine is deeper in colour and fruit and has more intensity than that of BROUILLY. Best producers: Lacondemine★, O Ravier★, Ch. Thivin (Zaccharie Geoffray★★), Viornery★.

CÔTE CHALONNAISE See Bourgogne-Côte Chalonnaise.

CÔTE DE NUITS *Côte d'Or, Burgundy, France*
This is the northern part of the great CÔTE D'OR and is *not* an AC. Almost entirely red wine country, the vineyards start in the southern suburbs of Dijon and continue south in a narrow swathe to below the town of NUITS-ST-GEORGES. The villages are some of the greatest wine names in the world – GEVREY-CHAMBERTIN, VOUGEOT and VOSNE-ROMANEE etc.

CÔTE DE NUITS-VILLAGES AC *Côte de Nuits, Burgundy, France*
Although not much seen, the wines (mostly red) are often good, not very deep in colour but with a nice cherry fruit. Best producers: (reds) D Bachelet★, Chopin-Groffier★, J-J Confuron, JADOT, JAYER-GILLES★, RION★, P Rossignol★. Best years: (reds) (2004) **03** 02 **01 99**.

CÔTE D'OR *Burgundy, France*
Europe's most northern great red wine area and also the home of some of the world's best dry white wines. The name, meaning 'golden slope', refers to a 48km (30-mile) stretch between Dijon and Chagny which divides into the CÔTE DE NUITS in the north and the CÔTE DE BEAUNE in the south.

CÔTE ROANNAISE AC *Loire Valley, France*
Small AC in the upper Loire producing mostly light reds and rosés from Gamay. A new wave of producers here and in neighbouring Côtes du Forez are on a quality drive. Non-appellation whites can be good. Best producers: A Demon, Fontenay★, M Lutz, M & L Montroussier, R Sérol★; (Côtes du Forez) Clos de Chozieux, Cave des Vignerons Foreziens, Verdier-Logel★.

CÔTE-RÔTIE AC *Rhône Valley, France*
The Côte-Rôtie, or 'roasted slope', produces one of France's greatest red wines. On its vertiginous slopes, the Syrah manages to balance super ripeness with freshness, and the small amount of white Viognier sometimes included in the blend gives an unexpected exotic fragrance. Lovely young, it is better aged for 8 years. Best producers: G Barge★★, Bernard★, P & C Bonnefond★★, Bonserine★, B Burgaud★, Clusel-Roch★★, CUILLERON★★, DELAS★★, Duclaux★★, Gallet★, Garon★, J-M Gérin★★, GUIGAL★★, JABOULET★, JAMET★★, Jasmin★★, S Ogier★, ROSTAING★, Tardieu-Laurent★★, Vidal-Fleury★, F Villard★, Vins de Vienne★★. Best years: (2004) 03 01 00 99 **98 97 95 94 91 90 89 88**.

COTEAUX D'AIX-EN-PROVENCE AC *Provence, France*
The first AC in the South to acknowledge that Cabernet Sauvignon can enormously enhance the traditional local grape varieties such as Grenache, Cinsaut, Mourvèdre, Syrah and Carignan. The reds can age. Some quite good fresh rosé is made, while the whites, mostly still traditionally made, are pleasant but hardly riveting. Best producers: Ch. Bas★, les Bastides★, des Béates★★, Beaupré★, Calissanne★, J-L COLOMBO (La Côte Bleue★), Fonscolombe★, Pontet Bagatelle★, Revelette★, Vignelaure★. Best years: (reds) (2003) **01 00 99 98 97 96**.

COTEAUX DE L'ARDÈCHE, VIN DE PAYS DES *Rhône Valley, France*
Increasingly good varietal red wines made from Cabernet Sauvignon, Syrah, Merlot or Gamay and dry, fresh white wines from Chardonnay, Viognier or Sauvignon Blanc. Best producers: Vignerons Ardechois, Colombier, DUBOEUF, G Flacher, Louis LATOUR, Pradel, ST-DESIRAT, Vigier.

COTEAUX DE L'AUBANCE AC *Loire Valley, France* Smallish AC north of COTEAUX DU LAYON AC, enjoying a renaissance for its sweet or semi-sweet white wines made from Chenin Blanc. Top sweet wines are now labelled Sélection de Grains Nobles, as in ALSACE. Best producers: Daviau/Bablut★★, Deux Moulins★, Haute Perche★, Montgilet/V Lebreton★★, RICHOU★★. Best years: 2004 03 02 01 **99 97 96 95 93 90**.

COTEAUX CHAMPENOIS AC *Champagne, France* Still wines from Champagne. Fairly acid with a few exceptions, notably from Bouzy and Aÿ. The best age for 5 years or more. Best producers: Paul Bara★, BOLLINGER★, Egly-Ouriet★, H Goutorbe, LAURENT-PERRIER, Joseph Perrier, Ch. de Saran★ (MOET & CHANDON). Best years: 2003 02 00 **99 98 96 95 90**.

COTEAUX DU LANGUEDOC AC *Languedoc, France*
Large and increasingly successful AC situated between Montpellier and Narbonne, producing around 73 million bottles of beefy red and tasty rosé wines. Twelve 'crus', including Montpeyroux, Quatourze and Cabrières, have historically been allowed to append their names to the AC – these are in the process of being delineated by climate and soil type. La CLAPE,  Grès de Montpellier and PIC ST-LOUP have already been officially recognized. Best producers: l'Aiguelière★, Aupilhac★, Calage★, Clavel★, la Coste★, Exindre★, Grès St-Paul★, Henry, Lacroix-Vanel★, Mas Cal Demoura, Mas des Chimères★, MAS JULLIEN★, PEYRE ROSE★★, Poujol★, PRIEURE DE ST-JEAN DE BEBIAN★★, Puech-Haut★, St-Martin de la Garrigue★, Terre Megère★. Best years: 2003 **01 00 99 98 96**.

COTEAUX DU LAYON AC *Loire Valley, France* Sweet wine from the Layon Valley, south of Angers. The wine is made from Chenin Blanc grapes that, ideally, are attacked by noble rot. In great years like 1996, and from a talented grower, this can be one of the world's exceptional sweet wines. A Sélection de Grains Nobles classification, as in ALSACE, now exists for top sweet wines. Seven villages are entitled to use the Coteaux du Layon-Villages AC and put their own name on the label, and these wines are definitely underpriced for the quality. Three sub-areas, BONNEZEAUX, Chaume Premier Cru and QUARTS DE CHAUME, have their own ACs. Best producers: P Aquilas★★, P Baudouin★★★, BAUMARD★★, Bergerie★★, Bidet★, Breuil★, Cady★★, P Delesvaux★★★, Forges★★, Guimonière★★, Ogereau★, Passavant★, Pierre-Bise★★, J Pithon★★★, J Renou★★, Roulerie★★, Sablonnettes★★, Sauveroy★, Soucherie/P-Y Tijou★★, Yves Soulez★★, Touche Noire★. Best years: 2004 03 02 01 **99 97 96 95 90 89 88 85 83 76**.

COTEAUX DU LYONNAIS AC *Beaujolais, Burgundy, France* Good, light, BEAUJOLAIS-style reds and a few whites and rosés from scattered vineyards between Villefranche and Lyon. Drink young.

COTEAUX DU TRICASTIN AC *Rhône Valley, France* Bright, fresh, sometimes full, reds and rosés with attractive juicy fruit. Only a little of the nutty white is made but is worth looking out for. Drink it young. Best producers: Décelle, Grangeneuve★, Lônes, St-Luc★, la Tour d'Elyssas, Vieux Micocoulier. Best years: 2004 **03 01 00 99 98**.

COTEAUX VAROIS AC *Provence, France* North of Toulon, this is an area to watch, with new plantings of classic grapes to improve quality. Best producers: Alysses★, Bremond, Calisse★, Chaberts, Deffends★, Garbelle, Routas★, St-Estève, St-Jean-le-Vieux, St-Jean-de-Villecroze★, Triennes★. Best years: 2004 **03 01 99**.

CÔTES DE BERGERAC AC See Bergerac AC.

CÔTES DE BOURG AC *Bordeaux, France* The best red wines are earthy but blackcurranty and can age for 6–10 years. Very little white is made; most of it is dry and dull. Best producers: Brulesécaille★, Bujan★, FALFAS★, Fougas★, Garreau, Guerry, Haut-Guiraud, Haut-Macô★, Macay, Mercier★, Nodoz★, ROC DE CAMBES★★, Rousset, Tauriac co-op, Tayac★, Tour de Guiet. Best years: 2003 02 **01 00 99 98 96 95**.

CÔTES DE CASTILLON AC *Bordeaux, France* Area east of ST-EMILION that has surged in quality in recent years. There's still good value for prices are beginning to climb. The best wines are full and firm with a fresh finish. Best producers: Dom. de l'A★, Aiguilhe★★, Belcier, Cap-de-Faugères★, la Clarière Laithwaite, Clos l'Eglise★, Clos Les Lunelles (from 2001), Clos Puy Arnaud★, Côte-Montpezat★, Poupille★, Robin★, Veyry★, Vieux-Ch.-Champs-de-Mars★. Best years: 2003 02 **01 00 99 98 96 95**.

CÔTES DE DURAS AC *South-West France* AC between ENTRE-DEUX-MERS and BERGERAC, with good, fresh, grassy reds and whites from traditional BORDEAUX grapes. Drink young. Best producers: Clos du Cadaret, Duras co-op, Grand Mayne, Lafon, Landerrouat co-op, Laulan, Mouthes le Bihan★, Petit Malromé. Best years: (reds) 2003 **01 00 98**.

CÔTES DE FRANCS See Bordeaux-Côtes de Francs.

CÔTES DU FRONTONNAIS AC *South-West France* From north of Toulouse, some of the most distinctive reds – often juicy and positively silky in texture – of South-West France. Négrette is the chief grape, but certain producers coarsen it with Cabernet, which rather defeats the object. Best producers: Baudare, Bellevue-la-Forêt★, Cahuzac★, la Colombière, Ferran, Flotis, Laurou, Montauriol, la Palme, Plaisance, le Roc★, St-Louis. Best years: 2003 **01 00 98 96**.

CÔTES DE GASCOGNE, VIN DE PAYS DES *South-West France* This is Armagnac country, but the tangy-fresh, fruity white table wines are tremendously good. Best producers: Aurin, Brumont, GRASSA★, de Joy, Producteurs PLAIMONT★, St-Lannes.

CÔTES DU JURA AC *Jura, France* Jura's regional AC covers a variety of wines, including specialities *vin jaune* and *vin de paille*. Savagnin makes strong-tasting whites and Chardonnay some good dry whites and CREMANT DU JURA. Reds and rosés can be good from Pinot Noir, but from local Poulsard and Trousseau the wines can be a bit odd. Drink young. Best producers: Arlay★★, Berthet-Bondet★, Bourdy★★, Chalandard★, Clavelin★, Durand-Perron★, Ch. de l'Étoile★, Joly★, A Labet★★, J Maclé★★, Reverchon★, Rijckaert★★, Rolet★★, A & M Tissot★.

CÔTES DU LUBÉRON AC *Rhône Valley, France* Production is dominated by the co-ops east of Avignon. The light, easy wines are refreshing and for drinking young. Best producers: Bonnieux co-op, Ch. la Canorgue, la Citadelle★, Fontenille★, Ch. de l'Isolette★, la Tour-d'Aigues co-op, Ch. des Tourettes, Val Joanis, la Verrerie★. Best years: (2004) **03 01 00 99 98**.

CÔTES DU MARMANDAIS AC *South-West France* The red wines are fairly successful BORDEAUX lookalikes; Syrah is also permitted. Best producers: Beaulieu, Cave de Beaupuy, Cocumont co-op, Elian Da Ros (Chante Coucou, Clos Baquey★).

CÔTES DE MONTRAVEL AC See Montravel AC.

CÔTES DE PROVENCE AC *Provence, France* Large AC mainly for fruity reds and rosés to drink young. Whites are improving. Best producers: Barbanau★, la Bernarde★, Commanderie de Peyrassol★, la Courtade★★, Coussin Ste-Victoire★, Dragon★, Féraud★, Galoupet★, des Garcinières★, Gavoty★, Grand Cros, Mauvanne★, Minuty★, Ott★, Rabiega★, Réa Martin★, RICHEAUME★, Rimauresq★, Roquefort★★, Maîtres Vignerons de St-Tropez, Sorin★, Élie Sumeire★.

CÔTES DU RHÔNE AC *Rhône Valley, France* AC for the whole RHONE VALLEY. Over 90% is red and rosé, mainly from Grenache, with some Cinsaut, Syrah, Carignan and Mourvèdre to add warm southern personality. Modern winemaking has revolutionized the style; today's wines are generally juicy, spicy and easy to drink, ideally within 5 years. Most wine is made by co-ops. Best producers: (reds) Amouriers★, d'Andézon★, les Aphillanthes★, A Brunel★, CLAPE★, COLOMBO★, Coudoulet de BEAUCASTEL★, Cros de la Mûre★, Estézargues co-op★, Fonsalette★★, FONT DE MICHELLE★, Gramenon★★, Grand Moulas★, Grand Prebois★, GUIGAL★, Hugues★, JABOULET, la Janasse★, LIONNET★, J-M Lombard★, Mas de Libian★, Mont-Redon★, la Mordorée★, REMEJEANNE★, M Richaud★, St-Estève★, ST-GAYAN, Ste-Anne★, Santa Duc★, Tardieu-Laurent★, Tours★, Vieux-Chêne★; (whites) CLAPE★, P Gaillard★, REMEJEANNE★, Ste-Anne★. Best years: (reds) **2004 03 01 00 99.**

CÔTES DU RHÔNE-VILLAGES AC *Rhône Valley, France* AC covering 16 villages in the southern COTES DU RHONE that have traditionally made superior wine (especially CAIRANNE, Rasteau, Beaumes-de-Venise Séguret, Valréas, Sablet, Visan). The are spicy reds that can age well. Best producers: (reds) Achiary★, Amouriers★, Beaurenard★, Bressy-Masson★, de Cabasse★, Cabotte★, Chapoton★, D Charavin★, Charbonnière★, Chaume-Arnaud★, Combe★, Coriançon★, Cros de la Mûre★, Espigouette★, Les Goubert, Estézargues co-op★, Gourt de Mautens★★, Gramenon★, Grand Moulas★, Grand Veneur★, la Janasse★, Pélaquié★, Piaugier★, Rasteau co-op★, REMEJEANNE★, ST-GAYAN★, Ste-Anne★, la Soumade★, Tours★, Trapadis★, Verquière★. Best years: (reds) (2004) 03 **01 00 99 98 95.**

CÔTES DU ROUSSILLON AC *Roussillon, France* ROUSSILLON's catch-all AC, dominated by co-ops. It's a hot area, and much of the wine is baked and dull. But there's a lively and expanding bunch of estates doing surprisingly good things with white and exciting things with reds. Best producers: (reds) Vignerons Catalans, la CASENOVE★, CAZES★, Chênes★, J-L COLOMBO★, Ferrer-Ribière★, Força Réal, GAUBY★★, Jau, Joliette, Laporte★, Mas Crémat★, Piquemal★, Olivier Pithon★, Rivesaltes co-op, Sarda-Malet★. Best years: (reds) 2003 **01 00 99 98 96.**

CÔTES DU ROUSSILLON-VILLAGES AC *Roussillon, France* Wines from the best sites in the northern COTES DU ROUSSILLON. Villages Caramany Latour-de-France, Lesquerde and Tautavel may add their own name. Best producers: Agly co-op, Vignerons Catalans, CAZES★, Chênes★, Clos des Fées★, Fontanel★, Força Réal, Gardiés★, GAUBY★★, Jau, Mas Amiel★, Mas Crémat★, Schistes★. Best years: (reds) (2003) **01 00 99 98 96.**

CÔTES DE ST-MONT VDQS *South-West France* A good VDQS for firm but fruity reds and some fair rosés and dry whites. Best producer: Producteurs PLAIMONT.

CÔTES DE THONGUE, VIN DE PAYS DES *Languedoc, France* Zone north-east of Béziers. Many dull red quaffers, but dynamic estates can produce excellent results. Best producers: l'Arjolle★, Bellevue, les Chemins de Bassac★, Condamine l'Evêque, Croix Belle.

CÔTES DU VENTOUX AC *Rhône Valley, France* AC with vineyards on the slopes of Mt Ventoux. When well made, the red wines can have a lovely juicy fruit, or in the case of JABOULET and Pesquié, some real stuffing. Best producers: Anges★, Bedoin co-op, Brusset, Cascavel, La Croix des Pins★, Goult/Cave de Lumières★, JABOULET★, Pesquié★, St-Didier/Cave Courtoise★, Valcombe★, la Verrière, la Vieille Ferme. Best years: (reds) 2004 **03 01 00 99**.

CÔTES DU VIVARAIS AC *Rhône Valley, France* In the northern Gard and Ardèche, typical southern Rhône grapes (Grenache, Syrah, Cinsaut, Carignan) produce mainly light, fresh reds and rosés for drinking young. Best producers: Vignerons Ardechois, Gallety, Vigier.

COTNARI *Romania* The warm mesoclimate of this hilly region, close to the border with Moldova, encourages noble rot, and it was once – but not now – on a footing with TOKAJI. Cotnari's principal local varieties are Grasa, Tamiîoasă, Francusa and Fetească Albă.

CÔTTO, QUINTA DO *Douro DOC and Port DOC, Douro, Portugal* Table wine expert in Lower DOURO. Basic red and white Quinta do Côtto are reasonable, and its Grande Escolha★★ is one of Portugal's best reds, oaky and powerful when young, rich and cedary when mature. Best years: (Grande Escolha) 2000 **97 95 94 90 87 85**.

COULY-DUTHEIL *Chinon AC, Loire Valley, France* Large merchant house responsible for 10% of the CHINON AC. Best wines are Clos de l'Écho★, Clos de l'Écho Crescendo★ and Clos de l'Olive★. Top négociant blend is la Baronnie Madeleine★, which combines tasty raspberry fruit with a considerable capacity to age. Also sells a range of other Touraine wines. Best years: (reds) 2004 03 02 **01 00 97 96 95 90 89**.

PIERRE COURSODON *St-Joseph AC, Rhône Valley, France* Family-owned domaine producing rich, oaked ST-JOSEPH★ from very old vines. The red wines need up to 5 years before they show all their magnificent cassis and truffle and violet richness, especially the top wine, La Sensonne★★. Whites are good, too. Best years: (reds) (2004) 03 **02** 01 **00 99 98 97 95 94 91 90 89 88**.

CH. COUTET★★ *Barsac AC, 1er Cru Classé, Bordeaux, France* BARSAC'S largest Classed Growth property has been in great form in recent years, and with its finesse and balance is once again a classic Barsac. Extraordinarily intense Cuvée Madame★★★ is made in exceptional years. Best years: 2003 02 01 **99 98 97 96 95 90 89 88**.

CRAGGY RANGE *Hawkes Bay, North Island, New Zealand* Exciting new venture managed by viticulturist Steve Smith; it suffered a severe blow last year with the death of its brilliant young winemaker, Doug Wisor. Premium HAWKES BAY wines include stylish Les Beaux Cailloux Chardonnay★★, a bold Cabernet blend called The Quarry★★, a rich Merlot blend known as Sophia★★ and the flagship Le Sol Syrah★★★. Also top Pinot Noirs★★ from MARTINBOROUGH; restrained yet intense Avery Sauvignon Blanc★ and tangy Rapaura Road Riesling★ from MARLBOROUGH; elegant Chardonnay★ and Merlot★, both from the Seven Poplars Vineyard in Hawkes Bay. Best years: (Syrah) (2004) 02 **01**.

CRASTO, QUINTA DO *Douro DOC and Port DOC, Douro, Portugal* Well-situated property belonging to the Roquette family. Very good traditional LBV★★ and Vintage★★ port and thoroughly enjoyable red DOURO★, especially Reserva★★ and varietal Touriga Nacional★★. Flagship reds Vinha da Ponte★★ and Maria Teresa★★ can reach ★★★. Best years: (port) 2000 99 97 **95 94**; (Reserva red) (2003) 01 **00 99 98**; (Ponte) 2000; (Maria Teresa) 2001.

119

CRÉMANT D'ALSACE AC *Alsace, France* Good CHAMPAGNE-method sparkling wine from Alsace, usually made from Pinot Blanc. Reasonable quality, if not great value for money. Best producers: BLANCK★, Dopff au Moulin★, Dopff & Irion, J Gross★, Kuentz-Bas, MURE★, Ostertag★, Pfaffenheim co-op, P Sparr★, A Stoffel★, TURCKHEIM co-op★.

CRÉMANT DE BOURGOGNE AC *Burgundy, France* Most Burgundian Crémant is white and is made either from Chardonnay alone or blended with Pinot Noir. The result, especially in ripe years, can be full, soft, almost honey-flavoured – if you give the wine the 2–3 years' aging needed for mellowness to develop. Best producers: A Delorme, Lucius-Grégoire, Parigot-Richard, Simonnet-Febvre; and the co-ops at Bailly★ (the best for rosé), Lugny★, St-Gengoux-de-Scissé and Viré.

CRÉMANT DE DIE AC *Rhône Valley, France* AC for traditional-method fizz made entirely from the Clairette Blanche grape. Less aromatic than CLAIRETTE DE DIE. Best producers: Jacques Faure, J-C Raspail.

CRÉMANT DU JURA AC *Jura, France* AC for fizz from Jura. Largely Chardonnay-based, with Poulsard for the pinks. Best producers: Ch. de l'Étoile★, la Pinte, Pupillin co-op★.

CRÉMANT DE LIMOUX AC *Languedoc-Roussillon, France* Sparkling wine made from a blend of Chardonnay, Chenin Blanc, Mauzac and Pinot Noir; the wines generally have more complexity than BLANQUETTE DE LIMOUX. Drink young. Best producers: l'Aigle★, Antech, Fourn★, Guinot, Laurens★, Martinolles★, SIEUR D'ARQUES★, Valent.

CRÉMANT DE LOIRE AC *Loire Valley, France* The AC for CHAMPAGNE-method sparkling wine in Anjou and Touraine, with more fruit and yeast character than those of VOUVRAY and SAUMUR. The wine is good to drink as soon as it is released and can be excellent value. Best producers: BAUMARD★, Berger Frères★, Brizé★, Fardeau★, la Gabillière★, Girault, GRATIEN & MEYER★, Lambert★, Langlois-Château★, Michaud★, Oisly-et-Thésée co-op★, Passavant★.

CRIOTS-BÂTARD-MONTRACHET AC See Bâtard-Montrachet AC.

CRISTOM *Willamette Valley AVA, Oregon, USA* Named after the owners' children, Chris and Tom, this winery, nestled in the Eola Hills, makes fine Pinot Noir. Two of the outstanding reserve Pinot Noirs are from Marjorie Vineyard★★ and Jessie Vineyard★★★. Good white wines include Chardonnay from Celilo Vineyard★ (in WASHINGTON), Pinot Gris and Viognier. Best years: (Pinot Noir) (2004) (03) 02 01 **00 99 98**.

CROFT *Port DOC, Douro, Portugal* Owned by the Fladgate Partnership (along with TAYLOR and FONSECA) since 2001, these wines are showing distinct improvements, especially at basic level. Vintage ports ★★ have traditionally been elegant, rather than thunderous. Single-quinta Quinta da Roêda★★ is fine in recent vintages. Best years: (Vintage) 2000 94 **91 77 70 66 63 55 45**; (Roêda) 1997 **95 83**.

CROZES-HERMITAGE AC *Rhône Valley, France* The largest of the northern Rhône ACs. Ideally, the pure Syrah reds should have a full colour and a strong, clear, black fruit flavour. You can drink them young, but in ripe years from a hillside site the wine improves greatly for 2–5 years. The best whites are fresh and clean. In general drink white Crozes young, before the floral perfume disappears. Best producers: (reds) A Belle★★, CHAPOUTIER★, Y Chave★ (Tête de Cuvée★★), Colombier★, Combier★ (Clos des Grives★★), DELAS★, O Dumaine★, Entrefaux★, L Fayolle★, Ferraton★, GRAILLOT★★, JABOULET★, Murinais★,

Pavillon-Mercurol★, Pochon★ (Ch. Curson★★), Remizières★★, G Robin★, Rousset★, M Sorrel★, Tardieu-Laurent★★, Vins de Vienne★; (whites) Y Chave★, Colombier★, Combier★★, Dard et Ribo★, DELAS★, O Dumaine★, Entrefaux★ (Cuvée des Pends★★) Ferraton★, GRAILLOT★, JABOULET★, Martinelles, Pochon★ (Ch. Curson★★), Remizières★, M Sorrel★★. Best years: (reds) 2004 **03 01 00** 99 98 97 96 95 90 89.

DR CRUSIUS *Traisen, Nahe, Germany* Dr Peter Crusius produces Rieslings from the Traiser Bastei★ and SCHLOSSBOCKELHEIMer Felsenberg★ vineyards which manage to be rich, clean and flinty at the same time. Best years: (2004) 03 02 01 **00 99 98**.

YVES CUILLERON *Condrieu AC, Rhône Valley, France* With wines like Cuilleron's you can understand CONDRIEU's fame and high prices. Les Chaillets Vieilles Vignes★★★ is everything wine made from Viognier should be: opulent and rich, with perfumed honey and apricot aromas. La Petite Côte★★ is also exceptional, and the late-harvest les Ayguets★★★ is an extraordinary sweet whirl of dried apricots, honey and barley sugar. Cuilleron also makes ST-JOSEPH reds★★ and whites★★ and tiny quantities of ripe, dark, spicy COTE-ROTIE★★. A joint venture, les Vins de Vienne, with partners Pierre Gaillard and François Villard, produces Vin de Pays des COLLINES RHODANIENNES Sotanum★★ (100% Syrah) and Taburnum★ (100% Viognier) from ancient terraces just north of Vienne. Best years: (Condrieu) 2004 **03 02 01** 00 99 98 96.

CULLEN *Margaret River, Western Australia* One of the original and best MARGARET RIVER vineyards, established by Diana and Kevin Cullen and now run by their talented winemaker daughter Vanya. Superb Chardonnay★★★ is complex and satisfying; the Semillon-Sauvignon blend★★ marries nectarines with melon and nuts. The Cabernet Sauvignon-Merlot★★★ is gloriously soft, deep and scented; this wine is now justifiably regarded as one of Australia's greats. Mangan Malbec-Petit Verdot-Merlot★★ is delicious. Best years: (Cabernet Sauvignon-Merlot) 2003 02 01 00 **99 98 97 96** 95 94 92 91 90 86 84 82.

CURICÓ, VALLE DE *Valle Central, Chile* Most of the big producers here have planted Cabernet Sauvignon, Merlot, Chardonnay and Sauvignon Blanc. The long growing season provides good fruit concentration. Best producers: Echeverría★★, MONTES★, SAN PEDRO★, Miguel TORRES★★, VALDIVIESO★.

CUVAISON *Napa Valley AVA, California, USA* Cuvaison's red wines include tasty, focused Merlot★★, sound Cabernet Sauvignon★ and delicate Pinot Noir★. Decent Chardonnay; silky Reserve Chardonnay★ is worth seeking out. Best years: (Merlot) (2002) 01 **99 98** 97 96 94 91 90.

CVNE *Rioja DOCa, Rioja, Spain* Compañía Vinícola del Norte de España is the full name of this firm, but it's usually known as 'coonay'. Viña Real★ is one of RIOJA's few remaining well-oaked whites; the Viña Real Reserva★ and Gran Reserva★ reds can be rich and meaty, and easily surpass the rather commercial Crianzas; the top Imperial Gran Reserva★ is long-lived and impressive. Real de Asúa★ is a new premium red. Best years: (reds) (2001) **98 96 95 94 91 90** 89 87 86 85.

DIDIER DAGUENEAU *Pouilly-Fumé AC, Loire Valley, France* Didier Dagueneau is a much-needed innovator and quality fanatic in a complacent region. His wines generally benefit from 4 or 5 years' aging and, although at times unpredictable, are generally intense and complex. The range starts with En Chailloux★★ and moves up through flinty Buisson Renard★★ to top-quality barrel-fermented Silex★★ and Pur Sang★★. Best years: 2004 03 02 **01 00 99 98 97**.

121

ROMANO DAL FORNO *Valpolicella DOC, Veneto, Italy* VALPOLICELLA
Superiore★★ from Monte Lodoletta vineyard, outside the Valpolicella
Classico area, is a model of power and grace; AMARONE★★★ and RECIOTO
DELLA VALPOLICELLA★★★, from the same source, are even more voluptuous.
Best years: (Amarone) (2004) (03) (01) (00) 97 **96 95 93 91 90 88 85**.

LUIGI D'ALESSANDRO, TENIMENTI *Cortona DOC, Tuscany, Italy*
Formerly known as the Fattoria di Manzano, the vineyards have
benefited from massive investment. From the 2000 vintage, Il
Bosco★★ and the 'second' wine, Vescovo II★, are both 100% Syrah.
The white Fontarca★ blends Chardonnay with varying amounts of
Viognier. Best years: (Il Bosco) (2004) (03) 01 00 **99 98 97 96 95**.

DALLA VALLE *Napa Valley AVA, California, USA* Stunning hillside winery,
producing some of NAPA's most esteemed Cabernets. Foremost among
them is Maya★★★, a magnificent blend of Cabernet Sauvignon and
Cabernet Franc. The straight Cabernet Sauvignon★★★ is almost as
rich. Cabernet-based reds drink well at 10 years, but will keep for 20
or more. Best years: (Maya) (2001) 00 99 98 97 96 **95** 94 **91 90**.

DÃO DOC *Beira Alta, Portugal* Dão has steep slopes ideal for vineyards,
and a great climate for growing local grape varieties, yet it's only just
beginning to realize its potential for characterful red and white wines.
Best producers: (reds) Caves ALIANÇA, Boas Quintas (Fonte do Ouro★),
Quinta de Cabriz★ (Virgilio Loureiro★★), Quinta das Maias★, Quinta da
Pellada (Tinta Roriz, Touriga Nacional★), Quinta da Ponte Pedrinha★,
Quinta dos ROQUES★★, Quinta de Sães★, Caves SAO JOAO★, SOGRAPE★
(Quinta dos Carvalhais★★); (whites) Quinta de Cabriz, Quinta das
Maias★, Quinta dos ROQUES★, Quinta de Sães★, SOGRAPE★. Best years:
(reds) (2004) 03 01 00 **99 97 96 95**.

D'ARENBERG *McLaren Vale, South Australia* Chester Osborn makes
blockbuster Dead Arm Shiraz★★, Footbolt Old Vine Shiraz★, Custodian
Grenache★ and other blends from low-yielding old vines. These are big,
brash, character-filled wines, and are continually being joined by more
new ideas. Best years: (Dead Arm Shiraz) (2004) (03) 02 01 00 **97 96 95**.

DARTING *Bad Dürkheim, Pfalz, Germany* Helmut Darting makes full,
richly fruity wines from sites in BAD DURKHEIM (Spielberg), Ungstein
(Herrenberg Riesling Spätlese★★) and WACHENHEIM (Mandelgarten). Best
years: (2004) 03 02 01 00 **99 98 97 96**.

RENÉ & VINCENT DAUVISSAT *Chablis AC, Burgundy, France* CHABLIS at
its most complex – refreshing, seductive and beautifully structured,
with the fruit balancing the subtle influence of mostly older oak. Look
for la Forest★★, the more aromatic Vaillons★★★ and the powerful les
Clos★★★. Best years: (2004) 03 02 00 **99 98 97 96 95 92 90 89**.

MARCO DE BARTOLI *Sicily, Italy* Marco De Bartoli is most noted for a
dry, unfortified MARSALA-style wine called Vecchio Samperi – his idea of
what Marsala was before the English merchant, John Woodhouse, first
fortified it for export. Particularly fine is the 20-year-old Ventennale –
dry, intense and redolent of candied citrus peel, dates and old, old
raisins. Also excellent MOSCATO PASSITO DI PANTELLERIA Bukkuram★★.

DE BORTOLI *Riverina, New South Wales, Australia* Large, family-owned
winery producing a truly sublime botrytized Noble One Semillon★★★.
Most of the RIVERINA reds and whites are merely decent, but varieties
like Petit Verdot, Cabernet Franc and Durif can produce good results.
In the YARRA VALLEY De Bortoli is crafting some fine Chardonnay★,
Shiraz★★, Cabernet★ and Pinot Noir★★. Best years: (Noble One) (2004)
03 02 **00 98 96 95 94 93 90 87 85 84 82**.

DEHLINGER *Russian River Valley AVA, California, USA* Outstanding Pinot Noir★★★ from vineyards in the cool RUSSIAN RIVER region a few miles from the Pacific, best at 5–10 years old. Also mouthfilling Chardonnay★★ and bold, peppery Syrah★★. Recent vintages of Cabernet★★ and Bordeaux Blend★★ (Cabernet-Merlot) reflect a surge in quality. Best years: (Pinot Noir) 2002 01 **00 99 98 97 96 95 94**.

MARCEL DEISS *Alsace AC, Alsace, France* Jean-Michel Deiss is fanatical about distinctions of *terroir* and, controversially for Alsace, his top wines are now blends, named according to the vineyard – Grands Crus Altenberg, Mambourg and Schoenenbourg are all ★★★. These are outstanding wines of huge character, often with some residual sugar. Pinot Noir Burlenburg★★ is vibrant and delicious. Even basic Riesling St-Hippolyte★ and Pinot Blanc Bergheim are delightful. Best years: (Grand Cru blends) 2002 01 **00 99**.

DELAS FRÈRES *Rhône Valley, France* Rapidly improving merchant (owned by ROEDERER) selling wines from the entire RHONE VALLEY, but with its own vineyards in the northern Rhône. Single-vineyard wines include dense, powerful red HERMITAGE★★ (les Bessards★★★), which needs a decade or more to reach its peak, perfumed COTE-ROTIE la Landonne★★ and ST-JOSEPH Ste-Epine★★. The CROZES-HERMITAGE Tour d'Albon★★ is a good bet, as is the COTES DU RHONE St-Esprit. Look out for the aromatic CONDRIEU★★. Best years: (premium reds) 2004 03 01 00 99 **98 97 96 95 94 91 90 89 88 85 78**.

DELATITE *Central Victoria, Australia* The Ritchies' high-altitude vineyard, in sight of VICTORIA's snowfields, grows delicate, aromatic Riesling★★ and Gewürztraminer★★; there is also subtle Chardonnay★ and extravagantly fruity reds. The Pinot Noir★ is perfumed, and Devil's River★ is a smart, minty BORDEAUX blend. Best years: (Riesling) 2002 01 **00 99 97 96 94 93 87 86 82**.

DELEGAT'S *Henderson, Auckland, North Island, New Zealand* One of New Zealand's largest family-run wineries, specializing in Chardonnay (Reserve★), Cabernet, Merlot (Reserve★) and Sauvignon Blanc from the HAWKES BAY and MARLBOROUGH (under Oyster Bay★ label) regions. Best years: (Chardonnay) (2004) **02 00**.

DELILLE CELLARS *Yakima Valley AVA* DeLille Cellars produces BORDEAUX-style wines from some of the better vineyards in YAKIMA VALLEY . The flagship is Chaleur Estate Red★★, a powerful, ageworthy blend of classic Bordeaux varietals. Chaleur Estate Blanc★★ (Semillon and Sauvignon Blanc) has a GRAVES-like character, albeit with a tad more alcohol. The second wine, D2★, short for Deuxième, is an early-drinking red. A Syrah labelled Doyenne★ shows promise. Best years: (Chaleur Estate Red) 2002 **99 97 94**.

DE MARTINO/SANTA INÉS *Maipo, Chile* Old-established winery and now one of MAIPO's rising stars, led by winemaker Marcelo Retamal, producing robust, concentrated red wines. Single Vineyard Carmenère★★ is one of Chile's best examples of this grape; De Martino Gran Familia Cabernet Sauvignon★★ is dense and complex. Single Vineyard Sauvignon Blanc★ is the most important white.

DENBIES *Surrey, England* UK's largest vineyard with 106ha (262 acres) of vines, planted on chalky slopes outside Dorking. First vintage 1989. Wines have been erratic over the years but now, with winemaker Marcus Sharp, they have reached a new plateau of quality with remarkably attractive whites and lively, refreshing rosé. Pinot Noir-based Redlands can be good too.

DE TRAFFORD *Stellenbosch WO, South Africa*   David Trafford is a leading
exponent of new-wave Chenin Blanc; at his
mountainside boutique winery he crafts two
versions, both barrel-fermented on their own
yeast: rich, ageworthy STELLENBOSCH Chenin
Blanc★ and minerally, concentrated WALKER
BAY Chenin Blanc★. A dessert-style Straw
Wine★★ is honey-tinged and succulent.
Among the reds, both Cabernet Sauvignon★
and Merlot★ are classically styled and built
to age. Shiraz★★, brimming with spicy
richness, remains remarkably elegant for its
size. Best years: (reds) 2003 02 01 **00 99 98**.

DEUTZ *Champagne AC, Champagne, France*   This small company has
been owned by ROEDERER since 1993 and considerable effort and
investment have turned a good producer into an excellent one. The
non-vintage Brut★★ is now regularly one of the best in Champagne,
often boasting a cedary scent, while the top wines are the classic
Blanc de Blancs★★, the weightier Cuvée William Deutz★★ and the
de luxe vintage blanc de blancs Amour de Deutz★★. Deutz also
makes good fizz in New Zealand. Best years: (1998) 96 **95 93 90 89 88**.

DÉZALEY *Lavaux, Vaud, Switzerland*   The top wine commune in the
VAUD, making surprisingly powerful, mineral wines from the Chasselas
grape. Best producers: Louis Bovard★, Conne, Les Frères Dubois★, J D
Fonjallaz (l'Arbalète)★, Pinget★, J & P Testuz.

D F J VINHOS *Portugal*   In the early 1990s, UK wine shippers D & F
began working with one of Portugal's most innovative winemakers,
José Neiva; in 1999 this relationship evolved into D F J Vinhos. The
Bela Fonte brand includes varietal reds Baga, Jaen★ and Touriga
Franca★ and a white Bical, all from BEIRAS. Other labels include
Segada from the RIBATEJO, Manta Preta★ from ESTREMADURA, Pedras do
Monte★ from TERRAS DO SADO, Monte Alentejano from the ALENTEJO and
an ALGARVE red, Esplanada. At the top end are the Grand'Arte reds,
including an intensely fruity, peppery Trincadeira★★ and beefy
Alicante Bouschet. Three new prestige wines from the DOURO
(Escada★), ALENQUER (Francos★) and RIBATEJO (Consensus★).

DIAMOND CREEK *Napa Valley AVA, California, USA*   Small estate
specializing in Cabernet: Volcanic Hill★★★, Red Rock Terrace★★,
Gravelly Meadow★★. Traditionally huge, tannic wines that, when
tasted young, I swear won't ever come round. Yet there's usually a
sweet inner core of fruit that envelops the tannin over 10–15 years;
recent releases show wonderful perfume and balance even in their
youth. Best years: (2002) 01 00 99 98 97 96 95 94 **92** 91 90 **87 86 84**.

DIEL, SCHLOSSGUT *Burg Layen, Nahe, Germany*   Armin Diel has
become one of the leading producers of classic-style Rieslings. Spätlese
and Auslese from Dorsheim's top sites are regularly ★★. Best years:
(2004) 03 02 01 00 **99 98 97 96 95 93 90**.

DISTELL *Stellenbosch, South Africa*   South Africa's largest wine company
is steadily building up export-friendly brands, and some of the allied
wineries – such as Neethlingshof★, STELLENZICHT★ and Durbanville
Hills★ – are performing well. The Fleur du Cap range is improving,
whites especially; Pongrácz★ Cap Classique fizz is also a promising
label. Two wineries in PAARL, Nederburg and Plaisir de Merle★, are run
separately. Nederburg is starting to create a buzz with some

unconventional blends as well as trademark botrytized dessert Edelkeur★, sold only through an annual auction. Plaisir de Merle lacks consistency, though its best wines are good in an international style.

CH. DOISY-DAËNE★★ *Sauternes AC, 2ème Cru Classé, Bordeaux, France*
A consistently good property in BARSAC (although it uses the SAUTERNES AC for its wines) and unusual in that the sweet wine is made exclusively from Sémillon. It ages well for 10 years or more. The extra-rich Extravagant★★★ is produced in exceptional years. Doisy-Daëne Sec★ is a good, perfumed, dry white. Drink young. Best years: (sweet) 2003 02 01 **99 98 97 96 95 90 89**; (dry) (2004) **02 01**.

CH. DOISY-VÉDRINES★★ *Sauternes AC, 2ème Cru Classé, Bordeaux, France* Next door to DOISY-DAENE, Doisy-Védrines is a richly botrytized wine, fatter and more syrupy than most BARSAC wines. Like its neighbour, it also sells its wines under the SAUTERNES AC. Best years: (sweet) 2003 02 01 **99 98 97 96 95 90 89 88 86 85 83**.

DOLCETTO One of Italy's most charming native grapes, producing, for the most part, purple wines bursting at the seams with fruit. Virtually exclusive to PIEDMONT and LIGURIA, it is DOC in 7 Piedmontese zones, with styles ranging from intense and rich in Alba, Ovada and Diano d'Alba, to lighter, more perfumed versions in Acqui and Asti. The most serious, longest lasting wines are from Dogliani. Usually best drunk within 1–2 years, traditionally vinified wines can last 10 years or more. Best producers: (Alba) Alario★★, ALTARE★★, Boglietti★★, Bongiovanni★★, Bricco Maiolica★★, Brovia★★, Elvio Cogno★★, Aldo CONTERNO★★, Conterno-Fantino★★, B Marcarini★, Bartolo MASCARELLO★, Giuseppe MASCARELLO★★, Paitin★, Pelissero★★, PRUNOTTO★, Albino Rocca★★, SANDRONE★★, Vajra★★, Vietti★, Gianni Voerzio★, Roberto VOERZIO★; (Dogliani) M & E Abbona★, Chionetti★★, Luigi Einaudi★★, Pecchenino★★, San Fereolo★★, San Romano★.

DÔLE *Valais, Switzerland* Red wine from the Swiss VALAIS that must be made from at least 51% Pinot Noir, the rest being Gamay. Dôle is generally a light wine – the deeper, richer (100% Pinot Noir) styles have the right to call themselves Pinot Noir. Most should be drunk young, and can be lightly chilled in summer. Best producers: M Clavien, J Germanier, Caves Imesch, Mathier, Caves Orsat.

DOMAINE CARNEROS *Carneros AVA, California, USA* Very successful TAITTINGER-owned sparkling wine house. The vintage Brut★ now matches, if not surpasses, Taittinger's fizz from Champagne. Also vintage-dated Le Rêve★★★ and delightful Pinot Noirs★★.

DOMAINE CHANDON *Yarra Valley, Victoria, Australia* MOET & CHANDON's Aussie offshoot makes fine Pinot Noir-Chardonnay fizz. Non-vintage Brut, Cuvée Riche and sparkling red Pinot-Shiraz★, and vintage Brut★★, Rosé★★, Blanc de Blancs★, Blanc de Noirs★, YARRA VALLEY Brut★★ and a Tasmanian Cuvée★, plus new vintage ZD★★ (Zero Dosage). Table wines, often at ★★ quality, under the Green Point label. The Green Point name is also used on fizz for export markets.

DOMAINE CHANDON *Napa Valley AVA, California, USA* California's first French-owned (MOET & CHANDON) sparkling wine producer has shown remarkable consistency and good quality with reasonably priced non-vintage bubblies. Reserve★ bottlings are rich and creamy. Blanc de Blancs★ is made entirely from CARNEROS Chardonnay. Étoile★★ is an aged de luxe wine, and is also made as a flavourful Rosé★★.

DOMAINE DROUHIN OREGON *Willamette Valley AVA, Oregon, USA*
Burgundy wine merchant Robert DROUHIN bought 40ha (100 acres) in OREGON in 1987, with plans to make fine Pinot Noir on New World land, with an Old World philosophy. The regular Pinot Noir★ is lean but attractive, and the de luxe Pinot Noir Laurène★★ is supple, voluptuous and one of Oregon's finest. Pinot Noir Louise★★ is a selection of the finest barrels in the winery. Also good Chardonnay Arthur★. Best years: (Pinot Noir) (2004) (03) 02 01 **00 99 98 97 96 94 93**.

DOMAINE SERENE *Willamette Valley AVA, Oregon, USA* Ken and Grace Evenstad purchased 17ha (42 acres) of land in the WILLAMETTE VALLEY in 1989, naming the property after their daughter, Serene. Devoted to Pinot Noir and Chardonnay, they have established a fine reputation. The full-bodied Pinot Noir Evenstad Reserve★★ is aged in French oak and has striking black cherry and currant flavours. The Chardonnay Côte du Soleil★★, made from Dijon clones, has a rich apple and hazelnut character. Best years: (Pinot Noir) (2004) (03) 02 01 **00 99 98**.

DOMAINE VISTALBA *Argentina* French-owned company whose Fabre Montmayou winery in LUJAN DE CUYO, with vineyards at 1150m (3770ft) above sea level, produces impressive Malbec★. The almost black, chocolate-and-damsons Grand Vin★★ is a blend of Malbec with Cabernet Sauvignon and Merlot.

DOMECQ *Jerez y Manzanilla DO and Rioja DOCa, Spain* The largest of the sherry companies, best known for its refreshing fino, La Ina★. At the top of the range, dry Amontillado 51-1A★★★, Sibarita Palo Cortado★★★ and Venerable Pedro Ximénez★★ are spectacular. Domecq also makes light, elegant RIOJA, Marqués de Arienzo★.

DOMINUS★★ *Napa Valley AVA, California, USA* Owned by Christian MOUEIX, director of Bordeaux superstar PETRUS. Wines are based on Cabernet with leavenings of Merlot and Cabernet Franc. Its reputation was marred by excessively tannic early releases, but recent wines are mellow and delicious. Best years: (2002) 01 00 99 97 96 **95 94 93 90**.

DONAULAND *Niederösterreich, Austria* Amorphous 2814ha (6920-acre) wine region on both banks of the Danube, stretching from just north of Vienna west to St Polten. Best are the dry Grüner Veltliners from the Wagram area. Best producers: Josef Bauer★, Karl Fritsch★, Leth★, Bernhard Ott★★, Wimmer-Czerny★.

DÖNNHOFF *Oberhausen, Nahe, Germany* Helmut Dönnhoff is the quiet winemaking genius of the NAHE, conjuring from a string of top sites some of the most mineral dry and naturally sweet Rieslings in the world. The very best are the subtle, long-lived wines from the Niederhäuser Hermannshöhle★★★ vineyard. Eiswein★★★ is equally exciting. Best years: (Hermannshöhle Riesling Spätlese) (2004) 03 02 01 00 **99 98 97 96 95 94 93 90**.

DOURO DOC *Douro, Portugal* As well as a flood of PORT and basic table wine, some of Portugal's top, soft-textured red wines come from here. Quality can be superb when the lush, scented fruit is not too smothered by new oak barrels. Whites are less interesting, and are best young, but reds may improve for 10 years or even more. Best producers: (reds) Caves ALIANCA (Quinta dos Quatro Ventos★★), Maria Doroteia Serôdio Borges (Fojo★★), BRIGHT BROTHERS (TFN★), Quinta da Brunheda★, Chryseia★★, Quinta do COTTO (Grande Escolha★★), Quinta do CRASTO★★ (Ponte★★, Maria Teresa★★), FERREIRA★ (Barca Velha★★, Quinta da Leda★★), Quinta da Gaivosa★, NIEPOORT★★★, Quinta do NOVAL★, Pintas★★, Poeira★★, Quinta do Portal (Grande Reserva★),

Quinta de Roriz★★, Quinta de la ROSA★, SOGRAPE, Quinta do Vale Dona Maria★★, Quinta do Vale Meao★★, Quinta do Vale da Raposa★, Vallado★. Best years: (reds) (2004) 03 01 **00 97 95.**

DOW *Port DOC, Douro, Portugal* The grapes for Dow's Vintage PORT★★★ come mostly from the Quinta do Bomfim, which is also the name of the excellent single quinta★★★. Dow ports are relatively dry compared with those of GRAHAM and WARRE (the 2 other major brands belonging to the Symington family). There are some excellent aged tawnies★★. Impressive young port has also been produced under the Quinta Senhora da Ribeira★★ label from the 40ha (100-acre) vineyard opposite VESUVIO since 1998. Best years: (Vintage) 2000 97 94 **91 85 83 80 77 70 66 63 60 55 45**; (Bomfim) 1999 98 95 **92 87 86 84** (single quinta) 2001 99 98 **96 95 92 87 86.**

DROMANA ESTATE *Mornington Peninsula, Victoria, Australia* After 20 years at the helm, founders Garry and Margaret Crittenden have left to start Crittenden at Dromana, using the original vineyard, winery and restaurant which they still own. Their son, Rollo, stays on as winemaker at Dromana Estate which is now a publicly listed company that also owns David Traeger, Mornington Estate, Yarra Valley Hills and the Garry Crittenden 'i' range. The fragrant, restrained Pinot Noir★ and complex Reserve Chardonnay★★ are best from the Mornington Estate range, while the 'i' range, mainly made from King Valley fruit, is of special interest, particularly Sangiovese★, Nebbiolo★, Barbera and Arneis★, and future releases will reach ★★ quality. Best years: (Reserve Chardonnay) (2003) **02 01 00 99 98 97.**

JOSEPH DROUHIN *Beaune, Burgundy, France* One of the best Burgundian merchants, with substantial vineyard holdings in CHABLIS and the COTE D'OR, and DOMAINE DROUHIN OREGON. Drouhin makes a consistently good, if expensive, range of wines from all over Burgundy. Look for BONNES-MARES★★, ROMANEE-ST-VIVANT★★★, BEAUNE Clos des Mouches (red★★ and white★★★), le MUSIGNY★★★ and le MONTRACHET★★★ from the Dom. du Marquis de Laguiche. Drouhin offers fine value in Chablis and less glamorous Burgundian ACs, such as RULLY★ and ST-AUBIN★. The BEAUJOLAIS is always good, but overall Drouhin's whites are (just) better than the reds. Quality reds and whites should be aged for at least 5 years, often better nearer 10. Best years: (2004) 03 02 01 00 99 96 **95 93 90**.

PIERRE-JACQUES DRUET *Bourgueil AC, Loire Valley, France* A passionate producer of BOURGUEIL and small quantities of CHINON. Druet makes 4 Bourgueils – les Cent Boisselées★, Cuvée Beauvais★★, Cuvée Grand Mont★★ and Vaumoreau★★ – each a complex expression of the Cabernet Franc grape. Best aged for at least 3–5 years. Best years: (top cuvées) 2004 03 02 **01 00 99 97 96 95 90 89 88 85.**

DRY CREEK VALLEY AVA *Sonoma, California, USA* Best known for Sauvignon Blanc, Zinfandel and Cabernet Sauvignon, this valley runs west of ALEXANDER VALLEY AVA, and similarly becomes hotter moving northwards. Best producers: DRY CREEK VINEYARD★, Duxoup★, FERRARI-CARANO★★, GALLO (Zinfandel★, Cabernet Sauvignon★), Michel-Schlumberger★, Nalle★, Pezzi King★, Preston★, Quivira★, Rafanelli (Zinfandel★★). Best years: (reds) (2002) (01) **00 99 98 97 96 95 94 91.**

DRY CREEK VINEYARD *Dry Creek Valley AVA, California, USA* An early advocate of Fumé Blanc★, Dave Stare remains faithful to the brisk racy style and also makes a serious Reserve★ which improves with aging. DCV3★ (sometimes ★★) is from original plantings and displays subtle notes of fig and herb. A drink-young Chardonnay (Reserve★) is attractive, but the stars here are red Meritage★, Merlot★ and Old Vine Zinfandel★★. Best years: (Old Vine Zin) (2002) (01) **00 99 97 96 95 94 91**.

DRY RIVER *Martinborough, North Island, New Zealand* Low yields and an uncompromising attitude to quality at this tiny winery have created some of the country's top Gewürztraminer★★★ and Pinot Gris★★, an intense but almost too ripe Pinot Noir★★, sleek Chardonnay★★ and powerful, long-lived Craighall Riesling★★★. Excellent Syrah★★ is made in tiny quantities. Best years: (Craighall Riesling) (2004) **01 00 99 98 96**; (Pinot Noir) **2001 00 99 96**.

GEORGES DUBOEUF *Beaujolais, Burgundy, France* Known as the King of Beaujolais, Duboeuf is responsible for more than 10% of the wine produced in the region. Given the size of his operation, the quality of the wines is good. Duboeuf also makes and blends wine from the Mâconnais (ST-VERAN★), the RHONE VALLEY and the LANGUEDOC. His BEAUJOLAIS NOUVEAU is usually reliable, but his top wines are those he bottles for independent growers, particularly Jean Descombes★★ in

MORGON, Dom. des Quatre Vents★ and la Madone★ in FLEURIE and Dom. de la Tour du Bief★ in MOULIN-A-VENT.

DUCKHORN *Napa Valley AVA, California, USA* Best known for its very chunky, tannic Merlot★ (Estate Merlot★★) – now, thankfully, softer and riper. The Cabernet Sauvignon★ and Sauvignon Blanc★ provide easier drinking. Under the Goldeneye label there is also a ripe, oaky Pinot Noir★. Paraduxx is a Zinfandel-Cabernet blend; Decoy is the budget line. Best years: (Merlot) (2002) 01 **99 98 97 96 95 94 91 90 86**.

CH. DUCRU-BEAUCAILLOU★★★ *St-Julien AC, 2ème Cru Classé, Haut-Médoc, Bordeaux, France* Traditionally the epitome of ST-JULIEN, mixing charm and austerity, fruit and firm tannins. Vintages from the mid-1980s to 1990 were flawed; back on form since 94. Second wine: la Croix de Beaucaillou. Best years: 2003 02 01 00 **99** 98 96 **95 94 85 83 82**.

DUJAC *Morey-St-Denis AC, Côte de Nuits, Burgundy, France* Owner Jacques Seysses' estate is based in MOREY-ST-DENIS, with some choice vineyards also in CHAMBOLLE-MUSIGNY, ECHEZEAUX and GEVREY-CHAMBERTIN. The wines are all perfumed and elegant, including a small quantity of Morey-St-Denis★ white wine, but the outstanding Dujac bottlings are the Grands Crus – Échézeaux★★★, CLOS DE LA ROCHE★★★, BONNES-MARES★★★ and CLOS ST-DENIS★★★ – all of which need to age for a decade or more. From 2000 he and son Jeremy have made some négociant cuvées under the label Dujac Fils et Père. Best years: (Grands Crus) (2004) 03 02 01 00 **99** 98 96 **95 93 91 90 89**.

DUNN VINEYARDS *Howell Mountain AVA, California, USA* Massive, concentrated, hauntingly perfumed, long-lived Cabernet Sauvignon★★★ is the trademark of Randy Dunn's HOWELL MOUNTAIN wines. His NAPA VALLEY Cabernets★★ are less powerful but still scented. Best years: (2001) (00) 99 97 96 95 94 93 **92** 91 90 **88 87 86 85 84 82**.

DURIF See Petite Sirah.

JEAN DURUP *Chablis, Burgundy, France* The largest vineyard owner in CHABLIS, Jean Durup is a great believer in unoaked Chablis, which tends to be clean without any great complexity. Best are the Premiers Crus Fourchaume★ and Montée de Tonnerre★★. Wines appear under a variety of labels, including l'Eglantière, Ch. de Maligny and Valéry.

ÉCHÉZEAUX AC *Grand Cru, Côte de Nuits, Burgundy, France* The Grands
Crus of Échézeaux and the smaller and more prestigious Grands-
Échézeaux are sandwiched between the world-famous CLOS DE VOUGEOT
and VOSNE-ROMANEE. Few of the 80 growers here have really made a
name for themselves, but there are some fine wines with a smoky,
plum richness and a soft texture that age well over 10–15 years to a
gamy, chocolaty depth. Best producers: R Arnoux★★, BOUCHARD PERE ET
FILS★★, Cacheux-Sirugue★★★, DROUHIN★★, DUJAC★★★, R Engel★★★,
GRIVOT★★★, A-F GROS★★★, JAYER-GILLES★★★, Mugneret-Gibourg★★★,
Dom. de la ROMANEE-CONTI★★★, E Rouget★★★. Best years: (2004) 03 02
01 **00** 99 98 **97** 96 **95 93 90**.

DOM. DE L'ECU *Muscadet Sèvre-et-Maine, Loire Valley, France* One of the
finest producers in MUSCADET, Guy Bossard's biodynamically run estate
also produces GROS PLANT DU PAYS NANTAIS white, a velvety red vin de
pays Cabernet blend and a refreshing sparkler, Ludwig Hahn. It is his
Muscadet, though, that stands out, especially the top cuvées from
different soil types: Gneiss, Orthogneiss★ and fuller-bodied, minerally
Granite★★. Best years: (Granite) 2004 03 **02 01 00**.

EDEN VALLEY See Barossa, pages 58–9.

CH. L'ÉGLISE-CLINET★★★ *Pomerol AC, Bordeaux, France* A tiny 5.5ha
(13-acre) domaine in the heart of POMEROL, l'Église-Clinet has a very old
vineyard – one of the reasons for the depth and elegance of the wines.
The other is the winemaking ability of owner Denis Durantou. The wine
is expensive and in limited supply, but worth seeking out. It can be
enjoyed young, though the best examples should be cellared for 10 years
or more. Best years: 2003 02 01 00 **99 98 97 96 95 94 93 90 89 86 85**.

EIKENDAL *Stellenbosch WO, South Africa* Consistent quality, despite
further winemaker changes. An elegant, balanced Chardonnay★ with
proven aging ability, a light-textured but tasty Merlot★ and an
occasional powerful Reserve Cabernet★ have been the best wines to
date. Best years: (Chardonnay) **2004 03 02 01 00 99 98 97**.

ELGIN WO *South Africa* This high-lying ward within the Overberg
District is being targetted by some of the Cape's leading winemakers,
and it plays host to an increasing number of vineyards. Summer cloud
helps to keep temperatures reasonable, creating the right conditions
for pure-fruited Sauvignon Blanc, Chardonnay, Riesling and Pinot
Noir. Best producers: Paul Cluver★, Neil ELLIS★★.

ELK COVE *Willamette Valley AVA, Oregon, USA* Back in 1974, Elk Cove
was one of the pioneers of the WILLAMETTE VALLEY. Today the Campbell
family produces Pinot Noir★★, Pinot Gris★, Riesling and tiny amounts
of Syrah and dessert Gewürztraminer. The Reserve Pinot Noirs –
Roosevelt★★, Windhill★ and La Bohème★ – now compete with the
elite from the state. Best years: (Pinot Noir) (2004) (03) 02 **01 00 99 98**.

NEIL ELLIS *Stellenbosch WO, South Africa* A leading winemaker and
négociant, renowned for powerful, invigorating Groenekloof
Sauvignon Blanc★★ and striking STELLENBOSCH reds (blackcurranty
Cabernet Sauvignon★★ and supple Cabernet-Merlot★). An aggively
single-vineyard Shiraz★ and Cabernet★★ (both from Jonkershoek
Valley fruit), and a subtly delicious Chardonnay★★ from cool ELGIN,
confirm his versatility. Best years: (Cabernet) 2002 **01 00 99 98 97**;
(whites) **2004 03 02 01 00**.

ERNIE ELS *Stellenbosch WO, South Africa* Jean Engelbrecht's joint
venture with his golfing friend Ernie Els has resulted in a stylish
BORDEAUX blend under the Ernie Els★ label. A second wine, Engelbrecht

Els, blends Shiraz with the Bordeaux quintet (Cabernets Sauvignon and Franc, Merlot, Malbec and Petit Verdot) in a more accessible yet seriously built style. Best years: (Ernie Els) **2002 01 00**.

ELTVILLE *Rheingau, Germany* Large wine town, making some of the RHEINGAU's most racy Rieslings. Best producers: J Fischer, Langwerth von Simmern★. Best years: (2004) 03 02 01 00 **99 98 97 90**.

EMILIA-ROMAGNA *Italy* This region is divided into the western zone of Emilia, best known for LAMBRUSCO, and the eastern zone of Romagna, where Sangiovese is dominant. See also Colli Bolognesi, Colli Piacentini.

EMRICH-SCHÖNLEBER *Monzingen, Nahe, Germany* Although Monzingen is not the most prestigious of NAHE villages, Werner Schönleber has steadily brought his 14ha (35-acre) property into the front ranks. His vigorous, spicy Rieslings are consistently ★ to ★★ and his Eisweins are ★★★. Best years: (2004) 03 02 01 00 **99 98 97 95**.

ENATE *Somontano DO, Aragón, Spain* Enate and VIÑAS DEL VERO seem to be slugging it out for supremacy in the SOMONTANO DO. Barrel-fermented Chardonnay★ is rich, buttery and toasty, Gewürztraminer★ is exotic and convincing. Imported grape varieties also feature in the red Crianza, Reserva★ (100% Cabernet Sauvignon), Reserva Especial★★ (Cabernet-Merlot) and blockbuster Enate Merlot-Merlot★. Best years: (reds) 2001 00 **99 98 96 95 94**.

ENTRE-DEUX-MERS AC *Bordeaux, France* This AC increasingly represents some of the freshest, snappiest dry white wine in France. In general, drink the latest vintage, though better wines will last a year or two. Sweet wines are sold as PREMIÈRES CÔTES DE BORDEAUX, St-Macaire, LOUPIAC and STE-CROIX-DU-MONT. Best producers: Bel Air, BONNET, de Fontenille★, Launay, Marjosse★, Moulin-de-Launay, Nardique-la-Gravière★, Ste-Marie★, Tour-de-Mirambeau★, Toutigeac★, Turcaud★.

ERBACH *Rheingau, Germany* Erbach's famous Marcobrunn vineyard is one of the top spots for Riesling on the Rhine. The village wines are elegant; those from Marcobrunn more powerful and imposing. Best producers: Jakob Jung★, Knyphausen★, SCHLOSS REINHARTSHAUSEN★, Schloss Schönborn★, Langwerth von Simmern★. Best years: (2004) 03 02 01 00 **99 98 97 96 94 93**.

ERBALUCE DI CALUSO DOC *Piedmont, Italy* Usually a dry or sparkling white from the Erbaluce grape, but Caluso Passito, where the grapes are semi-dried before fermenting, can be a fine sweet wine. Best producers: (Caluso Passito) Cieck★, Ferrando★, Orsolani★.

ERDEN *Mosel, Germany* Middle MOSEL village with the superb Prälat and Treppchen vineyards. Wines are rich and succulent with a strong mineral character. Best producers: Christoffel★★, Dr LOOSEN★★★, Mönchhof★★, Peter Nicolay★. Best years: (2004) 03 02 01 **99 97 95 94 93**.

ERMITAGE Swiss name for the Marsanne grape. Mostly found in the central VALAIS, where it produces a range of wines from dry to lovely honeyed dessert wines (called Flétri). Best producers: Dom. du Mont d'Or★, A Mathier★, Caves Orsat (Flétri★), Provins.

ERRÁZURIZ *Aconcagua, Chile* American winemaker Ed Flaherty brought consistency to this producer's wine. Flaherty is in charge of SEÑA and Arboleda, which were joint ventures with MONDAVI but are now back in Chilean hands, while Errázuriz has Francisco Baettig at the helm. The top label is Don Maximiano Founder's Reserve★, a red blend from Aconcagua, also the source of La Cumbre★ Syrah. Merlot★ and fruity Sangiovese are always reliable. CASABLANCA yields a simple Pinot Noir and a rich 'Wild Ferment' Chardonnay★ and Pinot Noir★. Best years: (reds) 2004 **03 02 01**.

ESPORÃO *Reguengos DOC, Alentejo, Portugal* Huge estate in the heart of the ALENTEJO, where Australian David Baverstock produces a broad range of wines. Principal labels are Esporão (red★★ and white★ Reservas), Vinha da Defesa★, Monte Velho and Alandra, and there are some delightful varietals: Trincadeira★, Aragonês★★, Cabernet Sauvignon★, Touriga Nacional★, Syrah★ and Alicante Bouschet★. Best years: (reds) (2004) **01 00**.

EST! EST!! EST!!! DI MONTEFIASCONE DOC *Lazio, Italy* TREBBIANO-based white accorded its undeserved reputation because of an old tale of a bishop's servant sent ahead to scout out good wines; he gave this one the thumbs-up code three times. Perhaps it had been a long day. Best producers: Bigi (Graffiti), FALESCO (Poggio dei Gelsi★), Mazziotti (Canuleio★).

CH. DES ESTANILLES *Faugères AC, Languedoc, France* The Louisons know that quality begins in the vineyard. Their best site is the Clos de Fou, with its very steep schistous slope planted with Syrah; the grape 'dominates' the Prestige cuvée★★ (i.e. 100% – but the AC regulations do not allow them to say so). Also a wood-fermented and aged rosé, plus fine COTEAUX DU LANGUEDOC white★. Best years: (reds) 2003 **01 00**.

ESTREMADURA *Portugal* Portugal's most productive region, occupying the western coastal strip and with an increasing number of clean, characterful wines. The leading area is ALENQUER, promoted to DOC status along with Arruda, Óbidos and Torres Vedras, and there are also the IPRs of Alcobaça and Encostas d'Aire. However, much of the wine, including some of the region's best, is simply labelled as Vinho Regional Estremadura. Spicy, perfumed reds are often based on Castelão, but Cabernet Sauvignon, Syrah, Touriga Nacional and Tinta Roriz contribute to top examples, which can benefit from 4 or 5 years' aging. Top producers also make fresh, aromatic whites. Best producers: Companhia Agricola Sanguinhal, Quinta da Cortezia★★/ALIANCA, D F J VINHOS (Francos★, Grand'Arte Touriga Nacional★), Quinta de Pancas★★, Quinta do Monte d'Oiro★★, Casa SANTOS LIMA★. See also Bucelas. Best years: (reds) (2004) 03 **01 00**.

L'ÉTOILE AC *Jura, France* A tiny area within the COTES DU JURA which has its own AC for whites, mainly Chardonnay and Savagnin, and for *vin jaune*. Fizz now comes under the CREMANT DU JURA AC. Best producers: Ch. l'Étoile★, Geneletti★, Joly★, Montbourgeau★, Quintigny★.

CH. L'ÉVANGILE★★ *Pomerol AC, Bordeaux, France* A neighbour to PETRUS and CHEVAL BLANC, this estate has been wholly owned and managed by the Rothschilds of LAFITE-ROTHSCHILD since 1999. The wine is quintessential POMEROL – rich, fat and exotic. Recent vintages have been very good, but expect further improvement as the Rothschild effect intensifies. Best years: 2002 00 **99** 98 **96** 95 94 93 90 89 88 85 83 82.

EVANS & TATE *Margaret River, Western Australia* This is now one of Australia's largest producers; in spite of the expansion, the quality of the MARGARET RIVER wines has never been better: figgy Chardonnay, crisp Sauvignon-Semillon★, nutty Semillon★★, blackcurranty Cabernet-Merlot★ and concentrated Cabernet Sauvignon★ and Shiraz★. Best years: (Redbrook Cabernet Sauvignon) (2002) (01) **99**.

131

EYRIE VINEYARDS *Willamette Valley AVA, Oregon, USA* One of the pioneering Pinot Noir producers in OREGON, but frequently the wines can be withdrawn and thin. Chardonnay shows nice varietal fruit, while the popular Pinot Gris flies off the shelves. Best years: (Pinot Noir Reserve) (2003) (02) **01 00 99 98**.

FAIRVIEW *Paarl WO, South Africa* Owner Charles Back believes South Africa's strength, especially in warmer areas, lies with Rhône varieties. These are expressed in the Goats do Roam range, a spoof on COTES DU RHONE. The red features Pinotage with Rhône varieties such as Grenache, Cinsaut, Mourvèdre and Syrah; a spicy rosé is lightly

oaked; and a lovely white★ is blended from Grenache Blanc, Clairette and Crouchen with a splash of Muscat. The French authorities are not amused but fans on both sides of the Atlantic can't get enough. Fine Shiraz★★ (Solitude★★, Beacon Block★★), Carignan★, Malbec★, Merlot★★, Cabernet Sauvignon★ and Pinotage★ (Primo★) and promising new all-Italian varietal blend, Agostinelli. Good whites include Semillon★ (Oom Pagel★★) and Viognier★. Back also owns SPICE ROUTE. Best years: (Shiraz) 2004 03 **02 01 00 99 98 97 96**.

JOSEPH FAIVELEY *Nuits-St-Georges AC, Côte de Nuits, Burgundy, France* This Burgundian merchant makes impressive but severely tannic red wines that demand aging (CORTON★★, CHAMBERTIN-Clos-de-Bèze★★★, Mazis-Chambertin★★), principally from its own substantial vineyard holdings. In lesser wines, the fruit may not hold out against the tannin, and even aging may not help. The much cheaper MERCUREY reds★ from the Côte Chalonnaise can be attractive, if on the lean side. Whites from Mercurey★ and RULLY★, and the oak-aged BOURGOGNE Blanc represent reasonably good value. Best years: (top reds) (2004) 03 02 01 99 98 **97** 96 **95 93 90 89**; (whites) (2004) 03 02 **00 99**.

FALERNO DEL MASSICO DOC *Campania, Italy* Falernian was one of the ancient Romans' star wines. The revived DOC, with a white Falanghina and reds from either Aglianico and Piedirosso or from Primitivo, looks promising. Best producers: Michele Moio★, Villa Matilde★ (Vigna Camarato★★). Best years: (reds) (2004) (03) 01 **00 99 97 95**.

FALESCO *Lazio, Italy* Property of the phenomenal Cotarella brothers: Renzo is ANTINORI's technical director (so responsible for SOLAIA, TIGNANELLO, etc.); Riccardo is today's most high-profile consultant enologist, working all over Italy from Piedmont to Sicily. Located at Montefiascone, the town of EST! EST!! EST!!!, their Poggio dei Gelsi★ is considered best of the genre, but they are better known for their Merlot Montiano★★, the essence of smooth if somewhat soulless modernity. Best years: (Montiano) (2004) (03) 01 **00 99 98 97 96 95 94**.

CH. FALFAS★ *Côtes de Bourg AC, Bordeaux, France* Biodynamic estate making concentrated, structured wine that needs 4–5 years to soften. Le Chevalier★ is an old-vines cuvée. Best years: 2003 02 **01 00 99 98**.

CH. DE FARGUES★★ *Sauternes AC, Cru Bourgeois, Bordeaux, France* Property run by the Lur-Saluces family, who until 1999 also owned Ch. d'YQUEM. The quality of this fine, rich wine is more a tribute to their commitment than to the inherent quality of the vineyard. Best years: 2001 99 **98 97 96 95 90 89 88 86 83**.

FAUGÈRES AC *Languedoc, France* Faugères, with its vineyards in the schistous hills north of Béziers in the Hérault, produces red wines whose ripe, soft, rather plummy flavour marks them out from other LANGUEDOC reds. Best producers: Abbaye Sylva Plana★, ALQUIER★, Léon Barral★, Chenaie★, ESTANILLES★, Faugères co-op, Fraisse, Grézan, Haut-Fabrègues, la Liquière★, Moulin de Ciffre★, Ollier-Taillefer (Cuvée Castel Fossibus★). Best years: 2003 **01 00 99 98 96**.

FAUSTINO *Rioja DOCa, País Vasco and Rioja, and Cava DO, Spain* Family-owned and technically very well equipped, this RIOJA company makes fair Reserva V and Gran Reserva I red Riojas, as well as a more modern, oak-aged red, Faustino de Autor, and fruit-driven Faustino de Crianza. But they could try harder. Best years: (reds) 2001 **99 98 96 95 94 92 91 90**.

FEILER-ARTINGER *Rust, Neusiedlersee, Burgenland, Austria* Father and son Hans and Kurt Feiler make elegant Ausbruch dessert wines★★★. Their dry whites are ★. Solitaire★★ is a suave red blend of Merlot with Blaufränkisch and Zweigelt. Best years: (sweet whites) (2004) (03) 02 01 00 **99 98 96 95 94 91**; (Solitaire) (2004) 03 02 01 00 **99 98 97**.

LIVIO FELLUGA *Colli Orientali del Friuli DOC, Friuli-Venezia Giulia, Italy* A younger generation has continued the great work of Livio Felluga, at this large Friuli estate. Merlot-Cabernet blend Vertigo★★, raspberryish straight Merlot Riserva Sossò★★, white Pinot Grigio★, Picolit Riserva★★ and Tocai Friulano★ are all class acts. Shàrjs★ combines Chardonnay with Ribolla and oak, but there's more to stimulate the palate in Terre Alte★★, an aromatic blend of Tocai, Pinot Bianco and Sauvignon. Best years: (whites) (2004) 02 **01 00 99 98 97 96**.

FELSINA, FATTORIA DI *Chianti Classico DOCG, Tuscany, Italy* Full, chunky CHIANTI CLASSICO★★ wines which improve with several years' bottle age. Quality is generally outstanding; most notable are the single-vineyard Riserva Rancia★★★ and (under the regional IGT Toscana) Sangiovese Fontalloro★★★. Also good are Chardonnay I Sistri★★ and Cabernet Maestro Raro★★. Best years: (Fontalloro) (2004) (03) 01 00 **99 98 97 95 93 90 88 85**.

FELTON ROAD *Central Otago, South Island, New Zealand* Runaway success with vineyards in the old goldfields of Bannockburn. Intensely fruity, seductive Pinot Noir★★ is surpassed by limited quantities of concentrated, complex Block 3 Pinot Noir★★★ and the equally limited edition Block 5★★★. Three classy Rieslings (all ★★) cover the range from dry to sweet. Mineral, citrus unoaked Chardonnay★★ is one of New Zealand's best; barrel-fermented Chardonnay★★ also impresses. Best years: (Pinot Noir) **2003 02 01 00 99 98 97**.

FENDANT *Valais, Switzerland* Chasselas wine from the steep slopes of the VALAIS. Good Fendant should be slightly *spritzig*, with a nutty character. However, the average Fendant is overcropped, thin and virtually characterless. Best drunk *very* young. Best producers: Chappaz, Jacques Germanier, Gilliard, Caves Imesch, Maye, Caves Orsat.

FERNGROVE *Great Southern, Western Australia* Ambitious new winery based in Frankland River, where it has 285ha (700 acres) of vines (along with 140ha/345 acres at Mount Barker). The quality potential in Frankland River is unquestioned, being sunny yet cool. Lack of water is a limiting factor, but that also means yields are naturally limited and flavours intensified. So far Riesling is excellent (Cossack★★) and Chardonnay very good (Butterfly★★). Shiraz, Cabernet Sauvignon, Merlot and Malbec all show great potential.

FERRARI *Trento DOC, Trentino, Italy* Founded in 1902, the firm is a leader for sparkling wine. Consistent, classy wines include Ferrari Brut★, Maximum Brut★, Perlé★, Rosé★ and vintage Giulio Ferrari Riserva del Fondatore★★, aged 8 years on its lees and an Italian classic.

FERRARI-CARANO *Dry Creek Valley AVA, California, USA* Balanced, elegant Chardonnay; the regular bottling★★ has delicious apple-spice fruit, while the Reserve★★ is deeply flavoured with more than a touch of oak. Fumé Blanc★ is also good. Red wines are equally impressive, including Siena★★ (Sangiovese-Cabernet Sauvignon), Trésor★★ (a BORDEAUX blend), Syrah★, Merlot★ and Zinfandel★. Reds can improve for 5–10 years. Best years: (reds) (2002) 01 **00 99 97 96 95**.

FERREIRA *Port DOC, Douro DOC, Douro, Portugal* Old PORT house owned by SOGRAPE. Ferreira is best known for excellent tawny ports: creamy, nutty Quinta do Porto 10-year-old★ and Duque de Braganza 20-year-old★★. The Vintage Port★★ is increasingly good. Ferreira's unfortified wine operation, known as Casa Ferreirinha, produces Portugal's most sought-after red, Barca Velha★★; made from DOURO grape varieties (mainly Tinta Roriz), it is produced only in the finest years – just 12 vintages since 1953. Marginally less good years are now sold as Casa Ferreirinha Reserva★ (previously Reserva Especial). Quinta da Leda reds★★ are also fine. Best years: (Vintage) 2000 97 95 94 **91** 85 83 82 78 77 70 66 63; (Barca Velha) **1995** 91 85 83 82 81 78.

CH. FERRIÈRE★★ *Margaux AC, 3ème Cru Classé, Haut-Médoc, Bordeaux, France* The smallest Classed Growth in MARGAUX, Ferrière was bought by the Merlaut family, owners of Ch. CHASSE-SPLEEN, in 1992. It is now managed by Claire Villars, and the ripe, rich and perfumed wines are among the best in Margaux AC. Best years: 2003 02 01 00 **99** 98 **96 95**.

FETZER VINEYARDS *Mendocino County, California, USA* Important winery balancing quality and quantity. Basic wines are good, with a tasty Syrah★; Barrel Select bottles are usually ★. Bargain-priced Valley Oaks line is good value. Also a leader in organic viticulture with the Bonterra range: Chardonnay★, Viognier★, Merlot★, Roussanne★, Zinfandel★, Cabernet Sauvignon and Sangiovese. Best years: (Barrel Select reds) (2002) (01) **99 98 97 96 94**.

FIANO Exciting, distinctive, low-yielding southern Italian white grape variety. Best producers: (Molise) Di Majo Norante; (Fiano di Avellino DOC in CAMPANIA) Colli di Lapio★, Feudi di San Gregorio★★, MASTROBERARDINO★, Terredora di Paolo★, Vadiaperti★; (others) L Maffini (Kràtos★★), PLANETA (Cometa★★), Settesoli (Inycon★).

CH. DE FIEUZAL *Pessac-Léognan AC, Cru Classé de Graves, Bordeaux, France* One of the most up-to-date properties in the region. The red★ is drinkable almost immediately, but has the structure to age. Less than 10% of the wine is white★★, but this gorgeous, perfumed (and ageworthy) wine is the star performer. Second wine (red and white): l'Abeille de Fieuzal. Best years: (reds) 2003 00 98 96 **95 94 90 89 88 87** 86 85 83 82; (whites) (2004) 02 01 00 **99 98 96 95 94 93 90 89 88 85**.

CH. FIGEAC★★ *St-Émilion Grand Cru AC, 1er Grand Cru Classé, Bordeaux, France* Leading property whose wine traditionally has a delightful fragrance and gentleness of texture. There is an unusually high percentage of Cabernets Franc and Sauvignon (70%) in the wine, making it more structured than other ST-EMILIONS. After an unconvincing run of vintages from the mid-1980s, recent vintages have been far more like the lovely Figeac of old. Second wine: la Grangeneuve de Figeac. Best years: 2003 02 01 00 99 98 **95 90 89**.

FINGER LAKES AVA *New York State, USA* Cool region in central NEW YORK STATE. Riesling, Chardonnay and sparkling wines are the trump cards here, with Pinot Noir and Cabernet Franc successful among the reds. Best producers: Chateau Lafayette Reneau★, FOX RUN★, Dr Konstantin FRANK★, Heron Hill, LAMOREAUX LANDING★, Red Newt, Swedish Hill, Wagner, Hermann J Wiemer★.

FITOU AC *Languedoc-Roussillon, France* One of the success stories of the 1980s. Quality subsequently slumped, but with the innovative MONT TAUCH co-op taking the lead, Fitou is once again an excellent place to seek out dark, herb-scented reds. Best producers: Abelanet, Bertrand-Berge★, Lerys★, Milles Vignes, MONT TAUCH co-op★, Nouvelles★, Rochelière, Rolland, Roudène★. Best years: 2003 **01 00 99 98 96**.

FIXIN AC *Côte de Nuits, Burgundy, France* Although it's next door to GEVREY-CHAMBERTIN, Fixin rarely produces anything really magical. The wines are often sold as COTE DE NUITS-VILLAGES. Best producers: Champy★, Pierre Gelin★, Alain Guyard★, Dominique Laurent★★, Naddef★. Best years: (reds) (2004) 03 02 **01 00 99 96**.

FLEURIE AC *Beaujolais, Burgundy, France* The best-known BEAUJOLAIS Cru, Fleurie reveals the happy, carefree flavours of the Gamay grape at its best, plus heady perfumes and a delightful juicy sweetness. But demand has meant that too many wines are overpriced and dull. Best producers: J-M Aujoux★, M Chignard★, Clos de la Roilette★, Daumas★, Depardon★, Depres★, DUBOEUF (single domaines★), Fleurie co-op★, Métrat★, A & M Morel★, Verpoix★, Vissoux/P-M Chermette★★.

CH. LA FLEUR-PÉTRUS★★ *Pomerol AC, Bordeaux, France* Like the better-known PETRUS and TROTANOY, this is owned by the dynamic MOUEIX family. Unlike its stablemates, it is situated entirely on gravel soil and tends to produce tighter wines with less immediate fruit but considerable elegance and cellar potential. Among POMEROL's top dozen properties. Best years: 2003 01 00 **99 98 97 96 95 94 93 90 89 88 85 82**.

FLORA SPRINGS *Napa Valley AVA, California, USA* Best known for red wines such as Cabernet Reserve★★, a BORDEAUX blend called Trilogy★★ and Merlot★★. Chardonnay Reserve★★ tops the whites, and Soliloquy★, a barrel-fermented Sauvignon Blanc, has attractive melon fruit. The winery also works with Italian varietals: a weighty Pinot Grigio★ and a lightly spiced Sangiovese★ are consistent successes. Best years: (Trilogy) (2002) (01) 00 99 97 **96 95 94 91**.

FLOWERS *Sonoma Coast AVA, California, USA* Small producer whose estate vineyard, Camp Meeting Ridge, a few miles from the Pacific Ocean, yields wines of great intensity. The Camp Meeting Ridge Pinot Noir★★★ and Chardonnay★★★ are usually made with native yeasts and offer wonderful exotic aromas and flavours. Wines from purchased fruit with a SONOMA COAST designation are ★★ in quality. Best years: (Chardonnay) 2001 **00 99 98 97 96**; (Pinot Noir) 2001 **00 99 98 97 96**.

TENUTE AMBROGIO & GIOVANNI FOLONARI *Tuscany, Italy* A few years ago the Folonari family, owners of the giant RUFFINO, split asunder and these two brothers went their own way. Their properties/brands include Cabreo (Sangiovese-Cabernet Il Borgo★, Chardonnay La Pietra★) and Nozzole (powerful, long-lived Cabernet Il Pareto★★) in CHIANTI CLASSICO, plus VINO NOBILE estate Gracciano-Svetoni, Campo del Mare in BOLGHERI and BRUNELLO producer La Fuga.

135

FONSECA Port DOC, Douro, Portugal   Owned by the same group as TAYLOR (Fladgate Partnership), Fonseca makes ports in a rich, densely plummy style. Fonseca Vintage★★★ is magnificent, the aged tawnies★★ uniformly superb. Fonseca Guimaraens★★ is the name of the 'off-vintage' wine, but off vintages here are equal to all but the best offerings of other houses. Bin No. 27★ is one of the best examples of a premium ruby port. Quinta do Panascal is the 3rd vintage label. Best years: (Vintage) 2000 97 94 92 **85 83 77 75 70 66 63 55**.

JOSÉ MARIA DA FONSECA Terras do Sado, Portugal   Go-ahead company making a huge range of wines, from fizzy Lancers Rosé to serious reds. Best include Vinya★ (Syrah-Aragonez), Domingos Soares Franco Private Collection★, and Garrafeiras with codenames like CO★★, RA★★ and TE★★. Optimum★★ is top of the range. Periquita is the mainstay, with Clássico★ made only in the best years. Also SETUBAL made mainly from the Moscatel grape: 5-year-old★ and 20-year-old★★. Older vintage-dated Setúbals are rare but superb.

DOM. FONT DE MICHELLE Châteauneuf-du-Pape AC, Rhône Valley, France   CHATEAUNEUF-DU-PAPE reds★★, in particular Cuvée Étienne Gonnet★★, and whites★ that are stylish but still heady, with richness and southern herb fragrance – and not too expensive. Best years: (Étienne Gonnet red) (2004) 03 01 00 99 98 **97 95 94 90 89**.

FONTANAFREDDA Barolo DOCG, Piedmont, Italy   One of the largest PIEDMONT estates, based in the old BAROLO hunting lodge of the King of Italy. As well as Barolo Serralunga d'Alba★, it also produces several single-vineyard Barolos (La Delizia★★), a range of Piedmont varietals, 4 million bottles of ASTI and a good dry sparkler, Contessa Rosa. Best years: (Barolo) (2004) (03) 01 **00** 99 **97 90 89 88 85**.

FONTERUTOLI, CASTELLO DI Chianti Classico DOCG, Tuscany, Italy   This eminent estate has belonged to the Mazzei family since the 15th century. The focus is on CHIANTI CLASSICO Riserva★★, along with excellent SUPER-TUSCAN Siepi★★★ (Sangiovese-Merlot). Belguardo★ is a new venture in the MAREMMA, with IGT and MORELLINO DI SCANSANO wines.

FONTODI Chianti Classico DOCG, Tuscany, Italy   The Manetti family has built this superbly sited estate into one of the most admired in the CHIANTI CLASSICO area, with excellent *normale*★★, richer Riserva★★ and fine Riserva Vigna del Sorbo★★. SUPER-TUSCAN Flaccianello della Pieve★★★, produced from a single vineyard of old vines, has served as a shining example to other producers of how excellent Sangiovese can be without the addition of other varieties. Two varietals, Pinot Nero and Syrah★★, are made under the Case Via label. Best years: (Flaccianello) (2004) (03) 01 **00** 99 **98 97 95 93 90 88 85**.

FORADORI Teroldego Rotaliano DOC, Trentino, Italy   Producer of dark, spicy, berry-fruited wines, including a regular TEROLDEGO ROTALIANO★ and barrique-aged Granato★★. Foradori's interest in Syrah is producing excellent results, both in the varietal Ailanpa★★ and the smoky, black-cherry lushness of Cabernet-Syrah blend Karanar★. Best years: (Granato) (2004) (03) 01 **00** 99 **98** 96 93.

FORST Pfalz, Germany   Village with 6 individual vineyard sites, including the Ungeheuer or 'Monster'; wines from the Monster can indeed be quite savage, with a marvellous mineral intensity and richness in the best years. Equally good are the Kirchenstück, Jesuitengarten, Freundstück and Pechstein. Best producers: BASSERMANN-JORDAN★★, von BUHL★, BURKLIN-WOLF★★, MOSBACHER★★, WEGELER★, Werlé★, WOLF★★. Best years: (2004) 03 02 01 **99 98 97 96 94**.

FOX CREEK *McLaren Vale, South Australia* Impressive, opulent, superripe MCLAREN VALE reds. Reserve Shiraz★★ and Reserve Cabernet Sauvignon★★ have wowed the critics; JSM (Shiraz-Cabernets)★★ is rich and succulent; Merlot★★ is a little lighter but still concentrated and powerful. Vixen sparkling Shiraz★ is also lip-smacking stuff. Whites are comparatively ordinary, albeit fair value for money.

FOX RUN VINEYARDS *Finger Lakes AVA, New York State, USA* A leader in crafting a regional style from Dry Riesling★, as well as a reliable producer of complex, ALSACE-style Gewürztraminer★ and an elegant Reserve Chardonnay★. There are also spicy, attractive reds from Pinot Noir and Cabernet Franc, and a complex, fruit-forward red Meritage.

FRANCIACORTA DOCG *Lombardy, Italy* CHAMPAGNE-method fizz made from Pinot and Chardonnay grapes. Still whites from Pinot Bianco and Chardonnay and reds from Cabernet, Barbera, Nebbiolo and Merlot are all DOC with the appellation Terre di Franciacorta. Best producers: BELLAVISTA★★, CA' DEL BOSCO★★, Fratelli Berlucchi★, Guido Berlucchi★, Castellino★, Cavalleri★, La Ferghettina★, Enrico Gatti★, Monte Rossa★, Il Mosnel★, Ricci Curbastro★, San Cristoforo★, Uberti★, Villa★.

FRANCISCAN *Napa Valley AVA, California, USA* Consistently good wines at fair prices, from the heart of the NAPA VALLEY. The Cuvée Sauvage Chardonnay★★ is a blockbusting, savoury mouthful, and the Cabernet Sauvignon-based meritage Magnificat★ is very attractive. Estancia is a separate label, with remarkably good-value Chardonnay★ and Pinot Noir★ from CENTRAL COAST and Cabernet Sauvignon★ from ALEXANDER VALLEY, as well as its own Meritage★. Franciscan also owns Mount Veeder Winery, where lean but intense Cabernet Sauvignon★★ of great mineral depth and complexity is made.

DR KONSTANTIN FRANK *Finger Lakes AVA, New York State, USA* The good doctor was a pioneer of vinifera grapes in the FINGER LAKES region of New York State in the 1960s. Now under the direction of his son, Willi, and grandson Fred, the winery continues to spotlight the area's talent with Riesling★. There's also some nice Chateau Frank fizz.

FRANKEN *Germany* 6000ha (14,820-acre) wine region specializing in dry wines. Easily recognizable by their squat, green Bocksbeutel bottles (familiar because of the Portuguese wine Mateus Rosé). Silvaner is the traditional grape variety, although Müller-Thurgau now predominates. The most famous vineyards are on the hillsides around WURZBURG and IPHOFEN.

FRANSCHHOEK WO *South Africa* Huguenot refugees settled in this picturesque valley, encircled by breathtaking mountain peaks, in the 17th century. Many wineries and other landmarks still bear French names. Semillon is a local speciality (a few vines are 100 years old), though the valley is today carving a reputation for a diverse range of reds. Cabrière Pinot Noir★, La Motte Shiraz★ and Stony Brook Cabernet Sauvignon Reserve★ are among the most promising. Best producers: Graham BECK★, BOEKENHOUTSKLOOF★★, Cabrière Estate★, Cape Chamonix★, La Motte★, La Petite Ferme, L'Ormarins, Stony Brook. Best years: (reds) 2002 01 00 99 98 97.

FRASCATI DOC *Lazio, Italy* One of Italy's most famous whites, frequently referred to as Rome's quaffing wine. The wine may be made from Trebbiano or Malvasia or any blend thereof; the better examples have a higher proportion of Malvasia. Good Frascati is worth seeking out, most notably Vigna Adriana★★, from Castel de Paolis. Other

137

light, dry Frascati-like wines come from neighbouring DOCs in the hills of the Castelli Romani and Colli Albani, including Marino, Montecompatri, Velletri and Zagarolo. Best producers: Casale Marchese★, Castel de Paolis★★, Colli di Catone★, Piero Costantini/Villa Simone★, Fontana Candida★, Zandotti★.

FREIXENET *Cava DO, Cataluña, Spain* The second-biggest Spanish sparkling wine company (after CODORNIU) makes the famous Cordon Negro Brut CAVA in a vast network of cellars in Sant Sadurní d'Anoia. Freixenet also owns the Castellblanch, Segura Viudas, Conde de Caralt and Canals & Nubiola Cava brands as well as PENEDES winery René Barbier. Its international expansion has gathered pace in recent years with interests in CHAMPAGNE, CALIFORNIA, Australia and BORDEAUX.

FRESCOBALDI *Tuscany, Italy* Florentine company selling large quantities of inexpensive blended CHIANTIS, but from its own vineyards (some 800 ha/1980 acres in total) it produces good to very good wines at Nipozzano (especially CHIANTI RUFINA Castello di Nipozzano Riserva★★ and Montesodi★★), Tenuta di Pomino★, and CASTELGIOCONDO★ in BRUNELLO DI MONTALCINO. Best years: (premium reds) (2004) (03) 01 **00 99 98 97 95 93 90 88 85**.

FRIULI GRAVE DOC *Friuli-Venezia Giulia, Italy* DOC in western Friuli covering 19 wine types. Good affordable Merlot, Refosco, Chardonnay, Pinot Grigio, Traminer and Tocai. Best producers: Borgo Magredo★, Le Fredis★, Di Lenardo★, Orgnani★, Pighin★, Pittaro★, Plozner★, Pradio★, Russolo★, Vigneti Le Monde★, Villa Chiopris★, Vistorta★. Best years: (whites) (2004) **02 01 00 98**.

FRIULI ISONZO DOC *Friuli-Venezia Giulia, Italy* Classy southern neighbour of COLLIO with wines of outstanding value. The DOC covers 20 styles, including Merlot, Chardonnay, Pinot Grigio and Sauvignon. The best from neighbouring Carso DOC are also good. Best producers: (Isonzo) Borgo San Daniele★, Colmello di Grotta★, Sergio & Mauro Drius★★, Masùt da Rive★ (Silvano Gallo), Lis Neris-Pecorari★★, Pierpaolo Pecorari★★, Giovanni Puiatti★, Ronco del Gelso★★, Tenuta Villanova★, Vie di Romans★★; (Carso) Castelvecchio, Edi Kante★★. Best years: (whites) (2004) 03 **02 01 00 99 98 97**.

FRIULI-VENEZIA GIULIA *Italy* North-east Italian region bordering Austria and Slovenia. The hilly DOC zones of COLLIO and COLLI ORIENTALI produce some of Italy's finest whites from Chardonnay, Pinot Bianco, Pinot Grigio, Sauvignon and Tocai, and excellent reds mainly from Cabernet, Merlot and Refosco. The DOCs of Friuli Aquileia, FRIULI ISONZO, Friuli Latisana and FRIULI GRAVE, in the rolling hills and plains, produce good-value wines.

FROMM *Marlborough, South Island, New Zealand* Small winery where low-yielding vines and intensively managed vineyards are the secret behind a string of winning white wines, including fine Burgundian-style Clayvin Vineyard Chardonnay★★, German-style Riesling★★ and Riesling Auslese★. Despite its success with whites, Fromm is perhaps best known for intense, long-lived reds, including Clayvin Vineyard Pinot Noir★★★, Fromm Vineyard Pinot Noir★★ and a powerful, peppery Syrah★★. Best years: (Pinot Noir) (2003) **02 01 00 99 98**.

FRONSAC AC *Bordeaux, France* Small area west of POMEROL making good-value Merlot-based wines. The top producers have taken note of the feeding frenzy in neighbouring Pomerol and sharpened up their act accordingly, with finely structured wines, occasionally perfumed, and better with at least 5 years' age. Best producers: Carolus, Dalem★, la Dauphine★, Fontenil★, la Grave★, Haut-Carles★, Magondeau Beausite, Mayne-Vieil (Cuvée Aliénor★), Moulin-Haut-Laroque★, Puy Guilhem, la Rivière★, la Rousselle★, Tour du Moulin, les Trois Croix★, la Vieille Cure★, Villars★. Best years: 2003 **01** 00 **98 97 96 95 94** 90 **89** 88.

FUMÉ BLANC See Sauvignon Blanc.

RUDOLF FÜRST *Bürgstadt, Franken, Germany* Paul Fürst's dry Rieslings★★ are unusually elegant for a region renowned for its earthy white wines, while his Burgundian-style Spätburgunder (Pinot Noir) reds★★ and barrel-fermented Weissburgunder (Pinot Blanc) whites★★ are some of the best in Germany. Sensual, intellectual wines with excellent aging potential. Best years: (dry Riesling) (2004) 03 02 01 **99 98 97 94 93;** (reds) (2004) 03 02 01 **00 99 98 97**.

JEAN-NOËL GAGNARD *Chassagne-Montrachet AC, Côte de Beaune, Burgundy, France* Now run by Gagnard's daughter Caroline Lestimé, who consistently makes some of the best wines of CHASSAGNE-MONTRACHET, particularly Premiers Crus Caillerets★★★ and Morgeot★★. Top wine is rich, toasty BATARD-MONTRACHET★★★. All whites are capable of extended cellaring. Reds★ are good, but not in the same class. Best years: (whites) (2004) 03 02 01 **00 99 98 97 95**.

GAILLAC AC *South-West France* The whites, mainly from Mauzac and Ondenc, with their sharp but attractive green apple bite, are rather stern but, from a decent producer, can be extremely refreshing. Sweet whites are getting better. Some more serious reds are made, which require some aging. The star of Gaillac at the moment is the fizz, ideally not quite dry and packed with fruit. Drink as young as possible. Best producers: Albert, Bosc-Long, Causses-Marines★, Clément Termes, Escausses, de Gineste★, Labarthe★, Labastide-de-Lévis co-op, Mas Pignou, PLAGEOLES★★, Rotier★, Técou co-op★, des Terrisses★.

GAJA *Barbaresco DOCG, Piedmont, Italy* Angelo Gaja brought about the transformation of PIEDMONT from an old-fashioned region that Italians swore made the finest red wine in the world yet the rest of the world disdained, to an area buzzing with excitement. He introduced international standards and charged staggeringly high prices, thus giving other Piedmont growers the chance to get a decent return for their labours. Into this fiercely conservative area, full of fascinating grape varieties but proudest of the native Nebbiolo, he introduced French grapes like Cabernet Sauvignon (Darmagi★★), Sauvignon Blanc (Alteni di Brassica★) and Chardonnay (Gaia & Rey★★). He has also renounced the Barbaresco and Barolo DOCGs for his best wines! Gaja's traditional strength has been in single-vineyard wines from the BARBARESCO region: his Sorì San Lorenzo★★★, Sorì Tildìn★★★ and Costa Russi★★★, now sold under the LANGHE DOC, are often cited as Barbaresco's best of the modern style. Only one premium bottling of Barbaresco★★★ is now made. Sperss★★★ and Conteisa★★★ – from BAROLO, but sold as Langhe DOC wines – are also outstanding. Barbera Sitorey★ and Nebbiolo-based Langhe Sito Moresco★ are less exciting. Gaja has also invested in BRUNELLO DI MONTALCINO (Pieve Santa Restituta) and BOLGHERI (Cà Marcanda). Best years: (Barbaresco) (2004) (03) 01 00 99 **98 97** 96 **95 93** 90 89 **88** 85 82 79 78 71 61.

GALICIA *Spain* Up in Spain's hilly, verdant north-west, Galicia is renowned for its Albariño whites. There are 5 DOs: RIAS BAIXAS can make excellent, fragrant Albariño, with modern equipment and serious winemaking; Ribeiro DO has also invested heavily in new equipment, and better local white grapes such as Treixadura are now being used, as is the case with Godello in the mountainous Valdeorras DO. Some young reds from the Mencía grape are also made there and in the Ribeira Sacra DO. Monterrei DO is technically backward but shows some potential with its native white grape, Doña Blanca. Most wines are best drunk young.

E & J GALLO *Central Valley, California, USA* Gallo, the world's second-largest wine company – and for generations a byword for cheap, drab wines – has made a massive effort to change its reputation and our attitudes since the mid-1990s. This began with the release of Sonoma Estate Chardonnay and Cabernet Sauvignon, and their success led to the establishment of Gallo of Sonoma★★, a new label for varietals such as Zinfandel and Cabernet Sauvignon from DRY CREEK VALLEY and ALEXANDER VALLEY and Chardonnay from several vineyards. New vineyards in RUSSIAN RIVER VALLEY have been planted to Pinot Noir and Pinot Gris. Even so, Gallo continues to produce oceans of ordinary wine, under labels such as Turning Leaf, Gossamer Bay and Garnet Point, that is just beginning to show an upturn in quality. About time too. More interesting are small-volume brands Anapamu (CENTRAL COAST Chardonnay), Rancho Zabaco (SONOMA COUNTY wines) and Indigo Hills (MENDOCINO wines). Gallo also owns the Frei Brothers and MacMurray Ranch brands. In 2002, Gallo acquired Louis M Martini in NAPA VALLEY, adding vital acreage to its north coast holdings, and also bought Mirassou. Gallo bought CENTRAL COAST winery Bridlewood in 2004.

GALLUCCIO FAMILY WINERIES/GRISTINA *Long Island, New York State, USA* Gristina was acquired in 2000 by Vincent Galluccio, who expanded facilities and plantings, and hired famed enologist Michel Rolland as consultant. Stars are the elegant Chardonnay★ and cherry-vanilla Merlot. Best years: (reds) (2002) **01 00 98**.

GAMAY The only grape allowed for red BEAUJOLAIS. In general Gamay wine is rather rough-edged and quite high in raspy acidity, but in Beaujolais, so long as the yield is not too high, it can achieve a wonderful, juicy-fruit gluggability, almost unmatched in the world of wine. Elsewhere in France, it is successful in the Ardèche and the Loire and less so in the Mâconnais. In Switzerland it is blended with Pinot Noir to create DOLE. There are occasional plantings in Canada, New Zealand, Australia, South Africa and even England, which could become interesting.

GARD, VIN DE PAYS DU *Languedoc, France* Mainly reds and rosés from the western side of the RHONE delta. Most red is light, spicy and attractive. Rosés can be fresh when young, and with modern winemaking, whites can be good. Best producers: des Aveylans★, Baruel★, Cantarelles★, Coste Plane, Grande Cassagne★, Guiot★, Mas des Bressades★.

GARGANEGA Italian white grape from the VENETO in north-east Italy; main component of SOAVE. Grown on hillsides, it can have class, but its reputation is tainted by excessive yields from the Veronese plain.

GARNACHA BLANCA See Grenache Blanc.

GARNACHA TINTA See Grenache Noir.

GATTINARA DOCG *Piedmont, Italy* One of the most capricious of Italy's
top red wine areas. The Nebbiolo wines should be softer and lighter
than BAROLO, with a delicious, black plums, tar and roses flavour if
you're lucky. Drink within 10 years. Vintages follow those for Barolo.
Best producers: Antoniolo★, S Gattinara, Nervi★, Travaglini★.

DOM. GAUBY *Côtes du Roussillon-Villages AC, Roussillon, France* Gérard
Gauby used to make burly but very tannic wines; now his wines are
softer but marvellously concentrated. Highlights include powerful
COTES DU ROUSSILLON-VILLAGES Vieilles Vignes★★ and Syrah-dominated la
Muntada★★ as well as a gorgeously seductive vin de pays Le Soula★★.
Best years: (reds) (2003) 02 **01 00 99 98 97 96**.

GAVI DOCG *Piedmont, Italy* Fashionable and often overpriced, this
Cortese-based, steely, lemony white can age up to 5 years, providing it
starts life with sufficient fruit. La Scolca's Spumante Brut Soldati★ is an
admirable sparkling wine. Best producers: Battistina★, Bergaglio★,
Broglia★, La Chiara★, CHIARLO★, FONTANAFREDDA, La Giustiniana★★, Pio
Cesare, San Pietro★, La Scolca★, Tassarolo★, Villa Sparina★.

CH. GAZIN★★ *Pomerol AC, Bordeaux, France* One of the largest
châteaux in POMEROL, situated next to the legendary PETRUS. The wine,
traditionally a succulent, sweet-textured Pomerol, seemed to lose its
way in the 1980s but is now showing real richness and a very
individualistic character under the management of owner Nicolas de
Bailliencourt. Best years: 2003 01 00 **98 97 96 95 94 90 89 88**.

GEELONG *Victoria, Australia* Cool-climate, maritime-influenced region
revived in the 1960s after destruction by phylloxera in the 19th
century. Can be brilliant; potentially a match for the YARRA VALLEY.
Impressive Pinot Noir, Chardonnay, Riesling, Sauvignon and Shiraz.
Best producers: BANNOCKBURN★, By Farr★, Idyll, Scotchmans Hill★.

GEISENHEIM *Rheingau, Germany* Village famous for its wine school,
where the Müller-Thurgau grape was bred in 1882. Geisenheim's
most famous vineyard is the Rothenberg, which produces strong,
earthy wines. Best producers: Johannishof★, WEGELER, von Zwierlein.
Best years: (2004) 03 02 01 **99 98 97 96**.

GEROVASSILIOU *Macedonia AO, Greece* Bordeaux-trained Evángelos
Gerovassiliou has 40ha (100 acres) of vineyards and a modern winery
in Epanomi in northern Greece. High-quality fruit results in Syrah-
dominated Domaine Gerovassiliou red★ and some fresh, modern whites,
including a fine Viognier★ that lacks a little perfume but has fantastic
fruit, barrel-fermented Chardonnay and Fumé, and the Domaine
Gerovassiliou★ white, a most original Assyrtiko-Malagousia blend.

GEVREY-CHAMBERTIN AC *Côte de Nuits, Burgundy, France* The wines of
Gevrey-Chambertin have at times proved disappointing, but a new
generation of growers has restored the reputation of Gevrey as a source
of well-coloured, firmly structured, powerful, perfumed wines that
become rich and gamy with age. Village wines should be kept for at least
5 years, Premiers Crus and the 8 Grands Crus for 10 years or more,
especially CHAMBERTIN and Clos-de-Bèze. The Premier Cru Clos St-Jacques
is worthy of promotion to Grand Cru. Best producers: D Bachelet★★,
L Boillot★, A Burguet★★, B CLAIR★★★, P Damoy★★, DROUHIN★,
C Dugat★★★, B Dugat-Py★★, DUJAC★★, S Esmonin★★, FAIVELEY★★,
Fourrier★★, Geantet-Pansiot★★, JADOT★★, Philippe Leclerc★★,
Denis MORTET★★★, Rossignol★, J Roty★★, ROUSSEAU★★★, Sérafin★★,
J & J-L Trapet★★. Best years: (2004) 03 02 01 **00 99 98 96 95 93 90**.

GEWÜRZTRAMINER *Gewürz* means spice, and the wine certainly can be spicy and exotically perfumed, as well as being typically low in acidity. It is thought to have originated in the village of Tramin, in Italy's ALTO ADIGE, and the name Traminer is used by many producers. In parts of Germany and Austria it is known as Clevner and in Switzerland it is called Heida or Paien. It makes an appearance in many wine-producing countries; quality is mixed and styles vary enormously, from the fresh, light, florally perfumed wines produced in Alto Adige to the rich, luscious, late-harvest ALSACE VENDANGE TARDIVE. Best in France's ALSACE and also good in Austria's Styria (STEIERMARK) and New Zealand.

GEYSER PEAK *Alexander Valley AVA, California, USA* Australian winemaker Daryl Groom's mainstream wines tend to be accessible, fruity and not too serious. Typical are the fruity SONOMA COUNTY Cabernet★ and Merlot★ – ripe, juicy and delicious upon release. The Reserve Alexandre★★, a BORDEAUX-style blend, is made for aging, and the Reserve Shiraz★★ has a cult following. Block Collection features limited production, single-vineyard wines. Best years: (Alexandre) (2002) (01) 00 99 **98** 97 **94 91**.

GIACONDA *Beechworth, Victoria, Australia* In spite of (or perhaps because of) Giaconda's tiny production, Rick Kinzbrunner is one of Australia's most influential winemakers. Because of his success, BEECHWORTH has become one of the country's most exciting viticultural regions. His tightly structured, minerally, savoury Chardonnay★★★ is one of Australia's best, the Pinot Noir★★★ is both serious and beautiful, the Cabernet★ is ripe, deep and complex, while the Warner Vineyard Shiraz★★ successfully pursues a deep, gamy HERMITAGE style. Because the grapes were affected by bushfires, only the late-ripening Cabernet will be released from the 2003 vintage. Best years: (Chardonnay) (2004) 02 01 **00 99 98 96 93 92**.

BRUNO GIACOSA *Barbaresco DOCG, Piedmont, Italy* One of the great winemakers of the LANGHE hills, still basically a traditionalist, though he has reduced maturation time for his BARBARESCOS and BAROLOS to a maximum of 4 years. Superb Barbarescos Asili★★★, Santo Stefano★★★ and Rabaja★★★, and Barolos including Rocche di Falletto★★★ and Falletto★★. Also excellent Dolcetto d'Alba★, ROERO Arneis★, MOSCATO D'ASTI★★ and sparkling Extra Brut★★.

GIESEN *Canterbury and Marlborough, South Island, New Zealand* A large winery that played a significant part in putting CANTERBURY on the map with a string of fine sweet and dry Rieslings. Has now bought 400ha (1000 acres) of vineyard in MARLBOROUGH and seems intent upon producing vast quantities of budget-priced Sauvignon Blanc rather than stellar Riesling. Best years: (Sauvignon Blanc) **2003 01 00**.

GIGONDAS AC *Rhône Valley, France* Gigondas wines, mostly red and made mainly from Grenache, have fistfuls of chunky personality. Most drink well with 5 years' age; some need a little more. Best producers: la Boussière★★, Brusset★★, Cassan★★, Cayron★★, Clos des Cazaux★★, Clos du Joncuas★★, Cros de la Mûre★★, DELAS★, des Espiers★★, Font-Sane★★, Fourmone★, les Goubert★, Gour de Chaule★, Grapillon d'Or★★, GUIGAL★, JABOULET★, Longue-Toque★, Montvac★★, Moulin de la Gardette★★, les Pallières★, Piaugier★, Raspail-Ay★★, Redortier★★, St-Cosme★★, ST-GAYAN★, Santa-Duc★★, Tardieu-Laurent★★, la Tourade★★, Trignon★★. Best years: 2004 03 01 00 **99 98 97 95 94 90**.

CH. GILETTE★★ *Sauternes AC, Bordeaux, France* These astonishing wines are stored in concrete vats as opposed to the more normal wooden barrels. This virtually precludes any oxygen contact, and it is oxygen that ages a wine. Consequently, when released at up to 30 years old, they are bursting with life and lusciousness. Best years: **1985 83 82 81 79 78 76 75 70 67 61 59 55 53 49**.

GIPPSLAND *Victoria, Australia* Diverse wineries along the southern Victoria coast, all tiny but with massive potential. Results can be erratic, occasionally brilliant. Nicholson River's BURGUNDY-style Chardonnay can sometimes hit ★★. Bass Phillip Reserve★★ and Premium★★ Pinot Noirs are among the best in Australia, with a cult following. McAlister★, a red BORDEAUX blend, has also produced some tasty flavours. Best producers: Bass Phillip★★, McAlister★, Nicholson River★.

VINCENT GIRARDIN *Santenay AC, Côte de Beaune, Burgundy, France* The best grower in SANTENAY and now a thriving négociant, with an establishment in MEURSAULT★★. Bright, glossy reds from Santenay★★, MARANGES★ and CHASSAGNE-MONTRACHET★★ are surpassed by excellent VOLNAY★★ and POMMARD Grands Épenots★★★. Chassagne-Montrachet whites (Morgeot★★, Caillerets★★★) are perfectly balanced with good fruit depth. CORTON-CHARLEMAGNE★★★ is exceptional. He has now taken over the moribund Henri Clerc estate in PULIGNY-MONTRACHET. Best years: (reds) (2004) 03 02 **01** 99 **96**; (whites) (2004) 03 02 01 **00 99**.

GISBORNE *North Island, New Zealand* Gisborne, with its hot, humid climate and fertile soils, delivers both quality and quantity. Local growers have christened their region 'The Chardonnay Capital of New Zealand' and Gewürztraminer and Chenin Blanc are also a success. Good reds, however, are hard to find. Best producers: MILLTON★★, MONTANA. Best years: (Chardonnay) (2004) **02 00 98**.

GIVRY AC *Côte Chalonnaise, Burgundy, France* Important COTE CHALONNAISE village. The reds have an intensity of fruit and ability to age that are unusual in the region. There are some attractive, fairly full, nutty whites, too. Best producers: Bourgeon★, Chofflet-Valdenaire★, B CLAIR★, Joblot★★, F Lumpp★★, Parize★, Ragot★, Sarrazin★. Best years: (reds) (2004) 03 02 **99 96**; (whites) (2004) 03 02 00 **99**.

GLAETZER *Barossa Valley, South Australia* Colin Glaetzer has been one of the BAROSSA VALLEY's most enthusiastic and successful winemakers for decades. He made his reputation working for other people, and now he and his son Ben are making tip-top Barossa wines under the family label. Fine Semillon★, juicy Grenache-Mourvèdre★ and rich, superripe Bishop Shiraz★★ (from 30–60 year-old-vines) and Glaetzer Shiraz★★ (from 80-year-old vines). Ben also makes Amon-Ra Shiraz, as well as cult McLaren Vale Mitolo★★ and exciting reds and whites for the Heartland★★ label. Best years: (Bishop Shiraz) 2002 01 **99 98 96**

GLEN CARLOU *Paarl WO, South Africa* Started by the Finlaysons in the 1980s and now owned by Donald HESS. David Finlayson remains as winemaker. Elegant standard Chardonnay★ and richer toasty Reserve★★ version, the spicy, silky Pinot Noir★, Grand Classique★★, a red BORDEAUX blend with excellent aging potential, and a rich, spicy Shiraz★★. Best years: (Chardonnay) 2004 **03 02 01 00** 99 98 97.

CH. GLORIA★ *St-Julien AC, Cru Bourgeois, Haut-Médoc, Bordeaux, France* An interesting property, created out of tiny plots of Classed Growth land scattered all round ST-JULIEN. Generally very soft and sweet-centred, the wine nonetheless ages well. Second wine: Peymartin. Best years: 2003 02 **01** 00 **98 96 95 90 89 88 86**.

GOLAN HEIGHTS WINERY *Golan Heights, Israel*   Israel's leading quality wine producer. Cool summers, high-altitude vineyards and modern winemaking with kosher standards have resulted in good Sauvignon Blanc and Cabernet Sauvignon★, balanced, oaky Chardonnay★ and good bottle-fermented fizz★. Yarden is the top label.

GOLDMUSKATELLER   Moscato Giallo, a strain of Muscat Blanc à Petits Grains, is known as Goldmuskateller in the ALTO ADIGE. Here and else-where in Italy's north-east, sometimes under the name Fior d'Arancio, it makes scented wines in dry, off-dry and sweet (*passito*) styles. Best producers: Bolognani★, LAGEDER★, Obermoser, Vignalta.

GOLDWATER ESTATE *Waiheke Island, Auckland, New Zealand*   Kim and Jeanette Goldwater established the first vineyard on WAIHEKE ISLAND, the vineyard paradise an hour out from Auckland. Top wines are intense, long-lived Cabernet-Merlot★★ and Esslin Merlot★★, made in an elegant, cedary style with considerable depth and structure. Zell Chardonnay★★ from Waiheke looks exciting. Also attractive New Dog Sauvignon Blanc★ and Roseland Chardonnay★ from MARLBOROUGH fruit. Best years: (Waiheke reds) (2004) 02 **00 99 96**.

GONZÁLEZ BYASS *Jerez y Manzanilla DO, Andalucía, Spain*   Tio Pepe★, the high-quality fino brand of this huge firm, is the world's biggest-selling sherry. The old sherries are superb: intense, dry Amontillado del Duque★★★; 2 rich, complex olorosos, sweet Matusalem★★ and medium Apóstoles★★; treacly Noé Pedro Ximénez★★★. One step down is the Alfonso Dry Oloroso★. The firm pioneered the rediscovery of single-vintage (non-solera) dry olorosos★★ and palos cortados★★.

GRAACH *Mosel, Germany*   Important Middle MOSEL wine village with 4 vineyard sites, the most famous being Domprobst (also the best) and Himmelreich. A third, the Josephshöfer, is wholly owned by the von KESSELSTATT estate. The wines have an attractive fullness to balance their steely acidity, and great aging potential. Best producers: von

KESSELSTATT★, Dr LOOSEN★★, Markus Molitor★, J J PRUM★★, S A PRUM★, Max Ferd RICHTER★, Willi SCHAEFER★★★, SELBACH-OSTER★★, Weins-Prüm★. Best years: (2004) 03 02 01 00 **99** 98 **97 96 95 94 90**.

GRACIANO   Rare, low-yielding but excellent Spanish grape, traditional in RIOJA, NAVARRA and Extremadura. It makes dense, highly structured, fragrant reds, and its high acidity adds life when blended with low-acid Tempranillo. Two wineries, CONTINO and Viña Ijalba, offer varietal examples. In Portugal it is called Tinta Miúda. Also grown by BROWN BROTHERS in Australia.

GRAHAM'S *Port DOC, Douro, Portugal*   Part of the Symington empire, making rich, florally scented Vintage Port★★★, sweeter than DOW's and WARRE's, but with the backbone to age. In non-declared years makes a fine vintage wine called Malvedos★★. Six Grapes★ is one of the best premium rubies, and 10-year-old★ and 20-year-old★ tawnies are consistently good. Best years: (Vintage) 2000 97 94 91 **85 83 80 77 75 70 66 63 60**; (Malvedos) 2001 99 **95 92 90**.

ALAIN GRAILLOT *Crozes-Hermitage AC, Rhône Valley, France* Excellent estate producing powerfully concentrated, rich, fruity reds. The top wine is CROZES-HERMITAGE la Guiraude★★, but the regular Crozes-Hermitage★★ is wonderful too, as are the ST-JOSEPH★★ and a lovely fragrant white Crozes-Hermitage★. Keep top reds for at least 5 years. Best years: (la Guiraude) 2004 03 **01 00 99 96 95 90 89**.

GRAMPIANS AND PYRENEES *Victoria, Australia* Two adjacent cool-climate regions in central western VICTORIA. Both produce some of Australia's most characterful Shiraz, as well as distinguished Riesling, subtle Pinot Gris and savoury Chardonnay. Best producers: BEST'S★, Blue Pyrenees, Dalwhinnie★★, MOUNT LANGI GHIRAN★★, Redbank★, SEPPELT★★, Taltarni. Best years: (Shiraz) 2003 02 **01 99 98 97 96 94 91 90**.

CH. GRAND-PUY-DUCASSE★ *Pauillac AC, 5ème Cru Classé, Haut-Médoc, Bordeaux, France* After great improvement in the 1980s, form dipped in the early 90s but recovered again in 95. Approachable after 5 years, but the wines can improve for considerably longer. Second wine: Artigues-Arnaud. Best years: 2003 02 **01** 00 **96 95 90 89 88 86 85**.

CH. GRAND-PUY-LACOSTE★★ *Pauillac AC, 5ème Cru Classé, Haut-Médoc, Bordeaux, France* Classic PAUILLAC, with lots of blackcurrant and cigar-box perfume. As the wine develops, the flavours mingle with the sweetness of new oak into one of Pauillac's most memorable taste sensations. Second wine: Lacoste-Borie. Best years: 2003 02 01 00 **99** 98 **97** 96 **95 94 93 90 89 88 86 85 83 82**.

GRANDS-ÉCHÉZEAUX AC See Échézeaux AC.

GRANGE★★★ *Barossa Valley, South Australia* In 1950, Max Schubert, chief winemaker at PENFOLDS, visited Europe and came back determined to make a wine that could match the great BORDEAUX reds. Undeterred by a lack of Cabernet Sauvignon grapes and French oak barrels, he set to work with BAROSSA Shiraz and barrels made from the more pungent American oak. Initially ignored and misunderstood, Schubert eventually achieved global recognition for his wine, a stupendously complex, thrillingly rich red that only begins to reveal its magnificence after 10 years in bottle. Produced using only the best grapes, primarily from the Barossa, CLARE and MCLAREN VALE, it is traditionally acknowledged as Australia's greatest red. Best years: (2000) 99 98 96 94 (92) 91 90 **88 86 84 83 80 78 76 71 67 66 63 62 55 53 52**.

DOM. DE LA GRANGE DES PÈRES *Vin de Pays de l'Hérault, Languedoc, France* With only 500 cases produced each year, demand is high for the meticulously crafted unfiltered red★★. The white★★ is produced in even smaller quantities. Best years: (red) (2003) 02 01 00 **99 98 97 96**.

GRANGEHURST *Stellenbosch WO, South Africa* Boutique winery with a focused 3-wine range. Pinotage★ is modern, the Cabernet-Merlot★★ has a more Bordeaux-ish appeal, while Nikela★, a blend of all 3 varieties, is owner/winemaker Jeremy Walker's answer to the Cape blend. Best years: (Cabernet-Merlot) 2001 **00 99 98 97 95 94 93 92**.

GRANS-FASSIAN *Leiwen, Mosel, Germany* LEIWEN owes its reputation largely to Gerhard Grans. Both sweet and dry Rieslings have gained in sophistication over the years: Spätlese★★ and Auslese★★ from TRITTENHEIMer Apotheke are particularly impressive. Eiswein is ★★★ in good vintages. Best years: (2004) 03 02 01 **99 98 97 96 95 93**.

YVES GRASSA *Vin de Pays des Côtes de Gascogne, South-West France* Innovative COTES DE GASCOGNE producer, who transformed Gascony's thin raw whites into some of the snappiest, fruitiest, almost-dry wines in France. Grassa also makes oak-aged★ and late-harvest★ styles.

ALFRED GRATIEN *Champagne AC, Champagne, France* This small company makes some of my favourite CHAMPAGNE. Its wines are made in wooden casks, which is very rare nowadays. The non-vintage★★ blend is usually 4 years old when sold, rather than the normal 3 years. The vintage★★★ is deliciously ripe and toasty when released but can age for another 10 years. The prestige cuvée, Cuvée Paradis★★, is non-vintage. Best years: (1997) 96 **95 92 91 90 89 88 85**.

GRATIEN & MEYER *Loire Valley, France* Owner of Champagne house Alfred GRATIEN, Gratien & Meyer is in turn owned by German sparkling wine company Henkell & Söhnlein. In the Loire the company's reputation rests on its Champagne-method SAUMUR MOUSSEUX, particularly its attractively rich, biscuity Cuvée Flamme★ and the Cuvée Flamme Rosé★. Also a producer of still white Coteaux de SAUMUR, red SAUMUR-CHAMPIGNY and a little CRÉMANT DE LOIRE★.

GRAVES AC *Bordeaux, France* The Graves region covers the area south of Bordeaux to Langon, but the generally superior villages in the northern half broke away in 1987 to form the PESSAC-LEOGNAN AC. In the southern Graves, a new wave of winemaking has produced plenty of clean, bone-dry white wines with lots of snappy freshness, as well as more complex soft, nutty barrel-aged whites, and some juicy, quick-drinking reds. Sweet white wines take the Graves Supérieures AC; the best make a decent substitute for the more expensive SAUTERNES. Best producers: Archambeau★, Ardennes★, le Bonnat, Brondelle★, Chantegrive★, Clos Floridène★★, l'Hospital, Léhoul★, Magence, Magneau★, Rahoul★, Respide-Médeville★, St-Robert★, Seuil, Vieux-Ch.-Gaubert★, Villa Bel Air★; (sweet) Clos St-Georges, Léhoul. Best years: (reds) **2001 00 98 96 95 90**; (dry whites) (2004) **02 01 00 98 96 95**; (sweet whites) 2003 02 **01 99 98 97 96 95 90 89**.

GRAVNER *Friuli-Venezia Giulia, Italy* Josko Gravner, FRIULI's most zealous winemaker, sets styles with his wood-aged wines. Along with prized and high-priced Chardonnay★★, Sauvignon★★ and Ribolla Gialla★, he combines 6 white varieties in Breg★★. Reds are Rosso Gravner★ (predominantly Merlot) and Rujno★★ (Merlot-Cabernet Sauvignon).

GREAT SOUTHERN *Western Australia* A vast, cool-climate region encompassing the sub-regions of Mount Barker, Frankland River, Denmark, Albany and Porongurup. Mount Barker has been particularly successful with Riesling, Shiraz and Cabernet; Frankland River with Riesling, Chardonnay, Shiraz and Cabernet; Denmark with Chardonnay and Pinot Noir; Albany with Pinot Noir; Porongurup with Riesling. Vineyard plantings have boomed in the past 5 years, especially in Frankland River. Best producers: Alkoomi★, FERNGROVE★, Forest Hill, Frankland Estate★, Garlands★, Gilberts★★, Goundrey, Harewood, HOUGHTON★★, HOWARD PARK★★, Jingalla, PLANTAGENET★★, West Cape Howe★.

GRECHETTO Italian grape centred on UMBRIA, the main component of ORVIETO DOC, also making tasty, anise-tinged dry white varietals. Occasionally used in VIN SANTO in TUSCANY. Best producers: Antonelli, Barberani-Vallesanta★, Caprai, FALESCO★, Palazzone, Castello della SALA.

GRENACHE BLANC A common white grape in the south of France, but without many admirers. Except me, that is, because I love the pear-scented wine flecked with anise that a good producer can achieve. Low-yield examples take surprisingly well to oak. Generally best within a year of the vintage, although the odd old-vine example can age attractively. Grown as Garnacha Blanca in Spain.

GRENACHE NOIR   Among the world's most widely planted red grapes – the bulk of it in Spain, where it is called Garnacha Tinta. It is a hot-climate grape and in France it reaches its peak in the southern RHONE, especially in CHATEAUNEUF-DU-PAPE, where it combines great alcoholic strength with rich raspberry fruit and a perfume hot from the herb-strewn hills. It is generally given more tannin, acid and structure by blending with Syrah, Mourvèdre, Cinsaut or other southern French grapes. It can make wonderful rosé in TAVEL, LIRAC and COTES DE PROVENCE, as well as in NAVARRA in Spain. It takes centre stage in ARAGON's Calatayud, Campo de Borja and CARINENA, and forms the backbone of the impressive reds of PRIORAT; in RIOJA it adds weight to the Tempranillo. It is also the basis for the *vins doux naturels* of BANYULS and MAURY. Also grown in CALIFORNIA and SOUTH AUSTRALIA, where it has only recently been accorded much respect as imaginative winemakers realized there was a great resource of century-old vines capable of making wild and massively enjoyable reds. In South Africa it is used mainly in Rhône-style blends. See also Cannonau.

GRGICH HILLS CELLAR *Rutherford AVA, California, USA*   Mike Grgich was winemaker at CHATEAU MONTELENA when its Chardonnay shocked Paris judges by finishing ahead of French versions in the famous 1976 tasting. At his own winery he makes ripe, tannic Cabernet★, plummy Merlot★ and a huge, old-style Zinfandel★, but it is his big, ripe Chardonnay★★ that is one of NAPA's best-selling high-priced wines. Best years: (Chardonnay) (2003) 02 01 **00 99 98 97 95 94 91**.

GRIOTTE-CHAMBERTIN AC   See Chambertin AC.

JEAN GRIVOT *Vosne-Romanée AC, Côte de Nuits, Burgundy, France*   Étienne Grivot has settled in to his own interpretation of his father's traditional styles, and has made brilliant wines since 1995, especially RICHEBOURG★★★ and NUITS-ST-GEORGES les Boudots★★. Expensive. Best years: (2004) 03 02 01 **00 99 98 97 96 95**.

GROS *Burgundy, France*   Brilliant COTE DE NUITS wines from various members of the family, especially Anne Gros, Michel Gros, Gros Frère et Soeur and Anne-Françoise Gros. Look out for CLOS DE VOUGEOT★★★, ECHEZEAUX★★★ and RICHEBOURG★★★ as well as good-value HAUTES-COTES DE NUITS★. Best years: (2004) 03 02 01 **00** 99 98 **97** 96 **95** 93 **90**.

GROS PLANT DU PAYS NANTAIS VDQS *Loire Valley, France*   Gros Plant can be searing stuff, but this acidic wine is well suited to the seafood guzzled in the region. Look for a *sur lie* bottling and drink the youngest available. Best producers: Brochet, les Coins, l'ECU, la Grange, Saupin.

GROSSET *Clare Valley, South Australia*   Jeffrey Grosset is a perfectionist, crafting tiny quantities of hand-made wines. A Riesling specialist, he bottles Watervale★★★ separately from Polish Hill★★★; both are supremely good and age well. Cabernet blend Gaia★★ is smooth and seamless. Also outstanding Piccadilly (ADELAIDE HILLS) Chardonnay★★★ and very fine Pinot Noir★★ and Semillon-Sauvignon★★. Best years: (Riesling) 2004 03 **02 01 00 99 98** 97 96 94 93 92 90.

GROVE MILL *Marlborough, South Island, New Zealand*   Export-focused producer. Full-bodied Sauvignon Blanc, rich, smooth Chardonnay★ and fruity Riesling, but I generally find the wines not dry enough to be completely convincing.

CH. GRUAUD-LAROSE★★ *St-Julien AC, 2ème Cru Classé, Haut-Médoc,*
Bordeaux, France One of the largest ST-JULIEN estates, now owned by
the same family as CHASSE-SPLEEN and HAUT-BAGES-LIBERAL. Until the
1970s these wines were classic, cedary St-Juliens. Since the early 80s,
the wines have been darker, richer and coated with new oak, yet have
also shown an unnerving animal quality. They're certainly impressive,
but it is hard to say whether the animal or the cedar will prevail after
20 years or so of aging in bottle. Second wine: Sarget de Gruaud-
Larose. Best years: 2003 02 01 00 **99 98 97** 96 **95 94 93 90 89 88 86 85**.

GRÜNER VELTLINER Austrian grape, also grown in the Czech Republic,
Slovakia and Hungary. It is at its best in Austria's KAMPTAL, KREMSTAL
and the WACHAU, where the soil and cool climate bring out all the
lentilly, white-peppery aromas. Styles vary from light and tart to
savoury, mouthfilling yet appetizing wines equalling the best in Europe.

GUELBENZU *Spain* Family-owned bodega making good Guelbenzu
Azul★, from Tempranillo, Cabernet and Merlot, and rich concentrated
Evo★, mostly from Cabernet Sauvignon. Lautus★★ is made from old
vines and incorporates Garnacha in the blend. Guelbenzu has estates
in both NAVARRA and ARAGON; the wines are non-DO and are labelled as
Vinos de la Tierra de la Ribera del Queiles. Best years: (Evo) 2001 **00 99
98 97 96 95 94**.

GUIGAL *Côte-Rôtie AC, Rhône Valley, France* Marcel Guigal is among
the most famous names in the RHÔNE, producing wines from his own
vineyards in CÔTE-ROTIE under the Château d'Ampuis★★★ label as well
as the Guigal range from purchased grapes (Côte-Rôtie Brune et
Blonde is ★★ since 1998). La Mouline, la Turque and la Landonne all
rate ★★★ in most critics' opinions. Well, I have definitely had
profound wines from La Landonne and La Mouline, and to my
surprise and delight, the considerable new oak aging had not dimmed
the classic Côte-Rôtie beauty and fragrance. However, Guigal is
uniquely talented; lesser producers using this amount of new oak
rarely manage to save the balance of the wine. CONDRIEU★★ (la
Doriane★★★) is wonderfully fragrant. HERMITAGE★★ is also good, ST-
JOSEPH★★ improving, as are the COTES DU RHÔNE★★ (red and white) and
chunky GIGONDAS★. Also owns J-L Grippat and Dom. de Vallouit. Best
years: (top reds) (2004) 03 01 00 99 **98 97 95 94** 91 90 89 88 85 83 82 78.

CH. GUIRAUD★★ *Sauternes AC, 1er Cru Classé, Bordeaux, France* Since
the 1980s this SAUTERNES estate has returned to the top-quality fold,
High price reflects the fact that only the best grapes are selected and
50% new oak used each year. Keep best vintages for 10 years or more.
Second wine (dry): G de Guiraud. Best years: 2003 02 01 **99 98 97 96
95 90 89 88 86**.

GUNDERLOCH *Nackenheim, Rheinhessen, Germany* Fritz and Agnes
Hasselbach's estate has become one of Germany's best. Sensationally
concentrated and luscious Beerenauslese★★★ and Trockenbeeren-
auslese★★★ dessert Rieslings are expensive for RHEINHESSEN, but worth
it. Dry and off-dry Rieslings, at least ★, however, are good value. Late-
harvest Spätlese and Auslese are ★★ year in, year out. Best years:
(2004) 03 02 01 00 **99 98 97 96 95 93 92 90 89**.

GUNDLACH-BUNDSCHU *Sonoma Valley AVA, California, USA* Family-
owned winery, founded in 1858. From the Rhinefarm Vineyards come
outstanding juicy, fruity Cabernet Sauvignon★★, rich and tightly

structured Merlot★★, Zinfandel★ and Pinot Noir★. Whites include Chardonnay★, attractive Riesling and lush Gewürztraminer★★. The Bundschu family also operates the boutique winery Bartholomew Park, which specializes in Cabernet blends.

FRITZ HAAG *Brauneberg, Mosel, Germany* MOSEL grower with vineyards in the BRAUNEBERGER Juffer and Brauneberger Juffer Sonnenuhr. Pure, elegant Rieslings at least ★★ quality, Auslese reaching ★★ or ★★★. Best years: (2004) 03 02 01 **99 98 97 96 95 90 88 85**.

REINHOLD HAART *Piesport, Mosel, Germany* Theo Haart produces sensational Rieslings – with blackcurrant, peach and citrus aromas – from the great Piesporter Goldtröpfchen vineyard. Ausleses are usually ★★★, but 2003 suffered a bit from heat stress. Best years: (2004) 02 01 00 **98 97 96 95 94 93 90**.

HAMILTON RUSSELL VINEYARDS *Walker Bay WO, South Africa* Anthony Hamilton Russell is fanatical about reflecting the farm's terroir in his Pinot Noir and Chardonnay. Pinot Noir★ has pure fruit and is well structured, while Chardonnay★ maintains the house style of minerally restraint. Pinotage (Southern Right★ and new Ashbourne★)

is another focus. A zingy, easy-drinking Sauvignon Blanc appears under the Southern Right label. Best years: (Pinot Noir) (2004) **03 02 01 00 99 98 97 96 95**; (Chardonnay) 2004 **03 02 01 00 99 98 97 96**.

HANDLEY *Mendocino County, California, USA* Outstanding producer of sparkling wines, including one of California's best Brut Rosés★ and a delicious Blanc de Blancs★★. An aromatic Gewürztraminer★★ is one of the state's finest. Two bottlings of Chardonnay, from the DRY CREEK VALLEY★ and ANDERSON VALLEY★, are worth seeking out. The Anderson Valley estate Pinot Noirs (regular★, Reserve★★) are in a lighter, more subtle style. A new Syrah★ is excellent. Best years: (Pinot Noir Reserve) 2001 00 **99 98 96**.

HANGING ROCK *Macedon Ranges, Victoria, Australia* Highly individual, gutsy sparkling wine, Macedon Cuvée★★ stands out at John and Anne (née TYRRELL) Ellis's ultra-cool-climate vineyard high in the Macedon Ranges. Tangy estate-grown 'The Jim Jim' Sauvignon Blanc★★ is mouthwatering stuff, while HEATHCOTE Shiraz★★ is the best red.

HARDY WINE COMPANY *McLaren Vale, South Australia* Despite the takeover of BRL Hardy by American giant Constellation, wines under the Hardys flagship label so far still taste reassuringly Australian. Varietals under the Siegersdorf, Nottage Hill and Tintara (Shiraz★★, Grenache★) labels are among Australia's most reliably good gluggers. Top of the tree are the commemorative Eileen Hardy Shiraz★★★ and Thomas Hardy Cabernet★★★, both dense reds for hedonists. Eileen Hardy Chardonnay★★ is more elegant and focused than it used to be. Also 'ecologically aware' Banrock Station, inexpensive Insignia wines, good-value Omni sparkling wine and top-quality Arras fizz★★. Best years: (Eileen Hardy Shiraz) 2002 01 00 98 **97** 96 **95** 93 88 87 81 79 70.

HARLAN ESTATE *Oakville AVA, California, USA* Estate in the western hills of OAKVILLE, whose BORDEAUX blend has become one of CALIFORNIA's most sought-after reds. Full-bodied and rather tannic, Harlan Estate★★★ offers layers of ripe black fruits and heaps of new French oak. Rough upon release, the wine is built to develop for 10 years.

HARTENBERG ESTATE *Stellenbosch WO, South Africa* Consultant Alberto Antonini is helping this winery to turn the corner. Shiraz★ (Gravel Hill★★) leads the field; Merlot★, Cabernet and Pinotage also perform well in the warm Bottelary Hills. Whites include a firm, flavoursome Chardonnay and an off-dry, limy Riesling★. Best years: (premium reds) **2002 01 00 98 97 96 95**.

HARTFORD FAMILY *Russian River AVA, California, USA* Very limited-production wines from RUSSIAN RIVER and SONOMA COAST fruit bear the Hartford Court label. Pinot Noirs include the stylish Marin County★★ and massive Arrendell Vineyard★★★. Seascape Vineyard Chardonnay★★ has textbook cool-climate intensity and acidity. Hartford label wines are blended from various sources. Sonoma Coast bottlings of Chardonnay★ and Pinot Noir★ are deeply flavoured and good value. Old-vine Zinfandels include Highwire★ and Fanucchi-Wood Road★★.

HARTWELL *Stags Leap District AVA, Napa Valley, California, USA* Wine collector Bob Hartwell has been producing a gloriously fruity and elegant Cabernet Sauvignon★★★ from his small vineyard in the Stags Leap District since 1993. Recently, an equally supple Merlot★★ and lower-priced Mistique★ have been added. Best years: (Cabernet Sauvignon) (2002) 01 **00 99 98 97 96 94**.

HATTENHEIM *Rheingau, Germany* Fine RHEINGAU village with 13 vineyard sites, including a share of the famous Marcobrunn vineyard. Best producers: SCHLOSS REINHARTSHAUSEN★★, Schloss Schönborn★. Best years: (2004) 03 02 01 00 **99 98 96 95 94 93 90**.

CH. HAUT-BAGES-LIBÉRAL★ *Pauillac AC, 5ème Cru Classé, Haut-Médoc, Bordeaux, France* Little-known PAUILLAC property that has quietly been gathering plaudits for some years now: loads of unbridled delicious fruit, a positively hedonistic style – and its lack of renown keeps the price just about reasonable. The wines will age well, especially the latest vintages. Best years: 2003 02 01 00 **99 98 96 95 94 93 90**.

CH. HAUT-BAILLY★★ *Pessac-Léognan AC, Cru Classé de Graves, Bordeaux, France* The softest and most charming among the GRAVES Classed Growths, which has been on good form right through the 1990s. Drinkable very early, but ages well. Second wine: la Parde-de-Haut-Bailly. Best years: 2003 02 01 00 **99** 98 96 **95 93 90 89 88 86 85 83 82**.

CH. HAUT-BATAILLEY★ *Pauillac AC, 5ème Cru Classé, Haut-Médoc, Bordeaux, France* Despite being owned by the Borie family of DUCRU-BEAUCAILLOU, this estate has produced too many wines that are light, pleasant, attractively spicy, but lacking real class and concentration. Recent vintages have shown improvement and the wine is becoming a bit more substantial. Best years: 2003 02 00 **99 96 95 90 89 85 83 82**.

CH. HAUT-BRION *Pessac-Léognan AC, 1er Cru Classé, Graves, Bordeaux, France* The only Bordeaux property outside the MEDOC and SAUTERNES to be included in the 1855 Classification, when it was accorded First Growth status. The excellent gravel-based vineyard is now part of Bordeaux's suburbs. The red wine★★★ almost always deserves its status. There is also a small amount of white★★★ which, at its best, is magically rich yet marvellously dry, blossoming out over 5–10 years. Second wine: (red) Bahans-Haut-Brion. Best years: (red) 2003 02 01 00 99 98 96 **95 94 93 90 89 88 86 85**; (white) 2003 02 01 00 **99 98 96 95**.

CH. HAUT-MARBUZET★★ *St-Estèphe AC, Cru Bourgeois, Haut-Médoc, Bordeaux, France* Impressive ST-ESTEPHE wine with great, rich, mouthfilling blasts of flavour and lots of new oak. Best years: 2003 02 01 00 **99** 98 **97 96 95 94 93 90 89 88 86 85 83 82**.

HAUT-MÉDOC AC *Bordeaux, France*   The finest gravelly soil is here in the
southern half of the MEDOC peninsula; this AC covers all the decent
vineyard land not included in the 6 village ACs (MARGAUX, MOULIS, LISTRAC,
ST-JULIEN, PAUILLAC and ST-ESTEPHE). Wines vary in quality and style. Best
producers: Beaumont, Belgrave★, Bernadotte★, Cambon la Pelouse★,
Camensac★, CANTEMERLE★, Charmail★, Cissac★, Citran★, Coufran, la
LAGUNE★, Lanessan★, Malescasse★, Maucamps★, Peyrabon★, Sénéjac★,
SOCIANDO-MALLET★★, la   Tour-Carnet★,   la   Tour-du-Haut-Moulin★,
Villegeorge. Best years: 2003 02 **01 00 96 95 94 90 89 88 86 85.**

HAUT-MONTRAVEL AC   See Montravel AC.

HAUTES-CÔTES DE BEAUNE AC See Bourgogne-Hautes-Côtes de Beaune AC.

HAUTES-CÔTES DE NUITS AC See Bourgogne-Hautes-Côtes de Nuits AC.

HAWKES BAY *North Island, New Zealand*   One of New Zealand's most
prestigious wine regions. The high number of sunshine hours, moderately
predictable weather during ripening and a complex array of soil patterns
make it ideal for a wide range of winemaking styles. Traditionally known
for Cabernet Sauvignon and, particularly, Merlot, it has recently produced
some superb Syrahs. Free-draining Gimblett Gravels area is especially
promising. Best producers: Alpha Domus★★, CHURCH ROAD★, Clearview★,
CRAGGY RANGE★★, Esk Valley★★, Matariki★, MATUA VALLEY★, MORTON ESTATE★,
Newton-Forrest★, NGATARAWA★, C J PASK★, Sacred Hill★, SILENI★, Stonecroft★,
TE MATA★★, Trinity Hill★, Unison★★, Vidal★★, VILLA MARIA★★. Best years:
(premium reds) **2002 00 99 98 96 95 94.**

HEATHCOTE *Central Victoria, Australia*   A recent breakaway from the
BENDIGO region. Its unique feature is the deep russet Cambrian soil,
formed more than 600 million years ago, which is found on the best
sites and is proving ideal for Shiraz. Established wineries include Jasper
Hill★★, Heathcote★★ and Wild Duck Creek★, while BROWN BROTHERS
and TYRRELL'S (Rufus Stone★★ is outstanding) have extensive new
vineyards. Best years: (Shiraz) 2003 02 **01 00 97 96 95 94 91 90.**

HEDGES CELLARS *Columbia Valley AVA, Washington State, USA*   Top
wines here are Cabernet-Merlot blends using fruit from prime Red
Mountain AVA vineyards: Three Vineyards★ is powerful and
ageworthy, with bold tannins but plenty of cassis fruit; Red Mountain
Reserve★ shows more polish and elegance. CMS★ (Cabernets-Merlot-
Syrah) forms the bulk of the production. White Fumé-Chardonnay is
crisp and lively. Best years: (reds) (2003) (02) 01 **00 99 98.**

DR HEGER *Ihringen, Baden, Germany*   Joachim Heger specializes in
powerful, dry Grauburgunder (Pinot Gris), Weissburgunder (Pinot
Blanc) and red Spätburgunder (Pinot Noir)★, with Riesling a sideline.
Grauburgunder from the Winklerberg★★ is serious stuff, while his
Yellow Muscat vines deliver powerful dry wines and rare but fabulous
TBA. Best years: (white) (2004) 03 02 **01 00 98 97 96.**

CHARLES HEIDSIECK *Champagne AC, Champagne, France*   Charles
Heidsieck, owned by Rémy Cointreau, is the most consistently fine of
all the major houses, with vintage★★★ Champagne only declared in
the very best years. The non-vintage★★, marked with a bottling date
(for example, Mis en Cave en 2000), is regularly of vintage quality;
these age well for 5 years. Best years: **1995 90 89 88 85 82.**

HEITZ CELLARS *Napa Valley AVA, California, USA*   Star attraction here is
the Martha's Vineyard Cabernet Sauvignon★★. Many believe that
early bottlings of Martha's Vineyard are among the best wines ever

produced in CALIFORNIA. After 1992, phylloxera forced the replanting of Martha's Vineyard and although bottling only resumed in 1996, the 1997 vintage★★★ is exceptional. Heitz also produces a Bella Oaks Vineyard Cabernet Sauvignon★, a Trailside Vineyard Cabernet★ and a straight Cabernet★ that takes time to understand but can be good. Grignolino Rosé is an attractive picnic wine. Best years: (Martha's Vineyard) 1997 96 **92** 91 **86 85 75**.

HENRIOT *Champagne AC, Champagne, France* In 1994 Joseph Henriot bought back the name of his old-established family company. Henriot CHAMPAGNES have an austere clarity – no Pinot Meunier is used. The range includes non-vintage Brut Souverain★ and Blanc de Blancs★, vintage Brut★★ and Rosé★ and de luxe Cuvée des Echanteleurs★★. Best years: (1998) 96 **95 90 89 88 85**.

HENRIQUES & HENRIQUES *Madeira DOC, Madeira, Portugal* The wines to look for are the 10-year-old★★ and 15-year-old★★ versions of the classic varieties. Vibrant Sercial and Verdelho, and rich Malmsey and Bual are all fine examples of their styles. Henriques & Henriques also has vintage Madeiras★★★ of extraordinary quality.

HENRY OF PELHAM *Niagara Peninsula VQA, Ontario, Canada* Winery making concentrated wines from low-yielding vines. Best are Reserve Chardonnay★, Proprietor's Reserve Riesling★, Riesling Icewine★ and a Cabernet-Merlot blend. Best years: (Riesling Icewine) 2003 **02 00 99 98**.

HENSCHKE *Eden Valley, South Australia* Fifth-generation winemaker Stephen Henschke and his viticulturist wife Prue make some of Australia's grandest reds from old vines. HILL OF GRACE★★★ is stunning. Mount Edelstone Shiraz★★, Cyril Henschke Cabernet★★, Johann's Garden Grenache★, Henry's Seven★ Shiraz blend and Keyneton Estate★ are also top wines. The whites are full and intensely flavoured too, led by the seductive, perfumed Julius Riesling★★, toasty yet fruity Louis Semillon★★ and Croft Chardonnay★. Best years: (Mount Edelstone) (2002) 01 99 **96 94 92 91 90 88 86 84 82 78 72 62 59 56**.

HÉRAULT, VIN DE PAYS DE L' *Languedoc, France* A huge region, covering the entire Hérault *département*. Red wines predominate, based on Carignan, Grenache and Cinsaut, and most of the wine is sold in bulk. But things are changing. There are lots of hilly vineyards with great potential, and MAS DE DAUMAS GASSAC★★ is merely the first of many exciting reds from the region. The whites are improving, too. Best producers: Bosc, Capion★, la Fadèze, GRANGE DES PERES★★, Jany, Limbardié★, MAS DE DAUMAS GASSAC★★, Marfée.

HERMITAGE AC *Rhône Valley, France* Great Hermitage, from steep vineyards above the town of Tain l'Hermitage in the northern RHONE, is revered throughout the world as a rare, rich red wine – expensive, memorable and classic. Not all Hermitage achieves such an exciting blend of flavours, but the best growers, with mature red Syrah vines, can create superbly original wine, needing 5–10 years' aging even in a light year and a minimum of 15 years in a ripe vintage. White Hermitage, from Marsanne and Roussanne, is less famous but the best wines, made by traditionalists, can outlive the reds, sometimes lasting as long as 40 years. Best producers: A Belle★★, CHAPOUTIER★★, J-L CHAVE★★★, Y Chave★★, Colombier★, COLOMBO★, DELAS★★ (Bessards★★★), B Faurie★★, L Fayolle★, Ferraton★, GUIGAL★★, JABOULET (la Chapelle★), Remizières, J-M Sorrel★, M Sorrel★★, TAIN L'HERMITAGE co-op★★, Tardieu-Laurent★★, les Vins de Vienne★★. Best years: (reds) 2004 03 01 00 99 98 **97 96 95 94 91 90 89 88 85 83 78**.

THE HESS COLLECTION *Mount Veeder AVA, California, USA* NAPA VALLEY
producer known for its Cabernet Sauvignon★ (Reserve★★), which
shows all the intense lime and black cherry originality of its MOUNT
VEEDER fruit, without coating it with impenetrable tannins. Hess Estate
Cabernet★ is excellent value. Chardonnay★ is ripe with tropical fruit
and balanced oak. Budget label: Hess Select. Best years: (Cabernet)
(2002) 01 00 **99 98 97 96 95 94 91 90**.

HESSISCHE BERGSTRASSE *Germany* Small (455ha/1125-acre), warm
region near Darmstadt. The co-op, Bergsträsser Winzer dominates, but
better wines, especially lovely Eiswein★★ is made by the Staatsweingut.
Riesling is still the most prized grape.

HEURIGER *Austria* Fresh, young wine drunk in the many family-run
taverns in the Viennese hills. These taverns are, not surprisingly,
known as Heurigen.

HEYL ZU HERRNSHEIM *Nierstein, Rheinhessen, Germany* Organic
estate whose main strength is substantial dry whites from the
Riesling, Weissburgunder (Pinot Blanc) and Silvaner grapes. However,
Auslese and higher Prädikat wines of recent vintages have been of ★★
– and sometimes ★★★ – quality. Only wines from the top sites
(Brudersberg, Pettenthal, Hipping, Oelberg) carry the vineyard
designation. Other high-quality dry wines are sold under the
'Rotschiefer' name. Best years: (2004) 03 02 01 **99 98 97 96 93 90**.

HEYMANN-LÖWENSTEIN *Winningen, Mosel, Germany* A leading estate
of the Lower MOSEL. Its dry Rieslings are unusually full-bodied for the
region; those from the Röttgen and Uhlen sites can reach ★★. Also
powerful Auslese. Best years: (2004) 03 02 01 **00 99 98 97 95 94**.

HIDALGO *Jerez y Manzanilla DO, Andalucía, Spain* Hidalgo's Manzanilla
La Gitana★★ is deservedly one of the best-selling manzanillas in Spain.
Hidalgo is still family-owned, and only uses grapes from its own
vineyards. Brands include Mariscal★, Fino Especial and Miraflores,
Amontillado Napoleon★★, Oloroso Viejo★★ and Jerez Cortado★★.

HILL OF GRACE★★★ *Eden Valley, South Australia* A stunning wine with
dark, exotic flavours made by HENSCHKE from a single plot of Shiraz. The
Hill of Grace vineyard was first planted in the 1860s, and the old vines
produce a powerful, structured wine with superb ripe fruit, chocolate,
coffee, earth, leather and the rest. Can be cellared for 20 years or more.
Best years: (2002) (01) 99 98 97 96 95 94 **93 92 91 90 88 86 85 82 78 72**.

HILLTOP *Neszmély, Hungary* Under chief winemaker Akos Kamocsay, this
winery provides fresh, bright wines, especially white, at friendly prices.
Indigenous varieties such as Irsai Oliver and Cserszegi Füszeres line up
with Gewürztraminer, Sauvignon Blanc★, Pinot Gris and Chardonnay.
Hilltop also produces a good but controversial TOKAJI.

HILLTOPS *New South Wales, Australia* Promising high-altitude cherry-
growing region with a small but fast-growing area of vineyards
around the town of Young. Good potential for reds from Cabernet
Sauvignon and Shiraz. Best producers: Chalkers Crossing,
Demondrille, Grove Estate, MCWILLIAM'S (Barwang★), Woodonga Hill.

FRANZ HIRTZBERGER *Wachau, Niederösterreich, Austria* One of the
WACHAU's top growers. Hirtzberger's finest wines are the concentrated,
elegant Smaragd Rieslings from Singerriedel★★★ and Hochrain★★.
The best Grüner Veltliner comes from the Honivogl site★★★. Best
years: (Riesling Smaragd) (2004) 03 02 01 **00 99 98 97 95 94 93 92 90**.

HOCHHEIM *Rheingau, Germany* Village best known for having given the English word 'Hock' for Rhine wine, but with good individual vineyard sites, especially Domdechaney, Hölle (hell!) and Kirchenstück. Best producers: Joachim Flick, Franz KUNSTLER★★, W J Schäfer. Best years: (2004) 03 02 01 99 **98 97 96 94 93 92 90**.

HOLLICK *Coonawarra, South Australia* Ian Hollick makes a broader range of good wines than is usually found in COONAWARRA: irresistible sparkling Merlot★ (yes, *Merlot*), subtle Chardonnay★, tobaccoey Cabernet-Merlot★ and richer Ravenswood Cabernet Sauvignon★. Also attractive Sauvignon-Semillon and good limy Riesling★. Best years: (Ravensood) (2004) (03) (02) 01 00 **99** 98 **96** 94 93 91 90 88.

DOM. DE L'HORTUS *Pic St-Loup, Coteaux du Languedoc AC, Languedoc, France* From a first vintage in 1990, Jean and Marie-Thérèse Orliac have created one of this region's leading estates. Bergerie de l'Hortus Cuvée Classique★, a ready-to-drink unoaked Mourvèdre-Syrah-Grenache blend, has delightful flavours of herbs, plums and cherries. Big brother Grande Cuvée★★ needs time for the fruit and oak to come into harmony. The white Grande Cuvée★ is a Chardonnay-Viognier blend. Best years: (Grande Cuvée red) (2003) **01 00 99 98 97 96**.

HOSPICES DE BEAUNE *Côte de Beaune, Burgundy, France* Scene of a theatrical auction on the third Sunday in November each year, the Hospices is an historical foundation which sells the wine of the new vintage from its holdings in the COTE D'OR to finance its charitable works. Pricing reflects charitable status rather than common sense, but the auction trend is regarded as an indicator of which way the market is likely to move. Much depends on the skills of the Hospices' wine-making, which has been variable, as well as on the maturation and bottling which are in the hands of the purchaser of each lot.

CH. L'HOSPITALET *Côteaux du Languedoc La Clape, Languedoc, France* With his purchase of this domaine in La CLAPE, Gérard Bertrand has entered the big time in the Languedoc. Best wines are the red Extrème★ and red and white Summum★. He also produces one of the top Vin de Pays d'Oc, Cigalus★★, with 50% Cabernet Sauvignon, as well as Les Matins d'Aurore MINERVOIS, a blend of Syrah and Grenache. Best years (Hospitalet Extrème): 2003 01 **00**.

HOUGHTON *Swan District, Western Australia* WESTERN AUSTRALIA'S biggest winery, owned by HARDY, sources fruit from its own outstanding vineyards and from growers in premium regions. The budget-priced Line range includes the popular, flavoursome 'White Burgundy'★ (called HWB in the EU), good Semillon-Sauvignon Blanc★ and Chenin Blanc; also recently improved Chardonnay and Cabernet. Moondah Brook Cabernet★★ and Shiraz★★ are a leap up in quality and even better value. Houghton has had enormous success with its regional range: a Riesling★★ and Shiraz★★ from Frankland River; a MARGARET RIVER Cabernet★★; and some of the best wines yet seen from the emerging PEMBERTON region. The dense, oaky Gladstones Shiraz★★★ and the powerful, lush Jack Mann Cabernet Sauvignon★★★ have also contributed to the burgeoning profile of Houghton. Best years: (Jack Mann) (2003) (02) 01 99 98 **96 95 94**

HOWARD PARK *Margaret River, Western Australia* Howard Park now has wineries at Denmark in GREAT SOUTHERN (for whites) and at MARGARET RIVER (for reds). The classic Cabernet Sauvignon-Merlot★★★ and occasional Best Barrels Merlot★★ are matched by intense, floral Riesling★★ and supremely classy Chardonnay★★. The Scotsdale

154

Shiraz★★ and Leston Cabernet★ are part of a range of regional reds. The Madfish label is good for Shiraz★, Sauvignon-Semillon★ and unwooded Chardonnay★. Best years: (Cabernet-Merlot) (2004) (03) 02 01 99 **96 94 92 91 90 88 86**; (Riesling) 2004 03 02 01 **97 95 92 91 89 86**.

HOWELL MOUNTAIN AVA *Napa Valley, California, USA* NAPA's north-eastern corner is noted for powerhouse Cabernet Sauvignon and Zinfandel as well as exotic, full-flavoured Merlot. Best producers: BERINGER (Merlot★★), DUCKHORN★, DUNN★★★, La Jota★★, Liparita★, PINE RIDGE (Cabernet Sauvignon★), Viader★★★. Best years: (reds) (2002) (01) 00 99 98 97 96 **95 94 91 90**.

HUADONG WINERY *Shandong Province, China* The first producer of varietal and vintage wines in China, Huadong received massive investment from its former multinational joint owners (Allied Domecq) as well as state support. Money, however, can't change the climate, and excessive moisture from the summer rainy season causes problems. Even so, Riesling and Chardonnay (under the Tsingtao label) are not at all bad and Cabernet Sauvignon and Chardonnay in special 'feng shui' bottles are pretty tasty.

HUET L'ECHANSONNE *Vouvray AC, Loire Valley, France* Complex, traditional VOUVRAY that can age for decades, produced using biodynamic methods. Three excellent sites – le Haut-Lieu, Clos du Bourg and le Mont – yield dry★★, medium-dry★★ or sweet★★★ wines, depending on the vintage. New investment from American Anthony Hwang is supporting Noël Pinguet's efforts to raise quality yet another notch. Also very good Vouvray Mousseux★★. Best years: 2004 03 02 **01 00 99 98 97 96 95 93 90 89 88 85 76 64 61 59 47**.

HUGEL *Alsace AC, Alsace, France* Best wines are sweet ALSACE VENDANGE TARDIVE★★ and Sélection de Grains Nobles★★★. The Tradition wines are rather dull, but Jubilee wines can be ★★. Best years: (Vendange Tardive Riesling) (2001) 00 **98 97 96 95 90 89 88 83 76**.

HUNTER VALLEY *New South Wales, Australia* NEW SOUTH WALES' oldest wine region overcomes a tricky climate to make fascinating, ageworthy Semillon and rich, buttery Chardonnay. Shiraz is the mainstay for reds, aging well but often developing a leathery overtone; Cabernet is occasionally successful. Premium region is the Lower Hunter Valley; the Upper Hunter has few wineries but extensive vineyards. Best producers: Allandale★, BROKENWOOD★★, De Iuliis★, Hope★, LAKE'S FOLLY★, LINDEMANS★★, Margan Family, MCWILLIAM'S★★, Meerea Park★, ROSEMOUNT★, ROTHBURY★, Thomas★★, TOWER★, Keith Tulloch★, TYRRELL'S★★. Best years: (Shiraz) 2002 00 99 **98 97 96 94 91**.

HUNTER'S *Marlborough, South Island, New Zealand* One of MARLBOROUGH's stars, with fine, if austere, Sauvignon★★, savoury, Burgundian Chardonnay★, vibrant Riesling★ and sophisticated Pinot Noir★. Also attractive fizz★. Best years: (Chardonnay) 2003 **01 00**.

CH. DU HUREAU *Saumur-Champigny AC, Loire Valley, France* The Vatan family produces an exemplary range of silky SAUMUR-CHAMPIGNY reds. The basic red★ is deliciously bright and fruity. Special cuvées Lisagathe★★ and Fevettes★★ need a bit of time. Jasmine-scented white SAUMUR★★ is exceptional in top years. Decent fizz and occasional sweet Coteaux de Saumur, too. Best years: (top reds) 2004 03 02 **01 00 99 97 96 95**.

INNISKILLIN *Niagara Peninsula, Ontario, Canada* One of Canada's leading wineries, producing good Pinot Noir★ and Cabernet Franc, beautifully rounded Klose Vineyard Chardonnay★ and rich Vidal Icewine★★ and Riesling Icewine★. Another Inniskillin winery is in the OKANAGAN VALLEY in British Columbia. Best years: (Vidal Icewine) 2003 02 **00 99 98 97 95 94 92**.

IPHOFEN *Franken, Germany* One of the 2 most important wine towns in FRANKEN for dry Riesling and Silvaner. Both are powerful, with a pronounced earthiness. Best producers: JULIUSSPITAL★, Johann Ruck★, Hans Wirsching★. Best years: (2004) 03 02 **01 00 99 98 97 94**.

IRANCY AC *Burgundy, France* This northern outpost of vineyards, just south-west of CHABLIS, is an unlikely champion of the clear, pure flavours of the Pinot Noir grape. But red Irancy can be delicate and lightly touched by the ripeness of plums and strawberries, and can age well. Best producers: Bienvenu, J-M BROCARD, Cantin, A & J-P Colinot★, Delaloge, Patrice Fort★. Best years: (2004) **03 02 99**.

IRON HORSE VINEYARDS *Sonoma County, California, USA* Outstanding sparkling wines with vintage Brut★★ and Blanc de Blancs★★ delicious on release but highly suitable for aging. The Brut LD★★★ (Late Disgorged) is a heavenly mouthful of sparkling wine – yeasty and complex. Wedding Cuvée★ blanc de noirs and Brut Rosé★ complete the line-up. Table wines include a lovely Pinot Noir★★, a barrel-fermented Chardonnay★ and a seductive Viognier★★.

IROULÉGUY AC *South-West France* A small AC in the Basque Pyrenees. Cabernet Sauvignon, Cabernet Franc and Tannat give robust reds that are softer than MADIRAN. Whites are made from Petit Courbu and Manseng. Best producers: Arretxea★, Brana★, Etxegaraya, Ilarria★, Irouléguy co-op (Mignaberry★). Best years: (reds) 2003 **01 00 98 97 96** .

ISABEL ESTATE *Marlborough, South Island, New Zealand* Grapegrowers (for CLOUDY BAY) turned winemakers Michael and Robyn Tiller are blazing a trail with Sauvignon Blanc★★ that equals the country's best. Aromatic, plum-and-cherry Pinot Noir★★, stylish, concentrated Chardonnay★★ and aromatic Riesling★ and Pinot Gris★ complete the impressive line-up. Best years: (Pinot Noir) (2003) **01 00 99 98**.

ISOLE E OLENA *Chianti Classico DOCG, Tuscany, Italy* Paolo De Marchi has long been one of the pacesetters in CHIANTI CLASSICO. His Chianti Classico★★★, characterized by clean, elegant and spicily perfumed fruit, excels in every vintage. The powerful SUPER-TUSCAN Cepparello★★★, made from 100% Sangiovese, is the top wine. Excellent Syrah★★, Cabernet Sauvignon★★★, Chardonnay★★ and VIN SANTO★★★. Best years: (Cepparello) (2004) (03) 01 00 99 **98 97 96 95 93 90 88**.

CH. D'ISSAN★ *Margaux AC, 3ème Cru Classé, Haut-Médoc, Bordeaux, France* This loosely moated property has disappointed me far too often in the past but pulled its socks up in the 90s. When successful, the wine can be one of the most delicate and scented in the MARGAUX AC. Best years: 2003 02 01 00 **99 98 96 95 90 89 85**.

PAUL JABOULET AÎNÉ *Rhône Valley, France* During the 1970s, Jaboulet led the way in raising the world's awareness of the great quality of RHONE wines, yet during the 80s the quality faltered, and though many of the wines are still good, they are no longer the star in any appellation. Best wines are top red HERMITAGE la Chapelle★ (this was a ★★★ wine in its heyday) and white Chevalier de Stérimberg★★. CROZES-HERMITAGE Thalabert★ is famous, but occasional release Vieilles Vignes★★ is much better nowadays, as are whites Mule Blanche★ and

Raymond Roure★. Attractive CORNAS Dom. St-Pierre★, reliable COTES DU RHONE Parallèle 45, good value COTES DU VENTOUX★ and sweet, perfumed MUSCAT DE BEAUMES-DE-VENISE★★. Best years: (la Chapelle) 2004 03 01 99 98 **97 96 95 94 91 90 89 88 78**.

JACKSON ESTATE *Marlborough, South Island, New Zealand* An established grapegrower with vineyards in MARLBOROUGH's most prestigious district, Jackson Estate turned its hand to winemaking in 1991, making tangy, appley Sauvignon Blanc★★ that improves with a little age, restrained Chardonnay and Pinot Noir★ and complex traditional-method fizz★. Best years: (Sauvignon Blanc) **2005 04 03 02 01 00**.

JACQUESSON *Champagne AC, Champagne, France* Top-class small producer that distanced itself further from the crowd by making its non-vintage a one-off that will change each year. Cuvée No 728★★ is based on the 2000 harvest. Cuvée 729★★, based on the 2001 harvest, was launched in January 2005. Cuvées that follow will represent the best possible blend from each harvest. The vintage Blanc de Blancs★★ and vintage Signature Brut★★★ are classic wines. Best years: (1997) 96 95 **93 90 89 88 85**.

LOUIS JADOT *Beaune, Burgundy, France* A leading merchant based in Beaune with a broad range matched only by DROUHIN, and with rights to some estate wines of the Duc de Magenta★★. Jadot has extensive vineyard holdings for red wines, but it is the firm's whites that have earned its reputation. Excellent in Grands Crus like BATARD-MONTRACHET★★★ and CORTON-CHARLEMAGNE★★, but Jadot also shows a more egalitarian side by producing good wines in lesser ACs like ST-AUBIN★ and RULLY★. Recent developments have included the purchase of top vineyards in the Beaujolais region, such as Ch. de Jacques★ in MOULIN-A-VENT. Best years: (top reds) (2004) 03 02 01 **00** 99 **98 97 96 95 93 90**.

JAMET★★★ *Côte-Rôtie AC, Rhône Valley, France* Jean-Paul and Jean-Luc Jamet are 2 of the most talented growers of COTE-ROTIE. Since they took over from their brilliant father, the wines, led by the marvellous Côte Brune, have actually improved. They age well for a decade-plus. Best years: 2004 03 01 00 99 **98 97 96 95 94 91 90 89 88**.

JARDIN See Jordan, South Africa.

JARDIN DE LA FRANCE, VIN DE PAYS DU *Loire Valley, France* This vin de pays covers most of the LOIRE VALLEY, and annual production often exceeds 80 million bottles – mostly of white wine, from Chenin Blanc and Sauvignon Blanc, and usually fairly cheap to buy. There is an increasing amount of good Chardonnay made here, as well as one or two pricy appellation-busting reds. Is the era of the super-Loires dawning? Best producers: Ampelidae, BOUVET-LADUBAY, Adéâ Consules, l'ECU, Henry Marionnet, RAGOTIERE.

JASNIÈRES AC *Loire Valley, France* Tiny AC north of Tours making long-lived, bone-dry whites from Chenin Blanc. Sweet wine may be made in good years. Best producers: Bellivière★★, J Gigou★★. Best years: 2004 03 02 **01 99 97 96 95 93 92 90 89**.

ROBERT JAYER-GILLES *Côte de Nuits, Burgundy, France* Expensive but sought-after wines, heavily dominated by new oak. Good ALIGOTE★, wonderful HAUTES-COTES DE NUITS Blanc★★, and sensuous reds, including ECHEZEAUX★★★ and NUITS-ST-GEORGES les Damodes★★. Best years: (top reds) (2004) 03 02 00 99 **97 96 95**.

JEREZ Y MANZANILLA DO/SHERRY See pages 158–9.

157

JEREZ Y MANZANILLA DO/SHERRY

Andalucía, Spain

The Spanish now own the name outright. At least in the EU, the only wines that can be sold as sherry come from the triangle of vineyard land between the Andalucian towns of Jerez de la Frontera (inland), and Sanlúcar de Barrameda and Puerto de Santa María (by the sea). New agreements signed by the EU are phasing out such other appellations as South African Sherry.

The best sherries can be spectacular. Three main factors contribute to the high quality potential of wines from this region: the chalky-spongy albariza soil where the best vines grow, the Palomino Fino grape – unexciting for table wines but potentially great once transformed by the sherry-making processes – and a natural yeast called flor. All sherry must be a minimum of 3 years old, but fine sherries age in barrel for much longer. Sherries must be blended through a solera system. About a third of the wine from the oldest barrels is bottled, and the barrels topped up with slightly younger wine from another set of barrels and so on, for a minimum of 3 sets of barrels. The idea is that the younger wine takes on the character of older wine, as well as keeping the blend refreshed.

MAIN SHERRY STYLES

Fino and manzanilla Fino sherries derive their extraordinary, tangy, pungent flavours from flor. Young, newly fermented wines destined for these styles of sherry are deliberately fortified very sparingly to just 15–15.5% alcohol before being put in barrels for their minimum of 3 years' maturation. The thin, soft, oatmeal-coloured mush of flor grows on the surface of the wines, protecting them from the air (and therefore keeping them pale) and giving them a characteristic sharp, pungent tang. The addition of younger wine each year feeds the flor, maintaining an even layer. Manzanillas are fino-style wines that have matured in the cooler seaside conditions of Sanlúcar de Barrameda, where the flor grows thickest and the fine, salty tang is most accentuated.

Amontillado True amontillados are fino sherries that have continued to age after the flor has died (after about 5 years) and so finish their aging period in contact with air. These should all be bone dry. Medium-sweet amontillados are concoctions in which the dry sherry is sweetened with mistela, a blend of grape juice and alcohol.

Oloroso This type of sherry is strongly fortified after fermentation to deter the growth of flor. Olorosos therefore mature in barrel in contact with the air, which gradually darkens them while they develop rich, intense, nutty and raisiny flavours.

Other styles Manzanilla pasada is aged manzanilla, with greater depth and nuttiness. Palo cortado is an unusual, deliciously nutty, dry style somewhere in between amontillado and oloroso. Sweet oloroso creams and pale creams are almost without exception enriched solely for the export market. Sweet varietal wines are made from sun-dried Pedro Ximénez or Moscatel.

See also individual producers.

BEST PRODUCERS
AND WINES

Argüeso (Manzanilla San León, Manzanilla Fina Las Medallas).

BARBADILLO (Manzanilla Eva, Solear Manzanilla Fina Vieja, Amontillado Príncipe, Amontillado de Sanlúcar, Cuco Oloroso Seco, Palo Cortado Obispo Gascon).

Delgado Zuleta (Manzanilla Pasada La Goya).

Díez Mérito (Don Zoilo Imperial Amontillado, Imperial Fino, Victoria Regina Oloroso).

DOMECQ (Amontillado 51-1A, Sibarita Palo Cortado, Fino La Ina, Venerable Pedro Ximénez).

El Maestro Sierra.

Garvey (Palo Cortado, Amontillado Tio Guillermo, Pedro Ximénez Gran Orden).

GONZALEZ BYASS (Tio Pepe Fino, Matusalem Oloroso Muy Viejo, Apóstoles Oloroso Viejo, Amontillado del Duque Seco y Muy Viejo, Noé Pedro Ximénez, Oloroso Viejo de Añado).

HIDALGO (Amontillado Napoleon, Oloroso Viejo, Manzanilla La Gitana, Manzanilla Pasada, Jerez Cortado).

LUSTAU (Almacenista single-producer wines, Old East India Cream, Puerto Fino).

OSBORNE (Amontillado Coquinero, Fino Quinta, Bailén Oloroso, Solera India Oloroso, Pedro Ximénez).

Rey Fernando de Castilla.

Sánchez Romate (Pedro Ximénez Cardenal Cisneros).

VALDESPINO (Amontillado Coliseo, Amontillado Tio Diego, Amontillado Don Tomás, Cardenal Palo Cortado, Inocente Fino, Oloroso Don Gonzalo, Pedro Ximénez Solera Superior).

Williams & Humbert (Pando Fino, Manzanilla Alegria).

159

JERMANN *Friuli-Venezia Giulia, Italy* Silvio Jermann produces non-DOC Chardonnay★, Sauvignon Blanc★, Pinot Bianco★ and Pinot Grigio★. Deep, long-lived Vintage Tunina★★ is based on Sauvignon-Chardonnay but includes Ribolla, Malvasia and Picolit. Barrel-fermented Chardonnay★★ is labelled 'Were dreams, now it is just wine'. Vinnae★ is based on Ribolla; Capo Martino★ is also a blend of local varieties. The wines are plump but pricy.

JOHANNISBERG *Rheingau, Germany* Probably the best known of all the Rhine wine villages, with 10 vineyard sites, including the famous Schloss Johannisberg. Best producers: Prinz von Hessen★, Johannishof★★, Schloss Johannisberg★. Best years: (2004) 03 02 01 **99 98 97 96 90**.

KARL H JOHNER *Bischoffingen, Baden, Germany* Johner specializes in new oak-aged wines from his native BADEN. The vividly fruity Pinot Noir★ and Pinot Blanc★ are excellent, the Chardonnay SJ★★ is one of Germany's best examples of this varietal, and the rich, silky Pinot Noir SJ★★ can be one of Germany's finest reds. Best years: (Pinot Noir SJ) (2004) 03 02 01 **00 99 98 97 93**.

JORDAN *Alexander Valley AVA, Sonoma, California, USA* Ripe, fruity Cabernet Sauvignon★ with a cedar character rare in California. The Chardonnay★ is balanced and attractive. J★ fizz is an attractive mouthful, now made independently by Judy Jordan's J Wine Co. Best years: (Cabernet) (2002) (01) 00 **99 97 96 95 94 91 86**.

JORDAN *Stellenbosch WO, South Africa* Meticulously groomed hillside vineyards, with a variety of aspects and soils. Chardonnays (regular★ with creamy complexity; Nine Yards★★ with classic New World tones) head a strong white range. Cabernet Sauvignon★, Merlot★ and BORDEAUX blend Cobblers Hill★ are understated but deepen with a little age. Sold under the Jardin label in the USA. Best years: (Chardonnay) (2004) **03 02 01 00 99 98 97**; (Cobblers Hill) **2002 01 00 99 98 97**.

TONI JOST *Bacharach, Mittelrhein, Germany* Peter Jost has put the MITTELRHEIN on the map. From the Bacharacher Hahn site come some delicious, racy Rieslings★ including well-structured Halbtrockens★; Auslese★★ adds creaminess without losing that pine-needle scent. Best years: (2004) 03 02 01 **99 98 97 96 94 90**.

J P VINHOS *Terras do Sado, Portugal* Forward-looking operation, using Portuguese and foreign grapes with equal ease. Quinta da Bacalhôa★ is an oaky, meaty Cabernet-Merlot blend; Tinto da Ânfora★ a rich and figgy ALENTEJO red (Grande Escolha★★ version is powerful and cedary); and Cova da Ursa★ a toasty, rich Chardonnay, if now more subdued than previously. Portugal's finest sparkling wine, vintage-dated Loridos Extra Bruto★, is a pretty decent Champagne lookalike, made from Chardonnay. SÓ (which means 'only' in Portuguese, as in 'only Syrah') is characterful if atypical. Also decent Moscatel de SETUBAL★.

JULIÉNAS AC *Beaujolais, Burgundy, France* One of the more northerly BEAUJOLAIS Crus, Juliénas is attractive, 'serious' Beaujolais which can be big and tannic enough to develop in bottle. Best producers: G Descombes★, DUBOEUF★, P Granger★, Ch. de Juliénas★, J P Margerand★, R Monnet★, Pelletier★, B Santé★. Best years: 2004 **03 00**.

JULIUSSPITAL *Würzburg, Franken, Germany* A 16th-century charitable foundation known for its dry wines – especially Silvaners from IPHOFEN and WURZBURG. Look out for the Würzburger Stein vineyard wines, sappy Müller-Thurgau, grapefruity Silvaners★★ and petrolly Rieslings★★. Back on form since 1999, after curiously disappointing 1998 and 97 vintages. Best years: (2004) 03 02 **01 00 99 94**.

JUMILLA DO *Murcia and Castilla-La Mancha, Spain* Jumilla's reputation is for big alcoholic reds, but fruity reds from Monastrell (Mourvèdre) show the region's potential. Whites are mostly boring. Best producers: Casa de la Ermita, Hijos de Juan Gil, Luzón★, Agapito Rico, Julia Roch (Casa Castillo★★). Best years: 2003 **01 00 99 98 96**.

JURA See Arbois, Château-Chalon, Côtes du Jura, Crémant du Jura, l'Étoile.

JURANÇON AC *South-West France* The sweet white wine made from late-harvested and occasionally botrytized grapes can be heavenly, with floral, spicy, apricot-quince flavours. The dry wine, Jurançon Sec, can be ageworthy. Best producers: Bellegarde★, Bru-Baché★★, Castera★, CAUHAPE★★, Clos Lapeyre★, Clos Thou★, CLOS UROULAT★★, Larrédya★, Souch★. Best years: (sweet) (2003) 02 **01 00 99 98 96 95**.

JUVÉ Y CAMPS *Cava DO and Penedès DO, Cataluña, Spain* Ultra-traditional and expensive, but unusually for a CAVA outfit most of the grapes come from its own vineyards. Fruitiest CAVA is Reserva de la Familia Extra Brut★, but the rosé and the top brand white Cava Gran Juvé are also good. Ermita d'Espiells is a neutral, dry white wine.

KAISERSTUHL *Baden, Germany* A 4000ha (10,000-acre) volcanic stump rising to 600m (2000ft) and overlooking the Rhine plain and south BADEN. Best producers: BERCHER★★, Bickensohl co-op, Dr HEGER★★, Karl H JOHNNER★★, Franz Keller★, Königsschaffhausen co-op, Salwey★. Best years: (dry whites) (2004) 02 01 **99 98 97 96**.

KALLSTADT *Pfalz, Germany* A warm climate combined with the excellent Saumagen site results in the richest dry Rieslings in Germany. These, and the dry Weissburgunder (Pinot Blanc) and Muskateller (Muscat), can stand beside the very best from ALSACE. Pinot Noir is also showing it likes the chalk soil. Best producer: KOEHLER-RUPRECHT★★★. Best years: (2004) 03 02 01 **00 99 98 97 96 95 93 90**.

KAMPTAL *Niederösterreich, Austria* 3870ha (9560-acre) wine region centred on the town of Langenlois, making some impressive dry Riesling and Grüner Veltliner. Best producers: BRUNDLMAYER★★★, Ehn★★, Hiedler★, Hirsch★, Jurtschitsch★, Fred Loimer★★, Schloss Gobelsburg★★. Best years: (2004) 03 02 01 **00 99 98 97 95**.

KANONKOP *Stellenbosch WO, South Africa* Beyers Truter, now at BEYERSKLOOF, still casts a friendly consulting eye over Abrie Beeslaar, his successor at this senior-statesman estate. This ensures a smooth continuation of style to the traditional, long-lived red wines. Muscular, savoury BORDEAUX blend Paul Sauer★★ really does mature for 10 years or more. A straight Cabernet Sauvignon★ adds to this enviable red wine reputation; Pinotage★★, from 50-year-old vines, is indelibly associated with the estate. Best years: (Paul Sauer) 2001 **00 99 98 97 96 95 94 92 91**.

KARTHÄUSERHOF *Trier, Ruwer, Germany* Top Ruwer estate which has gone from strength to strength under Christoph Tyrell and winemaker Ludwig Breiling. Rieslings combine aromatic extravagance with racy brilliance. Most wines are now ★★, some Auslese and Eiswein ★★★. Best years: (2004) 03 02 01 99 **97 95 94 93 90 89**.

KATNOOK ESTATE *Coonawarra, South Australia* Chardonnay★★ has consistently been the best of the fairly expensive whites here, though Riesling★ and Sauvignon★★ are pretty tasty, too. Well-structured Cabernet Sauvignon★ and treacly Shiraz★ lead the reds, with flagship Odyssey Cabernet Sauvignon★★ and Prodigy Shiraz★★, reaching a higher level. Best years: (Odyssey) (2003) 02 01 00 99 **98 97 96 94 92 91**.

KÉKFRANKOS See Blaufränkisch.

KELLER *Flörsheim-Dalsheim, Rheinhessen, Germany* Klaus Keller and son Klauspeter are the leading winemakers in the hill country of RHEINHESSEN, away from the Rhine riverbank. They produce a range of varietal dry wines and naturally sweet Rieslings, including succulent Spätlese★ and Auslese★★ from the Dalsheimer Hubacker site. Astonishing TBA★★★ from Riesling and Rieslaner. Best years: (2004) 03 02 01 00 **99 98**.

KENDALL-JACKSON *Sonoma County, California, USA* Jess Jackson founded KJ in bucolic Lake County in 1982 after buying a vineyard there; the operation has since grown to over 4 million cases. Early success was driven by off-dry Vintner's Reserve Chardonnay, but lately the wines have become more challenging. Today's Chardonnays are barrel fermented and oak aged. The three tiers above the Vintner's Reserve line are the Grand Reserve (blends of three appellations); Highland Estates★ (with specific terroir characteristics) and a top level, Stature★★, which started in 2001 with a single meritage-style red wine from Napa Valley. Kendall-Jackson also owns other wineries in California including La Crema (Chardonnay★, Pinot Noir★★) and value-priced Pepi, as well as Chile (Calina), Australia (Yangarra Estate in MCLAREN VALE) and Bordeaux (Château Lassegue in ST-EMILION).

KENWOOD *Sonoma Valley AVA, California, USA* Owned by Gary Heck of Korbel sparkling wine fame, this winery has always represented very good quality at reasonable prices. The Sauvignon Blanc★ highlights floral and melon flavours with a slightly earthy finish, while the Massara Merlot★ offers nice complexity in a subtle style. The range of Zinfandels is impressive (Jack London★★, Mazzoni★, Nuns Canyon★), while the flagship red remains the long-lived Artist Series Cabernet Sauvignon★★. Best years: (Zinfandel) (2002) 01 **00 99 98 97 96 95 94**.

VON KESSELSTATT *Trier, Mosel, Germany* Good Riesling Kabinett★ and rich, fragrant Spätlese★ and Auslese★★ wines from some top sites at GRAACH (Josephshöfer) in the MOSEL, Scharzhofberg in the Saar and Kasel in the Ruwer, but I feel they could do even better. Best years: (2004) 03 02 01 **99 98 97**.

KIEDRICH *Rheingau, Germany* Small village whose top vineyard is the Gräfenberg, giving long-lived, mineral Rieslings. Wines from Sandgrub and Wasseros are also often good. Best producers: Knyphausen★, WEIL★★★. Best years: (2004) 03 02 01 **99 98 97 96 95 94 93 90**.

KING ESTATE *Oregon, USA* OREGON's biggest producer of Pinot Gris and Pinot Noir. Both are made in a user-friendly style but the Pinot Noir is inconsistent. Reserve Pinot Gris★ and Reserve Pinot Noir offer greater depth. Domaine Pinot Noir is a selection of the best barrels and can be good. Best years: (Reserve Pinot Noir) (2004) (03) 02 **01 00 99**.

CH. KIRWAN★ *Margaux AC, 3ème Cru Classé, Haut-Médoc, Bordeaux, France* This MARGAUX estate has shown considerable improvement since the mid-1990s. Investment in the cellars, more attention to the vineyards and the advice of consultant Michel Rolland has produced wines of greater depth and class. Second wine: Les Charmes de Kirwan. Best years: 2003 02 01 00 98 96 **95**.

KISTLER *Sonoma Valley AVA, California, USA* One of California's hottest Chardonnay producers. Wines are made from many different vineyards (Kistler Vineyard, Durell Vineyard and Dutton Ranch can be ★★★; McCrea Vineyard and the ultra-cool-climate Camp Meeting Ridge Vineyard ★★). All possess great complexity with good aging potential. Kistler also makes a number of single-vineyard Pinot Noirs★★ that go from good to very good. Best years: (Kistler Vineyard Chardonnay) (2003) (02) 01 **00 99 98 97 95 94 91 90.**

KLEIN CONSTANTIA *Constantia WO, South Africa* A South African showpiece where winemaker Adam Mason is showing good results after his first year here. The area's aptitude for white wines is reflected in Sauvignon Blanc★ (usually crisp and tangy, though sometimes too ripe), decent Chardonnay, attractive off-dry Riesling★ and Vin de Constance★, a Muscat dessert wine based on the 18th-century CONSTANTIA. In reds, New World-style Shiraz★ looks promising. Best years: (Vin de Constance) **2000 99 98 97 96 95 94 93 92 91 90.**

KNAPPSTEIN *Clare Valley, South Australia* In 1995 Tim Knappstein quit the company, now owned by Lion Nathan, to focus on his own KNAPPSTEIN LENSWOOD VINEYARDS, high in the ADELAIDE HILLS. However, the Knappstein brand is still a market leader, with good Riesling★ and Gewürztraminer★, subtly-oaked Semillon-Sauvignon★, Cabernet-Merlot and Chardonnay, plus the premium Enterprise pair, Shiraz★ and Cabernet Sauvignon★. Best years: (Enterprise Cabernet Sauvignon) (2004) (03) 02 01 **00 99 98.**

KNAPPSTEIN LENSWOOD VINEYARDS *Adelaide Hills, South Australia* Tim and Annie Knappstein sold their KNAPPSTEIN Winery in 1995, but with Lenswood have since exceeded their old reputation with a string of good Sauvignon Blanc★, Chardonnay★ and Pinot Noir★. The Palatine★ is a Cabernet-Merlot-Malbec blend. Best years: (Pinot Noir) (2004) 03 **00 99 98 97 96 95.**

EMMERICH KNOLL *Unterloiben, Wachau, Niederösterreich, Austria* Since the late 1970s, some of the greatest Austrian dry white wines. His rich, complex Riesling and Grüner Veltliner are packed with fruit and rarely fail to reach ★★ quality, with versions from both the Loibenberg and Schütt sites ★★★. They repay keeping for 5 years or more. Best years: (Riesling Smaragd) (2004) 03 02 01 00 **99 98 97 96 95 94 93 92 90.**

KOEHLER-RUPRECHT *Kallstadt, Pfalz, Germany* Bernd Philippi makes powerful, very concentrated dry Rieslings★★★ from the KALLSTADTer Saumagen site, the oak-aged botrytized Elysium★★ and Burgundian-style Spätburgunder (Pinot Noir)★. Philippi is also co-winemaker at Mont du Toit in South Africa. Best years: (Saumagen Riesling) (2004) 03 02 01 **00 99 98 97 96 95 90.**

ALOIS KRACHER *Illmitz, Burgenland, Austria* Unquestionably Austria's greatest sweet winemaker. Nouvelle Vague wines are aged in barriques while Zwischen den Seen wines are spared oak. The Scheurebe Beerenauslesen and TBAs, and the Welschrieslings, Chardonnay-Welschrieslings and Grande Cuvée are all ★★★. Since 1997 Kracher has also made first-rate red wines. Best years: (whites) (2004) 02 01 00 99 **98 96 95 94 93 91 81.**

KREMSTAL *Niederösterreich, Austria* 2175ha (5375-acre) wine region around the town of Krems, producing some of Austria's best whites, particularly dry Riesling and Grüner Veltliner. Best producers: Malat★★, Mantlerhof★, Sepp Moser★, Nigl★★, NIKOLAIHOF★★, Franz Proidl★, Salomon★★. Best years: (2004) 03 02 01 **00 99 98 97 95.**

KRUG *Champagne AC, Champagne, France*   Serious CHAMPAGNE house making seriously expensive wines. The non-vintage Grande Cuvée★★ used to knock spots off most other de luxe brands in its rich, rather over-the-top traditional style. Under new owners LVMH, the style seems to have changed dramatically: it's fresher, leaner, more modern – good, but that's not why I buy Krug. Also an impressive vintage★★, a rosé★★ and ethereal single-vineyard Clos du Mesnil★★★ Blanc de Blancs. Best years: **1990 89 88 85 82 81 79**.

PETER JAKOB KÜHN *Oestrich, Rheingau, Germany*   During the late 1990s Kühn was the rising star of the RHEINGAU, frequently making headlines with his substantial dry Rieslings and full, juicy Spätlese. These wines are usually ★★. Best years: (2004) 03 02 **01 99** 98 **97 96 94**.

KUMEU/HUAPAI *Auckland, North Island, New Zealand*   A small but significant viticultural area north-west of Auckland. The 11 wineries profit from their proximity to New Zealand's largest city. Most producers make little or no wine from grapes grown in their home region. Best producers: COOPERS CREEK★, Harrier Rise, KUMEU RIVER★★, MATUA VALLEY★, NOBILO. Best years: (reds) (2004) 02 **00 99 98 96**.

KUMEU RIVER *Kumeu, Auckland, North Island, New Zealand*   This family winery has been transformed by New Zealand's first Master of Wine, Michael Brajkovich, with adventurous, high-quality wines: a big, complex, award-winning Chardonnay★★★ (Maté's Vineyard★★★), softly stylish Merlot★, complex oak-aged Pinot Gris★ and a newly released premium Merlot-Malbec blend called Melba★★. Only Pinot Noir disappoints so far. Best years: (Chardonnay) **2002 00 99 98 96**.

KUNDE ESTATE *Sonoma Valley, California, USA*   The Kunde family have grown wine grapes in SONOMA COUNTY for at least 100 years; in 1990 they started producing wines, with spectacular results. The Chardonnays are all impressive – Kinneybrook★★, Wildwood★★ and the powerful, buttery Reserve★★. The Century Vines Zinfandel★★ gets rave reviews, as does the peppery Syrah★★, the zesty Sauvignon Blanc★★ and the explosively fruity Viognier★★. Best years: (Zinfandel) (2002) 01 **00 99 97 96 94**.

FRANZ KÜNSTLER *Hochheim, Rheingau, Germany*   Gunter Künstler makes some of the best dry Rieslings in the RHEINGAU – powerful, mineral wines★★, with the Hölle wines often ★★★. The sweet wine quality has been erratic lately, but the best are fantastic. Powerful, earthy and pricy Pinot Noir. Best years: (2004) 03 02 01 **99 98 97 96 94** **90**.

KWV *Paarl WO, South Africa*   The flagship Cathedral Cellar line-up heads a large range. Best are the bright-fruited, well-oaked Triptych★ (Cabernet-Merlot-Shiraz), rich bold Cabernet Sauvignon★ and modern-style Pinotage. Among whites, barrel-fermented Chardonnay shows pleasing fruit/oak balance. Topping everything, and made in very limited quantities, is the single-vineyard Perold, a very ripe, slick, international-style Shiraz lavishly adorned with new American oak. PORT-style fortifieds remain superb value, particularly Vintage★★.

LA ROSA *Cachapoal, Rapel, Chile*   Old family operation rejuvenated by talented winemaker José Ignacio Cancino. The La Palma unoaked Chardonnay★ is pure apricots and figs, and the La Palma Merlot is a delightful easy-drinking style. The La Capitana★ and Don Reca★ labels are a step up in quality and always terrific value.

CH. LABÉGORCE-ZÉDÉ ★ *Margaux AC, Bordeaux, France* Although not situated on the best MARGAUX soil, this property has been cherished and improved by Luc Thienpont from POMEROL. The wine isn't that perfumed, but is well poised between concentration and finesse. Age for 5 years or more. Second wine: Domaine Zédé. A third wine, Z de Zédé, is a simple BORDEAUX AC. Best years: 2003 02 01 00 **99** 98 **96 95 94** 90 89.

LABOURÉ-ROI *Nuits-St-Georges AC, Burgundy, France* Price-conscious merchant, which has lost much of its previous consistency. Now also owner of the emerging merchant Nicolas POTEL. The CHABLIS★ and MEURSAULT★ are very correct wines, and NUITS-ST-GEORGES★, CHAMBOLLE-MUSIGNY★, GEVREY-CHAMBERTIN★, BEAUNE★ and VOLNAY★ can be good.

LADOIX AC *Côte de Beaune, Burgundy, France* Most northerly village in the COTE DE BEAUNE and one of the least known. The village includes some of the Grand Cru CORTON, and the lesser vineyards may be sold as Ladoix-Côte de Beaune or COTE DE BEAUNE-VILLAGES. Reasonably priced reds, quite light in colour and a little lean in style, from several good growers. Best producers: (reds) Cachat-Ocquidant★, Chevalier, E Cornu★, Prince Florent de Merode★, A & J-R Nudant★; (whites) E Cornu, R & R Jacob★, VERGET★. Best years: (reds) (2004) 03 02 **99 96**.

MICHEL LAFARGE *Côte de Beaune, Burgundy, France* The doyen of VOLNAY, with some outstanding red wines, notably Volnay Clos des Chênes★★★, Volnay Clos du Château des Ducs★★★ (a monopole) and less fashionable BEAUNE Grèves★★. BOURGOGNE Rouge★ is good value. Top wines may seem a little lean at first, but will age up to 10 years or more. Best years: (top reds) (2003) 02 99 98 **97** 96 **95 93** 91 90.

CH. LAFAURIE-PEYRAGUEY★★ *Sauternes AC, 1er Cru Classé, Bordeaux, France* One of the most improved SAUTERNES properties of the 1980s and now frequently one of the best Sauternes of all, sumptuous and rich when young, and marvellously deep and satisfying with age. Best years: 2003 02 01 **99 98 97** 96 **95** 90 89 88 86 85 83.

CH. LAFITE-ROTHSCHILD★★★ *Pauillac AC, 1er Cru Classé, Haut-Médoc, Bordeaux, France* This PAUILLAC First Growth is frequently cited as the epitome of elegance, indulgence and expense. Late 90s vintages have been superb, with added depth and body to match the wine's traditional finesse. Second wine: les Carruades de Lafite-Rothschild. Best years: 2003 02 01 00 99 98 **97** 96 **95 94 90 89 88 86 85** 82.

CH. LAFLEUR★★★ *Pomerol AC, Bordeaux, France* Using some of POMEROL's most traditional winemaking, this tiny estate can seriously rival the great PETRUS for texture, flavour and aroma. But a high percentage of Cabernet Franc (50%) makes this a more elegant style of wine. Best years: 2003 01 00 99 98 **97 96 95 94 93 90 89** 88.

LAFON *Meursault AC, Côte de Beaune, Burgundy, France* One of Burgundy's current superstars, with prices to match. From biodynamic viticulture Dominique Lafon produces rich, powerful Meursaults that spend as long as 2 years in barrel and should age superbly in bottle. As well as excellent MEURSAULT, especially Clos de la Barre★★, les Charmes★★★ and les Perrières★★★, Lafon makes a tiny amount of le MONTRACHET★★★ and some really individual and exciting red wines from VOLNAY★★ (Santenots du Milieu★★★) and MONTHELIE★★. Lafon also owns a MACON★ domaine. Best years: (whites) (2004) 03 02 00 99 **97 95 93 92**; (reds) (2004) 03 02 99 98 **97** 96 95 93 **91 90**.

CH. LAFON-ROCHET★ *St-Estèphe AC, 4ème Cru Classé, Haut-Médoc, Bordeaux, France* Good-value, affordable Classed Growth claret. Recent vintages have seen an increase of Merlot in the blend, making the wine less austere. Delicious and blackcurranty after 10 years. Best years: 2003 02 01 00 **99** 98 96 **95 94 90 89 88 86 85**.

ALOIS LAGEDER *Alto Adige DOC, Trentino-Alto Adige, Italy* Leading producer in ALTO ADIGE, making good, medium-priced varietals and pricy estate and single-vineyard wines such as Löwengang Cabernet★ and Chardonnay★★, Sauvignon Lehenhof★★, Cabernet Cor Römigberg★★, Pinot Noir Krafuss★, Pinot Bianco Haberlehof★ and Pinot Grigio Benefizium Porer★. Also owns the historic Casòn Hirschprunn estate, source of excellent Alto Adige blends. White Contest★★ is based on Pinot Grigio and Chardonnay, with small amounts of Marsanne and Roussanne. The red equivalent, Casòn★★, is Merlot-Cabernet based; a second red, Corolle★, and white Etelle★ show similar style.

LAGO DI CALDARO DOC *Trentino-Alto Adige, Italy* At its best a lovely, barely red, youthful glugger from the Schiava grape, tasting of strawberries and cream and bacon smoke. However, far too much Caldaro is overproduced. Known in German as Kalterersee. Kalterersee Auslese (Lago di Caldaro Scelto) is not sweet, but has 0.5% more alcohol. Best producers: Caldaro co-op★, LAGEDER★, Prima & Nuova/Erste & Neue★, San Michele Appiano co-op, Schloss Sallegg★.

CH. LAGRANGE★★ *St-Julien AC, 3ème Cru Classé, Haut-Médoc, Bordeaux, France* Since the Japanese company SUNTORY purchased this large estate in 1983 it has become a single-minded wine of good fruit, meticulous winemaking and fine quality. Second wine: les Fiefs de Lagrange. Best years: 2003 02 01 00 **99** 98 96 **95 94 93 90 89 88**.

LAGREIN Highly individual black grape, planted only in Italy's TRENTINO-Alto Adige region, producing, when not over-oaked, deep-coloured, brambly, chocolatey reds called Lagrein Dunkel, and full-bodied yet attractively scented rosé (known as Kretzer). Best producers: Colterenzio co-op (Cornell★), Graziano Fontana★, Franz Gojer★, Gries co-op★, Hofstätter★, LAGEDER★, Laimburg★, Muri-Gries★, J Niedermayr★, I Niedriest★, Plattner-Waldgries★, Hans Rottensteiner★, Santa Maddalena co-op★, Simoncelli★, Terlano co-op★★, Thurnhof★★, Tiefenbrunner★, Zemmer★.

CH. LAGREZETTE *Cahors AC, South-West France* Splendid CAHORS estate owned by Alain-Dominique Perrin, boss of luxury jewellers Cartier. The modern cellars are overseen by enologist Michel Rolland. There's supple, fruity Moulin Lagrezette, oak-aged Chevaliers and Ch. Lagrezette★, Cuvée Dame Honneur★ and le Pigeonnier★★ are sometimes produced, mainly from Auxerrois. Best years: 2001 **00 99**.

CH. LA LAGUNE★ *Haut-Médoc AC, 3ème Cru Classé, Haut-Médoc, Bordeaux, France* The closest MÉDOC Classed Growth to Bordeaux city. The best vintages are full of the charry, chestnut warmth of good oak and a deep, cherry-blackcurrant-plum sweetness which, after 10 years or so, becomes outstanding claret. Just off the pace recently. Second wine: Moulin de la Lagune. Best years: 2003 01 00 **98 96 95 94 90 89 88 86 85 83 82**.

LAKE'S FOLLY *Hunter Valley, New South Wales, Australia* Charismatic founder Dr Max Lake sold the winery to Perth businessman Peter Fogarty in 2000; the vineyard has been revitalized and the wines, under Rodney Kempe, have reached new levels of excellence and consistency. In best years, austere Chardonnay★★ ages slowly to a masterly antipodean yet Burgundy-like peak. The red★ is rich, complex and fleshy. Best years: (red) (2003) 02 01 00 99 **98 97 96 93 91 89 85 83 81**; (white) (2003) 02 01 **00 99 98 97 96 94 92 91**.

LALANDE-DE-POMEROL AC *Bordeaux, France* To the north of its more famous neighbour POMEROL, this AC produces full, ripe wines with an unmistakable mineral edge that are very attractive to drink at 3–4 years old, but age reasonably well too. Even though they lack the concentration of top Pomerols, the wines are not particularly cheap. Best producers: Annereaux★, Bertineau St-Vincent★, Borderie Mondésir★, Clos de l'Église, la Croix-St-André★, les Cruzelles, la Fleur de Boüard★★, Garraud★, Grand Ormeau★, Haut-Chaigneau, Haut-Surget, les Hauts Conseillants, Jean de Gué★, Perron-La-Fleur, Sergant, la Sergue★, Tournefeuille, Viaud. Best years: 2003 **01 00 99 98 96 95**.

LAMBRUSCO *Emilia-Romagna, Italy* 'Lambrusco' refers to a family of black grape varieties, grown in 3 DOC zones on the plains of Emilia and 1 around Mantova in LOMBARDY, but it is the screwcap bottles of non-DOC Lambrusco that made the name famous, even though some contain no wine from Lambrusco grapes at all. Proper Lambrusco is a dry or semi-sweet fizzy red with high acidity to partner the rich local foods, such as rich, buttery cheese sauces and salami, and is worth trying (especially Lambrusco di Sorbara and Grasparossa di Castelvetro). Best producers: Barbieri, Barbolini, F Bellei★, Casali, Cavicchioli★, Chiarli, Vittorio Graziano★, Oreste Lini, Stefano Spezia, Venturini Baldini.

LAMOREAUX LANDING *Finger Lakes AVA, New York State, USA* One of the most important wineries in FINGER LAKES. Its Chardonnay Reserve★ is a consistent medal winner, and the Pinot Noir★ is arguably the region's best. Merlot★ and Cabernet Franc★ are also attractive, as are Riesling★ and good, quaffable fizz. Best years: 2003 **02 01 00 99**.

LANDMARK *Sonoma County, California, USA* This producer concentrates on Chardonnay and Pinot Noir. Chardonnays include Overlook★★ and the oakier Damaris Reserve★★ and Lorenzo★★. Tropical-fruited Courtyard Chardonnay★ is lower-priced. Pinot Noirs – from Kastania Vineyard★★ in the SONOMA COAST AVA and Grand Detour★★ from Sonoma Mountain AVA – are beautifully focused.

LANGHE DOC *Piedmont, Italy* Important DOC covering wines from the Langhe hills around Alba. The range of varietals such as Chardonnay, Barbera and Nebbiolo embrace many former vino da tavola blends of the highest order. Best producers: (reds) ALTARE★★, Boglietti (Buio★★), Bongiovanni (Falletto★★), CERETTO★★, CHIARLO★, Cigliuti★★, CLERICO★★, Aldo CONTERNO★★, Conterno-Fantino (Monprà★★), Luigi Einaudi★, GAJA★★★, A Ghisolfi★★, Marchesi di Gresy (Virtus★★), F Nada (Seifile★★), Parusso (Bricco Rovella★★), Rocche dei Manzoni (Quatr Nas★), Vajra★, Gianni Voerzio (Serrapiu★★), Roberto VOERZIO★★. Best years: (reds) (2004) (03) **01 00 99 98 97 96 95 93 90**.

CH. LANGOA-BARTON ★★ *St-Julien AC, 3ème Cru Classé, Haut-Médoc, Bordeaux, France* Owned by the Barton family since 1821, Langoa-Barton is usually, but not always, lighter in style than its ST-JULIEN stablemate LEOVILLE-BARTON, but it is still extremely impressive and reasonably priced. Drink after 7 or 8 years, although it may keep for 15. Second wine: Réserve de Léoville-Barton (a blend from the young vines of both Barton properties). Best years: 2003 02 01 00 **99** 98 **96 95** 90 89 88 86 85 83 82.

167

LANGUEDOC-ROUSSILLON *France* This vast area of southern France, running from Nîmes to the Spanish border and covering the *départements* of the GARD, HERAULT, Aude and Pyrénées-Orientales, is still a source of undistinguished cheap wine, but is also one of France's most exciting wine regions. The transformation is the result of better grape varieties, modern winemaking and ambitious producers, from the heights of GRANGE DES PERES to very good local co-ops. The best wines are the reds, particularly those from CORBIERES, COTEAUX DU LANGUEDOC, MINERVOIS and PIC ST-LOUP, and some new-wave Cabernets, Merlots and Syrahs, as well as the more traditional *vins doux naturels*, such as BANYULS, MAURY and MUSCAT DE RIVESALTES; but we are now seeing exciting whites as well, particularly as new plantings of Chardonnay, Marsanne, Roussanne, Viognier and Sauvignon Blanc mature. See also Bouches-du-Rhône, Collioure, Costières de Nîmes, Côtes du Roussillon, Côtes de Thongue, Fitou, Muscat de Frontignan, Muscat de St-Jean-de-Minervois, Oc, Rivesaltes, Roussillon, St-Chinian.

LANSON *Champagne AC, Champagne, France* Lanson International produces Besserat de Bellefon, Gauthier, Massé and Alfred Rothschild as well as its flagship Lanson brand; it also has an important own-label business. Non-vintage Lanson Black Label ★ is reliably tasty and, like the rosé ★ and vintage ★★ wines, especially de luxe Noble Cuvée ★★, improves greatly with aging. Best years: 1996 **95 93 90 89 88 85 83 82**.

MICHEL LAROCHE *Chablis AC, Burgundy, France* Dynamic CHABLIS producer, with good St Martin Vieilles Vignes ★ and impressive Grand Cru Les Clos ★★★. One of the first Burgundians to use screwtop closures. Also owns MAS LA CHEVALIERE in the Languedoc. Best years: (Chablis) (2004) 03 **02 00 99 96**.

CH. LASCOMBES *Margaux AC, 2ème Cru Classé, Haut-Médoc, Bordeaux, France* One of the great underachievers in MARGAUX, with little worth drinking in the 1980s and 90s. New American ownership and investment might make the difference – there have been improvements since 2001, but there's still work to do. Best years: 2003 02 01 00 **96 95 90 89**.

CH. DE LASTOURS *Corbières AC, Languedoc, France* Large CORBIERES estate, with some exciting wines. There is a white, but the best wines are the reds – particularly concentrated old Grenache-Carignan Ch. de Lastours ★, fruity Cuvée Simone Descamps ★ and oaky la Grande Rompue ★. Best years: (reds) 2003 **01 00 99 98 96**.

CH. LATOUR ★★★ *Pauillac AC, 1er Cru Classé, Haut-Médoc, Bordeaux, France* Latour's reputation is based on powerful, long-lasting classic wines. Strangely, in the early 1980s there was an attempt to make lighter, more fashionable wines, with mixed results. The late 80s saw a return to classic Latour, much to my relief. Its reputation for making fine wine in less successful vintages is well deserved. After 30 years in British hands it returned to French ownership in 1993. Second wine: les Forts de Latour. Best years: 2003 02 01 00 99 98 **97** 96 **95 94 93 90 89 88 86**.

LOUIS LATOUR *Beaune, Burgundy, France* Merchant almost as well known for his COTEAUX DE L'ARDECHE Chardonnays as for his Burgundies. Latour's white Burgundies are much better than the reds, although the red CORTON-Grancey ★★ can be very good. Latour's oaky CORTON-CHARLEMAGNE ★★, from his own vineyard, is his top wine, but there is also good CHEVALIER-MONTRACHET ★★, BATARD-MONTRACHET ★★ and le MONTRACHET ★★. Even so, as these are the greatest white vineyards in Burgundy, there really should be more top performances. Best years: (top whites) (2004) 03 02 **00 99 97 95**.

CH. LATOUR-MARTILLAC *Pessac-Léognan AC, Cru Classé de Graves, Bordeaux, France* The vineyard here is strictly organic, and has many ancient vines. The deep, dark, well-structured reds★ improved considerably in the 90s. Whites★ are thoroughly modern and of good quality. Good value as well. Best years: (reds) 2003 02 01 00 98 **96 95 90 88 86 85 83**; (whites) (2004) 02 **01 00 99 98 96 95 94 93 90 89 88**.

CH. LATOUR-À-POMEROL ★★ *Pomerol AC, Bordeaux, France* Directed by Christian MOUEIX of PETRUS fame, this property makes luscious wines with loads of gorgeous fruit and enough tannin to age well. Best years: 2003 01 00 **99 98 96 95 94 90 89 88 85 83 82**.

LATRICIÈRES-CHAMBERTIN AC See Chambertin AC.

LAUREL GLEN *Sonoma Mountain AVA, California, USA* Owner/winemaker Patrick Campbell makes only Cabernet★★ at his mountaintop winery. This is rich wine with deep fruit flavours, aging after 6–10 years to a perfumed, complex BORDEAUX style. Counterpoint is a label for wine that does not make it into the top-level Cabernet. Terra Rosa is made from bought-in wine and bargain-label Reds has been made from wines from Chile and Argentina. Best years: (2002) 01 **99 98 97 96 95 94 91 90**.

LAURENT-PERRIER *Champagne AC, Champagne, France* Large, family-owned CHAMPAGNE house, offering flavour and quality at reasonable prices. Non-vintage★ is light and savoury; the vintage★★ is delicious, and the top wine, Cuvée Grand Siècle★★★, is among the finest Champagnes of all. Non-vintage rosé★ is good and vintage Grand Siècle Alexandra★★★ is excellent. Best years: 1996 **95 93 90 88 85 82**.

L'AVENIR *Stellenbosch WO, South Africa* Pinotage★★ is the forte of irrepressibly enthusiastic winemaker François Naudé, though Chenin Blanc★, Cabernet★ and Chardonnay★ are also stylish and well made. Best years: (Pinotage) **2003 02 01 00 99 98 97 96 95**.

CH. LAVILLE-HAUT-BRION★★★ *Pessac-Léognan AC, Cru Classé de Graves, Bordeaux, France* One of the finest white PESSAC-LEOGNANS, with a price tag to match. Fermented in barrel, it needs 10 years or more to reach its savoury but luscious peak. Best years: (2004) 03 02 01 00 **99 98 97 96 95 94 93 90 89 85**.

DOMAINE CONSTANTIN LAZARIDI *Drama, Greece* At this state-of-the-art, Bordeaux-inspired winery, winemaker Vasilis Tsaktsarlis makes good use of indigenous and international varieties. Fresh gooseberry Amethystos white★ (Sauvignon Blanc, Semillon and Assyrtiko); a fascinatingly intense experimental Viognier★ with a stunning, oily, peach kernel finish; tasty Château Julia Chardonnay★; and the fine Amethystos Cava★, an oak-aged Cabernet from very low yields.

LAZIO *Italy* Region best known for FRASCATI, Rome's white glugger. There are also various bland whites from Trebbiano and Malvasia, such as EST! EST!! EST!!! DI MONTEFIASCONE. The region's best are red wines based on Cabernet and Merlot or Sangiovese from the likes of Castel de Paolis (Quattro Mori★★), Paolo di Mauro (Vigna del Vassallo★★), Cerveteri co-op (Tertium★) and Falesco (Montiano★★), as well as wines from Casale del Giglio★, Pietra Pinta★ and Trappolini★.

LEASINGHAM *Clare Valley, South Australia* A wing of HARDY, Leasingham is one of CLARE VALLEY's largest wineries, and is well respected. Bin 56 Cabernet-Malbec★ and Bin 61 Shiraz★, once bargains, are rising in price, while Classic Clare Shiraz★★ and Cabernet★ are high-alcohol, heavily oaked, overpriced blockbusters; Bastion Shiraz-Cabernet★ is better value. Riesling★★ can be among Clare's best. Sparkling Shiraz★★ is excellent.

L'ECOLE NO 41 *Columbia Valley AVA, Washington State, USA* The velvety and deeply flavoured Seven Hills Merlot★ from this winery can be good, as can the Cabernet Sauvignon★; a BORDEAUX blend called Apogee★★ from the Pepper Bridge vineyard in WALLA WALLA is more interesting. The best wines are the Semillons: a rich, woody, barrel-fermented★ version and exciting single-vineyard Fries Vineyard Semillon★★ and Seven Hills Vineyard Semillon★★. The Chardonnay★ is pleasant, if simple. Best years: (top reds) (2004) (03) 02 01 **00 99**.

LEDA *Castilla y León, Spain* Small winery launched by a bunch of young wine professionals, including the sons of Mariano García (of VEGA SICILIA and MAURO fame). It has taken the country by storm with its profound red Viñas Viejas★★ from very old Tempranillo vines in small plots throughout the Duero region. Best years: 2001 00 99 **98**.

LEEUWIN ESTATE *Margaret River, Western Australia* MARGARET RIVER'S high flier, with pricy Chardonnay (Art Series★★★) that gets Burgundy lovers drooling. Art Series Cabernet Sauvignon★★ (sometimes ★★★) has improved dramatically since 1998 and exhibits superb blackcurrant and cedar balance. Art Series Riesling★★ is complex and fine, and look out for exceptional Shiraz★★ to come. New labels Prelude and Siblings give Leeuwin pleasure at lower prices. Best years: (Art Series Chardonnay) (2003) 02 01 00 **99 98 97 96 95 94 92 90 87**.

DOM. LEFLAIVE *Puligny-Montrachet AC, Côte de Beaune, Burgundy, France* Famous white Burgundy producer with extensive holdings in some of the greatest vineyards of PULIGNY-MONTRACHET, including les Pucelles★★★, Chevalier-MONTRACHET★★★, BATARD-MONTRACHET★★★ and a tiny slice of LE MONTRACHET★★★. After a disappointing patch, Anne-Claude Leflaive has taken the family domaine right back to the top using biodynamic methods. These extraordinarily fine wines can age for 20 years and are understandably expensive. More reasonably priced wines are due from a new venture in the Mâconnais. Best years: (2004) 03 02 01 00 99 **97** 96 **95**.

OLIVIER LEFLAIVE *Puligny-Montrachet AC, Côte de Beaune, Burgundy, France* Former co-manager of Dom. LEFLAIVE, négociant Olivier Leflaive specializes in crisp, modern white wines from the COTE D'OR and the COTE CHALONNAISE, but standards are far from consistent. Lesser ACs – ST-ROMAIN★, MONTAGNY★, ST-AUBIN★, RULLY★ – offer good value, but the rich, oaky BATARD-MONTRACHET★★★ is the star turn of winemaker Franck Grux. Best years: (top whites) (2004) **03** 02 00 **99 97**.

PETER LEHMANN *Barossa Valley, South Australia* BAROSSA doyen Lehmann buys grapes from many local growers and owns the superb Stonewell vineyard, which contributes to his best Shiraz★★★. Juicy, old-fashioned, fruit-packed reds include Grenache-Shiraz★, Mentor★★ and Eight Songs Shiraz★★. Also lemony Semillon★★ and Chenin★, and dry, long-lived Eden Valley Riesling★★. Bought by California-based Donald HESS in 2003. Best years: (Stonewell Shiraz) (2003) (02) 01 **99 98 96 94 93 92 91 90 89**.

JOSEF LEITZ *Rüdesheim, Rheingau, Germany* Some of the best dry and off-dry Rieslings in RUDESHEIM, especially from the Berg Rottland★★ and Berg Schlossberg★ sites. Many wines offer excellent value for money. Best years: (2004) 03 02 01 00 **99** 98 **97 96** 94.

LEIWEN *Mosel, Germany* This unspectacular village has become a hotbed of the MOSEL Riesling revolution. Nowhere else in the region is there such a concentration of dynamic estates and new ideas. Best producers: GRANS-FASSIAN★★, Carl Loewen★★, Josef Rosch★, St Urbans-Hof★, Heinz Schmitt★. Best years: (2004) 03 02 01 **99 98 97 95 93**.

LEMBERGER See Blaufränkisch.

LENZ WINERY *Long Island AVA, New York State, USA* A leading LONG ISLAND winery going from strength to strength. The Merlot★ is elegant and powerful with soft, balanced tannins; dry Gewürztraminer★ is spicy and tasty. In good vintages the Pinot Noir★ has deep, ripe fruit. Chardonnay★ is mostly good and Cabernet Franc is appealing. Brut-style sparkling wine★ is hard to find, but worth the search. Best years: (Merlot) **2000 99 98 97 96 95**.

LEONETTI CELLAR *Washington State, USA* The Cabernet Sauvignon★★ and Merlot★★ produced here are immense, with concentrated fruit and enough tannin to chew on but not be blasted by. The tiny production is usually sold out within hours. Sangiovese★ is also pretty interesting. Best years: (Cabernet) (2003) 02 01 **00 99 98 97**.

CH. LÉOVILLE-BARTON★★★ *St-Julien AC, 2ème Cru Classé, Haut-Médoc, Bordeaux, France* Made by Anthony Barton, whose family has run this ST-JULIEN property since 1826, this fine claret is a traditionalist's delight. Dark, dry and tannic, and not overly oaked, the wines are often underestimated, but over 10–15 years they achieve a lean yet sensitively proportioned beauty rarely equalled in Bordeaux. Moreover, they are never overpriced. Second wine: Réserve de Léoville-Barton. Best years: 2003 02 01 00 **99** 98 96 **95 94 93** 90 89 88 86 85 83 82.

CH. LÉOVILLE-LAS-CASES★★★ *St-Julien AC, 2ème Cru Classé, Haut-Médoc, Bordeaux, France* The largest of the 3 Léoville properties, making wines of startlingly deep, dark concentration. I now find them so dense and thick in texture that it is difficult to identify them as ST-JULIEN. Jean-Hubert Delon has maintained the same rigorous attitude toward quality since the death of his father, Michel, in 2000. Second wine: Clos du Marquis. Best years: 2003 02 01 00 99 98 96 **95 94 93 90 89 88 86 85 83 82**.

CH. LÉOVILLE-POYFERRÉ★★ *St-Julien AC, 2ème Cru Classé, Haut-Médoc, Bordeaux, France* Since the 1986 vintage Didier Cuvelier has gradually increased the richness of the wine without wavering from its austere style. A string of excellent wines in the 90s frequently show more classic ST-JULIEN style than those of illustrious neighbour LEOVILLE-LAS-CASES. Second wine: Moulin-Riche. Best years: 2003 02 01 00 **99** 98 96 **95 94 90 89 86 85 83 82**.

DOM. LEROY *Vosne-Romanée AC, Côte de Nuits, Burgundy, France* In 1988 Lalou Bize-Leroy bought the former Dom. Noëllat in VOSNE-ROMANEE, renaming it Domaine Leroy, which should not be confused with her négociant house, Maison LEROY, or her personal estate, Dom. d'Auvenay. Here she produces fiendishly expensive, though fabulously concentrated, wines with biodynamic methods and almost ludicrously low yields from top vineyards such as CHAMBERTIN★★★, CLOS DE VOUGEOT★★★, MUSIGNY★★★, RICHEBOURG★★★ and ROMANEE-ST-VIVANT★★★. Best years: (top reds) 2003 02 01 **00** 99 98 **97** 96 **95** 90 89.

MAISON LEROY *Auxey-Duresses AC, Côte de Beaune, Burgundy, France* Négociant tucked away in the back streets of AUXEY-DURESSES, Leroy co-owns Dom. de la ROMANEE-CONTI, though is no longer involved in its management. However, its own cellar contains an extraordinary range of gems, often terrifyingly expensive, dating back to the 1940s and before. Best years: (reds) **1990 85 71 59 49 47 45**.

LIEBFRAUMILCH *Pfalz, Rheinhessen, Nahe and Rheingau, Germany*
Sweetish and low in acidity, Liebfraumilch has a down-market image. It can come from the PFALZ, RHEINHESSEN, NAHE or the RHEINGAU and must be made of 70% Müller-Thurgau, Kerner, Riesling and Silvaner grapes.

LIGURIA *Italy* Thin coastal strip of north-west Italy, running from the French border at Ventimiglia to the Tuscan border. Best-known wines are the Cinqueterre, Colli di Luna, Riviera Ligure di Ponente and Rossese di Dolceacqua DOCs.

LIMESTONE COAST *South Australia* Newly defined zone for south-east of South Australia, including COONAWARRA, PADTHAWAY, Mount Benson, Penola, Robe and Wrattonbully, and plantings near Mount Gambier, Bordertown and Lucindale. New vineyards in this far-flung area have Coonawarra-like terra rossa soil with great potential. Southcorp, Beringer Blass, YALUMBA, HARDY and ORLANDO are all involved.

LIMOUX AC *Languedoc, France* The first AC in the LANGUEDOC to allow Chardonnay and Chenin Blanc, which must be vinified in oak. Production is dominated by the SIEUR D'ARQUES co-op. From 2003 a red Limoux AC was introduced, made from a minimum 50% Merlot. Best producers: Dom. d'Antugnac★, SIEUR D'ARQUES★.

LINDEMANS *Murray Darling, Victoria, Australia* Large, historic company that is a key part of Southcorp and has suffered from their corporate chaos, but beefy winemaking chief Greg Clayfield seems determined to pull things round – in COONAWARRA at least. Wines come from various regions. Best include HUNTER VALLEY Shiraz (Steven Vineyard★); classic Hunter Semillon★★; mineral COONAWARRA St George Cabernet★★; spicy Limestone Ridge Shiraz-Cabernet★★; and Pyrus★★ – a BORDEAUX blend. Also an impressive, if oaky, PADTHAWAY Chardonnay★ and the mass-market Bin Series reds and whites. Best years: (Hunter Shiraz) 2004 00 99 98 **96 94 91** 87 86 83 82 80 79; (Hunter Semillon) 2004 99 98 97 **96 94 91** 90 89 87 86 80 79; (Coonawarra reds) (2004) (03) 02 **01 99** 98 96 94 91 90 88 86.

JEAN LIONNET *Cornas, Rhône Valley, France* Jean Lionnet produces dense, tannic CORNAS★★ in a fairly modern style. The emphasis here is on new oak aging. Because the wines can seem closed when young, it's worth waiting for 6–7 years, especially for his Dom. de Rochepertuis★★. Lionnet also produces impressive COTES DU RHONE★ from his younger Cornas vines, and a little white ST-PERAY★. Best years: (Rochepertuis) 2004 03 01 00 **99 98 97 96 95 94 91 90 89**.

LIRAC AC *Rhône Valley, France* Underrated AC between TAVEL and CHATEAUNEUF-DU-PAPE. Reds have the dusty, spicy fruit of Châteauneuf without quite the intensity. They age well but are delicious young. Refreshing rosé has lovely strawberry fruit, and whites can be good – drink them young before the perfume goes. Best producers: Amido★, Aquéria★, Bouchassy★, la Genestière, Joncier★, Lafond-Roc-Epine★★, Maby, Mont-Redon★, la Mordorée★★, Pélaquié★, Roger Sabon★★, St-Roch★, Ségriès★, Tavel co-op★. Best years: 2004 03 **01 00 99 98 97 96**.

CUVÉE DE LA REINE DES BOIS

Domaine de la Mordorée

2001

L I R A C
APPELLATION LIRAC CONTROLEE

RED RHÔNE WINE
Mis en Bouteille au Domaine
DELORME, PROPRIÉTAIRES RÉCOLTANTS 30126 TAVEL
PRODUCT OF FRANCE

LISTRAC-MÉDOC AC *Haut-Médoc, Bordeaux, France*   Set back from the
Gironde and away from the best gravel ridges of the HAUT-MEDOC,
Listrac wines can be good without ever being thrilling, and are
marked by solid fruit, a slightly coarse tannin and an earthy flavour.
More Merlot is now being used to soften the style. **Best producers:** Cap
Léon Veyrin, CLARKE, Ducluzeau, Fonréaud, Fourcas-Dupré★, Fourcas-
Hosten, Fourcas-Loubaney, Grand Listrac co-op, Mayne-Lalande★,
Saransot-Dupré. **Best years:** 2003 **01 00 96 95 90 89 88 86 85.**

LOIRE VALLEY *France*   The Loire river cuts right through the heart of
France. The middle reaches are the home of world-famous SANCERRE and
POUILLY-FUME. The region of TOURAINE makes good Sauvignon Blanc and
Gamay, while at VOUVRAY and MONTLOUIS the Chenin Blanc makes some
pretty good fizz and still whites, ranging from sweet to very dry. The Loire's
best reds are made in SAUMUR-CHAMPIGNY, CHINON and BOURGUEIL, mainly
from Cabernet Franc, with ANJOU-VILLAGES improving fast. Anjou is famous
for rosé, but the best wines are white, either sweet from the Layon Valley
(now also a source of exciting dry white ANJOU), or dry from SAVENNIERES.
Near the mouth of the river around Nantes is MUSCADET. See also Anjou
Blanc, Anjou Rouge, Bonnezeaux, Cabernet d'Anjou, Cheverny, Côte
Roannaise, Coteaux de l'Aubance, Coteaux du Layon, Crémant de Loire,
Gros Plant du Pays Nantais, Jardin de la France, Jasnières, Menetou-Salon,
Pouilly-sur-Loire, Quarts de Chaume, Quincy, Reuilly, Rosé de Loire, St-
Nicolas-de-Bourgueil, Saumur, Saumur Mousseux.

LOMBARDY *Italy*   Lombardy is a larger consumer than producer. Many
of the best grapes, especially from OLTREPO PAVESE, go to provide base wine
for Italy's *spumante* industry. However, there are some interesting wines in
OLTREPO PAVESE, VALTELLINA, LUGANA and high-quality sparkling and still wines
in FRANCIACORTA.

LONG ISLAND AVA *New York State, USA*   Long Island encompasses 3
AVAs: the Hamptons; North Fork; and the broader Long Island AVA.
People have likened growing conditions to BORDEAUX, and the long
growing season, combined with a maritime influence, does produce
similarities. Certainly Merlot and Cabernet Franc are the best reds,
with Chardonnay the best white. **Best producers:** BEDELL★, Channing
Daughters, GALLUCCIO/GRISTINA, LENZ★, Macari, Martha Clara, Palmer★,
Paumanok★, Pellegrini★, Pindar, Raphael, Schneider★, Wölffer★. **Best**
years: (reds) **2001 00 98 97 95.**

DR LOOSEN *Bernkastel, Mosel, Germany*   Loosen's estate has portions
of some of the MOSEL's most famous vineyards: Treppchen and
Prälat in ERDEN, Würzgarten in URZIG, Sonnenuhr in WEHLEN,
Himmelreich in GRAACH and Lay in BERNKASTEL. Most of the wines
achieve ★★, and Spätlese and Auslese from Wehlen, Ürzig and
Erden frequently ★★★. His simple Riesling is excellent, year in year
out. A joint venture with CHATEAU STE MICHELLE in WASHINGTON is
proving exciting. **Best years:** (2004) 03 02 01 00 **99 98 97 96 95 94 93**
92 90. See also J L Wolf.

LÓPEZ DE HEREDIA *Rioja DOCa, Rioja, Spain*   Family-owned RIOJA
company, still aging wines in old oak casks. Younger red wines are
called Viña Cubillo★, and mature wines Viña Tondonia★ and Viña
Bosconia★. Good, oaky whites, especially Viña Gravonia★. **Best years:**
(Viña Tondonia) 1996 95 **94 93 91 87 86 85 76 54.**

LOUPIAC AC *Bordeaux, France* A sweet wine area across the Garonne
river from BARSAC. The wines are attractively sweet without being
gooey. Drink young in general, though they can age. Best producers:
Clos Jean★, Cros★, Loupiac-Gaudiet, Mémoires★, Noble★, Ricaud, les
Roques★. Best years: 2003 02 **01 99 98 97 96 95 90 89 88 86**.

CH. LA LOUVIÈRE *Pessac-Léognan AC, Bordeaux, France* The star of
PESSAC-LEOGNAN's non-classified estates, its reputation almost entirely
due to André Lurton. Well-structured reds★ and fresh, Sauvignon-
based whites★★ are excellent value. Best years: (reds) 2003 02 01 00 98
96 95 90 89 88; (whites) (2004) 03 02 **01 00 99 98 96 95 94 93**.

STEFANO LUBIANA *Tasmania, Australia* Rising star on the Tasmanian
wine scene. Vintage★★ and non-vintage★ sparkling wines rank with
the best in Australia, the Chardonnay★ is restrained and elegant, the
Sauvignon Blanc shows greengage and passionfruit characters while
the Pinot Noir★ has weight, concentration and a velvety texture.

LUGANA DOC *Lombardy, Italy* Dry white (occasionally sparkling) from
the Trebbiano di Lugana grape. Well-structured wines from the better
producers can develop excitingly over a few years. Best producers: Ca'
dei Frati★★, Ottella★, Provenza★, Visconti★, Zenato★.

LUJÁN DE CUYO *Mendoza, Argentina* The first DO in Argentina,
declared in 1989, with an average altitude of 1000m (3200 ft), Luján
de Cuyo's reputation lies in its magnificent old Malbec vines. Best
producers: Luigi BOSCA, CATENA★★, Cobos★, DOMAINE VISTALBA★, Dominio
del Plata, Finca la Anita, TERRAZAS DE LOS ANDES★★, WEINERT★★.

LUNGAROTTI *Torgiano DOC, Umbria, Italy* Leading producer of TORGIANO.
The Torgiano Riserva (Vigna Monticchio★★) is now DOCG. Also makes
red San Giorgio★ (Cabernet-Sangiovese) and Chardonnay Palazzi★.

LUSSAC-ST-ÉMILION AC *Bordeaux, France* Much of the wine from this
AC, which tastes like a lighter ST-EMILION, is made by the first-rate local
co-op and should be drunk within 4 years of the vintage; certain
properties are worth seeking out. Best producers: Barbe-Blanche★,
Bel-Air, Bellevue, Courlat, la Grenière, Lyonnat★, Mayne Blanc, des
Rochers★, Vieux-Ch.-Chambeau. Best years: 2003 **01 00 98 96 95 90**.

EMILIO LUSTAU *Jerez y Manzanilla DO, Andalucía, Spain* Specializes in
supplying 'own-label' wines to supermarkets. Quality is generally good,
and there are some real stars at the top, especially the Almacenista
range★★: very individual sherries from small, private producers.

CH. LYNCH-BAGES *Pauillac AC, 5ème Cru Classé, Haut-Médoc, Bordeaux,
France* I am a great fan of Lynch-Bages red★★★ – with its almost
succulent richness, its gentle texture and its starburst of flavours, all
butter, blackcurrants and mint – and it is now one of PAUILLAC's most
popular wines. No longer underpriced but it's still worth the money.
Impressive at 5 years, beautiful at 10 and irresistible at 20. Second
wine: Haut-Bages-Avérous. White wine: Blanc de Lynch-Bages★. Best
years: (reds) 2003 02 01 00 **99** 98 96 **95 94 90 89 88 86 85 83 82**.

LE MACCHIOLE *Bolgheri, Tuscany, Italy* Eugenio Campolmi died
prematurely in 2002, having established Le Macchiole as one of the
leading quality estates of the new TUSCANY. Mainstay is Paleo Rosso★★,
a pure Cabernet (from 2001 100% Cabernet Franc). Best known is the
Merlot Messorio★★, while Scrio★★ is one of the best Syrahs in Italy.
Best years: (2004) (03) 01 **00 99 98 97 96 95**.

MÂCON AC *Mâconnais, Burgundy, France* The basic Mâconnais AC, but
most whites in the region are labelled under the superior MACON-VILLAGES
AC. The wines are rarely exciting. Chardonnay-based Mâcon Blanc,

especially, is a rather expensive basic quaffer. Drink young. Mâcon Supérieur has a slightly higher minimum alcohol level. **Best producers:** Bertillonnes, Bruyère, DUBOEUF, LAFON★.

MÂCON-VILLAGES AC *Mâconnais, Burgundy, France* Mâcon-Villages should be an enjoyable, fruity, fresh wine for everyday drinking, but because it is made from Chardonnay, the wines are often overpriced. The name can be used by 43 villages, which may also append their own name, as in Mâcon-Lugny. Co-ops dominate production. Best villages: Chaintré, Chardonnay, Charnay, Clessé, Davayé, Igé, Lugny, Prissé, la Roche Vineuse, St-Gengoux-de-Scissé, Uchizy, Viré. **Best producers:** D & M Barraud★★, A Bonhomme★★, Bret Bros★★, Deux Roches★, E Gillet★, la Greffière★★, LAFON★, J-J Litaud★, Jean Manciat★, O Merlin★★, Rijckaert★, Roally★, Robert-Denogent★★, Saumaize-Michelin★, J Thévenet★★, Valette★★, VERGET★★, J-J Vincent★. **Best years:** (2004) **03 02 00**. See also Viré-Clessé.

MACULAN *Breganze DOC, Veneto, Italy* Fausto Maculan makes an impressive range under the Breganze DOC, led by Cabernet-Merlot blend Fratta★★ and Cabernet Palazzotto★, along with excellent reds★★ and whites★★ from the Ferrata vineyards, but his most impressive wines are sweet Torcolato★★ and outstanding Acininobili★★★, made mainly from botrytized Vespaiolo grapes.

MADEIRA DOC *Madeira, Portugal* The subtropical holiday island of Madeira seems an unlikely place to find a serious wine. However, Madeiras are very serious indeed and the best can survive to a great age. The wine was internationally famous by the 17th century, but modern Madeira was shaped by the phylloxera epidemic 100 years ago, which wiped out the vineyards. Replantation was with hybrid and non-vinifera vines greatly inferior to the 'noble' and traditional Malvasia (or Malmsey), Boal (or Bual), Verdelho and Sercial varieties. There are incentives to replant with noble grapes, but progress is slow (having now crept up to 15% of total plantings). The typically burnt, tangy taste of inexpensive Madeira comes from the process of heating in huge vats. The better wines are aged naturally in the subtropical warmth. All except dry wines are fortified early on and may be sweetened with fortified grape juice before bottling. Basic 3-year-old Madeira is made mainly from Tinta Negra Mole, whereas higher-quality 5-year-old, 10-year-old, 15-year-old and vintage wines (from a single year, aged in cask for at least 20 years) tend to be made from 1 of the 4 'noble' grapes. Colheita is an early-bottled vintage Madeira, which can be released after spending 5 years in wood (7 years for Sercial). **Best producers:** Barbeito, Barros e Souza, H M Borges, HENRIQUES & HENRIQUES, Vinhos Justino Henriques, MADEIRA WINE COMPANY, Pereira d'Oliveira.

MADEIRA WINE COMPANY *Madeira DOC, Madeira, Portugal* This company ships more than half of all Madeira exported in bottle. Among the brand names are Blandy's, Cossart Gordon, Leacock and Miles. Now controlled by the Symington family from the mainland. Big improvements are taking place in 5-, 10- and 15-year-old wines, including a tasty 5-year-old (a blend of Malvasia and Bual) called Alvada★. The vintage wines★★★ are superb.

MADIRAN AC *South-West France* The gentle hills of Vic-Bilh, north of Pau, have seen a steady revival of the Madiran AC. Several of the best producers use new oak and micro-oxygenation, and this certainly helps to soften the rather aggressive wine, based on the tannic Tannat

175

grape. Best producers: Aydie★★, Barréjat★, Berthoumieu★, Bouscassé★★, Capmartin★, CHAPELLE LENCLOS★★, du Crampilh★, Caves de Crouseilles, Laffitte-Teston★, MONTUS★★, Producteurs PLAIMONT, Viella★. Best years: (2003) 02 01 00 **98 97 96 95 94 90**.

CH. MAGDELAINE★★ *St-Émilion Grand Cru AC, 1er Grand Cru Classé, Bordeaux, France* Dark, rich, aggressive wines, yet with a load of luscious fruit and oaky spice. In lighter years the wine has a gushing, easy, tender fruit and can be enjoyed at 5–10 years. Owned by the quality-conscious company of MOUEIX. Best years: 2003 01 00 **99** 98 **96 95 90 89 88 85 82 75**.

MAIPO, VALLE DEL *Valle Central, Chile* Birthplace of the Chilean wine industry and increasingly encroached upon by Chile's capital, Santiago. Cabernet is king and many of Chile's premium-priced reds come from here. Good Chardonnay is produced from vineyards close to the Andes. Best producers: ALMAVIVA★★★, Antiyal★★, CARMEN★, Casa Rivas★★, CLOS QUEBRADA DE MACUL★★, CONCHA Y TORO★★, DE MARTINO/SANTA INES★, El Principal★, Haras de Pirque★, SANTA CAROLINA, SANTA RITA★, TARAPACA.

MAJELLA *Coonawarra, South Australia* The Lynn family are long-term grapegrowers turned successful winemakers. A trademark lush, sweet vanillin oakiness to the reds is always balanced by dense, opulent fruit. The profound Malleea (Cabernet-Shiraz)★★★ is the flagship, while the Cabernet Sauvignon★★ (a succulent, fleshy cassis bomb) and the Shiraz★★ are almost as good and very reasonably priced.

MÁLAGA DO *Andalucía, Spain* Málaga is a curious blend of sweet wine, alcohol and juices (some boiled up and concentrated, some fortified, some made from dried grapes) and production is dwindling. The label generally states colour and sweetness. The best are intensely nutty, raisiny and caramelly. A 'sister' appellation, Sierras de Málaga, was created in 2001 to include wineries outside the city limits of Málaga. Best producers: Gomara★, López Hermanos★★, Telmo RODRIGUEZ★★.

CH. MALARTIC-LAGRAVIÈRE★ *Pessac-Léognan AC, Cru Classé de Graves, Bordeaux, France* A change of ownership in 1997 and massive investment in the vineyard and cellars have seen a steady improvement here since the 1998 vintage. The tiny amount of white★ is made from 100% Sauvignon Blanc and usually softens after 3–4 years into a lovely nutty wine. Best years: (reds) 2003 02 01 00 **99** 98 **97 96 90 89**; (whites) (2004) 03 02 **01 00 99 98 96 95 94**.

MALBEC A red grape, rich in tannin and flavour, from South-West France. A major ingredient in CAHORS wines, where it is known as Auxerrois, it is also planted in the LOIRE where it is called Côt. However, it is at its best in Chile and especially in Argentina, where it produces lush-textured, ripe, perfumed, damsony reds. In California, Australia and New Zealand it sometimes appears in BORDEAUX-style blends. In South Africa it is used both in blends and for varietal wines.

CH. MALESCOT ST-EXUPÉRY★ *Margaux AC, 3ème Cru Classé, Haut-Médoc, Bordeaux, France* Once one of the most scented, exotic reds in Bordeaux, a model of perfumed MARGAUX. In the 1980s Malescot lost its reputation as the wine became pale, dilute and uninspired, but since 1995 it has begun to rediscover that cassis and violet perfume and return to its former glory. Best years: 2003 02 01 00 **99** 98 96 **95 90**.

MALVASIA This grape is widely planted in Italy and is found there in many guises, both white and red. In Fruili, it is known as the Malvasia Istriana and produces light, fragrant wines of great charm, while in TUSCANY, UMBRIA and the rest of central Italy it is used to improve the blend for wines like ORVIETO and FRASCATI. On the islands, Malvasia is used in the production of rich, dry or sweet wines in Bosa and Cagliari (in SARDINIA) and in Lipari off the coast of SICILY to make really tasty, apricotty sweet wines. As a black grape, Malvasia Nera is blended with Negroamaro in southern PUGLIA and with Sangiovese in CHIANTI. Variants of Malvasia also grow in Spain and mainland Portugal. On the island of MADEIRA it produces sweet, varietal fortified wine, usually known by its English name: Malmsey.

LA MANCHA DO *Castilla-La Mancha, Spain* Spain's vast central plateau is Europe's biggest delimited wine area. Since 1995, DO regulations have allowed for irrigation and the planting of new, higher quality grape varieties, including Viura, Chardonnay, Cabernet Sauvignon, Merlot and Syrah; and also banned new plantings of the simple white Airén grape. Whites are never exciting but nowadays are often fresh and attractive. Reds can be light and fruity, or richer. To the east, the top-notch red wine region of Ribera del Júcar has now seceded from La Mancha, to form its own DO. Best producers: Ayuso, Vinícola de Castilla (Castillo de Alhambra, Señorío de Guadianeja★), Blas Muñoz★, Rodriguez & Berger (Santa Elena), Torres Filoso (Arboles de Castillejo★), Casa de la Viña.

DOM. ALBERT MANN *Alsace AC, Alsace, France* Powerful, flavoursome and ageworthy wines from a range of Grand Cru vineyards, including intense, mineral Rieslings from Furstentum★★ and Rosenberg★★ and rich Furstentum Gewurztraminer★★. Impressive range of Pinot Gris culminates in some astonishingly concentrated Sélections de Grains Nobles. Basic wines are increasingly stylish. Best years: (Sélection de Grains Nobles Gewurztraminer) 2002 01 00 98 **97 94 89**.

MARANGES AC *Côte de Beaune, Burgundy, France* AC right at the southern tip of the COTE DE BEAUNE. Slightly tough red wines of medium depth which are mainly sold as COTE DE BEAUNE-VILLAGES. Less than 5% of production is white. Best producers: B Bachelet★, M Charleux★, Contat-Grangé★, DROUHIN, GIRARDIN★. Best years: (reds) (2004) **03 02 99**.

MARCASSIN *Sonoma County, California, USA* Helen Turley focuses on cool-climate Chardonnay and Pinot Noir. Incredible depth and restrained power are the hallmarks here. Tiny quantities of single-vineyard Chardonnays from Alexander Mountain Upper Barn, Hudson Vineyard, Lorenzo Vineyard, Three Sisters Vineyard and Marcassin Vineyard (the last three from SONOMA COAST) often rank ★★★. Best years: (2001) **00 99 98 97 96 95**.

MARCHE *Italy* Adriatic region producing increasingly good white VERDICCHIO and reds from Montepulciano and Sangiovese led by ROSSO CONERO and ROSSO PICENO. Good international varietals such as Cabernet, Chardonnay and Sauvignon Blanc under the Marche IGT are becoming more common, as well as blends with the native grapes. The best include Boccadigabbia's Akronte★★ (Cabernet), Oasi degli Angeli's Kurni★★ (Montepulciano), Umani Ronchi's Pelago★★ (Montepulciano-Cabernet-Merlot), La Monacesca's Camerte★★ (Sangiovese-Merlot) and Le Terrazze's Chaos★★ (Montepulciano-Merlot-Syrah).

MARCILLAC AC *South-West France*   Strong, dry red wines (and a little rosé), largely made from a local grape, Fer. The reds are rustic but full of fruit and should be drunk at 2–5 years old. Best producers: Michel Laurens, Marcillac-Vallon co-op, Jean-Luc Matha, Philippe Teulier.

MAREMMA *Tuscany, Italy*   The name given to the Tuscan Tyrrhenian coast, notably the southern part, which was only discovered wine-wise in the early 1970s, thanks to SASSICAIA. DOCs include (south to north): Capalbio, Parrina, Bianco di Pitigliano, MORELLINO DI SCANSANO, Montecucco, Monteregio di Massa Marittima, Val di Cornia, BOLGHERI. And of course there's IGT Maremma Toscana. In these climes, compared with inland, Sangiovese comes softer and jammier, the Bordeaux grapes thrive and vintages count for much less.

MARGARET RIVER *Western Australia*   Planted on the advice of agronomist John Gladstones from the late 1960s, this coastal region quickly established its name as a leading area for Cabernet, with marvellously deep, BORDEAUX-like structured reds. Now Chardonnay, concentrated and opulent, vies with Cabernet for top spot, but there is also fine grassy Semillon, often blended with citrus-zest Sauvignon. Neglected Shiraz is beginning to bloom. Best producers: Arlewood★★, Brookland Valley★★, CAPE MENTELLE★★, CULLEN★★★, Devil's Lair★★, EVANS & TATE★, Gralyn★, HOWARD PARK★★, LEEUWIN ESTATE★★★, MOSS WOOD★★, PIERRO★★, SANDALFORD★★, Suckfizzle★★, VASSE FELIX★, Voyager Estate★★, Xanadu. Best years: (Cabernet-based reds) 2002 **01 00 99 98 96 95 94 91 90**.

MARGAUX AC *Haut-Médoc, Bordeaux, France*   AC centred on the village of Margaux but including Soussans and Cantenac, Labarde and Arsac. Gravel banks dotted through the vineyards mean the wines are rarely heavy and should have a divine perfume after 7–12 years. Best producers: (Classed Growths) BRANE-CANTENAC★★, Dauzac★, FERRIERE★★, Giscours★, ISSAN★, KIRWAN★, LASCOMBES, MALESCOT ST-EXUPERY★, MARGAUX★★★, PALMER★★, PRIEURE-LICHINE★, RAUZAN-SEGLA★★, Tertre★; (others) ANGLUDET★, Bel-Air Marquis d'Aligre★, la Gurgue★, LABEGORCE-ZEDE★, Monbrison★, SIRAN★. Best years: 2003 02 01 00 **99 96 95 90**.

CH. MARGAUX★★★ *Margaux AC, 1er Cru Classé, Haut-Médoc, Bordeaux, France*   Frequently the greatest wine in the MEDOC. Has produced almost flawless wines since 1978, and inspired winemaker Paul Pontallier continues to produce the best from this great *terroir*. Also some delicious white, Pavillon Blanc★★, from Sauvignon Blanc, but it must be the most expensive BORDEAUX AC wine by a mile. Second wine: Pavillon Rouge★★. Best years: (reds) 2003 02 01 00 **99** 98 96 **95 94 93** 90 89 88 86 85 83 82; (whites) 2002 **01 00 99 98 96 95 94 90**.

MARIAH *Mendocino Ridge AVA, Mendocino County, California, USA*   Boutique winery producing Zinfandel from a vineyard at 600m (2000ft) overlooking the Pacific Ocean. The wines have cherry fruit and naturally high acidity. Mariah Vineyard Zinfandel★★ is the flagship; Poor Ranch★ is lighter but quite elegant. A tiny amount of fruit-forward Syrah★ is also made. Best years: (Zinfandel) (2001) **00 99**.

MARLBOROUGH *South Island, New Zealand*   Marlborough, a wide, flat, pebbly plain around the town of Blenheim, has enjoyed such spectacular success as a quality wine region that it is difficult to imagine that the first commercial vines were planted as recently as 1973. Its long, cool and relatively dry ripening season, cool nights and free-draining stony soils are the major assets. Its snappy, aromatic Sauvignon Blanc first brought the region fame worldwide. Fine-flavoured Chardonnay, steely Riesling, elegant CHAMPAGNE-method fizz and luscious botrytized wines are other successes. Pinot Noir is now establishing a strong regional identity. Best producers: CELLIER LE BRUN, CLOUDY BAY★★, Forrest Estate★★, FROMM★★, GROVE MILL, HUNTER'S★, ISABEL★★, JACKSON ESTATE★, Lawson's Dry Hills★, MONTANA, Nautilus★, SAINT CLAIR★, SERESIN★, Stoneleigh, VAVASOUR★★, VILLA MARIA★★, WITHER HILLS★★. Best years: (Chardonnay) **2003 01 00 99 98 97**; (Pinot Noir) **2003 01 00 99 98 97**; (Sauvignon Blanc) **2005 04 03 01 00**.

MARQUÉS DE CÁCERES *Rioja DOCa, Rioja, Spain* Go-ahead RIOJA winery making crisp, aromatic, modern whites★ and rosés★, and fleshy, fruity reds (Reservas★) with the emphasis on aging in bottle, not barrel. There is also a luxury red, Gaudium★. Best years: (reds) 2001 99 **98 96 95 94 92 91 90 89 87 85 82 78**.

MARQUÉS DE GRIÑÓN *Castilla-La Mancha, Spain* From his estate at Malpica, near Toledo, now with its own Dominio de Valdepusa DO, Carlos Falcó (the eponymous Marqués) produces some sensational wines: minty Dominio de Valdepusa Cabernet Sauvignon★★, Petit Verdot★★, Syrah★★ and the top wine, Eméritus★★, a blend of the 3 varieties. The joint venture with the Arco/BERBERANA group, which developed the Marqués de Griñón wines from RIOJA★, is now being phased out. Best years: (Eméritus) 2001 00 **99 98 97**.

MARQUÉS DE MURRIETA *Rioja DOCa, Rioja, Spain* The RIOJA bodega that most faithfully preserves the traditional style of long aging. Ultra-conservative, yet sporting glistening new fermentation vats and a Californian bottling line. The splendidly ornate Castillo de Ygay★★ label now includes wines other than the Gran Reserva. There's also a more modern-styled, upmarket cuvée, Dalmau★★, and a delicious Mazuelo★ varietal. Whites are dauntingly oaky, reds packed with savoury mulberry fruit. Best years: (reds) 2001 00 **99 96 95 94 92 91 89 87 85 68 64**.

MARQUÉS DE RISCAL *Rioja DOCa, País Vasco and Rueda DO, Castilla y León, Spain* A producer which has restored its reputation for classic pungent RIOJA reds (Reserva★). Expensive, Cabernet-based Barón de Chirel★★ is made only in selected years. Increasingly aromatic RUEDA whites★. Best years: (Barón de Chirel) **1996 95 94**.

MARSALA DOC *Sicily, Italy* Fortified wines, once as esteemed as sherry or Madeira. A taste of an old Vergine (unsweetened) Marsala, fine and complex, will show why. Today most is sweetened. Purists say this mars its delicate nuances, but DOC regulations allow for sweetening Fine and Superiore versions. Best producers: DE BARTOLI★★, Florio (Baglio Florio★, Terre Arse★), Pellegrino (Soleras★, Vintage★).

MARSANNAY AC *Côte de Nuits, Burgundy, France* Village almost in Dijon, best known for its pleasant but quite austere rosé. Reds are much better, frequently one of Burgundy's most fragrant wines. Best producers: R Bouvier★, P Charlopin★★, B CLAIR★★, Collotte★, Fougeray de BeaucIair★, Geantet-Pansiot★, JADOT, MEO-CAMUZET★, D MORTET★★, J & J-L Trapet★. Best years: (reds) (2004) **03 02 99**.

MARSANNE Undervalued grape yielding rich, nutty wines in the northern Rhône (HERMITAGE, CROZES-HERMITAGE, ST-JOSEPH and ST-PERAY), often with the more lively Roussanne. Also used in PIC ST-LOUP and other Languedoc wines, and performs well in Australia at MITCHELTON and TAHBILK. As Ermitage, it produces some good wines in Swiss VALAIS.

MARTINBOROUGH *North Island, New Zealand* A cool, dry climate, free-draining soil and a passion for quality are this region's greatest assets. Mild autumn weather promotes intense flavours balanced by good acidity in all varieties: top Pinot Noir and complex Chardonnay, intense Cabernet, full Sauvignon Blanc and honeyed Riesling. Best producers: ATA RANGI★★, DRY RIVER★★, MARTINBOROUGH VINEYARD★★, Nga Waka★, PALLISER ESTATE★★, Te Kairanga★. Best years: (Pinot Noir) **2001 00 99 98 97 96**.

MARTINBOROUGH VINEYARD *Martinborough, North Island, New Zealand* Famous for Pinot Noir★★ but also makes impressive Chardonnay★, spicy Riesling★, creamy Pinot Gris★ and luscious botrytized styles★★ when vintage conditions allow. Winemaker Claire Mulholland has brought added elegance to the often-blockbuster wines of this high-flying producer. Best years: (Pinot Noir) **2001 00 99 98 97**.

MARTÍNEZ BUJANDA *Rioja DOCa, País Vasco, Spain* Family-owned firm that makes some of the best modern RIOJA. Whites and rosés are young and crisp, reds★ are full of fruit *and* age well. The single-vineyard Finca Valpiedra★★ is a major newcomer. The family has now purchased a large estate in La MANCHA, Finca Antigua. Best years: (reds) 2001 **98 96 95 94 92 91 90 87 86 85**.

MARZEMINO This red grape of northern Italy's TRENTINO province makes deep-coloured, plummy and zesty reds that are best drunk within 3–5 years. Best producers: Battistotti★, La Cadalora★, Cavit★, Concilio Vini★, Isera co-op★, Letrari★, Mezzacorona, Eugenio Rosi★, Simoncelli★, Spagnolli★, De Tarczal★, Vallarom★, Vallis Agri★.

MAS BRUGUIÈRE *Pic St-Loup, Coteaux du Languedoc AC, Languedoc, France* One of the top domaines in PIC ST-LOUP. The basic red★ has rich, spicy Syrah character, while La Grenadière★★ develops buckets of black fruit and spice after 3 years. Calcadiz is an easy-drinking red from young vines. Aromatic, fruity and refreshingly crisp Roussanne white Les Mûriers★. Best years: (reds) 2003 **01 00 99 98**.

MAS LA CHEVALIÈRE *Vin de Pays d'Oc, Languedoc, France* State-of-the-art winery created by Chablis producer Michel LAROCHE in the early 1990s. Innovative wines include La Croix Chevalière★, a blend of Syrah, Grenache and Mourvèdre, and Mas la Chevalière Rouge★, from the estate vineyard. Best years: 2003 **01 00 99 98**.

MAS DE DAUMAS GASSAC *Vin de Pays de l'Hérault, Languedoc, France* Aimé Guibert proves that the HERAULT, normally associated with cheap table wine, can produce great, ageworthy reds. The tannic yet rich Cabernet Sauvignon-based red★ and Emile Peynaud★★ and the fabulously scented white★★ (Viognier, Muscat, Chardonnay and Petit Manseng) are impressive, if expensive. Sweet Vin de Laurance★★ is a triumph. Best years: (reds) (2003) 02 01 00 99 **98 97 96 95 94 93 90**.

MAS JULLIEN *Coteaux du Languedoc AC, Languedoc, France* Olivier Jullien makes fine wines in the COTEAUX DU LANGUEDOC. The red Mas Jullien generally rates★★, while the États d'Ame★ is more forward and fruit driven. White Les Vignes Oubliées★ is also good stuff. Best years: (reds) (2003) 02 01 **00 99 98 97 96**.

BARTOLO MASCARELLO *Barolo DOCG, Piedmont, Italy* One of the great producers of BAROLO★★★, Bartolo Mascarello died in 2005; his daughter Maria Teresa has run the winery since the early 1990s. Though proudly traditional, the wines have an exquisite perfume and balance. The Dolcetto★ and Barbera★ can need a little time to soften. Best years: (Barolo) (2004) (03) 01 00 **99 98 97** 96 **95 93 90 89 88 86 85 82 78**.

GIUSEPPE MASCARELLO *Barolo DOCG, Piedmont, Italy* The old house of Giuseppe Mascarello (now run by grandson Mauro) is renowned for dense, vibrant Dolcetto d'Alba (Bricco★★) and intense Barbera (Codana★★), but the pride of the house is BAROLO from the Monprivato★★★ vineyard. A little is now produced as a Riserva, Cà d'Morissio★★★, in top years. Small amounts are also made from the Bricco, Santo Stefano di Perno and Villero vineyards. Best years: (Monprivato) (2004) (03) 01 00 **99 98 97** 96 **95 93 91 90 89 88 85 82 78**.

MASI *Veneto, Italy* Family firm, one of the driving forces in VALPOLICELLA. Brolo di Campofiorin★ (effectively if not legally a *ripasso* Valpolicella) is worth looking out for, as is AMARONE (Mazzano★★ and Campolongo di Torbe★★). Valpolicella's Corvina grape is also used in red blends Toar★ and Osar★. The wines of Serègo Alighieri★★ are also produced by Masi. Best years: (Amarone): (2004) (03) 01 00 **97 95 93 90 88 85**.

MASTROBERARDINO *Campania, Italy* This family firm has long flown the flag for CAMPANIA in southern Italy, though it has now been joined by others. Best known for red TAURASI★★ and white Greco di Tufo★ and Fiano di Avellino★. Best years: (Taurasi Radici) (2004) (03) 01 99 **97 96 95 93 90 89 88 85 83 82 81 79 68**.

MATANZAS CREEK *Sonoma Valley AVA, California, USA* Sauvignon Blanc★ is taken seriously here, and it shows in a complex, zesty wine; Chardonnay★★ is rich and toasty but not overblown. Merlot★★ has silky, mouthfilling richness. Limited-edition Journey Chardonnay★★ and Merlot★★ are opulent but pricy. In 2000 Jess Jackson (of KENDALL-JACKSON) gained control of the winery. Best years: (Chardonnay) (2002) 01 **00 99 98 97 96 95 91 90**; (Merlot) (2002) 01 **00 99 97 96 95 94 91 90**.

MATETIC VINEYARDS *San Antonio Valley, Chile* Matetic has been producing high-quality wines from the SAN ANTONIO Valley – especially under the EQ label – since it burst onto the scene in 2001. Exceptional, concentrated and scented Syrah★★, fleshy Pinot Noir★ and superripe Sauvignon Blanc★.

MATUA VALLEY *Auckland, North Island, New Zealand* In 2001 Matua became part of Beringer Blass, with the consequent introduction of an uninspired budget range. Top wines are still good, with whites more consistent than reds: sensuous, scented Ararimu Chardonnay★★, lush, strongly varietal Gewürztraminer★, a creamy oak-aged Sauvignon Blanc★, tangy MARLBOROUGH Sauvignon Blanc★ (Shingle Peak), fine Merlot★ and Ararimu Merlot-Cabernet Sauvignon★. Best years: (Ararimu Merlot-Cabernet) 2002 **00 98 96 94**.

CH. MAUCAILLOU★ *Moulis AC, Cru Bourgeois, Haut-Médoc, Bordeaux, France* Maucaillou shows that you don't have to be a Classed Growth to make high-quality claret. Expertly made by the Dourthe family, it is soft but classically flavoured. It is accessible early on but ages well for 10–12 years. Best years: 2002 **00 99 98 96 95 90 89**.

MAULE, VALLE DEL *Valle Central, Chile* The most southerly sub-region of Chile's CENTRAL Valley, with wet winters and a large day/night temperature difference. Over 40% of Chile's vines are planted here, with more than 8600ha (21,250 acres) of Cabernet Sauvignon.

Merlot does well on the cool clay soils, and there is some tasty Carmenère and Syrah. Whites are mostly Chardonnay and Sauvignon Blanc. Best producers: J Bouchon, Calina★ (KENDALL-JACKSON), Casa Donoso, Terra Noble.

MAURO *Castilla y León, Spain* After making a name for himself as VEGA SICILIA's winemaker for 30 years, Mariano García has propelled his family's estate to the forefront in Spain and abroad. Wines include Crianza★★, Vendimia Seleccionada★★ and Terreus★★★. Best years: (2002) 01 00 **99 98 97 96 95 94**.

MAURY AC *Roussillon, France* A *vin doux naturel* made mainly from Grenache Noir. This strong, sweetish wine can be made in either a young, fresh style (vintage) or the locally revered old *rancio* style. Best producers: Mas Amiel★★, la Coume du Roy★, Maury co-op★, Maurydoré★, la Pleiade★.

MAXIMIN GRÜNHAUS *Grünhaus, Ruwer, Germany* The best estate in the Ruwer valley and one of Germany's greatest. Dr Carl von Schubert vinifies separately the wines of his 3 vineyards (Abtsberg, Bruderberg and Herrenberg), making chiefly dry and medium-dry wines of great subtlety. In good vintages the wines are easily ★★★ and the Auslese will age for decades; even QbA and Kabinett wines can age for many years. Best years: (2004) 03 02 01 00 97 **95 94 93 92 90 89 88 85 83 79 75**.

MAZIS-CHAMBERTIN AC See Chambertin AC.

MAZOYÈRES-CHAMBERTIN AC See Chambertin AC.

McLAREN VALE *South Australia* Sunny maritime region south of Adelaide, producing full-bodied wines from Chardonnay, Sauvignon Blanc, Shiraz, Grenache and Cabernet. More than 60 small wineries, plus big boys HARDY, Southcorp and Beringer Blass. Best producers: Cascabel, CHAPEL HILL★★, CLARENDON HILLS★★, Coriole★, D'ARENBERG★★, FOX CREEK★★, HARDY★★, Kangarilla Road★, Maxwell★, Geoff MERRILL★, Pirramimma, REYNELL★★, ROSEMOUNT★, Tatachilla★, WIRRA WIRRA★★.

McWILLIAM'S *Riverina, New South Wales, Australia* Large family winery, whose Hanwood brand is a joint venture with California's E & J GALLO, delivering good flavours at a fair price. Best are the Mount Pleasant wines from the Lower HUNTER VALLEY: classic bottle-aged Semillons (Elizabeth★★★, Lovedale★★), buttery Chardonnays★ and special-vineyard Shirazes – Old Paddock & Old Hill, Maurice O'Shea (★★ in the best years) and Rosehill★. Classy liqueur Muscat★★ from RIVERINA, and good table wines from HILLTOPS Barwang★ vineyard. Best years: (Elizabeth Semillon) (2004) (03) 02 01 00 99 **98 97 96 95 94 87 86 84 83 79**.

MÉDOC AC *Bordeaux, France* The Médoc peninsula north of Bordeaux on the left bank of the Gironde river produces a good fistful of the world's most famous reds. These are all situated in the HAUT-MÉDOC, the southern, more gravelly half of the area. The Médoc AC, for reds only, covers the northern part. Merlot dominates in these flat clay vineyards and the wines can be attractive in warm years: dry but juicy. Best at 3–5 years old. Best producers: Bournac★, Escurac★, les Grands Chênes★, Greysac★, Goulée★, Lacombe-Noaillac★, Lafon★, Loudenne, les Ormes-Sorbet★, Patache d'Aux, POTENSAC★, Preuillac, Ramafort★, Rollan-de-By★, la Tour-de-By★, la Tour-Haut-Caussan★, la Tour-St-Bonnet★, Vieux-Robin. Best years: 2003 02 **01 00 96 95 90 89**.

MEERLUST *Stellenbosch WO, South Africa* Chris Williams, former assistant winemaker, took over in 2004, bringing a breath of youthful fresh air to this venerable estate. Expect some polishing rather than re-invention of the classic range, including the complex Rubicon★★, one of the Cape's first BORDEAUX blends; a refined Merlot★; impressive Chardonnay★★ and ripe Pinot Noir★. Best years: (Rubicon) 2001 **00 99 98 97 96 95 94 92 91**; (Chardonnay) **2001 00 99 98 97**.

ALPHONSE MELLOT *Sancerre AC, Loire Valley, France*   Ambitious white and red SANCERRE, made with obsessive attention to detail by Alphonse 'Junior', the 19th generation of the family. Dom. la Moussière★ is unoaked, with fresh, intense citrus flavours; the oaked Cuvée Edmond★ needs a few years to mature to a fascinating rich flavour. Red and white Génération XIX★★ are outstanding, with a fine balance of fruit and oak. Best years: (Edmond) 2004 03 02 **01 00 99 98 97 96 95**.

CHARLES MELTON *Barossa Valley, South Australia*   One of the leading lights in the renaissance of hand-crafted Shiraz, Grenache and Mourvèdre in the BAROSSA. Fruity Grenache rosé Rose of Virginia★, RHONE blend Nine Popes★★, heady, sumptuous Grenache★★, smoky Shiraz★★ and Sparkling Red★★ have all attained cult status. Cabernet Sauvignon is variable, but ★★ at best. Best years: (Nine Popes) (2004) 03 02 01 99 98 **96 95 94 91 90**.

MENDOCINO COUNTY *California, USA*   The northernmost county of the North Coast AVA. It includes cool-climate ANDERSON VALLEY, excellent for sparkling wines and a little Pinot Noir; and the warmer Redwood Valley AVA, with good Zinfandel and Cabernet. Best producers: Brutocao★, FETZER, Fife★, Goldeneye, HANDLEY★★, Husch, Lazy Creek★, McDowell Valley★, Navarro★★★, ROEDERER ESTATE★★, SCHARFFENBERGER CELLARS★. Best years: (reds) (2001) 00 **99 97 96 95 94 93 91 90**.

MENDOCINO RIDGE AVA *California, USA*   Established in 1997, this is one of the most unusual AVAs in California. Mendocino Ridge starts at an altitude of 365m (1200ft) on the timber-covered mountain tops of western MENDOCINO COUNTY. Because of the topography, the AVA is non-contiguous: rising above the fog, the vineyards are commonly referred to as 'islands in the sky'. Currently only 30ha (75 acres) are planted, primarily with Zinfandel. Best producers: Edmeades, MARIAH★, Greenwood Ridge★, STEELE★★.

MENDOZA *Argentina*   The most important wine province in Argentina, accounting for around 80% of the country's wine. Situated in the eastern foothills of the Andes, Mendoza's bone-dry climate produces powerful, high-alcohol reds. Just south of Mendoza city, Maipú and LUJAN DE CUYO are ideal for Malbec, Syrah and Cabernet Sauvignon. High-altitude regions nearer the Andes, such as UCO VALLEY, produce better whites, particularly Chardonnay. Best producers: ACHAVAL-FERRER★★, ALTOS LAS HORMIGAS★, Luigi BOSCA★, CATENA★★, Cobos★, Finca El Retiro★, Finca La Celia★, Nieto Senetiner (Cadus★★), NORTON★, Salentein★, TERRAZAS DE LOS ANDES★★, Familia ZUCCARDI★.

MENETOU-SALON AC *Loire Valley, France*   Extremely attractive, chalky-clean Sauvignon whites and cherry-fresh Pinot Noir reds and rosés from west of SANCERRE. Best producers: Chatenoy★, Chavet★, J-P Gilbert★, H Pellé★, du Prieuré★, J-M Roger★, J Teiller★, Tour St-Martin★.

MÉO-CAMUZET *Vosne-Romanée AC, Côte de Nuits, Burgundy, France*   Super-quality estate, run by Jean-Nicolas Méo. New oak barrels and luscious, rich fruit combine in superb wines, which also age well. CLOS DE VOUGEOT★★★, RICHEBOURG★★★ and CORTON★★ are the grandest wines, along with the VOSNE-ROMANEE Premiers Crus, aux Brulées★★, Cros Parantoux★★★ and les Chaumes★★. Fine NUITS-ST-GEORGES aux Boudots★★ and aux Murgers★★, and now also some less expensive négociant wines. Best years: (2004) 03 02 01 **00 99 97 96 95 93 90**.

MERLOT

Red wine without tears. That's the reason Merlot has vaulted from being merely Bordeaux's red wine support act, well behind Cabernet Sauvignon in terms of class, to being the red wine drinker's darling, planted like fury all over the world. It is able to claim some seriousness and pedigree, but – crucially – can make wine of a fat, juicy character mercifully low in tannic bitterness, which can be glugged with gay abandon almost as soon as the juice has squirted from the press. Yet this doesn't mean that Merlot is the jelly baby of red wine grapes. Far from it.

WINE STYLES

Bordeaux Merlot The great wines of Pomerol and St-Émilion, on the Right Bank of the Dordogne, are largely based on Merlot and the best of these – for example, Château Pétrus, which is almost 100% Merlot – can mature for 20–30 years. In fact there is more Merlot than Cabernet Sauvignon planted throughout Bordeaux, and I doubt if there is a single red wine property that does not have some growing, because the variety ripens early, can cope with cool conditions and is able to bear a heavy crop of fruit. In a cool, damp area like Bordeaux, Cabernet Sauvignon cannot always ripen, so the soft, mellow character of Merlot is a fundamental component of the blend even in the best, Cabernet-dominated, Médoc estates, imparting a supple richness and approachability to the wines, even when young.

Other European Merlots The south of France has briskly adopted the variety, producing easy-drinking, fruit-driven wines, but in the hot Languedoc the grape often ripens too fast to express its full personality and can seem a little simple and even raw-edged. Italy has long used very high-crop Merlot to produce a simple, light quaffer in the north, particularly in the Veneto, though Friuli and Alto Adige make fuller styles and there are some very impressive examples from Tuscany and as far south as Sicily. The Swiss canton of Ticino is often unjustly overlooked for its intensely fruity, oak-aged versions. Eastern Europe has the potential to provide fertile pastures for Merlot and so far the most convincing, albeit simple, styles have come from Hungary and Bulgaria, although the younger examples are almost invariably better than the old. Spain has developed good Merlot credentials since the mid-1990s.

New World Merlots Youth is also important in the New World, nowhere more so than in Chile. Chilean Merlot, mostly blended with Carmenère, has leapt to the front of the pack of New World examples with gorgeous garnet-red wines of unbelievable crunchy fruit richness that cry out to be drunk virtually in their infancy. California Merlots often have more serious pretensions, but the nature of the grape is such that its soft, juicy quality still shines through. The cooler conditions in Washington State have produced some impressive wines, and the east coast of the US has produced good examples from places such as Long Island. With some French input, South Africa is starting to get Merlot right, and in New Zealand, despite the cool, damp conditions, some gorgeous rich examples have been made. Only Australia seems to find Merlot problematic, but there are some fine exceptions from cooler areas, including some surprisingly good fizzes – red fizzes, that is!

184

20 Barrels
Merlot
2001
D.O. RAPEL VALLEY, CHILE

BEST PRODUCERS

France
Bordeaux (St-Émilion) ANGELUS, AUSONE, BEAU-SEJOUR BECOT, Clos Fourtet, MAGDELAINE, la Mondotte, TERTRE-ROTEBOEUF, TROPLONG-MONDOT; (Pomerol) le BON PASTEUR, Certan-de-May, Clinet, la CONSEILLANTE, l'EGLISE-CLINET, l'EVANGILE, la FLEUR-PETRUS, GAZIN, LATOUR-A-POMEROL, PETIT-VILLAGE, PETRUS, le PIN, TROTANOY.

Other European Merlots
Italy (Friuli) Livio FELLUGA; (Tuscany) AMA, AVIGNONESI, CASTELGIOCONDO, Ghizzano, Le MACCHIOLE, ORNELLAIA, Petrolo, San Giusto a Rentennano, TUA RITA; (Lazio) FALESCO; (Sicily) PLANETA.

Spain (Penedès) Can Ràfols dels Caus; (Somontano) ENATE.

Switzerland Gialdi (Sassi Grossi), Daniel Huber, Werner Stucky, Christian Zündel.

New World Merlots
USA (California) ARROWOOD, BERINGER, CHATEAU ST JEAN, DUCKHORN, FERRARI-CARANO, MATANZAS CREEK, MERRYVALE, NEWTON, Pahlmeyer, Paloma, SHAFER, STERLING; (Washington) ANDREW WILL, CANOE RIDGE, LEONETTI; (New York) BEDELL, LENZ.

Australia BRAND'S, CLARENDON HILLS, COLDSTREAM HILLS, Elderton, Heggies/YALUMBA, James Irvine, PARKER COONAWARRA ESTATE, PETALUMA, Tatachilla.

New Zealand CRAGGY RANGE, Esk Valley, GOLDWATER, C J PASK, VILLA MARIA.

South Africa SAXENBURG, STEENBERG, THELEMA, VEENWOUDEN, VERGELEGEN.

Chile CARMEN, CASA LAPOSTOLLE (Cuvée Alexandre, Clos Apalta), CASABLANCA (Santa Isabel), CONCHA Y TORO, CONO SUR (20 Barrels, Visión), ERRAZURIZ.

MERCUREY AC *Côte Chalonnaise, Burgundy, France* Most important of
the 4 main COTE CHALONNAISE villages. The red is usually pleasant and
strawberry-flavoured, sometimes rustic, and can take some aging.
There is not much white, but I like its buttery, even spicy, taste. Best at
3–4 years old. Best producers: (reds) FAIVELEY★, E Juillot★, M Juillot★★,
Lorenzon★★, F Raquillet★★, RODET★, de Suremain★★, de Villaine★★;
(whites) FAIVELEY (Clos Rochette★), Genot-Boulanger★, M Juillot★, O
LEFLAIVE★, Ch. de Chamirey★/RODET★. Best years: (reds) (2004) **03 02 01 99**.

MERLOT See pages 184–5.

GEOFF MERRILL *McLaren Vale, South Australia* High-profile winemaker
with an instinctive feel for wine. There's a nicely bottle-aged Reserve
Cabernet★ in a light, early-picked, slightly eccentric style, Reserve
Shiraz★ (Henley Shiraz★★) and Chardonnay★ (Reserve★★). Also a
moreish unoaked and ageworthy Bush Vine Grenache★★.

MERRYVALE *Napa Valley AVA, California, USA* A Chardonnay powerhouse
(Reserve★★, Silhouette★★, Starmont★★), but reds are not far behind,
with BORDEAUX-blend Profile★★ and juicy Reserve Merlot★★. Best
years: (Chardonnay) (2002) 01 **00 99 98 96 95**.

MEURSAULT AC *Côte de Beaune, Burgundy, France* The biggest and
most popular white wine village in the COTE D'OR. There are no Grands
Crus, but a whole cluster of Premiers Crus, of which Perrières, Charmes
and Genevrières stand out. The general standard is better than in
neighbouring Puligny. The golden wine is lovely to drink young but
better aged for 5–8 years. Virtually no Meursault red is now made. Best
producers: R Ampeau★★, M Bouzereau★★, Boyer-Martenot★★, Coche-
Debord★★, COCHE-DURY★★★, DROUHIN★, A Ente★★★, J-P Fichet★★,
V GIRARDIN★★, JADOT★★, P Javillier★★, François Jobard★★, Rémi
Jobard★★, LAFON★★, Matrot★★, Pierre Morey★★, G Roulot★★★. Best
years: (2004) 03 02 01 **00** 99 **97** 95 92.

CH. MEYNEY★ *St-Estèphe AC, Cru Bourgeois, Haut-Médoc, Bordeaux,
France* One of the most reliable ST-ESTEPHES, producing broad-
flavoured wine with dark, plummy fruit. Second wine: Prieur de
Meyney. Best years: 2003 02 01 00 **99 96 95 94 90 89 88**.

PETER MICHAEL WINERY *Sonoma County, California, USA* British-born
Sir Peter Michael has turned a country retreat into an impressive
winery known for its small-batch wines. Les Pavots★★ is the estate
red BORDEAUX blend, and Mon Plaisir★★ and Cuvée Indigène★ are his
top Chardonnays, both noted for their deep, layered flavours. Best
years: (Les Pavots) (2002) 00 **99 97 96 95 94 91 90**.

LOUIS MICHEL *Chablis AC, Burgundy, France* A prime exponent of
unoaked CHABLIS. The top Crus – Montmains★★★, Montée de
Tonnerre★★★ and les Clos★★★ – are wonderfully fresh and mineral, and
they age triumphantly. Best years: (top crus) (2004) 03 02 00 **99 97 95 90**.

MIDI *France* A loose geographical term, virtually synonymous with
LANGUEDOC-ROUSSILLON, covering the vast, sunbaked area of southern
France between the Pyrenees and the RHONE VALLEY.

MILLTON *Gisborne, North Island, New Zealand* Organic vineyard using
biodynamic methods, whose top wines include the sophisticated Clos
St Anne Chardonnay★★, botrytized Opou Vineyard Riesling★★ and
complex barrel-fermented Chenin Blanc★. Chardonnays and Rieslings
both age well. Best years: (whites) 2004 **02 00 98**.

MINER FAMILY VINEYARDS *Oakville AVA, California, USA* Dave Miner
has 32ha (80 acres) planted on a ranch 300m (1000 feet) above the
OAKVILLE valley floor. Highlights include yeasty, full-bodied

Chardonnay★ (Oakville Ranch★★, Wild Yeast★★) as well as intense Merlot★★ and Cabernet Sauvignon★★ that demand a decade of aging. Also a stylish Viognier★★ and a striking Rosé★ from purchased fruit.

MINERVOIS AC *Languedoc, France* Attractive, mostly red wines from north-east of Carcassonne, made mainly from Syrah, Carignan and Grenache. The local co-ops produce good, juicy, quaffing wine at reasonable prices, but the best wines are made by the estates: full of ripe, red fruit and pine-dust perfume, for drinking young. It can age, especially if a little new oak has been used. A village denomination, La Livinière, covering 4 communes, can be appended to the Minervois label. Best producers: (reds) Aires Hautes★★, Ch. Bonhomme★, Borie de Maurel★, Cabezac, CLOS CENTEILLES★★, Pierre Cros★, Fabas★, la Grave, Maris★, Piccinini★, Pujol, Rieux, Rouviole, Ste-Eulalie★, TOUR BOISEE★, Villerambert-Julien★. Best years: 2003 **01 00 99 98 96**.

CH. LA MISSION-HAUT-BRION★★★ *Pessac-Léognan AC, Cru Classé de Graves, Bordeaux, France* Traditionally I have found la Mission long on power but short on grace, but in the difficult years of the 1990s it showed impressive consistency allied to challenging intensity and fragrance. Best years: 2003 02 01 00 98 96 **95 94 93 90 89 88 85**.

MISSION HILL *Okanagan Valley VQA, British Columbia, Canada* Expansion in 2001 has allowed Kiwi winemaker John Simes to process grapes from extensive holdings in the OKANAGAN VALLEY. He has strengthened the red wines of late: excellent Chardonnay★★, Pinot Blanc★ and Pinot Gris★ are joined by Merlot★, Cabernet Sauvignon and Shiraz★, and a red blend, Oculus★★.

MITCHELL *Clare Valley, South Australia* Jane and Andrew Mitchell turn out some of CLARE VALLEY's most ageworthy Watervale Riesling★★ and a classy barrel-fermented Growers Semillon★. Growers Grenache★ is a huge unwooded and heady fruit bomb, if you're in the mood... Peppertree Shiraz★★ and Sevenhill Cabernet Sauvignon★ are plump, chocolaty and typical of the region.

MITCHELTON *Goulburn Valley, Central Victoria, Australia* Some of VICTORIA's most consistently fine Riesling (Blackwood Park★★), but Rhône varieties are also specialities here, alone (Viognier★) or in blends (Airstrip Marsanne-Roussanne-Viognier). Print Label Shiraz★★ and the Crescent Shiraz-Mourvèdre-Grenache are increasingly deep and structured. Best years: (Print Label) (2002) 01 00 **98 96 95 92 91 90**.

MITTELRHEIN *Germany* Small (525ha/1300-acre), northerly wine region. Almost 75% of the wine here is Riesling, but the Mittelrhein has been in decline over the last few decades as the vineyard sites are steep and difficult to work. The best growers (like Toni JOST★), clustered around Bacharach in the south and Boppard in the north, make wines of a striking mineral tang and dry, fruity intensity. Best years: (2004) 03 02 01 **99 98 90**.

MOËT & CHANDON *Champagne AC, Champagne, France* Moët & Chandon dominates the CHAMPAGNE market (more than 25 million bottles a year), and has become a major producer of sparkling wine in California, Argentina and Australia too. Non-vintage has started to exhibit distressing unreliability, and some releases during 2005 were really not acceptable. The vintage is released too young and, while pleasant, is hardly vintage quality. Interestingly, the vintage rosé★★ can show a rare Pinot Noir floral fragrance. Dom Pérignon★★★ is the de luxe cuvée. It can be one of the greatest Champagnes of all, but

187

you've got to age it for a number of years or you're wasting your money. Best years: (1999) 98 **96 95 93 92 90 88 86 85 82**.

MONBAZILLAC AC *South-West France* BERGERAC's leading sweet wine.
Most is light, pleasant, but forgettable, from the efficient co-op. However, an increasing number of estates are making wines of a richness to approach Sauternes, and the ability to age 10 years too. Best producers: l'Ancienne Cure★, Bélingard (Blanche de Bosredon★), la Borderie★, Grande Maison★, Haut-Bernasse, Haut-Montlong (Grande Cuvée), Theulet★, Tirecul-la-Gravière★★, Tour des Verdots★, Treuil-de-Nailhac★. Best years: 2003 02 **01 99 98 97 96 95**.

CH. MONBOUSQUET★ *St-Émilion Grand Cru AC, Bordeaux, France*
Gérard Perse, owner of Ch. PAVIE, has transformed this struggling estate on the Dordogne plain into one of ST-EMILION's 'super-crus'. Rich, voluptuous and very expensive, the wine is drinkable from 3–4 years but will age longer. Also a white Monbousquet (BORDEAUX AC). Best years: 2003 02 **01** 00 **99 98 97 96 95 94**.

ROBERT MONDAVI *Napa Valley, California, USA* Robert Mondavi is a Californian institution best known for open and fruity regular Cabernet Sauvignon★ and the Reserve Cabernet★★★, possessing enormous depth and power. A regular★ and a Reserve★★ Pinot Noir are velvety smooth and supple wines with style, perfume and balance. For many years the Mondavi signature white was Fumé (Sauvignon Blanc) with ★ Reserve, but in recent years Chardonnay★ (Reserve★★) has become the winery leader, although, as with most of the wines, I'd like a little more personality to shine through. In late 2004, Constellation Brands of New York acquired Mondavi, along with a 50% stake in OPUS ONE. Constellation said it plans to expand the so-called lifestyle wines, including the Private Selection and Woodbridge lines. Best years: (Cabernet Sauvignon Reserve) (2002) 01 00 99 98 97 **96 95 94 92 91 87 86 85 84**.

MONT TAUCH, LES PRODUCTEURS DU *Fitou, Languedoc-Roussillon, France* A big, quality-conscious co-op producing a large range of wines, from good gutsy FITOU★ and CORBIERES to rich MUSCAT DE RIVESALTES★ and light but gluggable Vin de Pays du Torgan. Top wines: Les Quatre★, Les Douze★. Best years: (Les Douze) 2003 **01 00** 99.

MONTAGNE-ST-ÉMILION AC *Bordeaux, France* A ST-EMILION satellite which can produce rather good red wines. The wines are normally ready to drink in 4 years but age quite well in their slightly earthy way. Best producers: Calon★, Corbin, Croix Beauséjour★, Faizeau★, Laurets, Montaiguillon, Négrit, Roc-de-Calon, Rocher Corbin, Roudier, Vieux-Ch.-St-André. Best years: 2003 **01 00 98 96 95 90**.

MONTAGNY AC *Côte Chalonnaise, Burgundy, France* Wines from this Côte Chalonnaise village can be rather lean, but are greatly improved now that some producers are aging their wines for a few months in new oak. Generally best with 2–5 years' bottle age. Best producers: S Aladame★★, BOUCHARD PERE ET FILS★, BUXY CO-op★, Davenay★, FAIVELEY, LATOUR★, O LEFLAIVE★, A Roy★, J Vachet★. Best years: (2004) **03 02**.

MONTALCINO See Brunello di Montalcino DOCG.

MONTANA *Auckland, Gisborne, Hawkes Bay and Marlborough, New Zealand* Montana Wine changed its name to Allied Domecq NZ in 2004. Since purchasing Corbans in 2000 the company has produced a staggering 50% of New Zealand's wine. Montana's MARLBOROUGH Sauvignon Blanc★ and GISBORNE Chardonnay are in a considerable way to thank for putting New Zealand on the international wine map. Estate bottlings of whites, particularly Ormond Estate Chardonnay★★, are also generally good. Montana is now one of the world's biggest producers of Pinot Noir★, and each vintage the quality improves and the price stays fair. Consistent Lindauer fizz and, with the help of the CHAMPAGNE house DEUTZ, austere yet full-bodied Deutz Marlborough Cuvée NV Brut★. CHURCH ROAD★, a small (by Allied Domecq standards) winery in HAWKES BAY, aims to produce premium reds. Corbans brands include the top-selling Stoneleigh Sauvignon Blanc★ and Riesling★ from Marlborough.

MONTECARLO DOC *Tuscany, Italy* Distinctive reds (Sangiovese with Syrah) and whites (Trebbiano with Sémillon and Pinot Grigio). Also Non-DOC Cabernet, Merlot, Pinot Bianco, Roussanne and Vermentino. Best producers: Buonamico★, Carmignani★, Montechiari★, La Torre★, Wandanna★. Best years: (reds) (2004) 03 **01 00 99 98 97 96 95 93**.

MONTEFALCO DOC *Umbria, Italy* Good Sangiovese-based Montefalco Rosso is outclassed by dry Sagrantino di Montefalco DOCG and glorious sweet red Sagrantino Passito from dried grapes. Best producers: (Sagrantino) Adanti★, Antonelli★, Caprai★★ (25 Anni★★★), Colpetrone★★. Best years: (Sagrantino) (2004) (03) 01 00 **99 98 97 95 93 90 88**.

MONTEPULCIANO Grape grown mostly in eastern Italy (unconnected with TUSCANY's Sangiovese-based wine VINO NOBILE DI MONTEPULCIANO). Can produce deep-coloured, fleshy, spicy wines with moderate tannin and acidity. Besides MONTEPULCIANO D'ABRUZZO, it is used in ROSSO CONERO and ROSSO PICENO in the MARCHE and also in UMBRIA, Molise and PUGLIA.

MONTEPULCIANO D'ABRUZZO DOC *Abruzzo, Italy* The Montepulciano grape's most important manifestation. Quality varies from the insipid or rustic to the concentrated and characterful. Best producers: Cataldi Madonna★, Contesa★, Cornacchia★, Filomusi Guelfi★, Illuminati★, Marramiero★, Masciarelli★★, A & E Monti★, Montori★, Nicodemi★, Umani Ronchi★, Roxan★, Cantina Tollo★, La Valentina★, Valentini★★, L Valori★, Ciccio Zaccagnini★. Best years: (2004) 03 **01 00 98 97 95 94 93 90**.

MONTEREY COUNTY *California, USA* Large CENTRAL COAST county south of San Francisco Bay in the Salinas Valley. The most important AVAs are Arroyo Seco, Chalone, Carmel Valley and Santa Lucia Highlands. Best grapes are Chardonnay, Riesling and Pinot Blanc, with some good Cabernet Sauvignon, Merlot in Carmel Valley and superb Pinot Noir in the Santa Lucia Highlands in the cool middle of the county. Best producers: Bernardus★★, CHALONE★★, Estancia★, Jekel★, Joullian★, Mer Soleil★, Morgan★★, TALBOTT★★, Testarossa★★. Best years: (reds) 2001 **00 99 97 96 95 94 93 90**.

MONTES *Curicó, Chile* One of Chile's pioneering wineries in the modern era, notable for innovative development of top-quality vineyard land on the steep Apalta slopes of COLCHAGUA and the virgin country of Marchigue out toward the Pacific. Sauvignon Blanc★ (Leyda★★) and Chardonnay★ (Alpha★★) are good and fruit-led; all the reds are more austere and need bottle age. From the 2001 vintage, top-of-the-line Montes Alpha M★★ is beginning to shine. The most impressive wines, however, are two Syrahs; Montes Alpha★★, and Montes Folly★★, a massive red from the Apalta slopes.

MONTEVERTINE *Tuscany, Italy* Based in the heart of CHIANTI CLASSICO, Montevertine is famous for its non-DOC wines, particularly Le Pergole Torte★★★. This was the first of the SUPER-TUSCANS made solely with Sangiovese, and it remains one of the best. A little Canaiolo is included in the excellent Il Sodaccio★★ and Montevertine Riserva★★. Best years: (Le Pergole Torte) (2004) (03) 01 00 **99 98 97 95 93 90 88 85**.

MONTHELIE AC *Côte de Beaune, Burgundy, France* Attractive, mainly red wine village lying halfway along the COTE DE BEAUNE behind MEURSAULT and VOLNAY. The wines generally have a lovely cherry fruit and make pleasant drinking at a good price. Best producers: Boussey, COCHE-DURY★, Darviot-Perrin★, P Garaudet★, R Jobard★, LAFON★★, O LEFLAIVE★, Monthelie-Douhairet★, G Roulot★★, de Suremain★. Best years: (reds) (2004) 03 02 99 **98 96**; (whites) (2004) **03 02 00**.

MONTILLA-MORILES DO *Andalucía, Spain* Sherry-style wines that used to be sold almost entirely as lower-priced sherry substitutes. However, the wines *can* be superb, particularly the top dry amontillado, oloroso and rich Pedro Ximénez styles. Best producers: Alvear (top labels★★), Aragón, Gracia Hermanos, Pérez Barquero★, Toro Albalá★★.

DOM. DE MONTILLE *Côte de Beaune, Burgundy, France* Brought to fame by *Mondovino* star, Hubert de Montille, and now run by son Etienne. Consistent producer of stylish reds that demand aging, from VOLNAY (especially Mitans★★, Champans★★, Taillepieds★★★) and POMMARD (Pezerolles★★, Rugiens★★). Also top PULIGNY Les Caillerets★★★. Very expensive. Best years: (2004) 03 02 99 96 93 90 **85 83**.

MONTLOUIS AC *Loire Valley, France* On the opposite bank of the Loire to VOUVRAY, Montlouis makes similar styles (dry, medium, sweet and CHAMPAGNE-style fizz) but is often a touch more rustic. Mousseux, the green, appley fizz, is best drunk young. Still wines need 5–10 years, particularly the sweet Moelleux. Best producers: L Chatenay★, Chidaine★, Delétang★★, Levasseur-Alex Mathur★, des Liards/Berger★,Taille aux Loups★★. Best years: 2004 03 02 **01 99 97 96 95 90**.

MONTRACHET AC *Côte de Beaune, Burgundy, France* This world-famous Grand Cru straddles the boundary between the villages of CHASSAGNE-MONTRACHET and PULIGNY-MONTRACHET. Wines have a unique combination of concentration, finesse and perfume; white Burgundy at its most sublime. Chevalier-Montrachet, immediately above it on the slope, yields slightly leaner wine that is less explosive in its youth, but good examples become ever more fascinating with age. Best producers: G Amiot★★, M Colin★★★, DROUHIN (Laguiche)★★★, LAFON★★★, LATOUR★★, Dom. LEFLAIVE★★★, RAMONET★★★, Dom. de la ROMANEE-CONTI★★★, SAUZET★★, Thénard★★. Best years: (2004) 03 02 01 00 99 97 95 **92 90 89 85**.

MONTRAVEL AC *South-West France* Dry, medium-dry and sweet white wines from the western end of the BERGERAC region. Sweet ones from Côtes de Montravel AC and Haut-Montravel AC. Red Montravel, from 2001, is made from a minimum 50% Merlot. Best producers: le Bondieu, Masburel★, Moulin Caresse★, Perreau, Pique-Sègue, Puy-Servain★, le Raz. Best years: (sweet) 2002 **01 98 96 95**; (red) 2003 01.

CH. MONTROSE★★ *St-Estèphe AC, 2ème Cru Classé, Haut-Médoc, Bordeaux, France* A leading ST-ESTEPHE property, once famous for its dark, brooding wine that would take around 30 years to reach its prime. In the late 1970s and early 80s the wines became lighter, but Montrose has now returned to a powerful style, though softer than before. Recent vintages have mostly been extremely good. Second wine: la Dame de Montrose. Best years: 2003 02 01 00 **99** 98 96 **95 90 89 86**.

CH. MONTUS *Madiran AC, South-West France* Alain Brumont has led MADIRAN's revival, using 100% Tannat and deft public relations. The top wine is aged in new oak. He has 3 properties: Montus (Cuvée Prestige★★), Bouscassé (Vieilles Vignes★★) and Meinjarre. Montus and Bouscassé also make enjoyable dry PACHERENC DU VIC-BILH★, while Bouscassé has fine Moelleux★★. Best years: (Cuvée Prestige) (2003) 02 01 00 99 **98 97 96 95 94 93 91 90.**

MOON MOUNTAIN *Sonoma Valley AVA, California, USA* Formerly known as Carmenet, Moon Mountain specializes in intensely flavoured reds from mountain vineyards. Full-throttle Cabernet Franc★★ and Reserve Cabernet Sauvignon★★ can age for a decade. Reserve Sauvignon Blanc★★ from Edna Valley grapes features plenty of creamy oak. Note that Carmenet is now a brand of Beringer Blass and the wines are not related. Best years: (reds) (2002) (01) 00 99 98 97 **96 95 94.**

MORELLINO DI SCANSANO DOC *Tuscany, Italy* Morellino is the local name for the Sangiovese grape in the south-west of TUSCANY. The wines can be broad and robust, but the best are delightfully perfumed. Best producers: E Banti★, Belguardo★/FONTERUTOLI, Carletti/POLIZIANO (Lohsa★), Cecchi★, Il Macereto★, Mantellassi★, Morellino di Scansano co-op★, Moris Farms★★, Poggio Argentiera★★, Le Pupille★★. Best years: (2004) 03 **01 00 99 98 97 96 95 93 90.**

MOREY-ST-DENIS AC *Côte de Nuits, Burgundy, France* Morey has 5 Grands Crus (Clos des Lambrays, CLOS DE LA ROCHE, CLOS ST-DENIS, Clos de Tart and a share of BONNES-MARES) as well as some very good Premiers Crus. Basic village wine is sometimes unexciting, but from a quality grower the wine has good fruit and acquires an attractive depth as it ages. A tiny amount of startling nutty white wine is also made. Best producers: Pierre Amiot★, Arlaud★★, Dom. des Beaumonts, CLAIR★★, Dom. du Clos de Tart★★, DUJAC★★★, Dom. des Lambrays★★, H Lignier★★★, H Perrot-Minot★★, Ponsot★★, ROUMIER★★, ROUSSEAU★★, Sérafin★★. Best years: (2004) 03 02 01 **00 99 98 97 96 95 93 90.**

MORGENHOF *Stellenbosch WO, South Africa* A 300-year-old Cape farm grandly restored and run with French flair by owner Anne Cointreau-Huchon. The range spans Cap Classique sparkling to port styles. Best are a well-oaked, muscular Chenin Blanc, structured Merlot★ and the dark-berried, supple Première Sélection★, a BORDEAUX-style blend.

MORGON AC *Beaujolais, Burgundy, France* The longest-lasting of BEAUJOLAIS Crus, wines that should have structure, tannin and acidity to age well – the best normally come from the slopes of the Côte du Py. There are, however, many more Morgons, made in a commercial style for early drinking, which are nothing more than a pleasant, fruity – and pricy – drink. Best producers: N Aucoeur★, G Brun★, DUBOEUF (Jean Descombes★), M Jonchet★, M Lapierre★. Best years: 2003 **00.**

MORNINGTON PENINSULA *Victoria, Australia* Exciting cool-climate maritime region dotted with small vineyards. Chardonnay runs the gamut from honeyed to harsh; Pinot Noir can be very stylish in warm years. Best producers: DROMANA★, Kooyong★, Main Ridge★, Moorooduc★, Paringa Estate★★, Port Phillip Estate★, STONIER★★, T'Gallant★, Tuck's Ridge, Yabby Lake★. Best years: (Pinot Noir) 2003 02 **01 00 99 98 97 95 94.**

MORRIS *Rutherglen, Victoria, Australia* Historic winery, ORLANDO-owned, with David Morris making old favourites like Liqueur Muscat★★ and Tokay★★ (Old Premium★★★), 'ports', 'sherries' and robust table wines from Shiraz★, Cabernet★, Durif★ and Blue Imperial (Cinsaut).

DENIS MORTET *Gevrey-Chambertin AC, Côte de Nuits, Burgundy, France*
Denis Mortet joined the ranks of great producers with brilliant 1993s. Early vintages are deep coloured and powerful. Now he is adding finesse. Various cuvées of GEVREY-CHAMBERTIN★★★ and tiny amounts of CHAMBERTIN★★★ itself. Best years: (2004) 03 02 01 **00 98 97** 96 **95 93**.

MORTON ESTATE *Katikati, North Island, New Zealand* Morton started in the tiny town of Katikati, but has since established a second winery in HAWKES BAY, its principal grape source. It produces New Zealand's most expensive Chardonnay, Coniglio★★★, a limited-production Burgundy dead-ringer. Also robust, complex Black Label Chardonnay★★, rich and gamy Black Label Merlot★, the best Hawkes Bay Pinot Noir★ yet, berries and cedar Black Label Merlot-Cabernet Sauvignon★★ and good fizz★★. Best years: (Black Label Chardonnay) 2002 **00 98 96 95**.

GEORG MOSBACHER *Forst, Pfalz, Germany* This small estate makes dry white and dessert wines in the village of FORST. Best of all are the dry Rieslings★★ from the Forster Ungeheuer site, which are among the lushest in Germany. Delicious young, but worth cellaring for more than 3 years. Best years: (2004) 03 02 01 **99 98 97** 96 **94 93**.

MOSCATO D'ASTI DOCG *Piedmont, Italy* Utterly beguiling, delicately scented, gently bubbling wine, made from Moscato Bianco grapes grown in the hills between Acqui Terme, Asti and Alba in north-west Italy. The DOCG is the same as for ASTI, but only select grapes go into this wine, which is frizzante (semi-sparkling) rather than fully sparkling. Drink while they're bubbling with youthful fragrance. Best producers: Araldica/Alasia★, ASCHERI★, Bava★, Bera★★, Braida★, Cascina Castlèt★, Caudrina★★, Giuseppe Contratto★, Coppo★, Cascina Fonda★, Forteto della Luja★, Icardi★, Marenco★, Beppe Marino★, La Morandina★, Marco Negri★, Perrone★, Cascina Pian d'Or★, Saracco★★, Scagliola★, La Spinetta★★, I Vignaioli di Santo Stefano★.

MOSCATO PASSITO DI PANTELLERIA DOC *Sicily, Italy* Powerful dessert wine made from the Muscat of Alexandria, or Zibibbo, grape. Pantelleria is a small island south-west of SICILY, closer to Africa than it is to Italy. The grapes are picked in mid-August and laid out in the hot sun to dry and shrivel for a couple of weeks. They are then crushed and fermented to give an amber-coloured, intensely flavoured sweet Muscat. The wines are best drunk within 5–7 years of the vintage. Best producers: Benanti★, D'Ancona★, DE BARTOLI★★, Donnafugata (Ben Ryé★), Murana★, Nuova Agricoltura co-op★, Pellegrino.

MOSEL-SAAR-RUWER *Germany* A collection of vineyard areas on the Mosel and its tributaries, the Saar and the Ruwer, amounting to 11,240ha (27,770 acres). The Mosel river rises in the French Vosges before forming the border between Germany and Luxembourg. In its first German incarnation in the Upper Mosel the light, tart Elbling grape holds sway, but with the Middle Mosel begins a series of villages responsible for some of the world's very best Riesling wines: PIESPORT, BRAUNEBERG, BERNKASTEL, GRAACH, WEHLEN, URZIG and ERDEN. The wines are not big or powerful, but in good years they have tremendous slatiness and an ability to blend the greenness of citrus leaves and fruits with the golden warmth of honey. Great wines are rarer in the lower part of the valley as the Mosel swings round into Koblenz, although WINNINGEN is an island of excellence. The Saar can produce wonderful, piercing wines in villages such as Serrig, Ayl, OCKFEN and Wiltingen. Ruwer wines are slightly softer; the estates of MAXIMIN GRUNHAUS and KARTHAUSERHOF are on every list of the best in Germany.

MOSS WOOD *Margaret River, Western Australia* Seminal MARGARET RIVER winery at the top of its form. Supremely good, scented Cabernet★★★ needing 5 years' age to blossom, classy Chardonnay★★, pale, fragrant Pinot Noir★ and crisp, fruity but ageworthy Semillon★★. Range is expanding with excellent Ribbon Vale★★ and other single-vineyard wines. Best years: (Cabernet) (2003) 02 01 00 **99 98 96 95 94 91 90 85**.

J P MOUEIX *Bordeaux, France* As well as owning PETRUS, la FLEUR-PETRUS, MAGDELAINE, TROTANOY and other properties, the Moueix family runs a thriving merchant business specializing in the wines of the right bank, particularly POMEROL and ST-EMILION. Quality is generally high.

MOULIN-À-VENT AC *Beaujolais, Burgundy, France* Potentially the greatest of the BEAUJOLAIS Crus, taking its name from an ancient windmill that stands above Romanèche-Thorins. The granitic soil yields a majestic wine that with time transforms into a rich Burgundian style more characteristic of the Pinot Noir than the Gamay. Best producers: L Champagnon★, DUBOEUF (single domaines★), Ch. des Jacques★, Ch. du Moulin-à-Vent★, Dom. Romanesca★, P Sapin (Le Vieux Domaine). Best years: **2003 00 99**.

MOULIS AC *Haut-Médoc, Bordeaux, France* Small AC within the HAUT-MEDOC. Much of the wine is excellent – delicious at 5–6 years old, though good examples can age 10–20 years – and not overpriced. Best producers: Anthonic, Biston-Brillette, Brillette, CHASSE-SPLEEN★, Duplessis, Dutruch-Grand-Poujeau, Gressier-Grand-Poujeaux, MAUCAILLOU★, Ch. Moulin-à-Vent, POUJEAUX★★. Best years: 2003 02 **01** 00 **96 95 94 90 89 88**.

MOUNT HORROCKS *Clare Valley, South Australia* Stephanie Toole has transformed this label into one of the CLARE VALLEY's best, with taut, minerally, limy Riesling★★ from a single vineyard in Watervale; classy, cedary Semillon★; complex, savoury Shiraz★; and a delicious sticky (dessert wine), the Cordon Cut Riesling★★, which shows varietal character with a satisfying lush texture.

MOUNT LANGI GHIRAN *Grampians, Victoria, Australia* This winery made its reputation with remarkable dark plum, chocolate and pepper Shiraz★★. Delightful Riesling★, honeyed Pinot Gris★ and melony unwooded Chardonnay★. Joanna★★ Cabernet is dark and intriguing. Best years: (Shiraz) 2003 02 01 99 **98 97 96 95 94 93 92 90 89**.

MOUNT MARY *Yarra Valley, Victoria, Australia* Classic property using only estate-grown grapes along BORDEAUX lines, with dry white Triolet★★ blended from Sauvignon Blanc, Semillon and Muscadelle, and Quintet (★★★ for committed Francophiles), from Cabernets Sauvignon and Franc, Merlot, Malbec and Petit Verdot, that ages beautifully. The Pinot Noir★★ is almost as good. Best years: (Quintet) (2002) 01 00 99 98 97 96 **95 94 93 92 91 90 88 86 84**.

MOUNT VEEDER AVA *Napa Valley, California, USA* Small AVA in south-west NAPA, with Cabernet Sauvignon and Zinfandel in an impressive, rough-hewn style. Best producers: Chateau Potelle★, Robert Craig★★, HESS COLLECTION★★, Lokoya★★, Mayacamas★, Mount Veeder Winery★.

MOURVÈDRE The variety originated in Spain, where it is called Monastrell. It dominates the JUMILLA DO and also Alicante, Bullas and Yecla. It needs lots of sunshine to ripen, which is why it performs well on the Mediterranean coast at BANDOL. It is increasingly important as a source of body and tarry, pine-needle flavour in the wines of

193

CHATEAUNEUF-DU-PAPE and parts of the MIDI. It is beginning to make a reputation in Australia and California, where it is sometimes known as Mataro, and is just starting to make its presence felt in South Africa.

MOUTON-CADET *Bordeaux AC, Bordeaux, France*   The most widely sold red BORDEAUX in the world was created by Baron Philippe de Rothschild in the 1930s. Blended from the entire Bordeaux region, the wine is an undistinguished drink – and never cheap. Also a white and rosé.

CH. MOUTON-ROTHSCHILD★★★ *Pauillac AC, 1er Cru Classé, Haut-Médoc, Bordeaux, France*   Baron Philippe de Rothschild died in 1988, having raised Mouton from a run-down Second Growth to its promotion to First Growth in 1973, and a reputation as one of the greatest wines in the world. It can still be the most magnificently opulent of the great MEDOC reds, but inexcusable inconsistency frequently makes me want to downgrade it. Recent vintages seem back on top form. When young, it is rich and indulgent on the palate, aging after 15–20 years to a complex bouquet of blackcurrant and cigar box. There is also a white wine, Aile d'Argent. Second wine: Petit-Mouton. Best years: (red) 2003 02 01 00 **99** 98 96 **95 90 89 88 86 85 83 82 70**.

MUDGEE *New South Wales, Australia*   Small, long-overlooked region neighbouring HUNTER VALLEY, with a higher altitude and marginally cooler temperatures. Major new plantings are giving it a fresh lease of life; ROSEMOUNT is leading the charge with generally impressive but overpriced Mountain Blue Shiraz-Cabernet★★ and the Hill of Gold range of varietals. Other producers are beginning to make the best use of very good fruit. Best producers: Abercorn, Farmer's Daughter, Huntington Estate★, Miramar★, ORLANDO (Poet's Corner★), ROSEMOUNT★.

MUGA *Rioja DOCa, Rioja, Spain*   A traditional family winery making high-quality, rich red RIOJA★, especially the Gran Reserva, Prado Enea★★. It is the only bodega in Rioja where every step of red winemaking is still carried out in oak containers. The modern Torre Muga Reserva★ marks a major stylistic change. The new top cuvée is Aro★★. Whites and rosés are good too. Best years: (Torre Muga Reserva) 2001 99 **98 96 95**.

MULDERBOSCH *Stellenbosch WO, South Africa*   Consistency is the hallmark of this white-dominated range from winemaker Mike Dobrovic. Sleek, gooseberry-infused Sauvignon Blanc★★ is deservedly a cult wine; drink young and fresh. Purity and intensity mark out the Chardonnay★★ and Steen op Hout★ (Chenin Blanc brushed with oak, and labelled Chenin for export markets). The handful of reds includes Faithful Hound Cabernet-Merlot, BORDEAUX-like but easy-drinking. Best years: (Chardonnay) **2003 02 01 00** 99 98 97 96.

MÜLLER-CATOIR *Neustadt-Haardt, Pfalz, Germany*   This PFALZ producer makes wine of a piercing fruit flavour and powerful structure unsurpassed in Germany, including ★★★ Riesling and Scheurebe; ★★ Rieslaner, Gewürztraminer, Muskateller and Pinot Noir; and Weissburgunder★. In 2002 veteran winemaker Hans-Gunter Schwarz retired and was replaced by Martin Tranzen. Let's hope for more of the same. Best years: (2004) 03 02 01 **99 98 97 96 94 93 92 90**.

EGON MÜLLER-SCHARZHOF *Scharzhofberg, Saar, Germany*   Some of the world's greatest – and most expensive – sweet Rieslings are this estate's Auslese, Beerenauslese, Trockenbeerenauslese and Eiswein, all ★★★. Regular Kabinett and Spätlese wines are pricy but classic. Best years: (2004) 03 02 01 99 97 **95 93 90 89 88 83 76 75 71**.

MÜLLER-THURGAU The workhorse grape of Germany, largely responsible for LIEBFRAUMILCH, with 18% of the country's vineyards (second to Riesling, with 21%). When yields are low it produces pleasant floral wines; but this is rare since modern clones are all super-productive. It is occasionally better in England – though a few good examples, with a slightly green edge to the grapy flavour, come from Switzerland, Luxembourg and Italy's ALTO ADIGE and TRENTINO. New Zealand used to pride itself on making the world's best Müller-Thurgau, but acreage is in terminal decline.

G H MUMM *Champagne AC, Champagne, France* Mumm's top-selling non-vintage brand, Cordon Rouge, disappointing in the 1990s, has improved since Dominique Demarville took over as winemaker in 1998. New owners Allied Domecq seem to be supporting his efforts at raising quality. Let's hope so, because there's still a way to go. Best years: (1998) **96 95 90 89 88 85 82**.

MUMM NAPA *Napa Valley AVA, California, USA* The California offshoot of Champagne house MUMM has always made good bubbly, but the style is now leaner and meaner, which is a pity. Cuvée Napa Brut Prestige is a fair drink; Blanc de Noirs★ is better than most pink Champagnes. Also elegant vintage-dated Blanc de Blancs★ and the flagship DVX★.

RENÉ MURÉ *Alsace AC, Alsace, France* The pride and joy of this domaine's fine vineyards is the Clos St-Landelin, a parcel within the Grand Cru Vorbourg and the label for all the top wines. Négociant wines appear under the René Muré and superior (and increasingly good) Côte de Rouffach labels. The Clos is the source of lush, concentrated wines from all the major varieties, with particularly fine Riesling★★ and Pinot Gris★★. The Muscat Vendange Tardive★★ is rare and remarkable, as is the opulent old-vine Sylvaner Cuvée Oscar★. The Vendange Tardive★★ and Sélection de Grains Nobles★★★ wines are among the best in Alsace. Best years: (Clos St-Landelin Riesling) 2004 03 02 **01 00 97 96 95 94 92 90**.

MURFATLAR *Romania* Region to the west of the Black Sea, producing excellent late-harvest wines (including botrytized versions) from Pinot Gris★, Chardonnay and Muscat Ottonel. Sparkling wines are being made, too. Murfatlar can also be a source of ripe, soft, low-acid reds.

ANDREW MURRAY VINEYARDS *Santa Barbara County, California, USA* Working with RHONE varieties, winemaker Andrew Murray has created an impressive array of wines. Rich, aromatic Viognier★ and Roussanne★★ as well as several Syrahs, including Roasted Slope★★ and Hillside Reserve★★. Espérance★ is a spicy blend patterned after a serious COTES DU RHONE. Best years: (Syrah) 2001 **00 99 98 97 96 94**.

MUSCADET AC *Loire Valley, France* Muscadet is the general AC for the region around Nantes in north-west France, with 3 better-quality zones: Muscadet Coteaux de la Loire, Muscadet Côtes de Grand Lieu and Muscadet Sèvre-et-Maine. Always buy wines matured *sur lie* for greater depth of flavour. Producers who make basic Muscadet AC are allowed higher yields but cannot use the term *sur lie* on the labels. Best drunk young and fresh, a perfect match for the local seafood – but the best age well. Best producers: Serge Bâtard★, Bidière, Michel David, Dorices★, l'ECU★, Gadais, V Günther-Chéreau★, Jacques Guindon★, la Haute-Févrie★, Hautes-Noëlles, Herbauges★, l'Hyvernière★, Luneau-Papin★, Metaireau★, Quatre Routes★, RAGOTIERE★, Sauvion★, la Touché★. Best years: (*sur lie*) 2003 **02 01 00 99**.

MUSCAT See pages 196–7.

MUSCAT

It's strange, but there's hardly a wine grape in the world which makes wine that actually tastes of the grape itself. Yet there's one variety which is so joyously, exultantly grapy that it more than makes up for all the others – the Muscat, generally thought to be the original wine vine. In fact there seem to be about 200 different branches of the Muscat family worldwide, but the noblest of these and the one that always makes the most exciting wine is called Muscat Blanc à Petits Grains (the Muscat with the small berries). These berries can be crunchily green, golden yellow, pink or even brown – as a result Muscat has a large number of synonyms. The wines they make may be pale and dry, rich and golden, subtly aromatic or as dark and sweet as treacle.

WINE STYLES

France Muscat is grown from the far north-east right down to the Spanish border, yet is rarely accorded great respect in France. This is a pity, because the dry, light, hauntingly grapy Muscats of Alsace are some of France's most delicately beautiful wines. It pops up sporadically in the Rhône Valley, especially in the sparkling wine enclave of Die. Mixed with Clairette, the Clairette de Die Tradition is a fragrant grapy fizz that deserves to be better known. Muscat de Beaumes-de-Venise is a delicious manifestation of the grape, this time fortified, fragrant and sweet. Its success has encouraged the traditional fortified winemakers of Languedoc-Roussillon, especially in Frontignan and Rivesaltes, to make fresher, more perfumed wines than the flat and syrupy ones they've produced for generations.

Italy Muscat, mainly Moscato Bianco, is grown in Italy for fragrantly sweet or (rarely) dry table wines in the north and for *passito*-style wines in the south (though Muscat of Alexandria is sometimes preferred below Rome). The most delicate Muscats in Italy are those of Asti, where the grape is called Moscato di Canelli. As either Asti or Moscato d'Asti, this brilliantly fresh fizz can be a blissful drink. Italy also has red varieties: the Moscato Nero for rare sweet wines in Lazio, Lombardy and Piedmont; and Moscato Rosa/Rosenmuskateller for delicately sweet wines in Trentino-Alto Adige and Friuli-Venezia Giulia. Moscato Giallo/Goldmuskateller (Orange Muscat) is often preferred to Moscato Bianco in the northeast.

Other regions Elsewhere in Europe, Muscat is a component of some Tokajis in Hungary, Crimea has shown how good it can be in the Massandra fortified wines, and the rich golden Muscats of Samos and Patras are among Greece's finest wines. As Muskateller in Austria and Germany it makes primarily dry, subtly aromatic wines. In Spain, Moscatel de Valencia is sweet, light and sensational value, Moscatel de Grano Menudo is on the resurgence in Navarra and it has also been introduced in Mallorca. Portugal's Moscatel de Setúbal is also wonderfully rich and complex. California grows Muscat, often calling it Muscat Canelli, but South Africa and Australia make better use of it. With darker berries, and called Brown Muscat in Australia and Muscadel in South Africa, it makes some of the world's sweetest and most luscious fortified wines, especially in the north-east Victoria regions of Rutherglen and Glenrowan in Australia.

BEST PRODUCERS

Sparkling Muscat

France (Clairette de Die) Achard-Vincent, Clairette de Die co-op, Georges Raspail.

Italy (Asti) G Contratto, Gancia; (Moscato d'Asti) Fratelli Bera, Braida, Caudrina, Saracco, La Spinetta.

Dry Muscat

Austria (Muskateller) Lackner-Tinnacher, POLZ, TEMENT.

France (Alsace) J Becker, Dirler-Cadé, Kientzler, Kuentz-Bas, Rolly Gassmann, Schléret, SCHOFFIT, Sorg, WEINBACH, ZIND-HUMBRECHT.

Germany (Muskateller) BERCHER, Dr HEGER, MULLER-CATOIR, REBHOLZ.

Spain (Alicante) Bocopa co-op; (Penedès) TORRES (Viña Esmeralda).

Italy (Goldmuskateller) LAGEDER.

Sweet Muscat

Australia (Liqueur Muscat) ALL SAINTS, Baileys, BROWN BROTHERS, Buller, Campbells, CHAMBERS, MCWILLIAM'S, MORRIS, SEPPELT, Stanton & Killeen, YALUMBA.

France (Alsace) E Burn, René MURE, SCHOFFIT; (Beaumes-de-Venise) Bernardins, Durban, Paul JABOULET, Pigeade; (Frontignan) la Peyrade; (Lunel) Lacoste; (Rivesaltes) CAZES, Jau.

Greece SAMOS co-op.

Italy (Goldmuskateller) Viticoltori Caldaro, Thurnhof; (Pantelleria) DE BARTOLI, Murana.

Portugal (Moscatel de Setúbal) J M da FONSECA, J P VINHOS.

South Africa KLEIN CONSTANTIA.

Spain (Navarra) Camilo Castilla, CHIVITE; (Terra Alta) Vinos Piñol; (Valencia) Gandía; (Alicante) Gutiérrez de la Vega, Enrique Mendoza, Primitivo Quiles; (Sierras de Málaga) Telmo RODRIGUEZ.

MUSCAT OF ALEXANDRIA Muscat of Alexandria rarely shines in its own right but performs a useful job worldwide, adding perfume and fruit to what would otherwise be dull, neutral white wines. It is common for sweet and fortified wines throughout the Mediterranean basin (in Sicily it is called Zibibbo) and in South Africa (where it is also known as Hanepoot), as well as being a fruity, perfumed bulk producer there and in Australia, where it is known as Gordo Blanco or Lexia.

MUSCAT DE BEAUMES-DE-VENISE AC *Rhône Valley, France* Delicious Muscat *vin doux naturel* from the southern Rhône. It has a fruity acidity and a bright fresh feel, and is best drunk young to get all that lovely grapy perfume at its peak. Best producers: Baumalric★, Beaumes-de-Venise co-op, Bernardins★★, Coyeux★, DELAS★, Durban★★, Fenouillet★, JABOULET★★, Pigeade★★, Vidal-Fleury★.

MUSCAT BLANC À PETITS GRAINS See Muscat.

MUSCAT DE FRONTIGNAN AC *Languedoc, France* Muscat *vin doux naturel* on the Mediterranean coast. Quite impressive but can be a bit cloying. Muscat de Mireval AC, a little further inland, can have a touch more acid freshness, and quite an alcoholic kick. Best producers: (Frontignan) Cave du Muscat de Frontignan, la Peyrade★, Robiscau; (Lunel) Lacoste★; (Mireval) la Capelle★, Mas des Pigeonniers, Moulinas.

MUSCAT DE LUNEL AC, MUSCAT DE MIREVAL AC See Muscat de Frontignan.

MUSCAT DE RIVESALTES AC *Roussillon, France* Made from Muscat Blanc à Petits Grains and Muscat of Alexandria, the wine can be very good from go-ahead producers who keep the aromatic skins in the juice for longer periods to gain extra perfume and fruit. Most delicious when young. Best producers: Baixas co-op (Dom Brial★, Ch. les Pins★), la CASENOVE★, CAZES★★, Chênes★, Fontanel★, Força Réal★, Jau★, Laporte★, MONT TAUCH co-op★, de Nouvelles★, Piquemal★, Sarda-Malet★.

MUSCAT DE ST-JEAN-DE-MINERVOIS AC *Languedoc, France* Up in the remote Minervois hills, a small AC for fortified Muscat made from Muscat Blanc à Petits Grains. Less cloying than some Muscats from the plains of LANGUEDOC-ROUSSILLON, more tangerine and floral. Best producers: Combebelle, CLOS BAGATELLE, Vignerons de Septimanie.

MUSIGNY AC *Grand Cru, Côte de Nuits, Burgundy, France* One of a handful of truly great Grands Crus, combining power with an exceptional depth of fruit and lacy elegance – an iron fist in a velvet glove. Understandably expensive. A tiny amount of BOURGOGNE Blanc is currently made from the Musigny vineyard by de VOGÜE★★. Best producers: DROUHIN★★★, JADOT★★★, D Laurent★★★, Dom. LEROY★★★, J-F Mugnier★★★, J Prieur★★, ROUMIER★★★, VOGÜE★★, VOUGERAIE★★★. Best years: (2004) 03 02 01 00 99 98 97 96 95 93 **90 89 88**.

NAHE *Germany* 4600ha (11,370-acre) wine region named after the River Nahe, which rises below Birkenfeld and joins the Rhine by BINGEN, opposite RUDESHEIM in the RHEINGAU. Riesling, Müller-Thurgau and Silvaner are the main grapes, but the Rieslings from this geologically complex region are considered some of Germany's best. The finest vineyards are those of Niederhausen and SCHLOSSBOCKELHEIM, situated in the dramatic, rocky Upper Nahe Valley, and at Dorsheim and Münster in the lower Nahe.

CH. NAIRAC★★ *Barsac AC, 2ème Cru Classé, Bordeaux, France* An established star in BARSAC which, by dint of enormous effort and considerable investment, produces a wine sometimes on a par with the

First Growths. The influence of aging in new oak casks, adding spice and even a little tannin, makes this sweet wine a good candidate for aging 10–15 years. Best years: 2003 02 01 **99 98 97 96 95 90 89 88**.

NAPA VALLEY See pages 200–1.

NAPA VALLEY AVA *California, USA*   An AVA designed to be so inclusive that it is almost completely irrelevant. It includes vineyards that are outside the Napa River drainage system – such as Pope Valley and Chiles Valley. Because of this a number of sub-AVAs have been and are in the process of being created; a few such as CARNEROS and STAGS LEAP DISTRICT are discernibly different from their neighbours, but the majority are similar in nature, and many fear that these sub-AVAs will simply dilute the magic of Napa's name. See also Howell Mountain, Mount Veeder, Napa Valley, Oakville, Rutherford.

NAVARRA DO *Navarra, Spain*   This buzzing region has increasing numbers of vineyards planted to Cabernet Sauvignon, Merlot and Chardonnay in addition to Tempranillo, Garnacha and Moscatel (Muscat). This translates into a wealth of juicy reds, barrel-fermented whites and modern sweet Muscats, but quality is still more haphazard than it should be. Best producers: Camilo Castilla (Capricho de Goya Muscat★★), CHIVITE★, Magaña★, Alvaro Marino★, Castillo de Monjardin★, Nekeas co-op★, Ochoa, Palacio de la Vega★, Príncipe de Viana★, Señorío de Otazu★. Best years: (reds) **2001 99 98 96 95 94**.

NEBBIOLO   The grape variety responsible for the majestic wines of BAROLO and BARBARESCO, found almost nowhere outside north-west Italy. Its name derives from the Italian for fog, *nebbia*, because it ripens late when the hills are shrouded in autumn mists. It needs a thick skin to withstand this fog, so often gives very tannic wines that need years to soften. When grown in the limestone soils of the Langhe hills around Alba, Nebbiolo produces wines that are only moderately deep in colour but have a wonderful array of perfumes and an ability to develop great complexity with age – rivalled only by Pinot Noir and Syrah. Barolo is usually considered the best and longest-lived of the Nebbiolo wines; the myth that it needs a decade or more to be drinkable has been dispelled by new-style Barolo, yet the best of the traditional styles are more than worth the wait. Barbaresco also varies widely in style between the traditional and the new. NEBBIOLO D'ALBA and ROERO produce lighter styles. The variety is also used for special barrique-aged blends, often with Barbera and/or Cabernet and sold under the LANGHE DOC. Nebbiolo is also the principal grape for reds of northern PIEDMONT – Carema, GATTINARA and Ghemme. In LOMBARDY it is known as Chiavennasca and is the main variety of the Valtellina DOC and VALTELLINA SUPERIORE DOCG wines. Outside Italy, rare good examples have been made in Australia, California and South Africa.

NEBBIOLO D'ALBA DOC *Piedmont, Italy*   Red wine from Nebbiolo grown around Alba, but excluding the BAROLO and BARBARESCO zones. Vineyards in the LANGHE and ROERO hills, by the Tanaro river, are noted for sandy soils that produce a fragrant, fruity style for early drinking, though some growers make wines that improve for 5 years or more. Best producers: Alario★, ASCHERI, Bricco Maiolica★★, CERETTO, Cascina Chicco★, Correggia★★, GIACOSA★, Giuseppe MASCARELLO★, Pio Cesare★, PRUNOTTO★, RATTI, SANDRONE★, Vietti★. Best years: (2004) 03 **01 00 99 98 97 96 95**.

NAPA VALLEY

California, USA

 From the earliest days of California wine, and through all its ups and downs, the Napa Valley has been the standard-bearer for the whole industry and the driving force behind quality and progress. The magical Napa name – derived from an Indian word for plenty – applies to the fertile valley itself, the county in which it is found and the AVA for the overall area, but the region is so viticulturally diverse that the appellation is virtually meaningless.

The valley was first settled by immigrants in the 1830s, and by the late 19th century Napa, and in particular the area around the communities of Rutherford and Oakville, had gained a reputation for exciting Cabernet Sauvignon. Despite the long, dark years of Prohibition, this reputation survived and when the US interest in wine revived during the 1970s, Napa was ready to lead the charge.

GRAPE VARIETIES

Most of the classic French grapes are grown and recent replantings have done much to match varieties to the most suitable locations. Cabernet Sauvignon is planted in profusion and Napa's strongest reputation is for varietal Cabernet and Bordeaux-style (or meritage) blends, mostly Cabernet-Merlot. Pinot Noir and Chardonnay, for both still and sparkling wines, do best in the south, from Yountville down to Carneros. Zinfandel is grown mostly at the north end of the valley. Syrah and Sangiovese are relatively new here.

SUB-REGIONS

The most significant vine-growing area is the valley floor running from Calistoga in the north down to Carneros, below which the Napa River flows out into San Pablo Bay. It has been said that there are more soil types in Napa than in the whole of France, but much of the soil in the valley is heavy, clayish, over-fertile, difficult to drain and really not fit to make great wine. Some of the best vineyards are tucked into the mountain slopes at the valley sides or in selected spots at higher altitudes.

There is as much as a 10° temperature difference between torrid Calistoga and Carneros at the mouth of the valley, cooled by Pacific fog and a benchmark for US Pinot Noir and cool-climate Chardonnay. About 20 major sub-areas have been identified along the valley floor and in the mountains, although there is much debate over how many have a real claim to individuality. Rutherford, Oakville and Yountville in the mid-valley produce Cabernet redolent of dust, dried sage and ultra-ripe blackcurrants. Softer flavours come from Stags Leap to the east. The higher-altitude vineyards of Diamond Mountain, Spring Mountain and Mount Veeder along the Mayacamas mountain range to the west produce deep Cabernets, while Howell Mountain in the north-east has stunning Zinfandel and Merlot.

See also CARNEROS AVA, HOWELL MOUNTAIN AVA, MOUNT VEEDER AVA, NAPA VALLEY AVA, OAKVILLE AVA, RUTHERFORD AVA, STAGS LEAP DISTRICT AVA; and individual producers.

VIADER

NAPA VALLEY

(2002) 01 **00 99 97 95 94 91 90 87 86**

BEST PRODUCERS

Cabernet Sauvignon and meritage blends
Abreu, Altamura, Anderson's Conn Valley, ARAUJO, Barnett (Rattlesnake Hill), BEAULIEU, BERINGER, Bryant Family, Burgess Cellars, Cafaro, Cakebread, CAYMUS, CHATEAU MONTELENA, Chateau Potelle (VGS), CHIMNEY ROCK, Cliff Lede, CLOS DU VAL, Clos Pegase, Colgin, Conn Creek (Anthology), Corison, Cosentino, Robert Craig, DALLA VALLE, Darioush, Del Dotto, DIAMOND CREEK, DOMINUS, DUCKHORN, DUNN, Elyse, Etude, Far Niente, FLORA SPRINGS, Forman, Freemark Abbey, Frog's Leap, Grace Family, Groth, HARLAN ESTATE, HARTWELL, HEITZ, HESS, Jarvis, La Jota, Ladera, Lewis Cellars, Livingston, Lokoya, Long Meadow Ranch, Long Vineyards, Markham, Mayacamas, MERRYVALE, Peter MICHAEL, MINER, MONDAVI, Monticello, Mount Veeder Winery/FRANCISCAN, NEWTON, NIEBAUM-COPPOLA, Oakford, OPUS ONE, Pahlmeyer, Paradigm, Robert Pecota, Peju Province (HB Vineyard), PHELPS, PINE RIDGE, Plumpjack, Pride Mountain, Quintessa, Raymond, Rombauer (Meilleur du Chai), Rudd Estate, Saddleback, St Clement, SCREAMING EAGLE, Seavey, SHAFER, SILVER OAK, SILVERADO, SPOTTSWOODE, Staglin Family, STAG'S LEAP WINE CELLARS, STERLING, Swanson, The Terraces, Philip Togni, Turnbull, Viader, Villa Mt Eden (Signature Series), Vine Cliff, Vineyard 29, Von Strasser, Whitehall Lane, ZD.

NELSON *South Island, New Zealand* A range of mountains separates Nelson from MARLBOROUGH at the northern end of South Island. Nelson is made up of a series of small hills and valleys with a wide range of mesoclimates. Pinot Noir, Chardonnay, Riesling and Sauvignon Blanc do well. Best producers: Greenhough★, NEUDORF★★, SEIFRIED★/Redwood Valley. Best years: (whites) **2004 03 02 01 00**.

NERO D'AVOLA The name of SICILY's great red grape derives from the town of Avola near Siracusa, although it is now planted all over the island. Its deep colour, high sugars and acidity make it useful for blending, especially with the lower-acid Nerello Mascalese, but also with Cabernet, Merlot and Syrah. On its own, and from the right soils, it can be brilliant, with a soft, ripe, spicy black-fruit character. Examples range from simple quaffers to many of Sicily's top reds.

NEUCHÂTEL *Switzerland* Swiss canton with high-altitude vineyards, mainly Chasselas whites and Pinot Noir reds and rosé. Best producers: Ch. d'Auvernier, Châteney, Montmillon, Porret.

NEUDORF *Nelson, South Island, New Zealand* Owners Tim and Judy Finn produce some of New Zealand's most stylish and sought-after wines, including gorgeous, honeyed Chardonnay★★★, rich but scented Pinot Noir★★, Sauvignon Blanc★★ and Riesling★. Best years: (Chardonnay) (2004) **02 01 00 99 98**; (Pinot Noir) (2003) **02 01 00 99 98**.

NEW SOUTH WALES *Australia* Australia's most populous state is responsible for about 25% of the country's grape production. The largest centres of production are the irrigated areas of RIVERINA and Murray Darling, Swan Hill and Perricoota on the Murray River, where better viticultural and winemaking practices and lower yields have led to significant quality improvements. Smaller premium-quality regions include the old-established HUNTER VALLEY, Cowra and higher-altitude MUDGEE, Orange and HILLTOPS. CANBERRA is an area of tiny vineyards at chilly altitudes, as is Tumbarumba at the base of the Snowy Mountains.

NEW YORK STATE *USA* Wine grapes were first planted on Manhattan Island in the mid-17th century, but it wasn't until the early 1950s that a serious wine industry began to develop in the state as vinifera grapes were planted to replace natives such as *Vitis labrusca*. Weather conditions, particularly in the north, can be challenging, but improved vineyard practices have made a good vintage possible in most recent years. The most important region is the FINGER LAKES in the north of the state, but LONG ISLAND is the most exciting; the Hudson Valley has a couple of good producers. Best producers: (Hudson Valley) Clinton, Millbrook★. See also Finger Lakes and Long Island.

NEWTON *Napa Valley AVA, California, USA* Spectacular winery and steep vineyards high above St Helena, now owned by French luxury giant LVMH. Cabernet Sauvignon★★, Merlot★★ and Claret★ are some of California's most pleasurable examples. Even better is the single-vineyard Cabernet Sauvignon Le Puzzle★★★. Newton pioneered the unfiltered Chardonnay★★★ style and this lush mouthful remains one of California's best. Age the Chardonnays for up to 5 years, reds for 10–15. Best years: (Cabernet Sauvignon) (2002) (01) 00 99 97 **96 95 94 91 90**.

NGATARAWA *Hawkes Bay, North Island, New Zealand* Viticulture here is
organic, with Chardonnay, botrytized Riesling and Cabernet-Merlot
produced under the premium Alwyn Reserve label. The Glazebrook
range includes attractive Chardonnay★ and Cabernet-Merlot★, both
of which are best drunk within 5 years. Best years: (reds) **2002 00 98**.

NIAGARA PENINSULA *Ontario, Canada* Sandwiched between lakes Erie
and Ontario, the Niagara Peninsula benefits from regular through-
breezes created by the Niagara escarpment, the cool climate bringing
out distinctive characteristics in the wine. Icewine, from Riesling and
Vidal, is the showstopper, with growing international acclaim.
Chardonnay leads the dry whites, with Pinot Noir, Merlot and
Cabernet Franc showing most promise among the reds. Best
producers: Cave Spring★, Chateau des Charmes★, HENRY OF PELHAM★,
INNISKILLIN★★, Konzelmann★, Reif Estate★, Southbrook★, Stoney Ridge,
THIRTY BENCH★. Best years: (icewines) 2003 02 **00 99 98**.

NIEBAUM-COPPOLA ESTATE *Rutherford AVA, California, USA* Movie
director Francis Ford Coppola has turned the historical Inglenook
Niebaum winery into an elaborate tourist destination. Rubicon★★, a
BORDEAUX blend, lacked grace in early vintages but has now taken on a
more exciting personality. It still needs 5–6 years of aging. Coppola
offers Zinfandel★ under the Edizione Pennino label and Cabernet Franc★
under Coppola Family Wines. Cask★★, a 100% Cabernet Sauvignon, is
a recent addition, while the Diamond series (especially Syrah and Claret)
are good buys. Best years: (Rubicon) (2002) 01 **00 99 97 96 95 94 91 86**.

NIEPOORT *Port DOC, Douro, Portugal* Remarkable small PORT shipper of
Dutch origin, run by the widely respected Dirk van der Niepoort.
Outstanding Vintage ports★★★, old tawnies★★★ and Colheitas★★★
and a single-quinta wine: Quinta do Passadouro★★. Unfiltered LBVs★★
are among the best in their class – intense and complex. The Vintage
Port second label is called Secundum★★, while Batuta★★★ and
Charme★★★ are already established as two of Portugal's leading reds.
Niepoort also produces fine red and white DOURO Redoma★★. Best
years: (Vintage) 2000 97 94 92 91 **87 85 82 80 77 70 66 63**.

NIERSTEIN *Rheinhessen, Germany* Both a small town and a large Bereich
which includes the infamous Grosslage Gutes Domtal. The town boasts
23 vineyard sites and the top ones (Pettenthal, Brudersberg, Hipping,
Oelberg and Orbel) are some of the best in the Rhine Valley. Best
producers: Heinrich Braun★, GUNDERLOCH★★, HEYL ZU HERRNSHEIM★★, ST
ANTONY★★, Schneider★. Best years: (2004) 03 02 01 99 98 **97 96**.

NIKOLAIHOF *Wachau, Niederösterreich, Austria* The Saahs family makes
some of the best wines in the WACHAU as well as in nearby Krems-Stein
in KREMSTAL, including steely, intense Rieslings from the famous
Steiner Hund vineyard, always ★★. An organic estate. Best years:
(2004) 03 02 01 **99 98 97 95 94 90**.

NOBILO *Kumeu/Huapai, Auckland, North Island, New Zealand* Wines
from New Zealand's second-largest winery range from medium-dry
White Cloud to single-vineyard varietals. Lush, intensely flavoured
Dixon Vineyard Chardonnay★★ is made only in selected years. Tangy
though restrained Sauvignon Blanc and a vibrant Chardonnay★ are
the top wines from MARLBOROUGH. In 1998 Nobilo bought Selaks, with
wineries in AUCKLAND and Marlborough (Drylands); since then they
have added the intense Drylands Marlborough Sauvignon Blanc★★,
Chardonnay★ and Riesling★ to their list. Nobilo is now part of
Constellation, the world's largest wine group.

NORTON *Luján de Cuyo, Mendoza, Argentina* Austrian-owned winery where reds impress more than whites, with good, chocolaty Sangiovese, soft, rich Merlot★ and good Barbera. Higher up the scale, Reserva reds are ripe and full, while top-of-the-line Privada★★ is drinkable young but well worth aging. Perfumed Torrontés★ and snappy Sauvignon Blanc★ are good whites.

NOVAL, QUINTA DO *Port DOC, Douro, Portugal* Owned by AXA-Millésimes, this immaculate property is the source of extraordinary Quinta do Noval Nacional★★★, made from ungrafted vines – some say the best vintage PORT made, but virtually unobtainable except at auction. Other Noval ports (including Noval Vintage★★★ and single-quinta Silval★★) are excellent too. Also fine Colheitas★★ and some stunning 40-year-old tawnies★★★. Best years: (Nacional) 2000 97 94 87 85 **70 66 63 62 60 31**; (Vintage) 2000 97 95 94 91 **87 85 70 66 63 60 31**.

NUITS-ST-GEORGES AC *Côte de Nuits, Burgundy, France* This large AC is one of the few relatively reliable 'village' names in Burgundy. Although it has no Grands Crus, many of its Premiers Crus (it has 38!) are extremely good. The red can be rather slow to open out, often needing at least 5 years. Minuscule amounts of white are made by Gouges★, l'Arlot, Chevillon and RION. Best producers: l'Arlot★★, R Arnoux★★, J Chauvenet★★, R Chevillon★★, J-J Confuron★★, FAIVELEY★★, H Gouges★★, GRIVOT★★, JAYER-GILLES★★, D Laurent★★, Lecheneaut★★, MEO-CAMUZET★★, A Michelot★★, Mugneret★★, Nicolas POTEL★★, RION★★, THOMAS-MOILLARD★★. Best years: (reds) (2004) 03 02 01 **00** 99 **98 97** 96 **95 93 90**.

NYETIMBER *West Sussex, England* Specialist bottle-fermented sparkling wine producer using classic CHAMPAGNE varieties. Original owners (Sandy and Stuart Moss from Chicago) sold to songwriter Andy Hill in 2001. New winemaker Dermot Sugrue (from the 2004 harvest) and Epernay-based enologist Jean-Marie Jacquinot (who has been there since the first 1992 vintage) continue to make exceptionally good wines with delicious toasty flavours and great length. Two wines are made: Classic Cuvée★★ (Chardonnay, Pinot Noir and Pinot Meunier) and Chardonnay-based Blanc de Blancs★★. Best years: **1996 95 94**.

OAKVILLE AVA *Napa Valley, California, USA* This region is cooler than RUTHERFORD, which lies immediately to the north. Planted primarily to Cabernet Sauvignon, the area contains some of NAPA's best vineyards, both on the valley floor (MONDAVI, OPUS ONE, SCREAMING EAGLE) and hillsides (HARLAN ESTATE, DALLA VALLE), producing wines that display lush, ripe black fruits and firm tannins. Best years: (Cabernet Sauvignon) (2002) (01) (00) **99 97 96 95 94 91 90**.

OC, VIN DE PAYS D' *Languedoc-Roussillon, France* Important Vin de Pays covering LANGUEDOC-ROUSSILLON. Problems of overproduction and consequently underripeness have dogged attempts to smarten up its reputation. Occasional fine red or white shows what can be done. Best producers: l'Aigle★, Clovallon★, J-L Denois★, l'HOSPITALET (Cigalus★★), J & F Lurton★, MAS LA CHEVALIERE, Ormesson★, Pech-Céleyran (Viognier★), Quatre Sous★, St-Saturnin★, SKALLI-FORTANT, VAL D'ORBIEU (top reds★), Virginie.

OCKFEN *Saar, Germany* Village with one famous individual vineyard site, the Bockstein. The wines can be superb in a sunny year, never losing their cold steely streak but packing in delightful full-flavoured fruit as well. Best producers: St Urbans-Hof★★, Dr Heinz Wagner★★, ZILLIKEN★★. Best years: (2004) 03 02 01 **99 97 95 93 90**.

OKANAGAN VALLEY *British Columbia, Canada* The oldest and most important wine-producing region of British Columbia and first home of Canada's rich, honeyed icewine. The Okanagan Lake helps temper the bitterly cold nights but October frosts can be a problem. Chardonnay, Pinot Blanc, Pinot Gris and Pinot Noir are the top-performers. South of the lake, Cabernet, Merlot and even Shiraz are now being grown successfully. Best producers: Blue Mountain★, Burrowing Owl★, Gehringer★, INNISKILLIN, MISSION HILL★, Quails' Gate, SUMAC RIDGE★, Tinhorn Creek. Best years: (reds) **2002 01 00 98**.

OLTREPÒ PAVESE DOC *Lombardy, Italy* Italy's main source of Pinot Nero, used mainly for sparkling wines that may be called Classese when made here by the CHAMPAGNE method, though base wines supply *spumante* industries elsewhere. The region supplies Milan's everyday wines, often fizzy, though still reds from Barbera, Bonarda and Pinot Nero and whites from the Pinots, Riesling and Chardonnay can be impressive. Best producers: Cà di Frara★, Le Fracce★, Frecciarossa★, Fugazza, Mazzolino★, Monsupello★, Montelio★, Vercesi del Castellazzo★, Bruno Verdi★. Best years: (reds) (2004) 03 **01 00 99 98 97 96 95**.

WILLI OPITZ *Neusiedlersee, Austria* The eccentric and publicity-conscious Willi Opitz produces a remarkable, unusual range of dessert wines from his 12ha (30-acre) vineyard, including red Eiswein. The best are ★★, but dry wines are simpler and less consistent.

OPUS ONE★★ *Oakville AVA, California, USA* Joint venture between Robert MONDAVI and the late Baron Philippe de Rothschild of MOUTON-ROTHSCHILD. The first vintage (1979) of the BORDEAUX-blend wine was released in 1983. At that time, the $50 price was the most expensive for any California wine, though others have reached way beyond it now. The various Opus bottlings have been in the ★★ range but have rarely reached the standard of the Mondavi Reserve Cabernet. Best years: (2002) 01 00 99 98 97 96 **95** 94 **93 92 91 90 86 85 84**.

DOM. DE L'ORATOIRE ST-MARTIN *Côtes du Rhône AC, Rhône Valley, France* Careful fruit selection in the vineyard is the secret of Frédéric and François Alary's concentrated Côtes du Rhône-Villages CAIRANNE reds and whites. Haut-Coustias white★ is ripe with peach and exotic fruit aromas, while the red★★ is a luscious mouthful of raspberries, herbs and spice. Top red Cuvée Prestige★★ is deep and intense with darkly spicy fruit. Best years: (Cuvée Prestige) 2004 03 **01 00 99 98 97 96 95**.

DOMAINE DE
L'ORATOIRE S.ᵗᵉ MARTIN

Cuvée Prestige
— 2001 —
CAIRANNE
CÔTES-DU-RHÔNE-VILLAGES
FRÉDÉRIC & FRANÇOIS ALARY

OREGON *USA* Oregon shot to international stardom in the early 1980s following some perhaps overly generous praise of its Pinot Noir, but it is only with the release of 5 fine vintages in a row – 1998 to 2002 – and some soul-searching by the winemakers about what style they should be pursuing that we can now begin to accept that some of the hype was deserved. Chardonnay can be quite good in an austere, understated style. The rising star is Pinot Gris which, in Oregon's cool climate, can be delicious, with surprising complexity. Pinot Blanc is also gaining momentum. The WILLAMETTE VALLEY is considered the best growing region, although the more BORDEAUX-like climate of the Umpqua and Rogue Valleys can produce good Cabernet Sauvignon and Merlot. Best producers: (Rogue, Umpqua) Abacela★, Bridgeview★, Calahan Ridge, Foris★, Henry Estate, Valley View Winery. Best years: (reds) (2002) 01 **00 99 98 96**.

ORLANDO *Barossa Valley, South Australia*   Australia's third-biggest wine company and the force behind export colossus Jacob's Creek is owned by Pernod-Ricard. It encompasses MORRIS, Russet Ridge, Wickham Hill, Gramp's, Richmond Grove and Wyndham Estate, and MUDGEE winery Poet's Corner, home of the Henry Lawson and Montrose brands. Top wines under the Orlando name include COONAWARRA reds St Hugo★ and Jacaranda Ridge★, and individualistic Eden Valley Rieslings St Helga★ and Steingarten★★, but Orlando has lacked strength at the premium end. Rich Centenary Hill BAROSSA Shiraz★★ might change that, as might renewed efforts in Mudgee. Jacob's Creek Reserve and Limited Release★★ wines are excellent. Basic Jacob's Creek Cabernet and Semillon-Chardonnay seem stretched, but Riesling★ and Grenache-Shiraz are fine. Best years: (St Hugo Cabernet) (2004) 03 02 01 **00 99 98 96 94 91 90 88 86**.

ORNELLAIA, TENUTA DELL' *Bolgheri, Tuscany, Italy*   This beautiful property in the heart of BOLGHERI was developed by Lodovico Antinori, brother of Piero, after he left the family firm, ANTINORI, to strike out on his own. Ornellaia★★★, a Cabernet-Merlot blend, bears comparison with neighbouring SASSICAIA. Also small amounts of outstanding Merlot, Masseto★★★. Bought by MONDAVI and FRESCOBALDI in 2002 and now owned 100% by Frescobaldi. Best years: (Ornellaia) (2004) (03) 01 **00 99 98 97 96 95 94 93 90 88**.

ORTENAU *Baden, Germany*   A chain of steep granitic hills between Baden-Baden and Offenburg, which produce the most elegant (generally dry) Rieslings in BADEN, along with fragrant, fruity, medium-bodied Spätburgunder (Pinot Noir) reds. Best producers: Laible★★, Männle, Nägelsförst★, Schloss Neuweier★.

ORVIETO DOC *Umbria, Italy*   Traditionally a lightly sweet (*abboccato*) white wine, Orvieto is now usually dry and characterless. In the superior Classico zone, however, the potential for richer, more biscuity wines exists. Not generally a wine for aging. There are also some very good botrytis-affected examples. Best producers: (dry) Barberani-Vallesanta★, La Carraia★, Decugnano dei Barbi★, Palazzone★, Castello della SALA★, Salviano★, Conte Vaselli★, Le Velette★; (sweet) Barberani-Vallesanta★, Decugnano dei Barbi★, Palazzone★, Castello della SALA★.

OSBORNE *Jerez y Manzanilla DO, Andalucía, Spain*   The biggest drinks company in Spain, Osborne does most of its business in brandy and other spirits. Its sherry arm in Puerto de Santa María specializes in the light Fino Quinta★. Amontillado Coquinero★, rich, intense Bailén Oloroso★★ and Solera India Oloroso★★ are very good indeed.

PAARL WO *South Africa*   Paarl is South Africa's second most densely planted district after Worcester, accounting for 16.4% of all vineyards. A great diversity of soil and climate favour everything from Cap Classique sparkling wines to sherry styles, but reds are setting the quality pace, especially Shiraz. Its white RHONE counterpart, Viognier, is also performing well. Wellington and FRANSCHHOEK are smaller designated areas (wards) within the Paarl district. Best producers: (Paarl) Boschendal, DISTELL (Plaisir de Merle★, Nederburg), FAIRVIEW★★, GLEN CARLOU★★, Rupert & Rothschild★, VEENWOUDEN★★, Welgemeend★; (Wellington) Diemersfontein★, Mont du Toit★. Best years: (premium reds) 2003 **02 01 00 99 98 97**.

PACHERENC DU VIC-BILH AC *South-West France*   Individual whites from an area overlapping the MADIRAN AC in north-east Béarn. The wines are mainly dry, but there are some medium-sweet/sweet late-harvest wines. Most Pacherenc is best drunk young. Best producers: Aydie★, Berthoumieu★, Brumont (Bouscassé★, MONTUS★), du Crampilh★, Damiens, Laffitte-Teston★, Producteurs PLAIMONT★, Sergent★, Viella. Best years: 2004 03 **02 01 00 97**.

PADTHAWAY *South Australia* This wine region has always been the alter-ego of nearby COONAWARRA, growing whites to complement Coonawarra's reds. Padthaway Sauvignon Blanc is some of Australia's tastiest, and LINDEMANS' Padthaway Chardonnay★ is a serious white. But today some excellent reds are made, especially by Henry's Drive; even GRANGE has included some Padthaway grapes. ORLANDO's premium Lawson's Shiraz★★ is 100% Padthaway, HARDY's Eileen Hardy Shiraz★★★ sometimes includes some Padthaway fruit. Best producers: Browns of Padthaway, Stonehaven★ (Hardy), Henry's Drive★★, LINDEMANS★, ORLANDO★, Padthaway Estate, SEPPELT.

BRUNO PAILLARD *Champagne AC, Champagne, France* Bruno Paillard is one of the very few individuals to have created a new CHAMPAGNE house over the past century. Paillard still does the blending himself. The non-vintage Première Cuvée★ is lemony and crisp, the Réserve Privée★ is a blanc de blancs; the vintage Brut★★ is a serious wine, and in 2000 he launched a de luxe cuvée, Nec Plus Ultra★★, a barrel-fermented blend of Grands Crus made in top vintages. Also owns Philipponnat and the great single-vineyard site, Clos des Goisses★★★. Best years: 1996 **95 90 89 88**.

ALVARO PALACIOS *Priorat DOCa, Cataluña, Spain* The young Alvaro Palacios was already a veteran with Bordeaux and Napa experience when he launched his boutique winery in the rough hills of southern CATALUÑA in the late 1980s. He is now one of the driving forces of the area's sensational rebirth. His expensive, highly concentrated reds (L'Ermita★★★, Finca Dofí★★, Les Terrasses★) from old Garnacha vines and a dollop of Cabernet Sauvignon, Merlot, Cariñena and Syrah have won a cult following. Best years: 2001 00 **99 98 97 96 95 94 93**.

PALETTE AC *Provence, France* Tiny AC just east of Aix-en-Provence. Even though the local market pays high prices, I find the reds and rosés rather tough and charmless. However, Ch. Simone manages to achieve a white wine of some flavour from basic southern French grapes. Best producers: Crémade, Ch. Simone★.

PALLISER ESTATE *Martinborough, North Island, New Zealand* State-of-the-art winery producing some of New Zealand's best Sauvignon Blanc★★ (certainly the best outside MARLBOROUGH) and Riesling★, with some impressive, rich-textured Pinot Noir★★. Exciting botrytized dessert wines appear in favourable vintages. Méthode★ fizz is also impressive. Best years: (Pinot Noir) **2001 00 99 98**.

CH. PALMER★★ *Margaux AC, 3ème Cru Classé, Haut-Médoc, Bordeaux, France* This estate was named after a British major-general who fought in the Napoleonic Wars, and is one of the leading properties in MARGAUX AC. The wine is wonderfully perfumed, with irresistible plump fruit. The very best vintages can age for 30 years or more. Second wine: Alter Ego (previously Réserve-du-Général). Best years: 2003 02 01 00 **99 98 96 95 90 89 88 86 85 83 82**.

CH. PAPE-CLÉMENT *Pessac-Léognan AC, Cru Classé de Graves, Bordeaux, France* The expensive red wine★★ from this GRAVES Classed Growth has not always been as consistent as it should be – but things settled down into a high-quality groove during the 1990s. In style it is mid-way between the refinement of HAUT-BRION and the firmness of la MISSION-HAUT-BRION. Pape-Clément also produces a small amount of a much-improved white wine★★. Second wine: (red) Clémentin. Best years: (reds) 2003 02 01 00 **99** 98 **97** 96 **95 90 89 88 86**; (white) (2004) 03 02 **01 00 99 98 96**.

PARELLADA This Catalan exclusivity is the lightest of the trio of white grapes that go to make CAVA wines in north-eastern Spain. It also makes still wines, light, fresh and gently floral, with good acidity. Drink it as young as possible, while it still has the benefit of freshness.

PARKER COONAWARRA ESTATE *Coonawarra, South Australia* Things have finally settled down following the death of founder John Parker; the estate has been bought by the Rathbone family who own Yering Station in the YARRA VALLEY and MOUNT LANGHI GHIRAN. The top label, cheekily named First Growth★★ in imitation of illustrious BORDEAUX reds, has enjoyed much critical acclaim. It is released only in better years. Second label Terra Rossa Cabernet Sauvignon★ is lighter and leafier. The Merlot★★ is among the best produced in Australia. Best years: (First Growth) (2004) (03) 02 01 99 **98 96 93 91 90**.

C J PASK *Hawkes Bay, North Island, New Zealand* Chris Pask made the first wine in the now-famous Gimblett Gravels area of HAWKES BAY and remains one of the district's larger vineyard owners. Winemaker Kate Radburnd is best known for her Reserve reds, including a rich and powerful Reserve Merlot★★ and elegant, long-lived Reserve Cabernet Sauvignon★. Best years: (reds) **2002 00 98**.

PASO ROBLES AVA *California, USA* A large AVA at the northern end of SAN LUIS OBISPO COUNTY. Cabernet Sauvignon and Zinfandel perform well in this warm region, and Syrah is gaining an important foothold. The Perrin family from Ch. de BEAUCASTEL selected this AVA to plant RHONE varieties for their California project, Tablas Creek, whose whites so far outshine the reds. Best producers: Adelaida★, Eberle★, Justin★, J Lohr★, Peachy Canyon★, Tablas Creek★, Wild Horse★.

LUIS PATO *Bairrada, Beira Litoral, Portugal* Leading 'modernist' in BAIRRADA, passionately convinced of the Baga grape's ability to make great reds on clay soil. He now labels his wines as BEIRAS after arguing with Bairrada's bosses. Wines such as the Vinhas Velhas★, Vinha Barrosa★★, Vinha Pan★★ and the flagship Quinta do Ribeirinho Pé Franco★★ (from ungrafted vines) rank among Portugal's finest modern reds, and some can reach ★★★ with age. Homenagem★★ combines Baga with Touriga Nacional from Quinta de Cabriz (DÃO). Good white, Vinha Formal★, is 100% Bical. Best years: (reds) (2004) 03 01 **00 97 96 95 92**.

PAUILLAC AC *Haut-Médoc, Bordeaux, France* The deep gravel banks around the town of Pauillac in the HAUT-MEDOC are the heartland of Cabernet Sauvignon. For many wine lovers, the king of red wine grapes finds its ultimate expression in the 3 Pauillac First Growths (LATOUR, LAFITE-ROTHSCHILD and MOUTON-ROTHSCHILD). The large AC also contains 15 other Classed Growths. The uniting characteristic of Pauillac wines is their intense blackcurrant fruit flavour and heady cedar and pencil-shavings perfume. These are the longest-lived of BORDEAUX's great red wines. Best producers: Armailhac★, BATAILLEY★, Clerc-Milon★, Duhart-Milon★, Fonbadet, GRAND-PUY-DUCASSE★, GRAND-PUY-LACOSTE★★, HAUT-BAGES-LIBERAL★, HAUT-BATAILLEY★, LAFITE-ROTHSCHILD★★★, LATOUR★★★, LYNCH-BAGES★★★, MOUTON-ROTHSCHILD★★★,

Pibran★, PICHON-LONGUEVILLE★★★, PICHON-LONGUEVILLE-LALANDE★★★, PONTET-CANET★★. Best years: 2003 02 01 00 96 **95 90 89 88 86 85 83 82**.

CH. PAVIE★★ *St-Émilion Grand Cru AC, 1er Grand Cru Classé, Bordeaux, France* Pavie has had its ups and downs in recent years, until a change of ownership in 1998 (it is now part of the same team as Pavie-Decesse★ and MONBOUSQUET★) has revitalized it. However, the wine has now become so super-rich and concentrated, it tastes like a caricature. I wish someone would tell the owner – less is more. Best years: 2003 02 01 00 **99 98 96 95 90 89 88 85 83 82**.

CH. PAVIE-MACQUIN★★ *St-Émilion Grand Cru AC, Grand Cru Classé, Bordeaux, France* This has become one of the stars of the ST-EMILION GRAND CRU since the 1990s. Management and winemaking are in the hands of Nicolas Thienpont (of BORDEAUX-COTES DE FRANCS) and Stéphane Derenoncourt, who consults to CANON-LA-GAFFELIERE and PRIEURE-LICHINE, among others. Rich, firm and reserved, the wines need 7–8 years and will age longer. Best years: 2003 02 01 00 99 98 **97** 96 **95 94 90**.

PÉCHARMANT AC *South-West France* Improving red wines from small AC north-east of BERGERAC. The wines are quite light in body but have a delicious, full, piercing flavour of blackcurrants and attractive grassy acidity. Good vintages easily last 10 years and match a good HAUT-MEDOC. Best producers: Beauportail, Bertranoux, Costes★, Grand Jaure, Haut-Pécharmant★, Métairie★, Tiregand★. Best years: 2003 01 **00 98 96 95**.

PEDROSA *Ribera del Duero DO, Castilla y León, Spain* Delightful, elegant reds★ (Pérez Pascuas Gran Reserva★), both young and oak-aged, from a family winery in the little hill village of Pedrosa de Duero. The wines are not cheap, but far less pricy than some stars of this fashionable region. Best years: (Pérez Pascuas) 2001 **96 95 94 91 90**.

PEGASUS BAY *Canterbury, South Island, New Zealand* Matthew Donaldson and Lynette Hudson make lush, mouthfilling Chardonnay★★, an almost chewy Pinot Noir★★ and its even richer big brother Prima Donna Pinot Noir★★, a powerful Sauvignon Blanc-Semillon★★ and a very stylish Riesling★★ – an impressive portfolio from this upcoming region. All will age well. Best years: (2004) **02 01 00 99 98**.

PEMBERTON *Western Australia* Exciting emergent region, deep in the karri forests of the south-west, full of promise for cool-climate Pinot Noir, Shiraz, Chardonnay, Merlot and Sauvignon Blanc. HOUGHTON lead the way thanks to the outstanding fruit coming from the vineyard they purchased a decade ago. Their regional range – sparkling Chardonnay-Pinot Noir★, Sauvignon Blanc★★, Chardonnay★★, but dull Merlot – has been highly successful. Best producers: HOUGHTON★★, Lillian, Merum, Phillips Estate★, Picardy★, Salitage★, Smithbrook.

PENEDÈS DO *Cataluña, Spain* The booming CAVA industry is based in Penedès, and the majority of the still wines are white, made from the Cava trio of Parellada, Macabeo and Xarel-lo, clean and fresh when young, but never exciting. Better whites are made from Chardonnay. The reds are variable, the best made from Cabernet Sauvignon and/or Tempranillo and Merlot. Best producers: Albet i Noya★, Can Feixes★, Can Ràfols dels Caus★ (Caus Lubis Merlot★★), Cavas Hill, JUVE Y CAMPS, Jean León★, Marques de Monistrol, Masía Bach★, Albert Milá i Mallofré, Puig y Roca★, Sot Lefriec★, TORRES★, Vallformosa, Jané Ventura★.

PENFOLDS *Barossa Valley, South Australia* Part of Australia's giant Southcorp group, Penfolds has proved that quality *can* go hand in hand with quantity; but since merging with ROSEMOUNT there has been a discernible dulling of the Penfolds palate. Still makes the country's most famous red wine, GRANGE★★★, and a welter of other reds such as Magill Estate★★, St Henri★, Bin 707 Cabernet★★, Bin 389 Cabernet-Shiraz★, Bin 28 Kalimna★ and Bin 128 Coonawarra Shiraz, but as you go further down the range to previously reliable wines like Koonunga Hill and Rawson's Retreat a dispiriting blandness enters in. There are signs of return to form with the 2002 vintage. Whites are led by overpriced Yattarna Chardonnay★★. Also makes tasty wooded Semillon★★, citrus Eden Valley Riesling★ and Rawson's Retreat Riesling. Thomas Hyland red and white are pretty good. Best years: (top reds) 2002 99 **98 96 94 91 90**.

PENLEY ESTATE *Coonawarra, South Australia* Kym Tolley, a member of the PENFOLD family, combined the names when he left Southcorp and launched Penley Estate in 1991. From 1997 Cabernet Sauvignon★★★ has been outstanding. Chardonnay and Hyland Shiraz can reach ★★; Merlot★ and fizz★ are also worth a try. Best years: (Cabernet) (2004) (03) 02 00 99 98 **96 94 93 92 91**.

PERNAND-VERGELESSES AC *Côte de Beaune, Burgundy, France* The little-known village of Pernand-Vergelesses contains a decent chunk of the great Corton hill, including much of the best white CORTON-CHARLEMAGNE Grand Cru vineyard. The red wines sold under the village name are very attractive when young, with a nice raspberry pastille fruit and a slight earthiness, and will age for 6–10 years. As no-one ever links poor old Pernand with the heady heights of Corton-Charlemagne, the whites sold under the village name can be a bargain. The wines can be a bit lean and dry to start with but fatten up beautifully after 2–4 years in bottle. Best producers: (reds) CHANDON DE BRIAILLES★★, C Cornu★, Denis Père et Fils★, Dubreuil-Fontaine★, Laleure-Piot★, Rapet★, Rollin★; (whites) CHANDON DE BRIAILLES★★, Dubreuil-Fontaine★, Germain, A Guyon, JADOT, Laleure-Piot★, J-M Pavelot★, Rapet★, Rollin★. Best years: (reds) (2004) **03** 02 **01** 99; (whites) (2004) **03** 02 **01** 00 99.

ANDRÉ PERRET *Condrieu AC, Rhône Valley, France* One of the top CONDRIEU growers, with 2 star cuvées: Clos Chanson★★ is direct and full, Coteau de Chéry★★★, made with some later-picked grapes, is musky, floral and rich. Impressive white and red ST-JOSEPH, notably Les Grisières★★ from old Syrah vines. Best years: (Condrieu) 2004 **03 01 00 99**.

JOSEPH PERRIER *Champagne AC, Champagne, France* In 1998 Alain Thiénot took a controlling interest in this CHAMPAGNE house. The NV Cuvée★ is biscuity and creamy, Prestige Cuvée Josephine★★ has length and complexity, but the much cheaper Cuvée Royale Vintage★★ is the best deal. Best years: (1998) 96 **95 90 89 88 85 82**.

PERRIER-JOUËT *Champagne AC, Champagne, France* Until 1999, Perrier-Jouët was owned by the Seagram group, and performance was generally lacklustre, although the vintage CHAMPAGNE could be quite good. Quality then got better: the Blason Rosé★ is charming and the de luxe vintage cuvée Belle Époque★★ is now very classy. Efforts to improve quality and consistency by the winemaker Hervé Deschamps have continued under the ownership (since 2001) of Allied Domecq. Best years: (1998) 97 96 **95 92 90 89 85 82**.

PESQUERA *Ribera del Duero DO, Castilla y León, Spain*　Tinto Pesquera
reds, richly coloured, firm, fragrant and plummy-tobaccoey, have long
been among Spain's best. Made by the small firm of Alejandro
Fernández, they are 100% Tempranillo and sold as Crianza and
Reserva★. Gran Reserva★★ and Janus★★★ are made in the best
years. Condado de Haza (Alenza★) is a separate estate. New ventures
in Zamora (Dehesa La Granja★) and La MANCHA (Vínculo). Best years:
(Pesquera Crianza) 2001 **99 96 95 94 93 92 91 90 89**.

PESSAC-LÉOGNAN AC *Bordeaux, France*　AC created in 1987 for the
northern (and best) part of the GRAVES region and including all the
Graves Classed Growths. The supremely gravelly soil tends to favour
red wines over the rest of the Graves. Now, thanks to cool
fermentation and the use of new oak barrels, this is also one of the
most exciting areas of France for top-class white wines. Best
producers: (reds) Brown, les Carmes Haut-Brion★, Dom. de
CHEVALIER★★, FIEUZAL★, HAUT-BAILLY★★, HAUT-BRION★★★, Larrivet Haut-
Brion★, LATOUR-MARTILLAC★, la LOUVIERE★, MALARTIC-LAGRAVIERE★, la
MISSION-HAUT-BRION★★★, PAPE-CLEMENT★★, SMITH-HAUT-LAFITTE★★, la
Tour-Haut-Brion★; (whites) Carbonnieux★, Dom. de CHEVALIER★★★,
Couhins-Lurton★★, FIEUZAL★, HAUT-BRION★★★, LATOUR-MARTILLAC★,
LAVILLE-HAUT-BRION★★★, la LOUVIERE★★, MALARTIC-LAGRAVIERE★, PAPE-
CLEMENT★★, Rochemorin★, SMITH-HAUT-LAFITTE★★. Best years: (reds)
2002 01 00 **99 98 96 95 90 89 88**; (whites) (2004) 02 **01 00 99 98 96 95**.

PETALUMA *Adelaide Hills, South Australia*　This public company, which
includes KNAPPSTEIN, MITCHELTON, STONIER and Smithbrook in WESTERN
AUSTRALIA, was founded by Brian Croser, probably Australia's most
influential winemaker. It was taken over by brewer Lion Nathan in
2001. CHAMPAGNE-style Croser★ is stylish but lean. Chardonnay★★
and COONAWARRA (Cabernet-Merlot)★★ are consistently fine and CLARE
Riesling★★ is at the fuller end of the spectrum and matures superbly.
Vineyard Selection Tiers Chardonnay★★★ is ridiculously expensive
but excellent. Best years: (Coonawarra) 2002 01 00 **99 97 94 91 90 88**.

PETIT VERDOT　A rich, tannic variety, grown mainly in Bordeaux's HAUT-
MEDOC to add depth, colour and violet fragrance to top wines. Late
ripening and erratic yield limit its popularity, but warmer-climate
plantings in Australia, California, Chile, Argentina, Spain and Italy are
giving exciting results.

CH. PETIT-VILLAGE★★ *Pomerol AC, Bordeaux, France*　This top POMEROL
wine is sterner in style than its neighbours. In general it is worth
aging the wine for 8–10 years at least. Best years: 2003 01 00 **99 98 96
95 94 90 89 88 85 82**.

PETITE ARVINE　A Swiss grape variety from the VALAIS, Petite Arvine has
a bouquet of peach and apricot, and develops a spicy, honeyed
character. Dry, medium or sweet, the wines have good aging
potential. Best producers: Chappaz★, Caves Imesch★, Dom. du Mont
d'Or★, Varone.

PETITE SIRAH　Used as a blending grape in California but used also for
varietal wines, Petite Sirah is often confused with the Durif of southern
France. At its best in California and Mexico, the wine has great depth
and strength; at worst it can be monstrously huge and unfriendly. Best

producers: L A CETTO★ (Mexico), De Loach★, FETZER, Fife, Foppiano, RAVENSWOOD★, RIDGE★★, Stags' Leap Winery★★, TURLEY★★.

CH. PÉTRUS★★★ *Pomerol AC, Bordeaux, France*   One of the most expensive red wines in the world (alongside other superstars from POMEROL, such as le PIN). The powerful, concentrated wine produced here is the result of the caring genius of Pétrus' owners, the MOUEIX family, who have maximized the potential of the vineyard of almost solid clay, although the impressive average age of the vines has been much reduced by recent replantings. Drinkable for its astonishingly rich, dizzying blend of fruit and spice flavours after a decade, but top years will age for much longer, developing exotic scents of tobacco and chocolate and truffles as they mature. Best years: 2003 02 01 00 99 98 96 **95 90 89 88 86 85.**

DOM. PEYRE ROSE *Coteaux du Languedoc AC, Languedoc, France*   Organic viticulture, ultra-low yields and total absence of oak are all marks of the individuality of Marlène Soria's wines. Syrah is the dominant grape in both the raisin- and plum-scented Clos des Cistes★★ and the dense, velvety Clos Syrah Léone★★. Best years: (reds) 2001 00 **99 98 97 96 95 94.**

CH. DE PEZ★ *St-Estèphe AC, Cru Bourgeois, Haut-Médoc, Bordeaux, France*   One of ST-ESTEPHE's leading non-Classed Growths, de Pez makes mouthfilling, satisfying claret with sturdy fruit. Slow to evolve, good vintages often need 10 years or more. Now owned by Champagne house ROEDERER. Best years: 2003 02 01 00 **99 98 96 95 90 89 88.**

PFALZ *Germany*   Germany's most productive wine region, with 23,420ha (57,870 acres), makes a lot of mediocre wine, but the quality estates are capable of matching the best that Germany has to offer. The Mittelhaardt has a reputation for Riesling, especially round the villages of WACHENHEIM, FORST and Deidesheim, though Freinsheim, KALLSTADT, Ungstein, Gimmeldingen and Haardt also produce fine Riesling as well as Scheurebe, Rieslaner and Pinot Gris. In the Südliche Weinstrasse the warm climate makes the area an ideal testing ground for Spät-, Weiss- and Grauburgunder (aka Pinots Noir, Blanc and Gris), as well as Gewürztraminer, Scheurebe, Muscat and red Dornfelder, the last often dark and tannic, sometimes produced with oak barrique influence. See also Bad Dürkheim.

JOSEPH PHELPS *Napa Valley AVA, California, USA*   Joseph Phelps' BORDEAUX-blend Insignia★★★ is consistently one of California's top reds, strongly fruit-driven with a lively spicy background. Phelps' pure Cabernets include Napa Valley★ and huge Backus Vineyard★★, beautifully balanced with solid ripe fruit. The Napa Merlot★ is ripe and elegant, with layers of fruit. Phelps was the first California winery to major on Rhône varietals, and makes an intense Viognier★ and complex Syrah★. A separate wine, Le Mistral, is a splendid Rhône red blend from Phelps' vineyards in MONTEREY COUNTY. Best years: (Insignia) (2002) 01 00 99 97 **96 95 94 93 91 85.**

CH. DE PIBARNON *Bandol AC, Provence, France*   Blessed with excellently located vineyards, Pibarnon is one of BANDOL's leading properties. The reds★★, extremely attractive when young, develop a truffly, wild herb character with age. Average white and a ripe, strawberryish rosé. Best years: (red) (2003) 01 00 99 98 **97 96 95 94 93 91 90 89.**

PIC ST-LOUP *Coteaux du Languedoc AC, Languedoc, France* This Cru, north of Montpellier, is one of the coolest growing zones in the MIDI and produces some of the best reds in the Languedoc. Syrah is the dominant variety, along with Grenache and Mourvèdre. Whites from Marsanne, Roussanne, Rolle and Viognier are showing promise. Best producers: Cazeneuve★, Clos Marie★, Ermitage du Pic St-Loup, l'Euzière★, l'HORTUS★, Lancyre★, Lascaux★, Lavabre★, MAS BRUGUIERE★, Mas de Mortiès★. Best years: (reds) **2001 00 99 98 96 95 93 90**.

FRANZ X PICHLER *Wachau, Niederösterreich, Austria* Austria's most famous producer of dry wines. Demand for his Rieslings and Grüner Veltliners far outstrips supply. Top wines Grüner Veltliner and Riesling 'M'★★★ (for monumental) and Riesling Unendlich★★★ (endless), an alcoholically potent but balanced dry Riesling, are amazing. Since 1997 he has teamed up with Szemes and TEMENT in BURGENLAND to make red Arachon★★. Best years: (Riesling/Grüner Veltliner Smaragd) (2004) 03 02 01 00 **99 98 97 95 94 93 92**.

CH. PICHON-LONGUEVILLE★★★ *Pauillac AC, 2ème Cru Classé, Haut-Médoc, Bordeaux, France* Despite its superb vineyards, Pichon-Longueville (called Pichon-Baron until 1988) wines were 'also-rans' for a long time. In 1987 the property was bought by AXA and Jean-Michel Cazes of LYNCH-BAGES took over the management. The improvement was immediate and thrilling. Cazes has now left, but most recent vintages have been of First Growth standard, with firm tannic structure and rich dark fruit. Cellar for at least 10 years, although it is likely to keep for 30. Second wine: les Tourelles de Pichon. Best years: 2003 02 01 00 **99 98 97** 96 **95 90 89 88 86 82**.

CH. PICHON-LONGUEVILLE-LALANDE★★★ *Pauillac AC, 2ème Cru Classé, Haut-Médoc, Bordeaux, France* The inspirational figure of May de Lencquesaing has led the property ever upwards through her superlative vineyard management and winemaking sensitivity. Divinely scented and lush at 6–7 years, the wines usually last for 20 at least. Recent years have been excellent. Second wine: Réserve de la Comtesse. Best years: 2003 02 01 00 **99** 98 **97** 96 **95 90 89 88 86 85 83 82 81**.

PIEDMONT *Italy* This is the most important Italian region for the tradition of quality wines. In the north, there is Carema, Ghemme and GATTINARA. To the south, in the LANGHE hills, there's BAROLO and BARBARESCO, both masterful examples of the Nebbiolo grape, and other wines from Dolcetto and Barbera grapes. In the Monferrato hills, in the provinces of Asti and Alessandria, the Barbera, Moscato and Cortese grapes hold sway. Recent changes in the system have created the broad DOCs of Langhe and Monferrato and the regionwide Piemonte appellation, designed to classify all wines of quality from a great range of grape varieties. See also Asti, Erbaluce di Caluso, Gavi, Moscato d'Asti, Nebbiolo d'Alba, Roero.

PIEROPAN *Veneto, Italy* Leonildo Pieropan produces exceptionally good SOAVE Classico★ and, from 2 single vineyards, Calvarino★★ and La Rocca★★. Excellent RECIOTO DI SOAVE Le Colombare★★ and opulent Passito della Rocca★★, a barrique-aged blend of Sauvignon, Riesling Italico and Trebbiano di Soave. Single-vineyard Soaves can improve for 5 years or more, as can the Recioto and other sweet styles.

PIERRO *Margaret River, Western Australia* Mike Peterkin makes a fair bit of Pierro Chardonnay★★★, yet still it is a masterpiece of power and complexity. The LTC Semillon-Sauvignon-Chardonnay blend★ is full with just a hint of leafiness, while Pinot Noir★ continues to improve as the vines age. Dark, dense Cabernets★★ is the serious, BORDEAUX-like member of the family. The Fire Gully range is sourced from a nearby vineyard. Best years: (Chardonnay) 2003 02 **01 00 99 97 96 94 93**.

PIESPORT *Mosel, Germany* The generic Piesporter Michelsberg wines, soft, sweet and easy- drinking, have nothing to do with the excellent Rieslings from the top Goldtröpfchen site. With their intense peach and blackcurrant aromas they are unique among MOSEL wines. Best producers: GRANS-FASSIAN★★, Reinhold HAART★★, Kurt Hain★, von KESSELSTATT★, Lehnert-Veit, St Urbans-Hof★. Best years: (2004) 03 02 01 00 **99 98 97 96 95 93 92 90**.

CH. LE PIN★★★ *Pomerol AC, Bordeaux, France* Now one of the most expensive wines in the world, with prices at auction overtaking those for PETRUS. The 1979 was the first vintage and the wines, which are concentrated but elegant, are produced from 100% Merlot. The tiny 2ha (5-acre) vineyard lies close to those of TROTANOY and VIEUX-CH.-CERTAN. Best years: 2002 01 00 **99 98 96 95 94 90 89 88 86 85 83 82 81**.

PINE RIDGE WINERY *Stags Leap District AVA, California, USA* Wines come from several NAPA AVAs, but its flagship Cabernet remains the supple, plummy STAGS LEAP DISTRICT★★. Andrus Reserve★★, a BORDEAUX blend, has more richness and power, while the HOWELL MOUNTAIN Cabernet★ offers intense fruit and structure for long aging. CARNEROS Merlot★ is spicy and cherry fruited, and Carneros Chardonnay★ looks good. Best years: (Stags Leap Cabernet) (2002) 01 00 99 97 **96 95 94 91**.

PINGUS, DOMINIO DE *Ribera del Duero DO, Castilla y León, Spain* Peter Sisseck's tiny vineyards and winery have attracted worldwide attention since 1995 due to the extraordinary depth and character of the cult wine they produce, Pingus★★★. Second wine Flor de Pingus★★ is also super. Best years: (Pingus) (2001) 00 **99 98 97 96 95**.

PINOT BIANCO See Pinot Blanc.

PINOT BLANC Wines have a clear, yeasty, appley taste, and good examples can age to a delicious honeyed fullness. In ALSACE it is taking over the 'workhorse' role from Sylvaner and Chasselas and is the mainstay of most CREMANT D'ALSACE. Important in northern Italy as Pinot Bianco and taken seriously in southern Germany and Austria (as Weissburgunder), producing imposing wines with ripe pear and peach fruit and a distinct nutty character. Also successful in Hungary, Slovakia, Slovenia and the Czech Republic and promising in CALIFORNIA, OREGON and Canada.

PINOT GRIGIO See Pinot Gris.

PINOT GRIS At its finest in ALSACE; with reasonable acidity and a deep colour the grape produces fat, rich wines that mature wonderfully. It is very occasionally used in BURGUNDY (called Pinot Beurot) to add fatness to a wine. As Pinot Grigio in northern Italy it produces popular yet boring dry whites but also some of the country's most exciting. Also successful in Austria and Germany as Ruländer or Grauburgunder, and as Malvoisie in the Swiss VALAIS. There are good Romanian and Czech examples, as well as spirited ones in Hungary (as Szürkebarát). In a crisp style, it is very successful in OREGON and showing promise in CALIFORNIA and OKANAGAN VALLEY. Becoming fashionable in New Zealand and cooler regions of Australia.

PINOT MEUNIER The most widely planted grape in the CHAMPAGNE region. An important ingredient in Champagne, along with Pinot Noir and Chardonnay – though it is the least well known of the three.

PINOT NERO See Pinot Noir.
PINOT NOIR See pages 216–17.

PINOTAGE A Pinot Noir x Cinsaut cross, conceived in South Africa in 1925 and covering 6.1% of the country's vineyards. Highly versatile; classic versions are full-bodied and well-oaked with ripe plum, spice and maybe some mineral, banana or marshmallow flavours. New Zealand and California have interesting examples. A little is also grown in New York, Canada, Brazil and Zimbabwe. Best producers: (South Africa) Graham BECK★, Bellingham (Premium★), BEYERSKLOOF★, Clos Malverne★, DeWaal★ (Top of the Hill★★), Diemersfontein★, FAIRVIEW★, GRANGEHURST★, HAMILTON RUSSELL (Southern Right★), Kaapzicht★, KANONKOP★★, L'AVENIR★★, Newton Johnson★, SIMONSIG★, SPICE ROUTE★★, Stony Brook★, Tukulu, WARWICK; (New Zealand) BABICH.

PIPER-HEIDSIECK *Champagne AC, Champagne, France* Quality has been quietly improving for some years. Non-vintage★ is now gentle and biscuity, and the vintage★★ is showing real class. They've recently launched a plethora of new cuvées: Sublime (demi-sec), Divin (blanc de blancs), Rosé Sauvage and Rare★★, a de luxe non-vintage blend. Best years: 1996 **95 90 89 85 82**.

PIPERS BROOK VINEYARD *Northern Tasmania, Australia* Keenly sought, well-made wines. Steely Riesling★★, classically reserved Chardonnay★★, fragrant Gewürztraminer★ and refreshing Pinot Gris★ are highlights, as well as increasingly good Pinot Noir (Reserve★, Blackwood★ and Lyre★★). Its traditional-method sparkling wine, Kreglinger (formerly Pirie) ★★, may achieve ★★★ with a little extra age. Ninth Island★, the second label, is good. Best years: (Riesling) 2004 03 02 **01 00 99 98 97 95 94 93 92 86 82**.

DOM. ROBERT PLAGEOLES *Gaillac, South-West France.* Both traditionalist and modernizer, Robert Plageoles has revived 14 ancient grape varieties, which he blends in his sweet Vin d'Autan★★. His dry wines include Mauzac, Ondenc and a bone-dry Mauzac Nature★ fizz.

PLAIMONT, PRODUCTEURS *Madiran AC, Côtes de St-Mont VDQS and Vin de Pays des Côtes de Gascogne, South-West France* This grouping of 3 Gascon co-ops is the largest, most reliable and most go-ahead producer of COTES DE GASCOGNE and COTES DE ST-MONT. The whites, full of crisp fruit, are reasonably priced and are best drunk young. The reds, especially Ch. St-Go★ and de Sabazan★, are very good too. Also good MADIRAN (Arte Benedicte) and PACHERENC DU VIC-BILH.

PLANETA *Sicily, Italy* Rapidly expanding, young and dynamic estate. Chardonnay★★ is already one of the best in southern Italy; Cabernet Sauvignon Burdese★★ and Merlot★★ are becoming some of Italy's most impressive; and rich, peppery Santa Cecilia★★ (Nero d'Avola) has star quality. The latest addition is a fascinating Sicilian version of FIANO, Cometa★★. Gluggable Cerasuolo di Vittoria★ and La Segreta red★ and white★ blends are marvellously fruity.

PINOT NOIR

There's this myth about Pinot Noir that I think I'd better lay to rest. It goes something like this. Pinot Noir is an incredibly tricky grape to grow and even more difficult grape to vinify; in fact Pinot Noir is such a difficult customer that the only place that regularly achieves magical results is the thin stretch of land known as the Côte d'Or, between Dijon and Chagny in France, where mesoclimate, soil conditions and 2000 years of experience weave an inimitable web of pleasure.

This just isn't so. The thin-skinned, early-ripening Pinot Noir is undoubtedly more difficult to grow than other great varieties like Cabernet or Chardonnay, but that doesn't mean that it's impossible to grow elsewhere – you just have to work at it with more sensitivity and seek out the right growing conditions. And although great red Burgundy is a hauntingly beautiful wine, many Burgundians completely fail to deliver the magic, and the glorious thing about places like New Zealand, California, Oregon, Australia and Germany is that we are seeing an ever-increasing number of wines that are thrillingly different from anything produced in Burgundy, yet with flavours that are unique to Pinot Noir.

WINE STYLES

France All France's great Pinot Noir wines do come from Burgundy's Côte d'Or. Rarely deep in colour, they should nonetheless possess a wonderful fruit quality when young – raspberry, strawberry, cherry or plum – that becomes more scented and exotic with age, the plums turning to figs and pine, and the richness of chocolate mingling perilously with truffles and well-hung game. Strange, challenging, hedonistic. France's other Pinots – in north and south Burgundy, the Loire, Jura, Savoie, Alsace and now occasionally in the south of France – are lighter and milder, and in Champagne its pale, thin wine is used to make sparkling wine.

Other European regions Since the 1990s, helped by good vintages, German winemakers have made considerable efforts to produce serious Pinot Noir (generally called Spätburgunder). Italy, where it is called Pinot Nero, and Switzerland (as Blauburgunder) both have fair success with the variety. Austria and Spain have produced a couple of good examples, and Romania, the Czech Republic and Hungary produce significant amounts of Pinot Noir, though of generally low quality.

New World Light, fragrant wines have bestowed upon Oregon the reputation for being 'another Burgundy'; but I get more excited about the sensual wines of the cool, fog-affected areas of California: the ripe, stylish Russian River Valley examples; the exotically scented wines of Carneros, Anderson Valley and Sonoma Coast; the startlingly original offerings from Santa Barbara County and Santa Lucia Highlands on east-facing slopes of western Monterey County.

New Zealand produces wines of thrilling fruit and individuality, most notably from Martinborough, Canterbury's Waipara district and Central Otago. In the cooler regions of Australia – including Yarra Valley, Adelaide Hills, North-East Victoria and Tasmania – producers are beginning to find their way with the variety. New Burgundian clones now reaching maturity bode well for South African Pinot Noir. Chile also has a few fine producers.

France *Burgundy* (growers)
B Ambroise, d'ANGERVILLE,
Comte Armand, D Bachelet,
G Barthod, J-M Boillot,
CHANDON DE BRIAILLES, R
Chevillon, CLAIR, J-J Confuron,
C Dugat, B Dugat-Py, DUJAC,
R Engel, H Gouges, GRIVOT,
Anne GROS, Michel LAFARGE,
LAFON, Dom. LEROY, H Lignier,
MEO-CAMUZET, Montille, Denis
MORTET, J-F Mugnier, Ponsot,
RION, Dom. de la ROMANEE-
CONTI, E Rouget, ROUMIER,
ROUSSEAU, TOLLOT-BEAUT, de
VOGUE; (merchants) DROUHIN,
FAIVELEY, V GIRARDIN, JADOT,
LABOURE-ROI, D Laurent, POTEL.

Germany BERCHER, FURST,
JOHNER, Meyer-Näkel, REBHOLZ.

Italy CA' DEL BOSCO, Hofstätter,
Marchesi Pancrazi, Castello
della SALA.

New World Pinot Noirs
USA (California) ACACIA, AU BON
CLIMAT, BYRON, CALERA, CHALONE,
Clos Pepe, Davis Bynum,
DEHLINGER, Dutton-Goldfield,
Merry Edwards, Etude, Gary
Farrell, FLOWERS, HARTFORD
FAMILY, KISTLER, La Crema,
LANDMARK, Littorai, MARCASSIN,
Morgan, Patz & Hall,
RASMUSSEN, ROCHIOLI,
SAINTSBURY, SANFORD, Siduri,
SWAN, Talley, WILLIAMS SELYEM;
(Oregon) ARGYLE, BEAUX FRERES,
CRISTOM, DOMAINE DROUHIN, Rex
Hill, Torii Mor, Ken WRIGHT.

Australia Ashton Hills, Bass
Phillip, Bindi, COLDSTREAM HILLS,
Curly Flat, Diamond Valley,
Freycinet, GIACONDA, KNAPPSTEIN
LENSWOOD, Kooyong, Paringa,
TARRAWARRA.

New Zealand ATA RANGI, DRY
RIVER, FELTON ROAD, FROMM,
ISABEL, MARTINBOROUGH
VINEYARD, NEUDORF, PALLISER
ESTATE, PEGASUS BAY, SERESIN,
VAVASOUR, WITHER HILLS.

South Africa BOUCHARD
FINLAYSON, HAMILTON RUSSELL.

Chile CONCHA Y TORO (Terrunyo),
CONO SUR (20 Barrels, Ocio),
Viña Leyda.

PLANTAGENET *Great Southern, Western Australia* Influential winery in the GREAT SOUTHERN region, contract-making wine for smaller outfits and producing its own flavourful range, notably spicy Shiraz★★, limy Riesling★★, melony/nutty Chardonnay★★, plump Pinot Noir★ and classy Cabernet Sauvignon★★. Omrah is the second label, made from bought-in grapes – Sauvignon Blanc★, Chardonnay★ and Shiraz★ stand out. Best years: (Cabernet Sauvignon) 2003 02 01 **98 97 96 95 94 93 91 90 86 85**.

POL ROGER *Champagne AC, Champagne, France* Makers of Winston Churchill's favourite CHAMPAGNE and for many years a great favourite of the British market. The non-vintage White Foil★ (now renamed Réserve) is biscuity and dependable rather than thrilling. Pol Roger also produces a vintage★★, a vintage rosé★★, a vintage Grand Cru Chardonnay★★ and a vintage Réserve Spécial★★ (50% Chardonnay). Its top Champagne, the Pinot-dominated Cuvée Sir Winston Churchill★★, is a deliciously refined drink. All vintage wines will improve with at least 5 years' keeping. Best years: (1998) 96 95 **93 90 89 88 86 85 82**.

POLIZIANO *Vino Nobile di Montepulciano DOCG, Tuscany, Italy* A leading light in Montepulciano. VINO NOBILE★★ is far better than average, especially the Riserva Vigna Asinone★★. SUPER-TUSCAN Le Stanze★★★ (Cabernet Sauvignon-Merlot) has been outstanding in recent vintages – the fruit in part coming from owner Federico Carletti's other estate, Lohsa, in MORELLINO DI SCANSANO. Best years: (Vino Nobile) (2004) (03) 01 **99 98 97 95 93 90**.

POLZ *Steiermark, Austria* Brothers Erich and Walter Polz are probably the most consistent producers of aromatic dry white wines in Styria. Few wines here fail to reach ★, and with Weissburgunder (Pinot Blanc), Morillon (Chardonnay), Muskateller and Sauvignon Blanc the combination of intensity and elegance frequently deserves ★★. Steierische Klassik indicates wines vinified without any new oak. Best years: (2004) 03 02 **01 00 99 97**.

POMEROL AC *Bordeaux, France* The Pomerol AC includes some of the world's most sought-after red wines. Pomerol's unique quality lies in its deep clay in which the Merlot grape flourishes. The result is seductively rich, almost creamy wine with wonderful mouthfilling fruit flavours: often plummy, but with blackcurrants, raisins and chocolate, too, and mint to freshen it up. Best producers: Beauregard★, Bonalgue, le BON PASTEUR★★, Certan-de-May★★, Clinet★★, Clos l'Église★, Clos René★, la CONSEILLANTE★★, l'EGLISE-CLINET★★★, l'EVANGILE★★, la FLEUR-PETRUS★★, GAZIN★★, Hosanna★ (previously Certan-Guiraud), LAFLEUR★★★, LATOUR-A-POMEROL★★, Montviel, Nénin★, PETIT-VILLAGE★★, PETRUS★★★, Le PIN★★★, TROTANOY★★, VIEUX-CHATEAU-CERTAN★★. Best years: 2001 00 98 **96 95 94 90 89 88 86 85 83 82**.

POMINO DOC See Chianti Rufina.

POMMARD AC *Côte de Beaune, Burgundy, France* The first village south of Beaune. At their best, the wines should have full, round, beefy flavours. Can age well, often for 10 years or more. There are no Grands Crus but les Rugiens Bas and les Épenots (both Premiers Crus) occupy the best sites. Best producers: Comte Armand★★★, J-M Boillot★★, Carré-Courbin★, Courcel★★, Dancer★, P Garaudet★, M Gaunoux★, V GIRARDIN★★, LAFARGE★★, Lejeune★, Montille★★, J & A Parent★, Ch. de Pommard★, Pothier-Rieusset★. Best years: (2004) 03 02 99 98 97 96 **95 93 90**.

POMMERY *Champagne AC, Champagne, France* High-quality CHAMPAGNE house now owned by Vranken, who have maintained the traditional Pommery style but have launched a brace of new non-vintage cuvées – Summertime blanc de blancs and Wintertime blanc de noirs – to go along with Brut Royal and Apanage★. Austere vintage Brut★ is delicious with maturity, and the prestige cuvée Louise, both white★★ and rosé★★, is the epitome of discreet, perfumed elegance. Best years: (1997) 96 95 **92 90 89 88 85 82**.

CH. PONTET-CANET★★ *Pauillac AC, 5ème Cru Classé, Haut-Médoc, Bordeaux, France* The vineyards of this property are located close to those of MOUTON-ROTHSCHILD. Since 1975, when the Tesserons of LAFON-ROCHET bought the property, there has been a gradual return to the typical PAUILLAC style of big, chewy, intense claret that develops a beautiful blackcurrant fruit. Now one of the best value of the Classed Growths. Best years: 2003 02 01 00 **99** 98 96 **95 94 90 89 86 85 83 82**.

PORT See pages 220–1.

NICOLAS POTEL *Burgundy, France* Energetic young *négociant* producing consistently fine wines at attractive prices. Particularly strong in his native VOLNAY★★ and in NUITS-ST-GEORGES★★, where he is based. Best years: (2004) (03) 02 **01 00 99**.

CH. POTENSAC★★ *Médoc AC, Cru Bourgeois, Bordeaux, France* Owned and run by the Delon family, of LEOVILLE-LAS-CASES, Potensac's fabulous success is based on quality, consistency and value for money. The wine can be drunk at 4–5 years, but fine vintages will improve for at least 10 years. Best years: 2002 **01 00 99 98 96 95 90 89 88 86**.

POUILLY-FUISSÉ AC *Mâconnais, Burgundy, France* Chardonnay from 5 villages, including Pouilly and Fuissé. After a period of poor value, there are now some committed growers producing buttery, creamy wines that can be delicious at 2 years but will often develop beautifully for up to 10. Best producers: D & M Barraud★★, Bret Bros, Corsin★★, C & T Drouin★, J-A Ferret★★, M Forest★, Ch. Fuissé★★, Guffens-Heynen (VERGET)★★, R Lassarat★★, Léger-Plumet★, R Luquet★, O Merlin★★, Robert-Denogent★★, Ch. des Rontets★★, Saumaize-Michelin★★, Valette★★★. Best years: (2004) 03 02 01 **00 99 97**.

POUILLY-FUMÉ AC *Loire Valley, France* Fumé means 'smoked' in French and a good Pouilly-Fumé has a pungent smell often likened to gunflint. The grape is Sauvignon Blanc, and the extra smokiness comes from a flinty soil called silex. Despite the efforts of a few producers, this is a disappointingly underperforming and overpriced AC. Best producers: Berthiers★, G Blanchet★, Henri Bourgeois★, A Cailbourdin★, J-C Chatelain★, Didier DAGUENEAU★★, Serge Dagueneau★, M Deschamps★, Ladoucette★, Landrat-Guyollot★, Masson-Blondelet★, M Redde★, Tinel-Blondelet★, Ch. de Tracy★. Best years: 2004 **03 02 00 99**.

POUILLY-LOCHÉ AC See Pouilly-Vinzelles AC.

POUILLY-SUR-LOIRE AC *Loire Valley, France* Light appley wines from the Chasselas grape from vineyards around Pouilly-sur-Loire, the town which gave its name to POUILLY-FUME. Drink as young as possible.

POUILLY-VINZELLES AC *Mâconnais, Burgundy, France* A small AC which, with its neighbour Pouilly-Loché (whose wines may be sold as Pouilly-Vinzelles), lies somewhat in the shadow of big brother POUILLY-FUISSE. Most wines come through the local co-operative, but there are now some good domaines offering ripe white wines from the steep east-facing slopes. Best producers: Cave des Grands Crus Blancs, la Soufrandière★★, Tripoz★, Valette★. Best years: (2004) 03 **02 01 00 99**.

PORT DOC

Douro, Portugal

The Douro region in northern Portugal, where the grapes for port are grown, is wild and beautiful, and now classified as a World Heritage site. Steep hills covered in vineyard terraces plunge dramatically down to the Douro river. Grapes are one of the few crops that will grow in the inhospitable climate, which gets progressively drier the further inland you travel. But not all the Douro's grapes qualify to be made into increasingly good port. A quota is established every year, and the rest are made into unfortified Douro wines.

Red port grapes include Touriga Franca, Tinta Roriz, Touriga Nacional, Tinta Barroca, Tinta Cão and Tinta Amarela. Grapes for white port include Codega, Malvasia Fina, Malvasia Rei, Rabigato and Gouveio. The grapes are partially fermented, and then *aguardente* (grape spirit) is added – fortifying the wine, stopping the fermentation and leaving sweet, unfermented grape sugar in the finished port.

PORT STYLES

Vintage Finest of the ports matured in bottle, made from grapes from the best vineyards. Vintage port is not 'declared' every year (usually there are 3 or 4 declarations per decade), but only during the second year in cask, if the shipper thinks the standard is high enough. It is bottled after 2 years, and may be consumed soon afterwards, as is not uncommon in the USA; at this stage it packs quite a punch. The British custom of aging for 20 years or more can yield exceptional mellowness. Requires decanting.

Single quinta A true single-quinta wine comes from an individual estate; however, many shippers sell their vintage port under a quinta name in years which are not declared as a vintage, even though it may be sourced from 2 or 3 different vineyards. It is quite possible for these 'off vintage' ports to equal or even surpass the vintage wines from the same house.

Aged tawny Matured in cask for 10, 20, 30 or even 40 years before bottling, older tawnies have delicious nut and fig flavours.

Colheita Tawny from a single vintage, matured in cask for at least 7 years – potentially the finest of the aged tawnies.

Late Bottled (Vintage) (LBV) Port matured for 4–6 years in vat, then usually filtered to avoid sediment forming in the bottle. Traditional unfiltered LBV has much more flavour and requires decanting; it can generally be aged for another 5 years or more.

Crusted Making a comeback, this is a blend of good ports from 2–3 vintages, bottled without filtration after 3–4 years in cask. A deposit (crust) forms in the bottle and the wine should be decanted.

Reserve (most can be categorized as Premium Ruby) has an average of 3–5 years' age. A handful represent good value.

Ruby The youngest red port with only 1–3 years' age. Ruby port should be bursting with young, almost peppery fruit, and there has been an improvement in quality of late, except at the cheapest level.

Tawny Cheap tawny is either an emaciated ruby, or a blend of ruby and white port, and is both dilute and raw.

White Only the best taste dry and nutty from wood-aging; most are coarse and alcoholic, best drunk chilled or with tonic water.

BEST PRODUCERS

Vintage BURMESTER, COCKBURN, CROFT, Delaforce, DOW, FERREIRA, FONSECA, GRAHAM'S, NIEPOORT, NOVAL (including Nacional), SMITH WOODHOUSE, TAYLOR, WARRE.

Single quinta BURMESTER (Quinta Nova de Nossa Senhora do Carmo), CHURCHILL (Agua Alta), COCKBURN (Quinta dos Canais), Quinta do CRASTO, CROFT (Quinta da Roêda), Delaforce (Quinta da Corte), DOW (Quinta do Bomfim), FONSECA (Guimaraens), GRAHAM'S (Malvedos), Martinez (Quinta da Eira Velha), NIEPOORT (Quinta do Passadouro), NOVAL (Silval), Quinta de la ROSA, SMITH WOODHOUSE (Madalena), TAYLOR (Quinta de Terra Feita, Quinta de Vargellas), Quinta Vale Dona Maria, Quinta do VESUVIO, WARRE (Quinta da Cavadinha).

Aged tawny Barros, BURMESTER, COCKBURN, DOW, FERREIRA, FONSECA, GRAHAM'S, Krohn, NIEPOORT, NOVAL, RAMOS PINTO, la ROSA, SANDEMAN, TAYLOR, WARRE.

Colheita Barros, BURMESTER, Feist, Krohn, NIEPOORT, NOVAL.

Traditional Late Bottled Vintage CHURCHILL, CRASTO, Infantado, NIEPOORT, NOVAL, RAMOS PINTO, la ROSA, SMITH WOODHOUSE, Vale da Mina, WARRE.

Crusted CHURCHILL, DOW.

Ruby COCKBURN, FERREIRA, FONSECA, GRAHAM'S, la ROSA, SANDEMAN, SMITH WOODHOUSE, TAYLOR, WARRE.

White CHURCHILL, NIEPOORT.

221

CH. POUJEAUX★★ *Moulis AC, Cru Bourgeois, Haut-Médoc, Bordeaux,*
France Poujeaux is one reason why MOULIS AC is attracting attention:
the wines have a delicious chunky fruit and new-oak sweetness.
Attractive at 6–7 years old, good vintages can easily last for 20–30
years. Best years: 2003 02 01 00 98 **96 95 94 90 89 88 86 85 83 82**.

PRAGER *Wachau, Niederösterreich, Austria* Toni Bodenstein is one of
the pioneers of the WACHAU, producing top dry Rieslings from the
Achleiten and Klaus vineyards★★★ and excellent Grüner Veltliners
from the Achleiten vineyard★★. Best years: (Riesling/Grüner Veltliner
Smaragd) (2004) 03 02 01 00 **99 98 97 96 95 93 90**.

PREMIÈRES CÔTES DE BLAYE AC *Bordeaux, France* An improving AC
on the right bank of the Gironde. The fresh, Merlot-based reds are
ready at 2–3 years but will age for more. Top red wines can be
labelled under the new, quality-driven Blaye AC from 2000. Best
producers: (reds) Bel-Air la Royère★, Gigault★, Les Grands Maréchaux,
Haut-Bertinerie★, Haut-Grelot, Haut-Sociando, Jonqueyres★, Loumède,
Mondésir-Gazin★, Montfollet, Roland la Garde★, Segonzac★, Tourtes;
(whites) Haut-Bertinerie★, Charron (Acacia★), Cave des Hauts de
Gironde, Tourtes (Prestige★). Best years: 2003 **01 00 98 96 95**.

PREMIÈRES CÔTES DE BORDEAUX AC *Bordeaux, France* Hilly region
overlooking GRAVES and SAUTERNES across the Garonne. For a long time
the AC was best known for its Sauternes-style sweet wines, particularly
from the communes of CADILLAC, LOUPIAC and STE-CROIX-DU-MONT, but the
juicy reds and rosés have now forged ahead. These are usually
delicious at 2–3 years old but should last for 5–6 years. Dry whites are
designated BORDEAUX AC. Best producers: (reds) Brethous, Carignan★,
CARSIN★, Chelivette, Clos Ste-Anne, Grand-Mouëys★, Haux, Jonchet,
Juge (Dupleich), Lamothe-de-Haux, Lezongars★, Plaisance★, Puy-
Bardens★, REYNON★, le Sens, Suau★. Best years: (reds) **2000 98 96 95**.

CH. PRIEURÉ-LICHINE★ *Margaux AC, 4ème Cru Classé, Haut-Médoc,*
Bordeaux, France Seriously underachieving property that saw
several false dawns before being sold in 1999. Right Bank specialist
Stéphane Derenoncourt of PAVIE-MACQUIN and CANON-LA-GAFFELIERE fame
is now the consultant winemaker, and hopefully the wine will return
at very least to its traditional gentle, perfumed style. Best years: 2003
02 01 00 **99 98 96 95 94 90 89 88 86 85 83 82**.

PRIEURÉ DE ST-JEAN DE BÉBIAN *Coteaux du Languedoc AC, Languedoc,*
France One of the pioneering estates in the MIDI, now owned by
former wine writer Chantal Lecouty and her husband. It took a dip in
the early 1990s but is once more back on form, producing an intense,
spicy, generous red★★, second wine La Chapelle de Bébian and a
barrel-fermented white. Best years: (red) 2001 **00 99 98 97 96 95**.

PRIMITIVO DI MANDURIA DOC *Puglia, Italy* The most important
appellation for PUGLIA's Primitivo grape, which has been enjoying a
renaissance of interest since it was found to be nearly identical to
California's Zinfandel. The best wines combine outstanding ripeness
and concentration with a knockout alcohol level. Good Primitivo is also
sold as IGT Primitivo del Tarantino. Best producers: Felline★★,
Pervini★★, Giovanni Soloperto. Best years: (2004) 03 **01 00 98 97**.

PRIMO ESTATE *Adelaide Plains, South Australia* Innovative Joe Grilli
stuck his winery in one of Australia's hottest climates but works
miracles with his own grapes and those from outlying areas. The
premium label is Joseph: Grilli adapts the Italian *amarone* method for
Moda Amarone Cabernet-Merlot★★ (★★★ with 10 years' age!) and

makes a dense, eye-popping Joseph Red fizz★. He also does a sensuous Botrytis Riesling La Magia★★, fabulous honeyed fortified Fronti★★★, surprising dry white La Biondina Colombard★, and cherry-ripe Il Briccone★, a Shiraz-Sangiovese blend – and superb olive oils★★★. Best years: (Cabernet-Merlot Joseph) 2002 01 **00 99 98 97 96 95 94 93 91 90**.

PRIORAT DOCa *Cataluña, Spain* A hilly, isolated district with very low-yielding vineyards planted on precipitous slopes of deep slate soil. Old-style fortified *rancio* wines used to attract little attention. Then in the 1990s a group of young winemakers revolutionized the area, bringing in state-of-the-art winemaking methods and grape varieties such as Cabernet Sauvignon to back up the native Garnacha and Cariñena. Their rare, expensive wines have taken the world by storm. Ready at 5 years old, the best will last much longer. The region was elevated to DOCa status in 2001. Best producers: Bodegas B G (Gueta-Lupía★), Capafons-Ossó★, Cims de Porrera★★, CLOS ERASMUS★★★, CLOS MOGADOR★★★, La Conreria d'Scala Dei★, Costers del Siurana (Clos de l'Obac★★), J M Fuentes (Gran Clos★★), Ithaca★, Mas Doix★★, Mas d'en Gil (Clos Fontà★★), Mas Martinet (Clos Martinet★★), Alvaro PALACIOS★★★, Pasanau Germans (Finca la Planeta★), Rotllan Torra★, Scala Dei★, VALL-LLACH★★. Best years: (reds) (2001) 00 99 **98 96 95 94 93 90**.

PROSECCO DI CONEGLIANO-VALDOBBIADENE DOC *Veneto, Italy* The Prosecco grape gives soft, scented wine made sparkling by a second fermentation in tank, though Prosecco can also be still, or *tranquillo*. Generally, however, it is a spumante or frizzante for drinking young. The Cartizze sub-zone near Valdobbiadene produces the most refined wines. Best producers: Adami★, Bernardi★, Bisol★, Carpenè Malvolti★, Le Colture★, Col Vetoraz★, Nino Franco★, La Riva dei Frati★, Ruggeri & C★, Tanorè★, Zardetto★.

PROVENCE *France* Provence is home to France's oldest vineyards but the region is better known for its beaches and arts festivals than for its wines. However, it seems even Provence is caught up in the revolution sweeping through the vineyards of southern France. The area has 5 small ACs (BANDOL, les BAUX-DE-PROVENCE, BELLET, CASSIS and PALETTE), but most of the wine comes from the much larger areas of the COTES DE PROVENCE, COTEAUX VAROIS, Coteaux de Pierrevert and COTEAUX D'AIX-EN-PROVENCE. Vin de Pays des BOUCHES-DU-RHONE is also becoming increasingly important. Provençal reds are generally better than whites and rosés.

J J PRÜM *Bernkastel, Mosel, Germany* Estate making some of Germany's best Riesling in sites like the Sonnenuhr★★★ in WEHLEN, Himmel-reich★★ in GRAACH and Lay★★ and Badstube★★ in BERNKASTEL. All have great aging potential. Best years: (2004) 03 02 01 99 **98 97 96 95 94 93 90 88 85 83 79 76 71**.

S A PRÜM *Wehlen, Mosel, Germany* There are a confusing number of Prüms in the MOSEL – the best known is J J PRUM, but Raimund Prüm of S A Prüm makes a decent second. The estate's most interesting wines are Riesling from WEHLENER Sonnenuhr, especially Auslese★★, but it also makes good wine from sites in BERNKASTEL★, GRAACH★ and Zeltingen★. Best years: (2004) 03 02 01 99 **97 95 93 90 88**.

PRUNOTTO *Barolo DOCG, Piedmont, Italy* One of the great BAROLO producers, now ably run by Albiera, the eldest of Piero ANTINORI's 3 daughters. Highlights include BARBERA D'ALBA Pian Romualdo★★, BARBERA D'ASTI Costamiòle★★, NEBBIOLO D'ALBA Occhetti★, Barolo

Bussia★★★ and Cannubi★★ and new BARBARESCO Bric Turot★★. Also good MOSCATO D'ASTI★, BARBERA D'ASTI Fiulot★ and ROERO Arneis★. Best years: (Barolo) (2004) (03) 01 00 **99 98 97 95 93 90 89 88 85**.

PUGLIA *Italy* This southern region is a prolific source of blending wines, but exciting progress has been made with native varieties: Uva di Troia in CASTEL DEL MONTE; white Greco for characterful Gravina, revived by Botromagno; and Verdeca and Bianco d'Alessano for Locorotondo. The red Primitivo, led by examples from producers under the ACCADEMIA DEI RACEMI umbrella, make a big impact (whether under the PRIMITIVO DI MANDURIA DOC or more general IGTs). But it is the Negroamaro grape grown on traditional bush-trained or *alberello* vines in the Salento peninsula that provides the best wines, whether red or rosé. Outstanding examples include Vallone's Graticciaia★★, Candido's Duca d'Aragona★★ and Taurino's Patriglione★★. Brindisi and SALICE SALENTINO are two good-value, reliable DOCs.

PUISSEGUIN-ST-ÉMILION AC *Bordeaux, France* Small ST-EMILION satellite AC. The wines are generally fairly solid but with an attractive chunky fruit and usually make good drinking at 3–5 years. Best producers: Bel-Air, Branda, Durand-Laplagne★, Fongaban, Guibeau-la-Fourvieille, Laurets, la Mauriane★, Producteurs Réunis, Soleil. Best years: 2003 **01 00** 98 96 95.

PULIGNY-MONTRACHET AC *Côte de Beaune, Burgundy, France* Puligny is one of the finest white wine villages in the world and adds the name of its greatest Grand Cru, le MONTRACHET, to its own. There are 3 other Grands Crus (BATARD-MONTRACHET, Bienvenues-BATARD-MONTRACHET and Chevalier-MONTRACHET) and 11 Premiers Crus. The flatter vineyards use the Puligny-Montrachet AC. Good vintages really need 5 years' aging, while Premiers Crus and Grands Crus may need 10 years and can last for 20 or more. Only about 3% of the AC is red wine. Best producers: J-M Boillot★★, CARILLON★★★, J Chartron★, G Chavy★, DROUHIN★★, A Ente★★, B Ente★, JADOT★★, Larue★★, LATOUR★, Dom. LEFLAIVE★★★ (since 1994), O LEFLAIVE★, P Pernot★★, Ch. de Puligny-Montrachet★, RAMONET★★, SAUZET★★. Best years: (2004) 03 02 **01 00 99 97 95**.

PYRENEES See Grampians and Pyrenees.

QUARTS DE CHAUME AC *Loire Valley, France* The Chenin Blanc grape finds one of its most rewarding mesoclimates here. Quarts de Chaume is a 40ha (100-acre) AC within the larger COTEAUX DU LAYON AC and, as autumn mists begin to curl off the river Layon, noble rot attacks the grapes. The result is intense, sweet wines which can last for longer than almost any in the world – although many can be drunk after 5 years. Best producers: BAUMARD★★★, Bellerive★★, Laffourcade★, Pierre-Bise★, J Pithon★★★, Plaisance★, Joseph Renou★★, Suronde★★. Best years: 2004 03 02 01 **99 97 96 95 90 89 88 85 83 76 71 70 69 61 59 47**.

QUEENSLAND *Australia* The Queensland wine industry is expanding fast and now produces more than TASMANIA. Here wine is closely linked to tourism. About 60 wineries perch on rocky hills in the main region, the Granite Belt, near the NEW SOUTH WALES border. New areas South Burnett (north-west of Brisbane), Mount Cotton, Mount Tamborine and Toowoomba are showing promise. Best producers: Albert River, Barambah Ridge, Boireann★, Robert Channon★, Clovely Estate, Heritage, Jimbour Station, Preston Peak★, Robinsons Family, Sirromet, Summit Estate.

QUERCIABELLA *Chianti Classico DOCG, Tuscany, Italy* This model of a modern CHIANTI producer serves up a gorgeously scented, rich-fruited CHIANTI CLASSICO★★. But it has made an even greater splash with its three SUPER-TUSCANS: BURGUNDY-like white Batàr★★ from Pinot Bianco and Chardonnay; tobaccoey, spicy Sangiovese-Cabernet blend Camartina★★★; and Palafreno★, a blend of Sangiovese and Merlot. Best years: (Camartina) (2004) (03) 01 **99 97 95 93 90 88**.

QUILCEDA CREEK *Washington State, USA* Tiny winery with a cult following for its mammoth, rich Cabernet Sauvignon★★★. The wine can be a bit overpowering, but it opens up to stunning effect after a while in the glass and it has good aging potential. Less expensive Columbia Valley Red★★ is a blend of Cabernets Sauvignon and Franc and Merlot. Best years: (Cabernet) (2003) 02 **01 00 99 98 97 96 95**.

QUINCY AC *Loire Valley, France* Intensely flavoured, dry white wine from Sauvignon Blanc vineyards west of Bourges. Can age for a year or two but always keeps an appealingly aggressive gooseberry flavour. Best producers: Ballandors★, H Bourgeois★, Mardon★, J Rouzé, Silice de Quincy, Troterau★. Best years: (2003) **02 01 00**.

QUINTARELLI *Valpolicella DOC, Veneto, Italy* Giuseppe Quintarelli is the great traditional winemaker of VALPOLICELLA. His philosophy is one of vinifying only the very best grapes and leaving nature to do the rest. His Classico Superiore★★ is left in cask for about 4 years and his famed AMARONE★★★ and RECIOTO★★ for up to 7 years before release. Alzero★★ is a spectacular Amarone-style wine made from Cabernets Franc and Sauvignon. Best years: (Amarone) (1999) (97) **95 93 90 88 85 83**.

QUPÉ *Santa Maria Valley AVA, California, USA* Owner/winemaker Bob Lindquist makes a gorgeously tasty Bien Nacido Syrah★★. His Reserve Chardonnay★★ and Bien Nacido Cuvée★★ (a Chardonnay-Viognier blend) have sublime appley fruit and perfume. A leading exponent of red and white RHONE-style wines, including Viognier★ and Marsanne★. Best years: (Syrah) 2002 01 **00 99 98 97 96 95 94 91 90**.

CH. DE LA RAGOTIÈRE *Muscadet Sèvre-et-Maine, Loire Valley, France* The inexhaustibly inventive Couillaud brothers claim to have salvaged the reputation of Muscadet in US restaurants with M★★, an old-vines wine matured *sur lie* for over 2 years. The standard Muscadet★ is elegant and built to last, too; lighter ones come from the Couillauds' other property, Ch. la Morinière. Vin de pays Chardonnay is a speciality (Auguste Couillaud★) and a host of experimental varieties appear under the Collection Privée label (Sauvignon Gris★). Les Zunics is an exciting, fragrant vin de table blend, and Melon-Chardonnay blend Chardet is very quaffable. Best years: (M) (2002) **01 99 97**.

RAÏMAT *Costers del Segre DO, Cataluña, Spain* Owned by CODORNIU, this large, irrigated estate makes pleasant but surprisingly lean wines from Tempranillo, Cabernet Sauvignon (Mas Castell vineyard★) and Chardonnay. Lively 100% Chardonnay CAVA and a new upscale red blend 4 Varietales. Best years: (reds) 2001 **00 99 98 97 96 95 94 92**.

RAMONET *Chassagne-Montrachet AC, Côte de Beaune, Burgundy, France* The Ramonets (Noël and Claude) produce some of the most complex of all white Burgundies from 3 Grands Crus (BATARD-MONTRACHET★★★,

225

Bienvenues-BATARD-MONTRACHET★★★ and le MONTRACHET★★★) and Premiers Crus including Ruchottes★★★, Caillerets★★★, Boudriotte★★, Vergers★★, Morgeot★★ and Chaumées★★★. If you want to spare your wallet try the ST-AUBIN★★ or the CHASSAGNE-MONTRACHET white★★ or red★★. Best years: (whites) (2004) 03 02 01 00 99 98 **97 95 92 90 89**.

JOÃO PORTUGAL RAMOS *Alentejo, Portugal* João Portugal Ramos is one of Portugal's foremost winemakers. He used to be a consultant to at least a dozen producers, but he is now making his mark with his own winery and vineyards. Smoky, peppery Trincadeira★★, spicy Aragonês (Tempranillo)★, powerful Syrah★ and intensely dark-fruited red blend Vila Santa★★ are all superb. Marquês de Borba★ is the label for everyday red and white wines, and a brilliant red Reserva★★ is also made. New World-style Tagus Creek looks set to impress. Best years: (2004) 01 **00 99 97**.

RAMOS PINTO *Douro DOC and Port DOC, Douro, Portugal* Innovative PORT company now owned by ROEDERER, making excellent premium Ruby (Collector Reserve★), complex, full-bodied Late Bottled Vintage★ and aged tawnies (10-year-old Quinta da Ervamoira★★ and 20-year-old Quinta do Bom Retiro★★★). Vintage Ports★★ are rich and early maturing. DOURO reds Duas Quintas (Reserva Especial★★) and Bons Ares★ (Reserva★) are variable and not cheap. Best years: (Vintage) 2000 97 **95 94 83**.

RAMPOLLA, CASTELLO DEI *Chianti Classico DOCG, Tuscany, Italy* One of the outstanding CHIANTI CLASSICO★★ estates. SUPER-TUSCAN Sammarco, sometimes ★★★, is mostly Cabernet with some Sangiovese, while the extraordinary Vigna d'Alceo★★★ adds Petit Verdot to Cabernet Sauvignon. Best years: (Sammarco) (2004) (03) 01 00 **99 98 97 95 90 88 85**; (Vigna d'Alceo) (2003) (01) (00) 99 **98 97 96**.

RANDERSACKER *Franken, Germany* Important wine village just outside the city of Würzburg in FRANKEN, producing excellent, medium-bodied dry Rieslings, dry Silvaners, spicy Traminer and piercingly intense Rieslaner. Best producers: JULIUSSPITAL★, Robert Schmitt★, Schmitt's Kinder★. Best years: (2004) 03 02 01 **00 99 98 97 94 93**.

RAPEL, VALLE DEL *Valle Central, Chile* One of Chile's most exciting red wine regions, Rapel covers both the Valle del Cachapoal in the north and the Valle de COLCHAGUA in the south. Both are the cradle of Chilean Carmenère. Best producers: Anakena, CASA LAPOSTOLLE★★, CONCHA Y TORO★★, CONO SUR★★, GRACIA★, LA ROSA★, MONTES★, MontGras, Torreón de Paredes, Viu Manent★, VOE★★.

KENT RASMUSSEN *Carneros AVA, California, USA* Burgundian-style Chardonnay★★ capable of considerable aging and a fascinating juicy Pinot Noir★★ are made by ultra-traditional methods. Also occasional delightful oddities like Alicante and Dolcetto under the Ramsay label. Best years: (Pinot Noir) (2003) (02) **01 00 99 98 95 94 91 90**.

RASTEAU AC *Rhône Valley, France* This single-village AC is for fortified Grenache red or white wine and a *rancio* version which is left in barrel for 2 or more years. However, much of the best wine from Rasteau is full-bodied dry red, which comes under the COTES DU RHONE-VILLAGES AC. Best producers: Beaurenard★, J Bressy★, Cave des Vignerons, Rabasse-Charavin, la Soumade★, du Trapadis★.

RENATO RATTI *Barolo DOCG, Piedmont, Italy* The late Renato Ratti led the revolution in winemaking in the Alba area with BAROLO and BARBARESCO of better balance, colour and richness and softer in tannins than the traditional models. Today his son Pietro and nephew

Massimo Martinelli produce sound Barolo★★ from the Marcenasco vineyards at La Morra, as well as good BARBERA D'ALBA (Torriglione★), Dolcetto d'Alba (Colombè★), NEBBIOLO D'ALBA (Ochetti★) and Monferrato DOC Villa Pattono★, a blend of Barbera and Freisa.

RAUENTHAL *Rheingau, Germany* Sadly, only a few producers live up to the reputation earned by this RHEINGAU village's great Baiken and Gehrn sites, for intense, spicy Rieslings. Best producers: Georg BREUER★★, Staatsweingut. Best years: (2004) 03 02 01 00 **99 98 97 96 94 93**.

CH. RAUZAN-SÉGLA★★ *Margaux AC, 2ème Cru Classé, Haut-Médoc, Bordeaux, France* A dynamic change of winemaking regime in 1982 and the purchase of the property by Chanel in 1994 have propelled Rauzan-Ségla up the quality ladder. Now the wines have a rich blackcurrant fruit, almost tarry, thick tannins and weight, excellent woody spice and superb concentration. Second wine: Ségla. Best years: 2003 02 01 00 **99** 98 96 **95 94** 90 89 88 86 85 83.

JEAN-MARIE RAVENEAU *Chablis AC, Burgundy, France* A fine grower in CHABLIS, producing beautifully nuanced wines from 3 Grands Crus (Blanchot★★★, les Clos★★★ and Valmur★★★) and 4 Premiers Crus (Montée de Tonnerre★★★, Vaillons★★, Butteaux★★★ and Chapelot★★), using a combination of old oak and stainless-steel fermentation. The wines can easily age for a decade or more. Best years: (top crus) (2004) 03 02 00 **99 98 97 95 92 90 89**.

RAVENSWOOD *Sonoma Valley AVA, California, USA* Joel Peterson, one of California's best-known Zin experts, established Ravenswood in 1976. During the lean years, when most Zinfandel was pink and sweet, he added an intense Chardonnay, a sometimes very good Cabernet Sauvignon★ and several tasty Merlots (Sangiacomo★★). But Zinfandel remains the trump card. Recent offerings seem to have lost some of their depth and pungency – and large-volume Vintners Reserve is dull – but Amador County★ and Lodi★ wines are tasty and sometimes outperform the Sonoma products (some single-vineyard wines can be ★★). The Constellation group purchased the winery in 2001. Best years: (Zins) (2002) **01 00 99 97 96 95 94 91 90**.

CH. RAYAS *Châteauneuf-du-Pape, Rhône Valley, France* The most famous estate in CHATEAUNEUF-DU-PAPE. Emmanuel Reynaud, nephew of the eccentric Jacques Reynaud, is running this estate in his uncle's inimitable rule-breaking style, producing usually exotically rich reds★★★ and whites★★ which also age well. Prices are not cheap and the wines are not consistent, but at its best Rayas is a thrilling one-off. The red is made entirely from low-yielding Grenache vines – the only such wine in the AC – while the white is a blend of Clairette, Grenache Blanc and (so rumour has it) Chardonnay. Second label Pignan can also be impressive. COTES DU RHONE Ch. de Fonsalette★★ is usually wonderful. Best years: (Châteauneuf-du-Pape) 2003 01 99 98 **96 95 94 91** 90 89 88 86; (whites) 2003 01 00 99 **98 97 96 95 94 91 90 89**.

REBHOLZ *Siebeldingen, Pfalz, Germany* This estate in the southern PFALZ produces fine dry Riesling★★, Weissburgunder★★ and Grau-burgunder★, all crystalline in their clarity, with vibrant fruit aromas. Top of the range are intensely mineral dry Riesling★★★ from the Kastanienbusch vineyard, powerful dry Gewürztraminer★★ and extravagantly aromatic, crisp, dry Muskateller★★. The sparkling wine★★, made from barrel-fermented Pinot varieties, is among Germany's most elegant. Also produces Germany's finest barrel-fermented Chardonnay★★ and most serious Spätburgunder★★ (Pinot

Noir) reds. Best years: (whites) (2004) 03 02 01 00 **99 98 97 96**; (reds) (2004) 03 02 01 00 **99 98 97 96**.

RECIOTO DELLA VALPOLICELLA DOC *Veneto, Italy* The great sweet wine of VALPOLICELLA, made from grapes picked earlier than usual and left to dry on straw mats until the end of January. The wines are deep in colour, with a rich, bitter-sweet cherryish fruit. Top wines age well for 10 years, but most are best drunk young. As with Valpolicella, the Classico tag is all important. Best producers: Accordini★, ALLEGRINI★★, Bolla (Spumante★★), Brigaldara★, BUSSOLA★★★, Michele Castellani★★, DAL FORNO★★★, MASI★, QUINTARELLI★★, Le Ragose★, Le Salette★, Serègo Alighieri★★, Speri★★, Tedeschi★, Tommasi★, Villa Monteleone★★, Viviani★. Best years: (2003) 01 **00 98 97 95 93 90**.

RECIOTO DI SOAVE DOCG *Veneto, Italy* Sweet white wine made in the SOAVE zone from dried grapes, like RECIOTO DELLA VALPOLICELLA. Garganega grapes give wonderfully delicate yet intense wines that age well for up to a decade. The best, ANSELMI's I Capitelli, is now sold as IGT Veneto. Best producers: ANSELMI★★, La Cappuccina★★, Cà Rugate★, Coffele★, Gini★★, PIEROPAN★★, Bruno Sartori★, Tamellini★★. Best years: (2003) 01 **00 98 97 95 93 90**.

DOM. DE LA RECTORIE *Banyuls AC and Collioure AC, Roussillon, France* Marc and Thierry Parcé are producing some of the leading wines in BANYULS and COLLIOURE. Collioure cuvées Coume Pascole★★ and le Seris★★ are made for keeping, while Banyuls Cuvée Parcé Frères★★ can be enjoyed for its youthful fruit or kept for future pleasure. The vin de pays Grenache Gris, Cuvée l'Argile★, is one of the best whites in ROUSSILLON. Best years: (Coume Pascole) (2003) 01 **00 99 98 97 96**.

RÉGNIÉ AC *Beaujolais, Burgundy, France* Most recent of the BEAUJOLAIS Crus, upgraded from BEAUJOLAIS-VILLAGES in 1988. In good years it is light, aromatic and enjoyable along the style of CHIROUBLES. A wine for drinking, not for keeping. Best producers: DUBOEUF★ (des Buyats★), H & J-P Dubost★, Rampon, Gilles Roux (de la Plaigne★).

DOM. LA RÉMÉJEANNE *Côtes du Rhône AC, Rhône Valley, France* First-class property on the west bank of the Rhône, making a range of strikingly individual wines. COTES DU RHONE-VILLAGES les Genèvriers★★ has the weight and texture of good CHATEAUNEUF-DU-PAPE, while COTES DU RHONE Syrah les Eglantiers★★ is superb. Both need at least 3–5 years' aging. Also good Côtes du Rhône les Chèvrefeuilles★ and les Arbousiers (red and white). Best years: (les Eglantiers) 2004 03 **01 00 99 98 96**.

REMELLURI *Rioja DOCa, País Vasco, Spain* Organic RIOJA estate producing red wines with far more fruit than usual and good concentration for aging – the best are ★★. There is also a delicate, barrel-fermented white blend★. Best years: (Reserva) 2001 99 **98 96 95 94 91 89**.

RETSINA *Greece* Resinated white (and rosé) wine common all over Greece – although both production and sales are falling. Poor Retsina is diabolical but the best are deliciously oily and piny. Drink young.

REUILLY AC *Loire Valley, France* Extremely dry but attractive Sauvignon from west of SANCERRE. Also some pale Pinot Noir red and Pinot Gris rosé. Best producers: H Beurdin★, Gerard Bigonneau. Best years: 2004 **03 02 01 00**.

REYNELL *McLaren Vale, South Australia* Pioneer John Reynell established Chateau Reynella in 1838. Now HQ of HARDY, wines are labelled Reynell in Australia but Chateau Reynella for export. Prices have shot up lately, but they're not unreasonable given the quality. Basket

Pressed Cabernet★★, Merlot★★ and Shiraz★★ are concentrated, tannic, ageworthy reds from low-yielding vines, some of which were planted in the 1930s. Best years: (reds) 2003 02 01 **00 98 96 95 94**.

CH. REYNON *Premières Côtes de Bordeaux AC, Bordeaux, France*
Property of enology professor Denis Dubourdieu. The dry whites, particularly the barrel-fermented Vieilles Vignes★, are delightful and the red★ has come on tremendously since 1997. In the same stable is the lovely GRAVES Clos Floridène★★, which is vinified at Reynon. Best years: (reds) 2003 01 **00 99 98**; (whites) (2004) **02 01 00 99 98 96 95**.

RHEINGAU *Germany* 3205ha (7920-acre) wine region on a south-facing stretch of the Rhine flanking the city of Wiesbaden, planted with 79% Riesling and 12% Spätburgunder (Pinot Noir). Traditionally considered Germany's most aristocratic wine region, both in terms of the racy, slow-maturing wines and because of the number of noble estate owners. But famous names here are no longer a guarantee of top quality, as a new generation of winemakers is now producing many of the best wines. See also Eltville, Erbach, Geisenheim, Hochheim, Johannisberg, Kiedrich, Rauenthal, Rüdesheim, Winkel. Best years: (2004) 03 02 01 **99 98 97 96 93 90**.

RHEINHESSEN *Germany* 26,450ha (65,358-acre) wine region to the south and west of Mainz. On the Rheinterrasse between Mainz and Worms are a number of very famous top-quality estates, especially at Bodenheim, Nackenheim, NIERSTEIN and Oppenheim. BINGEN, to the north-west, also has a fine vineyard area along the left bank of the Rhine. Riesling accounts for only 10% of the vineyard area; Weissburgunder (Pinot Blanc) is the rising star. Best years: (2004) 03 02 01 **00 99 98 97 96 90**.

RHÔNE VALLEY *France* The Rhône starts out as a river in Switzerland, ambling through Lake Geneva before hurtling southwards into France. In the area south of Lyon, between Vienne and Avignon, the valley becomes one of France's great wine regions. In the northern part vertigo-inducing slopes overhang the river and the small amount of wine produced is of remarkable individuality. The Syrah grape reigns here in COTE-ROTIE and on the great hill of HERMITAGE. ST-JOSEPH, CROZES-HERMITAGE and CORNAS also make excellent reds, while the white Viognier grape yields perfumed, musky wine at CONDRIEU and the tiny CHATEAU-GRILLET. In the southern part the steep slopes give way to hot, wide plains, with hills both in the west and east. Most of these vineyards are either COTES DU RHONE or COTES DU RHONE-VILLAGES, reds, whites and rosés, but there are also specific ACs, the best known being CHATEAUNEUF-DU-PAPE, GIGONDAS and the luscious, golden dessert wine, MUSCAT DE BEAUMES-DE-VENISE. See also Cairanne, Clairette de Die, Coteaux de l'Ardèche, Coteaux du Tricastin, Côtes du Lubéron, Côtes du Ventoux, Lirac, Rasteau, St-Péray, Tavel, Vacqueyras.

RÍAS BAIXAS DO *Galicia, Spain* The best of GALICIA's DOs, Rías Baixas is making some of Spain's best whites (apart from a few Chardonnays in the north-east). The magic ingredient is the characterful Albariño grape, making dry, fruity whites with a glorious fragrance and citrus tang. Drink young or with short aging. Best producers: Adegas Galegas★,

Agro de Bazán★★, Castro Martin, Quinta de Couselo, Granxa Fillaboa★★, Lagar de Fornelos★/La RIOJA ALTA, Lusco do Miño★★, Martin Códax★, Gerardo Méndez Lázaro (Do Ferreiro Cepas Vellas★★), Pazo de Barrantes★/MARQUES DE MURRIETA, Pazo de Señorans★, Bodegas Salnesur (Condes de Albarei★), Santiago Ruiz★, Terras Gauda★★.

RIBATEJO *Portugal* Portugal's second-largest wine region, now with its own DOC, straddles the river Tagus (Tejo). Hotter and drier than ESTREMADURA to the west, vineyards in the fertile flood plain are being uprooted in favour of less vigorous soils away from the river, though D F J VINHOS still believes in the quality of the original alluvial sites. There are 6 sub-regional DOCs. Best producers: (reds) Quinta da Alorna, BRIGHT BROTHERS, Casa Cadaval★, Quinta do Casal Branco (Falcoaria★), D F J Vinhos★, Caves Dom Teodosio, Quinta do Falcão, Falua (Reserva★), Fiuza, Quinta Grande, Horta da Nazaré, Quinta da Lagoalva★, Quinta de Santo Andre.

RIBERA DEL DUERO DO *Castilla y León, Spain* The dark, mouthfilling reds in this DO, from Tinto Fino (Tempranillo), sometimes with Cabernet Sauvignon and Merlot, are nowadays generally more exciting than those of RIOJA. But excessive expansion of vineyards and increase in yields may threaten its supremacy. Best producers: AALTO★★, Alión★★, Arroyo, Arzuaga★, Balbás★, Hijos de Antonio Barceló★, Briego★, Felix Callejo★, Cillar de Silos★, Convento San Francisco★, Hermanos Cuadrado García★, Dehesa de los Canónigos, Hacienda Monasterio★★, Emilio Moro★★, Pago de los Capellanes★★, Pago de Carraovejas★, Parxet, PEDROSA★, PESQUERA★★★, PINGUS★★★, Protos★, Teófilo Reyes, Rodero★, Telmo RODRIGUEZ★★, Hermanos Sastre★★, Tarsus★, Valduero★, Valtravieso, VEGA SICILIA★★★, Viñedos y Bodegas★. Best years: 2001 00 **99 96 95 94 91 90 89 86 85**.

BARONE RICASOLI *Chianti Classico DOCG, Tuscany, Italy* The estate where modern CHIANTI was perfected by Baron Bettino Ricasoli in the mid-19th century. The flagship wine is Castello di Brolio Chianti Classico★★; that labelled Brolio is effectively a second selection. Riserva Guicciarda★ is good value. SUPER-TUSCAN Casalferro★★ is a Sangiovese-Merlot blend. Best years: (Casalferro) (2004) 03 01 **00 99 98 97 95**.

DOM. RICHEAUME *Côtes de Provence AC, Provence, France* German-owned property, run on organic principles and producing impressively deep-coloured reds★ (Columelle★★) full of smoky spice and power. Best years: (Columelle) 2002 **01 00 99 98 97**.

RICHEBOURG AC *Grand Cru, Côte de Nuits, Burgundy, France* Rich, fleshy wine from the northern end of VOSNE-ROMANEE. Most domaine-bottlings are exceptional. Best producers: GRIVOT★★★, Anne GROS★★★, A-F GROS★★★, Hudelot-Noëllat★, Dom. LEROY★★★, T Liger-Belair, MEO-CAMUZET★★★, Dom. de la ROMANEE-CONTI★★★. Best years: (2004) 03 02 01 00 99 98 **97** 96 **95 93 91 90**.

DOM. RICHOU *Loire Valley, France* One of the most consistent and good value domaines in the LOIRE. Best are the ANJOU-VILLAGES Brissac Vieilles Vignes★★ and sweet COTEAUX DE L'AUBANCE les Trois Demoiselles★★. Rogeries★ is a good example of modern dry ANJOU BLANC. Best years: (les Trois Demoiselles) (2004) 03 02 **01 99 97 96 95 90 89 88**.

MAX FERD RICHTER *Mülheim, Mosel-Saar-Ruwer, Germany* Racy Rieslings from some of the best sites in the MOSEL, including WEHLENER Sonnenuhr★★, BRAUNEBERGer Juffer★★ and GRAACHer Domprobst★. Richter's Mülheimer Helenenkloster vineyard produces a magical

Eiswein★★★ virtually every year – although not in 1999. Best years: (2004) 03 02 01 **99 98 97 96 95 94 93 90**.

RIDGE VINEYARDS *Santa Cruz Mountains AVA, California, USA* Paul Draper's Zinfandels★★★, made with grapes from various sources, have great intensity and long life. Other reds, led by Monte Bello Cabernet★★★, show impressive personality. Three Valleys★★ is a fascinating blend, including Zinfandel and Petite Sirah. There's fine Chardonnay★★, too. Best years: (Monte Bello) (2002) 01 00 99 **98 97 95 94 93 92 91 90 87 85 84**.

RIDGEVIEW *West Sussex, England* Specialist sparkling wine producer using classic CHAMPAGNE varieties. Christine and Mike Roberts produce an excellent – and improving – range of wines. All wines are named after London areas: Cavendish★★ and Bloomsbury★★ are traditional 3-variety blends; Knightsbridge★ is a Blanc de Noirs; Fitzrovia★ is a Chardonnay-Pinot Noir rosé. Best years **00 99 98**.

RIECINE *Chianti Classico DOCG, Tuscany, Italy* Small estate in Gaiole making exquisite wines. Yields are low, so there is a great intensity of fruit and a superb definition of spiced cherry flavours. New American owners have retained English winemaker Sean O'Callaghan, who continues to fashion ever better CHIANTI CLASSICO★★, Riserva★★★ and barrique-aged La Gioia★★★. Best years: (La Gioia) (2004) (03) 01 **99 98 97 95 90 88 85**.

RIESLING See pages 232–3.

RIESLING ITALICO Unrelated to the great Riesling of the Rhine, this grape is widely planted in northern Italy, where it produces decent dry whites. As Olasz Rizling, it is highly esteemed in Hungary. Elsewhere in Europe it is known as Welschriesling; in Austria it makes some of the very best sweet wines, but tends to be rather dull as a dry wine.

CH. RIEUSSEC★★★ *Sauternes AC, 1er Cru Classé, Bordeaux, France* Apart from the peerless Ch. d'YQUEM, Rieussec is often the richest, most succulent wine of SAUTERNES. Cellar for at least 10 years. Dry white 'R' is inexplicably dull. Second wine: Clos Labère. Owned by LAFITE-ROTHSCHILD. Best years: 2003 02 01 **99 98 97 96 95 90 89 88 86 85 83**.

RIOJA DOCa *Rioja, Navarra, País Vasco and Castilla y León, Spain* Rioja, in northern Spain, is not all oaky, creamy white wines and elegant, barrel-aged reds, combining oak flavours with wild strawberry and prune fruit. Over half Rioja's red wine is sold young, never having seen the inside of a barrel, and most of the white is fairly anonymous. Wine quality, as could be expected from such a large region with more than 300 producers, is inconsistent but a bevy of ambitious new producers is changing the regional hierarchy and taking quality seriously. Best producers: (reds) ALLENDE★★, Altos de Lanzaga★★ (Telmo RODRIGUEZ), Amézola de la Mora, ARTADI★★, Baron de Ley★, BERBERANA★, Bodegas Bilbaínas, CAMPILLO★, CAMPO VIEJO★, Luis Cañas, CONTINO★★, El Coto★, CVNE, DOMECQ★, FAUSTINO★, Lan (Culmen★), LOPEZ DE HEREDIA★, MARQUES DE CACERES★, MARQUES DE MURRIETA★★, MARQUES DE RISCAL★★, Marqués de Vargas★★, MARTINEZ BUJANDA★★, Abel Mendoza★★, Montecillo★, MUGA★, Palacio, REMELLURI★★, Fernando Remírez de Ganuza★★, La RIOJA ALTA★★, RIOJANAS★, Roda★★, Benjamin ROMEO★★, Sierra Cantabria★★, Señorío de San Vicente★★, Viña Ijalba; (whites) CAMPO VIEJO★, CVNE★, LOPEZ DE HEREDIA★, MARQUES DE CACERES★, MARQUES DE MURRIETA★, MARTINEZ BUJANDA★★, Montecillo★, La RIOJA ALTA★, RIOJANAS★. Best years: (reds) 2001 **96 95 94 91 89 87 86 85 83 82 81 78**.

RIESLING

I'm sad to have to make this bald statement at the start, but I feel I must. If you have tasted wines with names like Laski Riesling, Olasz Riesling, Welschriesling, Gray Riesling, Riesling Italico and the like and found them bland or unappetizing – do not blame the Riesling grape. These wines have filched Riesling's name, but have nothing whatsoever to do with the great grape itself.

Riesling is Germany's finest contribution to the world of wine – and herein lies the second problem. German wines have fallen to such a low level of general esteem through the proliferation of wines like Liebfraumilch during the 1980s that Riesling, even true German Riesling, has been dragged down with it.

So what *is* true Riesling? It is a very ancient German grape, probably the descendant of wild vines growing in the Rhine Valley. It certainly performs best in the cool vineyard regions of Germany's Rhine and Mosel Valleys, and in Alsace and Austria. It also does well in Canada, New Zealand and both warm and cool parts of Australia, and it is widely planted in California and Italy. Plantings are declining in South Africa, although cool-climate producers are dedicating more energy to the variety, especially drier styles.

Young Rieslings often show a delightful floral perfume, sometimes blended with the crispness of green apples, often lime, peach, nectarine or apricot, sometimes even raisin, honey or spice depending upon the ripeness of the grapes. As the wines age, the lime often intensifies, and a flavour perhaps of slate, perhaps of petrol/kerosene intrudes. In general Rieslings may be drunk young, but top dry wines can improve for many years, and the truly sweet German styles can age for generations.

WINE STYLES

Germany These wines have a marvellous perfume and an ability to hold on to a piercing acidity, even at high ripeness levels, so long as the ripening period has been warm and gradual rather than broiling and rushed. German Rieslings can be bone dry, through to medium and even lusciously sweet, but if they are dry, they must be made from fully ripe grapes, otherwise the acidity is excessive and the wine's body insufficient. Styles range from crisp elegant Mosels to riper, fuller wines from the Pfalz and Baden regions in the south. The very sweet Trockenbeerenauslese (TBA) Rieslings are made from grapes affected by noble rot; for Eiswein (icewine), also intensely sweet, the grapes are picked and pressed while frozen.

Other regions In the valleys of the Danube in Austria, Riesling gives stunning dry wines that combine richness with elegance, but the most fragrant wines, apart from German examples, come from France's Alsace. The mountain vineyards of northern Italy, and the cool vineyards of the Czech Republic, Slovakia and Switzerland can show a floral sharp style. Australia is the southern hemisphere's world-class producer, with cool areas of South Australia, Victoria and Western Australia all offering superb – and different – examples. New Zealand's style is floral and fresh. South Africa's best examples so far are usually sweetly botrytized. The USA's finest are from New York and the Pacific Northwest. California is best at sweet styles, as is Canada with its icewines.

BEST PRODUCERS

Germany

Dry BASSERMANN-JORDAN, Georg BREUER, BURKLIN-WOLF, HEYMANN-LOWENSTEIN, KOEHLER-RUPRECHT, KUNSTLER, J LEITZ, MULLER-CATOIR, REBHOLZ, ST ANTONY, SAUER, J L WOLF.

Non-dry DIEL, DONNHOFF, GUNDERLOCH, HAAG, HAART, HEYMANN-LOWENSTEIN, JOST, KARTHAUSERHOF, von KESSELSTATT, KUNSTLER, Carl Loewen, Dr LOOSEN, MAXIMIN GRUNHAUS, MULLER-CATOIR, Egon MULLER-SCHARZHOF, J J PRUM, RICHTER, Willi SCHAEFER, SELBACH-OSTER, WEIL.

Austria

Dry Alzinger, BRUNDLMAYER, HIRTZBERGER, J Högl, KNOLL, Loimer, Nigl, NIKOLAIHOF, F X PICHLER, Rudi Pichler, PRAGER, Schmelz.

France

(Alsace) *Dry* P BLANCK, A Boxler, DEISS, Dirler-Cadé, HUGEL, Kientzler, Kreydenweiss, Kuentz-Bas, A MANN, MURE, Ostertag, SCHOFFIT, TRIMBACH, WEINBACH, ZIND-HUMBRECHT.

Non-dry Léon Beyer, DEISS, HUGEL, Ostertag, TRIMBACH, WEINBACH, ZIND-HUMBRECHT.

Australia

Tim ADAMS, Leo Buring, DELATITE, FERNGROVE, Frankland Estate, Gilberts, GROSSET, HENSCHKE, HOWARD PARK, LEEUWIN, MITCHELL, MITCHELTON, MOUNT HORROCKS, ORLANDO, PETALUMA, PIPERS BROOK, PLANTAGENET, Skillogallee, Geoff WEAVER, YALUMBA.

New Zealand

DRY RIVER, FELTON ROAD, FROMM, MILLTON, Mt Difficulty, Muddy Water, PEGASUS BAY, VILLA MARIA, Waipara West.

South Africa

Sweet Avontuur (Above Royalty), Neethlingshof.

USA

(Washington) CHATEAU STE MICHELLE (Eroica).

233

LA RIOJA ALTA *Rioja DOCa, Rioja, Spain* One of the best of the older RIOJA producers, making mainly Reservas and Gran Reservas. Its only Crianza, Viña Alberdi, fulfils the minimum age requirements for a Reserva anyway. There is a little good, lemony-oaky Viña Ardanza Reserva★ white. Red Reservas, Viña Arana★ and Viña Ardanza★★, age splendidly, and Gran Reservas, Reserva 904★★ and Reserva 890★★★ (made only in exceptional years), are among the very best of Rioja wines. Best years: (Gran Reserva 890) 1989 **87 85 82 81 78**.

RIOJANAS *Rioja DOCa, Rioja, Spain* Quality winery producing Reservas and Gran Reservas in 2 styles – elegant Viña Albina★ and richer Monte Real★ – plus the new, refined Gran Albina★★. White Monte Real Blanco Crianza★ is one of RIOJA's best. The whites and Reservas can be kept for 5 years after release, Gran Reservas for 10 or more. Best years: (Monte Real Gran Reserva) 1996 **95 94 91 89 87 85 83 82 81**.

RION *Nuits-St-Georges AC, Côte de Nuits, Burgundy, France* Patrice Rion was the winemaker at Dom. Daniel Rion from 1979 to 2000, making consistently fine but often austere reds such as VOSNE-ROMANÉE les Beaumonts★★ and les Chaumes★★, ECHEZEAUX★★ and CLOS DE VOUGEOT★★★. His own label brings rich, concentrated BOURGOGNE Rouge★★, CHAMBOLLE-MUSIGNY les Cras★★, and NUITS-ST-GEORGES Clos des Argillières★★ from his own vines plus, since 2000, a small négociant range. Best years: (top reds) (2004) 03 02 01 **00 99 97 96 95 93 90**.

RIVERA *Puglia, Italy* One of southern Italy's most dynamic producers. The CASTEL DEL MONTE Riserva Il Falcone★★ is an excellent, full-blooded southern red. Also a series of varietals under the Terre al Monte label, best of which are Aglianico★, Pinot Bianco and Sauvignon Blanc.

RIVERINA *New South Wales, Australia* Centred on the town of Griffith and irrigated by the waters of the Murrumbidgee River, the Riverina is an important source of reliable cheap quaffing wines. Many of Australia's best-known brands, from companies like HARDY, MCWILLIAM'S, ORLANDO, ROSEMOUNT and PENFOLDS, though not mentioning the Riverina on the label, are based on wines from here. The potential for quality is definitely there, but as yet no-one has really determined to separate the characterful from the acceptable. The exception is the range of remarkable sweet wines, generally ★ level, but led by Noble One Botrytis Semillon★★★ from DE BORTOLI. Other leading producers are Casella (Yellowtail), Lillypilly, Miranda and West End★.

RIVERLAND *Australia* This important irrigated region, responsible for about 12% of the national grape crush, lies along the Murray River in SOUTH AUSTRALIA near the border with VICTORIA. A great deal goes to cask wine and cheap quaffers but an increased awareness of quality has seen inferior varieties replaced and yields lowered. Here and there, wines of real character are emerging, including some remarkable reds from the Petit Verdot grape. Best producers: Angove's, HARDY (Banrock Station, Renmano), Kingston Estate, YALUMBA (Oxford Landing).

RIVESALTES AC *Languedoc-Roussillon, France* *Vin doux naturel* from a large area around the town of Rivesaltes. These fortified wines are some of southern France's best and can be made from an assortment of grapes, mainly white Muscat (when it is called MUSCAT DE RIVESALTES) and Grenache Noir, Gris and Blanc. A *rancio* style ages well. Best producers: la CASENOVE★, CAZES★★, Chênes★, Fontanel★, Força Réal★, GAUBY★, Ch. de Jau★, Joliette★, Laporte, Rivesaltes co-op, Sarda-Malet★, Terrats co-op, Trouillas co-op.

ROBERTSON WO *South Africa*   Hot, dry inland area with lime-rich soils, uncommon in the Cape, that are ideal for vines. Chenin Blanc and Colombard remain the major white wine varieties, though a quarter of all South Africa's Chardonnay also grows here, performing well for both still and increasingly for sparkling styles. Sauvignon is also good. Muscadel (Muscat Blanc à Petits Grains) yields a benchmark fortified wine, usually unoaked and released young. A red revolution is under way; Shiraz, Merlot and Cabernet have made an excellent start. Best producers: Graham BECK★, Bon Courage, De Wetshof, Robertson Winery, SPRINGFIELD ESTATE★, Van Loveren, Weltevrede, Zandvliet.

CH. ROC DE CAMBES★★ *Côtes de Bourg AC, Bordeaux, France*   François Mitjavile of TERTRE-ROTEBOEUF has applied enthusiasm and diligence to this property since he acquired it in 1988. Full and concentrated, with ripe dark fruit, this wine takes the COTES DE BOURG appellation to new heights. Best years: 2003 02 **01** 00 **99 98 97 96 95 94 93 91 90 89**.

J ROCHIOLI *Russian River Valley AVA, California, USA*   Well-known grape growers, the Rochioli family are equally good at winemaking, offering silky, black cherry Pinot Noir★★ and a richer, dramatic West Block Reserve Pinot★★. All wines are high quality, including a fine Sauvignon Blanc★★ and a range of cult Chardonnays★★. Best years: (Pinot Noir) 2003 02 **01** 00 **99 98 97 95 94**.

ROCKFORD *Barossa Valley, South Australia*   Wonderfully nostalgic wines from Robert O'Callaghan, a great respecter of the old vines so plentiful in the BAROSSA, who delights in using antique machinery. Masterful Basket Press Shiraz★★, Riesling★, Moppa Springs★ (a Grenache-Shiraz-Mourvèdre blend) and cult sparkling Black Shiraz★★★. Best years: (Basket Press Shiraz) 2003 02 01 **99 98 96 95 92 91 90 86**.

ANTONIN RODET *Mercurey AC, Côte Chalonnaise, Burgundy, France*   Merchant based in MERCUREY, specializing in COTE CHALONNAISE, but with an excellent range throughout Burgundy. Rodet owns or co-owns 5 domaines – Ch. de Rully★, Ch. de Chamirey★, Ch. de Mercey★, Dom. des Perdrix★ and Jacques Prieur★★ – which are the source of the best wines. BOURGOGNE Vieilles Vignes★ is one of the best inexpensive Chardonnays available. Also owns Dom. de l'Aigle in LIMOUX. Best years: (reds) (2004) 03 02 99 **97** 96; (whites) (2004) **03 02 00 99**.

TELMO RODRÍGUEZ *Spain*   The former winemaker for REMELLURI has formed a 'wine company' that is active throughout Spain. With a team of enologists and viticulturists, it forms joint ventures with local growers and manages the winemaking process. The results are often spectacular. Top wines: Molino Real★★ (Sierras de MALAGA), Alto Matallana★★ (RIBERA DEL DUERO), Altos de Lanzaga★★ (RIOJA), Dehesa Gago Pago La Jara★★ (TORO), Viña 105 (Cigales), Basa (RUEDA).

LOUIS ROEDERER *Champagne AC, Champagne, France*   Renowned firm making some of the best, full-flavoured CHAMPAGNES around. As well as the excellent non-vintage★★ and pale vintage rosé★★, it also makes a big, exciting vintage★★, delicious vintage Blanc de Blancs★★ and the famous Roederer Cristal★★★ and Cristal Rosé★★★, de luxe cuvées which are nearly always magnificent. Both the vintage and Cristal can usually be aged for 10 years or more; the non-vintage benefits from a bit of aging, too. Best years: (1999) (97) 96 95 **93 90 89 88 86 85**.

ROEDERER ESTATE *Anderson Valley AVA, California, USA*   Californian offshoot of Louis ROEDERER. The Brut★★ (sold in the UK as Quartet) is austere but impressive, a step back from the upfront fruit of many California sparklers, but it will age beautifully if you can wait. Lovely rosé★★, and the top bottling, L'Ermitage★★★, is stunning. Best years: (L'Ermitage) (1999) (97) (96) **94 92 91**.

ROERO DOC *Piedmont, Italy* The Roero hills lie across the Tanaro river from the LANGHE hills, home of BAROLO and BARBARESCO. Long noted as a source of supple, fruity Nebbiolo-based red wines to drink in 2–5 years, Roero has recently been turning out Nebbiolos of Barolo-like intensity from producers such as Correggia and Malvirà. Roero is also the home of the white Arneis grape. Best producers: (reds) G Almondo★, Ca' Rossa★, Cascina Chicco★, Correggia★★, Deltetto★★, Funtanin★, F Gallino★, Malvirà★★, Monchiero Carbone★, Angelo Negro★, Porello★. Best years: (reds) (2004) (03) 01 **00 99 98 97 96**. See also Arneis.

ROMAGNA *Emilia-Romagna, Italy* Romagna's wine production is centred on 4 DOCs and 1 DOCG. The whites are from Trebbiano (ineffably dull), Pagadebit (showing promise as both a dry and sweet wine) and Albana (ALBANA DI ROMAGNA can be dry or sweet). The best of the Sangiovese-based reds can rival good CHIANTI CLASSICO. Best producers: (Sangiovese) La Berta★, Castelluccio★★, L Conti★, Drei Donà-La Palazza★★, G Madonia★, San Patrignano co-op/Terre del Cedro★ (Avi★★), Tre Monti★, Zerbina★★.

LA ROMANÉE-CONTI AC *Grand Cru, Côte de Nuits, Burgundy, France* For many extremely wealthy wine lovers this is the pinnacle of red Burgundy★★★. It is an incredibly complex wine with great structure and pure, clearly defined fruit flavour, but you've got to age it 15 years to see what all the fuss is about. The vineyard covers only 1.8ha (4½ acres), which is one reason for the high prices. Wholly owned by Dom. de la ROMANEE-CONTI. Best years: (2004) 03 02 01 00 99 98 97 96 95 93 90 **89** 88 **85 78**.

DOM. DE LA ROMANÉE-CONTI *Vosne-Romanée AC, Côte de Nuits, Burgundy, France* This famous red wine domaine owns a string of Grands Crus in VOSNE-ROMANEE (la TACHE★★★, RICHEBOURG★★★, ROMANEE-CONTI★★★, ROMANEE-ST-VIVANT★★★, ECHEZEAUX★★★ and Grands-Échézeaux★★★) as well as a small parcel of le MONTRACHET★★★. The wines are ludicrously expensive but can be sublime – full of fruit when young, but capable of aging for 15 years or more to an astonishing marriage made in the heaven and hell of richness and decay. Best years: (reds) (2004) 03 02 01 00 99 98 97 96 95 93 90 **89 85 78**.

ROMANÉE-ST-VIVANT AC *Grand Cru, Côte de Nuits, Burgundy, France* By far the largest of VOSNE-ROMANEE's 6 Grands Crus. At 10–15 years old the wines should reveal the keenly balanced brilliance of which the vineyard is capable, but a surly, rough edge sometimes gets in the way. Best producers: l'Arlot★★, R Arnoux★★★, S Cathiard★★★, J-J Confuron★★★, DROUHIN★★★, Hudelot-Noëllat★★★, JADOT★★★, Dom. LEROY★★★, Dom. de la ROMANEE-CONTI★★★, THOMAS-MOILLARD★★. Best years: (2004) 03 02 01 00 99 98 **97** 96 95 **93 90**.

BENJAMIN ROMEO *Rioja DOCa, La Rioja, Spain* ARTADI's former winemaker launched his own estate with a collection of tiny old vineyards, and immediately caused a sensation with his velvety, Burgundian and yet powerful wines, Contador★★★, La Viña de Andrés Romeo★★ and La Cueva de Contador★★. Best years: (2002) 01 00.

ROQUES, QUINTA DOS *Dão DOC, Beira Alta, Portugal* Now the DAO's finest producer, the wines of 2 estates with quite different characters are made here. Quinta dos Roques red★ is ripe and supple, while Quinta das Maias★ is a smoky, peppery red. The top wines are the dos Roques Reserva★★, made from old vines and aged in 100% new oak, and Touriga Nacional★★. Both estates also have a decent dry white, especially Roques Encruzado★. Best years: (2004) 03 01 **00 97 96**.

ROSA, QUINTA DE LA *Douro DOC and Port DOC, Douro, Portugal* The Bergqvist family have transformed this property into a small but serious producer of both PORT and DOURO★ (Reserve★★) table wines. The Vintage Port★★ is excellent, as is unfiltered LBV★★, while Finest Reserve and 10-year-old tawny★ are also good. A special selection vintage port, Vale do Inferno★★, was made in 1999 and shows a lovely old vine intensity. Best years: (Vintage) 2000 97 96 95 94 **92 91**.

ROSÉ DE LOIRE AC *Loire Valley, France* Dry rosé from ANJOU, SAUMUR and TOURAINE. It can be a lovely drink, full of red berry fruits, but drink as young as possible and chill well. It's far superior to Rosé d'Anjou AC, which is usually sweetish, without much flavour. Best producers: Hautes Ouches, Passavant, St-Arnoud, Trottières.

ROSÉ DES RICEYS AC *Champagne, France* Still, dark pink wine made from Pinot Noir grapes in the southern part of the CHAMPAGNE region. Best producers: Alexandre Bonnet★, Devaux★, Guy de Forez, Morel.

ROSEMOUNT ESTATE *Hunter Valley, New South Wales, Australia* Winery buying and growing grapes in several regions to produce some of Australia's most popular wines, but many seem sweeter and flatter than before. Even top-level Show Reserves are far less focused. The flagship Roxburgh Chardonnay★ is undergoing a dramatic style change, which may or may not return it to a position of eminence among Aussie whites. Best of the other whites is Orange Vineyard Chardonnay★. Show Reserve reds are a bit stodgy, but dense Balmoral Syrah★ and GSM★★ (Grenache, Syrah, Mourvèdre) can be good. After an inspiring start in MUDGEE, the Hill of Gold range has dipped, though Mountain Blue Shiraz-Cabernet★★ can still be excellent. Best years: (Balmoral Syrah) (2003) 02 01 00 **98 97 96 94 92 91 90**.

ROSSO CÒNERO DOC *Marche, Italy* The best wines in this zone, on the Adriatic coast, are made solely from Montepulciano, and have a wonderfully spicy richness. Best producers: Fazi Battaglia★, Garofoli★ (Grosso Agontano★★), Lanari★ (Fibbio★★), Leopardi Dittajuti★, Malacari★, Mecella (Rubelliano★), Moroder★ (Dorico★★), Le Terrazze★ (Sassi Neri★★, Visions of J★★), Umani Ronchi★ (Cúmaro★★), La Vite (Adeodato★★). Best years: (2004) (03) 01 **00 98 97 95 90**.

ROSSO DI MONTALCINO DOC *Tuscany, Italy* The little brother of BRUNELLO DI MONTALCINO spends much less time aging in wood, enabling the wines to retain a wonderful exuberance of flavour. In lesser years the best Brunello grapes may cascade here, so off-years (like 2002) can be surprisingly good. Best producers: Altesino★, Argiano★, Caparzo★, Casanova di Neri★★, Ciacci Piccolomini d'Aragona★★, Col d'Orcia★, Collemattoni★, COSTANTI★, Fuligni★, Gorelli-Due Portine★, M Lambardi★★, Lisini★, Siro Pacenti★★, Agostina Pieri★★, Poggio Antico★, Il Poggione★, Poggio Salvi★, Salicutti★★, San Filippo-Fanti★, Talenti★, Valdicava★. Best years: (2004) 03 **02 01 00 99 98 97 95**.

ROSSO DI MONTEPULCIANO DOC *Tuscany, Italy* Some VINO NOBILE producers use this DOC in order to improve selection for the main wine; the best deliver delightfully plummy, chocolaty flavours. Best producers: La Braccesca★/ANTINORI, La Ciarliana★, Contucci★, Dei★, Del Cerro★, Il Faggeto★, Fassati★, Nottola★, POLIZIANO★, Salcheto★★, Valdipiatta★, Villa Sant'Anna★. Best years: (2004) 03 **01 99 98 97**.

ROSSO PICENO DOC *Marche, Italy* Often considered a poor relative of ROSSO CONERO, but it can be rich and seductive when the full complement (40%) of Montepulciano is used. Best producers: Boccadigabbia★ (Villamagna★★), Le Caniette★, Laurentina★, Saladini Pilastri★, Velenosi★. Best years: (2004) 03 **01 00 98 97 95 94 93 90**.

RENÉ ROSTAING *Côte-Rôtie AC, Rhône Valley, France* Modern, oaked, rich, ripe wines with deep colour and soft fruit flavours, from some of the best sites in COTE-ROTIE: classic Côte-Rôtie★, la Viallère★★, Côte Blonde★★ and la Landonne★★. There's a very good CONDRIEU★★ too. Best years: (top crus) 2004 03 01 00 99 **98 95 94 91 90 88**.

ROTHBURY ESTATE *Hunter Valley, New South Wales, Australia* Len Evans' brainchild (now part of Beringer Blass) has struggled to find its way in recent years, and despite a new winemaker, Neil McGuigan, still seems to be underperforming. Best of the bunch are Neil McGuigan Shiraz★ and Semillon★. HUNTER VALLEY Verdelho has life and zest; also inexpensive varietals from MUDGEE and Cowra (Chardonnay★).

GEORGES ROUMIER *Chambolle-Musigny AC, Côte de Nuits, Burgundy, France* Christophe Roumier is one of Burgundy's top winemakers, devoting as much attention to his vineyards as to cellar technique, believing in severe pruning, low yields and stringent grape selection. Roumier never uses more than one-third new oak. His best wine is often BONNES-MARES★★★, but his other Grands Crus include MUSIGNY★★★, Ruchottes-Chambertin★★ and CORTON-CHARLEMAGNE★★★. The best value are usually the village CHAMBOLLE★★ and an exclusively owned Premier Cru in MOREY-ST-DENIS, Clos de la Bussière★★. Best years: (reds) (2004) 03 02 01 00 99 98 **97** 96 **95 90 89 88**.

ROUSSANNE The RHONE VALLEY's best white grape, frequently blended with Marsanne. Roussanne is the more aromatic and elegant of the two, less prone to oxidation and with better acidity, but growers usually prefer Marsanne due to its higher yields. Now being planted in the MIDI. There are some examples in Savoie and Australia. While much of the Roussanne planted in California has been identified as Viognier, there are a few true plantings that produce fascinating wines.

ARMAND ROUSSEAU *Gevrey-Chambertin AC, Côte de Nuits, Burgundy, France* One of the most highly respected and important CHAMBERTIN estates, with vineyards in Chambertin★★★, Clos-de-Bèze★★★ (both exceptional), Mazis-Chambertin★★ and Charmes-Chambertin★★ as well as CLOS DE LA ROCHE★★★ in MOREY-ST-DENIS and GEVREY-CHAMBERTIN Clos St-Jacques★★★. The long-lived traditional wines are outstandingly harmonious, elegant, yet rich. Charles Rousseau has been making these great wines since 1959, though recent vintages have been slightly inconsistent. Best years: (2004) 03 02 00 99 96 **93 91 90 89 88 85**.

ROUSSILLON *France* The snow-covered peaks of the Pyrenees form a spectacular backdrop to the ancient region of Roussillon, now the Pyrénées-Orientales *département*. The vineyards produce a wide range of fairly priced wines, mainly red, ranging from the ripe, raisin-rich *vins doux naturels* to light, fruity-fresh vins de pays, and there are now some really exciting table wines, both white and red, being made in Roussillon, especially by individual estates. See also Banyuls, Collioure, Côtes du Roussillon, Côtes du Roussillon-Villages, Maury, Muscat de Rivesaltes, Rivesaltes.

RUCHOTTES-CHAMBERTIN AC See Chambertin AC.

RÜDESHEIM *Rheingau, Germany* Village producing silky, aromatic wines from some steep terraced vineyards directly on the bank of the Rhein (Berg Schlossberg, Berg Rottland, Berg Roseneck and Bischofsberg). Not to be confused with the NAHE village of the same name. Best producers: Georg BREUER★★, Johannishof★, Kesseler★, Josef LEITZ★★. Best years: (2004) 03 02 01 00 **99 98 97 96 94 90**.

RUEDA DO *Castilla y León, Spain* The RIOJA firm of MARQUES DE RISCAL launched the reputation of this white wine region in the 1970s, first by rescuing the almost extinct Verdejo grape, then by introducing Sauvignon Blanc. Fresh young whites have been joined by barrel-fermented wines aiming for a longer life, particularly at Castilla La Vieja and Belondrade y Lurton. Best producers: Alvarez y Diez★, Antaño (Viña Mocén★), Belondrade y Lurton★, Cerrosol (Doña Beatriz), Hermanos Lurton, MARQUES DE RISCAL★, Bodegas de Crianza Castilla La Vieja (Palacio de Bornos Vendimia Seleccionada★★), Javier Sanz Cantalapiedra★, Viñedos de Nieva★, Viños Sanz, Angel Rodríguez Vidal (Martinsancho★), Viña Sila★ (Naia, Naiades).

RUFFINO *Tuscany, Italy* Huge winemaking concern now partly owned by American giant Constellation Brands. Brothers Marco and Paolo Folonari continue to control production, making CHIANTI CLASSICO from Santedame★ and the classic Riserva Ducale Oro★★. SUPER-TUSCANS include promising Chardonnay, La Solatia★; Sangiovese-Cabernet-Merlot blend Modus★; Pinot Noir Nero del Tondo★; and the unique blend of Colorino and Merlot, Romitorio di Santedame★★. The Ruffino operation also includes VINO NOBILE estate Lodola Nuova, BRUNELLO Il Greppone Mazzi and Borgo Conventi in COLLIO. See also Folonari.

RUINART *Champagne AC, Champagne, France* Ruinart has a surprisingly low profile given the quality of its wines. Non-vintage★ is very good, as is Blanc de Blancs★★, but the top wines here are the supremely classy Dom Ruinart Blanc de Blancs★★★ and the Dom Ruinart Rosé★★★. Best years: (1999) (98) 96 **95 93 92 90 88 86 85 83 82**.

RULLY AC *Côte Chalonnaise, Burgundy, France* Best known for its still whites, often oak-aged. Reds are light, with a fleeting strawberry and cherry perfume. Most wines are reasonably priced. Best producers: (whites) d'Allaines★, J-C Brelière★, DROUHIN★, Dureuil-Janthial★, Duvernay, FAIVELEY★, V GIRARDIN★, JADOT★, Jaffelin★, O LEFLAIVE★, RODET★, Villaine★; (reds) A Delorme, Dureuil-Janthial★, Duvernay, la Folie, H & P Jacqueson★. Best years: (whites) (2004) **03 02**; (reds) (2004) **03 02**.

RUSSIAN RIVER VALLEY AVA *Sonoma County, California, USA* Beginning south of Healdsburg this valley cools as it meanders towards the Pacific. It is now challenging CARNEROS as the top spot in North Coast California for Pinot Noir and Chardonnay. Best producers: Davis Bynum★, DEHLINGER★★★, De Loach★, Dutton-Goldfield★★, Gary Farrell★★★, IRON HORSE★★, Merry Edwards★★, ROCHIOLI★★, SONOMA-CUTRER★, Rodney Strong★, Joseph SWAN★, Marimar TORRES★★, WILLIAMS SELYEM★★. Best years: (Pinot Noir) 2002 **01 00 99 97 95 94 93 91 90**.

RUST EN VREDE *Stellenbosch WO, South Africa* Jannie Engelbrecht now runs this red-only property; his son, Jean, has left with winemaker Louis Strydom to run the nearby ERNIE ELS cellar. Rust en Vrede★, a

Cabernet-Shiraz-Merlot blend reflecting the farm's terroir, Shiraz★, Merlot and Cabernet all benefit from young, virus-free vines, showing fine, soft tannins and fresh fruit. Best years: (Rust en Vrede estate wine) 2001 00 99 98 97 96 95 94.

RUSTENBERG *Stellenbosch WO, South Africa* Premier-league producer, headed in the cellar by local youngster Adi Badenhorst. New RHONE-oriented plantings have resulted in a delightful Viognier★ under the good-value Brampton label. Tradition is perpetuated in the majestic Peter Barlow★★ (Cabernet) and BORDEAUX-style blend John X Merriman★★. Also new-look yet classically styled single-vineyard Five Soldiers★ (Chardonnay). Best years: (Peter Barlow) 2003 02 01 99 98 97; (Five Soldiers) 2003 02 01 00 99 98 97.

RUTHERFORD AVA *Napa Valley, California, USA* This viticultural area in mid-NAPA VALLEY has inspired hours of argument over whether it has a distinct identity. The heart of the area, the Rutherford Bench, does seem to be a prime Cabernet Sauvignon zone, and many traditional Napa Cabernets have come from here and exhibit the 'Rutherford dust' flavour. Best producers: BEAULIEU★★, Cakebread, FLORA SPRINGS★★, Freemark Abbey, NIEBAUM-COPPOLA★★, Quintessa★, Staglin★★. Best years: (Cabernet) (2002) 01 00 99 97 96 95 94 93 91 90 86.

RUTHERGLEN *Victoria, Australia* This region in north-east VICTORIA is the home of heroic reds from Shiraz, Cabernet and Durif, and luscious, world-beating fortifieds from Muscat and Tokay (Muscadelle). Good sherry- and PORT-style wines. Best producers: (fortifieds) ALL SAINTS★, Buller★★, Campbells★★, CHAMBERS★★, MORRIS★★, Stanton & Killeen★★.

SAALE-UNSTRUT *Germany* Located in the former East Germany, Saale-Unstrut's 650ha (1600 acres) of vineyards have been extensively replanted since 1989, but these vineyards must mature before first-class wines can be produced. Weissburgunder (Pinot Blanc) is the most important quality grape. Best producers: Kloster Pforta, Lützkendorf★.

SACHSEN *Germany* Until recently one of Europe's forgotten wine regions (445ha/1100 acres) on the river Elbe in former East Germany. Now beginning to produce some good wines, the best being dry Riesling, Gewürztraminer, Weissburgunder (Pinot Blanc) and Grauburgunder (Pinot Gris) with snappy acidity and surprisingly high alcohol. Best producers: Schloss Proschwitz★, Schloss Wackerbarth★, Klaus Zimmerling★.

ST-AMOUR AC *Beaujolais, Burgundy, France* The most northerly of the BEAUJOLAIS crus, much in demand through the romantic connotation of its name. The granitic vineyards produce wines with great intensity of colour that may be initially harsh, needing a few months to soften. Best producers: l'Ancien Relais/André Poitevin, des Billards/Loron★, DUBOEUF★ (des Sablons★), des Duc★. Best years: 2003 00.

ST ANTONY *Nierstein, Rheinhessen, Germany* Dr Alex Michalsky runs one of RHEINHESSEN's finest estates, making dry and off-dry Rieslings (frequently ★★) with unusual power and richness from the top sites of NIERSTEIN. Occasional sweet Auslese and higher Prädikat wines are always expansive and luscious. All wines except the regular dry Riesling★ have at least 5 years' aging potential. Best years: (2003) 02 01 00 99 98 97 96 94 93 90.

WEINGUT
ST. ANTONY

Nierstein
2002
Oelberg

ST-AUBIN AC *Côte de Beaune, Burgundy, France*   Some of Burgundy's best-value wines. Good reds, especially from Premiers Crus like les Frionnes and les Murgers des Dents de Chien. Also reasonably priced, oak-aged whites. Best producers: d'Allaines★, Bernard Bachelet, D & F Clair★★, M Colin★★, DROUHIN★, JADOT★, H & O Lamy★, Lamy-Pillot★, Larue★★, O LEFLAIVE★, B Morey★, RAMONET★★, Roux★, G Thomas★. Best years: (reds) (2004) 03 02 **01** 99; (whites) (2004) **03 02** 00.

ST-BRIS AC *Burgundy, France*   Recently promoted appellation for Sauvignon Blanc; paradoxically, producing less interesting wines than a decade ago. Drink young. Best producer: J-H Goisot.

ST-CHINIAN AC *Languedoc, France*   Large AC covering strong, spicy red wines with more personality and fruit than run-of-the-mill HERAULT from hill villages set back from the coast. Best producers: Berloup co-op, Borie la Vitarèle★, CANET-VALETTE★★, Cazal-Viel★, CLOS BAGATELLE★, Combebelle, Jougla★, Mas Champart★, Maurel Fonsalade★, Moulin de Ciffre, Moulinier, Navarre, Rimbert★, Roquebrun co-op, Tabatau (Lo Tabataire) . Best years: 2003 **01** 00 99 98 96.

SAINT CLAIR *Marlborough, South Island, New Zealand*   A top performer thanks to some great vineyard sites that are now expressing themselves more forcefully than of old. Several Sauvignons are led by the intensely fruity Wairau Reserve Sauvignon Blanc★★. Omaka Reserve Chardonnay★ combines attractive citrus fruit flavours and sensitive winemaking, while various Pinot Noirs★ and lean but tasty Rapaura Road Reserve Merlot★ lead the reds. Best years: (whites) **2005** 04 03 01 00 99.

ST-DÉSIRAT, CAVE DE *St-Joseph, Rhône Valley, France*   St-Désirat is one of the best co-ops in the RHONE VALLEY. The intense, smoky red ST-JOSEPH★ is a bargain, as are local vins de pays.

ST-ÉMILION AC *Bordeaux, France*   The scenic Roman hill town of St-Émilion is the centre of Bordeaux's most historic wine region. The finest vineyards are on the plateau and *côtes,* or steep slopes, around the town, although an area to the west, called the *graves,* contains 2 famous properties, CHEVAL BLANC and FIGEAC. It is a region of smallholdings, with over 1000 properties, and consequently the co-operative plays an important part. The dominant early-ripening Merlot grape gives wines with a 'come hither' softness and sweetness rare in red BORDEAUX. St-Émilion AC is the basic generic AC, with 4 'satellites' (LUSSAC, MONTAGNE, PUISSEGUIN, ST-GEORGES) allowed to annex their name to it. The best producers, including the Classed Growths, are found in the more tightly controlled ST-EMILION GRAND CRU AC category. Best years: 2003 **01 00** 98 96 95 90 89 88 86 85.

ST-ÉMILION GRAND CRU AC *Bordeaux, France*   St-Émilion's top-quality AC, which includes the estates classified as Grand Cru Classé and Premier Grand Cru Classé. The 1996 Classification lists 55 Grands Crus Classés. It also includes most of the new wave of limited edition *vins de garage.* Best producers: (Grands Crus Classés) l'ARROSEE★★, Balestard-la-Tonnelle★, CANON-LA-GAFFELIERE★★, Clos de l'Oratoire★, la Clotte★, la Dominique★★, Grand Mayne★★, Grand Pontet★, Larmande★, Pavie-Decesse★, PAVIE-MACQUIN★★, Soutard★, la Tour Figeac★, TROPLONG-MONDOT★★; (others) Faugères★, Fleur Cardinale★, Fombrauge★, la Gomerie★, Gracia★, MONBOUSQUET★★, La Mondotte★★, Moulin St-Georges★, Quinault l'Enclos★, Rol Valentin★★, TERTRE-ROTEBOEUF★★, Teyssier, VALANDRAUD★★. Best years: 2003 **01** 00 **98 96** 95 90 89 88 86 85. See also St-Émilion Premier Grand Cru Classé.

ST-ÉMILION PREMIER GRAND CRU CLASSÉ *Bordeaux, France* The St-Émilion élite level, divided into 2 categories – 'A' and 'B' – with only the much more expensive CHEVAL BLANC and AUSONE in category 'A'. There are 11 'B' châteaux, with ANGELUS and BEAU-SEJOUR BECOT added in the 1996 Classification. Best producers: ANGELUS★★★, AUSONE★★★, BEAU-SEJOUR BECOT★★, Beauséjour★, BELAIR★, CANON★, CHEVAL BLANC★★★, Clos Fourtet★, FIGEAC★★, la Gaffelière★, MAGDELAINE★★, PAVIE★★. Best years: 2003 02 01 00 **99** 98 **96 95 90 89 88 86 85 83 82**.

ST-ESTÈPHE AC *Haut-Médoc, Bordeaux, France* Large AC north of PAUILLAC with 5 Classed Growths. St-Estèphe wines have high tannin levels, but given time (10–20 years) those sought-after flavours of blackcurrant and cedarwood do peek out. More Merlot has been planted to soften the wines and make them more accessible at an earlier age. Best producers: CALON-SEGUR★★, COS D'ESTOURNEL★★★, Cos Labory★, HAUT-MARBUZET★★, LAFON-ROCHET★, Lilian-Ladouys★, Marbuzet★, MEYNEY★, MONTROSE★★, les Ormes-de-Pez★, PEZ★, Phélan Ségur★. Best years: 2003 02 01 00 96 **95 94 90 89 88 86 85 83 82**.

DOM. ST-GAYAN *Gigondas AC, Rhône Valley, France* The Meffre family's holdings include some very old vines, which lend power to the GIGONDAS★ (★★ in top years). The other reds are usually good value. Best years: (Gigondas) 2004 03 01 00 **99 98 97 96 95 90**.

ST-GEORGES-ST-ÉMILION AC *Bordeaux, France* The best satellite of ST-EMILION, with lovely, soft wines that can nevertheless age for 6–10 years. Best producers: Calon, Griffe de Cap d'Or, Macquin St-Georges★, St-André Corbin, Ch. St-Georges★, Tour-du-Pas-St-Georges★, Vieux-Montaiguillon. Best years: 2003 **01 00 98 96 95 90**.

ST HALLETT *Barossa Valley, South Australia* Change is afoot at the home of the venerable Old Block Shiraz★★ and its Shiraz siblings Blackwell★ and Faith★. Following a merger with MCLAREN VALE's Tatachilla, then a joint takeover by ADELAIDE HILLS' Hillstowe, all 3 wineries were snapped up by brewer Lion Nathan. We've yet to see whether the wines – including the bargain Gamekeeper's Reserve★ red, Poacher's Blend★ white, EDEN VALLEY Riesling★ and The Reward Cabernet★★ – will suffer, but production is now centred on St Hallett, which may strain resources. Best years: (Old Block) (2003) 02 01 99 98 **96 94 93 91 90**.

ST-JOSEPH AC *Rhône Valley, France* Large, mainly red AC, on the opposite bank of the Rhône to HERMITAGE. Made from Syrah, the reds have mouthfilling fruit with irresistible blackcurrant richness. Brilliant at 1–2 years, they can last for up to 10. The white wines are usually pleasant and flowery to drink young, although an increasing number can age. Best producers: (reds) CHAPOUTIER★, J-L CHAVE★★, Chêne★★, L Chèze★, COLOMBO★, Courbis★, COURSODON★★, CUILLERON★★, DELAS★, E & J Durand★, Florentin★, P Gaillard★★, Gonon★, GRAILLOT★★, B Gripa★★, GUIGAL★★, JABOULET★, Monteillet★★, Paret★, A PERRET★★, C Pichon★, ST-DESIRAT CO-OP★, TAIN L'HERMITAGE CO-OP★, Tardieu-Laurent★★, G Vernay★, F Villard★★; (whites) CHAPOUTIER (Granits★★), Chêne★★, L Chèze★, Courbis★ (Royes★★), CUILLERON★★, DELAS★, Ferraton★, P Finon, G Flacher, Florentin★, P Gaillard★★, Gonon★★, B Gripa★, GUIGAL, JABOULET★, Monteillet★, A PERRET★, Trollat★, Villard★★. Best years: (reds) 2004 03 01 **00 99 98 97 96 95**; (whites) 2004 **03 00 99 98 97 96**.

ST-JULIEN AC *Haut-Médoc, Bordeaux, France* For many, St-Julien produces perfect claret, with an ideal balance between opulence and austerity and between the brashness of youth and the genius of maturity. It is the smallest of the HAUT-MEDOC ACs but almost all is first-rate vineyard land and quality is high. Best producers: BEYCHEVELLE★, BRANAIRE★★, DUCRU-BEAUCAILLOU★★★, GLORIA★, GRUAUD-LAROSE★★, LAGRANGE★★, LANGOA-BARTON★★, LEOVILLE-BARTON★★, LEOVILLE-BARTON★★★, LEOVILLE-LAS-CASES★★★, LEOVILLE-POYFERRE★★, ST-PIERRE★★, TALBOT★. Best years: 2003 02 01 00 **99** 98 **97** 96 **95 94 90** 89 88 86 85 83 82.

ST-NICOLAS-DE-BOURGUEIL AC *Loire Valley, France* An enclave of just under 500ha (1250 acres) within the larger BOURGUEIL AC, and similarly producing light wines from vineyards towards the river, sturdier bottles from up the hill. Almost all the wine is red and with the same piercing red fruit flavours of Bourgueil, and much better after 7–10 years, especially in warm vintages. Best producers: Y Amirault★, Clos des Quarterons★, L & M Cognard-Taluau★, Vignoble de la Jarnoterie, F Mabileau★, J-C Mabileau★, Dom. Pavillon du Grand Clos★, J Taluau★, Vallée★. Best years: 2004 03 02 01 **00 97 96 95 90** 89.

ST-PÉRAY AC *Rhône Valley, France* Rather hefty, CHAMPAGNE-method fizz from Marsanne and Roussanne grapes. Still white is usually dry, fragrant and mineral on the finish. Best producers: S Chaboud★, CLAPE★, COLOMBO (La Belle de Mai★), G Darona★, DELAS, Fauterie★, B Gripa★★, J Lemenicier★, LIONNET★, J-L Thiers★, TAIN L'HERMITAGE co-op, Tunnel★, A Voge★. Best years: 2004 **03 01 00 99 98 96 95**.

CH. ST-PIERRE★★ *St-Julien AC, 4ème Cru Classé, Haut-Médoc, Bordeaux, France* Small ST-JULIEN property making wines that have become a byword for ripe, lush fruit wrapped round with the spice of new oak. Drinkable early, but top vintages can improve for 20 years. Best years: 2003 02 01 00 **99 98 97 96 95 94 90** 89 88 86 83 82.

ST-ROMAIN AC *Côte de Beaune, Burgundy, France* Out-of-the-way village producing red wines with a firm, bittersweet cherrystone fruit and flinty-dry whites. Both are usually good value by Burgundian standards, but take a few years to open out. Best producers: (whites) Bazenet★, H & G Buisson, Chassorney★★, A Gras★★, O LEFLAIVE★, P Taupenot, VERGET★★; (reds) A Gras★. Best years: (whites) (2004) **03 02 00**; (reds) (2004) 03 02 99.

ST-VÉRAN AC *Mâconnais, Burgundy, France* Often thought of as a POUILLY-FUISSÉ understudy, this is gentle, fairly fruity, normally unoaked Mâconnais Chardonnay. Overall quality is good. Drink young. Best producers: D & M Barraud★, G Chagny, Corsin★★, Deux Roches★, B & J-M Drouin★, DUBOEUF★, G Guérin★, R Lassarat★, O Merlin★, Saumaize-Michelin★, J C Thévenet★★, J-L Tissier★, VERGET★, J-J Vincent★.

STE-CROIX-DU-MONT AC *Bordeaux, France* Best of the 3 sweet wine ACs that gaze jealously at SAUTERNES and BARSAC across the Garonne river (the others are CADILLAC and LOUPIAC). The wine is mildly sweet rather than splendidly rich. Top wines can age for at least a decade. Best producers: Crabitan-Bellevue, Loubens★, Lousteau-Vieil, Mailles, Mont, Pavillon★, la Rame★. Best years: 2003 02 **01 99 98 97 96 95**.

SAINTSBURY *Carneros AVA, California, USA* Deeply committed CARNEROS winery. Its Pinot Noirs★★ are brilliant examples of the perfume and fruit quality of Carneros; the Reserve★★★ and the exquisite Brown Ranch★★★ are deeper and oakier, while Garnet★ is a delicious lighter style. The Chardonnays★ are also impressive, best after 2–3 years. Best years: (Pinot Noir Reserve) (2002) 01 **00 99 98 97 96 95 94 91**.

SALA, CASTELLO DELLA *Orvieto DOC, Umbria, Italy* Belongs to the ANTINORI family, making good ORVIETO★ and outstanding oak-aged Cervaro★★★ (Chardonnay and a little Grechetto). Also impressive Pinot Nero★ and sweet Muffato della Sala★★.

SALAPARUTA, DUCA DI *Sicily, Italy*   Corvo is the brand name for Sicilian wines made by this firm. Red and white Corvo are pretty basic, but there are superior whites, Colomba Platino★ and Bianca di Valguarnera★, and 2 fine reds, Terre d'Agala★ and Duca Enrico★★.

SALICE SALENTINO DOC *Puglia, Italy*   One of the better DOCs in the Salento peninsula, using Negroamaro tempered with a dash of perfumed Malvasia Nera for ripe, chocolaty wines that acquire hints of roast chestnuts and prunes with age. Drink after 3–4 years, although they may last as long again. The DOCs of Alezio, Brindisi, Copertino, Leverano and Squinzano are similar. Best producers: Candido★, Casale Bevagna★, Leone De Castris★, Due Palme★, Taurino★, Vallone★★, Conti Zecca. Best years: (reds) (2004) (03) **01 00 98 97 96**.

SAMOS *Greece*   The island of Samos has a centuries-old reputation for rich, sweet, Muscat-based dessert wines. The Samos co-op's wines include pale green Samena, a dry white made from early-picked Muscat; deep gold, honeyed Samos Nectar★★, made from sun-dried grapes; apricotty Palaio★, aged for up to 20 years; and seductively complex Samos Anthemis★, fortified and cask-aged for up to 5 years.

SAN ANTONIO VALLEY *Chile*   This region is really in two parts – the more northerly San Antonio, and the more southerly Leyda. Closeness to the Pacific Ocean and the icy Humboldt Current decides whether you are best at snappy Sauvignon Blanc and fragrant Pinot Noir, or scented, juice-laden Syrah. There are half a dozen estates, but big companies like CONCHA Y TORO and MONTES are also making exciting wine from the region's fruit. Water shortage is a problem, but expect Leyda in particular to become a new CASABLANCA. Best producers: CASA MARIN★, Garcés Silva★, Viña Leyda★, MATETIC★.

SAN LEONARDO *Trentino, Italy*   Marchese Carlo Guerrieri Gonzaga runs this model estate, beneath the awe-inspiring mountains of southern Trentino, with cool aristocratic passion. A former winemaker at SASSICAIA, he has established his Cabernet-Merlot blend San Leonardo★★ as the northern equivalent of the famous Tuscan. Recently launched is an almost equally impressive Merlot called Villa Gresti★★. Best years: (2004) (03) 01 00 **99 97 96 95**.

SAN LUIS OBISPO COUNTY *California, USA*   CENTRAL COAST county best known for Chardonnay, Pinot Noir, a bit of old-vine Zinfandel, Syrah and Cabernet Sauvignon. There are 5 AVAs – Edna Valley, PASO ROBLES, SANTA MARIA VALLEY (shared with SANTA BARBARA COUNTY), Arroyo Grande Valley and York Mountain – each of which has already grown some outstanding grapes. Best producers: Claiborne & Churchill★, Eberle★, Edna Valley★★, Justin★★, Laetitia, J Lohr (Hilltop Cabernet Sauvignon★★), Meridian★, Norman★, Saucelito Canyon★, Savannah-Chanelle★, Talley★★, Wild Horse★. Best years: (reds) 2002 **01 00 99 98 97 95 94**.

SAN PEDRO *Curicó, Chile*   San Pedro is a giant operation and produced little of note before Jacques Lurton arrived as a consultant in 1994. He's gone now, but the French influence lingers in a new venture with ST-EMILION Ch. Dassault called Altaïr. The Cabernet Sauvignon-based Altaïr★★ is a superb, sophisticated red, while the second wine, Sideral, is chewy and ripe. San Pedro's 35 South range is pretty good, Castillo de Molina Reservas★ are ripe and full-bodied, and 1865 Malbec★★ and Cabernet★★ are excellent, powerful, dark-fruited reds. The new winery, Tabali, in Limarí Valley, may well produce the group's best wines yet.

SANCERRE AC *Loire Valley, France* White Sancerre can provide the perfect expression of the bright green tang of the Sauvignon grape, and from a good grower can be deliciously refreshing – as can the rare Pinot Noir rosé – but the very best also age well. Some growers produce a richer style using new oak. Pinot Noir reds from top producers are now a serious proposition. The wines are more consistent than those of neighbouring POUILLY. Prices reflect the appellation's enduring popularity. Best producers: F & J Bailly★, Balland-Chapuis★, H Bourgeois★★, H Brochard★, R Champault★, F Cotat★★, L Crochet★, Delaporte★, Gitton★, P Jolivet★, Serge Laloue★, A MELLOT★★, J Mellot★, P Millérioux★, H Natter★, A & F Neveu★, R Neveu★, V Pinard★★, J Reverdy★, P & N Reverdy★, Reverdy-Ducroux★, J-M Roger★, VACHERON★★, André Vatan★. Best years: 2004 **03 02 00 99 98 97 96 95**.

SANDALFORD *Swan Valley, Western Australia* One of Western Australia's original wineries (founded in 1840) and a pioneer of the MARGARET RIVER, where Sandalford planted a large vineyard in 1972. However, it generally underperformed until the arrival of winemaker Paul Boulden in 2001. His Rieslings★★ from Frankland River and Mount Barker are astonishing, as are his Margaret River Semillon★★ and Chardonnay★★. The reds are perhaps even better: gentle and full of red fruit flavours from Frankland River, and dark and classically ripe from Margaret River (Shiraz★★, Cabernet Sauvignon★★★). New reserve Cabernet The Prendiville★★★ raises the bar even further. Best years: (Cabernet Sauvignon) 2003 02 01 00 **99**.

SANDEMAN *Port DOC, Douro, Portugal and Jerez y Manzanilla DO, Spain* Now owned by SOGRAPE, but run by George Sandeman (seventh-generation descendant of the founder). Excellent aged tawnies: Imperial Reserve★ and 20-year-old★★. Vintage ports are more patchy. Vau Vintage★★ is the second label, for early drinking. Formerly famous sherries are in need of improvement and no longer associated with the PORT company. Best years: (Vintage) 2000 97 94 **66 63 55**.

LUCIANO SANDRONE *Barolo DOCG, Piedmont, Italy* Luciano Sandrone has become one of PIEDMONT's leading wine stylists, renowned for his BAROLO Cannubi Boschis★★★ and Le Vigne★★★, as well as BARBERA D'ALBA★★ and Dolcetto d'Alba★★, which rank with the best.

SANFORD *Santa Rita Hills AVA, California, USA* Richard Sanford planted the great Benedict vineyard in the Santa Ynez Valley in 1971, thus establishing SANTA BARBARA as a potentially top-quality vineyard region. Sanford now makes sharply focused, dark-fruited Pinot Noir★★, Chardonnay★★ and Sauvignon Blanc★. An estate vineyard planted west of Highway 101 is in the SANTA RITA HILLS, an area that subsequently burst on the Pinot Noir scene with some spectacular wines. Best years: (Pinot Noir) 2002 01 **00 99 98 97 96 95 94**.

SANGIOVESE Sangiovese has overtaken Trebbiano as the most widely planted grape variety in Italy, but it reaches its greatest heights in central TUSCANY. This grape has produced a wide range of sub-varieties that make generalization difficult. Much care is being taken in the current wave of replanting, whether in CHIANTI CLASSICO, BRUNELLO DI MONTALCINO or VINO NOBILE DI MONTEPULCIANO. Styles range from pale, lively and cherryish through vivacious, mid-range

Chiantis to excellent top Riservas and SUPER-TUSCANS. Some fine examples are also produced in ROMAGNA. California producers like ATLAS PEAK, SHAFER, Robert Pepi and SEGHESIO are having a go at taming the grape. Australia has good examples from King Valley in VICTORIA (Gary Crittenden, Pizzini) and MCLAREN VALE (Coriole). Also grown in Argentina and Chile, and both South Africa and New York's LONG ISLAND are trying it.

SANTA BARBARA COUNTY *California, USA* CENTRAL COAST county, north-west of Los Angeles, known for Chardonnay, Riesling, Pinot Noir and Syrah. The main AVAs are SANTA RITA HILLS, Santa Ynez Valley and most of SANTA MARIA VALLEY (the remainder is in SAN LUIS OBISPO COUNTY), all top areas for Pinot Noir. Best producers: AU BON CLIMAT★★, Babcock, Beckmen★, Brewer-Clifton★★, BYRON★★, Cambria, Foxen★★, Hitching Post★★, Lane Tanner★★, Longoria★, Melville★, Andrew MURRAY★★, Ojai★★, Fess Parker★, QUPE★★, SANFORD★★, Whitcraft★★, Zaca Mesa★. Best years: (Pinot Noir) 2002 **01 00 99 98 97 95 94**.

SANTA CAROLINA *Maipo, Chile* Long-established winery that is at last catching up with the modern world. You'll find fresh Reserva whites★ with good fruit definition, and substantial, ripe, if oaky, Barrica Selection reds★. Top of the range is the Cabernet-based VSC★.

SANTA CRUZ MOUNTAINS AVA *California, USA* A sub-region of CENTRAL COAST AVA. Notable for long-lived Chardonnays and Cabernet Sauvignons, including the stunning Monte Bello from RIDGE. Also small amounts of robust Pinot Noir. Best producers: BONNY DOON★★, David Bruce★★, Clos La Chance★, Kathryn Kennedy★★, Mount Eden Vineyards★★, RIDGE★★★, Santa Cruz Mountain Vineyard★.

SANTA MARIA VALLEY AVA *Santa Barbara County and San Luis Obispo County, California, USA* Cool Santa Maria Valley is coming on strong as a producer of Chardonnay, Pinot Noir and Syrah. Look for wines made from grapes grown in Bien Nacido vineyards by several small wineries. Best producers: AU BON CLIMAT★★, BYRON★★, Cambria, Foxen★★, Lane Tanner (Pinot Noir)★★, Longoria★, QUPE★.

SANTA RITA *Maipo, Chile* Long-established MAIPO giant, now revitalized under winemaker Andrés Ilabaca. Red blends such as superb Triple C★★ (Cabernet Franc, Cabernet Sauvignon, Carmenère) and Syrah-Cabernet Sauvignon-Carmenère★ show real flair. Floresta whites (Leyda Sauvignon★★) and reds – both single varietal★★ and blends★★ (expect ★★★ here soon) are tremendous. Casa Real★ is expensive and old fashioned.

SANTA RITA HILLS AVA *Santa Barbara County, California, USA* Established in 2002, this small AVA lies at the western edge of the Santa Ynez Hills in SANTA BARBARA COUNTY. Fog from the Pacific keeps temperatures cool. Pinot Noir is the primary grape (along with small amounts of Syrah and Chardonnay) and the wines have deeper colour, greater varietal intensity and higher acidity than others in the region. Best producers: Babcock, Brewer-Clifton★★, Fiddlehead★★, Lafond★, Melville★, SANFORD★★, Sea Smoke★★.

SANTENAY AC *Côte de Beaune, Burgundy, France* Red Santenay wines often promise good ripe flavour, though they don't always deliver it, but are worth aging for 4–6 years in the hope that the wine will open out. Many of the best wines, both red and white, come from les Gravières Premier Cru on the border with CHASSAGNE-MONTRACHET. Best producers: (reds) R Belland★★, D & F Clair★, M Colin★, J Girardin★,

V GIRARDIN★★, Monnot★, B Morey★★, L Muzard★★, N POTEL, Prieur-Brunet, Roux Père et Fils★; (whites) V GIRARDIN★, Jaffelin, René Lequin-Colin★. Best years: (reds) (2004) 03 02 **01 99**; (whites) (2004) **03 02 00**.

CASA SANTOS LIMA *Alenquer DOC, Estremadura, Portugal* A beautiful estate with an expanding range. Light, fruity and tasty Espiga reds and whites, spicy red★ and creamy, perfumed white Palha Canas, and red and white Quinta das Setencostas★. Also Touriz★ (from DOURO varieties), varietal Touriga Nacional★, Touriga Franca★, Trincadeira★ and Tinta Roriz★ and peachy, herby Chardonnay★.

CAVES SÃO JOÃO *Beira Litoral, Portugal* This company was a pioneer of cool-fermented, white BAIRRADA, and has made some very good Cabernet Sauvignons from its own vines. Rich, complex traditional reds include outstanding Reserva★★ and Frei João★ from Bairrada and Porta dos Cavalheiros★★ from DAO – they demand at least 10 years age to show their quality.

SARDINIA *Italy* Grapes of Spanish origin, like the white Vermentino and Torbato and the red Monica, Cannonau and Carignano, dominate production on this huge, hilly Mediterranean island, but they vie with a Malvasia of Greek origin and natives like Nuragus and Vernaccia. The cooler northern part favours whites, especially Vermentino, while the southern and eastern parts are best suited to reds from Cannonau and Monica, with Carignano dominating in the south-east. The wines used to be powerful, alcoholic monsters, but the current trend is for a lighter, modern, more international style. Foremost among those in pursuit of quality are ARGIOLAS, SELLA & MOSCA and the Santadi co-op. See also Carignano del Sulcis.

SASSICAIA DOC★★★ *Tuscany, Italy* Legendary Cabernet Sauvignon-Cabernet Franc blend. Vines were planted in 1944 to satisfy the Marchese Incisa della Rocchetta's thirst for fine red Bordeaux, which was in short supply during the war. The wine remained purely for family consumption until nephew Piero ANTINORI and winemaker Giacomo Tachis persuaded the Marchese to refine production practices and to release several thousand bottles from the 1968 vintage. Since then, Sassicaia's fame has increased as it proved itself to be one of the world's great Cabernets, combining a blackcurrant power of blistering intensity with a heavenly scent of cigars. It is the first Italian single-owner estate wine to have its own DOC, within the BOLGHERI appellation, from the 1995 vintage. Best years: (2004) (03) (01) **99 98 97 95 90 88 85 84 83 82 81 78 75 71 68**.

HORST SAUER *Escherndorf, Franken, Germany* Horst Sauer shot to stardom in the late 1990s. His dry Rieslings★★ and Silvaners★ are unusually juicy and fresh for a region renowned for blunt, earthy wines. His late-harvest wines are unchallenged in the region and frequently ★★★; they will easily live a decade, sometimes much more. Best years: (dry Riesling, Silvaner) (2004) 03 02 **01 00 99 98**.

SAUMUR AC *Loire Valley, France* Dry white wines, mainly from Chenin Blanc, with up to 20% Chardonnay. The reds are lighter than those of SAUMUR-CHAMPIGNY. Also dry to off-dry Cabernet rosé, and sweet Coteaux de Saumur in good years. Best producers: Château-Gaillard★, Clos Rougeard★★, Collier★, Filliatreau★, Guiberteau★, HUREAU★★, Langlois-Château★, R-N Legrand★, la Paleine★, Roches Neuves★, St-Just★, VILLENEUVE★★, Yvonne★★. Best years: (whites) 2004 03 **02 01 00**.

247

SAUMUR-CHAMPIGNY AC *Loire Valley, France* Saumur's best red wine. Cabernet Franc is the main grape, and in hot years the wine can be superb, with a piercing scent of blackcurrants and raspberries easily overpowering the earthy finish. Delicious young, it can age for 6–10 years. Best producers: Clos Rougeard★★, de la Cune, Filliatreau★, HUREAU★★, Lavigne, R-N Legrand★, Nerleux★, la Perruche★, Retiveau-Rétif★, Roches Neuves★★, St-Vincent★, VILLENEUVE★★, Yvonne★. Best years: 2004 03 **02 01 00 97 96**.

SAUMUR MOUSSEUX AC *Loire Valley, France* Reasonable CHAMPAGNE-method sparkling wines made mainly from Chenin Blanc. Adding Chardonnay and Cabernet Franc makes Saumur Mousseux softer and more interesting. Usually non-vintage. Small quantities of rosé are also made. Best producers: BOUVET-LADUBAY★, GRATIEN & MEYER★, Grenelle★, la Paleine★, la Perruche★, St-Cyr-en-Bourg co-op★.

SAUTERNES AC *Bordeaux, France* The name Sauternes is synonymous with the best sweet wines in the world. Sauternes and BARSAC both lie on the banks of the little river Ciron and are 2 of the very few areas in France where noble rot occurs naturally. Production of these intense, sweet, luscious wines from botrytized grapes is a risk-laden and extremely expensive affair, and the wines are never going to be cheap. From good producers the wines are worth their high price – as well as 14% alcohol they have a richness full of flavours of pineapples, peaches, syrup and spice. Good vintages should be aged for 5–10 years and often last twice as long. Best producers: Bastor-Lamontagne★, Clos Haut-Peyraguey★★, Cru Barréjats★, DOISY-DAENE★★, DOISY-VEDRINES★★, FARGUES★★, GILETTE★★, GUIRAUD★★, Haut-Bergeron★, les Justices★, LAFAURIE-PEYRAGUEY★★, Lamothe-Guignard★, Malle★, Rabaud-Promis★, Raymond-Lafon★★, Rayne-Vigneau★, RIEUSSEC★★★, Sigalas Rabaud★★, SUDUIRAUT★★, la TOUR BLANCHE★★, YQUEM★★★. Best years: 2003 02 01 **99 98 97 96 95 90 89 88 86 83**.

SAUVIGNON BLANC See pages 250–1.

SAUZET *Côte de Beaune, Burgundy, France* A producer with a reputation for classic, rich, full-flavoured white Burgundies, made in an opulent, fat style, but recently showing more classical restraint. Sauzet owns prime sites in PULIGNY-MONTRACHET★ and CHASSAGNE-MONTRACHET★ (Premiers Crus usually ★★), as well as small parcels of BATARD-MONTRACHET★★★ and Bienvenues-BATARD-MONTRACHET★★★. Best years: (2004) **03** 02 **00 99 97**.

SAVENNIÈRES AC *Loire Valley, France* Wines from Chenin Blanc, produced on steep vineyards south of Anjou. Usually steely and dry, although there's a spirit of experimentation abroad and some softer wines are being produced using new oak. The top wines usually need at least 8 years to mature, and can age for longer. There are 2 extremely good vineyards with their own ACs: la Coulée-de-Serrant and la Roche-aux-Moines. Best producers: BAUMARD★★, Clos de Coulaine★, CLOS DE LA COULEE-DE-SERRANT★★, Clos de Varennes★, Closel★★, Épiré★★, Forges★★, aux Moines★, Monnaie★, Pierre-Bise★★, P Soulez/Chamboureau★, P-Y Tijou★★. Best years: 2004 03 02 01 **00 99 97 96 95 93 90 89 88 85 83**.

SAVIGNY-LÈS-BEAUNE AC *Côte de Beaune, Burgundy, France* Large village with reds dominating; usually dry and lean, they need 4–6 years to open out. The top Premiers Crus, such as Lavières, Peuillets and La Dominode, are more substantial. The white wines show a bit of dry, nutty class after 2–3 years. The wines are generally reasonably priced. Best producers: S Bize★, Camus-Bruchon★★, Champy★, CHANDON DE BRIAILLES★★, B CLAIR★★, M Écard★★, J J Girard★, P Girard★, V GIRARDIN★, L Jacob★★, Dom. LEROY★★, C Maréchal★, J-M Pavelot★★, TOLLOT-BEAUT★★. Best years: (reds) (2004) 03 02 **99 98 97 96 95**.

SAVOIE *France* Savoie's high Alpine vineyards produce fresh, snappy white wines with loads of flavour, when made from the Altesse (or Roussette) grape. Drink them young. There are some attractive light reds and rosés, too, mainly from a group of villages south of Chambéry and, in hot years, some positively Rhône-like reds from the Mondeuse grape. Most of the better wines use the Vin de Savoie AC and should be drunk young or with 3–4 years' age. The 15 best villages, including Abymes, Apremont, Arbin, Chignin, Cruet and Montmélian, can add their own name to the AC name. Between Lyon and Savoie are the vineyards of the Vin du Bugey VDQS, which produce light, easy-drinking reds and whites. Best producers: Boniface★, Bouvet★, Charlin, Dupasquier★, Jacquin★, Magnin★, C Marandon★, Monin, Neyroud, Perret★, A & M Quénard★, R Quénard★, Ripaille★, Rocailles★, C Trosset★; (Bugey) Charlin. See also Seyssel.

SAXENBURG *Stellenbosch WO, South Africa* In-demand red wines, led by dense, burly Private Collection Shiraz★★ and an even richer, bigger Shiraz Select★★, plus excellent Cabernet★★ and Merlot★. Private Collection Sauvignon Blanc★★ and Chardonnay★ head the white range. Winemaker Nico van der Merwe has relinquished the winemaking reins at Swiss businessman Adrian Bührer's LANGUEDOC estate, Ch. Capion, to concentrate on these wines. Drink whites young; reds will improve for 5–8 years. Best years: (premium reds) 2002 **01 00 99 98 97 96 95**.

WILLI SCHAEFER *Graach, Mosel, Germany* Classic MOSEL wines: Riesling Spätlese and Auslese from the GRAACHer Domprobst vineyard have a balance of piercing acidity and lavish fruit that is every bit as dramatic as Domprobst's precipitous slope. Made in tiny quantities and extremely long-lived, they're frequently ★★★, as is the sensational Beerenauslese Schaefer produced in good vintages. Even his QbA wines are ★. Best years: (Riesling Spätlese, Auslese) (2004) 03 02 01 00 99 **98 97 96 95 94 93 92 90**.

SCHARFFENBERGER CELLARS *Anderson Valley AVA, California, USA* In 2004, Louis ROEDERER bought sparkling wine producer Pacific Echo from LVMH, reverting to its original name, Scharffenberger Cellars. Non-vintage Brut★★, with lovely toasty depth, exuberant Rosé★★, and vintage Blanc de Blancs★★ are all excellent.

SCHEUREBE Very popular Silvaner x Riesling crossing found in Germany's RHEINHESSEN and PFALZ. In Austria it is sometimes labelled Sämling 88. At its best in Trockenbeerenauslese and Eiswein. When ripe, it has a marvellous flavour of honey, exotic fruits and the pinkest of pink grapefruit.

SCHIOPETTO *Friuli-Venezia Giulia, Italy* The late Mario Schiopetto was one of the legends of Italian wine, pioneering the development of scented varietals and high-quality, intensely concentrated white wines from COLLIO. Outstanding are Tocai★★, Pinot Bianco★★ and Sauvignon★★, which open out with age to display fascinating flavours. New COLLI ORIENTALI vineyards Poderi dei Blumeri can only add further prestige.

SAUVIGNON BLANC

Of all the world's grapes, the Sauvignon Blanc is leader of the 'love it or loathe it' pack. It veers from being wildly fashionable to totally out of favour depending upon where it is grown and which country's consumers are being consulted. But Sauvignon is always at its best when full rein is allowed to its very particular talents, because this grape does give intense, sometimes shocking flavours, and doesn't take kindly to being put into a straitjacket. One difficulty with the grape is that it must be picked perfectly ripe. Sometimes Loire Sauvignon Blanc is associated with a pungent 'catty' smell. This is a sure sign that the fruit was not fully ripe when picked. On the other hand, if the grapes are too ripe, they begin to lose the acidity that makes the wines so irresistibly snappy and refreshing.

WINE STYLES

Sancerre-style Sauvignon Although it had long been used as a blending grape in Bordeaux, where its characteristic green tang injected a bit of life into the blander, waxier Sémillon, Sauvignon first became trendy as the grape used for Sancerre, a bone-dry Loire white whose green gooseberry fruit and slightly smoky perfume inspired the winemakers of other countries to try to emulate, then often surpass, the original model.

But Sauvignon is only successful where it is respected. The grape is not as easy to grow as Chardonnay, and the flavours are not so adaptable. Yet the range of styles Sauvignon produces is as wide as, if less subtly nuanced than, those of Chardonnay. It is highly successful when picked not too ripe, fermented cool in stainless steel, and bottled early. This is the Sancerre model followed by growers elsewhere. New Zealand is now regarded as the top Sauvignon country, and many new producers in places like Australia, South Africa, southern France, Hungary and Chile are emulating this powerful mix of passionfruit, gooseberry and lime.

Using oak Sauvignon also lends itself to fermentation in barrel and aging in new oak, though less happily than does Chardonnay. This is the model of the Graves region of Bordeaux, although generally here Sémillon would be blended in with Sauvignon to good effect.

New Zealand again excels at this style, and there are good examples from California, Australia, northern Italy and South Africa. In Austria, producers in southern Styria (Steiermark) make powerful, aromatic versions, sometimes with a touch of oak. In all these regions, the acidity that is Sauvignon's great strength should remain, with a dried apricots fruit and a spicy, biscuity softness from the oak. These oaky styles are best drunk either within about a year, or after aging for 5 years or so, and can produce remarkable, strongly individual flavours that you'll either love or loathe.

Sweet wines Sauvignon is also a crucial ingredient in the great sweet wines of Sauternes and Barsac from Bordeaux, though it is less susceptible than its partner Sémillon to the sweetness-enhancing 'noble rot' fungus, botrytis.

Sweet wines from the USA, South Africa, Australia and, inevitably, New Zealand range from the interesting to the out-standing – but the characteristic green tang of the Sauvignon should stay in the wine even at ultra-sweet levels.

BEST PRODUCERS

France
Pouilly-Fumé J-C Chatelain, Didier DAGUENEAU, Ladoucette, Masson-Blondelet, de Tracy; *Sancerre* H Bourgeois, F Cotat, L Crochet, A MELLOT, Pinard, J-M Roger, VACHERON; *Pessac-Léognan* Dom. de CHEVALIER, Couhins-Lurton, FIEUZAL, HAUT-BRION, LAVILLE-HAUT-BRION, SMITH-HAUT-LAFITTE.

Other European Sauvignons
Austria Gross, Lackner-Tinnacher, POLZ, TEMENT.

Italy Colterenzio co-op, Peter Dipoli, GRAVNER, Edi Kante, LAGEDER,, SCHIOPETTO, Vie di Romans, Villa Russiz.

Spain (Rueda) Alvarez y Diez (Mantel Blanco), MARQUES DE RISCAL, Javier Sanz; (Penedès) TORRES (Fransola).

New Zealand
CLOUDY BAY, Drylands, Forrest Estate, HUNTER'S, ISABEL, JACKSON ESTATE, Lawson's Dry Hills, NEUDORF, PALLISER, SAINT CLAIR, VAVASOUR, VILLA MARIA, WITHER HILLS.

Australia
Alkoomi, Bridgewater Mill, Brookland Valley, HANGING ROCK, HOUGHTON (PEMBERTON), KATNOOK ESTATE, Ravenswood Lane, SHAW & SMITH, Stella Bella, Tamar Ridge, Geoff WEAVER.

USA
California Abreu, ARAUJO, FLORA SPRINGS (Soliloquy), KENWOOD, KUNDE, Mason, MATANZAS CREEK, MONDAVI (Reserve Fumé), Murphy-Goode, Navarro, Quivira, ROCHIOLI, SPOTTSWOODE, St. Supery, Voss.

Chile
CASA MARIN, Casas del Bosque, CONCHA Y TORO (Terrunyo), Viña Leyda, MONTES (Leyda), SANTA RITA (Floresta), Tabalí/SAN PEDRO.

South Africa
Cape Point Vineyards, Neil ELLIS, Flagstone, Havana Hills, MULDERBOSCH, SAXENBURG, SPRINGFIELD ESTATE, STEENBERG, THELEMA, VERGELEGEN.

SCHLOSS LIESER *Lieser, Mosel, Germany* Since Thomas Haag (son of Wilhelm, of the Fritz HAAG estate) took over the winemaking in 1992 (and then bought the property in 1997), this small estate has shot to the top. MOSEL Rieslings★★ marry richness with great elegance. Best years: (2004) 03 02 01 **99 98 97 96 95**.

SCHLOSS REINHARTSHAUSEN *Erbach, Rheingau, Germany* Estate formerly owned by the Hohenzollern family, rulers of Prussia. Top sites include the great ERBACHer Marcobrunn. Interesting organic Weissburgunder-Chardonnay blend from Erbacher Rheinhell, an island in the Rhine. Good Rieslings (Auslese, Beerenauslese, TBA ★★) and Sekt★. Best years: (2004) 03 02 01 **99 98 97 96 95** 94 90.

SCHLOSS SAARSTEIN *Serrig, Mosel-Saar-Ruwer, Germany* Fine Saar estate with somewhat austere Riesling trocken; Serriger Riesling Kabinett★, Spätlese★ and Auslese★★ are better balanced, keeping the startling acidity but coating it with fruit, often with the aromas of slightly unripe white peaches. Saarstein makes the occasional spectacular Eiswein★★★. Best years: (2004) 03 02 01 **99 97 95** 93 92 90.

SCHLOSS VOLLRADS *Oestrich-Winkel, Rheingau, Germany* Wines at this historic estate are now made by Rowald Hepp. Quality has improved greatly this century, with some brilliant Eiswein★★ and TBA★★. Best years: (2004) 03 02 01 **99**.

SCHLOSSBÖCKELHEIM *Nahe, Germany* This village's top sites are the Felsenberg and Kupfergrube, but good wines also come from Mühlberg and Königsfels. Best producers: Dr CRUSIUS★, DONNHOFF★★★, Gutsverwaltung Niederhausen-Schlossböckelheim★. Best years: (2004) 03 02 01 **00 99 98 96 95**.

DOM. SCHOFFIT *Alsace AC, Alsace, France* One of the two main owners of the outstanding Rangen Grand Cru vineyard, also making a range of deliciously fruity non-cru wines. Top-of-the-tree Clos St-Théobald wines from Rangen are often ★★★ and will improve for at least 5–6 years after release, Rieslings for even longer. The Cuvée Alexandre range is essentially declassified ALSACE VENDANGE TARDIVE. Best years: (Clos St-Théobald Riesling) 2004 03 02 01 00 **99 98 97** 96 95 94.

SCHRAMSBERG *Napa Valley AVA, California, USA* The first CALIFORNIA winery to make really excellent CHAMPAGNE-style sparklers from the classic grapes. Though all releases do not achieve the same heights, these wines can be among California's best, and as good as most Champagne. The Crémant★ is an attractive sweetish sparkler, the Blanc de Noirs★★ and the Blanc de Blancs★ are more classic. Bold, powerful J Schram★★ is rich and flavoursome and increasingly good. Top of the line is the Reserve Brut★★. Vintage-dated wines can be drunk with up to 10 years' age.

SCREAMING EAGLE *Oakville AVA, California, USA* Real estate agent Jean Phillips first produced a Cabernet Sauvignon from her OAKVILLE valley floor vineyard in 1992. Made in very limited quantities, the wine is one of California's most sought-after Cabernets each vintage. Made by Heidi Peterson Barrett, winemaker for Grace Family Vineyards and Paradigm, the Screaming Eagle Cabernet Sauvignon★★★ is a huge, brooding wine that displays all the lush fruit of Oakville.

SEGHESIO *Sonoma County, California, USA* Having grown grapes in SONOMA COUNTY for a century, the Seghesio family is today known for its own Zinfandel. All bottlings, from Sonoma County★★ to the single-vineyard San Lorenzo★★ and Cortina★★, display textbook black fruit and peppery spice. Sangiovese from 1910 vines, known as Chianti

Station★, is one of the best in the state. Also look for crisp Italian whites such as Pinot Grigio★ and Arneis★.

SEIFRIED *Nelson, South Island, New Zealand* Estate founded in 1974 by Austrian Hermann Seifried and his New Zealand wife Agnes. The best wines include Sauvignon Blanc★, Gewürztraminer★ and botrytized Riesling★★. The Redwood Valley label is sometimes used in export markets. Best years: (whites) **2004 03 02 01 00 99**.

SELBACH-OSTER *Zeltingen, Mosel, Germany* Johannes Selbach is one of the MOSEL's new generation of star winemakers, producing very pure, elegant Riesling★★ from the Zeltinger Sonnenuhr site. Also fine wine from WEHLEN, GRAACH and BERNKASTEL. Best years: (2004) 03 02 01 00 **99 98 97 96 95 94 93 92 90**.

SELLA & MOSCA *Sardinia, Italy* Apart from the rich, port-like Anghelu Ruju★ made from semi-dried Cannonau grapes, this much-modernized old firm produces excellent dry whites, Terre Bianche★ (Torbato) and La Cala★ (Vermentino), and oak-aged reds, Marchese di Villamarina★★ (Cabernet) and Tanca Farrà★★ (Cannonau-Cabernet). Best years: (Marchese di Villamarina) (2004) 01 00 **97 95 93 92 90**.

SELVAPIANA *Chianti DOCG, Tuscany, Italy* This estate has always produced excellent CHIANTI RUFINA typical of the zone. But since 1990 it has vaulted into the top rank of Tuscan estates, particularly with the single-vineyard crus, Vigneto Bucerchiale★★★ and Fornace★★. VIN SANTO★★ is very good. Best years: (Bucerchiale) (2004) (03) 01 **99 98 95 93 91 90 88 85**.

SÉMILLON Found mainly in South-West France, especially in the sweet wines of SAUTERNES and BARSAC, because it is prone to noble rot (*Botrytis cinerea*). Also blended for its waxy texture with Sauvignon Blanc to make dry wine – almost all the great GRAVES Classed Growths are based on this blend. Performs well in Australia (aged Semillon from the HUNTER, BAROSSA and CLARE VALLEY can be wonderful) on its own or as a blender with Chardonnay (the accent over the é is dropped on New World labels). Sémillon is also blended with Sauvignon in Australia, New Zealand, California and WASHINGTON STATE. In warmer areas of South Africa it is used as a bulk blender; in cooler regions varietal wines are producing some outstanding results, often barrel-fermented, and, increasingly, in flagship blends with Sauvignon.

SEÑA★ *Valle del Aconcagua, Aconcagua, Chile* Owned by the Chadwick family (ERRAZURIZ), formerly in partnership with MONDAVI from CALIFORNIA, Seña is a Cabernet-based blend that has had its ups and downs. The 2002 vintage, however, seems to put things on the right track. Cellar for 5–10 years. Best years: (2002) 01 00 **99 97 96**.

SEPPELT *Barossa Valley, South Australia and Grampians, Victoria* Now part of Southcorp, Seppelt has headquarters in the BAROSSA – long the scene of its fortified wine production – and at Great Western in VICTORIA, where sparkling winemaking has a century-old tradition. Today's flagship wines are the St Peters Shiraz★★ (from vineyards at Great Western), the definitive Show Sparkling Shiraz★★★, the Original Sparkling Shiraz★ and the legendary 100-year-old Para Liqueur Tawny★★★. The DP range of fortifieds★★ have been rebadged once again, but are still top-notch. Sparkling whites range from the crowd-pleasing Great Western to the pristine, subtly yeasty Salinger★★, which remains among the top flight of Australian bubbly. Drumborg table wines from the super-cool Henty region stand out.

SERESIN *Marlborough, South Island, New Zealand* Film producer Michael
Seresin's winery has made a big impact on the MARLBOROUGH scene
with his range of stylish organic wines. Intense Sauvignon Blanc★ is
best within a year or two of the vintage, but creamy Chardonnay★★,
succulent Pinot Gris★ and rich, oaky Pinot Noir★ will age for up to 3
years. Best years: (Sauvignon Blanc) **2005 03 01 00**.

SETÚBAL DOC *Terras do Sado, Portugal* Fortified wine from the Setúbal
Peninsula south of Lisbon, which is called 'Moscatel de Setúbal' when
made from at least 85% Moscatel, and 'Setúbal' when it's not. Best
producers: José Maria da FONSECA★★, J P VINHOS★.

SEYSSEL AC *Savoie, France* Known for its feather-light, sparkling
wine, Seyssel Mousseux. With the lovely sharp, peppery bite of the
Molette and Altesse grapes smoothed out with a creamy yeast, it is an
ideal summer gulper. The still white is light and floral, and made only
from Altesse. Best producers: Mollex★, Varichon & Clerc.

SEYVAL BLANC Hybrid grape (Seibel 5656 x Rayon d'Or) whose disease
resistance and ability to continue ripening in a damp autumn make it
a useful variety in England, Canada and NEW YORK STATE and other
areas in the eastern US. Gives clean, sappy, grapefruit-edged wines
that are sometimes a very passable imitation of bone-dry CHABLIS.

SHAFER *Stags Leap District AVA, California, USA* One of the best NAPA
wineries, making unusually fruity Cabernet★★ and a Reserve-style
Hillside Select★★★. Merlot★★ and Firebreak★★ (Sangiovese-Cabernet)
are also exciting. Chardonnay★★★, from Red Shoulder Ranch, is
classic CARNEROS style. Beginning with the 1999 vintage, estate-grown
Relentless (Syrah) has been added to the line-up. Best years: (Cabernet
Hillside Select) (2002) (01) 00 99 **98 97 96 95 94 93 91 90 84**.

SHAW & SMITH *Adelaide Hills, South Australia*
Cousins Michael Hill Smith – Australia's
first MW – and winemaker Martin Shaw
had a runaway success with their tangy
Sauvignon Blanc★★ from the first vintage
in 1989. The range now includes

SHAW SMITH
2003
Sauvignon Blanc

Unwooded Chardonnay★, single-vineyard M3 Chardonnay★ (formerly
Reserve★) and Shiraz★. Best years: (M3 Chardonnay) (2004) **03 02 01 00**.

SHERRY See Jerez y Manzanilla DO, pages 158–9.

SHIRAZ See Syrah, pages 266–7.

SICILY *Italy* Sicily is emerging with a renewed spirit and attitude to wine
production. Those who lead the way, such as PLANETA, Duca di SALAPARUTA
and TASCA D'ALMERITA, have been joined by others, including Donnafugata,
the revitalized Spadafora and transformed Settesoli (headed by Diego
Planeta; Inycon★ is its excellent budget label). Other exciting estates
include Abbazia Santa Anastasia, especially noted for its Cabernet
Sauvignon-Nero d'Avola blend, Litra★★; Cottanera, for excellent varietal
Merlot (Grammonte★★), Mondeuse (L'Ardenza★★) and Syrah (Sole di
Sesta★★); Cusumano, for 100% Nero d'Avola (Sàgana★) and a Nero
d'Avola-Cabernet-Merlot blend (Noà★); Morgante, for another pure Nero
d'Avola (Don Antonio★★); Palari, for its Nerello Mascalese-Cappuccio
blend (Faro Palari★★); and Ceuso, for a Nero d'Avola-Merlot-Cabernet
blend (Ceuso Custera★). Firriato, aided by Kym Milne, also makes excellent
reds★ and whites★. See also Marsala, Moscato Passito di Pantelleria.

SIEUR D'ARQUES, LES VIGNERONS DU *Limoux AC and Blanquette de Limoux AC, Languedoc, France*   This modern co-op makes around 80% of the still and sparkling wines of LIMOUX. The BLANQUETTE DE LIMOUX★ and CREMANT DE LIMOUX★ are both reliable, but the real excitement comes with the Toques et Clochers Chardonnays★ (occasionally ★★). The co-op also makes a range of white and red varietal vins de pays and has a joint venture with Philippine de Rothschild (MOUTON CADET), Baron'arques, and with GALLO in California (Red Bicyclette).

SILENI *Hawkes Bay, North Island, New Zealand*   Established by millionaire Graeme Avery, with a view to making nothing but the best, this modern winery brings a touch of the NAPA VALLEY to HAWKES BAY. A sleek and stylish Chardonnay★ and ripe, mouthfilling Semillon★ both impress. Best so far is the EV Merlot-Cabernet Franc★★, a dense yet elegant red with a classy oak influence.

SILVER OAK CELLARS *Napa Valley, California, USA*   Only Cabernet Sauvignon is made here, with bottlings from ALEXANDER VALLEY★★ and NAPA VALLEY★★ grapes. Forward, generous, fruity wines, impossible not to enjoy young, yet with great staying power. Best years: (Napa Valley) (2002) (01) 00 **99 97 96 95 94 93 92 91 90 88 85 84.**

SILVERADO VINEYARDS *Stags Leap District AVA, California, USA*   The regular Cabernet Sauvignon★ has intense fruit and is drinkable fairly young; Limited Reserve★★ has more depth and is capable of some aging; a new STAGS LEAP DISTRICT Cabernet Sauvignon★★ displays the cherry fruit and supple tannins of this AVA. The Chardonnay★ has soft, inviting fruit and a silky finish. Also a fruity Merlot★ and a refreshing Sauvignon Blanc★. Best years: (Reserve Cabernet) (2002) 01 **99 95 94 91 90.**

SIMI *Alexander Valley AVA, California, USA*   Historic winery purchased by Constellation in 1999. Currently the ALEXANDER VALLEY Cabernet Sauvignon★, Chardonnay★ and Sauvignon Blanc★ attain fair standards; Chardonnay Reserve often reaches ★★. Best years: (reds) 2001 99 97 **95 94 91 90.**

SIMONSIG *Stellenbosch WO, South Africa*   The Malan family are recognized for experimenting with new varieties. Winemaker Johan Malan also confidently handles all the classics. His forte is reds: most notable are regular Shiraz and lavishly oaked Merindol Syrah; a delicious unwooded Pinotage and plusher Redhill Pinotage★; the svelte BORDEAUX-blend Tiara★; and bright-fruited Frans Malan Reserve★, a Cape blend of Pinotage, Cabernet Sauvignon and Merlot. Whites are sound if less exciting. Cap Classique sparklers, Kaapse Vonkel and Cuvée Royale, are biscuity and creamy.

CH. SIRAN★ *Margaux AC, Cru Bourgeois, Haut-Médoc, Bordeaux, France*   Owned by the same family since 1848, this estate produces consistently good claret – increasingly characterful, approachable young, but with enough structure to last for as long as 20 years. Second wine: Ch. Bellegarde. Best years: 2003 01 00 98 **96 95 90 89 86 85 83 82.**

SKALLI-FORTANT DE FRANCE *Languedoc-Roussillon, France*   Now one of the most important producers in the south of France, Robert Skalli was an early pioneer of varietal wines in the MIDI. Modern winemaking and the planting of international grape varieties were the keys to success. The Fortant de France brand includes a range of single-variety Vins de Pays d'OC. Grenache and Chardonnay are among the best, along with Reserve F Merlot and Cabernet Sauvignon.

CH. SMITH-HAUT-LAFITTE *Pessac-Léognan AC, Cru Classé de Graves,*
Bordeaux, France Large property best known for its reds★★, now
one of the most improved and innovative estates in PESSAC-LEOGNAN
since a change of ownership in 1990. There is only a little white★★★
(from 100% Sauvignon Blanc) but it is a shining example of tip-top
modern white Bordeaux. Best years: (reds) 2003 02 01 00 **99** 98 **96 95
94 90** 89; (whites) (2004) 03 02 **01 00 99 98** 96 95 94 93 92.

SMITH WOODHOUSE *Port DOC, Portugal* Underrated but consistently
satisfying PORT from this shipper in the Symington group. The
Vintage★★ is always worth looking out for, as is single-quinta
Madalena (made since 1995), and its Late Bottled Vintage Port★★ is
the rich and characterful, figgy, unfiltered type. Best years: (Vintage)
2000 97 94 92 **91 85 83 80 77 70 63**; (Madalena) 2001 99 98 **95**.

SOAVE DOC *Veneto, Italy* In the hilly Soave Classico zone near Verona,
the Garganega and Trebbiano di Soave grapes can produce ripe,
nutty, scented wines. Since 1992, the blend may include 30%
Chardonnay, and good examples are definitely on the increase. Soave
Superiore is now DOCG, but most of the private producers ignore it in
protest at the anomalous rules governing the denomination. Best
producers: Bertani★, Ca' Rugate★, La Cappuccina★, Coffele★★,
Gini★★, Inama★, MASI★, Pasqua/Cecilia Beretta★, PIEROPAN★★,
Portinari★, Prà★★, Suavia★★, Tamellini★. See also Anselmi, Recioto di
Soave DOCG.

CH. SOCIANDO-MALLET★★ *Haut-Médoc AC, Cru Bourgeois, Haut-*
Médoc, Bordeaux, France Owner Jean Gautreau has made this one
of BORDEAUX's star Crus Bourgeois. The wine shows every sign of
great red Bordeaux flavours to come if you can hang on for 10–15
years. Best years: 2003 02 01 00 **99** 98 **97** 96 **95 94 93 90 89 88 86 85
83 82**.

SOGRAPE *Portugal* Portuguese giant Sogrape can be credited with
revolutionizing quality in some of Portugal's most reactionary wine
regions. Mateus Rosé is still the company's golden egg, but Sogrape
makes good to very good wines, including VINHO VERDE, DOURO
(Reserva Tinto★), DAO and ALENTEJO (Vinha do Monte and Herdade
do Peso★★). A high-tech winery in DAO produces improved Duque
de Viseu★ and Grão Vasco reds and whites, as well as premium
wines under the Quinta dos Carvalhais label: varietal Encruzado★
(white) and reds Tinta Roriz★ and Touriga Nacional are promising
but inconsistent. A (red) Reserva★★ is a further step up.
Subsidiaries FERREIRA, SANDEMAN and Offley provide top-flight PORTS.
Also owns Finca Flichman in Argentina.

SOLAIA★★★ *Tuscany, Italy* One of ANTINORI'S SUPER-TUSCANS, sourced,
like TIGNANELLO, from the Santa Cristina vineyard. Solaia is a blend of
Cabernet Sauvignon, Sangiovese and Cabernet Franc. Intense, with
rich fruit and a classic structure, it is not produced in every vintage.
Best years: (2004) (03) 01 99 **98 97 95 94 93 91 90 88 86 85**.

SOMONTANO DO *Aragón, Spain* Up-and-coming region in the foothills
of the Pyrenees. Reds and rosés from the local grapes (Moristel and
Tempranillo) can be light, fresh and flavourful, and international
varieties such as Chardonnay and Gewürztraminer are already
yielding promising wines. An interesting development is the
rediscovery of the powerful native red grape, Parraleta. Best
producers: Blecua★★, ENATE★★, Lalanne★, Bodega Pirineos★, VINAS DEL
VERO★. Best years: (reds) 2001 **99 98 97 96 95 94**.

SONOMA COAST AVA *California, USA* A huge appellation, defined on its western boundary by the Pacific Ocean, that attempts to bring together the coolest regions of SONOMA COUNTY. It encompasses the Sonoma part of CARNEROS and overlaps parts of SONOMA VALLEY and RUSSIAN RIVER. The heart of the appellation are vineyards on the high coastal ridge only a few miles from the Pacific. Intense Chardonnays and Pinot Noirs are the focus. **Best producers:** FLOWERS (Camp Meeting Ridge★★★), HARTFORD FAMILY★★, KISTLER (Hirsch Pinot Noir★★★), Littorai (Hirsch Pinot Noir★★★), MARCASSIN★★, W H Smith★★, Wild Hog★.

SONOMA COUNTY *California, USA* Sonoma's vine-growing area is big and sprawling (some 60,000 acres), with dozens of soil types and mesoclimates, from the fairly warm SONOMA VALLEY and ALEXANDER VALLEY regions to the cool Green Valley and lower RUSSIAN RIVER VALLEY. The best wines are from Chardonnay, Sauvignon Blanc, Cabernet Sauvignon, Pinot Noir and Zinfandel. Often the equal of rival NAPA in quality and originality of flavours. See also Carneros, Dry Creek Valley, Sonoma Coast.

SONOMA-CUTRER *Russian River Valley AVA, Sonoma County, California, USA* Rich, oaky, but often overrated Chardonnays. Single-vineyard Les Pierres is the most complex and richest, often worth ★★; Cutrer can also have a ★★ complexity worth waiting for. Russian River Ranches★ can be rather ordinary, though is much improved in recent releases. Founder's Reserve★★, bottled in large formats, is made only in exceptional vintages. **Best years:** (2002) 01 00 99 **98 97 95**.

SONOMA VALLEY AVA *California, USA* The oldest wine region north of San Francisco, Sonoma Valley is situated on the western side of the Mayacamas Mountains, which separate it from NAPA VALLEY. Best varieties are Chardonnay and Zinfandel, with Cabernet and Merlot from hillside sites also good. **Best producers:** ARROWOOD★★, CHATEAU ST JEAN★, B R Cohn, Fisher★, GUNDLACH-BUNDSCHU★★, KENWOOD★, KUNDE★★, LANDMARK★★, LAUREL GLEN★★, MATANZAS CREEK★★, MOON MOUNTAIN★★, RAVENSWOOD★★, St Francis★, Sebastiani★. **Best years:** (Zinfandel) (2001) 00 99 98 97 96 95 94.

SOUTH AUSTRALIA Australia's biggest grape-growing state, with some 70,000ha (173,000 acres) of vineyards and almost half the country's total production. Covers many climates and most wine styles, from bulk wines to the very best. Established areas are ADELAIDE HILLS, Adelaide Plains, CLARE, BAROSSA and Eden Valleys, MCLAREN VALE, Langhorne Creek, COONAWARRA, PADTHAWAY and RIVERLAND. Newer districts creating excitement include Mount Benson and Wrattonbully, both in the LIMESTONE COAST zone.

SOUTH-WEST FRANCE As well as the world-famous wines of BORDEAUX, South-West France has many lesser-known, less expensive ACs, VDQS and Vins de Pays, over 10 *départements* from the Atlantic coast to LANGUEDOC-ROUSSILLON. Bordeaux grapes (Cabernet Sauvignon, Merlot and Cabernet Franc for reds; Sauvignon Blanc, Sémillon and Muscadelle for whites) are common, but there are lots of interesting local varieties as well, such as Tannat (in MADIRAN), Petit Manseng (in JURANÇON) and Mauzac (in GAILLAC). See also Bergerac, Buzet, Cahors, Côtes de Duras, Côtes du Frontonnais, Irouléguy, Monbazillac, Montravel, Pacherenc du Vic-Bilh.

SPÄTBURGUNDER See Pinot Noir.

SPARKLING WINES OF THE WORLD ▬▬

Made by the Traditional (Champagne) Method

Although Champagne is still the benchmark for top-class sparkling wines all over the world, the Champagne houses themselves have taken the message to California, Australia and New Zealand via wineries they've established in these regions. However, Champagne-method fizz doesn't necessarily have to feature the traditional Champagne grape varieties (Chardonnay, Pinot Noir and Pinot Meunier), and this allows a host of other places to join the party. Describing a wine as Champagne method is strictly speaking no longer allowed (only original Champagne from France is officially sanctioned to do this), but the use of a phrase like Traditional Method should not distract from the fact that these wines are still painstakingly produced using the complex system of secondary fermentation in the bottle itself.

STYLES OF SPARKLING WINE

France French fizz ranges from the sublime to the near-ridiculous. The best examples have great finesse and include appley Crémant d'Alsace, produced from Pinot Blanc and Riesling; often inexpensive yet eminently drinkable Crémant de Bourgogne, based mainly on Chardonnay; and some stylish examples from the Loire, notably in Saumur and Vouvray. Clairette de Die and Cremant de Limoux in the south confuse the issue by sometimes following their own idiosyncratic method of production, but the result is delicious.

Rest of Europe Franciacorta DOCG is a success story for Italy. Most metodo classico sparkling wine is confined to the north, where ripening conditions are closer to those of Champagne, but a few good examples do pop up in unexpected places – Sicily, for instance. Asti and Lambrusco are not Champagne-method wines. In Spain, the Cava wines of Cataluña offer an affordable style for everyday drinking. German Sekt comes in two basic styles: one made from Riesling grapes, the other using Champagne varieties. England is proving naturally suited to growing grapes for sparkling wine.

Australia and New Zealand Australia has a wide range of styles, though there is still little overt varietal definition. Blends are still being produced using fruit from many areas, but regional characters are starting to emerge. Cool Tasmania is the star performer, making some top fizz from local grapes. Red sparklers, notably those made from Shiraz, are an irresistible Australian curiosity with an alcoholic kick. Cool-climate New Zealand is coming up fast for fizz with some premium and pricy examples; as in Australia, some have Champagne connections.

USA In California, some magnificent examples are produced – the best ones using grapes from Carneros or the Anderson Valley. Quality has been transformed by the efforts of French Champagne houses. Oregon is also a contender in the sparkling stakes.

South Africa Cap Classique is the local name for the Champagne method. The best are very good and those from the limy soils of Robertson are starting to show particularly well, but generally there are problems with consistency.

See also individual producers.

BEST PRODUCERS

Australia BROWN BROTHERS, Cope-Williams, DOMAINE CHANDON (Green Point), Freycinet (Radenti), HANGING ROCK, HARDY, Stefano LUBIANA, Charles MELTON, PETALUMA (Croser), PIPERS BROOK (Kreglinger), ROCKFORD (Black Shiraz), SEPPELT, Taltarni (Clover Hill), Tamar Ridge, YALUMBA (Jansz), Yarrabank, Yellowglen.

Austria BRUNDLMAYER, Schlumberger.

France (Alsace) Ostertag; (Burgundy) Bailly co-op, Lugny co-op; (Die) J-C Raspail; (Limoux) SIEUR D'ARQUES; (St-Péray) Darona, B Gripa, J-L Thiers; (Saumur) BOUVET-LADUBAY, GRATIEN & MEYER; (Vouvray) CLOS NAUDIN, HUET.

Germany (Franken) Schloss Sommerhausen; (Pfalz) Bergdolt, REBHOLZ; (Rheingau) BREUER.

Italy (Franciacorta) BELLAVISTA, CA' DEL BOSCO; (Trento) FERRARI; (Sicily) TASCA D'ALMERITA.

New Zealand CELLIER LE BRUN, CLOUDY BAY (Pelorus), HUNTER'S, MONTANA (Deutz), MORTON ESTATE, Nautilus, PALLISER.

Portugal Caves ALIANCA, J P VINHOS.

South Africa Graham BECK, DISTELL (Pongrácz), Twee Jonge Gezellen, VILLIERA.

Spain (Cava) Can Ràfols dels Caus, CODORNIU, FREIXENET, JUVE Y CAMPS, Agustí Torelló.

UK CHAPEL DOWN, NYETIMBER, RIDGEVIEW, VALLEY VINEYARDS.

USA (California) S Anderson (by Cliff Lede Vineyards), DOMAINE CARNEROS, DOMAINE CHANDON, Gloria Ferrer, HANDLEY, IRON HORSE, J Wine, Laetitia, MUMM NAPA, ROEDERER ESTATE, SCHARFFENBERGER CELLARS, SCHRAMSBERG; (Oregon) ARGYLE.

259

SPICE ROUTE WINE COMPANY *Swartland WO, South Africa*   Owned by
Charles Back of FAIRVIEW. Big yet classically styled Flagship Pinotage★★
and Syrah★★, and a Merlot that is not quite as successful. Malabar★,
a polished blend of Shiraz, Merlot and Grenache, reflects its
Malmesbury *terroir*. Best years: (Flagship reds) **2002 01 00 99 98**.

SPOTTSWOODE *Napa Valley AVA, California, USA*   Replanted in the mid-
1990s, this beautifully situated 16ha (40-acre) vineyard west of St
Helena has not missed a beat since the winery opened in 1982. Deep,
blackberry- and cherry-fruited Cabernet Sauvignon★★★ is wonderful
to drink early, but is best at 5–10 years. Sauvignon Blanc★★ (blended
with a little Semillon and barrel fermented) is a sophisticated treat.
Best years: (Cabernet) (2002) 01 **00 99 98 97 96 95 94 91**.

SPRINGFIELD ESTATE *Robertson WO, South Africa*   Abrie Bruwer's
approach is strictly hands-off in his efforts to capture his vineyard's
terroir. Méthode Ancienne Chardonnay★★ is barrel fermented with
vineyard yeasts and bottled without any fining or filtration. Not every
vintage makes it! Cabernet Sauvignon is also made as Méthode
Ancienne★. The unwooded Wild Yeast Chardonnay★ and flinty, lively
Life from Stone Sauvignon Blanc★★ are also notably expressive. The
Cabernet Franc-Merlot-based Work of Time★ is the farm's first blend.

STAGS LEAP DISTRICT AVA *Napa County, California, USA*   Created in
1989, this is one of California's best-defined appellations. Located in
south-eastern NAPA VALLEY, it is cooler than OAKVILLE or RUTHERFORD to
the north, so the red wines here are more elegant in nature. A little
Sauvignon Blanc and Chardonnay are grown, but the true stars are
Cabernet Sauvignon and Merlot. Best producers: CHIMNEY ROCK★★,
CLOS DU VAL★★, HARTWELL★★, PINE RIDGE★★, SHAFER★★★, SILVERADO★★,
Robert Sinskey★★, STAG'S LEAP WINE CELLARS★★, Stags' Leap Winery★★.

STAG'S LEAP WINE CELLARS *Stags Leap District AVA, California, USA*
The winery rose to fame when its Cabernet Sauvignon came first at
the famous Paris tasting of 1976. Cabernet Sauvignon★★ can be
stunning, particularly the SLV★★★ from estate vineyards and the
Fay★★; the Cask 23 Cabernet Sauvignon★★ can be very good, but is
overhyped. After a dip in quality, late 1990s vintages were back on
form. A lot of work has gone into the Chardonnay★ and the style is
one of NAPA'S more successful. Sauvignon Blanc★ (Rancho
Chimiles★★) is intensely flavoured, with brisk acidity. Best years:
(Cabernet) (2003) (02) 01 00 99 98 **97 96 95 94 91 90 86**.

STEELE *Lake County, California, USA*   Owner/winemaker Jed Steele is a
master blender. He sources grapes from all over California and shapes
them into exciting wines, usually featuring vivid fruit with supple
mouthfeel. He also offers single-vineyard wines and has, in current
release, 4–6 Chardonnays, most ★★. His Zinfandels★★ and Pinot
Noirs★★ (CARNEROS, SANTA MARIA VALLEY) are often very good. Shooting
Star label provides remarkable value in a ready-to-drink style.

STEENBERG *Constantia WO, South Africa*   The oldest farm in the
CONSTANTIA valley is seeing great results from total vineyard replanting
in the early 1990s. Sauvignon Blanc Reserve★★, firmly established as
one of South Africa's best, is smoky and flinty with underlying fruit
richness; straight Sauvignon★★ is pure upfront fruit. Barrel-fermented
Semillon★★ matches them in quality. An irresistible, minty Merlot★★
has been joined by Catharina★, a blend featuring the Bordeaux
varieties with Shiraz and a dab of Nebbiolo, and exciting, smoky
Shiraz★★. Best years: (whites) **2004 03 02 01 00 99 98**.

STEIERMARK *Austria* This 3990ha (9815-acre) region (Styria in English) in south-east Austria is divided into 3 areas: Süd-Oststeiermark, Südsteiermark and Weststeiermark. It is the warmest of the Austrian wine regions, but the best vineyards are in cool, high-altitude sites. The tastiest wines are Morillon (unoaked Chardonnay, though oak is catching on), Sauvignon Blanc and Gelber Muskateller (Muscat). Best producers: Gross★, Lackner-Tinnacher★, POLZ★★, E Sabathi, Sattlerhof★, TEMENT★★, Winkler-Hermaden★.

STELLENBOSCH WO *South Africa* This district boasts the greatest concentration of wineries in the Cape, though is only third in vineyard area; the vineyards straddle valley floors and stretch up the many mountain slopes. Climates and soils are as diverse as wine styles; smaller units of origin – wards – are now being demarcated to more accurately reflect this diversity. The renowned reds are matched by some excellent Sauvignon Blanc and Chardonnay, as well as modern Chenin Blanc and Semillon. Best producers: BEYERSKLOOF★, Cordoba★, Delaire★, De Toren★, DE TRAFFORD★★, DeWaal★, Dornier★, EIKENDAL★, Neil ELLIS★★, ERNIE ELS★, Ken Forrester★, GRANGEHURST★★, HARTENBERG★, JORDAN★, KANONKOP★★, L'AVENIR★, Le Bonheur★, Le Riche★, MEERLUST★★, Meinert★, MORGENHOF★, Morgenster★, MULDERBOSCH★★, Neethlingshof★, Overgaauw★, RUST EN VREDE★, RUSTENBERG★★, SAXENBURG★★, SIMONSIG★, Stellenbosch Vineyards, STELLENZICHT★, THELEMA★★, VERGELEGEN★★, VILLIERA★, WARWICK★, Waterford★.

STELLENZICHT *Stellenbosch WO, South Africa* Winemaker Guy Webber aims for fruit and perfume rather than power in his wines. This is evident in his silky, lemony Semillon★, smoky, spicy Syrah★★ and, from the Golden Triangle range, intense, gooseberryish Sauvignon Blanc★ and bold, perfumed Pinotage★. Best years: (Syrah) **2002 01 00 99 98 97 95**.

STERLING VINEYARDS *Napa Valley AVA, California, USA* Merlot is the focus here, led by Three Palms★★ and Reserve★★, both impressively packed with ripe, dense fruit. Reserve Cabernet is now ★★, and the regular bottling is improving, as is Winery Lake Pinot Noir★. The Winery Lake Chardonnay★ delivers honey and apple fruit in an elegant package. Best years: (Three Palms) (2002) (01) 00 99 97 **96 94**.

STONIER *Mornington Peninsula, Victoria, Australia* The peninsula's biggest winery and one of its best, though Lion Nathan, via PETALUMA, now has a controlling interest. Reserve Chardonnay★★ and Reserve Pinot★★ are usually outstanding, and there are fine standard bottlings in warm vintages.

STONYRIDGE *Waiheke Island, Auckland, North Island, New Zealand* The leading winery on WAIHEKE ISLAND, Stonyridge specializes in reds made from Cabernet Sauvignon, Merlot, Petit Verdot, Malbec and Cabernet Franc. The top label, Larose★★★, is a remarkably BORDEAUX-like red of real intensity; it is one of New Zealand's most expensive wines. Best years: (Larose) (2004) **02 00 99 98 96 94**.

CH. SUDUIRAUT★★ *Sauternes AC, 1er Cru Classé, Bordeaux, France* Together with RIEUSSEC, Suduiraut is regarded as a close runner-up to d'YQUEM. Although the wines are delicious at only a few years old, the richness and excitement increase enormously after a decade or so. Seemed to be under-performing in the 1980s and mid-90s but now owned by AXA (see PICHON-LONGUEVILLE) and back on song. Best years: 2003 02 01 **99 98 97 96 95 90 89 88 86 82 81**.

SUPER-TUSCANS

Tuscany, Italy

The term 'Super-Tuscans', first used by English and American writers, has now been adopted by Italians themselves to describe the new-style red wines of Tuscany. The 1970s and 80s were a time when enormous strides were being made in Bordeaux, Australia and California, yet these changes threatened to bypass Italy completely because of its restrictive wine laws. A group of winemakers, led by Piero Antinori – who created the inspirational Tignanello and Solaia from vineyards within the Chianti Classico DOCG – abandoned tradition to put their best efforts and best grapes into creative wines styled for modern tastes.

Old large oak casks were replaced with French barriques, while Cabernet Sauvignon and other trendy varieties, such as Cabernet Franc, Merlot and Syrah, were planted alongside Sangiovese in vineyards that emerged with sudden grandeur as crus. Since the DOC specifically forbade such innovations, producers were forced to label their wines as plain Vino da Tavola. The 'Super-Tuscan' Vino da Tavolas, as they were quickly dubbed, were a phenomenal success: brilliant in flavour with an approachable, upfront style. Some found it hard to believe that table wines with no official credentials could outrank DOCG Chianti. A single mouthful was usually enough to convince them.

WINE STYLES
Sangiovese, the Cabernets and Merlot are the basis for most Super-Tuscans, usually in a blend. All also appear varietally, with Sangiovese forming the largest group of top-quality varietal Super-Tuscans. To some Sangiovese-based wines, a small percentage of other native varieties such as Colorino, Canaiolo or Malvasia Nera is added. Merlot for long played second fiddle to Cabernet Sauvignon but new plantings today are tending Merlot's way. Syrah is of growing importance, mostly varietally, but also in innovative new blends such as Argiano's Solengo. Super-Tuscan wines also show considerable differences in vinification and aging. Top wines are invariably based on ripe, concentrated grapes from a site with special attributes.

CLASSIFICATIONS
A law passed in 1992 has finally brought the Super-Tuscans into line with official classifications. Sassicaia now has its own DOC under Bolgheri. Chianti Classico's now independent DOCG could cover many a Sangiovese-based Super-Tuscan, but the majority are currently sold under the region-wide IGT Toscana alongside wines made from international varieties. There are also 3 sub-regional IGTs, but only a few producers use these.

See also BOLGHERI, CHIANTI CLASSICO, SASSICAIA, SOLAIA, SYRAH, TIGNANELLO; and individual producers.

(2004) (03) 01 **00 99 98 97 95 93 90 88 85**

BEST PRODUCERS

Sangiovese and other Tuscan varieties Badia a Coltibuono (Sangioveto), BOSCARELLI, CASTELLARE (I Sodi di San Niccolò), FELSINA (Fontalloro), FONTODI (Flaccianello della Pieve), ISOLE E OLENA (Cepparello), Lilliano (Anagallis), MONTEVERTINE (Le Pergole Torte, Il Sodaccio), Paneretta (Quattrocentenario, Terrine), Poggio Scalette (Il Carbonaione), Poggiopiano (Rosso di Sera), Querceto (La Corte), RIECINE (La Gioia), San Giusto a Rentennano (Percarlo), VOLPAIA (Coltassala).

Sangiovese-Cabernet and Sangiovese-Merlot blends Argiano (Solengo), BANFI (Summus), Colombaio di Cencio (Il Futuro), FONTERUTOLI (Siepi), Gagliole, Montepeloso (Nardo), QUERCIABELLA (Camartina), RICASOLI (Casalferro), Sette Ponti (Oreno), TIGNANELLO.

Cabernet Col d'Orcia (Olmaia), Fossi (Sassoforte), ISOLE E OLENA (Collezione), Le MACCHIOLE (Paléo Rosso), Nozzole (Il Pareto), RAMPOLLA (Sammarco, Vigna d'Alceo), SOLAIA.

Merlot AMA (L'Apparita), Le MACCHIOLE (Messorio), ORNELLAIA (Masseto), Petrolo (Galatrona), TUA RITA (Redigaffi).

Cabernet-Merlot blends ANTINORI (Guado al Tasso), BANFI (Excelsus), Capezzana (Ghiaie della Furba), ORNELLAIA (Ornellaia), Poggio al Sole (Seraselva), POLIZIANO (Le Stanze), Le Pupille (Saffredi), Trinoro, TUA RITA (Giusto di Notri).

SUHINDOL *Danube Plain Region, Bulgaria* One of Bulgaria's largest producers. New technology and judicious use of oak have improved quality enormously, in a rather international way, as the Craftsman's Creek, Copper Crossing and regional wines show. The Gamza and Gamza-Merlot blends are worth trying, and it is now developing some premium Cabernet and Merlot reds.

SUMAC RIDGE *Okanagan Valley VQA, British Columbia, Canada* Winemaker Mark Wendenberg produces excellent Sauvignon Blanc★ and Gewürztraminer Reserve★, fine Pinot Blanc and one of Canada's best CHAMPAGNE-method fizzes, Steller's Jay Brut★. Top reds include Cabernet Sauvignon, Cabernet Franc, Merlot, Pinot Noir and Meritage★.

SUNTORY *Japan* Red Tomi and sweet white Noble d'Or (made from botrytized grapes) are top brands for wine made exclusively from grapes grown in Japan. Classic varieties – Cabernets Sauvignon and Franc, Chardonnay, Semillon and Sauvignon – are also having success.

SUPER-TUSCANS See pages 262–3.

SWAN DISTRICT *Western Australia* The original WESTERN AUSTRALIA wine region and the hottest stretch of vineyards in Australia, spread along the fertile silty flats of Perth's Swan River. It used to specialize in fortified wines, but SOUTH AUSTRALIA and north-east VICTORIA do them better. New-wave whites and reds are fresh and generous. Best producers: Paul Conti, Faber, HOUGHTON★★, John Kosovich, Lamont★, SANDALFORD★★, Upper Reach.

JOSEPH SWAN VINEYARDS *Russian River Valley AVA, California, USA* The late Joseph Swan made legendary Zinfandel in the 1970s and was one of the first to age Zinfandel★★ in French oak. In the 1980s he turned to Pinot Noir★★ which is now probably the winery's best offering. Best years: (Zinfandel) (2002) (01) 99 **98 97 96 95 94 91**.

SYRAH See pages 266–7.

LA TÂCHE AC★★★ *Grand Cru, Côte de Nuits, Burgundy, France* Along with the ROMANEE-CONTI, the greatest of the great VOSNE-ROMANEE Grands Crus, owned by Dom. de la ROMANEE-CONTI. The wine has the rare ability to provide layer on layer of flavours; keep it for 10 years or you'll only experience a fraction of the pleasure you paid big money for. Best years: (2004) 03 02 01 00 99 98 97 96 95 93 90 **89** 88 **85 78**.

TAHBILK *Goulburn Valley, Central Victoria, Australia* Wonderfully old-fashioned family company making traditionally big, gumleafy/minty reds, matured largely in old wood. Reserve Shiraz (1860 Vines★) and Cabernet are full of character, even if they need years of cellaring. White Marsanne★★ is perfumed and attractive, as is a floral-scented Viognier★. Other whites tend to lack finesse. Best years: (1860 Vines) 1999 98 96 **95 94 92 91 90 86 82**.

TAIN L'HERMITAGE, CAVE DE *Hermitage, Rhône Valley, France* Progressive co-op producing good-value wines from throughout the northern Rhône. A go-ahead young winemaker produces surprisingly high quality, despite production of 500,000 cases annually. Modern, oaked winemaking is the style. Impressive CROZES-HERMITAGE les Hauts du Fief★, fine CORNAS★★ and both red and white ST-JOSEPH★ and HERMITAGE★★. Topping the range are an old-vine red Hermitage Gambert de Loche★★ and a fine Vin de Paille★★. Also still and sparkling ST-PERAY★. Best years: (top reds) 2004 03 01 00 **99 98 97 95**.

TAITTINGER *Champagne AC, Champagne, France* The top wine, Comtes de Champagne Blanc de Blancs★★★, can be memorable for its creamy, foaming pleasures and the Comtes de Champagne rosé★★ is elegant and oozing class. Ordinary non-vintage is soft and honeyed but has been inconsistent for a while. Prélude is a new attractive, fuller-bodied non-vintage style (50% Chardonnay, 50% Pinot Noir) made from 4 Grands Crus and aged for 4 years before release. Best years: (1998) 96 **95 92 90 89 88 86 85 82 79**.

CH. TALBOT★ *St-Julien AC, 4ème Cru Classé, Haut-Médoc, Bordeaux, France* Chunky, soft-centred but sturdy, capable of aging well for 10–20 years. There is also an interesting and good-value white wine, Caillou Blanc de Talbot★. Second wine: Connétable de Talbot. Best years: 2003 02 01 00 **99** 98 96 **95 90 89 88 86 85 83 82**.

TALBOTT *Monterey County, California, USA* This estate is known for its Chardonnays from vineyards in the Santa Lucia Highlands in MONTEREY COUNTY. Sleepy Hollow Vineyard★★, Cuvée Cynthia★★ and Diamond T Estate★★★ are all packed with ripe tropical fruit and ample oak. Kali Hart Chardonnay★ gives a taste of the style on a budget. Also Chardonnay and Pinot Noir under the Logan label.

TARAPACÁ *Maipo, Chile* No expense has been spared in recent vineyard and winery improvements at this long-established company, and the wine, too, is improving under the guidance of Sergio Correa. New oak still rather dominates the reds, but Reserve Syrah★ and Carmenère★ are good, as is basic Sauvignon Blanc. New single-vineyard MAIPO bottlings and the Viña Mar winery from CASABLANCA are uneven. Also owns the Misiones de Rengo label (Reserve Cabernet-Syrah★).

TARRAWARRA *Yarra Valley, Victoria, Australia* Founder Marc Besen wanted to make a MONTRACHET, and hang the expense. The wine-makers are on the right track: Tarrawarra Chardonnay★★ is deep and multi-faceted. Pinot Noir★★ is just as good, with almost COTE DE NUITS flavour and concentration. Tin Cows is a less pricy brand for both these grapes, plus Shiraz and Merlot. Best years: (Pinot Noir) 2003 02 **01 99 98 97 96 94 92**.

TASCA D'ALMERITA *Sicily, Italy* This estate in the highlands of central SICILY makes some of southern Italy's best wines. Native grape varieties give excellent Rosso del Conte★★ (based on Nero d'Avola) and white Nozze d'Oro★ (based on Inzolia), but there are also Chardonnay★★ and Cabernet Sauvignon★★ of extraordinary intensity and elegance. Almerita Brut★ (Chardonnay) is a fine CHAMPAGNE-method sparkler. Relatively simple Regaleali Bianco and Rosato are good value.

TASMANIA *Australia* Tasmania may be a minor state viticulturally, with only 1200ha (2965 acres) of vines, but the island has a diverse range of mesoclimates and sub-regions. The generally cool climate has always attracted seekers of greatness in Pinot Noir and Chardonnay, and good results are becoming more consistent. Riesling, Gewürztraminer and Pinot Gris perform well, but the real star here is fabulous premium fizz. Best producers: Apsley Gorge, Freycinet★★, HARDY (Bay of Fires★), Stefano LUBIANA★, Moorilla★, PIPERS BROOK★★, Providence, Tamar Ridge★, Wellington★. Best years: (Pinot Noir) **2002 01 00 99 98 97 95 94 93 92 91**.

TAURASI DOCG *Campania, Italy* MASTROBERARDINO created Taurasi's reputation; now the great potential of the Aglianico grape is being exploited by others, both within this DOCG and elsewhere in CAMPANIA. Drink at 5–10 years. Best producers: A Caggiano★★, Feudi di San Gregorio★★, MASTROBERARDINO★★, S Molettieri★, Struzziero, Terredora★. Best years: (2004) (03) 01 00 98 **97** 96 **94 93 92 90 89 88**.

SYRAH/SHIRAZ

 Syrah's popularity is rising fast and it now produces world-class wines in 3 countries: in France, where Hermitage and Côte-Rôtie are 2 of the world's great reds; in Australia, where as Shiraz it produces some of the New World's most remarkable reds; and now in California, too. And wherever Syrah appears it trumpets a proud and wilful personality based on loads of flavour and unmistakable originality.

When the late-ripening Syrah grape is grown in the coolest, most marginal areas for full ripening, such as Côte-Rôtie, it is capable of producing wines of immense class and elegance. However, producers must ensure low yields if they are to produce high-quality wines.

Syrah's spread round the warmer wine regions of the world is at last accelerating. Syrah's heartland – Hermitage and Côte-Rôtie in the Rhône Valley – comprises a mere 350ha (865 acres) of steeply terraced vineyards, producing hardly enough wine to make more than a very rarefied reputation for themselves. This may be one reason for its relatively slow uptake by growers in other countries who simply had no idea as to what kind of flavour the Syrah grape produced, so didn't copy it. But the situation is rapidly changing.

WINE STYLES
French Syrah The flavours of Syrah are most individual, but with modern vineyard practices and winemaking techniques they are far less daunting than they used to be. Traditional Syrah had a savage, almost coarse, throaty roar of a flavour. And from the very low-yielding Hermitage vineyards, the small grapes often showed a bitter tannic quality. But better selections of clones in the vineyard and improved winemaking have revealed that Syrah in fact gives a wine with a majestic depth of fruit – all blackberry and damson, loganberry and plum – some quite strong tannin, and some tangy smoke, but also a warm creamy aftertaste, and a promise of chocolate and occasionally a scent of violets. It is these characteristics that have made Syrah popular throughout the south of France as an 'improving' variety for its rather traditional red wines.
Australian Shiraz Australia's most widely planted red variety has become, in many respects, its premium varietal. Shiraz gives spectacularly good results when taken seriously – especially in the Barossa, Clare, Eden Valley and McLaren Vale regions of South Australia. An increasingly diverse range of high-quality examples are also coming from Victoria's warmer vineyards, more traditional examples from New South Wales' Hunter Valley and Mudgee, and exciting, more restrained styles from Western Australia's Margaret River and Great Southern regions, as well as cooler high-country spots. Flavours are rich, intense, thick sweet fruit coated with chocolate, and seasoned with leather, herbs and spice. And here in Australia it is often blended with Cabernet Sauvignon.
Other regions In California producers are turning out superb Rhône blends as well as varietal Syrahs modelled closely on Côte-Rôtie or Hermitage. In South Africa and Chile, more exciting varietal wines and blends appear every vintage. Italy, Spain, Portugal, Argentina and New Zealand are also beginning to shine, and even North Africa is having a go.

BEST PRODUCERS

France

Rhône ALLEMAND, F Balthazar, G Barge, A Belle, B Burgaud, CHAPOUTIER, J-L CHAVE, Y Chave, Chêne, CLAPE, Clusel-Roch, COLOMBO, Combier, Courbis, COURSODON, CUILLERON, DELAS, E & J Durand, B Faurie, Gaillard, J-M Gérin, Gonon, GRAILLOT, GUIGAL, JAMET, Jasmin, LIONNET, R Michel, ROSTAING, M Sorrel, Tardieu-Laurent, F Villard, les Vins de Vienne.

Languedoc Aiguelière, Boillot, GAUBY, Grès St-Paul, PEYRE ROSE.

Other European Syrah

Italy Bertelli, D'ALESSANDRO, FONTODI, Fossi, ISOLE E OLENA, Le MACCHIOLE, Poggio al Sole.

Spain Albet i Noya, Dehesa del Carrizal, MARQUES DE GRINON, Enrique Mendoza.

New World Syrah/Shiraz

Australia Tim ADAMS, BAROSSA VALLEY ESTATE, Jim BARRY (Armagh), BEST'S, BRANDS (Stentiford's Reserve), BROKENWOOD, CHAPEL HILL, CLARENDON HILLS, Coriole, Craiglee, Dalwhinnie, D'ARENBERG, Dutschke, FOX CREEK, GLAETZER, HARDYS, Heartland, Henry's Drive, HENSCHKE, Hewitson, HOUGHTON, Jasper Hill, Peter LEHMANN, Charles MELTON, MITCHELTON, MOUNT LANGI GHIRAN, PENFOLDS, PLANTAGENET, ROCKFORD, ST HALLETT, SEPPELT, TORBRECK, Turkey Flat, TYRRELL'S, VERITAS, WENDOUREE, The Willows, WIRRA WIRRA, WYNNS, YALUMBA, Zema.

New Zealand ATA RANGI, CRAGGY RANGE, DRY RIVER, FROMM, Stonecroft, Trinity Hill, Vidal.

South Africa BOEKENHOUTSKLOOF, FAIRVIEW, Sadie Family, SAXENBURG, SPICE ROUTE, STEENBERG, STELLENZICHT.

USA (California) ALBAN, ARAUJO, Cline, DEHLINGER, Dutton-Goldfield, Edmunds St John, Havens, Jade Mountain, Lewis, Andrew MURRAY, QUPE, Swanson, Thackrey, Truchard.

Chile ERRAZURIZ, Falernia, MONTES, MATETIC, Tabalí/SAN PEDRO.

267

TAVEL AC *Rhône Valley, France* Big, alcoholic rosé from north-west of
Avignon. Grenache and Cinsaut are the main grapes. Drink Tavel at
one year old if you want it cheerful, heady, yet refreshing, with food.
Best producers: Aquéria★, la Forcadière★, Genestière★, GUIGAL,
Montézargues★, la Mordorée★, Vignerons de Tavel, Trinquevedel★.

TAYLOR *Port DOC, Douro, Portugal* The aristocrat of the PORT industry,
300 years old and still going strong. Now part of the Fladgate
Partnership, along with FONSECA, CROFT and Delaforce. Its Vintage★★★
is superb; Quinta de Vargellas★★ is an elegant, cedary, single-quinta
vintage port made in the best of the 'off-vintages'. Quinta de Terra
Feita★★, the other main component of Taylor's Vintage, is also often
released as a single-quinta in non-declared years. Taylor's 20-year-
old★★ is a very fine aged tawny. First Estate is a successful premium
ruby. Best years: (Vintage) 2000 97 94 92 **85 83 80 77 75 70 66 63 60 55
48 45 27**; (Vargellas) 2001 99 98 **96 95 91 88 87 86 82 78 67 64 61**.

TE MATA *Hawkes Bay, North Island, New Zealand* HAWKES BAY's glamour
winery, best known for its reds, Coleraine★★ and Awatea★★, both based
on Cabernet Sauvignon with varying proportions of Merlot and Cabernet
Franc. Also outstanding is toasty Elston Chardonnay★★. Exceptional
vintages of all 3 wines might be aged for 5–10 years. Bullnose Syrah★
is an elegant, peppery red. Woodthorpe Viognier★ is a New Zealand first
for the variety. Best years: (Coleraine) **2002 00 98 96 95 94 91**.

TEMENT *Südsteiermark, Austria* Austria's best Sauvignon Blanc★★
(single-site Zieregg★★★) and Morillon (Chardonnay)★★. Both varieties
are fermented and aged in oak, giving power, depth and subtle oak
character. The Gelber Muskateller are unusually racy – perfect aperitif
wines. Red Arachon★★ is a joint venture with PICHLER and Szemes in
BURGENLAND. Best years: (Morillon Zieregg) (2004) 03 02 **01 00 99**.

TEMPRANILLO Spain's best native red grape can make wonderful wine
with wild strawberry and spicy, tobaccoey flavours. It is important in
RIOJA, PENEDES (as Ull de Llebre), RIBERA DEL DUERO (as Tinto Fino or Tinta
del País), La MANCHA and VALDEPENAS (as Cencibel), NAVARRA, SOMONTANO,
UTIEL-REQUENA and TORO (as Tinta de Toro). In Portugal it is found in the
DOURO, DAO and ESTREMADURA (as Tinta Roriz) and in ALENTEJO (as
Aragonez). Wines can be deliciously fruity for drinking young, but
Tempranillo also matures well, and its flavours blend happily with oak.
It is now being taken more seriously in Argentina, and new plantings
have been made in CALIFORNIA, OREGON, WASHINGTON (CAYUSE VINEYARDS),
Australia, Chile and South Africa.

TEROLDEGO ROTALIANO DOC *Trentino-Alto Adige, Italy* Teroldego is a
TRENTINO grape variety, producing mainly deep-coloured, grassy,
blackberry-flavoured wine from gravel soils of the Rotaliano plain. Best
producers: Barone de Cles★, M Donati★, Dorigati★, Endrizzi★,
FORADORI★★, Conti Martini★, Mezzacorona (Riserva★), Cantina Rotaliana★,
A & R Zeni★. Best years: (2004) (03) 01 00 **99 97 96 95 93 91 90**.

TERRAS DO SADO *Setúbal Peninsula, Portugal* Warm, maritime area
south of Lisbon. SETUBAL produces fortified wine. Many of the better reds
(based on Castelão), come from the Palmela DOC. A few good whites. Best
producers: (reds) Caves ALIANCA (Palmela Particular★), BRIGHT BROTHERS, D F J
VINHOS★, José Maria da FONSECA★★, Hero do Castanheiro★, J P VINHOS★, Pegôes
co-op★, Pegos Claros★★. Best years: (2004) 03 01 00 **99 97 96 95**.

TERRAZAS DE LOS ANDES *Mendoza, Argentina* Offshoot of the Chandon empire, and a terrific source of reds from high-altitude vineyards around LUJAN DE CUYO. Robust Gran Malbec★★ and the elegant yet powerful Gran Cabernet Sauvignon★★ are heading for ★★★ in the near future. A joint venture with CHEVAL BLANC of ST-EMILION has yielded Cheval des Andes★★★, a stunning Malbec-Cabernet Sauvignon blend.

TERRICCIO, CASTELLO DEL *Tuscany, Italy* Estate in the Pisan hills south of Livorno. Changes in philosophy seem to have taken top red Lupicaia★★ (Cabernet-Merlot) and less pricy Tassinaia★ (Sangiovese-Cabernet-Merlot) of much of their exciting, scented, potentially ★★★ personality. Rondinaia (Chardonnay)★★ and Con Vento (Sauvignon Blanc)★ are the most interesting whites. Capannino is a new, inexpensive red. Best years: (Lupicaia) (2003) (01) (00) 98 **97 96 95 94 93**.

CH. LE TERTRE-RÔTEBOEUF★★ *St-Émilion Grand Cru AC, Bordeaux, France* ST-EMILION's most exceptional unclassified estate. The richly seductive, Merlot-based wines sell at the same price as the Premiers Grands Crus Classés. Under the same ownership as the outstanding ROC DE CAMBES. Best years: 2003 02 01 00 **99** 98 **97 96 95 94 90 89 88 86 85**.

TEXAS *USA* From experimental plantings in 1975, Texas has become one of the major US wine-producing states. The state has 7 AVAs, of which Texas High Plains is most significant, more than 40 wineries, and some fine Chardonnay and Riesling. Thunderstorms are capable of destroying entire crops in minutes. Best producers: Alamosa, Becker, Cap Rock, Fall Creek, Llano Estacado, Messina Hof, Pheasant Ridge.

THELEMA *Stellenbosch WO, South Africa* This mountainside farm is one of the Cape's top wineries. Meticulous attention is paid to the vineyards, and winemaker Gyles Webb produces consistently good, leafy yet blackcurranty Cabernet Sauvignon★★, ripe fleshy Merlot★, spicy, accessible Shiraz, barrel-fermented Chardonnay★★, vibrant Sauvignon Blanc★★ and Riesling★. Best years: (Cabernet Sauvignon) **2002 01 00 99 98 97 96 95 94**; (Chardonnay) 2004 **03 02 01 00 99 98 97**.

THERMENREGION *Niederösterreich, Austria* This warm, 2150ha (5290-acre) region, south of Vienna, takes its name from the spa towns of Baden and Bad Vöslau. Near Vienna is the village of Gumpoldskirchen with its rich and sometimes sweet white wines. The red wine area around Baden produces large amounts of Blauer Portugieser together with improving examples of Pinot Noir and Cabernet. Best producers: Alphart, Biegler, Fischer★, Johanneshof★, Schellmann, Stadlmann★. Best years: (sweet whites) (2004) 03 02 01 **00 99 98**.

THIRTY BENCH *Niagara Peninsula VQA, Ontario, Canada* A collaboration of 3 winemakers, Thirty Bench is known for its excellent Rieslings, including Late Harvest and Icewine★, very good BORDEAUX-style red Reserve Blend★ and a fine barrel-fermented Chardonnay★.

DOM. THOMAS-MOILLARD *Nuits-St-Georges AC, Côte de Nuits, Burgundy, France* The label for wines from the family-owned vineyards of négociant Moillard-Grivot. The wines are not consistent across the range, but the best, including ROMANEE-ST-VIVANT★★★ and BONNES-MARES★★★, are very fine, in an old-fashioned, long-lived, robust style. Other good reds include NUITS-ST-GEORGES Clos de Thorey★★, BEAUNE Grèves★ and VOSNE-ROMANEE Malconsorts★★. Red and white HAUTES-COTES DE NUITS★ stand out at the simpler end of the range. Best years: (top reds) (2004) 03 02 01 **00** 99 98 **97** 96 95 **90**.

THREE CHOIRS *Gloucestershire, England* Martin Fowke makes a large range of wines from 30ha (74 acres) of vines, plus bought-in grapes. New Release is a fresh, fruity white, released in November of vintage year (as with BEAUJOLAIS NOUVEAU). Other successful wines are Bacchus, Schönburger and Sieggerebe varietals, plus Late Harvest dessert wine. Sparkling wines and Seyval-based wines are not always so tasty.

TICINO *Switzerland* Italian-speaking, southerly canton of Switzerland. The most important wine here is Merlot, usually soft and gluggable, but sometimes more serious with some oak barrel-aging. Best producers: Daniel Huber★, Monti, Werner Stucky★, Tamborini, Christian Zündel★. Best years: (2004) 03 02 **01 00 97 96**.

TIGNANELLO★★ *Tuscany, Italy* In the early 1970s, Piero ANTINORI employed the previously unheard-of practice of aging in small French oak barrels and used Cabernet Sauvignon (20%) in the blend with Sangiovese. The quality was superb, and Tignanello's success sparked off the SUPER-TUSCAN movement. Top vintages are truly great; lesser years are of decent CHIANTI CLASSICO quality. Best years: (2004) (03) (01) 00 **99 98 97 95 93 90 88 85**.

TINTA RORIZ See Tempranillo.

TOCAI FRIULANO Tocai Friulano is a north-east Italian grape producing dry, nutty, oily whites of great character in COLLIO and COLLI ORIENTALI, good wines in the Veneto's Colli Euganei – and lots of neutral stuff in Piave. Best producers: Borgo San Daniele★, Borgo del Tiglio★, Dorigo★, Drius★, Livio FELLUGA★, JERMANN★, Edi Keber★★, Miani★★, Princic★, Paolo Rodaro★, Ronchi di Manzano★, Ronco del Gelso★★, Russiz Superiore★★, SCHIOPETTO★★, Specogna★, Le Vigne di Zamò★★, Villa Russiz★.

TOKAJI *Hungary* Hungary's classic, liquorous wine of historical reputation, with its unique, sweet-and-sour, sherry-like tang, comes from 28 villages on the Hungarian–Slovak border. Mists from the Bodrog river ensure that noble rot on the Furmint, Hárslevelü and Muscotaly (Muscat Ottonel) grapes is a fairly common occurrence. Degrees of sweetness are measured in *puttonyos*. Discussions continue about traditional oxidized styles versus fresher modern versions. Best producers: Disznókő★★, Château Megyer★★, Oremus★, Château Pajzos★★, Royal Tokaji Wine Co★★, Istvan Szepsy (6 Puttonyos 95★★★, Essencia★★★), Tokaji Kereskedóház★. Best years: 2000 **99 97 93**.

TOLLOT-BEAUT *Chorey-lès-Beaune AC, Burgundy, France* High-quality COTE DE BEAUNE reds with lots of fruit and a pronounced new oak character. The village-level CHOREY-LES-BEAUNE★★, ALOXE-CORTON★★ and SAVIGNY-LES-BEAUNE★★ wines are all excellent, as is the top BEAUNE Premier Cru Clos du Roi★★. Whites are more variable, but at best delicious. Best years: (reds) (2004) 03 02 01 99 **98 97 96 95**.

TORBRECK *Barossa Valley, South Australia* Dave Powell specializes in opulent, well-structured reds from 60–120-year-old Shiraz, Grenache and Mataro (Mourvèdre) vines. Made in minute quantities, the flagship RunRig★★★, single-vineyard Descendant★★ and Factor★★ are all richly concentrated, powerful and complex Shiraz (the first two with a touch of Viognier).

TORBRECK
BAROSSA VALLEY
2001
RunRig
750mL   *grown & made by Torbreck Vintners, Roennfeldt Road, Marananga, S.A.*

The Steading★ and Juveniles★ are Grenache-Mataro-Shiraz blends (the latter unoaked) while the Woodcutters White (Semillon) and Red (Shiraz) are lightly oaked, mouth-filling quaffers.

TORGIANO DOC & DOCG *Umbria, Italy*   A zone near Perugia dominated by one producer, LUNGAROTTI. Lungarotti's basic Rubesco Torgiano★ is ripely fruity; the Torgiano Riserva DOCG Vigna Monticchio★★ is a fine black cherry-flavoured wine, aged for up to 8 years before release.

TORO DO *Castilla y León, Spain*   Mainly red wines, which are robust, full of colour and tannin, and pretty high in alcohol. The main grape, Tinta de Toro, is a variant of Tempranillo, and there is some Garnacha. In the late 1990s, the arrival of some of the top wineries in Spain gave the sleepy area a major boost. Best producers: Viña Bajoz★, Fariña★, Frutos Villar (Muruve★), Maurodos★★, Pintia★★/VEGA SICILIA, Telmo RODRIGUEZ★★, Toresanas/Bodegas de Crianza Castilla la Vieja★, Vega Saúco★, Vega de Toro/Señorío de San Vicente (Numanthia★★, Termanthia★★).

TORRES *Penedès DO, Cataluña, Spain*   Large family winery led by visionary Miguel Torres, making good wines with local grapes, (Parellada, Tempranillo) and international varieties. Viña Sol★ is a good, citrony quaffer, Viña Esmeralda★ (Muscat Blanc à Petits Grains and Gewürztraminer) is grapy and spicy, Fransola★★ (Sauvignon Blanc with some Parellada) is rich yet leafy, and Milmanda★ is a delicate, expensive Chardonnay. Successful reds are soft, oaky and blackcurranty Gran Coronas★ (Tempranillo and Cabernet), fine, relatively rich Mas la Plana★ (Cabernet Sauvignon), floral, perfumed Mas Borrás (Pinot Noir) and raisiny Atrium★ (Merlot). The top reds – Grans Muralles★★, from a blend of Catalan grapes, and Reserva Real★★, a BORDEAUX-style red blend – are interesting but expensive. Best years: (Mas la Plana) **1998 96 95 94 91 90 88 87 83 81 79 76**.

MARIMAR TORRES ESTATE *Sonoma County, California, USA*   The sister of Spanish winemaker Miguel TORRES has established her own winery in the cool Green Valley region of SONOMA COUNTY, only a few miles from the Pacific Ocean. She specializes in Chardonnay and Pinot Noir, the best of which are from the Don Miguel Vineyard. The Chardonnay★★ is big and intense, initially quite oaky, but able to age gracefully and interestingly for up to 10 years. Recent vintages of full-flavoured Pinot Noir★★ are the best yet. Best years: (2002) (01) **00 99 98 97 95 94**.

MIGUEL TORRES *Curicó, Chile*   Now producing its best ever wines: snappy Sauvignon Blanc★★, grassy, fruity Santa Digna rosé★, weighty, blackcurrant Manso de Velasco Cabernet★★, exciting, sonorous old-Carignan-based Cordillera★★ and the new Conde de Superunda★★, a tremendous, dense blend based on Cabernet and Tempranillo. Best years: (Manso) (2002) 01 **00 99**.

CH. LA TOUR BLANCHE★★ *Sauternes AC, 1er Cru Classé, Bordeaux, France*   This estate regained top form in the 1980s with the introduction of new oak barrels for fermentation, lower yields and greater selection. Full-bodied, rich and aromatic, it now ranks with the best of the Classed Growths. Second wine: Les Charmilles de la Tour Blanche. Best years: 2003 02 01 **99 98 97 96 95 90 89 88 86**.

CH. TOUR BOISÉE *Minervois AC, Languedoc, France*   Jean-Louis Poudou is a pioneer of the MINERVOIS. Top wines are the red Cuvée Marie-Claude★, aged for 12 months in barrel, the fruity Cuvée Marielle et Frédérique★, and the white Cuvée Marie-Claude★, with a hint of Muscat Blanc à Petits Grains for added aroma. Best years: (red) (2003) **01 00**.

CH. TOUR DES GENDRES *Bergerac AC, South-West France* Luc de Conti's BERGERACS are made with as much sophistication as the better Crus Classés of BORDEAUX. Generously fruity Moulin des Dames★ and the more serious la Gloire de Mon Père★★ reds are mostly Cabernet Sauvignon. Full, fruity and elegant Moulin des Dames★ white is a Bordeaux blend of Sémillon, Sauvignon Blanc and Muscadelle. Best years: (la Gloire de Mon Père) (2003) **01 00 99 98 96 95**.

TOURAINE AC *Loire Valley, France* General AC for Touraine wines in the central LOIRE. Most of the reds are from Gamay and in hot years these can be juicy, rustic-fruited wines. There is a fair amount of red from Cabernets Sauvignon and Franc, too, and some good Côt (Malbec). The reds are best drunk young. Fairly decent whites come from the Chenin Blanc but the best are from Sauvignon Blanc. These can be a good SANCERRE substitute at half the price. Drink at a year old, though Chenin wines can last longer. White and rosé sparkling wines are made by the traditional method, but are rarely as good as the best VOUVRAY and CRÉMANT DE LOIRE. Best producers: (reds and rosés) Ch. de Chenonceau★, Clos de la Briderie★, Corbillières, J-P Crespin/Ch. de l'Aulée, J Delaunay★, Robert Denis★, Ch. Gaillard, Marcadet★, Marionnet/la Charmoise★, Pavy★, Roche Blanche★; (whites) Acacias★, Ch. de Chenonceau★, Marcadet★, Marionnet/la Charmoise★, Michaud★, Octavie★, Oisly-et-Thésée co-op★, Pibaleau★, Pré Baron★, J Preys★, Roche Blanche★. Best years: (reds) 2004 **03 02 01 00 97 96**.

TOURIGA NACIONAL High-quality red Portuguese grape which is rich in aroma and fruit. It contributes deep colour and tannin to PORT, and is rapidly increasing in importance for table wines.

TOWER ESTATE *Hunter Valley, New South Wales, Australia* Len Evans' latest venture, in partnership with a syndicate that includes British super-chef Rick Stein, focuses on sourcing top-notch grapes from their ideal regions. So, there is powerful, stylish COONAWARRA Cabernet★★, top-flight BAROSSA Shiraz★★, fine floral CLARE Riesling★★, fruity ADELAIDE HILLS Sauvignon Blanc★★ and classic Semillon★★, Shiraz★ and Chardonnay★ from the HUNTER VALLEY.

TRAPICHE *Mendoza, Argentina* The fine wine arm of Peñaflor, Argentina's biggest wine producer, where winemaker Daniel Pi is making serious progress. Iscay★ is a powerful Merlot-Malbec blend made with the assistance of Pomerol guru, Michel Rolland. Broquel Malbec is black and spicy and there is punchy Sauvignon and melony Chardonnay.

TRÁS-OS-MONTES *Portugal* Impoverished north-eastern province, producing pretty rustic stuff. However, the Vinho Regional Trás-os-Montes/Terras Durienses covers a handful of good DOURO-sourced reds. Best producers: Quinta de Cidrô (Chardonnay★), RAMOS PINTO (Quinta de Bons Ares★), Valle Pradinhos.

TREBBIANO The most widely planted white Italian grape variety. As Trebbiano Toscano, it is the base for EST! EST!! EST!!! and any number of other neutral, dry whites, as well as much VIN SANTO. But there are other grapes masquerading under the Trebbiano name that aren't anything like as neutral. The most notable are the Trebbianos from LUGANA and ABRUZZO – both grapes capable of full-bodied, fragrant wines. Called Ugni Blanc in France, where it is primarily used for distilling, as it should be.

TRENTINO *Italy*   Region of northern Italy. The wines rarely have the verve or perfume of ALTO ADIGE examples, but can make up for this with riper, softer flavours, where vineyard yields have been kept in check. The Trentino DOC covers 20 different styles of wine, including whites Pinot Bianco and Grigio, Chardonnay, Moscato Giallo, Müller-Thurgau and Nosiola, and reds Lagrein, Marzemino and Cabernet. Trento Classico is a DOC for CHAMPAGNE-method fizz. Best producers: N Balter★, N Bolognani★, La Cadalora★, Castel Noarna★, Cavit co-op, Cesconi★★, De Tarczal★, Dorigati, FERRARI★★, Graziano Fontana★, FORADORI★★, Letrari★, Longariva★, Conti Martini★, Maso Cantanghel★, Maso Furli★, Maso Roveri★, Mezzacorona, Pojer & Sandri★, Pravis★, SAN LEONARDO★★, Simoncelli★, E Spagnolli★, Vallarom★, La Vis co-op. See also Teroldego Rotaliano.

DOM. DE TRÉVALLON *Provence, France*   Iconoclastic Eloi Dürrbach makes brilliant reds★★ (at best ★★★) – a tradition-busting blend of Cabernet Sauvignon and Syrah, mixing herbal wildness with a sweetness of blackberry, blackcurrant and black, black plums – and a tiny quantity of white★★★. Both are labelled Vin de Pays des BOUCHES-DU-RHONE. The reds age well, but are intriguingly drinkable in their youth. Best years: (reds) (2003) 01 00 **99 98 97 96**.

TRIMBACH *Alsace AC, Alsace, France*   An excellent grower/merchant whose trademark is beautifully structured, emphatically dry, subtly perfumed elegance. Top wines are Gewurztraminer Cuvée des Seigneurs de Ribeaupierre★★, Riesling Cuvée Frédéric Émile★★ and Riesling Clos Ste-Hune★★★. Also very good Vendange Tardive★★ and Sélection de Grains Nobles★★. Trimbach basics, however, are a touch unexciting for the price. Best years: (Clos Ste-Hune) (2002) (01) 00 99 98 97 **96 95 93 92 90 89 88 85 83 81 76**.

TRITTENHEIM *Mosel, Germany*   Important village with some excellent vineyard sites, notably the Apotheke (pharmacy) and Leiterchen (little ladder). The wines are sleek, with crisp acidity and plenty of fruit. Best producers: Ernst Clüsserath★, Clüsserath-Weiler★, GRANS-FASSIAN★★, Milz-Laurentiushof★. Best years: (2004) 03 02 01 **99 98 97 95 93**.

CH. TROPLONG-MONDOT★★ *St-Émilion Grand Cru AC, Bordeaux, France*   Consistently one of the best of ST-EMILION's Grands Crus Classés. The wines are beautifully structured and mouthfillingly textured for long aging. Best years: 2003 02 01 00 **99 98 97 96 95 94 90 89 88 86 85**.

CH. TROTANOY★★ *Pomerol AC, Bordeaux, France*   Another POMEROL estate (like PETRUS, LATOUR-A-POMEROL and others) which has benefited from the brilliant touch of the MOUEIX family. Back on form after a dip in the mid-1980s. Best years: 2003 01 00 **99 98 97 96 95 94 93 90 89 88 82**.

TUA RITA *Tuscany, Italy*   Since the early 1990s, this estate at Val di Cornia in the MAREMMA has established itself at the top of the Italian Merlot tree with Redigaffi★★; Cabernet-Merlot blend Giusto di Notri★★ is almost as renowned. Best years: (2004) (03) 01 **00 99 98 97 96 95**.

CAVE VINICOLE DE TURCKHEIM *Alsace AC, Alsace, France*   Important co-op with good basics in all varieties. The Reserve tier of all wines merits ★, while Brand★, Hengst★★ and Ollwiller★ bottlings are rich and concentrated. Reds, rosés and CREMANT D'ALSACE★ are consistent. Best years: (Grand Cru Gewurztraminer) 2000 **99 98 97 95 94 93 90 89**.

TURLEY *Napa Valley AVA, California, USA* Larry Turley specializes in
powerful Zinfandel and a small amount of Petite Sirah. His ultra-ripe
Zins★★, from a number of old vineyards, are either praised for their
profound power and depth or damned for their tannic, high-alcohol,
PORT-like nature. Petite Sirah★★ is similarly built. Best years: (Zins)
(2003) 02 01 **00 99 98 97 96 95 94**.

TURSAN VDQS *South-West France* These wines are made on the edge of
les Landes, the sandy coastal area south of Bordeaux. The white is the
most interesting: made from the Baroque grape, it is clean, crisp and
refreshing. Best producers: Baron de Bachen, Dulucq, Tursan co-op.

TUSCANY *Italy* Tuscany's rolling hills, clad with vines, olive trees and
cypresses, have produced wine since at least Etruscan times. Today, its
many DOC/DOCGs are based on the red Sangiovese grape and are led by
CHIANTI CLASSICO, BRUNELLO DI MONTALCINO and VINO NOBILE DI MONTEPULCIANO, as
well as famous SUPER-TUSCANS like ORNELLAIA and TIGNANELLO. White wines,
despite sweet VIN SANTO, and the occasional excellent Chardonnay and
Sauvignon, do not figure highly. See also Bolgheri, Carmignano, Maremma,
Montecarlo, Morellino di Scansano, Rosso di Montalcino, Rosso di
Montepulciano, Sassicaia, Solaia, Vernaccia di San Gimignano.

TYRRELL'S *Hunter Valley, New South Wales, Australia* Top-notch family-
owned company with prime Lower HUNTER vineyards, now expanding
into COONAWARRA, MCLAREN VALE and HEATHCOTE, with impressive results.
Comprehensive range, from good-value quaffers (Old Winery★, Lost
Block★) to excellent Vat 47 Chardonnay★★★ and Vat 9 Shiraz★.
Semillon is the speciality, with 4 single-vineyard wines (all ★★) – Lost
Block, Stevens, Belford and the rare HVD – and, best of all, the superb
Vat 1★★★. Best years: (Vat 1 Semillon) (2003) (02) 01 00 99 **98 97 96 95
94 93 92 91 90 89 87 86 77 76 75**; (Vat 47 Chardonnay) (2003) 02 01 **00
99 98 97 96 95 94 91 89**.

UCO VALLEY *Mendoza, Argentina* This valley, in the foothills of the
Andes, is an old secret of Argentine viticulture, newly rediscovered.
With vineyards at 1000–1500m (3200–4900 ft) above sea level, it's
Argentina's best spot for Chardonnays, especially from the Tupungato
area. Reds are also showing fascinating flavours – especially Merlot,
Malbec, Syrah and Pinot Noir. Best producers: ACHAVAL-FERRER★★,
CATENA★★, Clos de los Siete★★, Finca La Celia★, O Fournier★,
Salentein★, TERRAZAS DE LOS ANDES★★.

UGNI BLANC See Trebbiano.

UMATHUM *Frauenkirchen, Neusiedlersee, Burgenland, Austria* Resisting
the trend in Austria to produce heavily oaked blockbuster reds, Josef
Umathum emphasizes finesse and sheer drinkability. The single-
vineyard Ried Hallebühl★★ is usually his top wine, but the St Laurent
Vom Stein★ and the Zweigelt-dominated Haideboden★ sometimes
match it in quality. Best years: (reds) (2004) 03 01 00 **99 97 94**.

UMBRIA *Italy* Wine production in this Italian region is dominated by
ORVIETO, accounting for almost 70% of DOC wines. However, some of the
most characterful wines are reds from TORGIANO and MONTEFALCO. Latest
interest centres on international-style reds made by the ubiquitous
Riccardo Cotarella at estates such as Pieve del Vescovo (Lucciaio★★), La
Carraia (Fobiano★★), Lamborghini (Campoleone★★) and La Palazzola
(Rubino★★).

ÜRZIG *Mosel, Germany* Middle MOSEL village with the famous red slate Würzgarten (spice garden) vineyard tumbling spectacularly down to the river and producing marvellously spicy Riesling. Drink young or with at least 5 years' age. Best producers: Bischöfliche Weinguter★, J J Christoffel★★, Dr LOOSEN★★★, Mönchhof★★, Peter Nicolay★. Best years: (2004) 03 02 01 00 **99 98 97 96 95 94**.

UTIEL-REQUENA DO *Valencia, Spain* Renowned for its rosés, mostly from the Bobal grape. Reds, increasingly based on Tempranillo, are on the up. The groundbreaking Mustiguillo★★ winery now has its own appellation, Vinos de la Tierra Terrerazo. Best producers: Gandía, Bodegas Palmera (L'Angelet★), Schenk, Torre Oria, Dominio de la Vega.

DOM. VACHERON *Sancerre AC, Loire Valley, France* Unusually for a SANCERRE domaine, Vacheron is more reputed for its Pinot Noir reds than for its whites, but the whole range is currently on top form. Intense and expensive Belle Dame★★ red and Les Romains★★ red and white lead the way. The basic Sancerres – a cherryish red★ and a grapefruity white★ – have reserves of complexity that set them above the crowd. Best years: (Belle Dame) 2004 03 02 **01 00 99 98 96**.

VACQUEYRAS AC *Rhône Valley, France* Important COTES DU RHONE-VILLAGES commune with its own AC since 1990. Red wines account for 95% of production; dark in colour, they have a warm, spicy bouquet and a rich deep flavour that seems infused with the herbs and pine dust of the south. Lovely to drink at 2–3 years, though good wines will age for 10 years.
Best producers: Amouriers★, la Charbonnière★, Clos des Cazaux★, Couroulu★, DELAS★, Font de Papier★, la Fourmone★, la Garrigue★, JABOULET★,

Monardière★★, Montirius★★, Montmirail★, Montvac★, Sang des Cailloux★, Tardieu-Laurent★★, Ch. des Tours★, Vacqueyras co-op★, Verquière★. Best years: 2004 03 **01 00 99 98 97 95**.

VAL D'ORBIEU, LES VIGNERONS DU *Languedoc-Roussillon, France* This growers' association is one of France's largest wine exporting companies, selling in excess of 20 million cases of wine a year. Membership includes several of the MIDI's best co-ops (Cucugnan, Cuxac, Montredon, Ribauté) and individual producers (Dom. de Fontsainte, Ch. la VOULTE-GASPARETS). It also owns Cordier (BORDEAUX) and Listel, and markets the wines of Ch. de Jau and the excellent BANYULS and COLLIOURE estate, Clos de Paulilles. Its range of upmarket blended wines (Cuvée Chouette★, Chorus★, Elysices★, Réserve St-Martin, la Cuvée Mythique★) are a mix of traditional Mediterranean varieties with Cabernet or Merlot.

VALAIS *Switzerland* Swiss canton flanking the Rhône. Between Martigny and Sierre the valley turns north-east, creating an Alpine suntrap, and this short stretch of terraced vineyard land provides many of Switzerland's most individual wines from Fendant, Johannisberger (Silvaner), Pinot Noir and Gamay, and several stunning examples from Syrah, Chardonnay, Ermitage (Marsanne) and Petite Arvine. Best producers: Bonvin★, M Clavien★, J Germanier★, Didier Joris★, Mathier, Dom. du Mont d'Or★, Orsat, Provins Valais, Zufferey.

CH. DE VALANDRAUD★★ *St-Émilion Grand Cru AC, Bordeaux, France* The precursor of the 'garage wine' sensation in ST-EMILION, a big, rich, extracted wine from low yields, from grapes mainly grown in different parcels around St-Émilion. The first vintage was in 1991 and since then prices have rocketed. Best years: 2003 02 01 00 **99 98 97 96 95**.

VALDEPEÑAS DO *Castilla-La Mancha, Spain* Valdepeñas offers some of
Spain's best inexpensive oak-aged reds, but these are a small drop in
a sea of less exciting stuff. In fact, there are more whites than reds, at
least some of them modern, fresh and fruity. Best producers: Miguel
Calatayud, Los Llanos★, Luís Megía, Real, Félix Solís, Casa de la Viña.

VALDESPINO *Jerez y Manzanilla DO, Andalucía, Spain* The bodega has
been sold and we wait anxiously to see whether the superb quality of
sherries such as Inocente Fino★★, Palo Cortado Cardenal★★ and dry
amontillado Coliseo★★ is going to suffer.

VALDIVIESO *Curicó, Chile* Important winery, getting back on track after
a few lean years. Varietals are attractive and direct, Reserves from
cooler regions a definite step up, and some of the Single Vineyards are
excellent (Chardonnay★★, Malbec★★). Multi-varietal, multi-vintage
blend Caballo Loco★★ is always fascinating and new Eclat★★, based
on old Carignan, is chewy and rich.

VALENCIA *Spain* The best wines from Valencia DO are the inexpensive,
sweet, grapy Moscatels. Simple, fruity whites, reds and rosés are also good.
Alicante DO to the south produces a little-known treasure, the Fondillón
dry or semi-dry fortified wine, as well as a cluster of wines made by a few
quality-conscious modern wineries. Monastrell (Mourvèdre) is the main red
grape variety. Best producers: (Valencia) Gandía, Los Pinos★, Celler del
Roure★, Schenk, Cherubino Valsangiacomo (Marqués de Caro); (Alicante)
Bocopa★, Gutiérrez de la Vega (Casta Diva Muscat★★), Enrique
Mendoza★★, Salvador Poveda★, Primitivo Quiles★. See also Utiel-Requena.

VALL-LLACH *Priorat DOCa, Spain* This tiny winery, owned by Catalan
folk singer Lluís Llach, has joined the ranks of the best PRIORAT
producers with its powerful reds★★ dominated by old-vine Cariñena.
Best years: 2001 00 **99 98**.

VALLE D'AOSTA *Italy* Tiny Alpine valley sandwiched between PIEDMONT
and the French Alps in northern Italy. The regional DOC covers 17 wine
styles, referring either to a specific grape variety (like Gamay or Pinot Nero)
or to a delimited region like Donnaz, a northern extension of Piedmont's
Carema, producing a light red from the Nebbiolo grape. Perhaps the finest
wine from these steep slopes is the sweet Chambave Moscato. Best
producers: R Anselmet★, C Charrère/Les Crêtes★, La Crotta di Vegneron★,
Grosjean, Institut Agricole Regional★, Onze Communes co-op, Ezio Voyat★.

VALLEY VINEYARDS *Berkshire, England* 10ha (26 acres) planted with a
wide range of grape varieties. Owner Jon Leighton, with consultant
John Worontschak and winemaker Vince Gower, has, over the past
20 years, produced many stunning wines. The range includes toasty
oaky Fumé and fragrant Regatta whites; Ruscombe red; sparkling
Ascot and Heritage Brut; barrel-aged Clocktower Pinot Noir★.

VALPOLICELLA DOC *Veneto, Italy* This wine can range in style from a
light, cherryish red to the rich, PORT-like RECIOTO and AMARONE. Most of
the better examples are Valpolicella Classico from the hills and are
made predominantly from the Corvina grape. The most concentrated,
ageworthy examples are made either from a particular vineyard, or by
refermenting the wine on the skins and lees of the Amarone, a style
called *ripasso*, or by using a portion of dried grapes. Best producers:
Accordini★, ALLEGRINI★★, Bertani★, Brigaldara★, Brunelli★, BUSSOLA★★,

M Castellani★, DAL FORNO★★, Guerrieri-Rizzardi★, MASI★, Mazzi★, Pasqua/Cecilia Beretta★, QUINTARELLI★★, Le Ragose★, Le Salette★, Serègo Alighieri★, Speri★, Tedeschi★, Villa Monteleone★, VIVIANI★★, Zenato★, Fratelli Zeni★. Best years: (2004) 03 **01 00 97 95 93 90 88**.

VALTELLINA SUPERIORE DOCG *Lombardy, Italy*   Red wine produced on the precipitous slopes of northern LOMBARDY. There is a basic, light Valtellina DOC red, made from at least 70% Nebbiolo (here called Chiavennasca), but the best wines are made under the Valtellina Superiore DOCG as Grumello, Inferno, Sassella and Valgella. From top vintages the wines are attractively perfumed and approachable. Sfursat or Sforzato is a dense, high-alcohol red (up to 14.5%) made from semi-dried grapes. Best producers: La Castellina★, Enologica Valtellinese★, Fay★, Nino Negri★, Nera★, Rainoldi★, Conti Sertoli Salis★, Triacca★. Best years: (2004) (03) 01 **99 98 97 95 93 90 88 85**.

CH. VANNIERES *Bandol AC, Provence, France*   Leading BANDOL estate, owned by the Boisseaux family since the 1950s. Under a new winemaker, it has leapt into the top ranks. Wood has replaced cement tanks, wines are bottled unfiltered, and the percentage of Mourvèdre has gone from 50 to 95. Besides red Bandol★★, Vannières also produces COTES DE PROVENCE and Vin de Pays. Best years: 2003 01 00 98 **97 96 95**.

VASSE FELIX *Margaret River, Western Australia*   Decadently rich, profound Cabernet Sauvignon★ and oak-led Shiraz★. Flagship red is the powerful Heytesbury★★, with a Chardonnay★ to match. But I'm still waiting for Vasse Felix consistently to reach the next level up. Best years: (Heytesbury Cabernet Sauvignon) (2003) 02 01 **99 97 96 95**.

VAUD *Switzerland*   The Vaud's main vineyards border Lake Geneva (Lac Léman), with 5 sub-regions: la Côte, Lavaux, CHABLAIS, Côtes de l'Orbe-Bonvillars, Vully. Fresh light white wines are made from Chasselas; at DEZALEY it gains some real depth and character. Reds are from Gamay and Pinot Noir. Best producers: Henri Badoux, Louis Bovard★, Dubois, Massy, Obrist, J & P Testuz★.

VAVASOUR *Marlborough, South Island, New Zealand*   First winery in MARLBOROUGH's Awatere Valley, now enjoying spectacular success. One of New Zealand's best Chardonnays★★, a fine Pinot Noir★★ and palate-tingling, oak-aged Sauvignon Blanc★. Second label Dashwood also impresses, particularly with the tangy Dashwood Sauvignon Blanc★★. Best years: (Sauvignon Blanc) 2005 **03 01 00**.

VEENWOUDEN *Paarl WO, South Africa*   This PAARL winery is recognized as one of the Cape's best and most focused producers. The 3 reds are based on BORDEAUX varieties: sumptuous, well-oaked Merlot★★; firm and silky-fruited Veenwouden Classic★★; and Vivat Bacchus★, with a distinctive Malbec component. A tiny quantity of fine Chardonnay★ is also made. Best years: (Merlot, Classic) 2002 **00 99 98 97 96 95**.

VEGA SICILIA *Ribera del Duero DO, Castilla y León, Spain*   Among Spain's most expensive wines, rich, fragrant, complex and very slow to mature, and by no means always easy to appreciate. This estate was the first in Spain to introduce French varieties, and over a quarter of the vines are now Cabernet Sauvignon, two-thirds are Tempranillo and the rest Malbec and Merlot. Vega Sicilia Unico★★★ – the top wine – was traditionally given about 10 years' wood aging, but since 1982 this has been reduced to 5 or 6. Second wine: Valbuena★★. A subsidiary winery produces the more modern Alión★★, and the new Pintia★★ winery makes some of the most distinctive wines in TORO. Best years: (Unico) 1991 **90 89 87 86 85 83 82 81 80 79 76 75 74 70 68**.

VELICH *Neuseidlersee, Burgenland, Austria* Roland and Heinz Velich make Austria's most mineral and sophisticated Chardonnay★★ from old vines in the Tiglat vineyard. Also, since 1995, spectacular dessert wines of ★★ and ★★★ quality. Best years: (Tiglat Chardonnay) (2004) 03 02 01 **00 99 97 95**; (sweet whites) (2004) 02 01 00 **99 98 96 95 94 91**.

VENETO *Italy* This region takes in the wine zones of SOAVE, VALPOLICELLA, BARDOLINO and Piave in north-east Italy. It is the source of a great deal of inexpensive wine, but the Soave and Valpolicella hills are also capable of producing small quantities of high-quality wine. Other hilly areas like Colli Berici and Colli Euganei produce large quantities of dull staple varietal wines, but can offer the odd flash of brilliance. The great dry red of this zone is AMARONE. See also Bianco di Custoza, Prosecco di Conegliano-Valdobbiadene, Recioto della Valpolicella, Recioto di Soave.

VERDICCHIO DEI CASTELLI DI JESI DOC *Marche, Italy* Verdicchio, grown in the hills near the Adriatic around Jesi and in the Apennine foothills enclave of Matelica, has blossomed into central Italy's most promising white variety. When fresh and fruity it is the ideal wine with fish, but some Verdicchio can age into a white of surprising depth of flavours. A few producers, notably Garofoli with Serra Fiorese★★, age it in oak, but even without wood it can develop an almost Burgundy-like complexity. A little is made sparkling. Best producers: (Jesi) Brunori★, Bucci★★, Colonnara★, Coroncino★★, Fazi Battaglia★, Garofoli★★, Mancinelli★, Terre Cortesi Moncaro★, Monte Schiavo★★, Santa Barbara★, Sartarelli★★, Tavignano★, Umani Ronchi★, Fratelli Zaccagnini★; (Matelica) Belisario★, Bisci★, Mecella★, La Monacesca★★.

VERGELEGEN *Stellenbosch WO, South Africa* Winemaker André van Rensburg is making this historic farm one of the greats of the new century. His Sauvignon Blancs are already considered benchmarks: the regular bottling★★ is aggressive and racy, streaked with sleek tropical fruit; the single-vineyard Reserve★★ is flinty, dry and powerful. Topping both is the barrel-fermented white Vergelegen★★ – now settled into a Semillon-Sauvignon blend. There is also a ripe-textured, stylish Chardonnay Reserve★★. The reds are even more attention-grabbing. Vergelegen★★, a BORDEAUX blend, shows classic mineral intensity. Merlot★★ and Cabernet Sauvignon★★ are some of the best in South Africa. Since Van Rensburg's arrival in 1998, several of these wines are nudging ★★★ status. Best years: (premium reds) 2002 **01 00 99 98 95 94**; (premium whites) 2004 **03 02 01 00 99 98 97**.

VERGET *Mâconnais, Burgundy, France* A négociant house run by Jean-Marie Guffens-Heynen, an exuberant character with his own domaine. The Guffens-Heynen wines include excellent MACON-VILLAGES★★ and POUILLY-FUISSE★★. The Verget range has outstanding Premiers Crus and Grands Crus from the COTE D'OR, notably CHASSAGNE-MONTRACHET★★ and BATARD-MONTRACHET★★★. But beware, the wines are made in a *very* individualistic style. Best years: (2004) 03 02 **01 00 99**.

VERITAS *Barossa, South Australia* *In vino veritas* (In wine there is truth), say the Binder family. There's certainly truth in the bottom of a bottle of Hanisch Vineyard Shiraz★★★ or Heysen Vineyard Shiraz★★★, both blindingly good wines. The Shiraz-Mourvèdre★★ (known locally as Bulls' Blood) and Shiraz-Grenache★★ blends are lovely big reds; Cabernet-Merlot★★ is also good. Under the Christa-Rolf label, Shiraz-Grenache★ is good and spicy with attractive, forward black fruit.

VERMENTINO The best dry white wines of SARDINIA generally come from the Vermentino grape. Light, dry, perfumed and nutty, the best examples tend to be from the north-east of the island, where the Vermentino di Gallura zone is located. Occasionally it is made sweet or sparkling. Vermentino is also grown in LIGURIA and TUSCANY, though its character is quite different. It is believed to be the same as Rolle, found in many blends in LANGUEDOC-ROUSSILLON. **Best producers:** (Sardinia) ARGIOLAS★, Capichera★★, Cherchi★, Gallura co-op★, Piero Mancini★, Pedra Majore★, Santadi co-op★, SELLA & MOSCA★, Vermentino co-op★.

VERNACCIA DI SAN GIMIGNANO DOCG *Tuscany, Italy* Dry white wines – generally light quaffers – made from the Vernaccia grape grown in the hills around San Gimignano. It is debatable whether the allowance of up to 10% Chardonnay in the blend is a forward step. There is a San Gimignano DOC for the zone's up-and-coming reds, though the best SUPER-TUSCANS are sold as IGT wines. **Best producers:** Cà del Vispo★, Le Calcinaie★, Casale-Falchini★, V Cesani★, La Lastra (Riserva★), Melini (Le Grillaie★), Montenidoli★, G Panizzi★, Il Paradiso★, Pietrafitta★, La Rampa di Fugnano★, Guicciardini Strozzi★, Teruzzi & Puthod (Terre di Tufi★★), Casa alle Vacche★, Vagnoni★.

VESUVIO DOC *Campania, Italy* Red wines based on Piedirosso and whites from Coda di Volpe and Verdeca. The evocative name Lacryma Christi del Vesuvio is now only for superior versions. **Best producers:** Cantine Caputo, Cantina Grotta del Sole, MASTROBERARDINO.

VESÚVIO, QUINTA DO★★ *Port DOC, Douro, Portugal* A consistently top performer that appears only when the high quality can be maintained (and not just in officially declared years). A fine PORT, best with at least 10 years' age, but I still think its greatest strength is as the backbone of top vintage blends. **Best years:** 2001 00 99 98 97 **96 95 94 92 91 90**.

VEUVE CLICQUOT *Champagne AC, Champagne, France* Produced by the LVMH luxury goods group, these CHAMPAGNES can still live up to the high standards set by the original Widow Clicquot at the beginning of the 19th century, although many are released too young. The non-vintage is full, toasty and satisfyingly weighty, or lean and raw, depending on your luck; the vintage★★ used to be reliably impressive, but recent releases have shown none of the traditional Clicquot class. The de luxe Grande Dame★★★, however, is both powerful and elegant. Grande Dame Rosé★★★ is exquisite. **Best years:** 1998 96 95 **93 91 90 89 88 85 82**.

VICTORIA *Australia* Despite its relatively small area, Victoria has arguably more land suited to quality grape-growing than any other state in Australia, with climates ranging from hot Murray Darling and Swan Hill on the Murray River to cool MORNINGTON PENINSULA and GIPPSLAND in the south. The range of flavours is similarly wide and exciting. With more than 460 wineries, Victoria leads the boutique winery boom, particularly in Mornington Peninsula. See also Beechworth, Bendigo, Central Victoria, Geelong, Grampians and Pyrenees, Heathcote, Rutherglen, Yarra Valley.

VIEUX-CHÂTEAU-CERTAN★★ *Pomerol AC, Bordeaux, France* Slow-developing, tannic red with up to 30% Cabernet Franc and 10% Cabernet Sauvignon in the blend, which after 15–20 years finally

resembles more a fragrant refined MEDOC than a hedonistic POMEROL.
Best years: 2002 01 00 **99 98 96 95 90 89 88 86 85 83 82**.

VIEUX TÉLÉGRAPHE *Châteauneuf-du-Pape AC, Rhône Valley, France*
The vines are some of the oldest in CHATEAUNEUF and the Grenache-
based red★★★ is among the best modern-style wines produced in the
RHONE VALLEY. There is also a small amount of white★★, which is rich
and heavenly when very young. Good second wine, Vieux Mas des
Papes. Also owns la Roquette★ in Châteauneuf and les Pallières★ in
GIGONDAS. Best years: (reds) 2004 03 01 00 **99 98 97 96 95 90 89 88**.

VILLA MARIA *Auckland and Marlborough, New Zealand* Founder George
Fistonich also owns Esk Valley and Vidal (both in HAWKES BAY). Villa
Maria Reserve Merlot-Cabernet★★★, Reserve Merlot★★, Esk Valley
The Terraces★★★ and Vidal Merlot-Cabernet★★ are superb. Reserve
Chardonnay from Vidal★★ and Villa Maria★★ are power-packed
wines. The Villa Maria Reserve range includes 2 outstanding
MARLBOROUGH Sauvignon Blancs: Wairau Valley★★ and even more
concentrated Clifford Bay★★. Also from Marlborough, impressive
Riesling★ and stunning botrytized Noble Riesling★★★. New Syrahs
are among New Zealand's best. Best years: (Hawkes Bay reds) **2002 00
99 98**.

CH. DE VILLENEUVE *Saumur-Champigny AC, Loire Valley, France*
During the 1990s this property emerged as one of the best in the
region. The secret lies in low yields, picked when properly ripe. First-
class SAUMUR-CHAMPIGNY★, with concentrated, mineral Vieilles
Vignes★★ and le Grand Clos★★. Also good white, stainless steel-
fermented SAUMUR★ and barrel-fermented Saumur Les Cormiers★★.
Best years: 2004 03 02 **01 00 97 96**.

VILLIERA *Stellenbosch WO, South Africa* The speciality is Cap Classique
sparklers; stand-outs are Monro Brut★, and the additive-free Brut
Natural Chardonnay. Sauvignon Blanc (Bush Vine★), a consistent
Riesling★ and 2 delicious Chenin Blancs with different degrees of
oaking illustrate winemaker Jeff Grier's versatility with whites. Reds
include new Monro★, a sleek, structured Merlot-led Bordeaux blend,
and Cellar Door Cape Blend★ combining Merlot and Pinotage.

VIN SANTO *Tuscany, Italy* The 'holy wine' of TUSCANY can be one of the
world's great sweet wines – but it has also been one of the most
wantonly abused wine terms in Italy (in particular avoid anything
called *liquoroso*). Made from grapes either hung from rafters or laid on
mats to dry, the resulting wines, fermented and aged in small barrels
(*caratelli*) for up to 7–8 years, should be nutty, oxidized, full of the
flavours of dried apricots and crystallized orange peel, concentrated
and long. Also produced in UMBRIA and TRENTINO as Vin Santo. Best
producers: Castello di AMA★, AVIGNONESI★★★, Fattoria di Basciano★,
Bindella★★, Cacchiano★, Capezzana★★, Fattoria del Cerro★★, Corzano
& Paterno★★, FONTODI★★, ISOLE E OLENA★★★, Romeo★★, San Felice★★,
San Gervasio★★, San Giusto a Rentennano★★★, SELVAPIANA★★, Villa
Sant'Anna★★, Villa di Vetrice★, VOLPAIA★.

VIÑAS DEL VERO *Somontano DO, Aragón, Spain* SOMONTANO's largest
company. A buttery but mineral unoaked Chardonnay and its toasty
barrel-fermented counterpart★ are joined by more original whites
such as Clarión★, a blend of Chardonnay, Gewürztraminer and
Macabeo. Flavours have unfortunately been lightening up recently,
but top reds – Gran Vos★ (Merlot-Cabernet-Pinot Noir) and the red
blend★★ made by its subsidiary Blecua – still deliver the goods.

VINHO VERDE DOC *Minho and Douro Litoral, Portugal* 'Vinho Verde' can be red *or* white – 'green' only in the sense of being young. The whites are the most widely seen outside Portugal and range from sulphured and acidic to aromatic, flowery and fruity. One or two that fall outside the DOC regulations are sold as Vinho Regional Minho. Best producers: Quinta de Alderiz, Quinta da Aveleda, Quinta da Baguinha★, Encostas dos Castelos, Quinta da Franqueira★, Moncão co-op (Deu la Deu Alvarinho★, Muralhas de Moncão), Muros de Melgaço (Alvarinho★), Quintas de Melgaço, Palácio de Brejoeira, Dom Salvador, Casa de Sezim★, Quinta da Soalheira★, SOGRAPE (Gazela, Quinta de Azevedo★), Quinta do Tamariz (Loureiro★).

VINO NOBILE DI MONTEPULCIANO DOCG *Tuscany, Italy* The 'noble wine' from the hills around the town of Montepulciano is made from the Sangiovese grape, known locally as Prugnolo, with the help of a little Canaiolo and Mammolo (and increasingly, today, Merlot and Cabernet). At its best, it combines the power and structure of BRUNELLO DI MONTALCINO with the finesse and complexity found in top CHIANTI. Unfortunately, the best was a rare beast until relatively recently; improvement in the 1990s has been impressive. The introduction of what is essentially a second wine, ROSSO DI MONTEPULCIANO, has certainly helped. Best producers: AVIGNONESI★★, Bindella★, BOSCARELLI★★, La Braccesca★★/ANTINORI, Le Casalte★, La Ciarliana★, Contucci★, Dei★★, Del Cerro★★, Fassati★★, Il Macchione★, Nottola★★, Palazzo Vecchio★, POLIZIANO★★, Redi★, Romeo★, Salcheto★★, Trerose★ (Angelini★★), Valdipiatta★. Best years: (2004) (03) 01 **00 99** 97 95 93 90 88.

VIOGNIER Traditionally grown only in the northern RHONE, and a poor yielder, prone to disease and difficult to vinify. The wine can be delicious: peachy, apricotty with a soft, almost waxy texture, usually a fragrance of spring flowers and sometimes a taste like crème fraîche. New, high-yielding clones are now found in LANGUEDOC-ROUSSILLON, Ardèche and the southern Rhône as well as in Switzerland, California, Argentina, Chile, Australia and South Africa, where it is used in blends as well as producing some fine varietal wines.

VIRÉ-CLESSÉ AC *Mâconnais, Burgundy, France* Appellation created in 1998 out of 2 of the best MACON-VILLAGES. Controversially, the rules have outlawed wines with residual sugar, thus excluding Jean Thévenet's extraordinary cuvées. Best producers: Bonhomme★★, Bret Bros★, Merlin★, Michel★★, Rijckaert★, Cave de Viré★, Ch. de Viré★. Best years: (2004) **03 02 00.**

VIRGINIA *USA* Thomas Jefferson failed miserably at growing grapes at his Monticello estate, but his modern-day successors have created a rapidly growing and improving wine industry. Virginia now has more than 80 wineries and 6 AVAs. Aromatic Viognier and earthy Cabernet Franc show most promise. Best producers: Barboursville★, Chrysalis, Horton★, Linden★, Valhalla★, Veritas, White Hall★.

VIVIANI *Valpolicella, Veneto, Italy* Claudio Viviani's 9ha (22-acre) site is turning out some beautifully balanced VALPOLICELLA. The top AMARONE, Casa dei Bepi★★★, is a model of enlightened modernity, and the Valpolicella Classico Superiore Campo Morar★★ and RECIOTO★★ are of a similar quality. Best years: (2004) (03) 01 **00 97** 96.

VOE/VIÑEDOS ORGÁNICOS EMILIANA *Colchagua, Chile* New venture from the Guilisasti family, also main shareholders in CONCHA Y TORO, with leading winemaker Alvaro Espinoza contributing his biodynamic and organic approach to viticulture. Adobe★ is good entry-level range, Novas★★ range is even better, and red 5-variety blend Coyam★★ is one of Chile's most interesting wines. Expect 'super Coyam' called Nazca out soon. Best years: 2003 **02 01**.

ROBERTO VOERZIO *Barolo DOCG, Piedmont, Italy* One of the best of the new wave of BAROLO producers. Dolcetto (Priavino★) is successful, as is Vignaserra★★ – barrique-aged Nebbiolo with a little Cabernet – and the outstanding BARBERA D'ALBA Riserva Vigneto Pozzo dell'Annunziata★★★. Barriques are also used for fashioning his Barolo, but such is the quality and concentration of fruit coming from densely planted vineyards that the oak does not overwhelm. Single-vineyard examples made in the best years are Brunate★★, Cerequio★★★, La Serra★★ and new Riserva Capalot★★★. Best years: (Barolo) (2004) (03) 01 00 **99 98 97** 96 **95 93 91** 90 89 88 85.

COMTE GEORGES DE VOGÜÉ *Chambolle-Musigny AC, Côte de Nuits, Burgundy, France* De Vogüé owns substantial holdings in 2 Grands Crus, BONNES-MARES★★★ and MUSIGNY★★★, as well as in Chambolle's top Premier Cru, les Amoureuses★★★. Since 1990 the domaine has been on magnificent form. It is the sole producer of minute quantities of Musigny Blanc★★, but because of recent replanting the wine is now being sold as (very expensive) BOURGOGNE Blanc. Best years: (Musigny) (2004) 03 02 01 00 99 98 97 96 93 **92 91 90**.

VOLNAY AC *Côte de Beaune, Burgundy, France* Some of the most elegant red wines of the CÔTE DE BEAUNE; attractive when young, the best examples can age well. The top Premiers Crus are Caillerets, Champans, Clos des Chênes, Santenots and Taillepieds. Best producers: R Ampeau★★, d'ANGERVILLE★★, H Boillot★, J-M Boillot★★, J-M Bouley★, Carré-Courbin★★, COCHE-DURY★★, V GIRARDIN★★, LAFARGE★★★, LAFON★★★, Dom. Matrot★★, MONTILLE★★★, N POTEL★★, J Prieur★★, Roblet-Monnot★, J Voillot★★. Best years: (2004) 03 02 99 98 **97** 96 **95 93 91 90**.

VOLPAIA, CASTELLO DI *Chianti Classico DOCG, Tuscany, Italy* Light, perfumed but refined CHIANTI CLASSICO★ (Riserva★★). Two stylish SUPER-TUSCANS, Balifico★★ and Coltassala★★, are both predominantly Sangiovese. Sometimes good but not great VIN SANTO★.

VOSNE-ROMANÉE AC *Côte de Nuits, Burgundy, France* The greatest village in the CÔTE DE NUITS, with 6 Grands Crus and 13 Premiers Crus (notably les Malconsorts, aux Brûlées and les Suchots) which are often as good as other villages' Grands Crus. The quality of Vosne's village wine is also high. In good years the wines need at least 6 years' aging, but 10–15 would be better. Best producers: R Arnoux★★★, Cacheux-Sirugue★★, Sylvain Cathiard★★★, B CLAIR★★, B Clavelier★★, R Engel★★, GRIVOT★★★, Anne GROS★★★, A-F GROS★★, M GROS★★★, Haegelen-Jayer★★, F Lamarche★★, Dom. LEROY★★★, MEO-CAMUZET★★★, Mugneret-Gibourg★★, RION★★, Dom. de la ROMANÉE-CONTI★★★, E Rouget★★★, THOMAS-MOILLARD★. Best years: (2004) 03 02 01 **00** 99 98 **97** 96 **95 93 91** 90.

VOUGEOT AC *Côte de Nuits, Burgundy, France*   Outside the walls of CLOS DE VOUGEOT there are 11ha (27 acres) of Premier Cru and 5ha (12 acres) of other vines. Look out for Premier Cru Les Cras (red) and the Clos Blanc de Vougeot, first planted with white grapes in 1110. Best producers: Bertagna★★, Chopin-Groffier★★, C Clerget★, VOUGERAIE★★. Best years: (reds) (2004) 03 02 01 00 99 98 **97** 96 **95 93** 90.

DOM. DE LA VOUGERAIE *Burgundy, France*   An estate created by Jean Claude BOISSET in 1999 out of the numerous vineyards – often excellent but under-achieving – which came with Burgundy merchant houses acquired during his inexorable rise to prominence since 1964. Under the stewardship of Pascal Marchand, the wines are generally outstanding, notably Clos Blanc de VOUGEOT★★★, GEVREY-CHAMBERTIN les Évocelles★★, le MUSIGNY★★★ and VOUGEOT les Cras★★ reds. Best years: (reds) (2004) 03 02 01 **00 99**.

CH. LA VOULTE-GASPARETS *Corbières AC, Languedoc, France* CORBIERES with flavours of thyme and baked earth from old hillside vines. Good basic Voulte-Gasparets and more expensive Cuvée Réservée★ and Romain Pauc★★. Can be drunk young, but ages well. Best years: (Romain Pauc) (2003) **01 00 98 96**.

VOUVRAY AC *Loire Valley, France*   Dry, medium-dry, sweet and sparkling wines from Chenin grapes east of Tours. The dry wines acquire beautifully rounded flavours after 6–8 years. Medium-dry wines, when well made from a single domaine, are worth aging for 20 years or more. Spectacular noble-rot-affected sweet wines can be produced when conditions are right. The fizz is some of the LOIRE's best. Best producers: Aubuisières★★, Bourillon-Dorléans★★, Champalou★, CLOS NAUDIN★★, la Fontainerie★★, Ch. Gaudrelle★★, Gautier★★, Haute Borne★, HUET★★, Pichot★★, F Pinon★★, Taille aux Loups★, Vigneau Chevreau★. Best years: 2004 03 **02 01** 99 97 96 95 93 90 89 88 85 83 78 75 70.

WACHAU *Niederösterreich, Austria*   This stunning 1390ha (3435-acre) stretch of the Danube is Austria's top region for dry whites, from Riesling and Grüner Veltliner. Best producers: F HIRTZBERGER★★★, Högl★★, KNOLL★★★, NIKOLAIHOF★★, F X PICHLER★★★, PRAGER★★★, Schmelz★★, Freie Weingärtner WACHAU★. Best years: (2004) 03 02 01 **00** 99 98 97 95 94 93 92 90 88.

WACHAU, FREIE WEINGÄRTNER *Wachau, Niederösterreich, Austria* Co-op long producing fine WACHAU white wines, especially vineyard-designated Grüner Veltliners and Rieslings★★. Now sells its top wines under the name Domäne Wachau. Its brilliant winemaker left in 2003, and quality has dipped – temporarily, one hopes. Best years: (2004) 03 02 01 **99 98** 97 96 95.

WACHENHEIM *Pfalz, Germany*   Wine village made famous by the BURKLIN-WOLF estate, its best vineyards can produce rich yet beautifully balanced Rieslings. Best producers: Josef BIFFAR★, BURKLIN-WOLF★★, Karl Schaefer★, J L WOLF★★. Best years: (2004) 03 02 01 **99 98** 97 96 94 90.

WAIHEKE ISLAND *North Island, New Zealand*   GOLDWATER pioneered wine-making on this island in Auckland harbour in the early 1980s, and this tiny region is now home to over 30 winemakers. Hot, dry ripening conditions have made high-quality Cabernet-based reds that sell for high prices. Chardonnay is now appearing, together with experimental plots of Syrah and Viognier. Best producers: Fenton★★, GOLDWATER★★, Obsidian, STONYRIDGE★★★, Te Whau★. Best years: (reds) (2004) **02 00** 99 98 96.

WALKER BAY WO *South Africa*   This maritime district on the south coast is home to a mix of grape varieties, but the holy grail of the majority is Pinot Noir, with the hub of activity in the Hemel en Aarde (heaven and earth) Valley. Steely Sauvignon Blanc, minerally Chardonnay and refined Pinotage increase the area's credentials. Best producers: BOUCHARD FINLAYSON★, Bartho Eksteen, HAMILTON RUSSELL★, Newton Johnson★. Best years: (Pinot Noir) (2004) **03 02 01 00 99 98 97**.

WALLA WALLA VALLEY AVA *Washington State, USA*   Walla Walla has 63 of WASHINGTON's wineries, but 35 have only been producing wine since 1999. Similarly, vineyard acreage, although only 4% of the state total, has trebled since 1999 – and is still growing. If you think there's a gold-rush feel about this clearly exciting area you wouldn't be far wrong. Best producers: CANOE RIDGE, CAYUSE VINEYARDS★★, Dunham Cellars★, L'ECOLE NO 41★★, LEONETTI CELLAR★★★, Pepper Bridge Winery★, WOODWARD CANYON★★.

WARRE *Port DOC, Douro, Portugal*   Part of the Symington group, with top-quality Vintage PORT★★★ and a good 'off-vintage' port from Quinta da Cavadinha★★. LBV★★ is a very welcome traditional, unfiltered port. Warrior★ is a reliable ruby. Otima, a 10-year-old tawny, is improving. Best years: (Vintage) 2000 97 94 **91 85 83 80 77 70 66 63**; (Cavadinha) 2001 99 98 **95 92 90 88 87 86 82 78**.

WARWICK *Stellenbosch WO, South Africa*   Situated in the heart of prime red wine country, Warwick produces the complex Trilogy★ BORDEAUX-style blend and a refined, fragrant Cabernet Franc★. Old Bush Vine Pinotage is less consistent but, at best, is plummy and perfumed; Pinotage also plays a role in the Three Cape Ladies★ red blend, with Cabernet Sauvignon and Merlot. Whites are represented by an unwooded Sauvignon Blanc and full-bodied, lightly oaked Chardonnay★. Best years: (Trilogy) 2003 **02 01 00 99 98 97 96 95**.

WASHINGTON STATE *USA*   Second-largest premium wine-producing state in the US. The chief growing areas are in irrigated high desert, east of the Cascade Mountains, where the COLUMBIA VALLEY AVA encompasses the smaller AVAs of YAKIMA VALLEY, WALLA WALLA VALLEY and Red Mountain. Although the heat is not as intense as in CALIFORNIA, long summer days with extra hours of sunshine due to the northern latitude seem to increase the intensity of fruit flavours and result in both red and white wines of great depth. Cabernet, Merlot, Syrah, Chardonnay, Sauvignon Blanc and Semillon produce very good wines here.

GEOFF WEAVER *Adelaide Hills, South Australia*   Low-yielding vines at Geoff Weaver's Lenswood vineyard produce top-quality fruit, from which he crafts limy Riesling★★, crisply gooseberryish Sauvignon★★ and stylish cool-climate Chardonnay★★. Pinot Noir is promising.

WEGELER *Bernkastel, Mosel; Oestrich-Winkel, Rheingau; Deidesheim, Pfalz, Germany*   The Wegeler family's 3 estates are dedicated primarily to Riesling, and today dry wines make up the bulk of production. Whether dry or naturally sweet Auslese, the best merit ★★ and will develop well with 5 or more years of aging. The MOSEL estate achieves the highest standard; all the wines are at least ★. Best years: (Mosel-Saar-Ruwer) (2004) 03 02 01 **99 98 97 96 95 93 90 89**.

WEHLEN *Mosel, Germany*   Village whose steep Sonnenuhr vineyard produces some of the most intense Rieslings in Germany. Best producers: Kerpen, Dr LOOSEN★★★, J J PRUM★★★, S A PRUM★, Max Ferd

RICHTER★★, SELBACH-OSTER★★, WEGELER★, Dr Weins-Prüm★. Best years: (2004) 03 02 01 **99 98 97 95 94 93 90 89 88**.

ROBERT WEIL *Kiedrich, Rheingau, Germany* This estate has enjoyed huge investment from Japanese drinks giant SUNTORY which, coupled with Wilhelm Weil's devotion to quality, has returned it to the RHEINGAU's premier division. Majestic sweet Auslese, Beerenauslese and Trockenbeerenauslese Rieslings★★★, and dry Rieslings★ are crisp and elegant, although the regular wines have been a little disappointing in recent vintages. Best years: (2004) 03 02 01 **99 98 96 95 94 93 90**.

WEINBACH *Alsace AC, Alsace, France* This Kaysersberg estate is run by Colette Faller and her two daughters. The range is quite complicated. The lightest wines are named in honour of Mme Faller's late husband Théo★★. Ste-Cathérine★★ bottlings come from the Schlossberg and are late picked, though not technically Vendange Tardive; Laurence wines are from the non-cru Altenbourg. Superior bottlings in both ranges include the vineyard name, and the top dry wine is the special selection Ste-Cathérine Riesling Grand Cru Schlossberg L'Inédit★★★. Quintessence – a super-concentrated Sélection de Grains Nobles from Pinot Gris★★ or Gewurztraminer★★★ – is not produced every year. All the wines are exceptionally balanced and, while delightful on release, can age for many years. Best years: (Grand Cru Riesling) 2004 03 02 01 00 **99 98 97 96 95 94 93 92 90 89**. See also Alsace Vendange Tardive.

WEINERT *Mendoza, Argentina* Buying grapes from some of the oldest vineyards in LUJÁN DE CUYO, Weinert has built a reputation for Malbec. Its oxidative approach to winemaking creates complex, long-lived reds such as mocha and black cherry Gran Vino★★. Estrella (Star) Malbec★★ is an eccentric red released decades after the vintage.

WEISSBURGUNDER See Pinot Blanc.

WELSCHRIESLING See Riesling Italico.

WENDOUREE *Clare Valley, South Australia* Small winery using old-fashioned methods to make enormous, ageworthy reds★★★ from paltry yields off their own very old Shiraz, Cabernet, Malbec and Mataro (Mourvèdre) vines, plus tiny amounts of sweet Muscat★. Reds can, and do, age beautifully for 30 years or more. Best years: (reds) (2004) 03 02 01 99 98 96 **95 94 92 91 90 86 83 82 81 80 78 76 75**.

WESTERN AUSTRALIA Only the south-west corner of this vast state is suited to vines, the SWAN DISTRICT and Perth environs being the oldest and hottest area, with present attention (and more than 230 producers) focused on GREAT SOUTHERN, MARGARET RIVER, Geographe and PEMBERTON. The state produces just over 4% of Australia's grape crush but about 20% of its premium wines.

WIEN *Austria* Region within the city limits of Wien (Vienna). The best wines come from south-facing sites in Grinzing, Nussdorf and Weiden; and the Bisamberg hill east of the Danube. Best producers: Christ, Edlmoser, Mayer, Schilling, WIENINGER★★, Zahel. Best years: (2004) 03 **01 00 99**. See also Heuriger.

WIENINGER *Stammersdorf, Wien, Austria* Fritz Wieninger has risen above the parochial standards of many Viennese growers to offer a range of elegant, well-crafted wines from Chardonnay and Pinot Noir. The best range is often the Select★★, the pricier Grand Select★ being often over-oaked. Recent additions are brilliant white wines from the renowned Nussberg★★ vineyard. Best years: (2004) 03 01 **00 99 97**.

WILLAMETTE VALLEY AVA *Oregon, USA* This viticultural area is typical of OREGON's maritime climate. Wet winters, generally dry summers, and a so-so chance of long, cool autumn days provide sound growing conditions for cool-climate varieties such as Pinot Noir, Pinot Gris and Chardonnay. Dundee Hills, with its volcanic hillsides, is considered the best sub-region. Best producers: ADELSHEIM★, ARCHERY SUMMIT★, ARGYLE★, BEAUX FRERES★★, Cameron★, CRISTOM★, DOMAINE DROUHIN★, DOMAINE SERENE★★, ELK COVE★★, KING ESTATE, Rex Hill★, Torii Mor★, WillaKenzie★, Ken WRIGHT★. Best years: (reds) (2004) 03 02 **01 00 99 98**.

WILLIAMS SELYEM *Russian River Valley AVA, California, USA* Purchased in 1998 by John Dyson, a vineyard owner from New York; in recent years it looks as if the cult following for the Pinot Noirs★★, especially the J Rochioli Vineyard★★, has diminished somewhat. The wine has become relatively lighter in weight, sometimes very fruity and sometimes just a bit off the wall. Best years: (Pinot Noir) (2002) **01 00 99 98 97 96 95 94**.

WINKEL *Rheingau, Germany* RHEINGAU village whose best vineyard is the large Hasensprung but the most famous one is Schloss Vollrads – an ancient estate that does not use the village name on its label. Best producers: August Eser, Johannishof★★, SCHLOSS VOLLRADS★ (since 1999), WEGELER★. Best years: (2004) 03 02 01 **99 98 96 90**.

WINNINGEN *Mosel, Germany* A small group of dedicated growers have shown that the steep slopes of this little-known village, particularly the Ühlen and Röttgen sites, can produce excellent Rieslings, especially in a rich dry style, plus occasional TBAs. Best producers: Von Heddesdorf, HEYMANN-LOWENSTEIN★★, Reinhard Knebel★★. Best years: (2004) 03 02 01 **99 97 96**.

WIRRA WIRRA *McLaren Vale, South Australia* Consistent maker of whites with more finesse than is customary in the region; now reds are as good, too. Recent years have seen rapid expansion. Well-balanced Sauvignon Blanc★, ageworthy Semillon blend★, buttery Chardonnay★★ and soft reds led by delicious The Angelus Cabernet★★, chocolaty RSW Shiraz★★, decadent Original Blend Grenache-Shiraz★, and seductive Allawah BAROSSA Grenache★★. Best years: (The Angelus) 2003 02 01 00 99 98 **97 96 95 92 91 90**.

WITHER HILLS *Marlborough, South Island, New Zealand* This quality-focused winery was bought in 2002 by New Zealand brewing group Lion Nathan; talented founder/winemaker Brent Marris stays at least until 2005. A trio of stylish MARLBOROUGH wines – concentrated, pungent Sauvignon Blanc★★, fine, fruit-focused Chardonnay★★ and vibrant Pinot Noir★★ – allows Wither Hills to concentrate only on wines that perform with distinction in this region. Expect little change, at least while Marris remains at the helm. Best years: (Sauvignon Blanc) (2005) **03 01 00**.

J L WOLF *Wachenheim, Pfalz, Germany* Ernst Loosen, of Dr LOOSEN, took over this underperforming estate in 1996. A string of concentrated, mostly dry Rieslings★★ have won it a place among the region's top producers. Best years: (2004) 03 02 01 **00 99 98**.

WOODWARD CANYON *Walla Walla Valley AVA, Washington State, USA* Big, barrel-fermented Chardonnays (Celilo Vineyard★) were the trademark wines for many years, but today the focus is on reds, with a fine Artist Series★ Cabernet Sauvignon and Old Vines★★ (formerly Dedication) Cabernet Sauvignon leading the line-up. Merlot can be velvety and deeply perfumed. White and red★ BORDEAUX-style blends are labelled Charbonneau, the name of the vineyard where the fruit is grown. Best years: (Cabernet Sauvignon) (2003) 02 01 **00 99 98**.

KEN WRIGHT CELLARS *Willamette Valley AVA, Oregon, USA* Ken Wright produces more than a dozen succulent, single-vineyard Pinot Noirs. Bold and rich with new oak flavour, they range from good to ethereal, led by the Carter★★★, Savoya★★★, Shea★★, Guadalupe★★ and McCrone★★. Fine WASHINGTON Chardonnay from the Celilo Vineyard★★, expressive French clone OREGON Chardonnays from Carabella★ and McCrone★ and a zesty Pinot Blanc from Freedom Hill Vineyard★ make up the portfolio of whites. Best years: (Pinot Noir) (2004) 03 02 **01 00 99 98**.

WÜRTTEMBERG *Germany* 11,250ha (27,800-acre) region centred on the river Neckar. Two-thirds of the wine made is red, and the best comes from Lemberger (Blaufränkisch) or Spätburgunder (Pinot Noir) grapes. Massive yields are often responsible for pallid wines, especially from the locally popular Trollinger grape. However, a few of the many marvellously steep sites are now producing perfumed reds and racy Riesling. Best years: (reds) (2004) 03 02 01 **99 97 93**.

WÜRZBURG *Franken, Germany* The centre of FRANKEN wines. Some Rieslings can be great, but the real star is Silvaner. Best producers: Bürgerspital, JULIUSSPITAL★★, Staatlicher Hofkeller, Weingut am Stein★. Best years: (2004) 03 02 01 **00 99 97 94 93**.

WYNNS *Coonawarra, South Australia* Wynns' name is synonymous with COONAWARRA. It is now part of the giant Southcorp, but its personality seems to have suffered less than most of Southcorp's other brands and, except at the top end, prices remain fair. Attractive Chardonnay★ and delightful Riesling★. However, Wynns is best known for reds. The Shiraz★ and Black Label Cabernet Sauvignon★★ are both good. Top-end John Riddoch Cabernet Sauvignon★★ and Michael Shiraz★★ are deep, ripe, oaky styles, but less thrilling than they used to be. Best years: (John Riddoch) (2003) 99 96 **94 91 90 88 86 82**.

YAKIMA VALLEY AVA *Washington State, USA* This important valley lies within the much larger COLUMBIA VALLEY AVA. Yakima is planted mostly to Chardonnay, Merlot and Cabernet Sauvignon and has more than 40 wineries. Best producers: Chinook★, DELILLE CELLARS★, HEDGES CELLARS★, Hogue Cellars, Wineglass Cellars★.

YALUMBA *Barossa Valley, South Australia* Distinguished old firm, owned by the Hill-Smith family, making a wide range of wines under its own name, as well as Heggies Vineyard (restrained Riesling★, plump Merlot★★, opulent Viognier★ and botrytis Riesling★★), Hill-Smith Estate (Sauvignon Blanc★) and Pewsey Vale (fine Riesling★★ and Cabernet Sauvignon★). Flagship reds are The Signature Cabernet-Shiraz★★, Octavius Shiraz★★ and The Menzies Cabernet★★ and all cellar well. New premiums include Old Vine Grenache★★, Contour Riesling★★, Virgilius Viognier★★ and Shiraz-Viognier★. High quality quaffers like Y Series varietals★ (sometimes ★★) and Oxford Landing Chardonnay, Sauvignon★ and Cabernet-Shiraz are consistently impressive. Angas Brut remains big-volume enjoyable fizz, while TASMANIA's Jansz★ (Vintage★★) has added a class act to the flight. Museum Release fortifieds (Muscat★★) are excellent, but rare. Best years: (The Signature red) (2003) 02 01 00 99 98 **97 96 95 93 92 91 90 88**.

YARRA VALLEY *Victoria, Australia* With its cool climate, the Yarra is asking to be judged as Australia's best Pinot Noir region. Exciting also for Chardonnay and Cabernet-Merlot blends and as a supplier of base wine for fizz. Best producers: Arthur's Creek★, COLDSTREAM HILLS★★, DE BORTOLI★★, Diamond Valley★★, DOMAINE CHANDON/Green Point★, Métier, MOUNT MARY★★, St Huberts, Seville Estate★, TARRAWARRA★★, Yarra Burn★, Yarra Ridge, Yarra Yering★★, Yeringberg★, Yering Station★★.

CH. D'YQUEM★★★ *Sauternes AC, 1er Cru Supérieur, Bordeaux, France* Often rated the most sublime sweet wine in the world, Yquem's total commitment to quality is unquestionable. Despite a large vineyard (100ha/250 acres), production is tiny. Only fully noble-rotted grapes are picked, often berry by berry, and low yield means each vine produces only a glass of wine! This precious liquid is then fermented in new oak barrels and left to mature for 3½ years before bottling. It is one of the world's most expensive wines, in constant demand because of its richness and exotic flavours. A dry white, Ygrec, is made in some years. In 1999 LVMH won a 3-year takeover battle with the Lur-Saluces family, owners for 406 years. Best years: 2001 00 99 98 97 **96 95 94 93 91 90 89 88 86 83 82 81 80 79 76 75 71 70 67 62.**

ZILLIKEN *Saarburg, Mosel-Saar-Ruwer, Germany* Estate specializing in Rieslings★★ (Auslese, Eiswein often ★★★) from the Saarburger Rausch vineyard. Best years: (2004) 03 02 01 99 **97 95 94 93 90 89 88.**

ZIND-HUMBRECHT *Alsace AC, Alsace, France* Olivier Humbrecht is one of France's outstanding winemakers, with an approach that emphasizes the individuality of each site and each vintage. The family owns vines in 4 Grand Cru sites – Rangen, Goldert, Hengst and Brand – and these wines (Riesling★★, Gewurztraminer★★★, Pinot Gris★★ and Muscat★★) are excellent, as is a range of wines from specific vineyards and *lieux dits*, such as Gewurztraminer or Riesling Clos Windsbuhl★★★ and Pinot Gris Clos Windsbuhl or Clos Jebsal★★. ALSACE VENDANGE TARDIVE wines are almost invariably of ★★★ quality. Even basic Sylvaners★ and Pinot Blancs★★ are fine. Wines often have some residual sugar. Best years: (Clos Windsbuhl Gewurztraminer) (2003) 02 **01 00 99 98 97 96 95 94.**

ZINFANDEL CALIFORNIA's versatile red grape can make big, juicy, fruit-packed wine – or insipid, sweetish 'blush' or even late-harvest dessert wine. Some Zinfandel is now made in other countries, with notable examples in Australia and South Africa. Best producers: (California) Brown★★, Cline Cellars★★, Dashe★★, DRY CREEK VINEYARD★, FETZER★, Gary Farrell★★, MARIAH★, Martinelli★★, Nalle★★, Preston★, Rafanelli★★, RAVENSWOOD★, RIDGE★★★, Rosenblum★★, Saddleback★★, St Francis★★, SEGHESIO★★, Trinitas★★, TURLEY★★; (Australia) CAPE MENTELLE★★, Kangarilla Road, Nepenthe★★. See also Primitivo di Manduria.

FAMILIA ZUCCARDI *Mendoza, Argentina* One of Argentina's great success stories. Dynamic owner José Zuccardi saw the potential for export before his compatriots and set about creating a range of utterly enjoyable easy-drinking wines. Basic Santa Julia reds★ are very successful. Santa Julia Reserves and Familia Zuccardi 'Q'★ wines have improved dramatically since a new barrel-aging facility was installed.

GLOSSARY OF WINE TERMS

AC/AOC (APPELLA-TION D'ORIGINE CONTRÔLÉE) The top category of French wines, defined by regulations covering vineyard yields, grape varieties, geographical boundaries, alcohol content and production method. Guarantees origin and style of a wine, but not its quality.

ACID/ACIDITY Naturally present in grapes and essential to wine, providing balance and stability and giving the refreshing tang in white wines and the appetizing grip in reds.

ADEGA Portuguese for winery.

AGING An alternative term for maturation.

ALCOHOLIC CONTENT The alcoholic strength of wine, expressed as a percentage of the total volume of the wine. Typically in the range of 7–15%.

ALCOHOLIC FERMENTATION The process whereby yeasts, natural or added, convert the grape sugars into alcohol (Ethyl alcohol, or Ethanol) and carbon dioxide.

AMONTILLADO Traditionally dry style of sherry. *See* Jerez y Manzanilla in main A–Z.

ANBAUGEBIET German for growing region; these names will appear on labels of all QbA and QmP wines. There are 13 *Anbaugebiete*: Ahr, Baden, Franken, Hessische Bergstrasse, Mittelrhein, Mosel-Saar-Ruwer, Nahe, Pfalz, Rheingau, Rheinhessen, Saale-Unstrut, Sachsen and Württemberg.

AUSBRUCH Austrian Prädikat category used for sweet wines.

AUSLESE German and Austrian Prädikat cat-egory meaning that the grapes were 'selected' for their higher ripeness.

AVA (AMERICAN VITICULTURAL AREA) System of appellations of origin for US wines.

AZIENDA AGRICOLA Italian for estate or farm. It also indicates wine made from grapes grown by the proprietor.

BARREL AGING Time spent maturing in wood, usually oak, during which the wines take on flavours from the wood.

BARREL FERMENTA-TION Oak barrels may be used for fermentation instead of stainless steel to give a rich, oaky flavour to the wine.

BARRIQUE The *barrique bordelaise* is the traditional Bordeaux oak barrel of 225 litres (50 gallons) capacity.

BAUMÉ A scale measuring must weight (the amount of sugar in grape juice) to estimate potential alcohol content.

BEERENAUSLESE German and Austrian Prädikat category applied to wines made from 'individually selected' berries (i.e. grapes) affected by noble rot (*Edelfäule* in German). The wines are rich and sweet.

Beerenauslese wines are only produced in the best years in Germany, but in Austria they are a regular occurrence.

BEREICH German for region or district within a wine region or *Anbaugebiet*. Bereichs tend to be large, and the use of a Bereich name, such as Bereich Bingen, without qualification is seldom an indication of quality – in most cases, quite the reverse.

BIODYNAMIC VITI-CULTURE This approach works with the movement of the planets and cosmic forces to achieve health and balance in the soil and in the vine. Vines are treated with infusions of mineral, animal and plant materials, applied in homeopathic quantities.

BLANC DE BLANCS White wine made from one or more white grape varieties. Used especially for sparkling wines; in Champagne, denotes wine made entirely from the Chardonnay grape.

BLANC DE NOIRS White wine made from black grapes only – the juice is separated from

BOTTLE SIZES

CHAMPAGNE

Magnum	1.5 litres	2 bottles
Jeroboam	3 litres	4 bottles
Rehoboam	4.5 litres	6 bottles
Methuselah	6 litres	8 bottles
Salmanazar	9 litres	12 bottles
Balthazar	12 litres	16 bottles
Nebuchadnezzar	15 litres	20 bottles

BORDEAUX

Magnum	1.5 litres	2 bottles
Marie-Jeanne	2.25 litres	3 bottles
Double-magnum	3 litres	4 bottles
Jeroboam	4.5 litres	6 bottles
Imperial	6 litres	8 bottles

the skins to avoid extracting any colour. Most often seen in Champagne, where it describes wine made from Pinot Noir and/or Pinot Meunier.

BLENDING (assemblage) The art of mixing together wines of different origin, styles or age, often to balance out acidity, weight etc.

BODEGA Spanish for winery.

BOTRYTIS See noble rot.

BRUT French term for dry sparkling wines, especially Champagne.

CARBONIC MACERATION Winemaking method used to produce fresh fruity reds for drinking young. Whole (uncrushed) bunches of grapes are fermented in closed containers – a process that extracts lots of fruit and colour, but little tannin.

CAVE CO-OPÉRATIVE French for co-operative cellar, where members bring their grapes for vinification and bottling under a collective label. In terms of quantity, the French wine industry is dominated by co-ops. Often use less workaday titles, such as Caves des Vignerons, Producteurs Réunis, Union des Producteurs or Cellier des Vignerons.

CHAMPAGNE METHOD Traditional method used for all of the world's finest sparkling wines. A second fermentation takes place in the bottle, producing carbon dioxide which, kept in solution under pressure, gives the wine its fizz.

CHAPTALIZATION Legal addition of sugar during fermentation to raise a wine's alcoholic strength. More necessary in cool climates

where lack of sun produces insufficient natural sugar in the grape.

CHARTA A German organization founded to protect the image of the best Rheingau Rieslings in 1984, recognizable by a double-window motif on the bottle or label. The accent is on dry wines that go with food. Now merged with VDP to form VDP-Rheingau, but the Charta symbol remains in use.

CHÂTEAU French for castle, used to describe a variety of wine estates.

CHIARETTO Italian for a rosé wine of very light pink colour.

CLARET English for red Bordeaux wines, from the French *clairet*, which was traditionally used to describe a lighter style of red Bordeaux.

CLARIFICATION Term covering any winemaking process (such as filtering or fining) that involves the removal of solid matter either from the must or the wine.

CLONE Strain of grape species. The term is usually taken to mean laboratory-produced, virus-free clones, selected to produce higher or lower quantity, or selected for resistance to frost or disease.

CLOS French for a walled vineyard – as in Burgundy's Clos de Vougeot – also commonly incorporated into the names of estates (e.g. Clos des Papes), regardless of whether they are walled or not.

COLD FERMENTATION Long, slow fermentation at low temperature to extract maximum freshness from the grapes.

COLHEITA Aged tawny port from a single vintage.

See Port in main A–Z.

COMMUNE A French village and its surrounding area or parish.

CORKED/CORKY Wine fault derived from a cork which has become contaminated, usually with Trichloroanisole or TCA, and nothing to do with pieces of cork in the wine. The mouldy, stale smell is unmistakable.

COSECHA Spanish for vintage.

CÔTE French word for a slope or hillside, which is where many, but not all, of the country's best vineyards are to be found.

CRÉMANT French term for traditional-method sparkling wine from Alsace, Bordeaux, Burgundy, Die, Jura, Limoux, Loire and Luxembourg.

CRIANZA Spanish term for the youngest official category of oak-matured wine. A red Crianza wine must have had at least 2 years' aging (1 in oak, 1 in bottle) before sale; a white or rosé, 1 year.

CRU French for growth, meaning a specific plot of land or particular estate. In Burgundy, growths are divided into Grands (great) and Premiers (first) Crus, and apply solely to the actual land. In Champagne the same terms are used for whole villages. In Bordeaux there are various hierarchical levels of Cru referring to estates rather than their vineyards.

CRU BOURGEOIS French term for wines from the Médoc that are ranked immediately below the Crus Classés. Many are excellent value for money.

CRU CLASSÉ The Classed Growths are the aristocracy of Bordeaux, ennobled by the Classifications of 1855 (for the Médoc, Barsac and Sauternes), 1955, 1969, 1986 and 1996 (for St-Émilion) and 1947, 1953 and 1959 (for Graves). Curiously, Pomerol has never been classified. The modern classifications are more reliable than the 1855 version, which was based solely on the price of the wines at the time of the Great Exhibition in Paris, but in terms of prestige the 1855 Classification remains the most important. With the exception of a single alteration in 1973, when Ch. Mouton-Rothschild was elevated to First Growth status, the list has not changed since 1855. It certainly needs revising.

CUVE CLOSE A bulk process used to produce inexpensive sparkling wines. The second fermentation, which produces the bubbles, takes place in tank rather than in the bottle.

CUVÉE French for the contents of a single vat or tank, but usually indicates a wine blended from either different grape varieties or the best barrels of wine.

DÉGORGEMENT Stage in the production of Champagne-method wines when the sediment, collected in the neck of the bottle during *remuage*, is removed.

DEMI-SEC French for medium-dry.

DO (DENOMINACIÓN DE ORIGEN) Spain's equivalent of the French AC quality category, regulating origin and production methods.

DOC (DENOMINAÇÃO DE ORIGEM CONTROLADA) The top regional classification for Portuguese wines.

DOCa (DENOMINACIÓN DE ORIGEN CALIFICADA) Spanish quality wine category, intended to be one step up from DO. So far only Rioja and Priorat qualify.

DOC (DENOMINAZIONE DI ORIGINE CONTROLLATA) Italian quality wine category, regulating origin, grape varieties, yield and production methods.

DOCG (DENOMINAZIONE DI ORIGINE CONTROLLATA E GARANTITA) The top tier of the Italian classification system.

DOSAGE A sugar and wine mixture added to sparkling wine after *dégorgement* which affects how sweet or dry it will be.

EDELZWICKER Blended wine from Alsace in France, usually bland.

EINZELLAGE German for an individual vineyard site which is generally farmed by several growers. The name is preceded on the label by that of the village; for example, the Wehlener Sonnenuhr is the Sonnenuhr vineyard in Wehlen. The mention of a particular site should signify a superior wine. Sadly, this is not necessarily so.

EISWEIN Rare, chiefly German and Austrian, late-harvested wine made by picking the grapes and pressing them while frozen. This concentrates the sweetness of the grape as most of the liquid is removed as ice. *See also* Icewine.

ESCOLHA Portuguese for selection.

FILTERING Removal of yeasts, solids and any impurities from a wine before bottling.

FINING Method of clarifying wine by adding a coagulant (e.g. egg whites, isinglass or bentonite) to remove soluble particles such as proteins and excessive tannins.

FINO The lightest, freshest style of sherry. *See* Jerez y Manzanilla in main A–Z.

FLOR A film of yeast which forms on the top of fino sherries (and some other wines), preventing oxidation and imparting a unique tangy, dry flavour.

FLYING WINEMAKER Term coined in the late 1980s to describe enologists, many Australian-trained, brought in to improve the quality of wines in many underperforming wine regions.

FORTIFIED WINE Wine which has high-alcohol grape spirit added, usually before the initial fermentation is completed, thereby preserving sweetness.

FRIZZANTE Italian for semi-sparkling wine, usually made dry, but sometimes sweet.

GARAGE WINE *See* vin de garage.

GARRAFEIRA Portuguese term for wine from an outstanding vintage, with 0.5% more alcohol than the minimum required, and 2 years' aging in vat or barrel followed by 1 year in bottle for reds, and 6 months of each for whites. Also used by merchants for their best blended and aged wines. Use of the term is in decline as producers opt for the more readily recognized Reserva as an alternative on the label.

GRAN RESERVA Top category of Spanish wines from a top vintage, with at least 5 years' aging (2 of them in cask) for reds and 4 for whites.

GRAND CRU French for great growth.

Supposedly the best vineyard sites in Alsace, Burgundy, Champagne and parts of Bordeaux and should produce the most exciting wines.

GRANDES MARQUES Great brands – the Syndicat des Grandes Marques was once Champagne's self-appointed élite. It disbanded in 1997.

GROSSLAGE German term for a grouping of vineyards. Some are not too big, and have the advantage of allowing small amounts of higher QmP wines to be made from the grapes from several vineyards. But sometimes the use of vast Grosslage names (e.g. Niersteiner Gutes Domtal) deceives consumers into believing they are buying something special.

HALBTROCKEN German for medium dry. In Germany and Austria medium-dry wine has 9–18g per litre of residual sugar, though sparkling wine is allowed up to 50g per litre. But the high acid levels in German wines can make them seem rather dry and lean.

ICEWINE A speciality of Canada, produced from juice squeezed from ripe grapes that have frozen on the vine. *See also* Eiswein.

IGT (INDICAZIONE GEOGRAFICA TIPICA) The Italian equivalent of the French vin de pays. As in the Midi, both premium and everyday wines may share the same appellation. Many of the Super-Tuscan vini da tavola are now sold under a regional IGT.

IPR (INDICAÇÃO DE PROVENIÊNCIA REGULAMENTADA) The second tier in the Portuguese wine classification regulations, covering grape varieties,

yields and aging requirements.

KABINETT Term used for the lowest level of QmP wines in Germany.

LANDWEIN German or Austrian country wine; the equivalent of French vin de pays. The wine must have a territorial definition and may be chaptalized to give it more alcohol.

LATE HARVEST *See* Vendange Tardive.

LAYING DOWN The storing of wine which will improve with age.

LEES Sediment – dead yeast cells, grape pips (seeds), pulp and tartrates – thrown by wine during fermentation and left behind after racking. Some wines are left on the fine lees for as long as possible to take on extra flavour.

MALOLACTIC FERMENTATION Secondary fermentation whereby harsh malic acid is converted into mild lactic acid and carbon dioxide. Normal in red wines but often prevented in whites to preserve a fresh, fruity taste.

MANZANILLA The tangiest style of sherry, similar to fino. *See* Jerez y Manzanilla in main A–Z.

MATURATION Positive term for the beneficial aging of wine.

MERITAGE American term for red or white wines made from a blend of Bordeaux grape varieties.

MESOCLIMATE The climate of a specific geographical area, be it a vineyard or simply a hillside or valley.

MOELLEUX French for soft or mellow, used to describe sweet or medium-sweet wines.

MOUSSEUX French for sparkling wine.

MUST The mixture of grape juice, skins, pips and pulp produced after crushing (but prior to completion of fermentation), which will eventually become wine.

MUST WEIGHT An indicator of the sugar content of juice – and therefore the ripeness of grapes.

NÉGOCIANT French term for a merchant who buys and sells wine. A négociant-éléveur is a merchant who buys, makes, ages and sells wine.

NEW WORLD When used as a geographical term, New World includes the Americas, South Africa, Australia and New Zealand. By extension, it is also a term used to describe the clean, fruity, upfront style now in evidence all over the world, but pioneered in the USA and Australia.

NOBLE ROT (*Botrytis cinerea*) Fungus which, when it attacks ripe white grapes, shrivels the fruit and intensifies their sugar while adding a distinctive flavour. A vital factor in creating many of the world's finest sweet wines, such as Sauternes and Trockenbeerenauslese.

OAK The wood used almost exclusively to make barrels for fermenting and aging fine wines.

OECHSLE German scale measuring must weight (sugar content).

OLOROSO The darkest, most heavily fortified style of sherry. *See* Jerez y Manzanilla in main A–Z.

OXIDATION Overexposure of wine to air, causing loss of fruit and flavour. Slight oxidation, such as occurs through the wood of a barrel or during racking, is part of the aging process and, in wines of sufficient structure, enhances flavour and complexity.

PASSITO Italian term for wine made from dried grapes. The result is usually a sweet wine with a raisiny intensity of fruit. *See also* Moscato Passito di Pantelleria, Recioto di Soave, Recioto della Valpolicella and Vin Santo in main A–Z.

PERLWEIN German for a lightly sparkling wine.

PÉTILLANT French for a slightly sparkling wine.

PHYLLOXERA The vine aphid *Phylloxera vastatrix* attacks vine roots. It devastated European and consequently other vineyards around the world in the late 1800s soon after it arrived from America. Since then, the vulnerable *Vitis vinifera* has generally been grafted on to vinously inferior, but phylloxera-resistant, American rootstocks.

PRÄDIKAT Grades defining quality wines in Germany and Austria. These are (in ascending order) Kabinett (not considered as Prädikat in Austria), Spätlese, Auslese, Beerenauslese, the Austrian-only category Ausbruch, and Trockenbeerenauslese. Strohwein and Eiswein are also Prädikat wines. Some Spätleses and even a few Ausleses are now made as dry wines.

PREMIER CRU First Growth; the top quality classification in parts of Bordeaux, but second to Grand Cru in Burgundy. Used in Champagne to designate vineyards just below Grand Cru.

PRIMEUR French term for a young wine, often released for sale within a few weeks of the harvest. Beaujolais Nouveau is the best-known example.

QbA (QUALITÄTSWEIN BESTIMMTER ANBAUGEBIETE) German for quality wine from designated regions. Sugar can be added to increase the alcohol content. Usually pretty ordinary, but from top estates this category offers excellent value for money. In Austria *Qualitätswein* is equivalent to the German QbA.

QmP (QUALITÄTSWEIN MIT PRÄDIKAT) German for quality wine with distinction. A higher category than QbA, with controlled yields and no sugar addition. QmP covers 6 levels based on the ripeness of the grapes: *see* Prädikat.

QUINTA Portuguese for farm or estate.

RACKING Gradual clarification of a quality wine; the wine is transferred from one barrel or container to another, leaving the lees behind.

RANCIO A fortified wine deliberately exposed to the effects of oxidation, found mainly in Languedoc-Roussillon, Cataluña and southern Spain.

REMUAGE Process in Champagne-making whereby the bottles, stored on their sides and at a progressively steeper angle in *pupitres*, are twisted, or riddled, each day so that the sediment moves down the sides and collects in the neck of the bottle on the cap, ready for *dégorgement*.

RESERVA Spanish wines that have fulfilled certain aging requirements: reds must have at least 3 years' aging before sale, of which one must be in oak barrels; whites and rosés must have at least

2 years' age, of which 6 months must be in oak.

RÉSERVE French for what is, in theory at least, a winemaker's finest wine. The word has no legal definition in France.

RIPASSO A method used in Valpolicella to make wines with extra depth. Wine is passed over the lees of Recioto or Amarone della Valpolicella, adding extra alcohol and flavour, though also extra tannin and a risk of higher acidity and oxidation.

RISERVA An Italian term, recognized in many DOCs and DOCGs, for a special selection of wine that has been aged longer before release. It is only a promise of a more pleasurable drink if the wine had enough fruit and structure in the first place.

SEC French for dry. When applied to Champagne, it actually means medium-dry.

'SECOND' WINES A second selection from a designated vineyard, usually lighter and quicker-maturing than the main wine.

SEDIMENT Usually refers to residue thrown by a wine, particularly red, as it ages in bottle.

SEKT German for sparkling wine. The wine will be entirely German only if it is called Deutscher Sekt or Sekt bA. The best wines are traditional-method made from 100% Riesling or from 100% Weissburgunder (Pinot Blanc).

SÉLECTION DE GRAINS NOBLES A super-ripe category for sweet Alsace wines, now also being used by some producers of Coteaux du Layon in the Loire for the most concentrated wines. *See*

also Alsace Vendange Tardive in main A–Z.

SMARAGD The top of the three categories of wine from the Wachau in Austria, the lower two being Federspiel and Steinfeder. Made from very ripe and usually late-harvested grapes, the wines have a minimum of 12% alcohol, often 13–14%.

SOLERA Traditional Spanish system of blending fortified wines, especially sherry and Montilla-Moriles.

SPÄTLESE German for late-picked (therefore riper) grapes. Often moderately sweet, though there are dry versions.

SPUMANTE Italian for sparkling. Bottle-fermented wines are often referred to as *metodo classico* or *metodo tradizionale*.

SUPÉRIEUR French for a wine with a slightly higher alcohol content than the basic AC.

SUPERIORE Italian DOC wines with higher alcohol or more age potential.

SUR LIE French for on the lees, meaning wine bottled direct from the cask/fermentation vat to gain extra flavour from the lees. Common with quality Muscadet, white Burgundy, similar barrel-aged whites and, increasingly, commercial bulk whites.

TAFELWEIN German for table wine.

TANNIN Harsh, bitter, mouth-puckering element in red wine, derived from grape skins and stems, and from oak barrels. Tannins soften with age and are essential for long-term development in red wines.

TERROIR A French term used to denote the combination of soil, climate and exposure to the sun – that is, the natural physical environment of the vine.

TROCKEN German for dry. In most parts of Germany and Austria Trocken matches the standard EU definition of dryness – less than 9g per litre residual sugar.

TROCKENBEEREN-AUSLESE (TBA) German for 'dry berry selected', denoting grapes affected by noble rot (*Edelfäule* in German) – the wines will be lusciously sweet although low in alcohol.

VARIETAL Wine made from, and named after, a single or dominant grape variety.

VDP German organization recognizable on the label by a Prussian eagle bearing grapes. The quality of estates included is usually – but not always – high. Now merged with the Charta organization.

VDQS (VIN DÉLIMITÉ DE QUALITÉ SUPÉRIEURE) The second-highest classification for French wines, behind AC.

VELHO Portuguese for old. Legally applied only to wines with at least 3 years' aging for reds and 2 years for whites.

VENDANGE TARDIVE French for late harvest. Grapes are left on the vines beyond the normal harvest time to concentrate flavours and sugars. The term is traditional in Alsace. *See also* Alsace Vendange Tardive in main A–Z.

VIEILLES VIGNES French term for a wine made from vines at least 20 years old. Should have greater concentration than wine from younger vines.

VIÑA Spanish for vineyard.

VIN DE GARAGE Wines made on so small a scale they could be made in one's garage. Such wines may be made from vineyards of a couple of hectares or less, and are often of extreme concentration.

VIN DE PAILLE Sweet wine found mainly in the Jura region of France. Traditionally, the grapes are left for 2–3 months on straw (*paille*) mats before fermentation to dehydrate, thus concentrating the sugars. The wines are sweet but slightly nutty.

VIN DE PAYS The term gives a regional identity to wine from the country districts of France. It is a particularly useful category for adventurous wine-makers who want to use good-quality grapes not allowed under the frequently restrictive AC regulations. Many are labelled with the grape variety.

VIN DE TABLE French for table wine, the lowest quality level.

VIN DOUX NATUREL (VDN) French for a fortified wine, where fermentation has been stopped by the addition of alcohol, leaving the wine 'naturally' sweet, although you could argue that stopping fermentation with a slug of powerful spirit is distinctly unnatural.

VIN JAUNE A speciality of the Jura region in France, made from the Savagnin grape. In Château-Chalon it is the only permitted style. Made in a similar way to fino sherry but not fortified. Unlike fino, *vin jaune* usually ages well.

VINIFICATION The process of turning grapes into wine.

VINO DA TAVOLA The Italian term for table wine, officially Italy's lowest level of production, is a catch-all that until recently applied to more than 80% of the nation's wine, with virtually no regulations controlling quality. Yet this category also provided the arena in the 1970s for the biggest revolution in quality that Italy has ever seen, with the creation of innovative, DOC-busting Super-Tuscans. See Super-Tuscans in main A–Z.

VINTAGE The year's grape harvest, also used to describe wines of a single year. 'Off-vintage' is a year not generally declared as vintage. See Port in main A–Z.

VITICULTURE Vine-growing and vineyard management.

VITIS VINIFERA Vine species, native to Europe and Central Asia, from which almost all the world's quality wine is made.

VQA (VINTNERS QUALITY ALLIANCE) Canadian equivalent of France's AC system, defining quality standards and designated viticultural areas.

WEISSHERBST German rosé wine, a speciality of Baden.

WO (WINE OF ORIGIN) South African system of appellations which certifies area of origin, grape variety and vintage.

YIELD The amount of fruit, and ultimately wine, produced from a vineyard. Measured in hectolitres per hectare (hl/ha) in most of Europe and in the New World as tons/acre or tonnes/hectare. Yield may vary from year to year, and depends on grape variety, age and density of the vines, and viticultural practices.

WHO OWNS WHAT

The world's major drinks companies are getting bigger and, frankly, I'm worried. As these vast wine conglomerates stride across continents, it seems highly likely that local traditions will – for purely business reasons – be pared away, along with individuality of flavour. It's not all bad news: in some cases wineries have benefited from the huge resources that come with corporate ownership, but I can't help feeling nervous knowing that the fate of a winery rests in the hands of distant institutional investors. Below I have listed some of the names that crop up again and again – and will no doubt continue to do so, as they aggressively pursue their grasp of market share.

Other wine companies – which bottle wines under their own names and therefore feature in the main A–Z – are gradually spreading their nets. KENDALL-JACKSON of California, for example, owns wineries in Chile, Bordeaux and Australia. The HESS COLLECTION also in California, owns Peter LEHMANN in Australia and GLEN CARLOU in South Africa. GALLO, the second-biggest wine producer in the world, has agreements with SIEUR D'ARQUES in southern France, Leonardo Da Vinci winery in Tuscany, MCWILLIAM'S of Australia and Whitehaven of New Zealand. As well as the renowned Ch. MOUTON-ROTHSCHILD, the Rothschild family have other interests in France, are co-owners of OPUS ONE and, in partnership with CONCHA Y TORO, produce ALMAVIVA in Chile.

Cross-ownership is making it enormously difficult to know which companies remain independent, and the never-ending whirl of joint ventures, mergers and takeovers shows no signs of slowing down: the following can only be a snapshot at the time of going to press.

ALLIED DOMECQ UK-based group with a global wines and spirits portfolio, which includes New Zealand's MONTANA and Spain's Bodegas & Bebidas group (Age/Siglo and CAMPO VIEJO in Rioja, Tarsus in Ribera del Duero and Selentia in Chile). Brands include: ATLAS PEAK, Buena Vista, Callaway, CLOS DU BOIS, William Hill and MUMM NAPA (California); Balbi and Graffigna (Argentina); COCKBURN (port); DOMECQ and Harveys (sherry); Marques de Arienzo (Rioja); MUMM and PERRIER JOUET (Champagne). Allied Domecq is itself currently the subject of takeover talks, with Pernod Ricard, Constellation and Diageo all potential bidders.

AXA-MILLESIMES The French insurance giant AXA's subsidiary owns Bordeaux châteaux PETIT-VILLAGE, PICHON-LONGUEVILLE, Pibran, Cantenac-Brown and SUDUIRAUT, plus Dom. de l'Arlot in Burgundy, Ch. Belles Eaux in the Languedoc, TOKAJI producer Disznókö and port producer Quinta do NOVAL.

BERINGER BLASS The wine division of Foster's, the brewers, takes its name from California's BERINGER and Australia's Wolf BLASS. In May 2005 Foster's won control of Southcorp, Australia's biggest wine conglomerate. In California it owns, among others, CHATEAU ST JEAN, Chateau Souverain, Meridian, St Clement, Stags' Leap Winery. Australian brands include Annie's Lane, BAILEYS of Glenrowan, Ingoldby, Jamiesons Run, Metala, Mildara, Greg Norman, ROTHBURY ESTATE, Saltram (Mamre Brook), T'Gallant, Yarra Ridge, Yellowglen. Southcorp, which merged with Rosemount in 2001, brought with it brands such as Leo Buring, COLDSTREAM HILLS, Devil's Lair, Kaiser Stuhl, Killawarra, Matthew Lang, LINDEMANS, PENFOLDS, ROSEMOUNT ESTATE, Rouge Homme, Seaview, SEPPELT, Tollana, WYNNS. Beringer Blass also owns estates in Italy and MATUA VALLEY in New Zealand.

CONSTELLATION BRANDS The world's largest wine company was created in 2003 by the merger of US-based wine, beer and spirits group Constellation with Australia's BRL Hardy. In late 2004 Constellation paid out $1.36 billion for the prestigious Robert MONDAVI Winery, announcing that it planned to develop Mondavi's Woodbridge brand. Other US brands include Paul Masson, Almaden, Inglenook and Covey Run. The FRANCISCAN Estates division makes wines from its Oakville estate and also owns Estancia, Mount Veeder Winery, RAVENSWOOD and Simi in California, COLUMBIA WINERY in Washington and Veramonte in Chile. BRL Hardy had already looked outside Australia (where brands include HARDYS, Banrock Station, BAROSSA VALLEY ESTATE, HOUGHTON, LEASINGHAM, Moondah Brook, REYNELL, Stonehaven, Yarra Burn) to New Zealand's NOBILO (Selaks, White Cloud) – and in 2003 launched Shamwari ('Friendship') wines, a joint venture with Stellenbosch Vineyards of South Africa. UK drinks wholesaler Matthew Clark (which owns Stowells of Chelsea) is a division of Constellation Brands. Constellation also has a 40% stake in Italy's RUFFINO.

FREIXENET Spanish wine producer making a bid for global market share, with some of Spain's biggest names (including Castellblanch, Conde de Caralt, Segura Viudas, René Barbier) and wine companies in California and Mexico. It also owns the Champagne house of Henri Abelé, Bordeaux négociant/producer Yvon Mau and Australia's Wingara Wine Group (Deakin Estate, KATNOOK ESTATE, Riddoch Estate).

LVMH French luxury goods group Louis Vuitton-Moët Hennessy owns Champagne houses MOET & CHANDON (including Dom Pérignon), KRUG, Mercier, RUINART and VEUVE CLICQUOT, and has established DOMAINE CHANDON sparkling wine companies in California, Australia, Argentina and Spain. The purchase of Ch. d'YQUEM in 1999 was a major coup. It also owns CAPE MENTELLE and Mountadam in Australia, CLOUDY BAY in New Zealand, NEWTON in California, and promising Argentinian winery TERRAZAS DE LOS ANDES.

PERNOD RICARD The French spirits giant owns the ORLANDO Wyndham Group (Australia), with Jacob's Creek; Etchart (Argentina); Long Mountain (South Africa); and Georgian Wines and Spirits/GWS (Georgia).

INDEX OF PRODUCERS

Numbers in **bold** refer to main entries.

302

315

318

319

ACKNOWLEDGEMENTS

Editor Maggie Ramsay; *Assistant Editor* Julie Ross;
Cartographer Andrew Thompson; *Indexer* Angie Hipkin;
Production Sara Granger, Emily Toogood; *Photography* Nigel James;
Art Director Nigel O'Gorman; *Managing Editor* Anne Lawrance.

OLDER VINTAGE CHARTS *(top wines only)*

FRANCE

Alsace (vendanges tardives)	90	89	88	85	83	81	76	71	69	61
	10◊	9♦	8♦	8♦	9♦	7◊	10♦	9◊	8◊	9◊
Champagne (vintage)	90	89	88	86	85	83	82	81	76	
	9◊	8♦	9♦	7♦	8♦	7◊	10♦	7◊	9◊	

Bordeaux

Bordeaux	94	90	89	88	86	85	83	82	81	79
Margaux	7◊	10◊	8◊	7♦	8♦	8♦	9♦	8♦	7◊	6◊
St.-Jul., Pauillac, St-Est.	7◊	10◊	9◊	8♦	9♦	9♦	7♦	10♦	7◊	7◊
Graves/Pessac-L. (red)	6◊	8♦	8♦	8♦	6♦	8♦	8♦	9♦	7◊	7◊
St-Émilion, Pomerol	7◊	10◊	9◊	8♦	7♦	9♦	7♦	9♦	7◊	7◊

Bordeaux (cont.)	78	75	70	66	61	59	55	53	49	47
Margaux (cont.)	7♦	6◊	8♦	7◊	10♦	8◊	6◊	8◊	9◊	8◊
St.-Jul. etc. (cont.)	7♦	8◊	8♦	8◊	10♦	9◊	8◊	9◊	10◊	9◊
Graves etc. (R) (cont.)	8♦	6◊	8◊	8◊	10◊	9◊	8◊	8◊	10◊	9◊
St-Émilion etc. (cont.)	7♦	8◊	8♦	6◊	10◊	7◊	7◊	8◊	9◊	10◊
Sauternes	90	89	88	86	83	82	81	80	76	75
	10♦	9♦	9♦	9♦	9♦	5♦	6◊	7◊	8♦	8♦
Sauternes (cont.)	71	67	62	59	55	53	49	47	45	37
	8♦	9◊	8◊	9◊	8◊	8◊	10◊	10◊	9◊	10◊

Burgundy

Chablis	92	90	89	88	86	85				
	7◊	10♦	8◊	8◊	7◊	9◊				
Côte de Beaune (wh.)	93	92	90	89	88	86	85	82	79	78
	7♦	8♦	7◊	9♦	6◊	8◊	8◊	6◊	8◊	8◊
Côte de Nuits (red)	93	90	89	88	85	83	80	78	76	71
	9♦	9◊	7◊	8♦	9◊	6◊	6◊	10♦	6◊	8◊